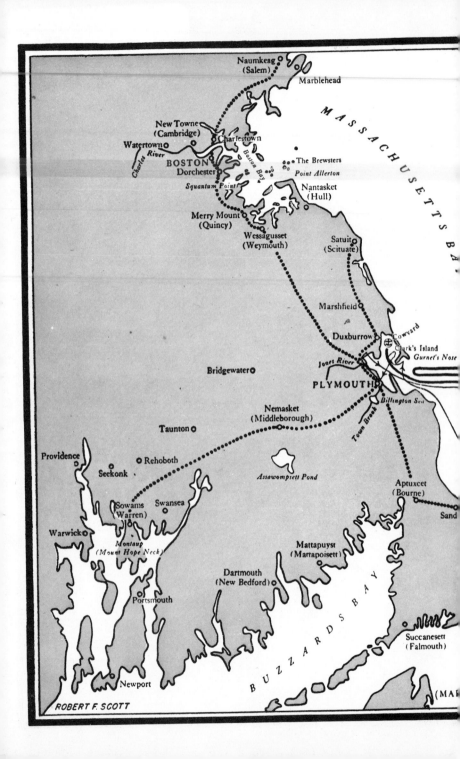

NaumkeAg
(Salem)

Marblehead

MASSACHUSETTS BAY

New Towne
(Cambridge)

Charlestown

Watertown

Charles River

BOSTON

Dorchester

Boston Bay

The Brewsters

Point Allerton

Squantum Point

Nantasket
(Hull)

Merry Mount
(Quincy)

Wessagusset
(Weymouth)

Satuit
(Scituate)

Marshfield

Duxburrow

Cowyard

Clark's Island

Gurnet's Nose

Jones River

PLYMOUTH

Bridgewater

Billington Sea

Town Brook

Nemasket
(Middleborough)

Taunton

Providence

Rehoboth

Seekonk

Assawompsett Pond

Aptuxcet
(Bourne)

Sowams
(Warren)

Swansea

Sand

Warwick

Montaup
(Mount Hope Neck)

Mattapuyst
(Mattapoisett)

Portsmouth

Dartmouth
(New Bedford)

BUZZARDS BAY

Succanesett
(Falmouth)

Newport

ROBERT F. SCOTT

(MA

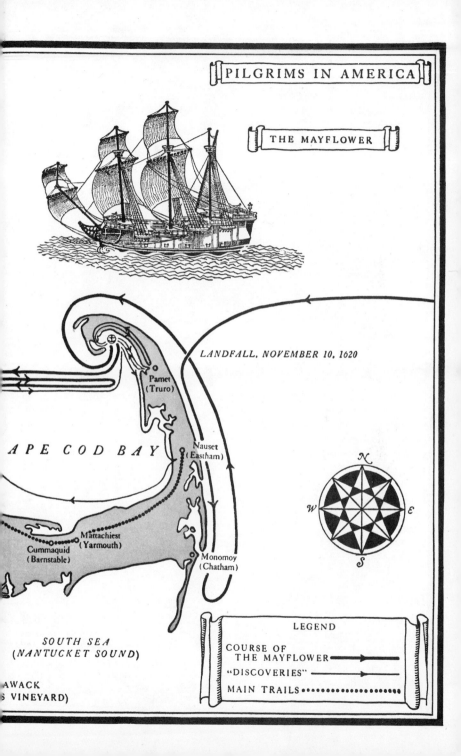

PILGRIMS IN AMERICA

THE MAYFLOWER

LANDFALL, NOVEMBER 10, 1620

Pamet
(Truro)

C A PE C O D B A Y

Nauset
(Eastham)

Mattachiest
(Yarmouth)

Cummaquid
(Barnstable)

Monomoy
(Chatham)

SOUTH SEA
(NANTUCKET SOUND)

AWACK
S VINEYARD)

N
W   E
S

LEGEND

COURSE OF
THE MAYFLOWER ⟶

"DISCOVERIES" ⟶

MAIN TRAILS ••••••••••

SAINTS
AND
STRANGERS

EDWARD WINSLOW

*(The sole authentic Pilgrim portrait,
painted at London in 1651)*

SAINTS
AND
STRANGERS

GEORGE F. WILLISON

Being the Lives of the Pilgrim Fathers
and Their Families,
with Their Friends and Foes;
and an Account of Their Posthumous
Wanderings in Limbo,
Their Final Resurrection
and Rise to Glory,
and the Strange Pilgrimages
of Plymouth Rock

TIME Reading Program Special Edition
TIME-LIFE BOOKS, ALEXANDRIA, VIRGINIA

Time-Life Books Inc.
is a wholly owned subsidiary of
TIME INCORPORATED

TIME Reading Program: *Editor*, Max Gissen

Library of Congress CIP data following page 565.

For information about any Time-Life book, please write:
Reader Information, Time-Life Books,
541 North Fairbanks Court, Chicago, Illinois 60611

to Toni and Malcolm

Contents

Editors' Preface

A more inept group of immigrants never set foot on an American shore. Fleeing England to establish a separate church of their own, they hired a North Sea skipper to take them to the Netherlands. He picked them off a dark beach one night, collected their money and delivered them right back to the English authorities. Extricating themselves from this setback, they reached Amsterdam. They lived there and in Leyden for 12 years in religious freedom and holy poverty. Then, putting aside fears of becoming "meate for ye fishes" or of losing their scalps to Indians whose practices caused "ye bowels of men to grate within them," some of them sailed off, in company with a group of fortune seekers, to establish a fishing colony in America. The remainder were to come over later. In America the pioneers discovered that they had forgotten to bring nets and small fishhooks, that none of their party knew the least thing about fishing and that once again they were "in ye briers."

This was in 1620, and these were the Pilgrim Fathers, "ye Saincts and Strangers," or churched and nonchurched members of the Old Colony they established at Plymouth. They are these days badly confused in people's minds with the dour Puritans, who came later to settle north of them on Massachusetts Bay and west of them in Connecticut. Henry Wadsworth Longfellow, whose own ancestors were Pilgrims, made mealy mouthed Puritans out of Myles Standish, John Alden and Priscilla Mullins—lusty Pilgrims all. But when the Pilgrims are allowed to speak out for themselves, as George Findlay Willison permits them to do so skillfully in *Saints and Strangers,* they reveal themselves as real people full of human juices. They were stubborn, opinionated and passionate, and much given to asking God stridently why they were afflicted with so many stubborn, opinionated and passionate foes, friends and bystanders.

Willison ranged through Pilgrim manuscripts, records and letters. Whenever he found the Saints bewailing their hardships, belaboring their foes, plotting against their financial backers or slyly altering the record about who struck first in a "huggery" with the Indians, he put it down in their own rich and vehement phrases. "Given to speaking their minds plainly," he notes, "they expressed themselves in the language of Marlowe and Shakespeare, in the torrential and often rafter-shaking rhetoric of Elizabethan England with no slightest regard for the proprieties and polite circumlocutions of a later day."

It was a time fit for thunderous prose. It was a time of war between religions, philosophies and ideologies. Men were being hanged in England for holding the views of the Pilgrims. But the Pilgrims' stubborn, often blockheaded bravery never broke. "Upon the slightest pretext, or none at all," Willison writes, "they rushed into the bitterest controversy about any and all kinds of things, sacred and profane, momentous or trivial, simple or abstruse, with a singular disregard of tolerance, candor, sound judgment, or even plain common sense." Again and again they hurled themselves and their wives and children into harebrained adventures, in confidence that God would help his "Saincts." "All great and honourable actions," one of them wrote, "are accompanied with great difficulties . . . and must be both enterprised and overcome with answerable courages."

Saints and Strangers good humoredly but unsentimentally examines the myths that have grown up around the Pilgrims.

Consider Plymouth Rock: "On the American horizon today," writes Willison, "Plymouth Rock looms like a Gibraltar. In our eyes it has become the symbol of a great faith and a greater hope, a mighty bulwark of freedom and democracy. No landmark on our shores has been more celebrated in song and story."

But did the Pilgrims really land on Plymouth Rock? Not, thinks Willison, unless the sailors blindly overlooked the sheltered mouth of Town Brook, a few oar pulls away.

What kind of harvest did the Pilgrims celebrate on that first Thanksgiving Day? A very poor one. Under the guidance of the Indians, who taught them to plant in hillocks and fertilize each hillock with dead fish, their American corn had come in fairly well. However, although most Pilgrims were brought up in "ye inocente trade of husbandrey," the acres devoted to the old familiar European crops of wheat, barley and peas failed completely. But at the banquet, which lasted three days, they ate venison, duck, goose (although turkeys aplenty ran wild in the woods, no mention is made of this bird), clams and other shellfish, eels, white bread, corn bread, leeks, watercress, with wild plums and dried berries for dessert—all of the venison and many of the other good things being provided by their Indian guests.

The Pilgrims loved good food, beer and "strong waters," especially after funerals, and in their first years of "hungrie bellies" they complained far less over the lack of food than over the necessity to drink ordinary water, which, Willison says, "they always regarded with suspicion as a prolific source of human ills." Nor were they, save on the Sabbath, the gloomy figures in dark grays of the myths. They ordinarily wore the rich russet brown and bright Lincoln green common among the English lower classes from which they sprang, and, Willison writes, "they passed no laws against 'gay apparel.'" Many of the Pilgrims had large and varied wardrobes. That of Ruling Elder William Brewster, one of the most exemplary of "ye Saincts," contained for wear on occasion "a red cap, a white cap, a quilted cap, a lace cap, a violet coat and '1 paire of greene drawers.'"

They did their best to keep a close watch on public morals. There were always people who had to sit shamefaced in the stocks for telling lies or shooting off their blunderbusses after dark when there were no proper targets (wolves or Indians) about. And there were husbands and wives who had to sit in stocks when their first-born came sooner, even a week sooner, than nine months after marriage. The Pilgrim Fathers did not have much faith in premature babies.

Himself a mild and scholarly man, little given to accepting myths or polite fictions for truth, the author of this book is only a generation away from Scotland on both sides of his family. Thus, with no forefathers among the *Mayflower* passengers or among those of the six other Pilgrim ships, he has no genealogical axes to grind. For all the coats of arms and even portraits that have been bestowed upon the plain people of the Pilgrim Company by their latter-day descendants he has nothing but laughter.

Willison was a machine gunner in World War I, a Rhodes scholar, a college professor, a writer of books and magazine articles. During the effervescent period of the New Deal he was one of the principal editors of the memorable American Guide Series of the Federal Writers' Project. It was then that he fell in love with the clamorous people who populate *Saints and Strangers.*

The affair began, he says, when he was working on the Massachusetts *Guide.* He discovered that he did not really know the Pilgrims. Much of what he had thought he knew turned out to be all wrong. Most of the things he found to be right had a charming quality that he had never suspected was there. It amused him that one of the greatest of "ye Saincts" was Squanto, the Indian, who guided them through their first years and died fervid in the faith. Willison set out to know them all better.

For five years, through most of World War II, he worked by day at a government job and by night disappeared into the libraries. His son and his wife saw little of him save when he dashed into the house with pages of notes to be typed. Then, after the book was finished in mid-1944, there was a long, frustrating delay. His publishers had used up all of their wartime paper ration on a bestseller, and so Willison's book was not published until August of 1945.

It received a shower of praise from literary critics and historians who reviewed it; from Pulitzer Prize winner Allan Nevins ("If it is as widely read as it deserves to be, it will weaken the grip of the Pilgrim-Puritan myth for half a dozen years"); from Pulitzer Prize winner Bernard De Voto ("I cannot remember that in our time any one else has written a general history of Plymouth at once full and fair, with justice done alike to the rigor and the passion of the Pilgrims, to their honor and dishonor, to their pettiness and obstinacy and belligerence and to their unsurpassed achievements"); from Pulitzer Prize winner Esther Forbes ("The book is a sheer joy to read because the vast work that went into assembling the facts has been so completely digested. . . . It was the Victorians who rescued the Pilgrims from obscurity and who named them, and now comes Mr. Willison to rescue them from the Victorians").

Nevertheless, George Willison is too good a historian to claim more for the Pilgrims than, in fact, they actually accomplished. They led no fight for religious freedom—they wanted only to replace one exclusive and intolerant creed with another. The Mayflower Compact was originally a device to insure minority rule—although, to be sure, it did establish a "civill body politick" and promised equal laws for all, which were extraordinary things to do at that time. Soon from the Pilgrim meetinghouse the New England town meeting would grow. And thereby, perhaps, the Pilgrims had a part in bequeathing to us rather more freedom in conscience and in politics than they would have cared for us to have.

—THE EDITORS

Author's Preface

More, perhaps, has been written about the Pilgrims than any other small group in our history. And yet they are still extravagantly praised for accomplishing what they never attempted or intended, and are even more foolishly abused for possessing attitudes and attributes quite foreign to them.

In the popular mind they are still generally confused—to their great disadvantage—with the Puritans who settled to the north of them around Boston Bay. Even Longfellow, who should have known better, dubbed Myles Standish "the Puritan Captain" and always referred to Priscilla Mullins as a "Puritan maid."

It is about time, I think, that the Pilgrims were allowed to tell their own story—and, so far as it can be readily and readably managed, in their own words. They were always quite able to speak for themselves, and never had any diffidence in doing so. They wrote marvelous letters, as fresh and crisp today as when penned three centuries ago. Though relatively few, their chronicles are remarkably rich in the very stuff of human life. They will stand forever as a bright clear mirror of all the hopes and fears that lie closest to men's hearts.

In essaying this group biography I am particularly indebted to the patient labors of three great Pilgrim scholars, all now dead—Henry Martyn Dexter, Edward Arber, and Charles Edward Banks. Without their years of exhaustive digging in musty archives to unearth every existing scrap of information about the Pilgrims and their families, many of the latter would still remain mere names.

On more personal grounds I am grateful to Fred Hamlin and Josef Berger for many thoughtful criticisms and suggestions; to Virginia Bass, who came to my rescue at a critical period; to Curtice Hitchcock, blessed with an exemplary patience beyond any of "ye saincts"; and above all, to T.H.W., who did most of the hard work in preparing the manuscript for press, saving me from many a slip, and always hopefully bore with me (even when bored stiff herself) during the long gestation of *Saints and Strangers*.

Lastly, I wish to thank the Massachusetts Historical Society for the Winslow portrait reproduced as the frontispiece; and the Library of Congress, the New York Public Library, the Yale University Library, and others for many courtesies and always excellent service.

Washington, D.C.   —GEORGE F. WILLISON
January 11, 1945

So they lefte that goodly & pleasante citie,
which had been their resting place near
12 years; but they knew they were pilgrimes,
& looked not much on those things, but lift{ed}
up their eyes to ye heavens, their dearest
cuntrie, and quieted their spirits.

—OF PLIMOTH PLANTATION

1

PLYMOUTH ROCK
AND THE
PILGRIM SAGA

The shore where true devotion
Shall rear no pillared shrine . . .

—JOHN PIERPONT

ON THE AMERICAN HORIZON TODAY PLYMOUTH ROCK LOOMS
like a Gibraltar. In our eyes it has become the symbol of a great
faith and a greater hope, a mighty bulwark of freedom and democracy. No landmark on our shores has been more celebrated in song
and story.

Yet this has not long been so.

For a century and a half after the landing of the Pilgrims the
rock lay unmarked, almost unnoticed. Until 1769, on the eve of
Independence, it was just another gray granite boulder, one more
troublesome bit of glacial debris littering a white arc of beach,
impeding development of a busy water front and cursed by many

as an obstacle to progress. For another century it was dragged, a broken and mutilated fragment, up and down the streets of Plymouth—first, to Town Square, to make a revolutionary holiday; then to Pilgrim Hall, as a museum piece, an altar of filial piety. Restored at length to the beach and enshrined below a box of bones, presumably Pilgrims', embedded in the domed ceiling of an elaborate Victorian stone canopy, the rock enjoyed a half century of comparative quiet and repose before it was snatched up again, in our day, and dumped where it has since remained, at tidewater, sheltered and quite overshadowed by a lustrous Grecian temple of Quincy granite. Here, much like a bear in a pit and not a great deal larger, it lies enclosed within a stout iron paling—dreaming perhaps of other days when it was not gathering moss, and peanuts and odd bits of lunch tossed at it by casual sightseers, and not being apostrophized by every hungry aspirant to public office.

Extraordinary in itself and with its own high significance, as will appear, the career of the rock throws a strange and arresting light upon the entire Pilgrim saga. That saga, now so central in our tradition, was wholly the creation of the nineteenth century, for the Pilgrims suffered quite as long from neglect as the rock, falling into almost complete oblivion. The two, in fact, emerged from the shadows of the past and belatedly rose to fame together. As late as 1820 they were known to few outside the town of Plymouth, in part because so little was known about them. Much of the Pilgrim story had been forgotten down the years; many indispensable documents had been lost and were still missing. Until 1849, for example, it was not known just where the original congregation had been formed and what were the home villages of its members.

And in the history and the saga of the Pilgrims, both curiously tangled tales, surely nothing is more curious than this—that their very name, "the Pilgrims," is little more than a century old, having come into common usage since 1840. Heterogeneous in origin, split even by religious differences, the Pilgrims had no name for themselves as a group. For generations they were known to their descendants merely as the Forefathers, a name preserved in the only holiday officially dedicated to their memory, Forefathers' Day, tardily instituted by Massachusetts in 1895.

The Pilgrims themselves were to blame in large part for the fog that so long obscured them, for they and their immediate descendants were singularly careless of their fame. Simple and humble folk of plebeian origin, they read no earth-shaking import into what they were doing. They erected no monuments to themselves and their prowess, leaving behind regrettably few memorials of any kind, whether inscribed on paper or in stone. Used to toil and hardship, many of them illiterate, few with any formal schooling, they performed as best they could the homely day-to-day tasks that had to be done, content to let history come after them. They did not even bother to keep town records until 1632, twelve years after the landing.

In the early years of settlement, it is true, they published two brief accounts of their initial trials and adventures—Mourt's *Relation* (1622), as it is known, obviously written by Governor William Bradford and Edward Winslow, and *Good Newes from New England* (1624), written by Winslow alone. Frankly designed as promotional literature to attract more settlers, both had exciting tales to tell. But they were only minor fragments of a fascinating story leading far back into the past and extending even farther forward into the future. Winslow later published *Hypocrisie Unmasked* (1646) and *New England's Salamander* (1647). Both were narrow controversial tracts and added little of consequence to the Pilgrim story.

Fortunately, there was one on the *Mayflower,* a member of the original congregation, who had a sense of history and an eye for the larger pattern in the flow of events. Fortunately, too, he had an eye for character and color, a sense of dramatic situation, apparently boundless energy, and a gifted hand at writing prose—a fine, full-bodied Elizabethan prose, strong and supple, studded with many brilliant turns of phrase, lighted now and again by a certain grim kind of humor and a flash of malicious wit. It was in 1630, as he himself tells us, that Governor Bradford sat down amid the distractions and burdens of office to begin what he called his "scribled Writings." These were necessarily "peeced up at times of leesure afterwards," for to the day of his death some thirty years later Bradford led a busy and usually bedeviled life at the center of affairs. By 1650, when he laid down his pen, he had piled up a manuscript of 270 folio pages, all patiently inscribed in his own neat hand. His chronicle, simply and modestly entitled *Of Plimoth Plantation,* related in graphic detail the story of the Pilgrims from 1606 to 1647, through the most critical and eventful period of their always eventful career.

Bradford enjoyed two great advantages usually denied the historian. He had been an actor in the scenes he described. Also, as chief of the inner council at Plymouth almost from the day of the landing, he knew what had been going on behind the scenes as well, and his pages reflect this. Many of his casual comments and almost unintended asides afford a startling flash of insight into what really occurred on occasion and the actual motives at work under the surface of events. Bradford was disingenuous at times. He was not above politic distortion of facts, and did not hesitate to suppress whole chapters in the history of his brethren—notably, their distressing stay at Amsterdam with the scandalous Ancient Brethren. More than once he misrepresented the sequence of events, cleverly transposing cause and effect, in an attempt to justify some dubious action. His remarks about those who opposed him or his brethren in any way are often unreliable and always savage. He never wearied of repeating against them the most slanderous gossip and libels. But for all that, Bradford is always an informed and usually a safe guide in exploring what, without him, would be a dark and hopelessly bewildering maze. One can scarcely write or speak a word about the Pilgrims without leaning heavily upon him. Every American conscious of his heritage, particularly of its democratic roots, is infinitely beholden to him.

But for two hundred years the world was little the wiser for anything that Bradford had written, for his history had a curious history of its own. As Bradford had not written for publication, his manuscript was handed down from father to son for several generations, with little or no appreciation of its unique worth. Some passages were copied into the church records by Nathaniel Morton, Bradford's nephew and secretary of the Old Colony, who also consulted it in compiling his rather dull and sketchy annals of the Forefathers, *New England's Memorial* (1669). Many years later Bradford's history passed into the hands of another early New England chronicler, the Reverend Thomas Prince, who published a few excerpts from it and then placed it on the shelves of the library he had fitted up for himself in the tower of the renowned Old South Church, Boston. Here the manuscript presumably remained until the American Revolution.

During the early years of that conflict the Old South was turned into a stable and a riding academy by the British, and after their evacuation of Boston an inventory of Prince's library revealed that Bradford's chronicle and other priceless old documents were missing. A search for them was made, and hopes of recovering them bounded up in 1793 when a manuscript volume of Bradford's letters suddenly came to light in a grocer's shop at Halifax, Nova Scotia, where its large folio pages were being used to wrap up pickles, soap, cheese, butter, and other small purchases. What little remained of it was rescued and published at Boston the next year, which stimulated more determined search for the other missing treasures. But when decade after decade passed without the discovery of a single clue, they were given up as irretrievably lost and written off as casualties of the Revolution.

But here, as so often in the Pilgrim story, chance had yet to speak the last word. In 1855, while thumbing through a book borrowed from a friend, a dull ecclesiastical work published in England almost ten years before, a student of Massachusetts history suddenly came upon several quoted passages attributed to an anonymous manuscript and instantly recognized that they could have been written only by Bradford. This promising lead was quickly followed up, and the long-lost manuscript was soon traced to its dusty hiding place. It was found—of all places—in the library of Fulham Palace, besides the Thames on the outskirts of London, one of the episcopal seats and long the favored summer residence of the bishops of London. How this loot from the Old South came into their possession has never been explained, and delicacy has precluded any too pressing inquiry. In any case, his then Lordship graciously allowed a transcript of *Plimoth Plantation* to be made, and with its publication at Boston early the next year the mists that had so long enshrouded the Pilgrims, blurring their features both as a group and as individuals, began to lift for the first time.

The year 1856 marks, in a real sense, the beginning of Pilgrim history.

Meanwhile, with consequences not altogether happy, the Pilgrim saga had taken shape and crystallized in the form in which it still persists as a cherished part of the American *mythos,* known to all of us from our days in school. Under the circumstances, it was necessarily compounded of some few scattered facts and quite as many random fancies, pieced out with legend, folklore, and odd bits of family tradition—some of which were very odd indeed, as will be seen. No wonder then that scarcely a detail in the saga is authentic in the sense that it is historically true.

Now a myth or saga, of course, has no need of such authenticity. Like any work of art or piece of fiction, it enjoys a kind of poetic license and can take great liberties with the facts without impairing in the slightest its essential validity and truth. It may be that George Washington did not chop down the cherry tree with his little hatchet. Only pedants are bothered by that. What if Davy Crockett did not actually perform all of the feats he so loved to boast about, and boasted about so well? The only important question is this—were they in character? And they were, obviously, for if anyone ever choked a grizzly to death with his bare hands, Davy was the man to do it.

Does it matter, then, if the Pilgrims did not first land on Plymouth Rock? Or even if, as seems likely, they never used it at all for such a purpose? That does not affect in any way its value as a symbol or as a useful pivot for the whole Pilgrim story. Nor does it much matter if the mythmakers had the Forefathers living in log cabins when the fact is that the log cabin, a foreign "invention," first appeared on our shores some years later in the settlements of the Swedes and Finns along the Delaware.

But it is something else again that the mythmakers so completely missed the essential character and spirit of the Pilgrims. Their portraits of the latter are little more than self-portraits, all done in the pale and sentimental manner of the nineteenth century at its worst. Under their brushes the Pilgrims appeared as a group of anemic Victorians doing a sort of pious charade in costumes out of grandmother's closet, which is the general impression of them that still persists. Nothing could be more unfortunate, for the popular and almost universal conception of the Pilgrims as a meek, drab, and uncomplaining lot, with eyes ever humbly fixed on the ground at their feet or turned tearfully upward toward the Pearly Gates in misty rapture, is a caricature at which the Pilgrims themselves would have been the first to laugh—and they were not much given to laughter, least of all when at their expense.

The Pilgrims were not nineteenth century pietists, or quietists. They were not pale plaster saints, hollow and bloodless. They were men—and women, too—of courage and conviction, strong and positive in their attitudes, prepared to sacrifice much for their principles, even their very lives. Far from being Victorians, they were children of another and a greater age, the Elizabethan, and in their lives reflected many of the qualities of that amazing age—its restlessness and impatience with old ways, its passionate enthusiasms, its eager curiosity and daring speculation in all fields, its boldness in action, its abounding and apparently inexhaustible energies.

Never did the Pilgrims quietly resign themselves to defeat, no matter what the odds against them. They launched themselves upon the most hazardous of ventures not once but many times, and no obstacle or untoward circumstance could stay them or divert them from their course. Far from being humble and soft-spoken, they were quick in their own defense, fond of controversy, and sharp of tongue, engaging in many a high-pitched quarrel with friends and foes alike, even among themselves. Given to speaking their minds plainly, they expressed themselves in the language of Marlowe and Shakespeare, in the torrential and often rafter-shaking rhetoric of Elizabethan England, with no slightest regard for the proprieties and polite circumlocutions of a later day. In denouncing the "whore at Rome," they meant just that.

The Pilgrims were Elizabethan, too, in their acceptance of the simpler joys of life. They practised no macerations of the flesh, no tortures of self-denial. They appreciated the pleasures of the table and of the bottle, liking both "strong waters" and beer, especially the latter, never complaining more loudly of their hardships than when necessity reduced them to drinking water, which they always regarded with suspicion as a prolific source of human ills. They were not monks or nuns in their intimate relations as their usually numerous families and more than occasional irregularities attest. Fond of the comforts of connubial bed and board, they married early and often and late, sometimes within a few weeks of losing a mate. Only on the Sabbath did they go about in funereal blacks and grays. Ordinarily they wore the russet browns and Lincoln green common among the English lower classes from which they sprang. Unlike their Puritan neighbors at Boston, with whom they are so often confused to their disadvantage, they passed no laws against "gay apparel." Many of the Pilgrims had large and varied wardrobes. That of Ruling Elder William Brewster, one of the most exemplary of "ye Saincts," contained for wear on occasion—though presumably not on the same occasion—a red cap, a white cap, a quilted cap, a lace cap, a violet coat, and "1 paire of greene drawers."

In still other respects the Pilgrims mirrored their age, which was one of great confusion and contention, not unlike our own, with two irreconcilable philosophies of life engaged in mortal combat. All of Europe had been in ferment for more than a century—ever since that fateful day in 1517 when Martin Luther had nailed his ninety-five theses to the door of Wittenberg Cathedral, blasting the autocratic pretensions of the Holy See and its many notorious "abuses." His bold defiance of the Pope, the overlord of Europe, still the King of Kings, shook Christendom to its foundations, releasing and giving direction to powerful latent forces that soon swept the continent in the great revolutionary movement known as the Reformation.

That movement was not wholly religious in character. It had profound social, economic, and political implications as well, a fact quickly sensed, to their great and growing alarm, by those in power everywhere. With one accord monarchs and lesser princes tried to stem the rising democratic tide by the most ruthless means, and with the usual lack of results in the long run.

In England the Pilgrims stood with their fellow-Separatists in the vanguard of this movement. For a time, to grind several axes of his own, Henry VIII had encouraged reform, but he soon called a halt. He was well pleased to have the Pope's wings clipped. But what was all this talk among the common people about their "rights" to independence of judgment in religious matters, to freedom of conscience? As if they had any "rights" but to do and believe exactly what they were told! Englishmen were sharply cautioned to behave accordingly—and no nonsense! Those who refused were locked up and the more stubborn sent to the stake or gallows. Prosecutions and persecutions became the order of the day. Yet such was the acceleration of the movement that within the Pilgrims' lifetime their co-religionists in England chopped off a king's head, deposed his "antichristian" bishops, and set up a revolutionary new state of their own—a Commonwealth, they significantly called it—under Oliver Cromwell.

News of this, when it came at last, was hailed in far-off Plymouth with shouts of triumph. Never was there better cause for celebration, exclaimed Bradford. Not only had he and his brethren had a "seede time." Beyond all expectation, they had "seene ye joyfull harvest." So why should they not "rejoyse, yea, and againe rejoyse, and say Hallelu-iah, salvation, and glorie, and honour, and power to be ye Lord our God, for true and righteous are his judgments. . . . Hallelu-iah!" Another of the Plymouth leaders, Edward Winslow, returned to England and remained there to forward the cause, dying at sea in its service. The Pilgrims played a vital part—and consciously so—in that great conflict of spiritual and material forces which so decisively shaped the world as we know it today.

That conflict centered on the fiercely contested right to freedom of conscience, merely one aspect of the still larger right to freedom of thought and speech. Stripped of theological trimmings, the issue as posed in the Pilgrims' day was this:

Was it right for the State to demand uniformity of belief? Should communion in an official church be compulsory?

Or were men entitled to independence of judgment in religious matters? Should all their beliefs be prescribed, or could they read the Bible for themselves and come to their own conclusions about its teachings?

If they could not worship as they wished in the established church, were they free to withdraw—secede, separate—and set up one of their own?

What was the purpose of the church anyway? And who rightfully spoke for it, the great body of believers or a priesthood appointed from above and quite beyond the control of those below?

Did a parish have to accept whatever pastor, good or bad, was imposed upon it? Or had every congregation the right, as the Pilgrims contended, to choose its own pastor and dismiss him for cause?

In short, was the "true" church a democratic or an autocratic institution?

From their varying responses to this central question can be determined the position of the several contending groups. Hostilities opened with each hurling at the others insufferably long and weighty sermons, huge tomes of carefully selected Scriptural texts, dull tracts, ill-natured squibs, and the grossest of personal abuse—religious controversy was never nice, and never less so than in Elizabethan England. The battle later shifted from the pulpit to the field, but in the beginning it was fought with theological phrases so abstruse and ecclesiastical concepts so nebulous that almost anything and everything could be read into them—and almost everything was. But it would be most superficial to conclude, as some Anglican and Roman apologists have done, that the battle fought with these ideological weapons was little more than a logic-choppers' brawl, a contest among hairsplitters all stridently eager to impose their own arbitrary definitions upon strange and empty words. Many of them were strange, all may now be empty, but the issues they clothed in the manner of the day were quite as real and vital as any that we now clothe differently.

Indeed, they were essentially the same issues. Men did not go unflinching to the stake or gallows—the Pilgrims did not wilfully choose exile and years of almost incredible hardship—Cromwell and his Independents did not lightly court death as rebels—merely for words. They were valiantly engaged, all of them, in a desperate struggle for a better order of things, for a more generous measure of freedom for all men, for a higher and nobler conception of life based upon recognition of the intrinsic worth and dignity of the individual.

To understand the Pilgrims and the heroic part they played in that epic struggle, it is necessary to go back with Bradford—and even beyond him—to "begine at ye very roote & rise of the same." And one would be well advised to follow Bradford also in his modest aim to tell the story "in a plaine stile, with a singuler regard unto ye simple trueth in all things."

Now, the "simple" truth in all things—or in anything, for that matter—is not always easy to discover. But the search is exciting and has its own rewards. It usually leads, as here, into unfamiliar but pleasant fields opening up unexpected new vistas. Or again it goes wandering off down some shady country lane or up some dark alley into many odd nooks and corners, occasionally even into an old closet or two harboring an unsuspected skeleton.

2

THE POSTMASTER
AT SCROOBY

... a meane Townlet

—JOHN LELAND

JUST OFF THE HISTORIC GREAT NORTH ROAD, ABOUT HALFWAY from London to the Scottish border, lies Scrooby, approximately in the center of England. The quiet hamlet stands on the banks of the River Ryton, within sight of its junction with the Idle, both sluggish small streams in the watershed of the Humber which drains the moors and fen lands of the middle eastern counties. As the countryside is rather poor, sparsely settled, and still somewhat isolated, the roar of modern life is scarcely an echo along Scrooby Water, as the Ryton was once known. Time, it would seem, has been timeless here. Apparently nothing has ever disturbed the tranquillity of this cluster of cottages and small houses, occupied largely by tenant farmers and field hands and their families. Like their fathers before them for generations they plow, plant, hoe, and harvest in season, with little to disturb the steady rhythm of their labors.

But Scrooby, however small and inconsequential, is larger and less isolated today than it was almost precisely four centuries ago when a traveler hurrying by noted it as a "meane Townlet," distinguished only by a small parish church, "well buildid" of cut stone, and a great manor house "of tymber." The latter stood beside the Ryton with a moat about it and was the property of the archbishopric of York, as it had been for almost a thousand years —for centuries before Domesday Book so recorded it in 1066.

With some forty rooms and apartments and its own private chapel, the manor house was palatial in its proportions if not in its appointments. It was of the characteristic half-timber construction of the period except for the main façade on the larger of two courtyards, which was of brick. Up this a flight of stone steps ascended to the heavy oak door that opened into the great baronial hall where the archbishops, like the lords of the realm they were in fact, held court in princely fashion on their rare visits to this poor and distant part of their see in the narrow northern tip of Nottinghamshire, which here lies tightly squeezed between Lincolnshire on one side and Yorkshire on the other.

Even more august personages came to grace the archiepiscopal palace from time to time. In 1503 Margaret Tudor, elder daughter of that old skinflint Henry VII, stopped here overnight while on her way north, trailing a magnificent equipage, to marry James IV of Scotland and mother the ill-starred Stuart breed that in time succeeded to the English throne. More than three-quarters of a century later, through a strange concatenation of circumstances, a humble youth brought up here at the manor was to have a promising career at Court ruined and the whole course of his life profoundly changed by becoming innocently entangled in the web of intrigue that always surrounded Margaret's fair and foolish granddaughter, Mary Queen of Scots. And that youth, grown to manhood, was to be harried out of the realm and pursued even into exile by Mary's "snivelling son," James I of England, the sixth of Scotland.

In the summer of 1530, while trying to hide away from the towering wrath of his gouty and lubricious master, Henry VIII, the great Cardinal Wolsey spent a quiet month here meditating upon the folly of ambition and the misspent energies of his life, anxiously watching the swift ebb tide of fortune that would sweep him away to utter disgrace and death before the year was out. Later, in 1541, came "good King Hal" himself with many great and merry gentlemen, and for a day Scrooby was virtually the capital of the realm. Still later Queen Elizabeth and James I passed by and noted the old manor house, now somewhat decayed. Both made efforts to secure it, planning to make it into a royal hunting lodge, for the district was still wild, with plenty of game usually to be found in the immediate neighborhood and if not there, then certainly in Sherwood Forest and the Robin Hood country only a few hours' ride to the south.

Of that ancient Scrooby nothing remains but the "well buildid" small church, St. Wilfred's, which still lifts its slender gray spire above the trees, and a few remnants of the old manorial walls. These have been preserved only because they chanced to be incorporated long ago in the construction of the "plain farm tenement" erected on the spot after the crumbling palace was demolished in 1637. On its front wall this farmhouse bears a memorial plaque, not to the lordly archbishops, not to Cardinal Wolsey, not even to Princess Margaret or any royal visitor, but to a humble commoner. It simply records the fact that here stood the old manor house

> where lived
>
> ### WILLIAM BREWSTER
>
> from 1588 to 1608, and where he organized the Pilgrim Church, of which he became the ruling elder, and with which, in 1608, he removed to Amsterdam, in 1609 to Leyden, and in 1620 to Plymouth, where he died
>
> April 16, 1644.

This tablet, like so much recorded of the Pilgrims, is misleading.[1] Brewster came to live at the manor as early as 1575, and it remained his home for thirty-three years, though he was absent for a time in the 1580's while at school and in his first employment. He came here as a lad of nine or ten, according to his own later reckoning, for neither the date nor the place of his birth is known. His mother's name was Prudence, the type of name favored by the religious radicals, but nothing more is known of her. If the boy had brothers and sisters, as is likely, their names have been lost, for his was an obscure family. Perhaps it had been living near by for some time as there were other Brewsters in the neighborhood. It may be that the boy's father and namesake was the William Brewster assessed for taxes in the parish in 1571.

This much at least is certain—in 1575 Archbishop Grindal of York, addressing him as "our trusty and well-beloved servant," commissioned the senior William Brewster as bailiff and receiver of Scrooby manor, an extensive lordship embracing hundreds of farms and many villages round about. As general overseer of the lordship, he had the duty of collecting manorial fees, "fines," and rents, and in minor disputes was empowered to sit as a magistrate. For his services he received the use of the manor seat and the fruits of its grounds. In addition, he was paid a nominal salary of £3 6s. 8d. ($165) a year.*

Though somewhat dilapidated, the old manorial establishment was still an imposing one when the Brewsters moved in. Many secondary buildings had recently been torn down, but there still stood within the moat several smaller houses, two or three large stables, kennels and dovecotes, a granary, blacksmith's shop, bake house, and brew house. As important as any were the stables, the bake house, and the brew house. Without them Brewster could not have become master of the local station on the royal post, for his commission required him to keep a tavern for the refreshment

---

* Monetary sums throughout have been roughly equated with the real value—i.e., purchasing power—of the 1940 dollar.[2]
For the current (January 1, 1945) dollar, add at least 20 per cent.

of the royal couriers and the occasional wayfarer along the Great North Road, which then ran through the hamlet close to the gates of the manor. Here, if possessed of the means, weary travelers could find comfortable quarters for the night after they had dined and wined in the great hall or, if they preferred, had filled up their skins with good old English ale from the brew house.[3] There must have been many a merry evening here, with the rafters ringing to song and laughter as a bright blaze roared in the great fireplaces, for Englishmen of the day were known throughout Europe for the staggering amounts of liquor they drank, for their "large tabling and belly cheer."

Some years later, when young Brewster had succeeded his father as "mine host," a guest noted that he had been charged 7s. ($17.50) for supper, bed, breakfast, and a caudle—a hot drink concocted of wine, egg, bread, sugar, and spices. On his return journey a few days later he paid 2s. for "burned sack, bread, beer, and sugar to wine," and 8s. for hire of a horse to carry him as many miles. With large profits from tavern and stables, with his postmaster's salary of £30 8s. 4d. ($1,525) a year, which was munificent for the time, with no rent to pay and all of his needs provided as bailiff-receiver of the manor, the older Brewster was a man of relative affluence and obvious consequence in the isolated countryside.

Here at the manor young Brewster spent the next five years of his life, roaming the woods and fields, exploring the fen lands, hunting and fishing, paddling in the moat or sailing boats on the placid Ryton, but not swimming. Elizabethans never swam and never bathed, having a pronounced distaste for water in all its uses. Sir Thomas More, author of *Utopia,* was a water-drinker, but all the Mores were regarded as eccentrics. Certainly, as the boy grew older, he was called upon more and more frequently to give his father a hand both in the tavern and in the stables where every postmaster was required to keep ready for instant use three "good and sufficient" horses with "furniture fit and belonging"— saddles, bridles, stout leather dispatch bags lined with baize, and three horns "to blow by the way." As the post served only official needs as these arose—private letters were sent by private messenger or chance travelers along the roads—there was no regular schedule of operations. A courier was apt to come riding in at any hour of the day or night to deliver a packet. Immediately upon its receipt, or within fifteen minutes at most, the packet had to be on its way again to the mournful winding of the horn, and the lad must have enjoyed the excitement and have taken some pride in helping his father perform his duties "with all good speed and diligence," as his commission from Queen Elizabeth required.

During these years, too, young Brewster somehow managed to acquire the rudiments of a formal education. This signified only that he had learned to read and write, parse a little Latin, sing the psalms, and endure much flogging, which was not merely incidental but quite systematic, being highly esteemed as the very essence of learning. At a time when not one child in ten received any schooling whatever, even in the larger cities, the Brewsters necessarily were at considerable pains and expense to provide their son with such an advantage in the lonely countryside. Where he received his schooling is not known, but his master may have been another Brewster in the neighborhood, one of the few university men in the district, the Reverend Henry Brewster, vicar at the hamlet of Sutton-cum-Lound a few miles to the southeast.[4]

Whatever the circumstances, the youth proved himself a likely scholar and in 1580, now an adolescent of fifteen, he packed up and left home, at once sad and elated, to enter the University of Cambridge. It was December and raw with the cold rains and blanket fogs of that season as he set off down the Great North Road, no doubt in company with a courier on his father's section of the post. Both were on horseback, for the state of the roads precluded other means of travel. The day of the stage coach had not yet arrived. There were scarcely a dozen in the kingdom; most of these were in London, where they wallowed along the miry streets at a snail's pace in the best of weather. As for the Great North Road so-called, it was little more than a trail, unfenced and ungraded. It wandered about open fields, around bogs, across streams, and through the woods with so little apparent aim or direction that none dared travel it more than a few miles from home without a guide.

As the riders jogged along the muddy track trying to maintain the post's stipulated average winter rate of five miles an hour, they kept a sharp lookout ahead and to both sides of the road, for highwaymen infested every part of England. The Queen had recently ordered all brush and undergrowth to be cleared away to a distance of two hundred feet on either side of main roads of travel, but with no appreciable decrease in larcenous and murderous assaults. Young Brewster was well aware of the danger, for the market town of Bawtry just above Scrooby on his father's section of the post was a notorious rendezvous of brigands and cutthroats. But his two or three days' journey to Cambridge was attended, so far as we know, with no greater excitement—and yet what could be more exciting!—than that experienced by every spirited and imaginative youth leaving home and going out into the world for the first time, determined to make a name for himself, certain that Destiny has reserved for him one of her brightest prizes.

Coming over the hill by Cambridge Castle, with a sudden breath-taking view of clustered spires and steepled towers in the distance, Brewster hastened down through Monk's Place to the Cam, across the Great Bridge, past St. Sepulchre's Church, and on up the High toward the gates of Peterhouse, one of the oldest of the fourteen colleges in the ancient walled town. He entered his name in the books on December 3, 1580. Unlike most sons of humble parents, he enrolled not as a poor sizar paying his way by doing menial chores and reading the Scriptures aloud at meal times, but as a pensioner—i.e., as one who could afford to pay *pensio,* or rent, for his lodgings and similar charges. The record of Brewster's university career consists of these two meager facts —the date of his matriculation, and his status. But the influences brought to bear upon him here are plain enough, for Cambridge opened a whole new world to the country boy from the Ryton.

Founded as theological seminaries, the colleges here and at Oxford were still monastic in regimen and spirit, as they were to remain almost down to our own day—if indeed they are yet wholly secularized. No one could become a fellow of a college and offer instruction unless he had taken holy orders. The entire curriculum had a religious cast, for the primary function of the universities was to provide the realm, particularly the rural parishes, with clergymen tolerably well rehearsed in administering the sacred rites, conducting the Sunday services with decorum, and defending whatever credo happened at the moment to be official.

But if theological in character, the universities were far from being models of simple piety. The *mores* of the time were not those of a later day, least of all among the clergy, and the colleges reflected this. Those at Cambridge were denounced by more than one contemporary critic as the "haunts of drones, the abodes of sloth and luxury, monasteries whose inmates yawn and snore, . . . leading their lives in vanity, folly, and idleness." And even friends of the university had to agree in part. The celebrated English physician, Dr. John Caius, founder and master of the college that still bears his name, had frequent cause to lament his students' passionate and apparently exclusive devotion to cards, dice, drink, gay apparel, and the strumpets of the town.

But under the surface, breaking through here and there to disturb conventional patterns, a spirit of revolt was seething. The heady wines of the Renaissance, the revolutionary doctrines of the Reformation, had everywhere quickened men's minds and hearts. Traditional attitudes and beliefs in all fields were ever more sharply challenged. As the light of open-minded inquiry was turned upon one hoary dogma after another, upon the whole musty mass of prejudice and superstition inherited from the Dark Ages, a refreshing breeze of skepticism began to stir even in the universities, always the jealous guardians of tradition. Soon the winds of controversy were whistling around academic cloisters, to the mounting distress of those who wished only to follow familiar routines, resentful at being disturbed in their quiet meditations and slumbers.

The storm first broke in the church with loud and increasingly insistent demands for reform. Even some of the orthodox were disposed to grant that religious affairs might be somewhat better ordered, that no harm would be done the church by some change in its doctrines, its rituals, and its form of organization. But what was "divine trueth" here, and what was "divillish errour," was not at all clear.

Before Henry VIII's break with Rome it had been easy enough to know right from wrong in these always somewhat esoteric matters. The truth—and there was no other—was precisely what the Pope pronounced it to be *ex cathedra,* one of the Vatican's more ancient pretensions though never explicitly formulated until 1870 when the doctrine of papal infallibility was proclaimed to a world perhaps somewhat less astonished than amused.

The Holy See and the English Crown had finally split on Henry VIII's inflexible resolve to divorce Catherine of Aragon and marry Anne Boleyn. But this was the occasion rather than the cause of the conflict, for the quarrel had long been smoldering. Politics rather than religion were involved, and for a time after the break there were no great doctrinal disputes. The English church, as envisaged by Henry, was to be a "purified" Catholic church, and it soon became quite apparent that purification was largely to consist of retaining within the kingdom the enormous ecclesiastical revenues that formerly had poured into the bottom-less coffers at Rome. Englishmen were to hold fast to their tradi-tional beliefs. They were to have no traffic with the rank heresies that had sprouted so luxuriantly since 1517 when "that stubborn monk," Martin Luther, had propounded his ninety-five theses in bold attack upon the established religious order.

After all, why should Englishmen have anything to do with such nonsense? Had not Henry himself exploded Luther's theses in his *Golden Book* published four years later, exposing his "damn-able and pestiferous" errors for what they were? Had not the Pope in gratitude bestowed upon him his proudest title, "Defender of the Faith," which is still emblazoned, ironically enough, upon the arms of the Crown? What if he—Henry!—had now been excom-municated as a heretic? It was ridiculous, of course, as anyone could see. The Pope was the heretic. It was he who had violated the ancient precepts of the Christian faith with his boundless pretensions and endless political intrigues. As simple duty required, Henry was prepared to live up to his proud title by defending that ancient faith against all who would defile it or subvert it, whether the Pope or any other. Henry was not a Protestant and did not propose to become one. Nor would he tolerate any in his kingdom. He looked with a jaundiced eye upon all reformers but those shrewd enough to see what few adjustments had to be made to strengthen him in his new and precarious position as Holy Father of his own church.

In 1539, after some delay, the shape of the new order of things was sketched in the Six Articles, "the whip with the six strings." The confessional was to be retained. So, too, were private masses. Priests were not to marry. Vows of chastity were eternal. Communion in both kinds was not obligatory. Lastly, as the very touchstone of orthodoxy, all had to believe, or at least profess to believe, in the doctrine of transubstantiation, an awful and ineffable mystery, the survival of a primitive blood rite. Under the proper auspices, wine and wafers became the blood and flesh of the Savior—not in any symbolic sense, but quite literally, for there was no heresy more "abhominable" than to hold the former view and men paid with their lives for espousing it.

Only two changes were countenanced by Henry. The worship of "idols" was forbidden, and images and shrines were systematically destroyed throughout the realm, always with an eye on the gold, silver, and precious jewels they contained which might go to swell the royal treasury. More important, every church was to install a Bible for public use. And it was not to be in Latin, but in English—a revolutionary innovation with consequences that have come thundering down the ages. For the first time Englishmen could examine Holy Writ for themselves and come to their own conclusions about it without benefit of clergy. Here was born the right to freedom of conscience, to independence of judgment, which the Pilgrims later so vehemently demanded, if not for all, at least for themselves.

Those in power quickly sensed the danger and cautioned that

the Bible was not to be read at mass, "nor afterwards for purposes
of discussion." Time and again Henry's bishops warned the devout
"against all crowding to read, or commenting on what is read."
Quite as if the tie with Rome had not been broken, the King
summed up the religious duties of his subjects in the command
that they were to go on "observing the holy bread and water,
creeping to the Cross, setting up of lights before the Corpus Christi,
bearing of candles, and the rest." Sir Thomas More and others of
distinction lost their heads, scores of humbler people were hanged
or burned, hundreds were thrown into filthy dungeons for refusing
to bend to the royal will in these and related matters.

At the same time Henry moved swiftly in another direction,
dissolving the monasteries and confiscating their huge estates, retaining some of the lands for the Crown, judiciously distributing
others among the nobility to quiet any objections from that quarter. A color of patriotism was lent these violent proceedings by
a not unreasonable doubt about the loyalty of the monastic orders.
These vast international brotherhoods owed allegiance only to
Rome and were directly governed from there. The monks in the
kingdom were justifiably regarded as agents of a hostile foreign
power, a sort of Fifth Column, for the Pope was a powerful temporal prince busily engaged at the moment in trying to persuade
neighboring Catholic monarchs to undertake a holy crusade against
"infidel" England. As an excommunicant, Henry was an outlaw,
in theory at least, and the Pope had formally released Englishmen
from their obedience to him. As the country was still largely
Roman in sympathy and belief, as it was to remain for almost
a half century, until the defeat of the Spanish Armada in 1588,
the situation had its grave and obvious dangers. Already there had
been two serious uprisings, one known as the Pilgrimage of Grace,
and in 1536 troops had marched through Scrooby on their way to
suppress it.

The church first began to assume a Protestant aspect under
Henry's sickly son, Edward VI, who came to the throne in 1546
as a boy of nine, with the powerful Duke of Somerset as Pro-

tector. Not allergic to new ideas, Somerset repealed the Six Articles. The first *Book of Common Prayer* appeared in 1549, largely the work of Thomas Cranmer, soon to be martyred, and a first step toward shaping a Protestant service was taken in 1552 with the publication of the Edwardian *Service Book*. But the course of reform abruptly halted a year later with the death of Edward, who was succeeded by his equally sickly half-sister, Mary, daughter of Henry and Catherine of Aragon.

A fervent and bigoted Catholic, Mary was determined to avenge the wrongs done her and her mother, as much to please God as herself. Again the Pope was recognized as the spiritual and temporal overlord of Europe. The Roman rite was reinstituted throughout the kingdom. Hundreds of Protestants—men, women, and children—were hanged or burned, fifty-four in Kent alone. Even the dead were dug up, solemnly placed on trial, convicted of heresy, and burned at the stake, together with their writings. Many Protestant leaders fled to the Continent, taking refuge in the Calvinist and Lutheran centers at Geneva, Basle, Frankfurt, and Strasbourg, where they imbibed far more radical doctrine than any yet heard in England. But their day of exile was short, for Mary died in agony in the fourth year of her reign, wasted by inherited disease, her dark mind clouded by fear that God had forsaken her for her sins. Just what these were she was not so sure, but she suspected that the chief was her failure to send more men, women, and children to the stake or gallows.

Under Queen Elizabeth, Anne Boleyn's spirited daughter, the reaction was as violent. Once more England broke with Rome and proscribed its rites. But in all else the Queen pursued a wary course from the start. On the one hand, she had reason to fear the Papists in the realm. The Pope was tiresomely denouncing her as a bastard with no legitimate claim to the throne, zealously forwarding by intrigue at every Catholic court in Europe the rival claims of Mary Queen of Scots, then also Queen of France. Jealous neighboring monarchs were only too willing to bend an ear to schemes of conquest thinly disguised as a crusade to restore "Christianity" in the only Protestant country in Europe. On the other hand, Elizabeth disliked the more ardent reformers, especially the radicals of the Calvinist school, fearing that they might provoke such civil war as had devastated the German states during the Peasants' War, which had burned itself out at last about thirty years before.

That war, to the alarm of every crowned head in Europe, had starkly revealed that the religious conflict was merely one aspect of a profound crisis—social, political, and economic—generated by the slow disintegration of the old feudal order. The institutional remains of that once pervasive order—its tight caste system, its elaborate and cumbersome hierarchy of authority, its monopolistic system of land ownership, its cramping restrictions on trade and manufacture, its antiquated fiscal methods, its frank contempt for the opinions and interests of the "lower orders"—all these and other crusty relics of the past were choking the growth of vigorous new groups pushing up in the social structure. Critics of the Church soon had pointed questions to ask also of the State. The assertion of the right to independence of judgment in one field led logically to its assertion in others.

If all men were equal before God, why not before the law? Could there be any true Christian brotherhood so long as a few enjoyed all of the good things of life through accident of birth while the many toiled laboriously from a half-starved cradle to a pauper's grave? In protest against manifest injustices, some of the religious radicals turned toward the equalitarianism and primitive communism of the early Christian church. This movement had gained considerable strength during the Peasants' War under the leadership of the Anabaptists, a name that quickly became anathema to those in authority everywhere. It was a period of great stress and strain throughout Europe. England was strewn with potentially explosive material, as Elizabeth was well aware, an obvious fact that escaped her Stuart successors and toppled them from the throne.

To maintain a delicate balance between implacably hostile forces, the Queen adopted the masterful policy of having no policy at all, now favoring one side, now the other, skillfully playing them against each other to keep both within bounds. She never came to a decision if she could possibly avoid it. When finally cornered, she always chose ground from which she could beat a hasty retreat. Elizabeth was the despair of her ministers, even of the great Lord Burghley, who usually favored her strategy, but her genius for procrastination saved both herself and the nation.

This strategy was reflected in religious affairs, which were further complicated by the Queen's divided mind about the main questions at issue. Unlike James I, her successor, who fancied himself as a theologue, she was simply not interested in abstractions of doctrine and dogma. So far as Protestantism was an assertion of national independence, she favored it. But she was certainly not pious and loathed solemn moralists, possessing in large measure the love of pomp and show, the wit and gaiety, the high animal spirits of the lusty age to which she gave her name. She openly dallied with one lover after another, had a taste for beer and "strong waters," swore like a trooper on occasion, and delighted in telling bawdy stories that left hardened men of the world gasping. So far as conventional religious observances were concerned, she conscientiously performed those that were expected of her, personally preferring the Roman Mass to the simpler Protestant service. She scandalized many by furnishing the royal chapel with rich gold plate, a massive crucifix, and two huge gilded candelabra with lighted tapers. As several foreign visitors noted, the royal service differed from the Roman only in this:—it was conducted in English, and the psalms were sung not to the organ merely, but to the blasts of cornets and trumpets and the heavy grunt of the sackbut, the Queen's one and somewhat singular contribution to the cause of reform.[5]

Pursuing her devious course, Elizabeth deposed many of the bishops whom she found in office. To offset any papal leanings among the others, she mitred some of the less radical Protestant leaders who had fled across the Channel in Mary's time. She quickly swung back again by ordering a revision of the Edwardian or Protestant *Service Book,* restoring the "Black Rubric," as kneeling at communion was termed by extreme anti-Papists. She then

intervened in the controversy raging about clerical vestments, the
hated "rags of Rome," temporarily silencing dispute by enforcing
a compromise. Only at communion was the cope to be worn.
Sunday services were to be conducted "in a comely surplice, with
sleeves." As a sop to the Protestants, priests were not to wear
"hattes but in their journeinge."

As Church and State were one, Elizabeth demanded absolute
uniformity of belief. No one could preach without a license. Above
all, there was to be no unlicensed printing, for that would be sure
to breed God knows what "seditious and hellish errours." Machinery to enforce uniformity already existed in the Court of High
Commission, a counterpart of the Court of the Holy Inquisition.
Dominated by the bishops, it shared the latter's supreme faith in
the stake and gallows as the surest means of spiritual conversion.

Though a relatively mild man of moderate views, Matthew
Parker, Archbishop of Canterbury, had two dissidents burned alive
in 1575. Hundreds of others were locked up in frightful dungeons
throughout the land at the order of the bishops. The latters'
authority was based not upon statutory law but the limitless royal
prerogative. They could summon and examine anyone at all, and
could and did condemn suspects upon no other evidence than
their own frightened and confused replies. If suspects hesitated to
answer from fear of incriminating themselves, punishment was
even more certain. The kingdom's vile and stinking prisons, incredible sinkholes of disease and vice, were filled with innocent
people lying helplessly awaiting the bishops' pleasure or displeasure, with no recourse whatever at law. The writ of habeas
corpus had yet to be devised to curb such arbitrary power and its
always arbitrary use.

"All power corrupts," a great historian once observed, "and
absolute power corrupts absolutely."

But do what they would or could, Elizabeth and her bishops
failed to silence the champions of the essentially democratic new
order of things being born from the womb of the old so painfully,
as new orders always are.

3

SEEDS OF
GRACE AND
VERTUE

... forsake & denie all ungodliness and
wicked fellowship...
—ROBERT BROWNE

AT CAMBRIDGE YOUNG BREWSTER FOUND HIMSELF AT THE VERY
center of the conflict. In spite of his youth he followed it with
some attention, it appears, early embracing the rebel cause, for it
was here, in Bradford's phrase, that he was "first seasoned with ye
seeds of grace and vertue."

On one side, a determined foe of all reform, stood the master of
his college, Dr. Andrew Perne, possessed of an elasticity of conscience seldom found outside academic circles. First a Catholic,
he had become a Protestant under Edward VI, reverted to Catholicism under Mary, and frantically embraced Protestantism again

under Elizabeth, thus managing to hold his mastership of Peter-house, which he ruled with a firm high hand. It was he who in Mary's reign had officiated at the trial and burning of the corpses of two long-buried Protestants, both men of mild views. Many of his students scorned Perne as the "old Turner," and certainly Brewster was among them. But the master of Peterhouse lived and died a power in the church, the intimate friend and adviser of John Whitgift, once a fellow of the college, now well on his way to becoming archbishop of Canterbury.

But there were many at Cambridge, both among the fellows and the students of the colleges, who were disturbed by the state of the church. True radicals in seeking the root of things, they dug into Scripture to discover just where "disorder" had first crept in. The more they dug and explored, the less warrant could they find for a great deal of current belief and observance. The originally simple Christian faith had been corrupted, they declared, by time and "human invention." The obvious need of the hour was to restore it to its "ancient purity"—or, as the Pilgrims later phrased it, "to its primitive órder, libertie, & bewtie." Such views upset the orthodox, and in 1565 Archbishop Parker denounced those who advanced them as "these precise men." The phrase was graphic and seemed to fit, and the reformers were soon known as the Precisians, somewhat later as the Puritans—so named, it should be observed, not for their moral code but for their theological doctrine.

The discontented had many telling points to make against the church. They particularly objected to the great host of "dumb" ministers who seldom or never preached. A sermon once a quarter or even once a month was not enough. Ministers should preach every Sunday, and "not to please the ears but move the heart." Pluralism had nominally been abolished by Henry VIII, but many clerics still held scores of pulpits and church livings, appearing only to collect their stipends. Country parishes frequently went for years without religious services of any kind. Those who en-joyed multiple livings defended themselves by arguing that there were insufficient educated men to go around, sneeringly asking critics if they would place cobblers and tailors in the pulpit.

"Yea!" came the sharp reply, "a great deale better were it so to do than place popishe Priestes, the devourers of Christe's Lambes. For their priest crafte is the wickedest occupation that ever was in the world, and the most craftie."

Under the circumstances it was no wonder that the English church was "a pache of popery, and a pudle of corruption." Was not the sign of the cross, hated as part of the Roman rite, still made over infants at baptism? Were not dispensations openly sold to those who could afford them? To dispense with publication of banns before marriage cost 10s. Eating flesh on fast days came higher at 40s. And did not the church still operate to its immense profit that elaborate fee and fine system known as the Indulgences, a primary cause of Luther's revolt and still a noisome scandal in the Roman church? Who dared deny that the higher clergy were brazenly making "merchandise of the Church of God?" They not only bestowed scores of benefices upon themselves and resided in none, but many were alienating their lands, wasting their woods, and disposing of ecclesiastical rights and revenues quite as if these were their personal property, with the result, as even the biographer of Archbishop Parker had to confess, that "the churchs ran greatly to decays, were kept filthy and nasty, and undecent for God's worship."

Even more devout churchmen were engaged in this nefarious traffic. Late in 1575, not long after he had commissioned the older Brewster as bailiff at Scrooby, Archbishop Grindal of York became archbishop of Canterbury and was succeeded by Edwin Sandys, a familiar name in Pilgrim annals. Sandys befriended the Brewsters and almost a half century later his sons performed several signal services for the Pilgrims. In 1582, while young Brewster was at Cambridge, Queen Elizabeth virtually commanded Sandys to grant her a long lease to Scrooby manor, desiring to make it a royal hunting lodge. If she had had her way, the Brewsters would have been evicted and there might have been no Pilgrim church; at least, its history would have been very different. But Elizabeth was balked when Sandys entered a moving plea of poverty. He was an old man, he said, and as he had labored long in the vineyard with no stain upon his conscience, the Queen should not now ask him to consent "to the ruine and spoil of this poor bishopric." Besides, he declared in a shrewd thrust that gave Elizabeth pause, the Papists would throw it in her teeth, "to the scandal of the Gospel."

It was a noble plea and it might still be moving had not Sandys hastened, as the Dean of York Cathedral complained, to distribute leases wholesale among the members of his family, granting each of his six sons large blocks of church property upon the most profitable terms. Scrooby manor fell to his second son, the later Sir Samuel, and to this day it remains in the hands of his heirs and assigns. When the Dean continued to protest, the Archibshop put on an air of injured innocence and professed his inability to understand what all the shouting was about. One would have thought, he said, that the Dean had been personally cheated. In any case, said Sandys, airily dismissing the subject, "I am bound in conscience to take care of my family"—and he did, cost the poor bishopric what it might.

Elizabeth's bishops were, by and large, a worldly and avaricious lot. Several were just plain rascals and had to be unseated for brazenly looting the parishes in their charge. The grossly sensual lives of others created scandal at a time when a Gargantuan love of the fleshpots, even among the clergy, scarcely caused comment. All lived in the greatest magnificence and luxury. On their travels the archbishops of Canterbury were accompanied with a great troop of white horse and hundreds of flunkeys in scarlet livery set off with gold chains and gold braid.

And such were the prelates who, to clothe their worldly pride and arrogance, clung so passionately to the "rags of Rome!", exclaimed the reformers with disgust. Churchmen, they said, should be distinguished "by their doctrines, not their garments; their conversation, not their dress; their purity of mind, not their adornment of person."

The Puritan animus against "gay apparel" originated here in

this dispute about clerical vestments. Anyone bedecked in silks and flounces must be as "antichristian" as a bishop. There were many at the time who belittled this controversy as trivial and illiberal on the Puritans' part. Many have since joined them in charging the latter with a "peevish forwardness and a zeal for discord." This is, at best, a very superficial view. At worst, it is the kind of special pleading employed at all times and all places by defenders of the status quo. The latter are always for peace and harmony and unity—but strictly on their own terms, of course. They have no use for "agitators" given to asking embarrassing questions, and are savage in their attack upon any and all not content to let well enough alone.

If clerical vestments were of no importance, as traditionalists pretended in this instance, why did they fight so fiercely to retain them? It was because they quite realistically appreciated their inestimable value as symbols, and the Puritans can hardly be blamed for likewise appraising them as just that—the flaunting banners of the old order. As the Pilgrims later declared, all this "popish & antichristian stuffe" merely encouraged the Papists "to hope againe for a day."

The reformers found increasing support throughout the realm, even in the most exalted circles. The Queen's ruling favorite, the highly decorative Earl of Leicester, was an avowed Puritan, as were the poets Spenser and Sir Philip Sidney, both with influence at Court. The great Lord Burghley, treasurer and virtually the prime minister of the land, more than once publicly urged a "reduction of the church to its former puritie" in spite of the Queen's jibes at him and "his brothers in Christ." Nothing ever said by the Puritans, even the most extreme, quite matched the vehement denunciation of the "abuses" uttered here at Cambridge in 1578 in a remarkable sermon by a distinguished and devout churchman, Dr. Laurence Chaderton, one of the inspired scholar-poets who later gave us the magnificent King James Version of the Bible.

The church was, he declared, mincing no words, "a huge masse of old and stinkinge workes, of conjuring, witchcraft, sorcery, charming, blaspheming the holy name of God, swearing and for-swearing, profaning of the Lord's Sabbothe, disobediance to supe-riours, contempt of inferiours; murther, Manslaughter, robberies, adulterye, Fornication, covenant-breaking, false witness-bearing, lieing . . ." It was filled with arrogant hypocrites and renegades. There was everywhere a crying need for honest and zealous pas-tors "to admonish, correct, suspende, and excommunicate such noysome, hurtfull, & monstruous beastes out of the house of God, without respect of persons."*

In their franker moments even some of the bishops agreed, but they always had some excuse to postpone action. Now was not the time for reform—and "now" never came. Besides, it would be necessary to retain certain "harmless" beliefs and ceremonies if "ye weake & ignorante" were not to be lost to the Lord. And there could be no question, of course, of touching the revenues of the higher clergy.

"When they that serve God's altar shall be exposed to poverty," growled Archbishop Whitgift in an aspersion on the early church and Christ himself, "then religion shall be exposed to scorn and become contemptible."

All in all, critics made little impression upon the "antichristian prelates" who more and more insistently demanded that all strictly conform and hold their tongues. Under increasing pressure many of the Puritans, especially those who were more comfortably situ-ated in life, began to give way and resign themselves to at least a nominal conformity, fearing to jeopardize their personal safety, their bread and butter, even their creature comforts. But those of greater faith and courage were determined to go on. If there was no place for them in the church, they would withdraw and estab-lish one of their own in which they might worship as they pleased. Come what might, they would defy the bishops, even the Queen, although from the first they protested their absolute loyalty to Elizabeth, declaring with some truth that they were far better

* Brewster thought so well of this sermon that he republished it at Leyden in later years.

subjects than most of those who prosecuted and persecuted them in her name.

Just before Brewster's arrival in Cambridge a great stir had been raised in the town by Robert Browne, a man of thirty at this time, a graduate of Corpus Christi College. The most creative religious thinker of his day, he was to exert a profound influence upon Brewster and all the Pilgrim leaders. He soon abandoned his advanced principles and rejoined the church, creeping "back into Egypt to live off the spoils of it," as a Pilgrim leader declared in rather lightly dismissing him as "a man of insinuating manners, but very unsteady in his views of men and things." Certainly, his was an always restless mind and its volatility in later years more than suggests mental derangement. But his leadership, however brief, laid the solid foundation upon which others were to build. So pervasive was his influence that all of the religious radicals, regardless of creed, were soon known as Brownists.

Returning to Cambridge in 1578 after an absence of six years, Browne created such a storm with his "forward" sermons that two years later he was forced to retire to Norwich, one of the most active Puritan centers. There he was soon jailed, on the complaint of the local bishop, for holding private meetings "of the vulgar sort of people . . . to the number of one hundred at a time." Appealing to Lord Burghley, a distant kinsman, Browne obtained his release, only to be jailed again by the bishop. Once more Burghley released him, again the bishop jailed him, whereupon "Troublechurch" Browne and his company seized the first opportunity to flee to Holland, blazing a trail that many were to follow. The exiles settled down at Middelburg, where in 1582 Browne published two works of the greatest consequence, *A Treatise of Reformation without Tarying for Anie* and *A Booke which Sheweth the Life and Manner of all True Christians.*

Formulating the basic principles upon which the revolutionary Independent movement took shape, giving clear and ringing expression for the first time to ideas that had been vaguely circulating for some time, Browne rejected Calvin's thesis that reform of the church had to wait until the state took action, a most unrealistic view at a time when Church and State were one. No, said Browne, the kingdom of God was "not to be begun by whole parishes, but rather by the worthiest, were they ever so few." In every parish these should withdraw from the church—secede, separate, as they had warrant to do by Scripture*—and organize themselves under a mutual covenant "to forsake & denie all ungodliness and wicked fellowship, and to refuse all ungodlie communion with Wicked Persons." This concept of a free covenant was borrowed from the execrated German Anabaptists and their descendants, the Dutch Mennonites, whom Browne had known at Norwich, for many of them had come to live there as workers in the woolen trade.

Every congregation so organized would select its own pastor and officers in a democratic manner, with all communicants having a vote. If other groups choose to follow, the several congregations were to remain quite independent. They might cooperate in a purely voluntary fellowship, but there were to be no bishops, no archbishops, no central organization or authority of any kind. There was no warrant for such things in the Bible. One could search the Holy Book from cover to cover without discovering anything remotely resembling the hierarchical structure of the Anglican church. Where in the Scripture, they asked, did one find rectors, vicars, rural deans, chaplains, chancellors, archdeacons, prebendaries, or bishops? One looked in vain, for these were "human inventions." The only "lawfull" form of the church was simplicity itself, said Browne, triumphantly pointing to I Corinthians 12.28:

> And God hath ordeined some in the Church: as first Apostles, secondly Prophets, thirdly teachers, then them that doe miracles; after them, the giftes of healing, helpers (deacons), gouvernours (elders), diversitie of tongues.†

* Paul: "Come out from among them, and be ye separate, saith the Lord, and touch not the unclean thing."
† So the verse reads in the Geneva or "Breeches" Bible of 1560, which was used by the Pilgrims and all of the Separatists. The passage appears in almost identical form in the King James Version of 1611 and the Revised Version of 1881.

For a more detailed description of their duties, the Brownists cited I Timothy 5. 17, and Romans 12. 6-8. But in elaborating their "Holy Discipline" they relied above all upon the unauthorized marginal notes—"human inventions" indeed!—that appeared beside these verses in the Geneva Bible.

The Holy Discipline was well named, being only for the holy, only for those who led unblemished lives. Browne refused to accept Calvin's doctrine that the "true" church should embrace the entire baptized population. He objected to such a sweeping inclusion of communicants "without regard to personal character." His was to be a "priesthood of believers," a church of "saincts," from which the irreligious were to be excluded, whether baptized or not. And the lives of the Saints, naturally, were to be subject to the closest scrutiny and to continuous review, for every act and word, and even every thought, weighed in the balance. Sharp and constant criticism both of oneself and others was enjoined as a positive religious duty. From this sprang that sometimes fruitful searching of soul and that often mean-spirited prying into the most intimate details of one another's lives which marked the Separatist churches without exception and caused almost all to founder—even Browne's, which was shattered within two years by bitter recriminations and dissensions. Returning to England, Browne made his peace with the bishops and blasted the Brownists, being rewarded with the rectorship at Achurch cum Thorpe, Northamptonshire. From 1591 to 1633, despised by Separatists and Puritans alike, he administered his office quite as if he had never denounced it as a "corruption."[1]

But Browne had planted seeds that were to sprout and flourish, and Cambridge in young Brewster's day was a principal seed bed. Many future martyrs were his contemporaries there, and several of them he must certainly have known at this time—notably, John Penry, his classmate at Peterhouse. Curiously, Penry and Brewster had entered Peterhouse on the same day and as the college was small, having not many more than a hundred students, their mutual interests may well have brought them together. In any case, Penry's later career was well known to Brewster, for many men played an intimate part in the lives of both. At this time Brewster may also have known Penry's friend, John Greenwood, a student at Corpus Christi, who, like Penry, was destined for the gallows.

At Trinity was John Udall—condemned to death in 1588, dying in prison four years later—one of whose "seditious" works Brewster republished thirty years later at Leyden. One of the fellows at Christ's was William Perkins, an eloquent preacher of the "forward" school, author of a catechism later used by the Pilgrims. Brewster especially had a high regard for him, reprinting a volume of his sermons and carrying eleven others with him to Plymouth.

And there was another at Christ's who, if not known to Brewster at this time, was to be closely associated with him some years later when their widely divergent paths met and joined for a time in Holland—to the profound regret of both. This was Francis Johnson, son of the mayor of Richmond, Yorkshire. He and his brother George, also at Christ's, were to bring scandal and shame upon a congregation with whom the Pilgrims worshiped for more than a year—a painful episode so disgraceful, so damaging to the entire Separatist cause, that the Pilgrims simply dropped it from their annals, and their sojourn at Amsterdam with the scandalous Ancient Brethren has remained a suppressed chapter in their history.

In his wanderings about Cambridge young Brewster may have glimpsed among the undergraduates the great "Kit" Marlowe, two years his senior, the passionate and precocious son of a Canterbury shoemaker, who would win immortality a few years later, when scarcely out of his teens, with two scintillating works of genius, *Tamburlaine the Great* (1587) and *Dr. Faustus* (1588). Like John Greenwood, his contemporary at Corpus Christi, Marlowe leaned toward heresy and was viciously assailed in later years for his "atheisticall" opinions, which probably reflected the mystic

views of Francis Kett, a fellow of the college, who was sent to
the stake.

And from a respectful distance, for their worlds lay poles apart,
Brewster may have noted a tall and handsome boy of his own age,
a student at Trinity, Robert Devereux, already Earl of Essex, in
whose veins coursed the blood of the noblest families in the realm.
As precocious in his way as Marlowe, Essex became, in 1587,
when not yet twenty, the lover of the Queen, then fifty-three—
the start of a meteoric career that carried him to a dazzling emi-
nence within a decade and almost overnight plunged him headlong to the executioner's block, a victim of his own incorrigible
addiction to feudal chivalry and romance. Brewster followed his
exploits with some attention, it appears, for one of the few contemporary historical works to find a place on the shelves of his
library at Plymouth was an account of the foolhardy Essex Rebellion as subtly garbled for official purposes by Lord Francis
Bacon, the moral philosopher, in a cool betrayal of the Earl, his
former patron and always loyal friend.

Brewster's interest in Essex and his tragic entanglement in court
intrigue may have come from remembering him at Cambridge.
More probably it had another inspiration, for Brewster had been
at the university only a few years when he himself was suddenly
translated to the glamorous world of London and to the still more
glamorous world of the Court—something that he can scarcely
have dreamed of in his wildest flights of fancy as a boy along
the Ryton. To whom he owed this promising turn of fortune
is not known, but it probably represents another of the many
services rendered the Brewsters by Archbishop Sandys and his
family. However arranged, late in 1582 or early in 1583, having
"attained some learning, viz. ye knowledge of ye Latine tongue,
& some insight in ye Greeke," Brewster left the university without taking a degree to enter the service of "that religious and
godly gentleman," Sir William Davison, one of Elizabeth's most
adroit and trusted diplomats. If Brewster's thoughts on his ride
up to Cambridge three years before had been exciting, they were

pale indeed beside the rainbow hopes that now possessed him as he rode up, an eager youth of seventeen, to the great city of London.

Although its population did not exceed 150,000, London was in truth a great city, even more the heart and brain of the kingdom than the modern metropolis sixty times its size. Here the contrasts and perplexing contradictions of Elizabethan England were at their sharpest—its extreme sensitivity to the slightest and most delicate movements of the human heart and mind, existing side by side with the most callous brutality and a delight in simply fiendish cruelty to man and beast alike; its high loyalties and despicable treacheries, often cradled in the same stout breast; its asceticism and love of the fleshpots; its intellectual clarity and gross superstitions; its equal applause of Shakespeare and the hangman in publicly drawing and quartering some poor wretch caught stealing a few pence; its artful and often exquisite splendor flowering in the midst of stupefying poverty and of simply nauseous filth, even at Court. The most resplendent lords and ladies crawled with vermin and performed their natural functions like barnyard fowl. Plague and the pox, both great and small, were endemic. Cities forbade the killing of kites and crows because they performed what little scavenging was done. There were no public sanitation facilities of any kind. Almost a century later Samuel Pepys could still complain, not of the fact, but of the casual manner in which William Penn's father, the testy old admiral, tossed the most stinking slops out his window to the peril of the latest finery that Pepys had donned with the hope of impressing the amiable but reluctant barmaid at *The Swan*.

Young Brewster, according to a misconception fostered by the Pilgrims and most of their historians, served Davison as his secretary. This is quite improbable, for he wanted the years, the training, the practical knowledge, and—above all—the social position for such a post, one traditionally reserved for sons of the gentry and nobility. Rather, his duties probably combined those of valet and confidential messenger, and in these he proved himself so faithful and discreet that his master "trusted him above all others that were aboute him," employing him on the most secret missions. Sir William, an avowed Puritan, quickly noted the youth's "wisdom & godliness," often drawing him aside to talk with him in private, altogether treating him much more like "a sonne than a servante."

From his humble post Brewster can have seen only the outermost fringes of life at Court. But he must have glimpsed many of the great figures of the day and learned much about them from conversations with his master and from gossip in the servants' hall. Davison no doubt spoke often of the powerful Lord Burghley, though young Brewster's fancy was perhaps more taken with that bold and swaggering Captain of the Guard whose post was always just outside his mistress' door—Sir Walter Raleigh, whose rise from rather humble origin had been so spectacular. An even bolder and fiercer spirit, Sir Francis Drake, had just come in on the *Pelican* after circling the globe and harrying the Spanish on the Seven Seas.

And there was, of course, that quintessence of Elizabethan England, the embodiment of all its qualities, a faithful mirror of its every mood—the Queen herself. Winsome as a girl, handsome as a younger woman, Elizabeth was now fifty, tall and rather gaunt, at once a formidable and fantastic creature as she swept through the great rooms at Whitehall in her stiff brocades and elaborate finery, her long white face set off with a black stubble of teeth and a hoodlike mass of brilliantly-dyed red hair. And through this lordly company—and as powerful as any—strode the Queen's "little black husband," Archbishop John Whitgift of Canterbury, a choleric bigot, who had recently succeeded the Brewsters' former patron at Scrooby, Edmund Grindal, immortalized as the "gentle Algrind" in Spenser's *Faerie Queene*. There was nothing gentle about Whitgift. Once a reformer himself, he was now vindictively and relentlessly pursuing his friends of earlier years, having no patience whatever with the rather conciliatory policy of his predecessors, seizing every opportunity to show his utter contempt for the "common sort of persons, particularly those that read the Bible." As Whitgift had been a fellow at

Peterhouse, one of the ineffable Dr. Perne's cronies, Brewster doubtless remarked him at this time and certainly had cause to remember him in later years when the iron hand of the "old Beelzebub of Canterbury" lay heavy upon the Pilgrims and all of the Separatists.

Across the Channel a menacing storm was gathering, one that became steadily more threatening until the air was cleared with the thundering defeat of the Spanish Armada four years later. In 1585, with the fall of Antwerp, Elizabeth decided to extend at least a gesture of aid to the Dutch Protestants so stoutly defending themselves against the armies of Spain, the sword of the Holy Inquisition. Some 6,000 English troops were dispatched to the Low Countries under the Earl of Leicester, with young Essex as General of the Horse. Brewster, too, shipped for Holland when the Queen, always a hard and shrewd bargainer, sent Sir William Davison to demand security for moneys advanced to the Dutch. The latter offered two towns and a castle as collateral, and in token of this handed over the keys to the gates of Flushing. These in turn were passed on to Brewster, who, so he liked to relate the story in later years, "kepte them under his pilow on which he slepte ye first night." About a year later, upon the completion of his mission, the Dutch presented Davison with a great gold chain. This, too, was entrusted to Brewster, and upon landing in England his master allowed him to wear it as the party rode in brilliant cavalcade up to London and through its streets to White-hall. Brewster shared in the triumph and in a sense was himself promoted when Elizabeth rewarded her always adept envoy by appointing him a principal Secretary of State, charged with the conduct of foreign affairs.

This colorful life of travel and adventure might have long continued, and the exciting whirl of it might have carried Brewster away to quite another destiny if Davison had not fallen victim to a necessity of State. Through messages decoded by one Thomas Phillipes, better known as "Morice, the Decipherer," Mary Queen of Scots was trapped in a conspiracy to assassinate Elizabeth by the hand of an English Catholic, and on a charge of treason was condemned to die. Her death warrant was signed by Davison, who was well aware of his royal mistress' unspoken desires. But Elizabeth, anxious to absolve herself from blame for the execution of her cousin, made Davison the scapegoat of the affair, pretending that he had exceeded his authority in signing the warrant without her express order. Tried for misprision and contempt in 1587, he was heavily fined and committed to the Tower of London for two years. Brewster loyally remained with him and tended his needs, performing "manie faithfull offices of servise in ye time of his troubles."

His master in disgrace, his own career in the great world at an end, Brewster left London in 1589 and returned to the sleepy hamlet of Scrooby. Now in his early twenties and with his father ailing, he took upon himself many of the latter's responsibilities as postmaster and bailiff-receiver of the manor, succeeding to both offices upon his father's death a year later. Court intrigue almost deprived him of the profitable postmastership, which was actually sold to another but soon restored to him through the good offices of Davison, always a loyal friend and patron. With an ample income thus assured, Brewster soon married, late in 1591 or early the next year. Though a woman of great courage and strength of character, as is evident from the wide influence she radiated in later years, his wife is a mere shadow occasionally falling across the pages of the day. Almost nothing is known about her. Her name was Mary;[2] she was a year or two younger than her husband, and died at Plymouth many years before him. On August 12, 1593, she bore the first of their children—a son named Jonathan, in due course a Pilgrim Father himself.

With his life at Cambridge and the Court still fresh in mind, recalling his travels and adventures, again shuddering with apprehension at the excitements of his master's trial and the dark days in the Tower, Brewster must have found the hush of life at Scrooby somewhat oppressive and his round of duties rather humdrum. It is obvious that collecting rents, tending his fields, running the local section of the post, and keeping his tavern never completely occupied him. And in want of newspapers—

the first in the kingdom did not appear till a half century later
—how eagerly he must have welcomed the occasional informed
traveler who stopped to spend the night, especially if he came
from London with news of the Court and what was going on
in the world outside. One may have remarked the rapidly rising
star of Essex, who was dashing from triumph to triumph. Another
may have noted after a round of the London theaters that the
great "Kit" Marlowe had a serious new rival in William Shak-
spear, or Shakespur—or something like that.

But other news was more to Brewster's taste, and all of it
was disquieting. Every day there were new prosecutions and persecutions, for the bishops were in a violently angry mood, occasioned
by the appearance of a series of tracts addressed to the "proud,
Popish, presumptuous, profane, paultrie, pestilent, and pernicious
Prelates." The first of these tracts had appeared in 1588, written
by a pretended archbishop who signed himself Martin Mar-prelate.
No one has yet convincingly established the identity of this first
great satirist in the English language whose biting wit and sovereign scorn of the Lords Spiritual soon had all England by the
ears. No pamphlets were ever more eagerly snatched up and
avidly read, and none ever caused a greater uproar. They brought
Puritanism out of the closet into the market place, and stripped
it of its sectarian air. Here was the first inspired literature of the
reform movement, and it struck deep.

The tracts had their immediate origin in a controversy precipitated in 1584 when a Puritan, one William Fulke, published a
short defense of three simple propositions, all of which the Pilgrims later embraced—every congregation had the right to (1)
choose its own pastor and other officers, (2) discipline its own
members, and (3) control all actions of its officers by approving
or rejecting their decisions. To ecclesiastics appointed from above
this was, of course, very disturbing doctrine, and Dean Bridges
of Salisbury took it upon himself to expose its fallacies and silence
forever the champions of such subversive nonsense. His self-
dedication was roundly applauded by churchmen and schoolmen,
for his scholarship was regarded as scarcely inferior to that of the

learned Thomas Bilson, subsequently Bishop of Winchester, who had recently proved so eloquently and with such a multitude of citations that the church had *always* been just what it was. The Anglican bishops had their authority directly from the Apostles and the Holy Ghost—indeed, from Adam, who had governed the church for precisely 930 years, with Seth as his assistant for the last five centuries. Seth had then gone on alone for 112 years, and from him the mantle of authority had descended, through Moses, directly to Archbishop Whitgift.

Dean Bridges hoped to do at least as well as Dr. Bilson, and at last he was ready after almost incredible labors. His reply to Fulke's pointed argument of less than forty pages was a massive quarto volume of 1,500 pages, now remembered only because it brought down upon his addled pate the cool contempt, scathing wit, broad learning, and deep human sympathies of Martin Mar-prelate. Citing chapter and verse in charging them with greed, malice, ignorance, and corruption, he stung the bishops to the quick, to the delight of many; the hierarchy replied with a roar of rage that grew louder as their bailiffs frantically rushed about in a vain effort to discover the author of the tracts and his secret wandering press. Whitgift had the Queen issue a proclamation against such "diffamatorie and fantasticall" writings aimed at promoting reform—or, as she called it, "monstruous & apparaunt Innovation." Complaints were also heard from a strange quarter.

"The Puritans are angry with me," Mar-prelate admitted, hastily adding, "I mean the Puritan preachers. And why? Because I am too open; because I jest."

These preachers had been upset by his wit and broad humor. He had committed the mistake, said one, of making "sin ridiculous, whereas it ought to be made odious." This solemn and pompous view has had its advocates in all ages. Most of the Pilgrims shared it, but Mar-prelate would have none of it. He had chosen his course deliberately, he said, because only thus could he get the great majority of men to read.

"Aye," he exclaimed, "for jesting is lawfull by circumstances, even in the highest matters . . . The Lord being the author both of mirth and gravity, is it not lawfull in itself for the Truth to use either of these ways?"

Already deep in Puritanism and as one who kept abreast of religious controversy to the end of his days, Brewster certainly knew of these tracts and probably read them at this time, for they passed quickly and secretly from hand to hand throughout the realm, particularly among the reformer groups. Undoubtedly he found a new and startling interest in them—an interest of curious significance in later years—when word came that his classmate at Peterhouse, John Penry, had been hanged at St. Thomas Watering, London, as the operator of the wandering Martinist press.[3]

A few months previously, in the spring of 1593, another of Brewster's contemporaries at Cambridge, John Greenwood, had gone to the gallows, together with Henry Barrow, one of the greatest of the early leaders of the Separation. Condemned for "devising and circulating seditious books," they had been granted a reprieve at the insistence of Lord Burghley, who protested that the blood of reformers who were essentially in agreement with the Protestant tenets of the Anglican church should not be the first to flow "in a land where no Papist has been touched for religion by death." But Archbishop Whitgift was "very peremptory" and demanded their immediate execution. Burghley flared up and gave Whitgift and the bishops "some round taxing words," subsequently carrying the matter to Elizabeth. But as no one seconded him in the Privy Council, the Queen's venomous "little black husband" finally had his way with Penry, Greenwood, and Barrow, immediately taking steps to jail hundreds of others.

Determined to crush all resistance, the bishops pushed through a reluctant Parliament the most nefarious act of Elizabeth's reign, aimed at the Brownists and "other Sectaries and disloyal persons." By this act, which was to run only for five years but was successively extended well into the reign of Charles I, any persons who absented themselves from the orthodox service for more than a month, or who attempted in any way to persuade others to do so, or who attended "any unlawful assemblies, conventicles, or meetings under colour or pretence of any Exercise of Religion," were to be imprisoned without bail until they pledged themselves to conform. If submission were not made within three months, they were to quit the realm on pain of death without benefit of clergy. If they ever returned, they were to be summarily executed.

Reporting the passage of this measure, Morice the Decipherer attributed it to the "malice of the Bishops . . . which hath procured them much hatred of the common people," adding details on the execution of Penry and "two of the principal Brownists, Barrowe and Greenwood . . . so as that Sect is in effect extinguished."

But Morice, for all his talents, was not apt at deciphering the future, for this was the beginning, not the end, of the Brownist movement and the Separation.

4

YE LORD'S
FREE PEOPLE

> . . . they would not submitte to their cere-
> monies, & become slaves to them & their
> popish trash, which have no ground in ye
> word of God, but are relikes of that man
> of sin.
>
> —WILLIAM BRADFORD

QUIETLY SETTLING DOWN AT SCROOBY, OBVIOUSLY RESIGNED
to spending the remainder of his life there, Brewster soon won
the friendship and respect of his neighbors and lived in "good
esteeme" among them, "espetially the godly & religious." As the
Pilgrims used the phrase, this meant that he frequented reformist
circles. He did much to forward the cause by his example and
by his tireless efforts in providing the villages round about with
good preachers, persuading others to assist in the work, he himself usually being "deepest in ye charge & sometimes above his
abillitie."

Though a strong and zealous Puritan, Brewster was far from

being sour of mien, solemn in manner, or harsh and intolerant in his views. On the contrary, he was "of a very cherfull spirite, very sociable & pleasante amongst his friends." Unlike so many of his brethren, who were apt to be contentious and stridently opinionated, he was peaceable by nature and soft-spoken, "of an humble and modest mind," given to deprecating his own ability and overrating that of others. Toward the poor and unfortunate he was "tender-harted," with an always open purse to ease their sufferings. Only those offended him who put on airs and carried themselves haughtily when they had nothing to "commend them but a few fine cloaths, or a litle riches more than others." Altogether a wise, discreet, and extraordinarily gentle man, Brewster did more in a year to advance the Christian faith and spread the even broader gospel of simple human kindliness than most men in a lifetime, patiently "doeing ye best he could, and walking according to ye light he saw, till ye Lord reveiled further unto him."

But whether Brewster was short or tall, thin or fat, dark or fair, handsome or ill-favored, will never be known. This is true, unfortunately, of all but one of the Pilgrims. The lone exception is Edward Winslow, many times a governor of Plymouth, who in a moment of vanity once sat for his portrait. For the rest, there is not a line in the records to indicate what the Pilgrims looked like in the flesh, not a word—with a single exception to be noted —about their personal appearance or physical characteristics. Only the soul had substance, so why bother with anything as ephemeral as the lineaments of the flesh? All that mattered was the eternal character, the heavenly essence—alas! so often corrupted and so cruelly tempted in this "vaell of tears."

Among Brewster's earliest allies was Richard Clyfton, the rector at Babworth, a village about six miles to the southeast. A "forward" preacher of the Puritan school, for years the only one in the district, he had been laboring in this unpromising corner of the vineyard since 1586 and exerted considerable influence throughout the countryside, attracting followers from miles around. Early every Sabbath morning and occasionally during the week the Brewsters, William and Mary—and little Jonathan, too, for it was never too early to begin the work of salvation—wound their way down the lane to sit at the feet of the "grave & reverend" Clyfton, a notable and long neglected figure in Pilgrim history. It was he who became the pastor of the original congregation. Enemies in later years pronounced him "a most simple and pietous teacher, . . . weak in the Scriptures, unable to convince his gainsayers, and careless to deliver his doctrine pure, sound, and plain." But this was largely malice, it appears, for Bradford and others testified that his "paines & dilligens" had been a means of converting many.*

And here one first glimpses, as a sickly and somewhat precocious boy, probably the ablest and certainly the most diversely gifted of the Pilgrim Fathers. Born at Austerfield, a hamlet two miles to the north, just across the River Idle in Yorkshire, William Bradford was the son and namesake of a prosperous yeoman who tilled many broad acres of his own, and others leased from the local gentry and the Crown. His wife was Alice Hanson, daughter of an enterprising local shopkeeper and farmer. Shortly after the birth of his son in 1589, the father died. Three years later the widow remarried and sent her young four-year-old to live with his grandfather, another William Bradford. Upon the latter's death in 1596 and his mother's the following year, the boy was taken in hand by his paternal uncles, Robert and Thomas, "who devoted him, like his ancestors, unto the affairs of husbandry."

Suffering an orphan's usual trials, Bradford spent a most unhappy childhood, which doubtless accounts in large part for the "soon and long" sickness that afflicted him in early years. To judge from his abounding health and inexhaustible energies in adult life, his illness was psychological in character, an emotional disturbance, passing away as he grew older. But painful as it was, Bradford came to regard it as a blessing in disguise, for it had kept him, he used to say, "from the vanities of youth." By the age of twelve he was deep in the Scriptures and made the acquaintance

---

* On the front end-papers appears a sketch map of the Scrooby district.

of a youth similarly preoccupied. The latter introduced him to the Puritans in the neighborhood, and every Sabbath the two boys walked eight miles to Babworth, by way of Scrooby, to enjoy Richard Clyfton's "illuminating Ministry," the first step in Bradford's "holy, prayerful, watchful, and fruitful Walk with God, wherein he was very exemplary."

But walking with God had its trials, too. Bradford's youthful pilot became a "profane and wicked apostate," having decided perhaps to taste the pleasures of the world before renouncing them, and all of Bradford's family violently objected to his course, arguing that if he continued to associate with "fantasticall schismatics," he would lose everything he prized—his lands, his reputation, his very soul. But prayer and meditation had convinced Bradford that he was on the right path, and in spite of all obstacles he went on alone, "nor could the wrath of his uncles, nor the scoff of his neighbors, now turned upon him as one of the Puritans, divert him from his pious inclinations." Fortunately, he soon fell under the gentle and knowing hand of William Brewster, who befriended the hapless orphan and virtually adopted him as his son, the beginning of a lifelong intimacy that decisively shaped the Pilgrim story.

Other converts in the neighborhood were of more immediate weight and influence. The village of Worksop, on the Ryton a few miles west of Babworth, began to take on a Puritan complexion in 1601 when Richard Bernard was appointed vicar there. His large congregation of a hundred or more persons shortly took a solemn vow, "sealed up with the Lord's supper, to forsake all known sin, to hear no more wicked or dumb ministers." The following year a more radical group began to meet with some regularity at Gainsborough, a sizeable town eight miles east of Scrooby, just across the Trent in Lincolnshire.

New hope was born in the breasts of reformers throughout the land in 1603 when Queen Elizabeth passed away in her seventieth year, gaunt and worn but still formidable, to be succeeded by James VI of Scotland, first-born of Mary Queen of Scots. The Puritans warmly welcomed James, for they expected great things of him. As he had been born and raised among the tough Presbyterian Scots who had overthrown the Episcopacy, surely the new King would put the hated Anglican bishops in their place. On his triumphal procession down the Great North Road, James passed by Scrooby manor, noting its "exceeding decay," and Brewster and the entire countryside turned out to cheer him and his brilliant equipage. The first of the Stuarts had scarcely received a new crown as James I of England when he was presented with the Millenary Petition so-called, signed by more than eight hundred reformist ministers, a tenth of all the clergy in the realm. The petitioners humbly begged the correction of the worst of the "abuses," finding particular fault with the continued use of papish vestments, want of weekly sermons by competent preachers, use of the ring in the marriage ceremony, inclusion of the Apocrypha in the Holy Book, and the generally lax and "profane" observance of the Sabbath.[1]

This last complaint is significant, revealing that Puritanism was assuming a moral as well as a doctrinal aspect. The manner of keeping the Sabbath first became a controversial issue about 1595 when the more extreme Puritans began to object, still largely on doctrinal grounds, to the gay and often riotous way in which Englishmen habitually spent their day of rest and devotion, a survival from Roman Catholic and still earlier pagan times when a holy day was always celebrated as a holiday. As the Puritans could find no warrant for this in Scripture, they demanded a return to the primitive Hebrew Sabbath with its prayers and fasting. Some of the more zealous went to fantastic lengths in declaring that to enjoy a wedding feast or any festivity on the Lord's Day was "as great a sin as for a Father to take a knife and cut his child's throat." It was but a step from this attitude to condemnation of worldly pleasure at any time, for Scripture contained no warrant for that, either.

As England was still Merrie England, boisterous and laughter-loving, much of the popular hostility toward Puritans was aroused by their glum disapproval of even the most innocent enjoyments. Most Englishmen were furious when they heard the Maypole on the village green cursed as "that Stynking Idol." The reformers were, most of them, far too smug and self-righteous in summarily consigning to hell all who did not share their narrow views. There is something a bit disingenuous in their pained surprise when enemies struck back at them, denouncing them as sour, bloodless, and stonyhearted bigots without a spark of emotion in them, incapable of any warm human feeling. "Aye," so a dramatist characterized one of them in a popular play, "he seem'd all Church, & his conscience was as hard as a pulpit." And so base and dishonest were these sniffling hypocrites that even the dirt under their fingernails "was Ill-got."

Acting upon the Millenary Petition, the King called the Hampton Court Conference early in 1604, taking a personal part in the proceedings, for he fancied himself as a theologue. Archbishop Whitgift had carefully seen to it as almost the last act of his life that the conference was packed against the reformers. Only four moderates were invited to attend, and these were left to cool their heels in an antechamber for days. When admitted at last, they were curtly asked what they wanted, and the bishops immediately created a diversion by falling upon them for daring to appear before His Majesty "in Turky gowns." Mercilessly badgered, misrepresented and insulted, with the King joining in the sneers and abuse, the Puritans refused to be provoked and behaved themselves very well, one of them even venturing at the first opportunity to make a restrained plea for liberty of conscience.

"I will none of that!" thundered James, and at mention of the Scottish church and its more democratic organization he worked himself into a characteristic fit of slobbering rage.

"A Scottish Presbytery . . . as well agreeth with a Monarchy as God and the Devill. Then Jack & Tom, & Will & Dick, shall meete and at their pleasure censure me, and my Councell, and all our proceedinges."

That explosive political issue had not yet been posed, but it must be said for James that he sensed the drift of the argument. It was impossible to confine the demand for freedom of conscience, for freedom of thought and speech, to the field of religion alone. Retreating from that issue, the Puritan delegates ended by asking merely that ministers should no longer be required to wear the surplice when conducting Sunday services.

"Away with all your snivelling!" cried the King, breaking up the conference with an ominous threat. He and his mother, he said, had been haunted from their cradles by a Puritan devil, and he feared it would not leave him till his grave. But he would put down such "malicious spirits" even at the cost of his crown.

"I will *make* them conform," he thundered, "or I will harry them out of the land!"

The conference achieved next to nothing in the way of reform though it incidentally accomplished two things of the greatest importance. First, at the suggestion of John Reynolds, one of the Puritan delegates, a new translation of the Bible was authorized, eventuating seven years later in the King James Version, one of the towering monuments in our literature, a poetic masterpiece that has colored the thought and speech of the English-speaking world for more than three centuries.

Second, hope of reforming the church from within was now dead. A rigid pattern had now been set which could not be broken short of revolution, as Cromwell and his Independents were to learn during the next reign. James immediately implemented the decisions of the conference by issuing new decrees commanding use of the Book of Common Prayer, full and unreserved acceptance of the Thirty-nine Articles, suppression of all private religious meetings, and obligatory communion in the Anglican church at least three times a year. Within twelve months more than three hundred clergymen were deprived of office for their obvious reluctance or flat refusal to obey these decrees. Again the tide of reform began to ebb under heavy pressure from above.

But Brewster and his friends about Scrooby were not intimidated. For "sundrie years, with much patience," they had borne the silencing of "godly & zealous preachers." Now their patience was exhausted. The time for half measures had passed, and they began looking "further into things by the light of ye word of God." The deeper they probed, following Browne's lead, the more apparent it became that the Anglican church was "a prophane mixture of persons & things," none having any "warrante in ye word of God, but the same that were used in poperie & still retained." That was why the church was filled with "base and beggerly ceremonies." Let the bishops follow them if they wished. As for themselves, they would not "become slaves to them & their popish trash."

For those "whose harts ye Lord had touched with heavenly zeale for his trueth" there was now, plainly, just one thing to do. And this they did!—shaking off "this yoake of antichristian bondage, and as ye Lord's free people joyned themselves (by a covenant of the Lord) into a church estate, in ye felowship of ye gospell, to walke in all his wayes made known or to be made known unto them, according to their best endeavors, whatsoever it should cost them, the Lord assisting them."

Though some set it earlier, the final break probably occurred in 1606 with the arrival in Gainsborough of John Smyth, a graduate of Cambridge, who had been preaching in the city of Lincoln for several years. A bold theorist, one of the most interesting and engaging figures of the early Separation, Smyth is known to history as the Se-Baptist, but at this time he was a thoroughgoing Brownist. Unlike others of the school, he gloried in the name, then a term of utmost reproach and abuse. Though later belittled and meanly assailed by his fellow-Separatists, Smyth was "a man of able gifts, & a good preacher," and for a time ministered to all of "ye Saincts" in the neighborhood who gathered at Gainsborough every Sabbath from widely separated parts of Lincolnshire, Nottinghamshire, and Yorkshire. In a sense, therefore, Smyth was the first Pilgrim pastor.[2]

But this congregation soon split into "2 distincte bodys or churches" for reasons of convenience, as Bradford tells us, and a new and smaller meeting was organized for those living in and around Scrooby. As its pastor, this congregation called Richard Clyfton, now a man of fifty, a patriarchal figure "with a great white beard," evidently notable in its dimensions, for this is the sole observation on personal appearance, the one bit of physical

description, in all the Pilgrim records. Much fault was later found
with Clyfton, but none ever challenged his sincerity or his courage
at this time in giving up his long career in the Anglican church
to join the lowly and harassed Separatists. No doubt this second
congregation was organized by Brewster, who during these and
later days was a "spetiall stay & help" to his brethren. Every Sabbath the congregation managed to meet secretly at one place or
another. With fine irony, it was usually in the archiepiscopal manor
house at Scrooby, perhaps occasionally in the tavern, which was
the largest room in the house, where the postmaster always entertained them "with great love, . . . making provission for them to
his great charge."

There now appears in the congregation, first as a humble private
member, "that famous & worthy man," John Robinson, the most
beloved and respected of the early company, a man of genuine
distinction in an age of great men. Ten years Brewster's junior,
just thirty at this time, Robinson was another of those "godlie &
painfull" students of divinity from Cambridge who were raising
such a stir in the world. Entering Corpus Christi College as a poor
sizar in 1592, he took his degree there four years later, pursuing his
studies under Thomas Jegon, brother of John Jegon, master of the
college. Made a fellow in 1597, he became reader in Greek in
1599, dean of the college the next year. Early in 1603 John Jegon
was named bishop of Norwich, and the mastership of Corpus
Christi fell to his brother Thomas, Robinson's tutor. Archbishop
Whitgift tried to intervene in favor of his chaplain, Dr. Carrier,
but the fellows of the college were too quick for him. A year later
Robinson resigned his fellowship in order to marry, and with his
bride departed for Norwich to become assistant minister of St.
Andrew's. At the university he had been deeply influenced by the
"forward" views of William Perkins, as Brewster had been before
him, and this influence continued at Norwich where Robinson
served under the Reverend Thomas Newhouse, an older man and
another of Perkins' ardent disciples.

Always an eager and sensitive soul, Robinson was increasingly
tortured by doubts about Anglican doctrine and ceremony. Nor-

wich had remained an active reformist center since the days when Robert Browne had preached there, but Robinson apparently was not associated in any way with the small Brownist congregation that still met in the city, continuing his work at St. Andrew's and being "worthily reverenced of all the city for the Grace of God in him." But he had been in office less than a year when he ran foul of the drastic new decrees issued as a result of the Hampton Court Conference and found himself one of the three hundred clergymen deprived of office in all parts of the realm for "branding the ceremonies." He continued to preach, however, until the authorities put a stop to it and excommunicated some of his followers, which was conclusive proof to him and others, as one of them boldly informed the local bishop, "what small hope there is of curing the Canker in your Church."

Now at the crossroads of his career, Robinson hesitated, reluctant to go forward, unwilling to turn back. At length, after wrestling with his soul for two years, he came to a decision which he resolutely followed without the slightest wavering to the end of his life.

"Had not the truth been in my heart as a burning fire, shut up in my bones," he once exclaimed when the anguish of these days was still upon him, "I had never broken the bonds of flesh and blood wherein I was so straightly tied, but had suffered the light of God to have been put out in mine own unthankful heart by other men's darkness."

The Scrooby congregation owed Robinson's presence largely to the fact that he happened to have been born nearby, in the hamlet of Sturton le Steeple, also the home of his wife, Bridget White, daughter of a large and well-to-do yeoman family that was to provide many members of the congregation both here and at Leyden with wives. It is probable that the Robinsons came here to live with Bridget's family after their expulsion from Norwich. By 1606 Robinson had become acquainted with Brewster and John Smyth, to be deeply influenced by both. The latter's influence appears to have been decisive, for it was Smyth, as many contemporaries noted, who finally resolved Robinson's doubts and led him to join the Separation. His conversion immensely strengthened the infant Scrooby congregation, which probably never numbered more than forty or fifty communicants. Although Robinson was overshadowed for a time by Clyfton, he rose rapidly from the ranks and was soon second in command as "teacher" of the group.[3]

For some years the local reformers had been annoyed and harassed by the authorities. But these troubles were "but as fleabitings" to those that now came upon them when they finally left the church and withdrew to meet illegally by themselves. The whole countryside was soon aroused against them, which can be readily understood without subscribing to Cotton Mather's usual extravagant nonsense in characterizing their neighbors as "most ignorant and licentious people." The simple truth is that most Englishmen, without really knowing much about either, hated and feared Puritans and Separatists alike, for the pulpit, the press of the day, thundered continuously against them. A Separatist, said one high-placed cleric, is "proud without learning, presumptuous without authoritie, zealous without knowledge, holy without Religion: in a word, a dangerous and malicious *Hypocrite*." Smug professors at Oxford and Cambridge heaped scorn upon the "absurd Brownists"; they were notoriously weak in judgment, if not actually feeble of mind, as shown by their "childish fallacies and other insolent attempts." Yet these same pundits unblushingly asserted, upon no authority whatever but their own vulgar prejudices, that the Separatists did not believe in capital punishment— in itself, evidently a capital crime—and not merely advocated but practised the communistic principles of the Anabaptists, who in turn had modeled their economy upon that of the early Christian church.

But those in power were really less disturbed by what the Separatists had to say than by the fact that they dared to speak at all, which directly challenged the aristocratic principle socalled. The religious rebels were, for the most part, quite definitely "lower class," not only socially but in actual legal status. And their masters were not disposed to allow them to forget this for a moment, contemptuously asking who gave a tinker's dam what "Symon the Saddler, Tomkins the Tailor, or Billy the Bellows-maker" might have to say on any subject. Their duty was plain and simple enough—to do and believe precisely what they were told. Let them leave thinking to their "betters"!

There was an immediate outcry in the neighborhood when the "upstarts" at Scrooby denounced the "base and beggerly cere-monies" of the church and boldly proclaimed that "ye lordly & tiranous power of ye prelats ought not to be submitted unto." Who were these prelates anyhow? And what was the source of their authority? "Bishops and elders are not lords over God's creation, as if the Church could not *be* without them." No, the "true" church was nothing more—and just as surely, nothing less —than the whole body of its communants, and in such a church nothing would or could be done "but with the people's privity and consent." Now, this was dangerous doctrine at any time, but especially in Stuart England with James I busily elaborating the doctrine of the divine right of kings.

The Scrooby congregation had been meeting less than a year when the authorities struck. Some members "were taken & clapt up in prison; others had their houses besett & watcht night and day, & hardly escaped their hands; and ye most were faine to flie & leave their howses & habitations, and the means of their livele-hood." A wave of terror swept the countryside. The daughter born to the Brewsters at this time was, significantly, named Fear.

Jailed as a "very daingerous" Brownist, Gervase Neville, grand-son of the High Sheriff of Nottinghamshire, was charged with making "contemptuous & scandalous" speeches and "frequenting of conventicles and the companie of others of his profession," a direct reference to the secret illegal meetings at Gainsborough and in the manor house at Scrooby. Warrants were also issued for Richard Jackson, Robert Rochester, and young Francis Jessop of Worksop, later of the Leyden congregation, brother-in-law of the Robinsons through his marriage to Bridget's younger sister, Frances. On the last day of September, 1607, Brewster resigned his postmastership, doubtless under pressure, and several months later was commanded to appear at York before the dread Court of High Commission for being "disobedient in matters of religion." The prisoners were fined £20 ($1,000) each, and were fortunate to escape so lightly.

Clyfton's congregation now began to think seriously of a plan that had been casually discussed before—flight to The Netherlands where there was, so they heard, "freedome of Religion for all men." John Smyth and his group had already fled Gainsborough and taken refuge in Amsterdam. Yet flight, too, involved suffering and hardship. It meant exile from the pleasant English countryside and the scenes that all had known since childhood. It meant leaving old friends and acquaintances, abandoning homes and farms that had been in their families for generations. It meant learning a strange new tongue and conforming to strange new ways. Furthermore, these farmer folk would have to learn new skills and trades to survive in one or another of the Dutch cities. They were faced with a heartbreaking choice. Under the circumstances it was only natural that many were hesitant, protesting that flight to a foreign land was "an adventure almost desperate, a case intolerable, & a miserie worse than death."

In the end the majority decided to hazard the risk, for it was evident that the congregation could not live "in any peaceable condition" at home. The migration from the district was led by an elderly country gentleman in Smyth's group, the Reverend Thomas Helwys, later a founder of the Baptist church. "If any brought oars, he brought sails," as John Robinson once said, and Helwys had reason to be forward in the matter, for his wife was lying in York Castle for refusing to take an oath in the form prescribed by law. But flight posed still another formidable obstacle, one more ground for prosecution, for "ye ports & havens were shut against them" under a law forbidding any subject to leave the realm without permission of the Crown. They would therefore have to escape by stealth and pay some shipmaster dearly for engaging in such illegal traffic.

Clyfton and his more ardent disciples quietly sold their lands and possessions for what they would bring, usually at great sacrifice, and after several vexatious and expensive delays set out on foot late in 1607 for the town of Boston, on The Wash, about sixty miles to the southeast, as long and difficult an undertaking as a transcontinental journey today. Arrangements were made for a ship to pick them up "at a conveniente place" nearby. But on the appointed day the vessel failed to appear. A night or two later, after much anxiety and tiresome fretting, the ship put in under cover of dark, and all hurriedly clambered on board—men, women, and children—heaving great sighs of relief, for at a time when a traveler was a rare object to be stared at and whispered about, the presence of so many strangers in Boston must have aroused considerable speculation and suspicion.

But the passengers' prayers of thanksgiving were quite premature. No sooner had the skipper of the vessel collected the money due him than he betrayed his charges into the hands of the local authorities and their "chatchpoule" officers, as he had arranged to do. Forcing the frightened company into open boats, the constables rifled their goods and persons, stripping the men to their shirts in their search for gold. "Yea!" exclaimed Bradford, "and ye women furder than became modestie." The prisoners were hustled into Boston to be made "a specktackle & wonder to ye multitude" and then jailed. A messenger was dispatched to London to inform the Privy Council, which apparently was not much interested, probably because the company was so weak and obscure. Four or five weeks later the magistrates released all but seven of the prisoners and ordered them to return to their homes. They would have been pleased enough to do this, but they now had no homes to go to. They returned to Scrooby nevertheless and found shelter in the neighborhood. Brewster, Clyfton, Robinson, and four others were bound over to stand trial. They were never indicted, however, and in time were released.

A few of the more timid, disheartened by the blows of fortune, now withdrew from the enterprise. But the majority persevered, and in the spring of 1608 a second attempt to escape was made

with the aid of a Dutch captain met at Hull. The business was
carefully arranged to prevent any untoward accidents or surprises.
Setting out on foot, the men struck out across country some forty
miles to the rendezvous on the east coast, somewhere between
Hull and Great Grimsby, at a lonely spot where there was a
"large commone a good way distante from any town." A bark was
hired to transport the women, children, and baggage. In good
time the bark sailed down the Ryton into the Idle, then into the
Trent, and finally into the broad estuary of the Humber, where it
tacked southeast along the coast, arriving at the rendezvous a day
early. This was a wise precaution, but as usually happened with
the Pilgrims, whose affairs almost never went as planned, their
foresight here led to their undoing. A stiff breeze blew up as the
bark came down the coast, "& ye sea being rough, and ye women
very sicke," the latter pleaded with the crew to put into a cove
hard by. The skipper put the helm over and ran before the wind,
only to run aground on a shoal. The bark was still stuck fast
in the mud the next morning when the Dutchman put in and
dropped anchor a mile or two down the coast. The men had meantime arrived and were anxiously pacing up and down the beach,
unable to reach the bark because of the treacherous swamps and
deep channels that lay between. Seeing how matters stood, the
captain suggested that the men come on board while waiting for
the tide to float the bark. A boat carried out half the men and was
about to put back for the others when the skipper caught sight
of a large mob approaching the beach, "both horse & foote, with
bills, & gunes, & other weapons, for ye countrie was raised to
take them."

"Sacramente!" swore the Dutchman—or so Bradford reported
his most un-Dutch oath—and having a fair wind, "waiged Ancor,
hoysed sayles, and away!" There was a wail of anguish and impotent rage from the men on board. Some of those on shore ran
for their lives, but most of them floundered out to the bark to aid
the women who were "weeping & crying on every side." Some
feared for their husbands on the ship, "others not knowing what

should become of them & their little ones, others againe melted in tears, seeing their pore litle ones hanging aboute them, crying for feare and quaking with cold."

Those at sea, it turned out, faced the greater danger, for a gale blew up and drove the ship far out into the North Sea, almost to the Norwegian coast. More than once the vessel almost foundered. As the wind roared through the rigging and angry waves swept across the deck, the frightened Scrooby farmers prayed fervently, "espetially some of them, and even without any great distraction when ye water ran into their mouthes & ears." One mountainous sea crashed into the ship and laid her on her beam ends almost under water, and for an awful moment or two it seemed that she was bound straight for the bottom.

"We sink, we sink!" cried the Dutchman and his crew.

"Yet Lord, thou canst save!" moaned the sick and battered Saints. "Yet Lord, thou canst save!"

And thereupon, so these Pilgrims reported, the ship righted herself. More than that, the gale quickly subsided and "ye Lord filled their afflicted minds with shuch comforts as every one cannot understand." At length, after being tossed about for two weeks on a voyage that ordinarily took a day or two, the vanguard of the Pilgrims landed at Amsterdam with only the coats on their backs, most of them without a penny in their pockets, the hearts of all heavy with anxiety about their loved ones at home.

The latter had not fared so badly. Seized by the mob, they had been hustled from town to town, from magistrate to magistrate, for no one knew what to do with them. After they had been "thus turmoyled a good while," they were released and again ordered to return to their homes. A few more of the timid now abandoned all idea of flight. But others "came on with fresh courage," resolved to get across to Holland by any means at all. This time they decided to slip away a few at a time rather than attempt to escape in a single large group, which it would have been wise to have done in the first place. Clyfton and Brewster stayed to the last to assist the weaker brethren across. The authorities apparently did not interfere in any way, being "wearied & tired" of these stiff-necked rebels, and one may well believe Bradford that they were "glad to be rid of them in ye end upon any termes."

By the summer of 1608 all of those choosing exile had succeeded in making their escape, "some at one time & some at another, and some in one place & some in another," their paths converging upon Amsterdam where at length they "mett togeather againe according to their desires, with no small rejoycing."

5

SCANDAL
IN BROWNISTS
ALLEY

> . . . more becoming the streets of Sodome
> than of Sion.
> —CHRISTOPHER LAWNE

SIMPLE AND UNSOPHISTICATED FOLK, USED TO THE "PLAINE countrie villages" along the Ryton and the Idle, the émigrés from Scrooby found The Netherlands quite overwhelming. They noted with awe its "many goodly and fortified cities, strongly walled and garded with troops of armed men, . . . and strongly flowing with abundance of all sorts of welth & riches." Amsterdam particularly impressed them. Somewhat larger and far more cosmopolitan than London, it was one of Europe's greatest cities, the center of many flourishing handicraft industries, a bustling and prosperous seaport with a far-flung maritime trade. Besides, it was a tolerant, friendly, and hospitable community. The new-comers had no reason here to fear the violence of neighbors or heavy-handed bailiffs, for Amsterdam was, as the bigoted every-where complained, "the Fair of all the Sects, where all the Pedlars of Religion have leave to vend their Toyes."

Yet, like all refugees, those from Scrooby had to contend with many hardships and disabilities. They could make little of the "uncouth" Dutch tongue. They found the people strange in their dress, stranger still in their customs and manners. Altogether, they stood amazed at a scene so foreign to them that "it seemed they were come into a new world"—as indeed they had, and they were ill equipped to meet it. For the most part, they had been schooled in "ye inocente trade of husbandrey," but that was of no use to them now. If they were to survive, they had quickly to find what employment they could in the least skilled and worst paid oper-ations of the textile, metal, leather, and other trades. William Bradford apprenticed himself to a French silk maker, and others did similarly. But labor as they would, it was not long before they saw "ye grimme & grisly face of povertie coming upon them like an armed man," and from this gaunt specter they could not fly as from James and his bishops but "must bukle & incounter." Though they met with many reverses, yet they always managed somehow to foil their adversary, for they were "armed with faith & patience against him, and all his encounters."

The group was small, wanting even the strength of numbers. Its exact size is unknown and can only be conjectured. There were the Robinsons, John and Bridget, with at least two small children, John and Bridget. William and Mary Brewster had arrived with Jonathan, now a youth of fifteen, and their two daughters, Patience and Fear, the latter a babe in arms. Though he was approaching twenty, Bradford was probably a member of this household. Richard Clyfton had been one of the last to come, arriving in August, 1608, with his wife Ann (Stuffen, of Worksop) and their three sons—Zachary, Timothy, and Eleazar, aged nine to nineteen.

And these are the only members of the emigrant group—indeed, with relatively few exceptions, the only members of the original Scrooby congregation—who are known by name. As that congregation had always been relatively small, certainly never exceeding fifty or sixty members, it may well be, contrary to what has always been assumed, that the Robinson, Brewster-Bradford, and Clyfton households—fifteen persons in all, with only six adults among them—constituted the larger part of those at Scrooby who in the end, after so many disheartening setbacks, retained both the will and the resources to effect their escape. And of these three households, only one—Brewster's—ever reached the New World!

In their initial bewilderment, the exiles accounted it a great boon to find in Amsterdam so many friends, both old and new, to welcome them and help smooth their path. John Smyth and his Gainsborough group, seventy or eighty strong, had arrived some months before and were busy getting settled. But of more comfort and aid, in the beginning at least, was another far larger group, the Brethren of the Separation of the First English Church at Amsterdam, better known as the Ancient Brethren. They had recently completed a large new meeting house on the Bruinistengange, or Brownists Alley, as the narrow lane in the heart of the old city is still known. With three hundred or more communicants, this was the most numerous and renowned of the Separatist congregations, being the magnet which had drawn both the Gainsborough and Scrooby groups to the city. Within a short time John Smyth organized a congregation of his own. Clyfton did not, probably because his flock was too small, and throughout their stay in Amsterdam they worshiped in the Bruinistengange. Though they did not formally join the Ancient Brethren, they took communion with them for more than a year, to the profound regret of both.

Brewster, Smyth, and possibly others had interesting and rather curious connections with this group. The nucleus of the famed and soon-to-be-infamous Ancient Brethren was that harassed London congregation which had fled the country after the execution in 1593 of its leaders—John Greenwood, Henry Barrow, and John Penry. This congregation, the first of consequence in the Separatist movement, had been organized in 1587 by John Greenwood, then an uncompromising Brownist, during one of his brief respites from prison. About a year previously a most remarkable incident had occurred, one of several such incidents if the records are to be credited. One day, while in the Clink, one of the foulest prisons in England, Greenwood had received an unexpected visit from a stranger who introduced himself as Henry Barrow. Obviously a "gentleman of a good house," as later described by Lord Francis Bacon, a kinsman, Barrow was just over thirty but looked older from the gay and dissipated life he had led at Cambridge and later in London, where he had been lackadaisically practising law for some years as a member of Gray's Inn.

Barrow introduced himself and humbly explained his mission. A few days before, he said, happening to pass a church in which a "forward" minister was preaching, he had stepped in from curiosity to hear him. Deeply moved and impressed, he began asking questions, being referred for more specific answers to Greenwood in the Clink. And here he was, wanting to know more about the reformers and their aims, a fateful moment in the history of the Separation. During the interview Barrow himself was seized and locked up, remaining in jail till his death seven years later.[1]

Barrow's life really began in the Clink where he made the most of his years of enforced leisure. He embraced the Holy Discipline and soon became one of its most eloquent champions and influential theorists. The question of church organization particularly concerned him. Should each of the Separatist churches be quite independent, as the Brownists advocated, or should they be subject to some measure of central direction and control? Recalling the fate of Robert Browne's church, which had been wrecked by internal disorders and dissensions, Barrow evolved and after a time brought Greenwood to accept a compromise between Brownism, with its extreme independency, and Calvinism, as represented by the Presbyterian church with its synods, assemblies, and other general governing agencies. The structure of the individual churches was not to be changed, but all were to be regulated by a representative assembly of elders democratically elected by each.

This was the chief of the Barrowist principles upon which English Congregationalism, as distinguished from the American, took shape.

At this time, too, Barrow began writing furiously against the "dull-headed, dogbolt priests," secretly collaborating with Greenwood in this. In 1590 he penned *A Briefe Discoverie of the False Church,* one of the volumes which Brewster chose to carry with him to Plymouth. The manuscript of this work was smuggled out of the Gatehouse, sheet by sheet, and across to Holland to be set in type by a Dutch printer at Dort. Similarly, Barrow and Greenwood published a number of tracts, which were smuggled back into England and sold in considerable numbers at 8d. a copy. Alarmed by this, the bishops issued a blast against such "seditious" publications, persuading Queen Elizabeth that her ambassador at The Hague should be instructed to look into the matter and put a stop to this "monstruous" business. The latter in turn enlisted the aid of an English clergyman living at Middelburg, the Reverend Francis Johnson, a choice with strange and quite unexpected results.

A graduate of Christ's College, Cambridge, where he had become a fellow in 1581, Francis Johnson had been at the university in Brewster's day. The latter may have known him there. In any case, Brewster and his brethren came to know him intimately here at Amsterdam, for he was now pastor of the Ancient Brethren. Curiously, too, Johnson had been the tutor of that engaging rebel, John Smyth, who probably had the first seeds of "errour" planted in him by Johnson, for in 1589 the latter had preached so militant a sermon against the "abuses" that the university authorities jailed him. Lord Burghley's protest against this arbitrary action secured his release. The heads of the colleges, prodded by Archbishop Whitgift, thereupon deprived him of his fellowship in a high-handed manner and ordered him to leave Cambridge, against the protests of some seventy fellows of the colleges, all good churchmen, several well on their way to being mitred. When Johnson challenged his expulsion and refused to leave Cambridge, he was again jailed. Finally, to be rid of him, the university officials persuaded him to accept a more remunerative post, and in 1590 Johnson sailed for Holland to minister to the needs of the English merchants of the staple at Middelburg.

Though a militant Puritan, Johnson was still opposed to Separatism and readily accepted the English ambassador's invitation to do some private snooping. Somehow, he soon nosed out the shop where Barrow's tracts were being printed. One happened to be on the press and Johnson patiently bided his time until the whole edition of 3,000 copies had been run off and then had it seized by the Dutch authorities. The latter were reluctant to act but did not dare jeopardize the little aid they were receiving from England in their desperate struggle against Spain. The tracts were burned, but out of the bonfire Johnson rescued two copies, one for himself, the other for a friend. One day, while casually thumbing through his copy, Johnson began to read and very soon, so Bradford told the story in later years, "met with something that began to work upon his spirit, which so wrought with him as drew him to this resolution, seriously to read over the whole book, the which he did once and again."

Profoundly moved and troubled in conscience, Johnson crossed to England and hastened to the Gatehouse to talk with Barrow, as the latter had hurried to the Clink six years previously to talk with Greenwood—and with strikingly similar results. Johnson embraced the Holy Discipline, resigned his post at Middelburg, and threw in his lot with the humble Separatists, rising rapidly to prominence among them.

A few months later, the congregation was reorganized upon a more formal basis. The members swore a solemn covenant to "walke with ye rest of them as long as they did walke in ye way of ye Lorde, & as farr as might be warranted by ye word of God." To the office of pastor the congregation called its latest convert, Francis Johnson, a tribute to his forceful personality and brilliant though erratic talents. John Greenwood, momentarily out of jail, became the "teacher." As elders, the company selected George Knyveton, an apothecary with a shop in Newgate Market, and

Daniel Studley, whose name was to become a stench in Pilgrim nostrils. Two deacons were also named, Nicholas Lee and Christopher Bowman, a young goldsmith recently released after spending four years in prison for drawing up a petition to the Queen in support of liberty of conscience.

Almost immediately complaints against these "Barrowish synagogues, . . . cages of franticke schismatics," began to reach the authorities, who promptly seized Johnson and Greenwood. Other prominent members were picked up from time to time, including Edward Boys, a prosperous haberdasher with a shop in Fleet Street. Then in March, 1593, some fifty members were taken at a clandestine service being conducted in the woods outside London by George Johnson, master of a school in Mincing Lane, one of Francis' younger brothers. The prisoners were herded for safe-keeping into a constable's house, where they defiantly resumed their interrupted devotions. Unrecognized among the worshipers was the most sought-after man in the realm, John Penry. Taking refuge for a time in Scotland, he had recently doubled back on his tracks, hotly pursued by Whitgift's spies and agents. Watching his opportunity, Penry now coolly walked out the door and disappeared, immediately drawing up a petition to the Privy Council in behalf of the prisoners. When his wife and other women presented it, the authorities' only reply was to arrest one of them.

Events moved swiftly to a tragic climax. Edward Boys and many others soon died of dread jail-fever and after a relentless pursuit of four years, the authorities finally trapped Penry and laid him up by the heels in the Poultry Compter. The next day Greenwood and Barrow were brought to trial, along with Elder Daniel Studley, Scipio Bellot, and Robert Bowle. All were sentenced to death for sedition. Studley's sentence was later commuted, but death claimed the others. Bellot and Bowle died in prison within a few months. Greenwood and Barrow went to the gallows after Lord Burghley had made a halfhearted effort to save them. Penry was next brought to trial and subjected to the vilest insults and abuse by the notorious Lord Chief Justice, John Popham, fond of boasting that he had been a highwayman in his younger days. Late in May, 1593, the bold and resourceful Penry was hanged, drawn, and quartered, carrying with him to the grave the secret of Martin Mar-prelate.

Francis Johnson and other leaders were kept under lock and key for years, but humbler members were released after a time. By 1595, acting upon Penry's advice, fifty or sixty of them had managed to flee the country, establishing themselves at Amsterdam. Here, in the absence of Pastor Johnson, they worshiped under another of the great leaders of the Separation, young Henry Ainsworth, not yet twenty-five, a gentle scholar whom the Pilgrims always greatly esteemed. Born at Swanton Morley, near Norwich, the son of a poor yeoman family, Ainsworth had entered Cambridge in 1588, leaving three years later without taking a degree, doubtless for reasons of conscience, for he was "a very learned man," as Bradford declared, "ready and pregnant in the Scriptures, . . . eminent in the knowledge of tongues." Drifting from Cambridge to London and into Separatist circles there, Ainsworth soon crossed to Ireland, returned to London, and shortly moved on to Amsterdam, finding work with a local bookseller as a porter, almost starving to death before his employer discovered the talents of his modest messenger boy. At Cambridge he had studied Hebrew with an old rabbi of the town. Learning of this, the bookseller put Ainsworth to work on the translations and exegeses that brought him wide fame as a scholar in his day. The Pilgrims used his translation of the Psalms for generations.

Henry Barrow had left the congregation what little remained of his once substantial fortune and contributions came occasionally from London and elsewhere, but the exiles were nevertheless "eaten up in a maner by deep povertie." To make matters worse, they soon antagonized the Dutch Reformed Church, Calvinist in doctrine, by gratuitously pointing out the "errours" in that church. Charged with being conceited and contentious, they were ordered to leave Amsterdam "for writing libels." At great cost and hardship they moved first to Kampen, then to Narden, and back to Amsterdam again after peace had been restored by Ainsworth.

Bitter strife had meantime broken out in London between

Francis Johnson and his brother George. In 1594, while still in the Clink, Francis had married Thomasine Boys, the dashing widow of the Fleet Street haberdasher who had died a martyr to the cause. Thomasine, it appears, was a true Elizabethan, gay and spirited, fond of jewelry, pretty clothes, and even a frilly extravagance or two. With a small fortune of her own to indulge her tastes, she was obviously the envy of poorer and plainer sisters in the congregation. Gossip about her seeped into the prisons and came to the ears of George Johnson in the Fleet, who took a very serious view of the matter, sharply rebuking his brother and his wife, demanding a pledge of instant reform. When nothing came of this, to the schoolmaster's pained surprise, he turned to the members of the congregation and insisted that they should command "better walking." Again he was disappointed, for the members were "loth & would not," which left George quite beside himself in impotent rage.

The breaking point came when Thomasine adopted Penry's oldest daughter, Deliverance, a child of five. This was more than George could bear. He would not, he shouted, stand idly by and see the innocent child corrupted by the pastor's wife, who was nothing but a "bouncing girl," as bad in her way as the wife of the Bishop of London. Why, she wore "3, 4 or 5 gold rings at once!" As for the "whalebones in her breast" and the busks she wore to point her shapely figure—well, said George, "many of ye Saincts are greeved." Let her remove her rings and "excessive deal of lace," take off her whalebone stays, exchange her "showish hat for a sober taffety or felt," and stop wearing musk and fancy white ruffs stiff with starch, "the Devill's liquor." Thomasine bluntly told George to mind his own business, but the latter went on hurling Scriptural texts and personal abuse at the pastor and his wife. Francis spiritedly replied in kind, and so the Millinery War continued, to the shame of all the Separatists.

A truce in this unseemly brawling was forced in 1597 when the quarreling brothers and Elder Studley, after five years in jail without trial, were ordered deported to America. They embarked with a company of settlers going out to found a colony at the mouth of the St. Lawrence. When one of the vessels foundered, the other put back and tied up at Southampton, where the prisoners made their escape and got away to Amsterdam. Shortly after their arrival the group was reorganized. Francis Johnson was retained as pastor. The office of "teacher," vacant since Greenwood's death, fell to Ainsworth. Studley and Knyveton continued as elders and were given two colleagues—Matthew Slade, a schoolmaster, soon excommunicated for daring to pray with the Dutch, and Jean de l'Ecluse, subsequently Bradford's brother-in-law. Giles Thorpe, a printer, was chosen as deacon to serve with Christopher Bowman, the goldsmith.

All seemed to be going well when the Millinery War flamed anew, occasioned by Thomasine's refusal to invite hungry and homeless George to live in the combination parsonage-meeting house which the congregation had rented on the Green Rampart. Again Scriptural texts and personal slanders flew thick and fast until Francis excommunicated his brother and publicly consigned him to the devil, with Ainsworth protesting such extreme measures. At this point the brothers' aged father was so ill-advised as to enter the fray, crossing from Yorkshire with the hope of restoring peace—a hope fervently shared by the Dutch, who were tired of the clamor. For his pains he, too, was publicly consigned to the devil by Francis. "Hath the like unnaturalness been read or heard of!" he exclaimed. It was enough to persuade even the most obtuse parents "to hold their children from learning and studying in the Universities." The shocked and disillusioned old man returned home, taking George with him, and the latter was promptly in trouble again. Jailed as a heretic, he soon died in Durham prison, waging the Millinery War to the last. Death overtook him on page 214 of the monumental work he devoted to the subject. Published at Amsterdam in 1603 and widely circulated, it was seized upon with glee by every enemy of the Separatists, "alias Brownists, the factious Brethren of these Times."[2]

The bishops and most orthodox Anglicans professed not to be surprised by all this, saying that it was just what one would expect

of people who had been "Amsterdamnified by brainlesse opinions."
They made a mockery of religion by reducing it to "frequent fasting and long prayers, which devour widdowes' houses." And who
were these "painted Sepulchres, whited walls," these Jonahs, these
"new-crept-in Caterpillers," this plague of Egyptian locusts consuming all in their course? One could readily tell them "by their
frequent and far fetcht sighes, the continuall elevation of their
eyes, their meager physiognomies, solitary countenances, sharp
noses, by the cut of their hayre, made even with the top of their
prick-ears; . . . by the broad hats and narrow ruffs which they
usually weare, the putting of their gloves under their girdles, and
the folding of their hands one within another. . . . They are double-
minded, hollow-hearted, and will as nimbly swallow up at a bite
another man's estate, as our Dutch will pills of butter, and never
purch for it. . . . A Pope and a Bishop are all one with them."

Most of this was patent nonsense, the usual obloquy heaped
upon the unorthodox in all ages. But it would be idle to deny the
frequent charge, true even of the Pilgrims at times, that the Separatists were a factious lot. Upon the slightest pretext, or none at
all, they rushed into the bitterest of controversy about any and
all kinds of things, sacred and profane, momentous or trivial,
simple or abstruse, with a singular disregard of tolerance, candor,
sound judgment or even plain common sense. The Ancient Brethren sinned especially in this respect and paid dearly for it.

The din of the Millinery War had scarcely died away before
a worse scandal had everybody by the ears. In 1604 the Reverend
Thomas White arrived with a dozen converts from his parish in
the west of England. Conflict immediately ensued. Withdrawing
to establish a short-lived church of his own, White took with him
not only his former parishioners but a group of dissatisfied Ancient
Brethren. Francis Johnson, always disposed to ascribe the meanest
and pettiest motives to his opponents, attributed White's withdrawal to his failure to be elected to an important office. The
latter made no immediate reply, withholding his fire until ready
to deliver a smashing broadside in the form of a small book,

lengthily entitled *A Discoverie of Brownisme: or, a Briefe Declaration of some of the Errours and Abhominations daily practised and increased among the English Company of the Separation . . . at Amsterdam in Holland.*

That church, said White, God had undoubtedly created "as a spectacle for others to beware of rash, heady, and contentious courses." The members of the congregation were notorious for their "disgracing, back-biting, & undermining one of another." In addition to being "giddy" in matters of religion, the Ancient Brethren were vicious and dishonest. White charged, naming names, that John Nicholas and others were unconscionably running up debts which they neither could nor would repay. Deacon Christopher Bowman was dubbed "Judas the Purse-Bearer" for allegedly swindling the poor in the congregation, specifically for having cheated them of half the alms given them by the magistrates of Narden when they were starving during their brief stay in that city. As for Daniel Studley, he was "fitter for the stewes than to be an elder in any Christian society." His affair with Mrs. Judith Holder was known to everybody, and "he never so much as denyed the matter of incest with his wife's daughter." Many outraged brethren wished to bring him to book, but even when they "had a matter as cleare as the sunne against him, yet durst they not deale with him for it," so great was his influence with Pastor Johnson.

And these, exclaimed White, were the men who accused others "of simplicitie, absurdity, inconstancy in turning their coates, of being hearers and not doers of the Word, of retayning open offenders, & so becoming cages of every uncleane bird!"

This broadside was much too damaging to go unanswered, and a suit for slander was brought against White by Ruling Elder Studley, seconded by Pastor Johnson, Deacon Bowman, Mrs. Judith Holder, and five others. After carefully reviewing the evidence, the Dutch magistrates pronounced in White's favor and assessed the costs of the trial against his accusers. This further damaged the good name of the church and the prestige of its leaders. It did not unseat the latter, however, and things went on much as before—or rather, from bad to worse, as soon became evident.

But White went too far, it seems, in dismissing the church as "brokerage of whores." After all, this was the congregation that Clyfton and his flock virtually joined when they began straggling into Amsterdam little more than a year later. They were aware of this public scandal, but probably regarded it as one more evidence of the satanic zeal of their enemies in fabricating malicious lies about all Separatists. But in this instance, "ye pure & unspotty'd Lambes of ye Lord" had fallen into very unpleasant company, as they quickly discovered, though one would never guess it from anything they ever said or wrote.

Francis Johnson, so Bradford once described him, was a good preacher, the "most solemn" of any he had known "in all his administrations," notably in baptism and the Lord's Supper. The passing years had evidently exacted their toll of Thomasine, who had become a "very grave" matron, "very modest both in her apparel and all her demeanour, ready to do any good works in her place and helpful to many, especially the poor." But the Pilgrims were particularly taken with Henry Ainsworth, who taught well "without tossing and turning his book." Ordinarily he was "very modest, amiable, and sociable," though in his writings Bradford found him "something smart in his style." The congregation was blessed with four "grave" elders, and the deacons were "able and godly." The church also had a deaconess, an "anciente Widow" well past sixty, who was "obeyed as a Mother in Israel." She visited the old and sick, collected alms for the needy, and altogether was an "ornament to her calling," especially during the services on the Sabbath—from eight in the morning till noon, and again from two to six in the afternoon—when she sat "in a conveniente place, . . . with a little birchen rod in her hand, and kept little children in great awe, from disturbing the Congregation."

"And truly," said Bradford many years later when time had effaced or at least blurred the memory of many untoward things, the Ancient Brethren were well officered and contained "many worthy men." And "if you had seen them in their bewty and order as we have done," he told the young men of Plymouth in the *First Dialogue* that he addressed to them, "you would have bin much affected therewith, we dare say."

The "dare say" was wisely prudential, to say the least.

Certainly, the "bewty and order" of the Ancient Brethren escaped Bradford and his brethren during their stay in Amsterdam. In fact, they had not been there long before they realized they were sitting on a volcano, and from ominous rumblings it was evident that a resounding explosion was not far off.

Trouble first broke out in an unexpected quarter, in John Smyth's group, among their old friends from Gainsborough, who had recently established themselves as the Brethren of the Separation of the Second English Church at Amsterdam. Open-minded and impulsive as a child, full of ideas and uncompromisingly bold in following them wherever they might lead, the always restless Smyth—"his instability and wantonness of wit," said John Robinson, "is his sin and our crosse"—had been pondering the true course of salvation and made several astonishing discoveries. The first dropped like a bombshell among the Separatists:

The Bible used by them was *not* the true word of God!

How could it be? asked Smyth. It was merely some fallible translator's imperfect attempt to reduce the "pure" revelation to English. It was plainly a "human invention," quite as tainted with human error as the Anglican prayer book or the Roman mass book. Only the Scriptures in the original Greek and Hebrew were admissible in the House of God!

Pursuing his argument, Smyth suddenly came to the edge of an awful abyss and looked over. Shuddering, he drew back before it was too late. No, he reassured himself, it was unthinkable! It simply could not be that the original Scriptures were also "man-made," a "human invention." God could have spoken in Greek and Hebrew, and quite obviously had done so. And yet— well, perhaps it would be better, after all, to dispense with the Book in the services and rely solely upon the Holy Ghost as it spoke directly from the heart. Let the preacher preach, the teacher teach, and the congregation pray and sing as the spirit moved them.

With this grave question solved, Smyth was off again and immediately stumbled upon an even more startling "trueth" that left him literally breathless. It seemed almost incredible that none had noted it before:

There was not a true Christian in all the world! And there had been none for many centuries!

Baptism was an act of faith, said Smyth, and not otherwise "lawfull." What was one to think, then, of the terrible practice of infant baptism which had prevailed in Christendom for more than a thousand years? Could a newborn babe confess its faith and ask to have its name enrolled in the Christian fellowship? It was ridiculous, even worse. Infant baptism, so Smyth informed Clyfton, was "the mark of the beast," and the stain should be eradicated. Steps should instantly be taken to see that "ye Saincts" at least were legitimately baptized.

Clyfton, Robinson, Brewster, Francis Johnson, Henry Ainsworth, and others remained distressingly blind to the crisis, to Smyth's pained surprise, which only convinced him the more that he and his congregation should lead the way. The problem they faced was a thorny and apparently insoluble one. How could anyone be baptized when there was no properly baptized person anywhere in the world to perform the rite? Smyth dug into Scripture and finally emerged with something that seemed to offer a solution. First, he and all the officers of the church resigned. Next, the congregation met and "unchurched" itself, which theoretically left the members without religious faith of any kind. Then, mustering texts to justify his course, Smyth proceeded to baptize himself and win a name for himself in history as the Se-Baptist, or the Self-Baptizer. Immediately Clyfton and his former friends began to chide him, firing at him from all sides, asking many sharp and perplexing questions. Was he a church, they asked, when he baptized himself? If not, what was the point of the proceedings? Anyone could pour plain water upon himself.

"Resolve me how you can baptize yourself into the church, being out of it," demanded Clyfton, "yea, and when there is no church!"

Smyth offered an elaborate defense and confidently went his way. Sharing the Brownist aversion to "dipping," he sprinkled his followers; they then assembled, organized themselves as a congregation, and elected Smyth and all former officers to the posts which they had held before. Again the church was just what it had been. Yet it was somehow very different—"purified," reformed, with everything at last in good order—until Smyth, still deep in the awful mysteries of theology, stood up one day to announce to a gasping congregation that the whole business had been a "damnable errour."

This opened a breach that was never closed. Most of the "new-washed companie" reiterated their faith in Smyth the Se-Baptist, throwing out Smyth the Skeptic, excommunicating him and thirty of his still devoted followers. The larger group, under the command of the Reverend Thomas Helwys, returned to England to establish in London one of the first Baptist churches in the realm. Smyth's group applied for membership in a local Mennonite congregation, pleading a desire "to get back into the true Church of Christ as speedily as may be." But the Mennonites were not eager to accept them, and Smyth and his dwindling company took refuge in Jan Munter's bakery, or Great Cake House, where the group held services and many of its members lived for five or six years.

In the eyes of Robinson, Brewster, and "some others of best discerning" in the Scrooby group, these contentions were serious enough, but it was also evident and far more alarming that "ye flames of contention were like to breake out in that ancient church itselfe (as afterwards lamentably came to pass)." For these and "some other reasons," to quote Bradford's summary phrase, the group thought it high time to be moving on again, though all knew it would be "much to ye prejudice of their outward estats, . . . as indeed it proved to be." In February, 1609, Robinson visited

Leyden and in behalf of his company asked the burgomasters for permission to settle in the city. They were "members of the Christian Reformed church," he said, "to the number of one hundred persons, men and women," and asked only to be allowed to carry on their trades "without being a burden in the least to any one." Their large number indicates quite clearly that the small Scrooby group had been joined in this project by three or four score of the more disaffected Ancient Brethren.

The Leyden burgomasters replied, plainly with an eye on the scene at Amsterdam, that they were pleased to welcome all "honest" persons, "provided such persons behave themselves." Suddenly, at the command of James I, the English ambassador intervened with a protest to the Leyden authorities against their "agreement with certain Brownists," intimating that the latter were fugitives from justice. Fortunately the Dutch were not as sensitive as before to pressure from their English allies, for their bitter struggle against Spanish domination was about to end in a long truce, formally signed just a few months later. Consequently, the enlightened burghers politely but firmly brushed aside the ambassador's protest and reiterated their settled policy to admit all honest persons regardless of their religious faith. They did not know whether the petitioners were Brownists or not, they said, and the inference was plain that they did not care. This silenced the English ambassador, and by May 1, 1609, the second leg of a long and trying pilgrimage had been completed—but not without casualties.

The "Saincts" lost their pastor, Clyfton abandoning his flock to remain with the Ancient Brethren, for which he was never forgiven and which he himself lived to regret. Ruling Elder Daniel Studley took the withdrawal as a personal insult. The seceding brethren, he raged, were "ignorant idiots, noddy Nabalites, dogged Doegs, faire-faced Pharisees, shameless Shemeites, malicious Machivillians." Francis Johnson and others were also angry at losing so large a part of the congregation, almost a third of the membership. This fanned old resentments to flame, new causes of conflict were born, and the church was soon wrecked by a final shattering explosion. John Robinson and his company had escaped not a moment too soon.

The bitter quarrels among the Ancient Brethren involved both doctrine and morals, for the first had been invoked to defend practices absolutely indefensible. Scandal again broke into a lurid blaze when several members withdrew from the congregation in disgust and blasted its leaders in an avidly read and widely quoted book, *The Prophane Schisme of the Brownists or Separatists, with the Impietie, Dissensions, and Lewd and Abhominable Vices of that Impure Sect,* written by Christopher Lawne and three colleagues. One need not credit their more extravagant statements to believe in the essential truth of their charges, especially as these were confirmed by events and the belated confession of the worst offender.

Lawne and his collaborators acknowledged that they were "unlearned" men, like most of those "taken in the net of Brownism." Yet they hoped their book would "not be disliked therefore, seeing we speak of nothing but what our own knowledge and experience hath taught us." They were inclined rather to pity than censure Richard Clyfton, "a most simple and piteous teacher," a mere "bond-slave unto St. Francis." As for the latter, the pastor's swift and shifty courses were "as the way of an Eagle, in the Ayre." But they reserved their utmost contempt for the "two principall pillars of that Rotten Separation," Elders Edward Benet and Daniel Studley. The former, a man of wealth and influence, played to Johnson the role of "King of Spaine unto the Pope," while the other regularly sat next to the pastor "in the usurped throne of their judgment, and eftsoones upon each occasion he whispers in St. Francis's ear, who bends & listens to him."

By all accounts Studley had traveled a long downward course since those days in London fifteen years before when he had been the trusted associate and confidant of Greenwood and Barrow. It was he who had smuggled out of prison, sheet by sheet, the writings for which the latter were hanged. Studley himself escaped the hangman only by grace of a commuted sentence. But in crossing to The Netherlands, or somewhere along the way, his character had suffered a marked sea change, and he was now a thorough reprobate—though a rather amusing one, it must be said, for he had a quick, impudent, and often disarming wit.

Studley's favorite was the much admired Mrs. Judith Holder, named by White as one of his paramours. The gay and toothsome Judith, though a great joy to some, was plainly a thorn in the flesh of others. When her husband was lying on what he presumed to be his deathbed, Judith sat beside him happily singing. When her spouse unexpectedly recovered, he had her summoned before the elders for "unnatural and unchristian behaviour." Sympathy was all on his side until Studley excepted, defending Judith's conduct on the ground that it was "a most holy and religious action to praise the Lord with songs in adversitie." A few months later, the Ruling Elder was caught hiding behind a large basket in her bedchamber. But it was innocent enough, he declared, for he had come on official business, to observe the "behaviour of G.P. who came thither after him." Only a few weeks passed before still another admirer, Geoffrey Whittaker, was taken in bed with Judith. Studley interceded and they escaped censure on his plea that Geoffrey had been performing a "simple dutie of Christian love," having come "but to comfort Judith Holder, being sicke, to keep her warme." But a somewhat different complexion was placed upon the matter not long after, when Geoffrey had to be excommunicated for publicly boasting that he had "laine with her night after night." Judith, too, had taxed the brethren's patience to the limit, and she was soon cast out.

Studley was also very fond of Marie May, "the victualler," who in her tavern used "to sing such Songs as is a shame to report (being more fit for a common Bawd, than for a person professing such pure Separation from the other Churches)." Marie had been excommunicated for lying with her husband before marriage, and many publicly charged that she had bribed Studley to wink at this by indulging him with "joynts of meat and bottles of wine." Anxiously seeking readmission to the church, Marie swore a mighty oath that if she ever got in again, "all the Devills in Hell could not get her out." Some gossip reported this—unfortunately, snooping and gossip steadily became a more integral part of the Holy Discipline—and Marie was once more called upon to explain. Studley saved her by persuading the eldership that Marie's was "a very holy speech, shewing her faith and hope of assistance from the Lord." But the Ruling Elder really surpassed himself in defending her when, "having been in a whore-house upon some occasion," she was observed crawling out a window "in a very untoward manner." Just as she was about to be tossed to the wolves, the chief of Bradford's four "grave" elders stepped forward and quoting Scripture, at which he was apt as the devil, pointed triumphantly to II Corinthians 2. 33, which deals with St. Paul's escape from his enemies in Damascus by climbing through a window in the city wall and using a basket to lower himself to the ground.

Studley's most recent attempt had been made upon the young daughter of Henry Ainsworth. This hastened the impending break between Ainsworth and Pastor Johnson, for the latter defended Studley in all things. In this instance, testimony against him was offered by four of the brethren, including Edward Tolwine, one of the first of the Separatists, a member of Robert Browne's original group, highly revered by all as one who had suffered greatly for the faith. Well past eighty, the disillusioned old man now withdrew from the congregation and soon died of a broken heart. Studley could not well enter a denial, but blandly excused everything by saying that he was merely interested in discovering the child's sex. And if the latter had not screamed, "who doubts but what he would have knowne whether she was man or woman?" exclaimed Lawne, who denounced Studley in good round Elizabethan phrases as "a beastly camel, . . a filthie Swine, . . a slipperie Eele, . . a hard shell-fish, . . a hypocritical Camelion, . . a Griffon, . . a Night-Crow, so often and so ordinarily haunting with other men's wives, at unseasonable times of the night, as namely Mistresses M., V., C., K., D., and divers others heretofore."

Nor was this the sum of the rogue's transgressions. The Ancient Brethren conducted a school—with Studley as master, it seems—

and parents of many children were soon complaining that "instead of catechising them and learning them to know God," he taught them "vaine, idle, and wicked songs" and other things "more becoming the streets of Sodome than of Sion." But the greatest weight was attached to his enormity in falling asleep "in time of publike worship, though an Elder, and sitting in a throne in a high and eminente place, whereby his offense became more offensive and notorious." In this, however, Studley had to yield to another of the brethren, one Richard Mansfield, later a deacon, who slept not only through the public service but "yet further, which is more strange, even when himselfe hath been praying at home with his familie." It would have been stranger still if his snores had been more readily distinguishable from the drone of interminable prayers.

And for daring to question the behavior of such men, exclaimed Lawne and his collaborators, they had been charged with "disloyalty" and hauled before Francis Johnson, who flew out at them in a great rage. "The first word he spake was a reproach; the second, railing also; the third was a lie; the fourth was a word of tyranny."[3]

These, then, were the "some other reasons" which induced Robinson and his company to be off before the storm broke in full fury. But the rock upon which the Ancient Brethren finally split was the interpretation of these five words from Matthew 18.17.—". . . tell it unto the Church." The passage was from Christ's injunction that if one of the faithful injured another and the matter could not be privately settled, it should be brought before the church for its decision. That seemed plain enough. But what was the church, and who spoke for it? The congregation, said Ainsworth, expressing the democratic Brownist and Barrowist view. The eldership, said Francis Johnson, rapidly moving away from his former convictions toward higher ground. As many of the congregation were now resolved to unseat them, Studley and other officers naturally sided with Johnson. With the two factions at loggerheads, Ainsworth suggested that Robinson and Brewster mediate the conflict. The latter offered a compromise which was accepted. But Johnson quickly broke the agreement by demanding that Ainsworth and his group migrate to Leyden, which they declined to do.

Late in 1610 the Ancient Brethren, once the pride of the Separatist movement, came to an inglorious end. Violating every principle of the church, the "Franciscans" arbitrarily excommunicated Ainsworth's group and seized the meeting house in the Bruinistengange, to which they had small legal and less moral right, forcing their opponents to meet for a time in a former Jewish synagogue a few doors down the street. The majority of the rank and file went with Ainsworth, but Johnson retained the loyalty and dubious talents of Studley, Deacon ("Judas the Purse-Bearer") Bowman, and all officers but two. One was Elder Jean de l'Écluse, recently married to Jacqueline May, elder sister of young Dorothy, soon to be Bradford's bride. L'Écluse was promptly denounced as an accomplished tippler and trencherman, and a notorious sot. In reply he offered to prove before a court of law that there was "probable murther, and approved whoredoms, maintained or suffered in M. Johnson's church." Litigation for possession of the meeting house, eventually awarded to the Ainsworthians, inspired new bitterness and even more slanderous recrimination, to the embarrassment not merely of Separatists but of Protestants everywhere.

When this split occurred, Clyfton was chosen as "teacher" in Ainsworth's stead. He immediately undertook to defend the "Franciscans" in general and Ruling Elder Daniel Studley in particular, asking the latter to frame his own reply to critics. What Clyfton was thinking of in publishing Studley's "Answer" is beyond comprehension. The latter blandly confessed almost everything charged against him, merely insisting that he had reformed since 1610. Even this was not true, and his brethren stripped him of office and threw him out at long last. Clyfton had no sooner published his defense of Studley than he had to retract it, "and that under his own hand, in writing." Four years later, in 1616, the Pilgrims' first pastor died in Amsterdam at the age of sixty-three, a broken and unhappy man, separated even from the Franciscans. After their ejection from the meeting house, the latter had moved on to Emden in the first step of a final pilgrimage that was to bring most of them to a fearful and tragic end far from home, on the tempestuous Atlantic, off the Virginia capes, a disaster that sent a cold chill down the spines of those at Leyden who were then contemplating a similar voyage. Francis Johnson was spared this last crushing blow, dying at Amsterdam early in 1618. The fate of that once "bouncing" girl, the engaging Thomasine, is lost in the mists of history.

Meanwhile, at the height of these commotions, poor John Smyth, the high-minded and simple-hearted, had died in obscurity, brought to his grave prematurely by want and hardship. After a modest service in the Great Cake House, his few remaining followers bore his corpse to the Niewe Kerk for burial. Now leaderless, they once more sought to join one of the local Mennonite churches and in 1615 they were admitted. For a time a separate English service was conducted for them in Jan Munter's bakery, but they were soon absorbed by the Dutch, leaving no trace of themselves as a group, or of Smyth's eager researches into the one "true" course of salvation.

Perhaps this was just as well, for in his later years Smyth had come to frown upon the rigidities of dogma and the fierce intolerance which these bred among the self-righteous and more precise. In his last work, published a year after his death in 1612, he divorced himself from all controversy about ceremony, ritual, and the outward forms of the church. If a man were a "penitent and faithful Christian," that was enough, he declared, and no church should require more. In particular he renounced the "vice" of sharply and generously censuring others, to which he and his brethren had been so addicted in what he described as the days of his "blind zeal and preposterous imitation of Christ." If any of his old friends were now disposed to charge him with inconstancy, "let them think of me as they please," he said. "I will every day, as my errours shall be discovered, confesse them & renounce them. . . .

I professe I have changed, and shall be readie still to change for the better."

Johnson and Clyfton found all of this "sad and woeful." Even John Robinson was "very hard" on the gentle soul who had led him to the light. But Smyth died content, at peace with himself and the world, happy at last in a "triumphant assurance of Salvation."

6

AT THE
GREEN GATE,
LEYDEN

... and many came unto them from diverse parts of England, so as they grew a large congregation.

—WILLIAM BRADFORD

THREE YEARS BEFORE SMYTH'S DEATH, IN 1609, JUST AS SPRING set the lovely Dutch countryside aglow with color, the pastorless Scrooby group and the "Machivillians" fleeing the Ancient Brethren said their farewells in Amsterdam, plainly without regret, and departed for Leyden. It lay only a short distance away to the southwest, about twenty-five miles by road. But as travel by water was easier and cheaper, Robinson and his company probably went the long way round—sailing up and out the Zuyder Zee and down the coast to the mouth of the Old Rhine, proceeding up the historic river six or seven miles to the quays at Leyden, their new home.

It was, they noted with delight, "a fair & bewtifull citie, and of a sweete situation." And with its fine old buildings and spotless houses, its broad streets paved with brick, its many green and shaded squares, its blue canals lined with lindens and spanned by many graceful stone bridges, it was indeed a beautiful city, one of the fairest of that or any other time—and the Pilgrims never forgot it. How many of them during that first awful winter at Plymouth must have looked back on it with a sigh, with perhaps even an occasional doubt, quickly suppressed, of the wisdom of exchanging its comforts and felicities for the heartbreaking wants of a raw outpost on the farthermost frontier.

Though far smaller than Amsterdam, being scarcely a third its size, and wanting the latter's great maritime traffic, Leyden was a busy city of 80,000 or more people, the flourishing center of handicraft industries offering many opportunities for employment. More important perhaps, it was one of the spiritual capitals of Protestant Europe by reason of its already famous university, founded in 1575 to commemorate the Leydeners' heroic defense of their homes, their lives, and their faith against the besieging armies of Spain, the sword of the Holy Inquisition. The newcomers found the Leydeners to be helpful and affable, though some fault was later found with them for the lighthearted way in which they spent the Sabbath. But all in all, Robinson and his group were pleased.

The company settled down around the Pieterskerk, or St. Peter's, formerly a Roman Catholic cathedral, a plain but massive structure in the center of the city. Close by, the university occupied a cluster of nondescript buildings, once the Convent of the White Nuns, housing students from all parts of Europe, many from England. It was a rather poor and crowded quarter, cut by many winding lanes and alleys. In one of these the Brewsters lived during their stay in Leyden, and until his marriage a few years later Bradford probably shared their house in the Stincksteeg, or Stink Alley—or Stench Lane, as some have more delicately put it. But the odors and fumes in the dank dark alley were anything but delicate, and the Brewsters soon lost a child here. In the group the rate of infant mortality ran high throughout these Leyden years, a reflection of the poverty in which most of the congregation lived.

A few of the richer later found means to establish small businesses of their own, largely as merchants, but in the beginning all were forced to work for wages. Bradford became a maker of fustian (corduroy or moleskin); young Jonathan Brewster, now sixteen, was a ribbon maker. The rest were variously employed as wool combers and carders, finishers of bombazine and other cloth, silk workers, felt makers, button makers, drapers, tailors, hatters, glovers, leather dressers, cobblers, metal workers, carpenters, cutlers, barbers, brewery workers, stone and brick masons, hod carriers, printers, block makers, pipe makers, and pump makers. All worked from sunrise to sundown for wages which, at best, barely provided subsistence and often touched the starvation level. William Brewster had a very hard time of it at first. His once ample means had been exhausted by his unstinting aid to the group. He had a large family, and as he was now getting on in years, was not as fit as others were for the general run of jobs, "espetially such as were toylesume & laborious." After a time, however, his fortunes began to mend when he "fell into a way (by reason he had ye Latine tongue)" of offering private lessons in English to students at the university. According to Bradford, the latter quickly acquired great facility in the language, for, *horribile dictu,* Brewster "drew rules to lerne it by, after ye Latine manner." But many came to study with him, Danes and Germans particularly, "some of them being great men's sonnes."

The group's initial struggle for mere existence was so all-absorbing that it virtually drops from sight for several years. Only an occasional glimpse is caught of a few individuals. Where the congregation met during this period is unknown. But it met regularly, there can be no doubt of that, probably in one or another of the members' houses until May, 1611, when it acquired a permanent place of worship in the Kloksteeg, or Bell Alley, with the purchase from one Heer van Poelgeest of a "spacious" old house which stood facing the south transept of the Pieterskerk. It was known as the Groenepoort, or Green Gate. As it served both as a meeting house and a parsonage, John and Bridget Robinson moved in with their maid, Mary Hardy, and three children—John, Bridget, and Isaac. Behind the house was a garden, and beyond this an open lot about fifty yards square, walled in on three sides and opening on the fourth to the Dark Canal, the Donckeregrafte. In this open lot were built many small houses to shelter the poorer members of the congregation. The Green Gate was a pleasant spot, but its acquisition entailed heavy sacrifices from all, for it cost them 8,000 guilders ($10,500), payable a fourth down and the remainder at 500 guilders a year, a considerable debt for so impoverished a congregation.

Settled at last after many difficulties, the company lived for many years "in a comfortable condition, injoying much sweete & delightefull societie & spirituall comforte togeather in ye wayes of God, under ye able ministrie and prudente governmente of Mr. John Robinson & Mr. William Brewster. . . . So as they grew in knowledge & other gifts & graces of ye spirit of God, & lived togeather in peace, & love, and holiness."

Here Robinson came into his own as a gentle, wise, and resourceful leader. He was very pleasant and courteous in manner, "towards his own people espetially," though on occasion he could be "very plain" with them. He despised hypocrites who inveighed against the sins of others and yet were "remisse in themselves and not so carefull to express a vertuous conversation." He likewise despised those who were "close and cleaving unto themselves, and retired from ye commone good." Peace and unity were his aims at all times so far as these could be achieved "with faith and a good conscience." Robinson preached three times a week, twice on the Sabbath and again on Thursday evenings, to the great comfort and content of his disciples. The latter held him "in precious estimation, as his worth & wisdom did deserve," for in addition to his "singuler abilities in divine things (wherin he excelled)," Robinson had a level head in business affairs and other worldly matters. Quick to sense hidden dangers, he skilfully led his flock around many a pitfall and in every way was a "commone father unto them."

Brewster, too, gave eminent satisfaction as ruling elder. He had a "singuler good gift of prayer" and was superlative, it was said, "in ripping up ye hart & conscience before God." His teachings were "very plaine & distincte," and they were pleasingly brief, for he used to say that "it were better for ministers to pray oftener, and devide their prears, than to be longe & tedious in ye same." His ears still ringing with the squabbles at Amsterdam, he took great care to keep the church in good order, preserve purity of doctrine, and suppress any errors that might creep in to disturb the peace. When contentions arose, which is bound to happen "even amongst ye best of men," as Bradford observed, they were "nipt in ye head betimes." Nor would Brewster tolerate any Studleys, for he quickly purged the church of all the "incurable & incorrigible."

The deacon of the church was Samuel Fuller, serge maker, apparently the leader of the seceding Ancient Brethren. To him had been addressed that alliterative letter in which Studley denounced his former brothers as "ignorant idiots," among other things. Named to the inner council of the church here, it would seem, to represent the large non-Scrooby majority among the communicants, Fuller appears for a time to have been the only deacon though he later had two able colleagues, both better known than he. Born at Redenhall, Norfolk, and now in his thirties, Fuller had been "bred a butcher," according to a later enemy, who probably was just being malicious about the fact that at Plymouth the deacon was the Pilgrims' "surgeon & physition," cutting and bleeding many. But "in his facultie, so otherwise," his brethren found him a "man godly, and forward to doe good."

The congregation here did not have a deaconess, perhaps in want of any suitably "anciente Widow." Certainly it was not in want of little birchen rods or an aversion to using them, for "ye Saincts" always believed in quite literally beating the devil out

of "impious" little children, out of "wretched little boys" especially, about whom there were grievous complaints at Plymouth.
Nor did the church fill the office of prophet, doubtless because of
the antics at Amsterdam of "Prophets" Thomas Cocky and Jacob
Johnson, another of Francis' younger brothers, who did not always
provide the enlightenment so confidently expected of them. They
spent most of their time in acrimonious debate, formally charging
each other with telling lies, which left the brethren bewildered
and quite at a loss to know whose was the true revelation.

On the Sabbath the congregation met early to enjoy the first
of two extended exercises—"the publick ordinances of praying
and preaching," as they were called. During the meeting the Saints
were not allowed to sit as they pleased in cozy little family groups.
As they filed in, the men took their seats on the hard wooden
benches to one side, the women sat apart across the aisle, while
the children were placed off by themselves under the stern and
restless eye of the deacons. This was known as "dignifying the
meeting," an institution carried to Plymouth where it persisted
for generations, almost down to the nineteenth century.

Having assembled bright and early on a Sabbath morning, at
least by eight o'clock, the Saints first prayed. During prayer the
members of the congregation stood up, not going down on their
knees, for kneeling was an "idolatrous" Roman practice. After the
opening prayer, often continuing for an hour or more, Pastor
Robinson took up his huge Geneva Bible and read a passage aloud
—always with comment and exposition, for mere "dumb reading"
was prohibited by the Holy Discipline. Next, a psalm was sung,
without instrumental music of any kind, for that also was proscribed by the Holy Discipline, which specifically banned the use
of the organ, "the Divill's bag-pipes."

Nor did the congregation have musical notation of any kind
to aid its singing. All tunes were sung from memory. Someone
set the pitch, usually one of the deacons, and all lifted their voices
together, with the men taking the lead in the song, which was
sung as a simple melody, for the Saints shared Calvin's aversion

to part singing as "frivolous and unbecoming the House of God."

At Amsterdam there had been loud complaints about the singing, even among the brethren. It was so bad, many protested, that "the congregation was made a laughing stocke to strangers who on occasion came to see them in their publike worship." The songs they sang—out of the Sternhold and Hopkins *Psalm Book* (1549)—were "of so harsh & hard a phrase," they said, "that they knew not what they meant, . . . neyther could they sing them with understanding."

Sharing their displeasure, Henry Ainsworth undertook to provide something better. His *Book of Psalmes: Englished both in Prose & Metre,* published at Amsterdam in 1612, was immediately adopted by the Saints at the Green Gate and later carried with them to Plymouth. Ainsworth's fame as a scholar was great, but his translation of the Psalms was so wretched that many critics insisted there must be two Ainsworths.[1]

After song came the sermon, which ordinarily lasted several hours and was preached not from a pulpit but a low dais supporting a simple wooden table. Here, in black clothes and black gloves, Robinson expounded his text with a quiet and moving eloquence, a deep human understanding, and a wealth of apt illustration that held his brethren spellbound, for the Green Gate pastor was not a bookish doctrinaire. He had a firm grasp of essentials, and a sharp perceptive eye gave his thought its breadth and depth.

For the meat of his observations, Robinson once remarked, he was beholden, above all, to the Holy Scriptures; "next, to the memorable sayings of wise and learned men which I have read or heard and carefully stored up as a precious treasure for mine own and others' benefit; and lastly, to the great volume of men's manners which I have diligently observed and from them gathered no small part thereof, having also had in the days of my pilgrimage special opportunities of conversing with persons of divers nations, estates, and dispositions, in great variety."

When the sermon was done, the congregation sang another song, and on appropriate occasions the sacraments were then administered. The deacons now came forward to pass the collection plates, and the morning exercise ended about noon with a benediction.

Early in the afternoon the congregation met again for a less formal exercise known as "prophecying." After the opening prayer Pastor Robinson or Ruling Elder Brewster chose a text, spoke to it briefly, and then opened the meeting for general discussion. Only the men could speak, for women had no voice in the church, in accord with the prohibition laid down by St. Paul. The Saints had taken John Smyth severely to task for his more liberal attitude in this matter. Not the least of his heresies, in their view, was his "errour" in allowing and even encouraging "females" to speak up in meeting, even in "censures" of wayward males, an unheard-of procedure!

More than anything else, it was this "prophecying" by laymen which scandalized the orthodox and led them to sneer at all Separatist preachers as "rude mechanick fellowes." But their snobbery only revealed their profound ignorance of Scripture, said Robinson, who pointed "to that which is written, Acts xiii. 14, &c., where Paul and Barnabas coming into the synagogue, the rulers, after the work of the ordinary ministry was ended (considering them not as apostles, which they acknowledged not, but only as men having gifts), sent unto them, that if they had any word of exhortation to the people, they should say on."

Here at Leyden it is possible to identify a few more of the original Scrooby congregation. Several of them may have been at Amsterdam though they do not appear in the record, which suggests that their flight was delayed until the removal to Leyden. There was Roger White, Bridget Robinson's brother, and Jane White, her youngest sister, who in 1611 was married here to Ralph Tickens, looking-glass maker of London, probably another of the Ancient Brethren. Later in the year Elizabeth Neal, "maid of Scrooby," became the bride of William Buckrum, block maker, of Ipswich. There were the two Mortons, George and Thomas, sons of a well-to-do Roman Catholic family at Harworth, a few miles up the Ryton from Scrooby, and their neighbor Francis

Cooke, of the hamlet of Blyth, all Pilgrim Fathers in time. A merchant at York before coming to Leyden, George Morton was married here in 1611 to Juliana Carpenter, sister of Deacon Fuller's wife.

There are five other possibilities. In 1610, Wybra(?)Hanson became the wife of a young fustian maker of Dover, William Pontus ("Pantes," the Dutch wrote it). William Brewster was a witness for the bride, who may have been related to Bradford and from the vicinity of Austerfield, for she bore his mother's family name. In any case, the "Pantes" belatedly appeared in Plymouth and are properly numbered among the Pilgrim company. Living with Brewster, as his wards, were two adolescents, Robert Peck and his sister Ann, from "Laundé" (probably Sutton-cum-Lound). Finally, there was Edward Southworth, with his brother Thomas. The former, a silk worker, was married here in 1613 to Alice Carpenter, the second Mrs. Bradford, another of the many daughters of Alexander Carpenter who had early crossed from the West of England—from the hamlet of Wrington, near Bath—to join the Ancient Brethren.[2]

And these, together with the Robinsons, the Brewsters, and William Bradford, comprise all of those at Leyden who can have been identified in any way with the surreptitious meetings at the old manor house beside the Ryton. All told, they number just twenty-one persons, including four small children. The dominance of the Scrooby group rested not upon its numbers but the leadership it provided. More particularly, it rested upon the character and abilities of Robinson and Brewster. That the church continued to grow in reputation and size till it numbered some three hundred members can be regarded in large measure as their personal triumph. No quarrels or scandals broke out here to mar the peace of Robinson's company, of which it can be truthfully said "to ye honour of God, & without prejudice to any, that such was ye true pietie, ye humble zeale, & fervent love of this people . . . towards God and his waies, and ye single hartednes & sinceir affection one towards another, that they came as near ye primative patterne of ye first churches as any other church of these later times has done."

The congregation took no formal name in Leyden. Nor was it
the only English church in the city. Another had been formed
about a year before its arrival. Popularly known as the Scottish
Church because of its Calvinist tenets and Presbyterian structure,
it was really an English-speaking unit of the Dutch Reformed
Church. The latter was not a state church, but it enjoyed special
privileges. The state paid the salaries of its ministers and assigned
each of its congregations a place to worship. The Scottish Church
had been given St. Catherine's Gasthuis, formerly a convent chapel,
which stood close to the Pieterskerk and the Green Gate. As Calvinism had been rejected alike by Browne and Barrow, Robinson's
company could not subscribe to many of its rival's beliefs and
practices, but there were here no such bitter clashes as at Amsterdam where the Ancient Brethren had continuously quarreled with
a similar church there. Here in Leyden, on the contrary, the two
English churches were soon so closely associated that it is often
difficult to distinguish between the members of one and the other.
On occasion, against all precedent and every precept of the Holy
Discipline, they even took communion together, an offense which
the Ancient Brethren punished with excommurication, expelling
Deacon Matthew Slade for so corrupting himself.

Robinson had earlier held such narrow self-righteous views,
but he now became far less rigid and intolerant. However deficient
non-Separatists might be in their grasp of the whole truth, he
brought himself to admit that any and all were Christians who
"grounded their practice upon the Word of God." He even allowed
that a man was not necessarily lost if he prayed, sang the Psalms,
or read the Scripture with members of the Church of England—
provided this were discreetly done in private. Only those were to
be shunned who, like the Anglican bishops, "hated Reformers and
Reformation, and went on in antichristian opposition to it and
persecution of it." As the members of the Dutch Reformed Church
were obviously of the elect, no harm could come of association
with them. Many in the congregation followed the practice of
young John Jenney, brewery worker from Norwich, later a Pilgrim
Father, who when business took him to other cities always attended

Dutch services "without any offence to the Church." Many of the Dutch and French-speaking Walloons came, in turn, to hear Robinson at the Green Gate, and not a few were converted and joined the final pilgrimage to the New World—notably, Philippe de la Noye (Delano), Godbert Godbertson (Cuthbert Cuthbertson), Moses Symonson (Simmons), Hester Mayhieu (Mrs. Francis Cooke), and Bridget van der Velde, who in 1615 married John Tilley from London, silk maker. The rival churches remained on the friendliest of terms, and within thirty years the Scottish Church, much the stronger of the two, absorbed what remained of Robinson's congregation after the partial exodus to Plymouth and its beloved pastor's untimely death, and thus became, as it were, its foster mother.

But in its day the company at the Green Gate more than held its own, winning many friends as it gradually identified itself with the life of the city. Many of the members became citizens of Leyden, principally for business reasons, for none but citizens could belong to the guilds which controlled all skilled employment and independent trades in the city. With characteristic foresight and decision, Bradford took out his citizenship papers in 1612 when he had just turned twenty-three. Five years later Jonathan Brewster likewise became a citizen. A half dozen other Pilgrim Fathers are to be found in this enterprising and less impoverished group. Among others, it included Isaac Allerton of London, a tailor, who rose rapidly to prominence at Plymouth and was second in command for years; his brother-in-law, Degory Priest of London, a hatter; a wool comber of Sandwich, Richard Masterson, later a deacon; Thomas Rogers, dealer in camlet; and John Turner, merchant.

Soon after becoming a citizen of Leyden, Bradford married. His bride was young Dorothy May, daughter of Henry May of Wisbeach, Cambridgeshire, who had been one of the Ancient Brethren since 1598 and was now an elder in Ainsworth's church. Dorothy's sister Jacqueline had married Jean de l'Écluse, formerly one of Francis Johnson's elders and now also with Ainsworth. Whether Marie May, "the victualler," Studley's friend, was a member of this family does not appear. Nor does it appear that there were two English families of that name at Amsterdam.

Tender in years and apparently of heart, for little is known of her but her tragic fate, Dorothy was just sixteen. Evidently Bradford had kept up rather close relations with some of the now divided Ancient Brethren, visiting them occasionally and having an opportunity to court Dorothy. Either that, or he had made his choice years before while at Amsterdam, when Dorothy was still a child of ten or eleven. However it was, Bradford now summoned her, and Dorothy came alone to the wedding, perhaps in virtual flight from the always sulphurous atmosphere at Amsterdam. Selling lands inherited at Austerfield, Bradford bought a small house on the Achtergracht, or Back Canal, and there established his girl bride. The son soon born to them was named John, probably for John Robinson, for the name was not traditional in the Bradford family.

During these years there was much marrying in the congregation, both among the young and the somewhat older. Death struck often at the Green Gate, and almost without exception widows and widowers manifested an eager desire to exchange their single blessedness for the conveniences, comforts, and innocent pleasures of marriage. So far as the women were concerned, this is not so difficult to understand, for at a time when all employment but domestic service was closed to them, the lot of a poor widow in a strange land was a hard and bitter one at best. As the choice of mates was narrow and largely restricted to the congregation, it was not long before most of the families were interrelated, one of the roots of the clannish spirit that so often bedeviled affairs at Plymouth.

In 1615, at the age of thirty-nine, John Robinson entered the University of Leyden as a student of theology and was immediately drawn into a controversy raging about the tenets of the Arminians. The views of this sect were anathema to Dutch Calvinists and English Brownists alike, for the Arminians held that Christ had made atonement for the sins of all mankind, both for Christians and non-Christians, though as "true" believers the former stood to profit most, of course, from his sacrifice. This was bad enough, but the Arminians went on to deny the doctrine of predestination, arguing that a soul bound for heaven might possibly slip from grace and land in hell. Such childish nonsense, such utter want of logic, was simply not to be borne.

With the university and city resounding to the clamor of the dispute—or of the disputants, at least—matters soon reached a pass where the advocates of one school refused to "hear ye other teach," which has a modern and familiar ring. Robinson, however, was an exception, listening with attention to all arguments, for he used to say "many times, both in writing and disputation, he knew he had sufficiently answered others, but many times not himself, and was ever desirous of *any* light."

With such an attitude, Robinson quickly learned the dodges and shifts of his adversaries, and he now "begane to be terrible to ye Arminians." Luther-like, the latters' champion posted a number of theses and dared anyone to debate them publicly with him. According to the story later told by Bradford and Winslow, Polyander and other renowned Calvinist professors at the university urged Robinson to step forward, but he was "loath, being a stranger." When they continued to importune him, he at length "condesended" and on the appointed day before a large assembly put his opponent "to an apparent non-plus," repeating the performance a second and then a third time for good measure, which "caused many to praise God that ye trueth had so famous a victory." The records of Leyden, unfortunately, are silent about all this, and in view of the temper of the times it seems quite unlikely that the Calvinists stepped aside and allowed the Brownists alone to enjoy the pleasure of slaughtering the Arminians.

In addition to all else, Robinson now began to write for publication, issuing one volume after another in defense of "ye trueth" against hydra-headed "errour." Like all of the reformers, he was an ardent proselytizer, burning with zeal to bring all men—all Englishmen especially—to the light. But how this could be accomplished was another question. There was no legal way of reaching the minds of Englishmen through the iron ring of censorship.

From Roman Catholic days the Anglican bishops had inherited almost limitless powers as "guardians of faith and morals." Without their approval, no book could be published or imported into the realm, an arbitrary power exercised through the law requiring that all publications be registered with the Company of Stationers, a conservative London guild directly under the thumb of the Church and the Court. None of the Tudors or Stuarts made any pretense of tolerating freedom of the press. In their eyes it was a hellish device to upset the divine and eternal order of things. But others construed God's will quite differently and were resolved to carry on the age-long fight for the right of all men to speak the truth as they saw it.

Late in 1616 or early the next year, doubtless after serious consideration of several dangerous risks involved, William Brewster managed with the help of friends to set up a publishing house. He was chiefly indebted to one of a family of Kentish gentry, Thomas Brewer, who was, as the English ambassador to The Netherlands later described him, "a Gentleman of a good house, both of land and living, which none of his [religious] profession in these parts are." A man of thirty-six, sixteen years Brewster's junior, Brewer had settled in Leyden several years previously, buying a large residence known as the Groenehuis, or Green House, just a few doors down Bell Alley from the Green Gate. Like Robinson, he enrolled in the university, as a student of literature, and his house appears to have become something of a social and intellectual center for the local English, particularly for the university students among them, several of whom lived in the Groenehuis. Many years later, after his return to Kent, Brewer was charged with encouraging others to preach "in houses, barns, and woods, that the Church of England is the Whore of Babilon, and the Synagogue of Satan, &c.," for which he was clapped into jail for fourteen years as a "perfect Brownist."

But in Leyden, at least, Brewer was not a Brownist. Rather, he was a Calvinist, a member of the Scottish Church, although on occasion he "walked in communion with Master Robinson and also with Master Ainsworth." Brewer and Brewster differed in their creeds, but they were loyal partners and worked well together. The former provided the necessary capital while the latter served as general manager and editor-in-chief. They established an office and print shop in Choir Alley, the Koorsteeg, now better known in its Latin form, Vicus Chorali, thanks to the Pilgrim Press, as it has come to be known in fairly recent years. While the offices faced on the Koorsteeg, they were really part of Brewster's house, occupying an irregular extension which ran back from the main house on the Stincksteeg. For business reasons it was obviously better to have a Choir Alley rather than a Stink Alley address. Besides, an ostensibly separate address might have its uses in case of trouble. So successful was the ruse that scholars have only recently discovered that the two addresses identified different ends of the same L-shaped house.

Several fonts of type and other necessary equipment were bought and installed in the print shop. There may have been a small hand press or two, but this is doubtful in light of subsequent events. Plates from the shop were probably carried out to Dutch printers to be run off in their larger and better equipped establishments, at once an economical and prudent procedure, for if the need for hasty concealment arose, it would be much easier to hide a case or two of type than a bulky hand press. From London the partners brought over a master printer named John Reynolds to take charge of mechanical operations. The latter brought along as his assistant or apprentice a youth "of a very active genius," twenty-two-year-old Edward Winslow, destined to be one of the most distinguished of the Pilgrim Fathers, serving Plimoth Plantation for years as its astute and resourceful ambassador-at-large.

According to a carefully cherished family tradition, Winslow was a young gentleman of "qualitie" who happened to fall in with the Leyden company while making the grand tour of the Continent—traditionally taken by sons of the upper classes—and overnight embraced the lowly Separatist way of life. It is quite evident, however, that he had already been trained in the printing craft and had previously known Reynolds, for shortly after his arrival he was a witness for his master at the latter's marriage.

Winslow had probably worked for Reynolds in London, where he had connections, his mother Magdalen (Oliver) being a Londoner. But Winslow had been born in the west of England, near Worcester, in the hamlet of Careswell, being the eldest of five sons and three daughters. Family tradition also has it that young Edward was the first of the Winslows to adopt radical Separatist ideas. If so, his family was remarkably ripe for conversion. A younger brother accompanied him on the *Mayflower* a few years later. Three others followed as quickly as they could, and all but one remained in Plymouth to father a numerous progeny.

Brewster and Reynolds, with Winslow assisting, were soon hard at work in their shop and made remarkably good speed with their cumbersome equipment. Within a few months they had issued three books. The first was in Dutch, a translation of *A Plaine and Familiar Exposition of the Tenne Commandements, with a Methodicall short Catechisme,* by Dod and Cleaver. The other two were in Latin—one, a now meaningless polemic against a certain Grevinchovius by Dr. William Ames, a Calvinist, subsequently associated with the university here; the second, a reprint of "plain and succinct" commentaries on the Proverbs by Thomas Cartwright, also a Calvinist, once a fellow of Peterhouse College, who had been driven from Cambridge by his former friend John Whitgift and later jailed by him for several years. There was nothing Brownist about any of these volumes, and they obviously represented Brewer's rather than Brewster's choice. All were dated 1617 and bore the imprint of the house:

> Lugduni Batavorum
> Apud Guiljelmum Brewsterum
> In vico Chorali

This, too, should be noted about these works. None was in English and none dealt with the controversial issues of the day, so that no exception could be taken to them if they happened to fall under the eye of an Anglican bishop. They were the only volumes to bear the house imprint, for the purpose of the press was not as innocent as it seemed. The three signed works were merely a blind to screen other more important activities, for the press had been founded, as the English ambassador at The Hague soon complained, "to print prohibited books to be vended underhand in His Majesty's kingdoms."

For two years all went well, and Brewster had "imployement inoughg" to the further mending of his worldly estate. The production of the press was considerable for the time, but just how many works it surreptitiously issued during its brief existence is uncertain. Students of the matter variously estimate the number from fifteen to eighteen, but their lists of probabilities are not identical beyond a certain point. All agree, however, about eight titles—the three signed works and five others which can be rather confidently ascribed to the Pilgrim Press, largely on the basis of circumstantial evidence brought to light after the Choir Alley shop got into trouble.[3]

According to Sir Dudley Carleton, the complaining English ambassador, Brewster later acknowledged publishing *De vera et genuina Jesu Christi Domini et Salvatoris nostri Religione* (1618), a not particularly objectionable book by an "English minister." After studying the type and ornament used in this book, expert Dutch printers hired by Sir Dudley Carleton declared that the Choir Alley shop was also the source of *De regimine Ecclesiae Scoticanae* and *Perth Assembly*, written by David Calderwood, an able Scottish minister and church historian. Sir Dudley, it appears, was also right in attributing to the press *A Confutation of the Rhemists' Translation, Glosses, and Annotations on the New Testament* (1618), written by Thomas Cartwright. Lastly, it appears that Brewster published John Robinson's *The People's Plea for the Exercise of Prophesy* (1618).

Ironically enough, it was a Calvinist work, the *Perth Assembly,* which brought the Pilgrim Press to grief and set in motion a chain of events which greatly influenced the congregation's decision to be on the move again. The book was a sharp attack on James I and his bishops for their tyrannical attempts to impose episcopacy upon the stubborn Scots, who had succeeded in establishing their own independent Presbyterian kirk in 1560. James had suppressed it in 1610, but the Scottish people were still fighting a bold rear guard action. Anticipating stiff resistance in the general assembly of the kirk summoned to meet in Perth in 1618, the hierarchy hoped to crush the opposition by ordering the arrest of its leader, David Calderwood. But the latter, anticipating this move, had gone into hiding and from a safe point of vantage closely watched the proceedings at Perth. Upon their conclusion, he immediately sat down to blast them as wholly illegal, totally null and void, and to advise his people to pay no attention to them. His manuscript was smuggled across to Leyden to be set in type by Brewster, and Calderwood himself soon slipped away to spend some time in Leyden, where he often worshipped at the Green Gate and came to hold Robinson in the highest admiration.

Copies of the *Perth Assembly,* packed into French wine vats to escape detection, were smuggled back into Scotland where they were secretly distributed and widely read. In April, 1619, a copy came to the notice of the authorities who "in deep resentment" denounced the work as an "atrocious and seditious libel." Suspicion fell upon an Edinburgh printer and bookseller, James Cathkin, and on a visit to London not long after, he was seized and hauled before His Majesty to be examined. James worked himself into a towering rage in trying to bully the prisoner into making a confession. When he failed, he remanded Cathkin to jail where the latter remained for several weeks, until the middle of July, when he was released upon receipt of some highly interesting information from abroad which turned the search in quite another direction.

Unaware of Cathkin's arrest, the English ambassador reported from The Hague that he had just picked up a most offensive book entitled *Perth Assembly,* "written with much scorn and reproach" of His Majesty and the bishops. So far as he could discover, wrote Sir Dudley Carleton, it had been published "by a certain English Brownist of Leyden, as are most of the Puritan books sent over of late days into England." In another dispatch later in the week, he positively identified the culprit as "one William Brewster, a Brownist, who hath been for some years an inhabitant and printer at Leyden." But the knave was no longer there, "having within these three weeks removed from thence and gone back to dwell in London, where he may be found out and examined." Sir Dudley was mistaken here, for Brewster had prudently slipped away at least three months before, shortly after the trouble began in Scotland.

At the King's command, a determined search for Brewster now began along both sides of the North Sea and the Channel. From Sir Dudley's dispatches it is evident that the ruling elder's brethren did everything possible to throw the authorities off the track. Within a short time the ambassador reported that Brewster was back again in Leyden. No, that was wrong. Nor was Brewster likely to return to his old haunts, for he had—which was not the fact—"removed from thence his family and goods." Sorry, but Brewster was in Leyden after all. Somebody had seen him on the streets there. No, he was not in Leyden. He was in Amsterdam preparing to move to the town of Leiderdorp, "thinking there to be able to print prohibited books without discovery." But the thoroughly bewildered ambassador promised, "I shall lay wait for him, both there and in other places."

Angry and disgusted by his envoy's fumbling efforts, the King commanded him "to deal roundly" with the Dutch authorities "for the apprehension of him, the said Brewster, as they tender His Majesty's friendship." Redoubling his efforts, Sir Dudley triumphantly reported three weeks later that Brewster had been caught at last, seized at Leyden while lying sick in bed. He had also arrested "one Brewer, of his profession, a Brownist, who was an assistant to him in his printing." Steps were being taken "to have their books and printing letters seized; as likewise to have them examined of all the books, as well Latin as English, they have printed for the space of eighteen months or two years past."

What was Sir Dudley's chagrin to have to report the next day that he was again mistaken, for the bailiff, "being a dull drunken fellow," had let Brewster slip and arrested the wrong man. Had not the ambassador been so dull himself, he would have suspected long since that he was nowhere near his quarry and was being

cleverly misled by false clues, for all this time Brewster appears
to have been safely concealed somewhere in England, probably at
Scrooby or in the neighborhood. Months before, in May, just after
the storm broke, a friend had reported his presence in London,
discreetly writing his brethren at Leyden, "Mr. B. is not well at this
time; whether he will come back to you or goe into ye north, I
yet know not."

In want of Brewster, the wrath of James and his clerics was
turned upon Thomas Brewer, who was locked up for some time in
the prison of the University of Leyden. The shop in Choir Alley
was raided and incriminating cases of type were found hidden in
the attic. The printers, Reynolds and Winslow, were not seized,
but the former considered it prudent to move on to Amsterdam
where he lived for several years. The company at the Green Gate
did everything possible to aid Brewer, seeking to obtain his release
on bail, as Sir Dudley complained, saying that the "whole company of Brownists doth offer caution for Brewer, and he being a
university man, the scholars are likewise stirred up by the Brownists to plead Privilege in that kind." But pressure from the King
blocked this.

When brought up for examination, Brewer protested that nothing had been published by the press after November, 1618. If true,
which it almost certainly was not, this would have absolved him
and Brewster from all blame for *Perth Assembly,* which was issued
early the next year. Dissatisfied with the little that could be
wormed out of Brewer, James "requested" that he be sent over
to London to be questioned there, saying that he would not punish
him "further than with a free Confession of his own misdemeanours and those of his complices," promising to hand him back
unharmed to the Dutch authorities. "And for the time to come,"
ran his sharp command to the ineffectual Sir Dudley, "you are
required to move the States [General] to take some strict order
through all their Provinces for the preventing of the like abuses
and licentiousness in publishing, printing, and vending underhand
such scandalous and libellous pamphlets."

The university authorities refused to surrender Brewer. After a time, however, largely through the influence of Polyander, a famed scholar who had contributed a preface to one of the signed works of the press, Brewer was persuaded to go voluntarily on the assurance of the English ambassador that he would be returned within three months and that the King would bear the entire expense. Robinson and several others of the congregation accompanied Brewer to Rotterdam, where the university beadle delivered him into the hands of Sir William Zouche, a member of the Privy Council. Storms delayed their departure for several weeks and the travelers whiled away the time as best they could, principally in the taverns of the town, to the great concern of Brewer's friends who were scandalized to "hear Sir William hath taught him to drink healths."

In London, where he was closely examined for weeks on end, Brewer proved to be quite as stubborn as the King and "did all that a silly creature could to increase his dissatisfaction," according to a dispatch to The Hague from Sir Robert Naunton, Secretary of State. "But I have beaten him from his asse," the latter informed Sir Dudley Carleton, "and have drawn something from him that hath in part contented His Majesty, who bade me tell you that he gives no credit to this fool's confident and improbable assertions and"—reiterating the King's chief concern at the moment—"that he will be very good friends with you if you can procure Brewster to be taken."

After two months of fruitless questioning, Brewer was released with the expectation that he would immediately return to Leyden where some very unpleasant work had been laid out for him. He was to be kept under lock and key until he promised "to do his uttermost in finding out Brewster—wherein I will not fail likewise, of all other endeavors," Sir Dudley assured his royal master. But this plan was knocked askew by the King's refusal to honor the pledge given by his ambassador that all of Brewer's expenses would be borne by the Crown, which touched parsimonious Jaimie in a tender spot. He declined to bear more than his expenses in England, refusing to pay his passage home, which left the prisoner free to follow his own devices. Perhaps suspecting what was in store for him, Brewer chose to remain in England for some time, not returning to Leyden until three years later, which defeated the design to use him as an informer. Now thoroughly discouraged, Sir Dudley Carleton made a few more feeble gestures before abandoning the hunt for Brewster. But he made sure that the type and other equipment seized in the Choir Alley shop remained impounded. This ended the brief but stormy career of the underground Pilgrim Press, as active as any in its day.

If Brewster had been caught, he might possibly have been hanged, as his friend Penry had been. At best, he could have expected no better fate than that suffered a few years later by Alexander Leighton, a Scottish minister, for publishing in The Netherlands a "libellous" attack upon the Anglican church, not half as sharp as *Perth Assembly.* Tried before the notorious Star Chamber, Leighton was sentenced to pay a fine of £100,000, to be whipped and pilloried in the presence of the Court, to have one ear sliced off and his nose split, to have branded upon his forehead the letters "SS" (stirrer of sedition), to be whipped and pilloried again "at some conveniente later time," to have his other ear cut off, and to be imprisoned for life in the stinking Fleet.

No wonder, then, that "Mr. B." was not feeling well at this time and took to his heels at the first alarm, quickly vanishing and remaining out of sight for some time, probably in England. In any case, he is not seen again until almost a year and a half later, when the *Mayflower,* after long and dangerous delays, is well out to sea on her "waighty vioage."

7

THE MERCHANT
ADVENTURERS

It doth often trouble me to thinke that in
this busines we are all to lerne and none to
teach. . . .
—ROBERT CUSHMAN

THE HUNT FOR BREWSTER PRECIPITATED ACTION IN A MATTER
which had been more or less seriously discussed before. Late in
1617, more than a year before the Pilgrim Press got into trouble,
a sudden restlessness had seized the company at the Green Gate.
The immediate cause of this is obscure. To all outward appearances Leyden was still regarded as a pleasant and permanent
refuge. More members of the congregation had become citizens
of Leyden. Others had recently bought houses in the town. Operations at the Choir Alley shop were now well under way and
going prosperously. There was as much marrying and remarrying

as before. Among others, young Edward Winslow found for himself a bride in the group, Elizabeth Barker, probably of Chester; and the recently widowed Deacon Fuller took a third and last wife, Bridget Lee. Families were large, for the most part, and went on growing larger quite as if all believed themselves securely anchored here for many years to come.

Yet a change of mood was evident and became increasingly marked. The leaders of the group were worried—above all, by the poverty in which most of the congregation lived. Many were getting on in years, feeling old age stealing upon them, and their "great & continuall labours, with other crosses and sorrows, hastened it before ye time." Even worse, they were compelled by their need to put their children to work, and the latter were "so oppressed by their hevie labours that, though their minds were free and willing, yet their bodies bowed under ye weight of ye same and became decreped in their early youth, the vigour of nature being consumed in ye very bud, as it were." Their situation aroused an uneasy fear that within a few years they would either scatter by reason of necessity or "sinke under their burdens, or both." Aware of their hardships, friends in England hesitated to come to them, and some at Leyden had already given up the bitter struggle and returned home. "Yea," said Bradford, they "preferred & chose ye prisons in England rather than this libertie in Holland, with these afflictions."

Many began to argue not unreasonably that if they could find a place where they might live more comfortably and still enjoy freedom of religion, they would have greater success in spreading the glad tidings of salvation. They could then hope to make converts of all those who "desired to injoye ye ordinances of God in their puritie." Then, too, they wished to retain their identity as an English group, having no desire to be absorbed by the Dutch, which was not a fanciful danger, for in the end that was the fate of the larger part of this and every other Separatist congregation in exile. But a more immediate danger was the seduction of their children by "ye great licentiousnes of youth in that countrie and ye manifold temptations of ye place." The younger "Saincts" had developed as yet no great resistance to the lures of Satan, allowing themselves to slide with alarming ease "into extravagante & dangerous courses, getting ye raines off their neks, & departing from their parents." But that was one of the penalties of living among the jolly, pleasure-loving Dutch. It surprised and pained those at the Green Gate to observe that, do what they would in a friendly way to reform them, the Dutch remained incorrigibly light-hearted. This was bad enough on week days, but it was intolerable on the Sabbath, which the Dutch insisted upon celebrating as a holiday (holy day), simply laughing and tossing off another pot of beer when told it should be endured grimly as a penance.

Such were the "weightie & solid" reasons which led Robinson's company to decide to be on the move again. But a story was soon circulating that the Dutch wanted them to get out, being "wearie of them." This was a lie, said Bradford indignantly, a gross slander "beleeved of few, being raised only by ye malice of some who laboured their disgrace." His brethren were respected throughout the city. Employers were eager to hire them "for their honestie & diligence," and if any were "known to be of that congregation, the Dutch (both bakers and others) would trust them in any reasonable matter when they wanted money," which was often. The malicious story about them might quickly have been forgotten if a Dutch ballad maker had not picked it up and turned it into a rhyme, published as a broadside, in which he pictured the local Brownist church as a little worm trying to destroy the great fair tree of the Dutch Reformed Church. John Robinson, unfortunately, took a very serious view of this *jeu d'esprit,* and promptly sat down to write *A Just and Necessarie Apologie* (1619). As Brewster's press was in trouble, it was probably published at Amsterdam by an old friend, Giles Thorpe, one of the Ancient Brethren and now an elder in Ainsworth's church.

If Robinson had set out deliberately to make matters worse, he could scarcely have done as well as he did. His usual discretion and good sense deserting him in his anger, he bluntly attacked the hierarchical structure of the Dutch church with its synods, assemblies, and other central governing agencies, citing against it the "true" Brownist principle of independent congregations, each a church in itself and accountable to no higher authority, cooperating with sister churches in a purely voluntary fellowship. Ministers in the Dutch church had too much power and were too pretentious. Only they could preach, whereas preaching was a lay function, for it was the province of the entire eldership to teach as well as govern. The administration of the sacred rites was the pastor's only distinctive function. Robinson went on to denounce the use of set prayers, even the Lord's Prayer. Anybody could read a prayer. It was altogether as puerile a performance as for a child "to read of a book or prayer (saying), Father, I prey you give me bread, or fish, or an egg." And the Dutch could not possibly be true Christians so long as they went on benightedly celebrating Easter and Christmas, for which there was no warrant in Scripture.

These were important matters, certainly, but the company at the moment was more seriously interested in other things. The majority had decided, "not out of any newfanglednes or other such like giddie humour," that it was time to be moving on. But there was no general agreement about where to go. Some favored establishing a colony in the New World. Many violently objected, however, citing their want of funds for so ambitious a venture, the hardships of a long voyage, the danger of perishing of starvation and disease, not to speak of the savagery of the Indians, a "cruell, barbarous, & most trecherous" people, whose practices were such that a mere recitation of them caused "ye bowels of men to grate within them."

The dangers were great, it was admitted, "but not desperate; the difficulties were many, but not invincible." Such a step should not be taken "rashly or lightly, as many have done, for curiosite or hope of gaine, &c." But their undertaking was not an ordinary one. "Their ends were good & honourable; their calling, lawfull & urgente; and therefore they might expecte ye blessing of God in their proceding. Yea, though they should lose their lives in this action, yet might they have comforte in the same . . . All great &

honourable actions are accompanied with great difficulties, and must be both enterprised and overcome with answerable courages."

Whatever else may be said of the Pilgrims, it must be granted their courage was always "answerable."

And never more than here, for they decided in spite of all to go to the New World. But this raised debate on another question. Quite a few had their eyes fixed on Guiana or some other spot along the tropical Caribbean coast of South America. In the works of Sir Walter Raleigh and other explorers they had read that the land was rich and blessed with a perpetual spring. They could live off the trees, and would require less substantial houses and few clothes, just enough for modesty. The less romantic wanted to go to Virginia. Against this it was argued that the Anglican church was already established in the colony, and they might be as harassed and persecuted there as they had been at home, "and it might be worse." In the end, after much discussion, the vote was for Virginia. Here the company hoped to live as a group apart, harboring the notion that they might succeed in petitioning the King to grant them "freedome of Religion" Late in the summer of 1617, two agents were dispatched to London to see what could be done.

One of these was Deacon Robert Cushman, of Canterbury, a wool comber by trade and apparently another of the dissident Ancient Brethren who had quit Johnson's church in disgust. When he was named a deacon at the Green Gate is not known. A man of some education and better off than most, Cushman had bought in 1611 a small house in Nuns Alley, close to the Pieterskerk. The following year he purchased a larger house, also in the Nonnensteeg, where in 1616 he lost his wife and one of two children, being left with a young son, Thomas, destined in time to succeed William Brewster as ruling elder. Now approaching forty, the deacon had just found himself another wife, the widow of a Canterbury shoemaker, Mary Singleton, of Sandwich. Leaving his nine-year-old son with her, he departed a month or two later for England where he remained almost continuously for three years on a very difficult and harassing assignment.

Cushman's colleague was Deacon John Carver, "a pious, faith-full, and very beneficial instrument," now famed as the first gov-ernor of Plimoth Plantation. But in spite of his fame, Carver remains a somewhat shadowy figure with many things about him unexplained. A prosperous merchant in his early fifties, several years Brewster's senior, he had been born at Doncaster, Yorkshire, ten miles up the Great North Road from Scrooby. Like so many in the group, he had found a wife at Sturton le Steeple, marrying Catherine White, eldest sister of Bridget Robinson, Jane Tickens, and Frances Jessop. Yet the Carvers, it seems, had not been mem-bers of the Scrooby congregation, perhaps because they had left the poor countryside to seek their fortune elsewhere. It also ap-pears that they had been in Leyden for some time, as they were reported living along the Dark Canal as early as May, 1609, just a week or two after the exodus from Amsterdam. But they cannot be identified as members of the congregation until 1616—when their names first suddenly appear in the records, occupying many a page thereafter, for the deacon rose rapidly to prominence.

If Carver had belonged to the church for some time, it is diffi-cult to account for the company's complete previous neglect of him and his talents, spiritual and golden. It may be that he had been living in Leyden as a resident merchant before the congrega-tion arrived, in which case he may have exercised through Robin-son, his brother-in-law, some influence upon the group's decision to come here. But whatever the circumstances, it is probable that the staid and prosperous Carver, like so many of the more respect-able of the time, held fast to purely reformist Puritan principles as long as he could, hesitating to throw in his lot with the despised Separatist radicals in spite of the pull of personal and family ties. Once he took the plunge, however, he never wavered in his course and was generally respected. Tradition has it that he was the richest man in the group, but he was "of singular Piety and Rare for humillitie which appeered (as otherwise) soe by his Great Condesendencye."

In England the two agents approached the First (or London) Virginia Company through an influential member, later the treasurer of the company, Sir Edwin Sandys, son of the old Archbishop of York who had been the Brewsters' patron at Scrooby.[1] Anxious to recruit colonists, the foundering Virginia Company encouraged Cushman and Carver to believe that it would not be difficult for them to obtain an assurance of freedom of religion and "have it confirmed under ye king's broad seale, according to their desires." In an attempt to conciliate James and the bishops, the two emissaries had brought along a confession of faith in the form of Seven Articles, quite obviously drawn up with tongue in cheek in an effort to minimize the differences between the Brownist and Anglican creeds. This disingenuous document was passed along to the Privy Council, which frankly voiced its suspicions and demanded less ambiguous information on many points. Forwarded to Leyden by Sir John Wolstenholme—or "Worssenham," as Bradford called him—this demand caused much uneasiness at the Green Gate.

Two statements were immediately drawn up and sent to London by Robinson and Brewster, "though it be greevious unto us," they complained, "that such unjust insinuations are made against us." The statements were enclosed in a letter addressed to Sabin Staresmore, a London Separatist, later a member of the Leyden congregation, who handed them to Wolstenholme. One enclosure was brief and confined to generalities, ending with the statement, evidently in reply to a specific question, that in its public profession of faith the congregation did not differ in any way from the French Reformed Church. But the second and longer enclosure listed "some small accidentall differences" between their practices and those of the French church with which, so they had just said, "we doe wholy and in all points agree." In reporting the interview Staresmore complained that he wished he had known what was in the enclosures, particularly the larger one, at which Wolstenholme "stuck so much."

"Who shall make them?" the latter inquired of Staresmore, referring to the ordination of ministers and elders.

"The power of making is in the church, to be ordained by the imposition of hands by the fittest instruments they have. It must either be in the church or from the Pope, and the Pope is Anti-christ."

"Ho!" cried Sir John, "what the Pope holds good, as in Holy Trinity, that we do well to assent to. But we will not enter into dispute now." Wolstenholme had been asked to use his own dis-cretion in deciding which of the two tricky statements should be submitted to the Privy Council. Having read both, he decided to use neither for fear they would spoil all.

"What good news have you for me to write tomorrow?" Stares-more asked as he took his leave.

"Very good news," said Wolstenholme, "for both His Majesty and the bishops have consented."

This was not true, unfortunately, though Sandys had brought the congregation's petition before the King through Sir Robert Naunton, Secretary of State, soon to direct the international man hunt for Brewster. James pronounced it a good and honest motion, inquiring of his minister, "What profits may arise in the parts to which they intend to go?"

"Fishing," he was told.

"So God have my soul, 'tis an honest trade! It was the Apostles' own calling."

James advised a conference with the bishops, but those at Ley-den decided against it, fearing dangerous complications. All in all, not much had been accomplished. So far as they could read the King's mind, he would not issue any document bearing the Great Seal to sanction their venture. But if they wished to go to Virginia without it, he "would connive at them & not molest them, provided they carried themselves peaceably." This "made a dampe in ye busines, and caused some distraction." A large number of the congregation now wished to drop the project, holding that no good could come of trying to build upon such a "sandie founda-tion." But others, including most of the leaders, thought otherwise. A piece of paper was no protection even if stamped with a "seale as broad as ye house flore." It could always be revoked at the King's pleasure. No, they would have to rely, as they had always done, upon the providence of God. But doubts persisted, and matters dragged along without apparent progress for more than a year.

At length, in the spring of 1619, Cushman and Brewster were sent to London "to end with ye Virginia Company as well as they could." Torn by dissensions, its treasury empty, the company was vainly trying to escape the bankruptcy which overtook it and ended its career five years later. Under the circumstances it proved to be very difficult to conduct any business with it, and in the midst of negotiations a most embarrassing complication arose— copies of *Perth Assembly* were discovered in Scotland. Though not yet suspected, Brewster quickly slipped away and left Cushman to carry on alone. The latter had only bad news to report to his anxious brethren. In some respects the most disturbing was the fearful catastrophe that had overtaken hundreds of their former friends among the Ancient Brethren, a disaster which cast an ominous shadow over the risky business they now had in hand.

Evicted from the Bruinistengange in 1613, Francis Johnson and his faction had removed to Emden, drifting back to Amsterdam four years later. Upon the pastor's death the next year, leadership passed to Elder Francis Blackwell, "a man well known" to most of those at the Green Gate. Sinking deeper and deeper into poverty, the Franciscans now turned their eyes toward the New World and decided to go to Virginia. Crossing to England, they promptly got themselves into trouble, as always. Arrested in a raid upon a private meeting, Blackwell "slipped his own neck out of ye collar" by betraying Sabin Staresmore, Cushman's friend, and Richard Masterson of Leyden, chancing to be in London, would have "tasted of ye same cupp" if Blackwell had known his address. At his trial Blackwell denied his Separatist principles and so dissembled that he "won ye bishops' favour (but lost ye Lord's)." Like Studley before him, Ruling Elder Blackwell argued that this was all to the good—"yea, for the best." As the archbishop in open court had solemnly blessed his voyage, he could now open a way to a better world for all the Separatists. "But if such events follow ye bishops' blessing," growled Bradford, "happie are they that escape ye same."

After many quarrels and squabbles the Franciscans, "packed togeather like herings," set sail in the fall of 1618, soon running into heavy storms which drove them far off their course. Their water ran short, "ye fluxe" broke out, the captain and other officers died, leaving none with any skill at navigation. Six months out from Gravesend, "after long seeking & beating aboute," they put into the mouth of the Chesapeake and dropped anchor off James-town. Of some two hundred passengers only fifty were alive, and these soon scattered. Blackwell and his chief lieutenant, "Judas the Purse Bearer" Bowman, now also an elder, had died at sea and been consigned to a watery grave. Such was the miserable end of the once proud and arrogant Franciscans.

"Heavie newes it is," wrote Cushman, "and I would be glad to hear how farr it will discourage." Their friends in London were not "discouraged much." Rather, they were inclined to draw the proper moral, agreeing with Robinson who had "once said, he thought we should hear no good of them." Still, the ways of Providence were strange, and the fate of their fellow Separatists had been a terrible one. "It doth often trouble me," said Cushman, "to thinke that in this busines we are all to lerne and none to teach."

The news of the disaster sent a cold chill of apprehension down the spines of many, but most took it in their stride. A month or so later—fortunately, before *Perth Assembly* was traced to Leyden—Cushman succeeded in obtaining a patent to a tract of land along the northern boundary of the Virginia colony. Presumably, the tract lay somewhere between the Delaware and Hudson rivers. For many reasons they had been counselled by friends in London to hide their identity, and the patent was taken out in the name of John Wincob, a "religious gentleman" in the household of Elizabeth de Clinton, Dowager Duchess of Lincoln. A preacher of the "forward" school, Wincob had signified his intention of accompanying them to Virginia. But when it came time to go, he declined. Nor was any use ever made of this patent which had cost them so much time, worry, and expense.

What the Pilgrims needed, after all, was not only a patent but free shipping, and this the Virginia Company was unable to offer in its bankrupt state. At this point, the directors of the New Netherlands Company came forward with a very generous offer. They would not only provide free transportation, but furnish each family with cattle if the congregation would settle at New Amsterdam, their trading post at the mouth of the Hudson, where they would enjoy, of course, complete freedom of religion as they had in Holland. Inspired with new hope, the leaders at the Green Gate opened negotiations which apparently went very well. In February, 1620, the directors of the company petitioned the Prince of Orange to assign two warships for the protection of the colonists en route and until they were safely settled at New Amsterdam, explaining that in Leyden there was a "certain English preacher, well versed in the Dutch tongue, who is well inclined to proceed thither to live, assuring the Petitioners that he has the means of inducing over four hundred families to accompany him thither, both out of this country and England, provided they would be guarded and protected from all violence on the part of other potentates"—which was to say, on the part of King James, the only monarch who challenged the Dutch right to the Hudson and was in a position to strike at them.

But these negotiations were suddenly broken off with the appearance at the Green Gate of a friend from London, an ironmonger named Thomas Weston, "who was well acquainted with some of them and a furtherer of them in their former proseedings." Weston warned them against relying too much upon the Virginia Company and advised them to break off with the New Netherlands Company, saying that he and his friends among the merchants of London would finance their venture. Let them prepare to go as soon as possible, and they should "neither feare wante of shipping nor money." Everything would be taken care of. A bold and restless spirit, a typical adventurer of the time, Weston was a man of many schemes and stratagems, having a hand in all kinds of affairs, licit and illicit. A year or two back he had been ordered to stop illegal trade in cloth with The Netherlands. He was always more apt at promise than performance, as the Pilgrims were to learn, but his brisk confidence and businesslike air imparted a new vigor to affairs which had been dragging along now for more than two years.

Weston asked the congregation to draw up a contract detailing the terms of agreement. This was done and he approved the draft before departing for London, where he immediately began organizing a joint stock company to finance the venture. About seventy members were induced to join. Some were country gentlemen, others were master craftsmen, but the majority were merchants. Almost all were Londoners, but two were of Leyden—Edward Pickering, merchant, a member of the congregation since 1612 at least, and that "perfect Brownist," Thomas Brewer, who was still dallying in England. A few of the merchant adventurers invested relatively large sums, as much as £500 ($25,000)*, but the average investment was small. With scarcely an exception they were induced to risk their money solely by hope of large and quick profits. They were simply not interested in the Separatists as such, having no desire whatever to establish the Holy Discipline in the New World. But they were interested in the as   .ance that the brethren at Leyden were, "for the body of them, ' industrious & frugall . . . as any company of people in the world," used to hardships and difficulties, as Robinson and Brewster had once pointed out. "We are well weaned from ye delicate milke of our mother countrie," they had said, and it was not with them "as with other men, whom small things can discourage, or small discontentments cause to wish themselves at home againe."

Weston took no steps to incorporate his company, which throughout its troubled career remained a voluntary association managed by an annually elected president and treasurer. Weston was the first president, while the treasury for some years was in

* See footnote p. 15.

the hands of James Sherley, a goldsmith, who lived on Crooked Lane not far from his shop at the sign of *The Golden Horseshoe* on London Bridge. Ordinary business was decided by majority vote. But in important matters all stockholders had to give their assent, which seriously impeded operations in the field and created a great deal of conflict and confusion.

At Leyden "ye Saincts" were busy ordering their affairs. As their means were limited, it was obvious that all could not go at once. It was therefore decided that only the "yongest and strongest part" should go, and only those who really wanted to go and came forward as volunteers. As the great majority of the congregation would have to come along later, it was agreed that Pastor Robinson should remain with them while Ruling Elder Brewster accompanied the smaller section. Each group was to be an "absolute church of themselves, . . . seeing in such a dangerous vioage, and a removall to such a distance, it might come to pass they should (for ye body of them) never meete againe in this world." Members of one church were to be members of the other "without any further dismission or testimoniall." If the expedition failed, the survivors were to be helped to return to Leyden by those who remained behind, and the latter also promised their departing brethren that if a settlement were established and "ye Lord gave them life, & means, & opportunitie, they would come to them as soone as they could."

At this time another change of plan was made. The Second (Plymouth) Virginia Company had just petitioned the Crown for permission to reorganize its affairs, primarily for the purpose of obtaining clear and undisputed title to the northern half of the territory embraced within the original Virginia grant. Also, in an obvious attempt to butter the King and the Prince of Wales, the petitioners asked royal sanction for a change in the name of their territory, requesting that it "be called—as by the Prince, His Highness, it hath been named—New England." Both requests were granted though some months passed before the new patent was issued, stamped with the Great Seal. Learning of this, Weston and the Leyden leaders swung to the view that the congregation should go to New England. For one thing, there was no Anglican church there, which was a sensible reason, but "cheefly for ye hope of present profite to be made by ye fishing that was found in that countrie." Many at the Green Gate agreed, for the illusion long persisted among these simple farmers-turned-artisans that they could become fishermen overnight and quickly master the lore of the sea.

This change of plan did not please everybody, however, and brought on new "distractions" both in London and Leyden. A number of the brethren and the merchant adventurers now withdrew from the venture. Some still favored Guiana, while others had their hearts set on Virginia. This debate upset those who had already sold their goods and put their money "into ye commone stock" to buy provisions, for during the turmoil they were "brought into a great streight, fearing what issue things would come to." But a sharp conflict with the merchant adventurers was their greatest worry. Cushman and Carver had been sent to London to deliver the finished draft of the articles of agreement and "to receive ye moneys & make provissions both for shipping & other things." They were strictly charged "not to exseede their commission." In particular, they were to make sure that everything was done in accord with the contract which Weston had seen and approved. But Weston and some of his partners now insisted upon amending the agreement "either for their better advantage, or rather for ye drawing on of others, as they pretended," which led to bitter recriminations on both sides and hard feelings that nothing could remove.

The altered agreement consisted of ten articles. By the terms of the contract the colony was to be conducted on a joint stock basis by the settlers and merchant adventurers for a period of seven years. The former were to contribute their labor while the latter contributed the capital funds. During this period all profits from "trade, traffick, trucking, working, fishing, or any means" were to be credited to the joint account or placed in the common store. Out of the latter the settlers were "to have their meate, drink, apparell, and all provissions." At the end of seven years all "capitall

& profits, viz., the houses, lands, goods, and chatles," were to be divided between the settlers and adventurers on the basis of the number of shares held by each. Shares were rated at £10 ($500), and anyone contributing that amount either in money or provisions received one. In addition, every settler was to receive in the final division a share for himself as a settler and a share also for every person sixteen years of age or older in his household— wife, servants, and older children. Youngsters of ten to sixteen were rated at a half share while the putative value of smaller fry was "50 acers of unmanured land."

There was no objection to any of these provisions on the part of those at Leyden. What angered them most was the deletion of two articles which they had written into the original contract. They sharply complained that their agents in London had exceeded their authority in agreeing to strike out these articles, one of which exempted from the final division the settlers' houses, "gardens, & home lotts." These would not be worth much, not more than £5 each, so that the merchant adventurers' half interest in them would amount to very little. Though the adventurers would receive no great profit, the divided interest would discourage the settlers. On the other hand, if the latter knew that the houses they built and the gardens they cleared were to be their own, they would diligently labor to improve them "with borrowed houres from their sleep." Equal objection was raised to deletion of a clause specifically authorizing the settlers to work two days a week as they saw fit "for ye more comforte of themselves and their families." If everybody had to work at all times for the merchant adventurers, why should anyone go to the trouble and expense of bringing along servants? Besides, it was intolerable to be forced to live seven years without a "day's freedome from task." The new contract was an insult, fitter for "theeves & bondslaves than honest men."

Cushman was roundly berated by his brethren for his hand in this. What in the world was he thinking of when he allowed the agreement to be changed in this drastic and disastrous manner? Poor Cushman patiently explained that the business would have completely collapsed if he had not consented. As it was, funds were short, and many of the adventurers—one with an investment of £500—had threatened to withdraw their money unless the requested changes were promptly made. There was no time to write Leyden for advice, said Cushman. But he had informed his colleague, John Carver, who had seen and approved the changes. Carver denied this, saying that he had been down at Southampton buying supplies and knew nothing about it. Anyway, said Cushman, there was nothing to be done about it now. He had saved the enterprise from shipwreck, and if his brethren did not want to go, let them stay home. The adventurers would be just as pleased.

"Doe they urge or egg us?" asked the deacon with growing annoyance. "If we will not goe, they are content to keep their moneys. Thus I have pointed at a way to loose these knots, which I hope you will consider seriously, and let me have no more stirre about them." Let the querulous at Leyden "not be too bussie answering matters before they know them. If I doe such things as I cannot give reasons for, it is like you have sett a foole about your busines and so turne ye reproffe to yourselves, & send another, and let me come againe to my Combes. . . . Only let us have quietnes and no more of these clamours."

But "quirimonies & complaints" continued to pour in upon Cushman, who finally lost his temper. He had done the best he could and no one could have done better under the circumstances, he would have the brethren know. Did they think he had no brains? No, but he might "exercise them therein," came a joint reply from Bradford, Winslow, Allerton, and Fuller speaking for the company. Even Robinson took a fling at poor Cushman, who was a "good man, & of spetiall abilities in his kind," he said, yet "most unfitt to deale for other men by reason of his singularitie and too great indifferencie for any conditions, and . . . (to speak truly) we have had nothing from him but termes & presumptions."

This quite upset the hapless deacon, badgered by other worries and now harassed on all sides. If his presence were not required in London to keep the sinking enterprise even half-afloat, he would come to Leyden, he said, and answer his critics. Both he and Weston were tired of their captious complaints, sick to death of "clamours

& jangling." On one occasion Weston had decided to abandon the business in disgust, thinking better of it the next day only because he knew that it would utterly ruin many of his more particular friends at Leyden. "Full litle did I expect these things which are now come to pass," exclaimed Cushman. If the question of the final ownership of houses and lots involved such a small sum, why did they raise such a rumpus about it? Why give the merchant adventurers an occasion to suspect them of being "worldly & covetous?" he asked. "I will not say what I have heard since these complaints first came over." The building of "good & faire houses" was not, as some seemed to think, their primary mission. "Our purpose," said Cushman, "is to build for ye presente such houses as, if need be, we may with litle greefe set afire and rune away by the lighte; our riches shall not be in pompe but in strength; if God send us riches, we will imploye them to provide more men, ships, munition, &c. You may see it amongst the best pollitiks, that a commonweale is readier to ebb than to flow when once fine houses and gay cloaths come in." Repent! the deacon warned his carping brethren, "or els goe not, lest you be like Jonas to Tarshis." And "if the company thinke me to be ye Jonas," he added, "let them cast me off before we goe." Though left with only the clothes on his back, he would be quite content to stay.

Affairs at Leyden, so Robinson informed Carver at this time, were "very pitiful." Many more had withdrawn from the enterprise out of one discontent or another, and there was scarcely a man who did not wish he "had againe his money in his purse." Things were so desperate that an attempt was made to recruit colonists at Amsterdam in Ainsworth's church and among a few remnants of the "Franciscans." This brought on new troubles and dissensions. "I had thought," Cushman protested, that "they would as soone have gone to Rome as with us, for our libertie is to them as ratt's bane and their rigour as bad to us as ye Spanish Inquisition. If any practice of mine discourage them, let them draw back; I will undertake they shall have their money againe presently paid here."

The Amsterdammers, evidently at their own request, did get their money back. But this left a major problem still unsolved, for so many of "ye Saincts" were now unable or unwilling to go that other recruits simply had to be found if the emigrants were to have sufficient strength to survive the trials and dangers of the wilderness. Anxious to protect their investments, the merchant adventurers solved the problem by signing up colonists in London, recruiting them at large without any regard to their religious beliefs. So long as a man was willing to work and strive to turn a profit for them, it was of no concern to the adventurers how he prayed. In fact, as some of them later complained, praying might seriously interfere with more important business.

To allay any suspicion or jealousy, these new recruits were given a spokesman to collaborate with Cushman and Carver in making arrangements for the voyage. The third agent so appointed was Christopher Martin, born at Great Burstead, Essex, apparently one of the more radical Puritans, for he and Solomon Prower, his stepson, had recently been in trouble with the authorities for challenging the current manner of catechizing. Named treasurer of the emigrant company by the adventurers, Martin immediately took a highhanded course. Carver was at Southampton buying supplies against the desires of Cushman and Weston, who wished to concentrate the business in London. And now Martin went down into Kent against the desires of all three and began buying up everything that took his fancy. A headstrong man of waspish temper, he refused to tell anybody what he was doing, scorning all advice and suggestion.

Weston was worried and greatly annoyed, saying that the voyage would never get under way with the three agents refusing to cooperate, "going up & downe, wrangling & expostulating." Carver wrote Cushman asking for £500, urging him to raise more money from the adventurers to meet the pressing needs of those at Leyden. Cushman somehow managed to send the large sum requested, but for any additional money, Carver was informed, "we may goe scratch for it." Weston would not give them another penny, nor would any of his partners, and they were in desperate need of some £300 or £400. "Counting upon 150 persons, there cannot be founde," said Cushman, "above £1,200 & odd moneys, . . . besids some cloath, stockings, & shoes." Martin was perfectly impossible, he added, "and to speake ye trueth, there is fallen amongst us a flatt schisme." In short, he said, unless there was an unexpected change in the complexion of things, "we that should be partners of humilitie and peace shall be examples of jangling & insulting."

Still, in spite of all, things went slowly forward. In June, 1620, the adventurers chartered a large vessel of 180 tons, "a fine ship," Cushman reported, having already engaged as pilot "one Mr. Clarke, who went last year to Virginia with a ship of kine." With Weston scoffing and laughing at them, the group in Leyden bought a smaller vessel of sixty tons, the *Speedwell,* which was to transport part of the company and stay in the New World for use there in "fishing and shuch other affairs as might be for ye good & benefite of ye colonie." As the ship was in bad condition, she had to be refitted at considerable expense. New and larger masts were stepped in, a new suit of sail was bought for her, and she was now lying at Delft Haven ready to depart for the rendezvous at South-ampton. Preparations for the long, hazardous journey still left much to be desired, many problems were yet unsolved, but with the summer already upon them and passing rapidly, it was obvious that if the company was to go at all, it was a question of now or never.

As the congregation usually did on important occasions, a "day of solleme humiliation" was proclaimed. Some time was spent in "powering out prairs to ye Lord with great fervencie, mixed with abundance of tears." Then Robinson rose to speak, taking his text from Ezra 8.21 and devoting most of the day to it "very profitably." His departing brethren never forgot his sermon. "I charge you before God and his blessed Angels to follow me no further than I follow Christ," he told them in his modest way, "and if God shall reveal anything to you by any other Instrument of his, be as ready to receive it as ever you were to receive any truth by my Ministry. . . . Be not loath to take another Pastor or Teacher, for the Flock that hath two Shepherds is not indangered, but secured by it."

After the services there was a feast at the Green Gate in honor of those about to depart. Tears were wiped away, and all enjoyed themselves eating and drinking, with "christian discourse" and song, pouring all of the agitation in their hearts and souls, all of their hopes and fears, into the mournful measures of the Psalms— "the sweetest melody that ever mine ears heard," so one of them remembered it thirty years later.

At long last, at sunrise on July 21, 1620, the Pilgrim vanguard set out for Delft Haven, about twenty miles to the south, on the Maas just a few miles below Rotterdam. They probably traveled by canal, and most of their friends at the Green Gate accompanied them. Other friends came from Leyden to see them off, and even from Amsterdam, almost fifty miles distant. Here they enjoyed another feast and "more christian discourse and other reall expressions of true christian love." That night was spent ashore, "with litle sleepe by ye most," and early the next morning they and their friends boarded the *Speedwell* to exchange a last farewell, and "truly dolfull was ye sight of that sad and mournfull parting, to see what sighs and sobbs and praires did sound amongst them, what tears did gush from every eye, & pithy speeches peirst each harte." Falling upon his knees, and everybody with him, Robinson gave them his blessing and "with watrie cheeks commended them with most fervente praiers to ye Lord, . . . and then with mutual imbrases and many tears, they tooke their leaves one of another, which proved to be ye last leave to many of them."

And so, in Bradford's eloquent and memorable phrase, the first company of "ye Saincts" left Leyden, "that goodly & pleasante citie which had been their resting place for near 12 years; but they knew they were pilgrimes, & looked not much on those things, but lift[ed] up their eyes to ye heavens, their dearest cuntrie, and quieted their spirits."

8

A
WAIGHTY
VIOAGE

Poore William Ring & myselfe doe strive
who shall be meate first for ye fishes; but we
looke for a glorious resurrection . . .

—Robert Cushman

WITH PENNONS FLYING BRAVELY AT THE MASTHEADS, THE
Speedwell slipped her hawsers, unfurled her bright new sails, and
moved slowly out into the broad channel of the Maas, her rails
crowded with excited but heavyhearted passengers frantically wav-
ing a last farewell to those still lining the quay—many suspecting
what proved to be the fact, that this was a final separation from
their loved ones, that they had seen old friends for the last time,
that never again in this life would they hold their wives and
laughing children in their arms. A salvo of cannon boomed from
the ship and the passengers fired a volley of small arms in parting
salute as the vessel got under way. Having a "prosperus winde,"

they were soon past the Hook of Holland and out in the North Sea, where Captain Reynolds set his course WSW to round the chalk cliffs at Dover and follow the coast to Southampton. This first leg of the long voyage was accomplished in good time though the *Speedwell* proved to be a cranky vessel, heeling far over and shipping water even in a moderate breeze, giving the skipper cause for concern and the passengers several good wettings.

Those on board constituted only a small part of the congregation, not a sixth of the Green Gate company, numbering less than fifty persons—and almost half of them were children. Many had brought along their entire families. There was Isaac Allerton, the tailor, with his wife Mary, big with child, and three small children —Bartholomew, Remember, and Mary (aged two), who lived to be the last survivor of this "waighty vioage," outliving even the Old Colony itself. With William White, wool comber, had come his wife Susanna (Fuller), also big with child, and a three-year-old son, Resolved. His wife Bridget (van der Velde) and their young daughter Elizabeth accompanied John Tilley, silk worker, of London. His brother Edward had sailed with his wife Ann and two small "cousins," Humility Cooper and "Henery" Samson; Thomas Blossom, of Cambridge, with his wife and two sons; and Thomas Tinker, sawyer and citizen of Leyden, with a now nameless wife and son. Mary Cushman had brought along her ten-year-old stepson, Thomas, planning to meet her husband in England where he was still swamped with troubles. Both of the Winslows were on board, Edward and Elizabeth, but they were childless, as was Catherine Carver. She, too, was to join her husband at Southampton and had with her young Desire Minter, daughter of Thomas Minter, citizen of Leyden and evidently of the congregation.

Some had decided to split their families. With her husband still hiding somewhere in England but planning to slip on board the *Speedwell* at Southampton, Mary Brewster, now a grandmother, had brought along her two youngest children, "Wrastle" or Wrestling (with the Devil) and Love (of God, presumably), boys of six and nine. Her two daughters, Fear and Patience, the former an adolescent, the latter a woman of twenty, were left behind at Leyden for a time, doubtless in care of their older brother Jonathan, now a man of twenty-seven, who delayed his departure for more than a year, perhaps because he had recently lost both his wife and only child. Though their son John was only a year younger than Wrestling Brewster, William and Dorothy Bradford decided to leave him behind, apparently with the Robinsons. The child never saw his mother again, nor his father for seven years, and his heartbreaking appeals and frightened cries at parting may have had something to do with Dorothy's tragic death a few months later.

Others had chosen to come with children and not with wives. Francis Cooke, wool comber, and Thomas Rogers, camlet merchant and citizen of Leyden, had each brought along a son, as had John Crackston, while John Turner, merchant and also a citizen of Leyden, had brought along two. Still others had embarked without wives or children—Degory Priest, the hatter; Deacon Samuel Fuller; Moses Fletcher, a smith; and John Goodman, married just a few months before. Altogether, so far as can be determined from available records, there were forty-six "Saincts" on the *Speedwell*—sixteen men, eleven women, and nineteen children—and not all of these reached the New World.

Putting in at Southampton, they dropped anchor alongside the *Mayflower,* which had been waiting here for some days, having sailed round from London about a week before with the emigrants recruited at large by the merchant adventurers. The two groups were not acquainted, but there was no time to stand on ceremony. After "mutuall congratulations, with other frendly entertainements, they fell to parley aboute their bussines," and they found a great deal to discuss. Affairs were in a mess. Cushman, Carver, and Martin were still at loggerheads, quarreling about supplies and the amended articles of agreement. Almost £700 had been spent here at Southampton, and "upon what I know not," exclaimed Cushman. "Mr. Martin saith he neither can nor will give any accounte of it, and if he be called upon for accounts, he crieth

out of unthankfullnes for his paines & care, that we are susspitious
of him, and flings away & will end nothing." For his part, Martin
charged Cushman with reducing the colonists to the status of
slaves, denouncing the adventurers as "bloudsuckers" for changing
the contract. The circumspect Carver declined to take sides, finding
fault with both Cushman and Martin.

To make matters worse, Thomas Weston now appeared on the
scene, coming down from London with the amended articles of
agreement to have them properly signed by leaders of the Leyden
group. The latter stubbornly refused to do so in spite of his
insistence, saying that he "knew right well that the articles were
not according to ye first agreemente, neither could they yeeld to
them without the consent of the rest that were behind." Weston
was "much offended" and departed in a huff, announcing that he
was through with the business. Henceforth, they could shift for
themselves.

This was a staggering blow, for they were desperately short of
funds, largely because of expensive repairs to the *Speedwell*. To
correct the faults she manifested in crossing from Holland, her rig
had been changed, and now it was necessary to change it again.
In addition to all else, this involved a loss of precious time, itself
a source of deep concern. It was now August, rather late to be
getting started, for it meant that they would run into heavy
equinoctial gales on the high seas and wintry weather at the far
end of their voyage, which would dangerously increase their difficulties in getting settled. Cushman warned them of this, making
a cogent point of it in defending his compromise with the adventurers. There was no time for long-winded arguments and stumbling over straws, he protested, for they had "already delayed
overlong in regard to ye season of ye year," which he feared—and
how right he was!—"they would find to their cost."

Under the circumstances, an attempt to appease the merchant
adventurers seemed wise, and a letter to London was drafted.

"Beloved freinds," they wrote somewhat acidly, "sory we are
that there should be occasion of writing at all unto you, partly
because we ever expected to see ye most of you here, but espetially

because there should any difference at all be conceived betweene us."

Again they reiterated that Cushman had never been empowered to amend the contract. But as the adventurers now plainly felt aggrieved, they would give way a little in their demand that settlers should be granted their houses and lots in the final division. Furthermore, if the adventurers failed to make a substantial profit during the life of the contract, they would consider extending it beyond the seven-year period. This should be sufficient to satisfy any reasonable persons, "espetially freinds" in a position to know their desperate needs.

"We are in shuch a streate at present," they declared, "as we are forced to sell away £60 worth of our provissions to cleare ye Haven, & withall put ourselves upon great extremities, scarce haveing any butter, no oyle, not a sole to mend a shoe, nor every man a sword to his side, wanting many muskets, much armoure, &c . . . Thus saluting all of you in love . . ."

Weston, for once, was as good as his word, refusing to give them another penny, turning a deaf ear to their pleas and promises. In the midst of these anxieties came a letter addressed to all of them from their beloved pastor, and it must have lightened the burden in many a troubled soul. He was sorry, he said, not to bear a part "in this first brunt." As it was, he could only offer some advice, not because he doubted their "godly wisdoms" but rather "to add some furder spurr of provocation unto them who rune allready, if not because you need it, yet because I owe it in love & dutie." They were to repent of all their sins, both known and unknown. They were to store up patience "against ye evill day, without which we take offence at ye Lord himselfe in his holy & just works." They were not to "shake the house of God . . . with unnecessarie novelties." They were to avoid the pursuit of private profit "as a deadly plague" and direct their efforts to "ye general conveniencie," putting down the self-regarding "as so many rebels against ye commone good." Above all, let them cultivate peace and harmony with all men, and especially among themselves.

"You are, many of you, strangers as to ye persons, so to ye

infirmities one of another," Robinson pointed out, "& so stande in need of more watchfullnes this way lest when shuch things fall out in men & women as you suspected not, you be inordinately affected with them, which doth require at your hands much wisdome & charitie for ye covering & preventing of incident offences that way"—words that the Plymouth Saints would have done well to recall on several occasions. In electing governors they should let their "wisdome & godlines appeare not only in chusing such persons as doe intirely love and will promote ye commone good, but also in yeelding unto them all due honour & obediance in their lawful administrations, not behoulding in them ye ordinarinesse of their persons." It was all very well for the foolish multitude to honor and follow "ye gay coate," he concluded, "but you know better things."

On August 5th, after an anxious delay of almost two weeks, the *Speedwell* was ready at last and tacked out of the harbor in the wake of the *Mayflower,* Captain Christopher Jones in command. To the day of departure, Cushman and others had nursed the hope that the adventurers would relent and send them more money. But no word came from Weston and his partners, not even a note of farewell, and to clear the port the hard-pressed colonists had to sell part of their meager stock of provisions, "some 3 or 4 score firkins of butter, which comoditie they might best spare, haveing provided too large a quantitie of that kind."

On board the two ships, crowding the rails for a last glimpse of the green shores of their homeland, were about 120 passengers, with perhaps ninety of these on the *Mayflower.* There was a governor on each—Cushman on the *Speedwell,* Martin on the *Mayflower*—"to order ye people by ye way, and to see to ye disposing of their provissions and shuch like affairs." The vessels went scudding along under a good stiff breeze, but after a few days at sea the *Speedwell* was "open and leakie as a sieve." At one place "ye water came in as at a mole hole." After a conference, Captains Reynolds and Jones decided to turn back, the two ships putting in at Dartmouth—and just in time, according to Cushman, for if the

Speedwell had "stayed at sea but 3 or 4 howers more, she would have sunke right downe." As the company worried and fretted, the vessel was again searched and mended "to their great charge & losse of time and a faire wind," which did nothing to improve the dispositions of either passengers or crew.

All were incensed at Christopher Martin, the sailors for his "ignorante bouldnes" in meddling in things he knew nothing about. Some were so infuriated that they openly threatened to "mischeefe him"; others talked of deserting. Nor did Martin get on any better with the "Saincts," whom he insulted and deeply offended, treating them with great "scorne & contempte, as if they were not good enough to wipe his shoes," exclaimed Cushman indignantly. "It would break your hart to see his dealing and ye mourning of our people ... They complaine to me, & alass! I can doe nothing for them; if I speake to him, he flies in my face as mutinous, and saith no complaints shall be heard or received but by himselfe, and saith they are frowarde & waspish, discontented people, & I doe ill to hear them ... Where is ye meek & humble spirite of Moyses? & of Nehemiah who reedified ye walls of Jerusalen & ye state of Israell? Is not ye sound of Rehoboam's braggs daly heard amongst us? ... Freind, if ever we make a plantation, God works a mirakle, especially considering how scante we shall be of victualls, and most of all ununited amongst ourselves, & devoyd of good tutors & regimente. Violence will break all."

Many of the passengers were now so upset and discouraged that they, too, were talking of deserting the expedition and returning home. To scotch this, Martin confined them to the narrow quarters of the ships and would not "suffer them to goe ashore least they should rune away." Cushman was as discouraged as any but philosophically resigned to his lot. "If I should write to you of all things which promiscuously forerune our ruine," he told his friend Edward Southworth, one of the brethren, "I should overcharge my weake head and greeve your tender hart; only this, I pray you, prepare for evill tidings of us every day ... I see not in reason how we shall escape even ye gasping of hunger starved

persons; but God can doe much, & his will be done . . . Poore
William Ring & myself doe strive who shall be meate first for ye
fishes; but we looke for a glorious resurrection."

Once more, after losing almost two weeks, the *Mayflower* and
Speedwell put to sea and stood off to the westward. Land's End
soon dropped from view in their foaming wake and they were
well out on the broad Atlantic, more than three hundred miles
from shore, when the skipper of the *Speedwell* began to complain
that his ship was "so leakie as he must bear up or sinke at sea, for
they could scarce free her with much pumping." After another
conference with Captain Jones, it was decided to turn back again,
the ships putting in at Plymouth. For a third time the ill-named
Speedwell was searched from stem to stern. Finding nothing
specific the matter with her, they were forced to attribute her
disabilities to "generall weaknes" and decided to go on without her.
The ship departed for London and after being refitted there proved
to be quite seaworthy, sailing on many a profitable voyage. This
later led Bradford to charge that the company had been victimized
by Captain Reynolds and his crew, who had signed a contract to
remain in the colony for a year and now sought means to break
it. But the main and probably the sole cause of the *Speedwell's*
troubles lay closer home—in the fact that the masts placed in her
when she was refitted at Delft Haven were much too large, as
Bradford himself admitted.

The dismissal of the *Speedwell* precipitated another painful
crisis. As the *Mayflower* could not accommodate all of the passengers, some of them had to remain behind, which meant "another
sad parting." Altogether, some twenty persons, about a sixth of
the company, had to turn back. They were, for the most part,
those who chose to do so "either out of some discontente or feare
they conceived of ye ill success of ye vioage, seeing so many crosses
befall & the year time so farr spente," or because they were bur-
dened with many young children. Thomas Blossom withdrew and
returned to Leyden with his wife and two sons. Cushman's friend,
William Ring, decided that fate might have something better in
store for him than becoming "meate for ye fishes." Those who

turned back were the weaker and "least useful" part of the company, according to Bradford, who maliciously singled out poor, harassed, long-suffering, and now thoroughly-disgusted Robert Cushman as chief of those whose courage had long ago deserted them, and "though it discover some infirmities in him (as who under temtation is free), yet after this he continued to be"—Cushman was a forgiving soul—"a spetiall instrumente for their good."

At length, on September 6th, having lost seven precious weeks since leaving London, the *Mayflower* once again put to sea and headed westward, favored by a "fine small gale." The roar of the wind in the rigging, the steady roll of the ship as she swung along at six or seven knots were reassuring but certainly not a pleasure at first, for, "according to ye usuall maner, many were afflicted with seasicknes." As the ship had only the crudest of conveniences and no sanitary facilities of any kind except the traditional bucket, as there was no provision for bathing or even cursory washing (even if it had been a practice of the time to indulge), the air in the narrow, crowded quarters below deck must have been nauseating at best and at worst simply staggering. The North Atlantic is always cold, and the passengers found it almost impossible to keep warm and dry. Except for an occasional hot dish, they lived on a monotonous and upsetting diet of hard tack, "salt horse," dried fish, cheese, and beer.

Yet the *Mayflower,* apple-cheeked, broad of beam, double-decked, with high superstructures—"castles"—fore and aft, was a fine ship, as Cushman had described her. She was also a "sweet" ship, having been engaged since 1616 in the Mediterranean wine trade, though she undoubtedly retained about her some trace of the years she had spent hauling fish, timber, turpentine, tar, and other smelly products from Norway. A stout chunky vessel of 180 tons, she was far above the average in size, being a fifth again as large as the three ships—the *Sarah Constant* (100 tons), *Goodspeed* (40 tons), and *Discovery* (20 tons)—in which Captain John Smith had set sail for Virginia with his company of "gentlemen" thirteen years before. She was more than seven times as big

as the two tiny craft, one of fifteen tons, the other of ten, in which
Champlain had explored the Gulf of St. Lawrence and the New
England coast in 1605. Yet any ocean voyage three centuries ago
was a trial and an heroic adventure in itself.

The *Mayflower* was packed to the gunwales, for 102 passengers
had been crammed on board with their goods and supplies. No
impression is more deeply imbedded in the popular mind, nothing
is more firmly woven into the American *mythos* than the notion
that these first Pilgrims were a homogeneous and united group,
all from Scrooby by way of Leyden, closely knit by family and
personal ties, by the hardships and dangers they had suffered
together, the hearts of each and all fired with a burning zeal to
found a church of their own in the wilderness. It is a pleasing
fancy, but the Pilgrims would have exploded it in the name of
"ye trueth." Only three of the company were from Scrooby—
William and Mary Brewster and William Bradford—and little
more than a third of those on board came from Leyden—forty-one,
to be exact, made up of seventeen men, ten women, and fourteen
children.

The others, the great majority, were "strangers," largely from
London and southeastern England. They were not Brownists;
neither were they Separatists of any rival school. On the contrary,
they were good members of the Church of England—not from
reasoned choice or any strong conviction perhaps, but simply
because they had been born and baptized in that faith. They were
content, like most of us, to accept the beliefs handed down to them
by their fathers. Christopher Martin and a few others belonged to
the Puritan wing of the church, it appears, but most of them were
as orthodox in their uncritical way as any Anglican bishop. They
had no intention of breaking with their cultural past and religious
faith. What they were seeking in the New World, like the tens
of millions who crossed the Atlantic after them, was not spiritual salvation but economic opportunity, a chance to better their
worldly lot, and for a time they stoutly resisted all attempts to
convert them to "ye trueth." This led to considerable irritation and
several loud explosions that almost wrecked New Plimoth, for the

smaller Leyden group was in command and made no secret of its firm resolve—and what chuckles must have come from the grave of old "Beelzebub of Canterbury" at this—to impose their religious views upon the majority whether the latter chose to accept the Holy Discipline or not.

But the passengers had one bond in common. All were lower class, "from the cottages and not the castles of England," a strong cohesive force at a time when society was still rigidly stratified, with rights and privileges concentrated at the top. There was not a drop of blue blood to be found anywhere among them in the *Mayflower,* as these Pilgrims were all too acutely aware from the poverty and other disabilities they suffered. They were of the common people and in conscious revolt against the aristocratic principle so-called, a fact which seems to have escaped some of their descendants with their proofs of "blood" and pathetic interest in coats of arms.

By an ironic twist of fate, it is among the "strangers" and not "ye saincts" that one finds the three Pilgrims who, thanks to Longfellow, have enjoyed the greatest posthumous fame—Myles Standish, John Alden, and Priscilla Mullins.* The last may possibly have been a Separatist on boarding the *Mayflower,* for Cushman had early outlined the venture to her father who was one of the first to sign up and pay in his money. Largely because of his name, tradition has it that William Mullins—or "Molines," as he wrote it—was a Huguenot and came from France to join the company. It is much more likely that his was merely one of many common English names of Norman origin. In any case, he had long been a shopkeeper at Dorking, Surrey, about thirty miles southwest of London, and from there departed for the New World. With him came his wife and two children, Joseph and Priscilla, a girl in her late teens and probably not half so prim as painted —and certainly not so affectedly coy, a revolting mannerism not of hers but of Longfellow's day.

Priscilla's future husband, John Alden, was a "hopfull yonge

* For the passengers on the *Mayflower,* see Appendix A, which, with Appendix B, constitutes a sort of *dramatis personae.*

man" of twenty from Harwich, Essex. His children remembered him as tall, blond, and very powerful in physique, one of the strongest men at Plymouth, qualities very useful in a hired man, as the company no doubt recognized in signing him up as such under a contract obliging him to remain in the colony for a year, at the end of which time he was free to go or stay as he chose. A cooper by trade, he was now carefully tending the Pilgrims' precious barrels of beer, plain water, and "strong water," which took up much space in the hold. But the Pilgrims had no such supply as that enjoyed by the Puritans who set sail for Massachusetts Bay ten years later on the good ship *Arabella,* which carried 10,000 gallons of wine, fourteen tuns of fresh water, and forty-two tuns of beer. Still, Alden had plenty to do keeping the barrels tight and sampling them occasionally to see that air was not getting in to spoil the contents.

Myles Standish was an older man, one of the middle generation, a hardened professional soldier of thirty-six or thereabouts, being four or five years Bradford's senior. Though now perhaps the best known of all the Pilgrims, at least by name, Standish remains something of an enigma, for much mystery still surrounds "Captaine Shrimpe," as he was dubbed by an enemy because he was short in stature, with red hair and a florid complexion, which flamed to crimson when he flew into a rage—which was often. No trace has been found of his parents, but he appears to have been born at Chorley, Lancashire, about 1584. According to tradition, he was early left an orphan and went off to the wars before he was twenty, shipping to The Netherlands with the troops sent by Queen Elizabeth to aid the Dutch against Spain. All English troops were withdrawn in 1609, and Lieutenant Standish presumably returned home with them. It is evident, however, that he had somewhere met John Robinson, either at Amsterdam or Leyden, or elsewere, and Robinson had taken his measure rather well, as later revealed when he delivered the Plymouth brethren a stinging rebuke for a bloody and dubious action. But Standish's life is virtually a blank page down to the day when he and his wife Rose stepped on the *Mayflower.*

Many years later, in his last will and testament, Standish asserted his claim to many large estates in Lancashire and on the Isle of Man, declaring himself the rightful heir of a rich and powerful house of landed gentry, the Standishes of Standish. It was a family with a distinguished military tradition, proud of its long line of warriors, and it is significant that the Pilgrim captain was named Myles, from the Latin *miles,* soldier. But modern scholars have quite clearly disproved Standish's claims to the lands that were, so he alleged, rightfully his "by lawfull Decent but Surruptuously Detained." They have discovered that the Standishes of Standish owned no properties in the parishes which the captain named, and that he had only the remotest connection with this family.

Yet this connection, remote as it is, may explain the most re-markable thing about the commander-in-chief of the small but formidable Pilgrim army. Alone of the Pilgrim leaders, he never joined the church at Plymouth. His name is conspicuously absent from its records and rolls. Nowhere is he listed among the com-municants. This is all the more startling because Plymouth early adopted the theocratic principle that no one could be a citizen, let alone a magistrate or officer shaping and executing policy, who was not a member of the church and a communicant in good standing. Why this signal exception? Can it be that the Pilgrims needed him and appreciated his success in organizing the defense of the colony, and for that reason were willing to overlook his religious scruples? And what were his scruples? No one knows, but it is interesting at least that the Standishes of Standish and all the branches of that family had never accepted Protestantism in any form, steadfastly adhering to their old Roman Catholic faith.

Among the "strangers" appeared others of note. There was James Chilton, a tailor of Canterbury, with his wife and their daughter Mary, the sprightly young miss who led the initial land-ing on Plymouth beach, according to a quite unfounded family tradition, and was the first to step foot on Plymouth Rock. Samuel Eaton of Bristol, a ship's carpenter, had with him his wife Sarah and their son Samuel, "a sucking child." The largest family on board was that of Stephen Hopkins of Wotton-under-Edge,

Gloucestershire, more recently of London. His wife Elizabeth, his second, had the care of three young children—Giles, Constance, and Damaris—and now at sea was delivered of another, appropriately named Oceanus. The "grave" Richard Warren of London, "a usefull instrumente," had an even larger family but had wisely decided to leave it at home. One of Edward Winslow's younger brothers, Gilbert, had joined the ship at Southampton, as had Peter Browne, ancestor of John Brown of Osawatomie, who came from Christopher Martin's home village, Great Burstead, Essex. Then there was John Billington of London, destined to win distinction as the only Pilgrim Father to be hanged. With him had come his wife Ellen and their two sons, John and Francis—"one of ye profanest families amongst them," exclaimed Bradford, "and I know not by what freinds shufled into their company."

Nor were the Saints and Strangers the only two distinct and often antagonistic groups on board. A third consisted of the hired men, five in all, under contract to remain in the colony for a year. They were not regarded as settlers or members of the company, sharing neither the rights nor responsibilities of the latter. In addition to Alden, the cooper, there were two ordinary seamen and two master mariners, Thomas English, who was to captain the long boat or shallop which the *Mayflower* was carrying between decks, and John Allerton, apparently not related to the other Allerton, having been hired to return to Leyden and help bring over those left behind. It was a major blow a few months later when both master mariners died.

There was a fourth and much larger group sharply set off from all the others—the indentured servants. These were not servants in our sense of the word. They were not housemaids, butlers, cooks, valets, or general flunkies to wait upon the personal needs of the Pilgrims. On the contrary, they were brought along to do the heaviest kind of labor. They were to fell trees, hew timbers, build houses, clear fields and plough them, tend crops, gather the harvest, and do whatever their masters ordered. During the period of their indenture, which usually ran for seven years, they were fed, clothed, and housed by their masters, but received no wages, being virtually slaves, and were frequently bought, sold, and hired out as such.

Eleven of the eighteen servants on board were strong young men, a sixth of the adult company. For the most part, they belonged to the Leyden group, which suggests that if the Saints were poor, the Strangers were still poorer. As befitted a man of his wealth, John Carver had four—for his wife, a boy and a maid; for himself, Roger Wilder and John Howland, "a lustie yonge man," who quickly made a name for himself at Plymouth. The William Whites had brought two, as had the Winslows, one being George Soule of Eckington, Worcestershire, who was destined, like Howland, to rise to some prominence after he had served his time. Lastly, Isaac Allerton and Deacon Samuel Fuller had one servant each. Among the Strangers only three had the means to transport bondslaves. Christopher Martin and William Mullins each had one, while Stephen Hopkins had two, Edward Dotey and Edward Leister, both of London. In this servant group were four small waifs by the name of More, poor orphans of London, who were living with Thomas Weston when they were dragged off quite as if they were debtors or criminals sentenced to be transported to the colonies. Encouraged by the Lord Mayor and the Bishop of London, this was a favored means of relieving the pressure of population in the poorer quarters of the city. One of the waifs was "put into" Winslow's household, a second into Carver's, while Richard More and a now nameless brother were given to the Brewsters. Only Richard was alive a few months later, living to a ripe old age, having changed his name to Mann along the way.

All of these—Saints and Strangers, hired hands and indentured servants, men, women, and children, down to babes in arms, even in embryo—should properly be numbered in the Pilgrim company. Though many are little more than names, though some have become anonymous ghosts, all are deserving of their meed of fame and honor.

On the pitching rolling vessel there was still another group and quite as important as any—the ship's officers and crew. The

latter numbered thirty or more seamen, by all accounts an ungodly
and intemperate lot, who worked under the sharp eye of a tough
old bosun given to mighty oaths which, though usually lost on the
"monkeys" in the rigging, always made the Saints wince. Hailing
from Rotherhithe, Surrey, Skipper Jones was close to forty and a
hard rough sea dog, as all skippers of the day had to be, but under
his quarterdeck manner he was really a kindly and reasonable
person and a more humane master than most. Under him were
four mates and a master gunner. The first officer, John Clarke, a
man of many adventures and always a good friend of the Pilgrims,
had been in the New World at least twice before. On his last
voyage, in 1619, he had gone to Virginia with a shipload of cattle
from Ireland.[1] The other mates were Andrew Williamson, John
Parker, and Robert Coffin, usually referred to as the "pilot."
Though the Pilgrims never once mentioned his name, it has been
discovered recently that there was a ship's doctor on board, Giles
Heale, who later had a profitable practice in London. Perhaps
Bradford and his brethren had no confidence in him, preferring
the ministrations and mysterious potions of their own "chirurgeon
& physition," Deacon Samuel Fuller.

Under fair skies and with a fresh breeze still blowing, September
passed. The *Mayflower* was now in mid-Atlantic and making
steady headway. But as week after week dragged on with nothing
to break the monotony of the voyage, tensions began to rise on
the crowded ship—between Saints and Strangers, masters and
servants, passengers and crew. The sailors loathed Christopher
Martin and all about him, and could not stomach the pious ways
of the Leyden group, "cursing them dayly with greevous execra-
tions." One of their worst tormentors, a huge brawny seaman,
used to taunt the weak and sick by saying that he expected to bury
half of them at sea and "make merry with what they had." When
they reproached him, no matter how gently, "he would curse &
swear most bitterly." But retribution was swift in coming. Stricken
himself one morning, this "proud & very profane yonge man" was
dead by afternoon and his body was the first to go over the side,
to the great astonishment of his wicked cronies, said Bradford,

and with a most salutary effect, for they saw that it was "ye just hand of God upon him."

Then, suddenly, the weather changed as fierce storms came roaring out of the west. For days at a time it was impossible to carry a yard of sail, the ship drifting under bare poles with the helmsman desperately trying to hold her into the wind as she wallowed through mountainous seas which often had her lying on her beam-ends. The pounding of heavy seas opened up many seams in the deck and superstructure, letting cascades of icy water down upon the ill and frightened passengers curled up in their narrow bunks below. Unable to endure it any longer in the stuffy hold, John Howland came on deck one day and was immediately swept overboard. The ship happened to be trailing some of the topsail halyards, and Howland managed to get hold of these and hang on, "though he was sundrie fadomes under water," till he was pulled in with a boat hook. He was "something ill with it, yet he lived many years after, and became a profitable member both in church & commone wealthe." The storm mounted to new fury and at length, with the report of a cannon, a main beam amidships cracked and buckled. Even the skipper was seriously concerned, and the Saints were simply terrified, remembering the fate of Francis Blackwell and his Franciscans who had come to grief just two years before because they, too, departed rather too late in the season for a safe voyage.

Fortunately, someone had brought along from Holland a "great iron scrue" which was used to force the cracked beam back into place where it was secured and reinforced with a timber braced against the lower deck. The sailors were muttering among themselves about the dangerous condition of the ship, and among the officers there was "great distraction & difference of opinion" about whether to turn back or not. Finally, after much discussion and a careful examination of his vessel, Captain Jones pronounced her strong and tight under water, even though leaky in her upper works, and "so they commited themselves to ye will of God & resolved to proseede."

November came, and six days later death struck for the first

time among the Pilgrims, claiming young William Butten, Deacon
Fuller's servant, whose remains were committed to the deep with
simple ceremony. Then on the 10th,[2] at dawn, "after longe beating
at sea," the lookout spied in the distance a faint dark line off the
starboard bow and shortly raised a cry that brought all running—
Land, ahoy!—and as the excited passengers crowded the rail, one
may well believe Bradford that they were "not a litle joyfull."

Their course had brought them to the wrist of Cape Cod, apparently to a point off the high bluffs at Truro. The ship stood in
toward shore, but after a conference with the skipper they tacked
about and stood off to the south'ard, for the Pilgrims were still
ostensibly bent on finding "some place aboute Hudson's river for
their habitation." Running close to shore, they followed this course
till noon when, at the sharp elbow of the Cape, off the present
town of Chatham, they suddenly "fell amongst deangerous shoulds
and roring breakers." They had stumbled into the treacherous
waters which had almost brought Champlain to grief in 1605 and
three years earlier had been christened Tucker's Terror by Captain Bartholomew Gosnold, who had tried fishing in these waters
and given the Cape its apt name. The *Mayflower* seemed to be
"in great danger, & ye wind shrinking upon them withall," the
helm was put hard over and they headed back up the coast, "happy
to gett out of those dangers," before nightfall. With a gentle
breeze blowing, the ship lay to in the open sea all that night, and
early the next morning—sixty-six days out of Plymouth, ninety-
eight out of Southampton, almost four months out of Delft Haven
—the Pilgrims rounded the curved tip of the Cape into what is
now Provincetown harbor, as fine and fair as any on the continent, large enough to shelter a fleet of a thousand sail.

And as the anchor went down with a rattle of chains and the
decks under foot were stable again, "no marvell if they were thus
joyefull, seeing wise Seneca was so affected with sailing a few miles
on ye coast of his owne Italy that he affirmed that he had rather
remaine twentie years on his way by land than pass by sea to any
place in a short time, so tedious & dreadfull was ye same . . ."

9

MUTINY
ON THE
MAYFLOWER

In ye name of God, Amen . . . at Cap-Codd ye 11 of November . . .

—OF PLIMOTH PLANTATION

THEIR EYES LONGINGLY FIXED ON TERRA FIRMA, ALL THE passengers were eager to leave the cramped ship and go ashore to stretch themselves if only for an hour or two. But there was some very serious business to be settled first. Affairs had taken an alarming turn. Leaders of the company had overheard ominous mutterings among some of the passengers as the ship came into the harbor. Now the bolder of these malcontents had become quite defiant, openly proclaiming that "when they came ashore, they would use their own libertie, for none had power to command them, the patente they had being for Virginia and not

New-england, which belonged to another Government, with which ye Virginia Company had nothing to doe."

Nor was this the end of these "discontents & murmurings amongst some, and mutinous speeches & carriags in others," for they continued at Plymouth until firmly put down by the governor and "ye better part, which clave faithfully togeather, in ye maine."

The names of these rebels have not been handed down. Bradford knew who they were, of course, but in his otherwise detailed chronicle he exhibits a curious reticence here, vaguely dismissing them as "some of the strangers." There was certainly a reason for his reticence, and it will bear looking into, for the mutiny has several important and dramatic aspects. Among other things, it gave us one of the great documents of American history.

Some ten years earlier, in 1609, another emigrant company had left England, with Virginia also as its destination, embarking in a fleet of nine ships under the command of Sir George Somers and Sir William Gates, who had recently been appointed governor of the colony and was going out to assume his post. A tropical hurricane struck the fleet and scattered it. Months later, cruelly battered and in sinking condition, some of the vessels limped into the Chesapeake and dropped anchor off Jamestown. But the admiral's flagship, the *Sea Venture,* was not among them. She had been wrecked off Bermuda, fortunately without loss of life. Those on board had scarcely crawled up the beach and dried themselves out before Gates and Somers commanded them to start building pinnaces to transport the company to its destination. There was much grumbling, with growing resistance on every hand, for the men argued that if forced to go on to Virginia, they "might well feare to be detained in that countrie by the authority of the Commander thereof, and their whole life to serve the turnes of the Adventurers with their travailes and labours."

The center of resistance, it later developed, lay in Governor Gates's own household, in the suite of his private chaplain who had brought with him "a Clarke to read the Psalms and Chapters on Sundays, . . . a fellow who had much knowledge of the Scriptures and could reason well therein." It was this humble clerk who, insidiously at first, then more openly, began "to advance substantial arguments, both civill and divine (the Scriptures falsely quoted), that it was no breach of honesty, conscience, nor Religion to decline from the obedience of the Governor or to refuse to go further, . . . since the authority ceased when the wracke was committed, and with it they were all then freed from the government of any man"—which was precisely what some on the *Mayflower* were contending under essentially similar conditions.

When the clerk boldly pushed his arguments from sedition to treason and began to preach organized resistance, he was promptly seized and brought before a court-martial on a charge of "Mutinie and Rebellion," together with three or four of his lieutenants in these divellish disquiets." All were convicted and sentenced to die. All were executed with the signal exception of the chief rebel, who succeeded in begging off and was finally pardoned because he "made so much moane, alleadging the Ruine of his wife and children in this his Trespasse."

The name of the Scripture-quoting, treason-plotting, loud-bemoaning "Clarke" was Stephen Hopkins.[1]

If this was not the Stephen Hopkins on the *Mayflower,* then several other curious things have to be explained. The matter of name, of course, may have been a mere coincidence, though a remarkable one under the circumstances. But was it also coincidence that the *Mayflower* rebels echoed the arguments, even the very phrases, of the Bermuda mutineers? Again, it is plain from the record that Stephen Hopkins, alone of the passengers on board, had been in the New World before. When the Pilgrims sent ashore their first exploring party, he was one of three named as a sort of general staff to assist Captain Standish with their "counsel and advise." As the Leyden group exercised command and was not at all disposed to share it, the only Stranger so honored was Hopkins, presumably because he knew the wilderness and the ways of the Indians. This he did, obviously. Tramping through the woods one day, the party came upon a clever contrivance which none could puzzle out until Hopkins came up and showed them how it worked, explaining that it was an Indian trap "to catch some deer." If not with the company that finally reached Virginia after surviving the shipwreck and "disquiets" at Bermuda, when had Hopkins acquired such knowledge? There is good reason to suppose that the argumentative clerk who so providentially escaped the hangman lived to become one of the ablest and apparently the most prolific of the Pilgrim Fathers, for his posterity is legion if one can credit the claims of all who profess to be his descendants.

But there is no reason to believe that Hopkins led the malcontents here as at Bermuda. Since those days he had come up in the world. No longer was he a lowly clerk, perhaps even an indentured servant, dependent upon a master's bounty and always at his beck and call. Now a master himself with servants of his own, he certainly would not have been pleased to hear them talking of using "their own libertie," arguing that they were now "freed from the government of any man." It is not unlikely, however, that rebellion centered in his household. Only three men on board had been in America before—the two mates, Clarke and Coffin, and himself—and during the long weeks at sea they must have whiled away many an hour telling the passengers of their adventures in the wild and mysterious land toward which they were bound, leaving their eager listeners breathless and often goggle-eyed with wonder. And what a story Hopkins could have made—and he was always rather gabby—of the shipwreck, the tyranny of Gates, his own determined opposition, what the men said and then what he said, the court-martial, and the last-minute reprieve! Nor would he have apologized for what he did, for Hopkins was more democratically inclined than any of the prominent Pilgrims and had no blind respect for authority as such, having many conflicts with the Plymouth magistrates in later years. He insisted upon selling liquor without a license and more than once was in trouble for his free and easy way with "inferiours," being heavily fined on one occasion for "allowing servants and such to sit in his house drinking and playing shovelboard."

There were many on board to listen attentively to such an exciting and provocative story. The poorer and humbler freemen (the "goodmen," as they were called) had no more desire than those at Bermuda "to serve the turnes of the Adventurers with their travailes and labours." The servants were only too eager to be free of their bonds, and the two groups represented a majority of the men in the company. Was it true that here in New England "none had power to command them?" As the question was discussed and argued, none can have listened more intently than Edward Dotey and Edward Leister, Hopkins' servants, both of whom were ambitious, high-spirited, and somewhat violent youths. It was they who, armed with cutlasses in one hand, knives in the other, fought Plymouth's first and last duel soon after landing, for which they were tied together by their heads and their heels until they cooled off. When his indenture expired, Leister abruptly departed for Virginia, having no taste for the company of the Saints. Dotey stayed on and became known as an aggressive and highly contentious character, ever involved in quarrels and lawsuits, being hauled into court more than once to answer charges of assault. Did these two play a leading role in the mutiny, citing against their master the arguments and the very words that he had used? How ironic it would be if Stephen Hopkins, once a viper himself in Governor Gates' household, now found to his dismay that he had inadvertently hatched several in the bosom of his own.

Whoever the leaders, mutiny was brewing on the *Mayflower,* and all the Pilgrim leaders were gravely concerned about it. If there was any talk of stringing up the rebels, the records make no mention of the fact. Perhaps there was none. The company obviously needed every able-bodied man it could muster for the tremendous task ahead. Masters may have considered it as foolish to sacrifice their servants as to kill an ox, or a horse, or any other valuable work animal, for attempting occasionally to kick over the traces. Still, something had to be done about the explosive situation. Mutiny could not simply be ignored. To meet the situation, those in command decided once again to rely upon the Word, drafting as formal and formidable a document as they knew how. The church covenants long in use among the Separatists plainly served as a model, and it was probably Brewster's handiwork in the main, for he had some acquaintance with "by these presents" and other bits of appropriate legal jargon from his days as post-master and receiver at Scrooby. As soon as the document was completed, the entire Pilgrim company was called together to hear it slowly read aloud, perhaps in the skipper's cabin on the poop deck, as painters have usually chosen to picture the scene attending the birth of the now celebrated Mayflower Compact.

"In ye name of God, Amen," it began. "We whose names are underwritten, the loyall subjects of our dread soveraigne Lord, King James, . . . doe by these presents solemnly & mutualy in ye presence of God, and one of another, covenant & combine ourselves togeather into a civill body politick, . . . and by vertue hereof to enacte, constitute, and frame such just & equall lawes, ordinances, acts, constitutions, & offices, from time to time, as shall be thought most meete & convenient for ye generall good of ye Colonie unto which we promise all due submission and obedience."

The covenant was first signed by those who had the right or had assumed the privilege of using the title of "Mr."—then pronounced "master," and often written so. Relatively the aristocrats of the company, there were twelve of this group, with Saints and Strangers equally represented. John Carver, the most substantial and respectable among them, signed first. He was followed by Bradford, Winslow, Brewster, and Allerton. Then came Standish, Deacon Fuller, Christopher Martin, William Mullins, William White, Richard Warren, and Stephen Hopkins. Next, the "goodmen" were asked to sign. Only twenty-seven responded; several either declined or were ailing. Lastly, no doubt with the hope that it might make them take their prescribed loyalty more seriously, a few of the servants were invited or commanded to sign—Edward Dotey, Edward Leister, and two others. The women were excluded, of course, for they were not free agents, being the legal chattels and servants of their lords—indentured for life, as it were.

For generations, ever since John Quincy Adams rescued it from oblivion in 1802, the Mayflower Compact has been hailed as a great charter of freedom, which it was. It did not apply to all, to be sure, and its promise of "just & equall lawes" was often more honored in the breach than the observance. But for its day it was an extraordinary document, a remarkable statement of revolutionary new principles, an important milestone in our long, hard, and often bloody ascent from feudalism, from that degrading "aristocratic" system of power and privilege for the few which had held Europe in irons for centuries, vestiges of which still remain to plague us. It is also the fashion, as every school child knows, to hail the compact in the most extravagant terms as the very cornerstone of American democracy, which it most certainly was not. As the circumstances of its birth reveal, it was conceived as an instrument to maintain the status quo on the *Mayflower,* to show inferiors in general and servants in particular their place and keep them there where they belonged—i.e. under the thumbs of their masters. As is evident from the merest glance at the history of Plymouth, the Pilgrim leaders did not believe in equalitarian democracy though they were moving in that direction. They favored a change in the hierarchical structure above them, but not below. That change in the foundations of society would come in due time, but long after the Pilgrims had gone to their rewards.

"American democracy was not born in the cabin of the *Mayflower,* or in the Boston town meeting," as has been well said by Mr. Samuel Eliot Morison, son of Massachusetts and her most distinguished historian, "but on the farming, fighting frontier of all the colonies, New England included."

Another matter had to be attended to before the historic first Pilgrim assembly adjourned. As it was now a "civill body politick," the company had to have officers duly authorized to act and speak for it. For the time being it was decided that one would suffice— a governor, to be chosen by popular election of the freemen, just as it had long been the custom of the Saints to choose a pastor. Apparently there was no electioneering by the rival factions, and the unanimous choice fell upon John Carver, "a man godly & well approved amongst them," whose real title to fame is not that he was the Pilgrims' first governor but rather the first colonial governor in the whole New World, perhaps the first of history, to be named by the colonists themselves in a free election. The pattern set here on the *Mayflower* on the day of her arrival continued throughout the life of the Plymouth colony, which from first to last chose to govern itself through officers named at regular annual elections, though it should be remembered that narrow limitations upon the right to vote denied many a voice in the direction of affairs.

The crisis on board had another significance which has been ill understood. From the Pilgrim description of events, the inference is plain that overnight they had abandoned all idea of going on to Virginia. But from all surrounding circumstance it can be seriously questioned whether they had entertained any such idea for some time. Weston had talked to them about New England and the profitable fisheries there, and they had spent some of their meager funds in buying hooks, seines, and salt. The Pilgrims explained their apparent change of plan by saying that Captain Jones refused to go on, and a half century later Nathaniel Morton, Bradford's nephew and secretary, asserted that he had received "late and certain intelligence"—which was never offered—that the skipper of the *Mayflower* had been bribed by the Dutch to keep the Pilgrims away from their settlements along the Hudson.[2]

The truth is, it would seem, that the company never intended to go beyond these shores. Among other things, New England offered this cardinal advantage—there was here no established government and no Anglican church, as in Virginia, so that the Saints would be free of interference in ordering their affairs as they chose. In England they had been in communication with Captain John Smith, known to fame for his few years in Virginia, though he spent the remainder of his life promoting the colonization of New England and is more deserving of fame on that account. It was Smith who gave New England its name while exploring its coast south from Maine in 1614, publishing his findings two years later in *A Description of New England*. This contained a remarkably accurate map of the region, which the Pilgrims had carefully studied and now had with them.

Before their departure Captain Smith had suggested that he be taken along as guide and adviser. But the Pilgrims declined, remarking that it was cheaper to buy his book than hire him. The result, said Smith tartly, was that "their humorous ignorances caused them for more than a year to endure a wonderful deal of misery with infinite patience, . . . thinking to find things better than I advised them."

Lastly, it is evident that the merchant adventurers knew of the company's real plans and had probably inspired them. When word came at length of the Pilgrims' whereabouts, far from their announced destination, Weston and his partners evinced no slightest surprise.

Nor did the Pilgrims ever offer them an explanation.

In this one matter at least, the Pilgrims and the merchant adventurers seem to have understood one another well enough, doubtless having agreed beforehand that the less said about it the better in view of possible complications with the King, the Privy Council, and the First Virginia Company from which they held a patent.

10

BABES
IN THE
WILDERNESS

...they had now no freinds to wellcome
them, nor inns to entertaine or refresh
their weatherbeaten bodys...
—WILLIAM BRADFORD

AND ONLY NOW, AFTER THE DISCONTENTED ON BOARD HAD
been given a solemn warning to watch their step—or as the
Saints usually phrased it, to "preserve better walking"—was anyone allowed to leave the ship. The first party ashore consisted of
sixteen armed men under orders to reconnoiter the neighborhood
and bring back badly needed supplies of wood and water. With
muskets primed and ready, the party marched inland several miles,
far enough to learn that they were on a slender hook of land
between Cape Cod Bay and the ocean. It reminded them of the
sand dune country in parts of Holland. Only this was better, they
reported, for it had a topsoil of "excellent black earth" and was

well wooded, though in most spots "open and without under-wood, fit either to go or ride in." They met no Indians and, more surprising, saw no signs of habitation. Nor did they find any fresh water. Returning soon to the beach, they pushed off for the *May-flower* with a boatload of juniper which, as it burned on com-forting fires, "smelled very sweet and strong," like frankincense itself to those who had lived for months in the smelly hold.

No work was done the following day, a Sabbath, which was quietly spent on board in prayer and meditation. The Pilgrims had much to be thankful for, and one and all, Saints and Strangers alike, "fell upon their knees & blessed ye God of heaven, who had brought them over ye vast & furious ocean, and delivered them from all ye periles & miseries thereof, againe to set their feete on ye firme and stable earth, their proper elemente." Yet as they looked about them, the prospect had little to assure even the most sanguine and stout of heart. It was clear from a casual glance or two that they had not come to an earthly paradise. With summer long since gone, all things bore "a wether-beaten face, and ye whole countrie, full of woods & thickets, represented a wild & savage heiw." Cold weather would be upon them any day now, and "they that know ye winter in that cuntrie know them to be sharp & violent, & subjecte to cruell & feirce storms, deangerous to travill to known places, much more to serch an unknown coast." They were hundreds of miles from the nearest settlement and could expect no aid from any quarter, least of all from the Indians who, as events proved, were "readier to fill their sids full of arrows than otherwise." Altogether, it was enough to give anyone pause, said Bradford, for "what could they see but a hidious & desolate wildernes, full of wild beasts & willd men? and what multituds there might be of them, they knew not." But their always "answerable" courage did not fail them.

The next day, November 13th, New England's first "blue" Monday, the women were early put ashore under an armed guard to do the family "wash, as they had great need." While they were beating, scrubbing, and rinsing heaps of dirty clothes and bedding, the children ran wildly up and down the beach under the watchful eye of the sentries. The men brought in the long boat stowed between decks on the *Mayflower* and beached her for repairs, for she had been badly battered and bruised by the storms at sea and her seams had been opened up "with the people's lying in her." As a gang went to work on the shallop under the direction of Francis Eaton, the ship's carpenter from Bristol, the rest prowled the beach and tidal flats in search of shellfish. Ravenous for fresh food, they made a great feast on tender soft-shell clams and succulent young quahogs, the now famed cherrystones of New England, and also put away many large mussels, "very fat," which was a grave error, as many another visitor to the Cape has since discovered, for the mussels made them deathly sick, causing all "to cast and scour."

Two days later, when it became evident that the shallop would not be ready for some time, the Pilgrim leaders decided that there could be no further delay in finding a place to settle. They could not afford to lose another day if they were to get a roof over their heads before the snow began to fly. Besides, the crew on the *Mayflower* and some of the officers were growling that the passengers and their goods should be dumped on the beach so that the ship might sail for home before all its stores were consumed. In coming into the harbor, the Pilgrims had noted what appeared to be a large river flowing into the bay about five miles down the coast, and it was now proposed that a party proceed overland to investigate. Because of the obvious dangers this was "rather permitted than approved," and the company called for volunteers. Sixteen men stepped forward and were put ashore, "with every man his musket, sword, and corselet, under ye command of Captain Myles Standish* . . . unto whom was adjoined, for counsel and advise, William Bradford, Stephen Hopkins, and Edward Tilley."

The party set off down the broad white beach and had gone about a mile when they saw five or six "salvages" approaching in the distance. When the Indians spied them, they darted into the

---

* Here, for the first time, the Captain's name appears in the Pilgrim records.

woods, whistling their dog after them. The Pilgrims hurried forward and plunged into the woods after them, about as foolish a thing as could have been done. But they wanted to see, they said, "if there might not be more of them lying in ambush." Fortunately, no trap had been laid for these babes in the wilderness, and they patiently plodded along following the tracks of the Indians all day without catching sight of them. Next morning, after a chill night spent in the open, they picked up the trail again, wandering up and down steep hills and deep valleys in what is now the township of Truro, at the wrist of the Cape. But they soon lost both the trail and themselves, "falling into shuch thickets as were ready to tear their cloaths & armore in peeces," suffering cruelly from "wante of drinke," for they had brought with them only a small bottle of *aqua vitae*—probably Holland gin. At length they found a spring of cool fresh water, and "in their great thirste," they said, it tasted "as pleasante unto them as wine or beer had been in for-times."

Coming out of the woods near the bay shore, they discovered several large clearings used by the Indians as cornfields. Here they noted several curious heaps of sand, and one in particular caught their eye. It was covered with grass mats and had an arched piece of wood at one end, a half-buried earthen pot at the other. Their curiosity aroused, they dug into this, turning up several rotted arrows and an old bow, which they carefully put back and covered with sand, rightly surmising that the Indians had buried one of their braves here and that "it would be odious unto them to ransack their sepulchres." Proceeding to the "river" which interested them, they were unable to determine from brief investigation whether it was a river or only a tidal inlet. Whatever it was, it had possibilities as a harbor and apparently would accommodate ships.

Luckily, the Pilgrims kept to the shore on their return and within a mile or two came to a high sandy hill rising steeply from the beach. At its base was a large meadow, and in it they again noted curious heaps of sand. One had been freshly made, and casting all scruples to the winds, they decided to excavate. A few feet down they came upon a large basket, "very handsomely and cunningly made." It held three or four bushels and was filled to the top with corn, "some in eares, faire and good, of diverce colours, which seemed to them a very goodly sight (haveing never seen any such before)." This they did not cover up and leave as they found it. First posting a guard to keep off any Indians who might object to their proceedings, they hauled the basket out of the ground. In their wanderings they had picked up a big iron kettle, obviously a ship's kettle "brought out from Europe," probably by some of the English or Breton fishermen who occasionally visited this coast. The Pilgrims filled up the kettle with corn and then stuffed their pockets with the yellow, red, and blue maize. Unable to carry all of it, they left the remainder in the basket and put it back in the ground, salving their consciences by saying that as soon as they met the Indians, they would "satisfie them for their corne." On their way to the ship they soon tired of carrying the heavy kettle and tossed it away, salvaging some of its contents. Back on the *Mayflower* at last, after being three days out, they put the corn into the common store "to be kept for seed," which made everybody "marvelusly glad." This was just plain larceny, of course, but the Pilgrims were inclined to regard it as another special providence of God. And in a sense it was, for without this seed corn they would have had no crops the next year, "as ye sequell did manyfest," and all would have starved to death. As it was, they just barely managed to squeeze through.

Ten days passed with the company in a dangerous state of indecision, with little going forward but the repair of the shallop. At last the boat was ready to sail, though not entirely mended, and it was decided to use her in sending a second expedition to Truro. It consisted of twenty-four Pilgrims and nine of the *Mayflower* crew, all under the command of Captain Jones, who had volunteered to go and had been named chief of the party "for his kindnes & forwardnes." It was a strong and well-armed group, large enough to strike hard if the Indians were up in arms about the theft of their corn. Bad weather forced the shallop to turn back, but the Pilgrims were anxious to proceed and insisted upon being put ashore, wading from the boat to the beach in icy water up to their hips. Many of those who soon died "took the original of their death here," for it "blowed and did snow all that day and night, and froze withal." Picked up by the shallop in the morning, they sailed to the river cursorily examined before—the Pamet River, as it was soon named for the local Indian tribe. It was not a river but a tidal estuary, they finally determined, and too shallow for ships though good for boats.

Disappointed here, the Pilgrims made straight for the meadow where they had struck buried treasure, at Corn Hill, as the spot was aptly named by them and is still known. Everything was covered with a thick blanket of snow, but they quickly located the sand heap which had not been entirely despoiled by those on the First Discovery. The ground was frozen hard, but they broke through with their cutlasses and short swords and soon had the sand flying, finding the corn where they had left it, being "very happie" that the Indians had not discovered their loss and removed the large basket, which was now quickly emptied of all it contained.

"We also digged in a place a little further off, and found a bottle of oil.

"We went to another place which we had seen before, and digged and found corn: viz., two or three baskets full of Indian wheat [maize], and a bag of beans . . .

"Whilst some of us were digging up this, some others found another heap of corn, which they digged up also.

"So as we had, in all, about ten bushels; which will serve us sufficiently for seed." The Indians needed it for the same purpose, but if this thought ever occurred to the Pilgrims, they brushed it aside, pleading their necessity.

"And sure it was God's good providence that we found this corn, for else we know not how we should have done. For we knew not how we should find or meet with any of the Indians, except it be to do us a mischief." This was adding insult to injury, for it was they and not the Indians who were up to mischief. "But the Lord is never wanting unto his in their greatest needs; let his holy name have all ye praise."

Loaded on the shallop, the corn was carried to the *Mayflower,* the Pilgrims following the next day after some more spade work, having dug into several mounds which they knew to be graves. In one they found the skeletons of a child and a man, the latter's skull with "fine yellow hair still on it and some of the flesh unconsumed." It was wrapped in a sailor's canvas cassock and a pair of cloth breeches, and in the grave were many bowls, trays, trinkets, a knife, a pack needle, strings of fine white beads, and two or three old iron things. Still musing upon the mystery of the yellow-haired man,[1] the Pilgrims closed the grave, having removed "sundrie of the prettiest things" to take away with them. In their meanderings they also stumbled upon several of the Indians' round huts, from which the occupants had evidently just fled. Nosing about, they found antlers, eagle claws, a piece of broiled herring, several chunks of venison, some tobacco seed, many wooden trays and dishes, thin and heavy mats, earthen pots, an English bucket without a handle, large baskets ingeniously made of crab shells, other baskets of fiber "curiously wrought with black and white in pretty works." Here, too, they took "some of the best things" away with them, making note of the fact that they "left the houses standing."

The report on the findings of this Second Discovery provoked lively debate on the *Mayflower* and led to an important decision. Many wanted to settle at Corn Hill immediately, arguing that it was a fertile, healthful, and easily defended site. It was close by, which would obviate the risks of exploring farther afield at this late season. While the harbor there left much to be desired, it offered safe anchorage for boats and was "like to be a place of good fishing." No cod had yet been caught, but every day they saw "great whales of the best kind for oil and bone," and Captain Jones had told them that with the proper gear they could have made £3,000 or £4,000 right here in the harbor, more than twice their debt to the merchant adventurers.

But others spoke against Corn Hill, citing its want of an adequate water supply. They would have to depend upon fresh-water ponds which might dry up in summer. If their town were built on the top of the hill for better defense, they would have to haul water and all their supplies up its steep slopes. Some suggested sailing away to the far side of Cape Ann, to what is now Ipswich, having heard that the harbor, land, and fishing were good there. But it was chance which finally decided that Corn Hill was not to be the Pilgrims' home in the New World. One of the mates, Robert Coffin, had been in these waters before, it so happened, and now told them of a good harbor directly across the bay in which he had once been—"Thievish Harbor," as they called it, because "one of the wild men with whom they had some trucking, stole a harping iron [harpoon] from them."

On December 6th, with Coffin at the tiller, eighteen men pushed off in the shallop to round the bay and have a look at "Thievish Harbor," or Plymouth, as it had been named by Captain John Smith six years previously. Ten of the Pilgrims had volunteered to go—of the Saints, Edward and John Tilley, Bradford, Winslow, and Governor Carver with his servant John Howland; of the Strangers, Captain Standish, Richard Warren, and Stephen Hopkins with one of his servants, Edward Dotey. It was bitterly cold, with a stiff breeze blowing, and the spray whipping across the open boat cut like a knife and froze their clothes till they were "like coates of iron." Many were "sick unto death." Edward Tilley and the master gunner fainted with the cold, but they held to their course, sailing south past Corn Hill and swinging round a sandy point into what is now Wellfleet Bay. Making for shore, they spotted in the distance ten or twelve Indians very busy doing something with a black object on the beach. As soon as the latter spied the boat, they became very excited, jumping about a good deal before they ran for the woods. The party spent the night on the beach, around a blazing fire in the center of a "barricado" built of logs, stakes, and pine boughs. Smoke from Indian fires was seen a few miles away, but nothing disturbed their slumbers that night.

In the morning some went back to the point where the Indians had been seen. The latter, they found, had been cutting up a huge black fish about fifteen feet long, covered "some 2 inches thike of

fat, like a hogg, . . . and fleshed like a swine." This was the Pilgrims' first acquaintance with the grampus or blackfish, alias the
Social or Howling Whale (*Globicephalus melas*), which was to
play so large a role in the lives of their descendants along the
Cape. Roaming the woods, they came upon a large burial ground
with a fence about it, "like a churchyard, with young spires
[saplings] four or five yards long, set as close one by another as
they could, two or three feet in the ground." They resisted temptation and "digged none of them up." They did some digging, however, and were disappointed to find nothing but parched acorns,
which they scorned. The shallop had been moved down the beach
a few miles to the mouth of a small stream, within the present
township of Eastham, and here the party threw up a barricade,
brought in firewood, ate a meager supper, posted sentries, and
soon fell asleep, to be startled about midnight by a "hideous &
great crie."

   "Arm, arm!" shouted one of the sentries as he came running into
the barricade. All jumped for their muskets and lined up along
the walls of the barricade. They could see nothing in the darkness
but blazed away nonetheless, and the "noys seased." Assured by
a sailor who had been in Newfoundland that the sound was merely
the howling of wolves, they were soon fast asleep, to be up before
daybreak. They first had prayers, as usual, and then began preparing breakfast. While waiting, some started carrying their things
down to the shallop, even their muskets, against the advice of
Standish and several others who protested that this was a dangerous
thing to do. There was now a streak of dawn in the east, and the
Pilgrims were just sitting down to breakfast when, "all on ye
sudain, they heard a great & strange crie, which they knew to be
the same voyces they had heard in ye night, though they varied
their notes."

   "Men, Indians, Indians!" And one of the sentries came dashing
into the barricade, followed by a shower of arrows.

   "Woach! Woach! Ha! Ha! Hach! Woach!" echoed terrifyingly
from the surrounding woods.

Fortunately, Standish had kept his flintlock by him, as had another man, and their fire gave the others time to get their clumsy matchlocks ready. Several of the men recklessly dashed toward the shallop to recover their guns, and with loud cries the Indians wheeled about to cut them off. Others of the party ran to their rescue, armed only with cutlasses. All soon got hold of their blunderbusses and "let flye amongst them, and quickly stopped their violence." But one "lustie man, and no less valiante," stoutly stood his ground close by and kept arrows whizzing through the barricade. Finally, after several shots had failed to dislodge him, Standish took careful aim and made bark and splinters fly about his ears, whereupon he "gave an extraordinary shrike, and away they went all of them." The Pilgrims went after them, chasing them about a quarter of a mile. Before turning back, they shouted after the Indians several times and shot off a piece or two in their direction—just to show them, they said, that they were "not affrade of them or any way discouraged."

This "huggery" at Nauset, in which by some miracle no one received even a scratch though their coats hanging in the barricade were shot through and through with arrows, was only the first of many desperate adventures on a day which those on this Third Discovery never forgot. As they pushed off for Plymouth, the weather was fair, but it soon began to snow and rain, with the wind steadily rising until by mid-afternoon it was blowing a gale. In the rough sea they "broake their rudder, & it was as much as 2 men could doe to steere her with a cupple of oares."

"Be of good cheer!" sang out Coffin after a time, saying that he now saw the harbor for which they were heading. As night was coming on, they ran up more sail to get in before dark, whereupon the mast broke in three pieces and went overboard with the sail "in a very grown sea." But they managed to cut the mast and sail away before capsizing, and with a flood tide sweeping them along, struck into the harbor and bore up to the north as directed by Coffin, who thought he recognized certain landmarks through the murk.

"Lord, be merciful unto us," he suddenly exclaimed as the shallop went scudding toward shore in a cove white with thunderous breakers, "for mine eyes have never seen this place before!"

"If you are men, about with her, or else we are all cast away!" shouted a sailor at one of the steering oars. All rowed with might and main, slowly pulling the shallop to safety and swinging round to the west where they found themselves at length in the lee of a wooded shore. As it was now quite dark, they could see nothing and decided to spend the night in the storm-tossed boat, partly in fear of another "huggery." But the wind soon shifted and it became so unbearably cold that First Officer Clarke resolved to go ashore even at the risk of drowning or being scalped. A few bolder spirits went with him and after a time they got a fire started, a welcome beacon in the night, and "ye rest were glad to come to them."

In the morning the Pilgrims learned that they were on an island in Plymouth harbor—Clark's Island, as they named it for the *Mayflower's* capable and kindly chief mate, who first stepped foot on it. The weather had cleared, but the Pilgrims decided to rest that day, being too exhausted to do more than dry out their stuff, clean their fouled muskets, and give "God thanks for his mercies, in their manifould deliverances." And as this was Saturday, "they prepared there to keepe ye Sabath," so two more days were lost.

Early on Monday, December 11th,* the Pilgrims sounded the harbor and discovered that it would accommodate ships. Going ashore for a hasty exploration, they found "diverse cornfeilds & litle runing brooks, a place (as they supposed) fitt for situation; at least, it was ye best they could find, and ye season & their presente necessitie made them glad to accepte of it." By the following day they were back on the *Mayflower* to report the news to the rest of the company, "which did much comforte their harts."

* The date is Old Style. For current New Style, add ten days. Thus Forefathers' Day, which commemorates the historic landing, is now (after much confusion) celebrated on December 21st. Britain and her colonies did not shift from the old Julian to the new Gregorian calendar until 1752, with curious effects upon the Pilgrim saga, as will be seen.

All had need of comfort, especially Bradford, who returned to learn that on the day after his departure his wife had been drowned. Young Dorothy had somehow fallen overboard while the ship was lying quietly at anchor, so the story has come down to us— and perhaps she did. But it is strange that there is not a word in the Pilgrim chronicles about the tragedy—not a phrase, as one expects, about her desperate struggle for life and her heartbreaking cries as attempts to rescue her failed. In his pocket notebook, under the heading of "Deaths," Bradford made this laconic entry— "Dec. 7. Dorothy, Wife to Mr. William Bradford"—and never mentioned her name again.

There undoubtedly was some reason for this as Bradford was not a hardhearted or callous man. If Dorothy had jumped overboard, that was reason enough, for at the time nothing was regarded as so heinous an offense against the laws of God and man as taking one's life. Nor would Dorothy have been the first or last to crack in terror of the "hideous & desolate wildernes." At her first sight of New England some ten years later, that stouthearted rebel, Anne Hutchinson, declared that her heart and spirit all but failed her, and that she would have fled in panic back to England had she not believed that God was about to destroy the kingdom for its sins and iniquities. Lady Arabella Johnson, who came with John Winthrop and his Puritans in 1630, soon languished and died, broken in spirit, overwhelmed by fear and horror of life on a wild frontier. To picture the forlorn lot or share the soul-searing experience of the pioneer women who first came to our shores is impossible for even the liveliest imagination today.

After a delay of three days, evidently spent in long-winded arguments pro and con, the *Mayflower* weighed anchor and headed for Plymouth. But with a stiff breeze blowing from the northwest, Captain Jones could not work his vessel into the harbor and stood off again for the Cape. Next day he made another try and just before the wind shifted back to the northwest, slipped between the long sandspits that almost enclosed the harbor and hauled round to the north, dropping anchor beyond Clark's Island, in what was later known as the Cow Yard, for a great cow whale once trapped and killed there.

And now it was Saturday again, to be spent in making preparations for the Sabbath. This edified the less impatient Saints no doubt, but some of the more "prophane" Strangers must have found it pretty trying.

11

NEW
PLIMOTH
PLANTED

Freind, if ever we make a plantation, God
works a mirakle ...
——ROBERT CUSHMAN

THIEVISH HARBOR IMPRESSED AND ENCOURAGED THE WEARY
passengers on the *Mayflower*. Though somewhat shallow, it was
a large and well-sheltered harbor, ringed with stately woods and
alive with waterfowl. Altogether, it was a "most hopefull place,"
all agreed, but the company had yet to make up its mind just
where to settle.

Early on Monday, December 18th, a party was sent ashore to
explore the environs, pushing off in the shallop under the command of Captain Jones, who was as anxious as any for some
decision to be reached so that he and his men might depart while
the ship still had sufficient stores to see them home. Heading for

the lower part of the harbor, the shallop put into the wide mouth
of a large brook which emptied into the bay between high steep
banks leading up to gently sloping clearings on both sides of the
stream. After looking about here, the Pilgrims marched seven or
eight miles up the beach along the edge of the woods, passing
other clearings where the Indians had planted corn, though obviously not for several years. But they saw "not an Indean nor an
Indean house," which somewhat puzzled them. In general, these
former yeomen noted, the soil was fairly good and "fat in some
places," supporting a thick cover of pine, walnut, beech, ash, birch,
hazel, and sassafras, which was then highly prized and of great
commercial value, for the pharmacopeia of the day prescribed it
as a sovereign cure for almost every ill the flesh is heir to. They
also found berries and herbs of many kinds—strawberry, rasp-
berry, sorrel, yarrow, liverwort, watercress, and "great store of
leeks and onions"—and for building purposes, plenty of sand and
gravel, and fine clay, "no better in the world, excellente for pots,
and will wash like soap; and great store of stone, though somewhat soft."

On the following day the Pilgrims again went ashore "to discover further," making for the upper part of the harbor where they
had remarked a large stream or tidal inlet. Sailing up this for several miles, they discovered it to be a "very pleasante river" and
named it for the patient skipper of the *Mayflower*. Here along the
Jones River, in what is now the village of Kingston, many wished
to settle. But others objected, arguing that it was too heavily
wooded to be cleared with ease, that it was exposed to attack and
inconveniently far from their fishing, their "principal profit." Led
by Bradford, this group spoke for Clark's Island on the ground that
it offered greater security from the Indians. The party crossed to
the island and found it secure enough but otherwise unsuitable,
which left the great problem of the moment no nearer solution
than it had been.

Matters simply could not go on like this, that was obvious, so
the next morning they "called on God for direction" and came to
this resolution—"to goe presently ashore againe" for another look

at the two most likely spots they had seen. As soon as a final report was received on these, the question was to be put to a vote, for they could not now take time, as one remarked and all agreed, "for further search or consideration, our victuals being much spente, especially our Beere, and it now being the 20th of December"—more than six weeks since they had touched the coast. After unprecedentedly brief discussion, the Pilgrims decided to "plant" on the high ground along the brook in the southern part of the harbor, just behind now famed Plymouth Rock, then and for generations thereafter an anonymous and often quite troublesome boulder. Here, so the report ran, "there is a great deale of Land cleared, and hath been planted with Corne three or four years agoe; and there is a very sweete brooke runnes under a hill side . . . where we may habour our boats and shallops exceeding well, and in this brooke much good fishe in their seasons; on the further side of the river also, much Corne ground cleared. In one field is a great hill on which we poynt to make a platforme & plant our Ordinance, which will command all round about." So there, at long last, they made their "randevous" and later in the day brought in twenty men to stay the night, "resolving in the morning to come all ashore and build houses."

A storm broke almost immediately, catching the men out in the open before they had time to put up any kind of shelter. In the morning the bay was so rough that it was noon before the shallop could get in to bring them food. With a gale now howling, the shallop had to be beached and was unable to return to the ship either that day or the next. At the height of the storm, with the *Mayflower* dragging at anchor and leaping about like a wild thing, Mary Allerton, the tailor's wife, was brought to bed and delivered of a son, "but dead borne." And now it was Saturday again. The quiet of the Sabbath was broken only by an Indian alarm when the more nervous of those ashore "heard the crie of some salvages, as they thought."

Work began in earnest on Monday, December 25th, which was Christmas, of course, but that made no difference to the Pilgrims—or at least not to the Saints, for they scorned Christmas

as a "human invention," another Roman "corruption," a survival
from heathen days, as indeed it was.[1] John Robinson had dealt
with the matter at some length in his *Just and Necessarie Apologie,*
in which he took the Dutch to task for many things. They were
not "true" Christians, he informed them, and never would be
until they ceased celebrating Christmas—and Easter, too, for that
matter. There was no warrant for either in Scripture. Christ had
not celebrated Easter, for obvious reasons. As for Christmas, Robinson admitted that he did not know just when Christ had been
born, but of one thing he was certain—"December 25th cannot
be the time."

And why celebrate the birth, he asked, and not the circum-
cision of the Savior?

Not interested in these esoteric matters, the Strangers were sad
not to enjoy the traditional rites and festivities of the season. But
all able-bodied men went ashore willingly enough this Christmas
morning, "some to fell timber, some to saw, some to rive, and
some to carry, so no man rested all that day." On the north bank
of the brook, just above the beach, they chose a site and laid the
foundations of their Common House. Close by, to house the "guard
of honour" now left ashore each night, they threw up a number
of temporary shelters, probably conical huts of branches and turf
much like those which they had seen used by charcoal burners in
England. Late in the afternoon, after another Indian alarm had
sent all running for their muskets, a guard was posted and most
in the working party returned to the *Mayflower.* On this day, it
so happened, the Pilgrims had been reduced at last "to drinking
water." But on board that evening there was a little Christmas
cheer, thanks to the skipper, who as a good Church of England
man did not share the Saints' scruples and broke out a barrel of
the ship's beer, inviting the Pilgrims to drink with him and his
mates, as his guests appreciatively noted.

But there was no good cheer for the men on shore who spent
a miserable night under the blasts of a "sore storm of wind &
raine" which continued to rage all the next day. Through the
Pilgrim chronicles runs the same melancholy theme week after

week, for months on end—". . . aboute noone, it began to raine
. . . at night, it did freeze & snow . . . still the cold weather continued . . . very wet and rainy, with the greatest gusts of wind
ever we saw . . . frost and foule weather hindered us much; this
time of the yeare seldom could we worke half the weeke." Then,
too, the ship was lying far out, almost a mile and a half distant.
As it could not safely be anchored closer, much time was lost in
going to and fro.

Yet slow progress was made and New Plimoth began to take
shape in the clearing. A short street—New England's first "Main
Street"—was laid out along the high north bank of Town Brook.
Long known merely as the Street, then as First and later as Broad
Street, now the famous Leyden Street, it climbed rather sharply
from the beach and ran several hundred yards to the foot of a
steep hill, soon named Fort Hill, for here Captain Standish immediately built a wooden platform on which to mount his cannon.
The lots staked off along the street were very narrow, being only
half a pole (about eight feet) wide and three poles deep. To
simplify the problem of providing living quarters quickly, the
company was reduced to nineteen household units by asking single
men and those without their wives to join some family of their
choice for a time. The amount of land granted each household
depended upon its size. It was entitled to a lot for every man,
woman, and child it contained. But assignment was for present
use only and did not convey permanent title. Heads of households
then drew lots to determine which site each should occupy. There
was no mad scramble here to grab the best locations and defend
them against all comers. There was none of the greedy over-
reaching, the fraud and bloody violence that everywhere marked
the frontier as it moved westward. New Plimoth was, in the beginning at least, a planned community, a cooperative commonwealth,
in which selfish personal aggrandizement and the pursuit of private
profit played no part.

The lot at the foot of the street above the Common House fell
to one of the Strangers, Peter Browne; the next, to William
Brewster and his large household, which included Bradford and

others. Here the street was intersected by a rough road, usually dignified as the Highway, which twisted its way down to the brook on one side and meandered off across the clearing on the other. Above this road, now Main Street, were the lots of John Billington, Isaac Allerton, Francis Cooke, and Edward Winslow. These tracts on the south side of the street ran back to the steep bank of the brook. Below it, bordering the stream, was a rich grassy flat, and here the Pilgrims had their first "gardens & meersteads," soon planting them with turnip, cabbage, parsnip, and other seeds brought from home.

The other side of the street was left open for a time and used as part of the Pilgrims' cornfields. But it was later staked off into lots. That at the foot of Fort Hill was given to Captain Standish so that he might quickly get to his post in time of danger. Just below, at the corner of the Street and the Highway, a large tract was reserved for the Governor's House. On the slope from the Highway to the beach were the plots of Stephen Hopkins, John Howland, and Deacon Samuel Fuller, the last on the edge of a high bank overlooking Plymouth Rock—Cole's Hill, as it came to be called for the popular owner of the pleasant and often boisterous tavern that long stood there.

Now and again, while at work in the clearing, the Pilgrims saw columns of smoke from Indian fires in the distance. But they had not yet caught sight of an Indian, which puzzled and rather worried them. Where were the savages? What were they doing? Resolved to find out, Captain Standish took three or four men and marched off to investigate, half hoping to meet with some of them. The party stumbled upon a few abandoned Indian huts but nothing else of interest, and returned empty-handed except for an "eagle," probably a fish hawk, shot along the way. In their ravenous hunger for fresh food the Pilgrims cooked and ate it, pronouncing it "excellente,... hardly to be discerned from mutton" —which to anyone acquainted with English mutton will seem not at all unlikely. It was a memorable occasion the next day when a sailor picked up on the beach a live herring, "which the Master had to his supper." This encouraged the Pilgrims to hope that they would "have plenty of fishe shortly." As yet they had "got but one cod," largely because these aspiring fishermen had failed to bring along proper gear, specifically wanting nets and small hooks.

Work was interrupted for several days and the company received a fright when Peter Browne and John Goodman mysteriously disappeared one noon time while off gathering thatch for the Common House. Governor Carver organized a searching party and beat the woods for them till dark. When no trace of the missing men was found the next day, the company mourned them as dead, "verilie thinking the Indeans had surprised them," a most disturbing thought.

But Goodman and Browne, it turned out, had merely been off hunting deer and having marvelous adventures. Near a pond their two dogs, a large mastiff bitch and a small spaniel, had raised a big buck which went bounding off into the woods, with the dogs barking after him and the men puffing along behind hopefully clutching their sickles. Soon winded and lost, they wandered about all afternoon in a cold drizzle that later turned to snow. Tired and hungry, chilled to the bone, they lay down on the frozen ground to get some sleep. Suddenly—and their hair stood on end—they were terrified to hear "two lyons roaring exceedingly, for a long time together." Leaping to their feet, they dashed for the nearest tree, intending to climb it in case of attack even though it would be "intollerable cold lodging." Momentarily expecting to be torn limb from limb, they paced up and down under the tree all night, but their only difficulty was with the mastiff bitch, who was not at all impressed and kept trying to break away and go for the "lyons." Next day, after much aimless wandering in the snow, the two hunters got their bearings at last and came stumbling into camp after dark, "readie to faint with travail & wante of victuals, and almost famished with cold." Goodman's shoes—and shoes were worth their weight in gold—had to be cut from his swollen frost-bitten feet.

Not long after, to exercise his lame feet, Goodman called his spaniel and wandered off again. As he was limping along the edge of the clearing, two wolves jumped out from the woods and made for the dog, which finally managed to escape and ran yelping to his master. Picking up a stick, Goodman threw it and hit one of the beasts, which sent both trotting away into the forest. But they immediately circled round and came back, this time approaching quite close in the boldest manner. Goodman snatched up a heavy stake and stood ready, whereupon the wolves "sat both on their tayles, grinning at him a good while"—perhaps recalling their howling success as "lyons." Still grinning, they "wente their way & left him," which is our last glimpse of the engaging Nimrod, John Goodman, who soon passed with so many of his friends to a premature and nameless grave, cut down by disease and the unaccustomed rigors of a New England winter. This winter was, as a matter of fact, rather a mild one as New England winters go. Otherwise there might have been no one left to tell the Pilgrim tale.

On January 14th, a Sabbath, "the wind being very great, they on shipboard spied their great new randevous on fire, which was to them a new discomfort." Unaware as yet of the return of Browne and Goodman late the night before, they were convinced that the Indians, growing bolder, had attacked and killed the party ashore before putting torch to the almost completed Common House, now pressed into service as a hospital, being "as full of beds as they could lie one by another." After some difficulty the shallop got in with a strong party to find that matters were not as bad as suspected, but serious enough. The fire had been caused by a spark flying up into the thatch which instantly burst into flame, dropping fiery embers upon the sick and causing consternation among them, for several open barrels of gunpowder and many charged muskets were lying about the room. The sick jumped from their beds and rushed these outside, "and if they had not risen with good speed, had been blown up with powder." Fortunately, the timbers of the roof held and little damage was done except to the poor patients who took another chill. Many lost irreplaceable clothing and other articles, the greatest loss being suffered by Carver and Bradford, both of whom were ailing and in bed when the fire started. Having caught cold on the Third

Discovery, Bradford had been complaining of his "ancles" for some time and just a few days previously, while at work in the clearing, had been so "vehemently taken with a grief & paine, and so shot to his huckle-bone" that it was feared he would instantly die. But he got a little better toward night and "in time, through God's mercie in the use of means, recovered."

On the following Sabbath the entire company on the *Mayflower* came ashore for the first time—but only for an hour or two— to enjoy religious services together under Ruling Elder Brewster, all crowding into the hurriedly repaired Common House. This structure, the largest in early Plymouth, was about twenty feet square, of wattle and daub construction with a high steep roof. Neither now nor later did the Pilgrims build log cabins, for the good reason that they did not know how. As already remarked, the log cabin, apparently so native to the American scene, is actually a foreign importation, Scandinavian in origin, first appearing on our shores about 1640 in the settlements of the Swedes and Finns along the Delaware.

Against the Common House was erected a lean-to in which to store tools and supplies. And now, as opportunity offered, the Pilgrims began building a few "small cottages," also of wattle and daub construction with steep thatched roofs, typically English in design. The company agreed that each family was to build its own house, "thinking by that course men would make more haste." But many things conspired to slow operations, and it was not until March 21st—four long months since the First Discovery, eight months to the day from the departure from Leyden—that the last of the Pilgrims left the *Mayflower* and came ashore "with much adoe" to live henceforth on "ye firme and stable earth, their proper elemente."

The delay in providing warm and adequate shelter was at once the cause and the effect of the "General Sickness" that threatened for a time to wipe out the Pilgrim company. Disease reached epidemic proportions and appears to have been a powerful combination of scurvy, pneumonia, and tuberculosis in a peculiarly virulent form, brought on by months of bad diet, cramped and unsanitary quarters, exposure and overexertion in all kinds of weather. Nothing so graphically reveals the appalling death rate as these simple notes from the old records:

> . . . this day [December 24th] dies Solomon Martin, the sixth & last who dies this month.

> Jan. 29th, dies Rose, the wife of Captaine Standish. N.B. This month eight of our number die.

> Feb. 21. Die Mr. William White, Mr. William Mullins, with two more; and the 25th dies Mary, the wife of Mr. Isaac Allerton. N.B. This month seventeen of our number die.

> March 24. Dies Elizabeth, the wife of Mr. Edward Winslow. N.B. This month thirteen of our number die. And in three months past dies halfe our company . . . Of a hundred persons, scarce fifty remain, the living scarce able to bury the dead.

Death struck quite as hard among the *Mayflower* crew, carrying off half the sailors, three of the mates, the master gunner, the bosun, and the cook. Many of these, the Pilgrims felt, deserved their fate, especially the bosun, a "prowd yonge man," who used to "curse & scofe at ye passengers." When Bradford was ill and pleaded for some beer, the bosun and others mocked him and swore that "if he were their owne father, he should have none." When Captain Jones heard of this, he intervened and promised "beere for them that had need of it" even though he were left with none for the voyage home. In the end the Saints softened even the hard heart of the bosun, caring for him in his illness after he had been deserted by his "boone companions in drinking & joyllity." The villain repented and publicly acknowledged his sins, but too late!

"O!" he confessed on his deathbed, "you, I now see, shew your love like Christians indeed one to another, but we let one another lye & dye like doggs."

The sick were violently physicked in the manner of the day

by Giles Heale, the ship's doctor, and Deacon Samuel Fuller, the Pilgrims' "physition-chirurgeon," who possessed a smattering of the lore that then passed for medical science. But their ministrations were of little avail. The Pilgrims thought so little of Giles Heale that they simply ignored him. Their records contain no slightest reference to him, and it was not until 1927 that scholars discovered his presence on the *Mayflower* and his profitable private practice subsequently in London.

Disease wiped out whole families among the Pilgrims—four, in fact, numbering twelve persons in all. One was that of Christopher Martin, the unpopular treasurer, whose accounts were found to be in great disorder, as Cushman had long ago warned they would be. When the worst was over, only three married couples remained unbroken. Mortality ran highest among the wives, only five of eighteen surviving. More than half the heads of households perished. Mortality also ran high among the single men, hired hands, and servants. Of the twenty-nine in these groups, nineteen died. Only the very young escaped to bring down the general average. Of seven daughters, none died; and of thirteen sons, only three. This may merely have been a coincidence, but it rather suggests that parents in general and mothers in particular sacrificed themselves for their children. Only one family escaped without a loss, and the fortunate ones were—of all people—the "prophane" Billingtons, which must have set some of the Saints to pondering God's inscrutable ways.

At the time of the Pilgrims' greatest distress only six or seven persons in all the company were strong enough to be up and around, and these hazarded their own health and their very lives in tending the sick and trying to comfort them, toiling day and night. They "fetched them woode, made them fires, drest them meat, made their beds, washed their lothsome cloaths, cloathed & uncloathed them; in a word, did all ye homly & necessarie offices for them which dainty & quesie stomacks cannot endure to hear named; and all this willingly & cherfully, without any grudging in ye least." Two of these were William Brewster and Myles Standish, "unto whom myselfe & many others," said Bradford in an eloquent and moving passage, "were much beholden in our low & sicke condition . . . And what I have said of these, I may say of many others who dyed in this general visitation, & others yet living, that whilst they had health, yea, or any strength continuing, they were not wanting to any that had need of them. And I doute not but their recompence is with ye Lord."

And all this while, with the company growing weaker and weaker, "ye Indeans came skulking about them."

12

YELLOW
FEATHER
THE BIG
CHIEF

That night we kepte good watch, but there
was no appearance of danger.

—MOURT'S *Relation*

FOR SOME TIME NOW THE INDIANS HAD BEEN CAUSING THE
Pilgrims steadily increasing concern, being a source of constant
nagging worry. Not because of anything they had done—but
precisely because they had done nothing, which seemed very suspicious and aroused much uneasy speculation.

Had the savages withdrawn at sight of them, retreating into
the wilderness to organize their forces and recruit allies with the
intention of returning in force to fall upon New Plimoth some
dark night with tomahawk and torch? With sickness rapidly
spreading and most of the company prostrate, another "huggery"

as at Nauset would prove fatal. Or were the savages contriving some diabolical trap, some skilfully laid ambush?

What puzzled the Pilgrims most was that weeks went by without sight of an Indian. Yet there were Indians in the neighborhood, as was evident from the columns of smoke from their fires occasionally seen in the distance. From the cleared cornfields and other things it was plain that Town Brook had recently been the center of a large Indian community. It had been wiped out in a great tragedy, as the Pilgrims soon learned, but in the beginning the mystery only sharpened their anxieties. So apprehensive were they, according to an old and probable tradition, that they secretly buried their dead at night on Cole's Hill, above Plymouth Rock, leveling off the graves and planting them with corn to hide their great and growing losses from the Indians.

One day late in January, six weeks after putting into the harbor, Captain Jones chanced to spy two Indians, the first that anyone had seen. They were intently watching the ship from Clark's Island near by and seeing themselves observed, quickly vanished, which did nothing to calm the Pilgrims' fears. Then, about two weeks later, they had cause for serious alarm. Out hunting water-fowl to feed the hungry, a Pilgrim was lying concealed in the reeds along the bank of a small stream several miles away when he was suddenly startled to see a dozen painted warriors marching by very near him, headed toward the plantation, and to hear sounds of many more in the woods behind. Slipping away as soon as possible, he hastened "with what speed he could" to give the alarm. All at work in the woods and the clearing dropped their tools and ran for their blunderbusses, tensely watching in all directions for an attack that did not come. Toward evening Standish and Francis Cooke cautiously returned to the woods to gather up their tools, but they were nowhere to be found. They had been carried off by the Indians who had crept up unobserved to the very edge of the clearing.

That unseen eyes were watching them from the dark rim of the forest was a profoundly disturbing thought and led the Pilgrims to keep stricter watch and look carefully to their muskets, "which with the moisture & raine were out of temper." A meeting was called in the Common House next morning "for the establishment of military Orders." Defense had been left a matter to be improvised on occasion, but it was now to be organized on a planned and formal basis so that each man would know his post and exact duties in time of danger. By popular vote the company chose Myles Standish as its Captain-General and "gave him authoritie of command in affayrs," and from this day till his death almost forty years later he continued to be the commander-in-chief of the small but formidable Pilgrim army, his voice carrying almost as much weight in the councils of state as that of the annually elected governor.

Standish's election was the only thing accomplished this day, for the meeting abruptly adjourned and broke up in some confusion with the startling appearance of two Indians just across the brook, on the summit of Strawberry Hill,* opposite Fort Hill. The fiercely painted braves made signs for the Pilgrims to come over, but the latter were suspicious and after arming themselves beckoned the Indians to come to them instead. The warriors were equally wary and suspicious, and at length Captain Standish and Stephen Hopkins volunteered to go across, taking a single musket with them. Wading the brook, they laid the musket on the ground "in signe of peace & to parley with them." Then they slowly and cautiously advanced, but the braves "would not tarrie their coming," taking to their heels and disappearing down the far slope of the hill, from behind which now came a great deal of noise, suggesting that a considerable force was marshaled there.

Their cannon, the Pilgrims agreed, had to be mounted without further delay. Captain Jones and his crew wrestled ashore a large three-inch piece known as a minion, weighing 1,200 pounds. On the beach, fouled by the weather, was lying a still larger piece, a saker, with an extreme range of 360 yards. Both were laboriously dragged across the clearing and up the precipitous slope of Fort Hill, where they were mounted on the wooden platform beside

---

* Since prosaically and somewhat stupidly renamed Watson's Hill.

two smaller cannon, known as bases, shooting a half-pound iron ball. All of these were clumsy pieces, short in range, hard to load, and uncertain of aim. When touched off, they were quite as likely to explode and kill the gun crew as hit a target at fifty paces. But the simple savages and the settlers themselves appear to have been quite impressed by the Pilgrim artillery with its reverberating booms.

Doubtless because of the General Sickness, a month passed before a meeting was called to conclude the business of military organization broken off before. The Pilgrims were just sitting down when they were again interrupted, and in the most astonishing manner. Armed with bow and arrows, a tall powerful warrior emerged from the woods, crossed the clearing, and came striding down the street toward the Common House where the meeting was in session, and would have walked right in had not some of the dumbfounded Pilgrims run out to intercept him. A moment later their amazement knew no bounds.

"Welcome," said the Indian, greeting them in English, smiling as the Pilgrims stared at him in blank surprise.

His name was Samoset, he said, and from him the Pilgrims learned many things they wished to know. But before answering their flood of questions, he asked for some beer. Having none, they gave him "strong water"—brandy, perhaps, or Holland gin— and "bisket, and butter, and cheese, & pudding, and a peece of mallard, all of which he liked well." Then they threw about him a long coat, a bright red horseman's coat—to keep him warm, they said, but rather to cool their own crimson blushes, it would seem, for he was stark naked except for a leather string about his waist "with a fringe about a span longe, or little more."

Samoset, strangely, was not a native of these parts but a "foreigner," like the Pilgrims themselves, having come some months before on a visit from Pemaquid, far up the Maine coast, where he was chief or sagamore of a sub-tribe of the Abnaki, or Wabenake, "people of the dawn." From him the Pilgrims learned that the Indian name for New Plimoth was Patuxet, meaning Little Bay or Little Falls, and he explained the mystery of the abandoned cornfields and why it was that no Indians had been seen for weeks. There were none to see, for a great tragedy had recently overwhelmed the Patuxet tribe. Four years previously, in 1617, a devastating plague—probably smallpox—had swept the forests of New England, spreading rapidly from the trading posts operated along the Maine coast during the fishing season. No part of the "white man's burden" has weighed more heavily upon the "dark" continents than his diseases—smallpox, tuberculosis, and syphilis, in particular—which have often been more effective than his superior arms in speeding conquest of the lands he has coveted. In this instance, the plague decimated many tribes and utterly destroyed others, wiping out the local Patuxet. For years their white skulls and bleaching bones were found in the neighborhood, "a sad spectakle to behould," but the Pilgrims were disposed to accept the tragedy philosophically, regarding it as another special providence of God who had not forgotten "His owne" in thus "opening up a way for them."[1] The Pilgrims, in any case, could thank their lucky stars that they did not have to contest possession of the ground with the Patuxet, in their day a large and formidable tribe.

"Free in speeche, so farr as he could express his mind, and of seemely carriage," Samoset spoke of the tribes round about, where they lived, how strong they were, and who ruled them. The overlord of the region, he said, was his friend Ousamequin (Yellow Feather), better known as Massasoit, the Big Chief, sachem of the Wampanoag, who lived off to the southwest on the shores of Narragansett Bay, about forty miles distant. Massasoit exercised vague dominion over all of the tribes here in the southeastern corner of New England, including those on Cape Cod, the most powerful of whom were the Nauset, a hundred strong. It was this warlike tribe, the Pilgrims discovered, that had fallen upon their exploring party in the "huggery" near the elbow of the Cape.

Samoset went on talking and spinning yarns for his fascinated audience most of the day. But as night came on, the Pilgrims began to get restive and rather plainly intimated to their guest that it was now time for him to leave. Samoset had other plans, however, and "was not willing to go," which placed his hosts in a quandary, for they dared not be too insistent about his departure. Still suspicious and uneasy, they "lodged him that night at Stephen Hopkins' house, & watched him." In the morning, giving him a knife, a bracelet, and a ring, they sent him on his way, having obtained his promise to return soon with some of the Wampanoag, who were to bring along whatever they had to trade.

As good as his word, the sagamore was back the next day with five husky braves, "each with a deere skin on him." They were warmly welcomed and entertained, and "did eate liberally," as the Pilgrims anxiously noted. Suddenly, to show their appreciation, the savages burst into weird song and began to dance "after their manner, like Anticks." But the Saints were not amused, quite definitely! On their calendar of sins "dauncing" of any kind bore a scarlet marking. Besides, it was the Sabbath which heightened the offense. But their grim countenances softened a bit when the Indians handed back the tools taken from the woods some weeks before and brought out three or four beaver skins. Though their hands were itching to get hold of these, the Pilgrims declined to "truck" for them on the Sabbath and dismissed the Indians as soon as they could, on the pretext that they could not waste time on petty trade, urging them to come back soon with every beaver pelt they had and they "would trucke for all." They said good-bye to Samoset along with the rest, but again he refused to go as he "either was sicke, or fayned himselfe so." Four days later, when the Indians had not returned, the Pilgrims impatiently sent Samoset after them. Departing for Sowams,* the main village of the Wampanoag, he cut quite a figure as he passed along the forest track in his latest gifts from the English—a pair of shoes and stockings, a shirt, and a hat.

Taking advantage of Samoset's absence, Captain Standish called another meeting to finish the business of military organization that had been so often interrupted. And so it was again when two Indians suddenly appeared—as before, on Strawberry Hill—and

* Now Warren, Rhode Island.

"made semblance of daring" them, rubbing their bowstrings and whetting the points of their arrows with a "show of defiance," making other "braving" gestures and some that were plainly obscene. With a single musketeer Captain Standish angrily splashed across Town Brook to put a stop to it, and the Indians soon withdrew, making horrible faces.

More determined than ever to complete their military organization and get everything in order, especially since the women and children had just come ashore, the Pilgrims met once again the next day. Business was just getting under way when, as if in a nightmare, two Indians appeared and sent all scurrying for their muskets. But there was no cause for alarm. It was Samoset again, who had come with a friend whom he introduced as Squanto, saying that he "had been in England & could speake better English than himselfe." The name of the now famous Squanto, or Tisquantum, appears on many a page of the Pilgrim records, but the company had no time at all for him now. Everybody was excited, for Samoset had come with the breath-taking news that the great chief Massasoit was at hand, with his brother Quadequina and most of their men.

The sachem presently appeared in barbaric splendor on the summit of Strawberry Hill, with sixty fiercely painted braves behind him—three times the Pilgrims' maximum force. It was an anxious moment. Through Samoset the Big Chief invited the Pilgrim leaders to come over for a powwow. The latter declined, inviting Massasoit to visit them instead, which he refused to consider. Things were at a rather dangerous impasse until young Edward Winslow asked and finally obtained permission to go on the first of the many diplomatic missions that he always adroitly carried out as the Pilgrims' ambassador-at-large. As tokens of friendship and good will, he carried with him for Quadequina a knife and a "Jewell to hange in his eare." To Massasoit he presented a pair of knives, a copper chain bearing a jewel, biscuits, butter, and "withall a Pot of strong water." The sachem was pleased but was most taken with Winslow's sword and steel corselet, saying that he wished to truck for them. Winslow put him off by launching into a long speech, with Squanto acting as interpreter, assuring Massasoit that King James honored him as a friend and ally, and saluted him with "words of love and peace," as did the Governor of New Plimoth, who wished to talk with him, truck with him, and make lasting peace with him as a close and friendly neighbor. Squanto "did not well expresse it," Winslow felt, but even so the speech impressed Massasoit and they fell to parleying. In the end it was arranged that Winslow should stay with Quadequina as a hostage while the Big Chief went to pay his respects to Governor Carver.

Leaving their bows and arrows behind, as had been agreed, twenty of his finest warriors accompanied Massasoit as he slowly and majestically advanced to Town Brook. Here he was met and saluted by a squad of Pilgrim musketeers, hurriedly rigged out in all the military finery available and all looking as martial and formidable as possible under the command of Captain Standish and Andrew Williamson, one of the *Mayflower* mates. The sachem, the latter noted, was exceptionally tall and powerful, "a very lustie man in his best years," and his braves were also big strapping fellows. In general, they were considerably taller than the whites; in particular, the Big Chief stood three or four heads higher than the Pilgrims' squat commander-in-chief. But "Captaine Shrimpe" showed no slightest sign of trepidation. Placing himself at the towering sachem's right, and with his awkward squad bringing up the rear, he escorted Massasoit and his men down the street through a lane of women and children all agape.

The Indians looked like English gypsies, they observed, "with little hair on their face or none at all"—which the heavily bearded whites might have regarded as another immodesty had not their faces been so heavily painted. Some were done in black, others in red, still others in yellow or white, and all were decorated with "crosses and other Antick workes." Massasoit's was a "sad mulberry," which seemed to be in character, for he appeared to be a man solemn and dignified, sparing of speech, grave in mien and manner. He was wearing a deerskin fastened over one shoulder, and his dress differed from his braves' only in the great chain of white bone beads about his neck. To this was fastened a long knife in front and a small leather tobacco pouch behind.

Every effort was made to impress the Big Chief, for upon him depended the vital question of war or peace, and throughout his reception Standish's hand is evident. With the Pilgrim guard of honor at his heels Massasoit was led to an almost completed house which had been hastily furnished for the occasion with a green rug and a few cushions. The sachem had no sooner settled himself than there was a great to-do outside—a loud blaring of brass and rolling of drums—and in the doorway appeared Governor Carver, with another Pilgrim squad under arms. Massasoit rose and kissed the Governor's hand, and Carver reciprocated, though privately noting that the Big Chief "looked greasily." Calling for a pot of hard liquor, Carver then drank to the sachem. The latter in turn lifted the pot and poured down a "great draughte," overdoing it somewhat, it appears, for it "made him sweate all the while after."

These pleasant formalities out of the way, Carver and Yellow Feather settled down to business, with Squanto and Samoset as interpreters and intermediaries. The peace treaty negotiated this day was a memorable one. A simple and explicit mutual assistance pact, quite free from the usual diplomatic double-talk, it relieved the Pilgrims of many anxieties, providing a sound and stable base for their foreign policy for many years. By the terms of this treaty, which was periodically renewed and never seriously strained down to Massasoit's death more than forty years later, the Pilgrims and the Wampanoag pledged themselves not to "doe hurte" to one another in any way. If the peace were broken by an Indian, he was to be sent to Plymouth for punishment; if the offender were a Pilgrim, he was to be sent to Sowams. Indians coming to visit Plymouth were to leave their arms behind, and the Pilgrims were to do likewise on their visits. If anyone "unjustly" attacked either party to the treaty, the other was to come immediately to its assistance. The pact was to apply to all tribes under the dominion of the Wampanoag, and Massasoit undertook "to certifie them of this."

After the Big Chief had placed his mark upon the document,

and Carver his signature, the Indians departed, being escorted with fitting ceremony as far as Town Brook where the governor and the sachem again embraced. Well pleased with the day's proceedings, the Pilgrims heaved a sigh of relief and relaxed, thinking the show was over. But upon his return to Strawberry Hill, the Big Chief sent his brother Quadequina and many of his men to sample the Pilgrims' hospitality. They "took kindlie" to their entertainment, several of the braves being so delighted, especially with the "strong water," that they announced that they would stay the night. The Pilgrims eventually got rid of them, allowing only Samoset and Squanto to remain, and at dusk Massasoit and his men, many with their squaws and children, moved off a short distance and encamped about a half mile away. During the night the Pilgrims "kepte good watch, but there was no appearance of danger."

Early the next morning Massasoit's warriors came streaming into town, eager to be wined and dined once more. The Pilgrims evaded the issue, and soon a messenger came from the Big Chief with an invitation to the Pilgrim leaders to visit his camp to be honored and entertained. Captain Standish and Isaac Allerton went "venterously" and enjoyed "three or four ground nuts, and some tobacco." Returning, they brought with them a large kettle which was filled with English peas and sent back to the Indians, "which pleased them very well, & so they wente their way."

Later that same day the Pilgrims called another meeting, their fifth on the matter, and at long last established a skeletal military organization. At the same time they took this occasion to pass their first civil legislation, enacting a few simple laws and ordinances such as were "thought behoofefull for their present estate and condition." Also, an election was held, for the New Year was only two days off. Under the old Julian calendar that was still in use among the English, the new year began not on January 1st but on March 25th. Again the Pilgrims chose as their governor the venerable and sagacious Carver, "a man well approved amongst them."

Their relations with the Indians were almost too successful, the Pilgrims soon felt, for hungry braves kept dropping in on them at all hours of the day and night, often with their wives and children, and all had insatiable thirsts and appetites. They were such a nuisance that a mission was sent to Massasoit to stop this "disorderly coming." Incidentally, the party was to explore the surrounding countryside and learn the way to Sowams in case they had to go for aid in a hurry. Edward Winslow and Stephen Hopkins were named for the task and departed with Squanto as guide, Samoset having since returned home. After many adventures the two Pilgrims arrived to find that the Big Chief was not at home. A messenger was sent for him, and upon his arrival the next morning the Pilgrims lifted their blunderbusses and greeted him with a salvo, which greatly frightened the Big Chief and all his people, especially the women and children. The Pilgrims always found it the very height of diplomacy to show off their firearms, which terrified the savages and held them in respectful awe for some time. Winslow then presented the sachem with a red horseman's coat, doubtless the one that had been thrown about Samoset, but now tricked out with a deal of lace. Donning it, the Big Chief strode up and down a good while, very proud of himself, as his men were also "to see their King so bravely attired."

The coat was a small token of the Pilgrims' boundless love and esteem, said Winslow in his best manner, and after more such persiflage circled round to the point. The Wampanoag came very often to the plantation and were always welcome, Winslow assured the Big Chief, "yet we, being but strangers as yet at Patuxet alias New Plimoth, and not knowing how our corne may prosper, can no longer give them such entertainment as we have done, and as we desire still to doe. Therefore, we ask you to hinder the multitude from oppressing us with themselves." Now, of course, if any of his people came with beaver skins to truck, that was another matter. They should come at any time—the oftener, the better. And if Massasoit were pleased to come himself, he would be most welcome, as would any of his special friends, and "to the end we may know them from others," said Winslow, "our Governour hath sent you a copper chain, desiring if any messenger shall come from you to us, we may know him from his bringing it with him, and hearken and give credit to his message accordingly." Winslow concluded by asking if they would trade some of their seed corn so that the planters might determine which grew best in the soil at Plymouth.

"My men will no more pester you as they have done," the Big Chief promised and then embarked upon an even longer speech than Winslow's, the latter finding it "very tedious." The sachem ended his harangue by assuring the Pilgrims that he was "King James his man," taking occasion to remark, however, that he was frankly puzzled by His Majesty, being quite at a loss to understand how he "could live without a wife."

As they had eaten nothing all day, the Pilgrims looked about hopefully for supper. None was offered and they went hungry to bed, Massasoit inviting them to share the royal couch with himself and his squaw. It was hard and uncomfortable, consisting of heavy planks and a few thin mats, and two big braves came in later and lay down on top of them. The Pilgrims, as Winslow complained, spent a wretched night, being "worse wearie of our lodging than our journey." In the morning Massasoit went fishing and about noon returned with two bass. These were thrown into a pot and boiled, but with forty famished braves to share the feast the Pilgrims felt emptier than before, hurrying to announce to their host that they must be going, saying that they wished to be back in Plymouth for the Sabbath. The sachem begged them to stay, but they could not be dissuaded, for they really feared that they might never get home, being faint and dizzy from fatigue, hunger, and want of sleep, "for what with bad lodging, the savages' barbarous singing (for they used to sing themselves asleep), lice & fleas indoors, and muskeetoes without," they had had no rest for two nights and were literally staggering on their feet.

Sending a runner ahead with instructions to bring back food from Plymouth and meet them along the way, Winslow and Hopkins took their leave of Massasoit, who seemed to be both "grieved & ashamed" of his poor entertainment. He offered to make amends if they would leave Squanto with him, saying that he would send him throughout his dominion "to procure trucke" for the planters—corn, skins, and whatever else they wanted.

The Pilgrims could not have asked for more, having already made a discovery of the greatest consequence. If they were regularly to obtain the supplies from home they so desperately needed, if they were ever to be free of the crushing burden of their debts, King Beaver and not the Sacred Cod would pay the ransom.

13

FORTUNE

. . . we are so far from want that we often
wish you partakers of our plenty.

—EDWARD WINSLOW

THE PILGRIMS WERE NOW ALTOGETHER ON THEIR OWN, QUITE
cut off from the outside world, with no hope of immediate aid
from any quarter. Their last tie with the homeland had been
broken early in the spring, with the belated departure of the
Mayflower on the 5th of April, 1621. Lining the shore to wave a
last farewell, many had wept disconsolately as Captain Jones
brought his ship round and tacked out of the harbor, never to be
seen on these shores again. The accommodating skipper had
delayed his departure far beyond his original intention, partly
because of sickness among the crew, but also at the desperate insistence of the Pilgrims who feared to be left alone before the

almost prostrate company had somewhat recovered its strength, thinking it "better to draw some more charge upon themselves & freinds than hazard all."

Nor was the roster of Pilgrim dead yet complete. About a week after the *Mayflower* sailed, while at work planting corn with "as many as were able," Governor Carver laid down his hoe, the day being unusually hot, and came in from the fields complaining "greatly of his head." He soon passed into a coma and "never spake more" till he died a day or two later, "whose death was much lamented and caused great heavines amongst them, as there was cause." A sage and deliberate graybeard of almost sixty, the patriarch of the company, Carver had won general respect and affection by his evenhanded course as governor, patiently listening to the grievances of all, doing much to allay the mutinous spirit that had threatened for a time to split the company. Mourned by Saints and Strangers alike, he was buried with simple ceremony "in ye best manner they could, with some vollies of shott by all that bore armes." His wife Catherine, "being a weak woman," did not long survive him, dying five or six weeks later—of a broken heart, said Deacon Fuller—snapping another close link with the Green Gate in Bell Alley, the home of her sister Bridget Robinson, and with the countryside along the Ryton where she had been born Catherine White at Sturton le Steeple.

With Carver's death the purple fell upon the ample shoulders of William Bradford, a man now of thirty-two, and with only an occasional break he carried the responsibilities of supreme command for more than thirty years, pulling the Pilgrims through many a tight and apparently hopeless situation by his inexhaustible energy, ready wit, and absolutely indomitable courage. As Bradford still felt in his huckle bone the effects of the "grief & paine" that had almost cost him his life, he asked for an aide. The company agreed and as the assistant governor selected another of the Saints, Isaac Allerton, the London tailor, who remained in office till his disgrace ten years later when he was caught fleecing his brethren, a great shock to "ye pure & unspottyed Lambes of ye Lord," who let out a roar of rage and drove him into exile.

The choice of Bradford as governor is an important milestone in Pilgrim history in several respects. For one thing, it signalized the fact that a younger generation had been edging slowly toward the front of the stage and was now ready to play a major role. Up to this time affairs had rested largely in the hands of Elder Brewster, Pastor Robinson, Deacon Cushman, and Deacon Carver, all of whom were getting on in years. Now this group was scattered—one was dead, another was in London, a third was in Leyden, and only Brewster was here at Plymouth. When these men spoke, they still commanded great respect and spoke with unchallenged authority. But their function increasingly became that of elder statesmen. The actual conduct of affairs, the day-by-day direction of operations, even important policy decisions, fell more and more to an able and diversely talented group of much younger men—to Governor Bradford, astute and practical, a far-sighted organizer and efficient administrator, to Assistant Governor Allerton, a shrewd and sharp trader, who took over the plantation's business dealings; to Captain Myles Standish, the squat and easily kindled "little chimney"; and to young Edward Winslow, just turned twenty-six, a governor in later years but now chiefly employed as an envoy on more delicate diplomatic missions. Winslow was suave and plausible—"a cunning, smooth-tongued fellow," said one critic—possessed of a nice sense of tact and the good sense to use it, rare qualities among the Pilgrims.

With the rise of this younger group a new vigor, an unaccustomed note of bold and sharp decision, began to manifest themselves in Pilgrim affairs. There was less backing and filling and long-winded debate, no more costly procrastination in taking action. Rather, decisions were often too hastily made on the spur of the moment. Blows were struck that were obviously ill-advised, and their serious and unexpected repercussions caught the Pilgrims dangerously off guard. Also, and more important, there appeared among the leaders a subtle shift of concern from purely spiritual to more secular matters. Not that the Holy Discipline was neglected—God forbid! But when a course of action was to be charted, there was a growing disposition to consider not only what was religiously "lawfull" but what was practically expedient and immediately profitable. This reflected a fact of the utmost significance, one that has always been overlooked, and its consequences have never clearly been appreciated.

Unlike all of the older leaders, not one in this younger group was an officer of the church. To this development—fortuitous and unpremeditated, it would seem, but no less important for that— can be attributed the blessing that at Plymouth the civil authority always retained supreme control both *de jure* and *de facto,* never abdicating to the church and allowing the professional religious to usurp its functions. In the Old Colony, from first to last, ministers ministered, performing their own proper services, but never ruled. Unlike the Puritan communities to the north, Plymouth was never priest-ridden—or pastor-ridden, if you will—having no John Cottons or Mathers, ambition-bitten father and demon-haunted son, to dictate public policy and lay down the law both civil and ecclesiastical. In the short-lived Pilgrim empire the "voice of God" thundering from the pulpit never succeeded in drowning out the voice of the people speaking through their popularly elected representatives and civil magistrates. The Saints and their disciples stuck to first principles, acting upon the belief that the church consisted primarily of the great body of communicants, and not of those temporarily ministering to their needs. They were often very hard on their pastors, taking them severely to task for many things, showing great independence in their acts and judgments, being quite unwilling to accept a new set of autocratic bishops under another name. Strictly speaking, Plymouth was never a theocracy —certainly not in the sense or to the degree that the Massachusetts Bay Colony was for generations.

But wise as Pilgrim policy was in this respect, the plantation owed its survival of early difficulties less to its chosen leaders than to a chance acquaintance who, it so happened, had been born and brought up on the spot—to Samoset's accomplished friend, Squanto, spared by a strange fate to become the last of the Patuxet.

In his extraordinary career Squanto had seen far more of the world than any of the Pilgrims. Carried to England in 1605 by the exploring party of Captain George Weymouth, he had returned in 1614 with Captain John Smith. Upon the latter's departure, one of his ships had been left behind with a Captain Thomas Hunt in command, under instructions to sail for home after he had loaded up with fish and obtained a cargo of beaver skins and other articles from the Indians. Hunt put in here at Patuxet and at several points along Cape Cod, pretending trade. But as soon as he had lured a number of Indians on board, he seized and bound them, and sailed away to sell them as slaves. Among others, he kidnapped twenty of the Patuxet, including Squanto, and seven of the Nauset, arousing in that warlike tribe a deep suspicion and hatred of the whites. The "huggery" on the Cape, seemingly so unprovoked, now appeared in a somewhat different light to the Pilgrims who, upon hearing the story, denounced Hunt as "a bad man, . . . a wretched man that cares not what mischiefe he doth for his own profit," and at their first opportunity they assured the Nauset that they would never think of doing them "any such injurie, though it would gain us all the skins in the countrie."[1]

Heading for Spain, Hunt sold the "poor silly salvages for rials of eight" in the slave market at Malaga. Most of his victims passed to an unknown fate, perhaps ending their days as curious blackamoors in North African harems, but a few fell into the hands of local friars who decided that what the grieving captives needed most was "to be instructed in the Christian faith." Squanto was one of these and after a time managed to get away to London where he lived for several years with a rich merchant, John Slanie, treasurer of the Newfoundland Company. Through him he met Captain Thomas Dermer and accompanied the latter when he set out in 1619 to explore New England. At the island of Monhegan, the chief English fishing station in Maine waters, Dermer took Samoset on board and sailed south, dropping anchor in Plymouth harbor just six months before the *Mayflower* arrived—Squanto to find that plague had exterminated his people, carrying off every last man, woman, and child, all of his family and friends, and he went to live with the Wampanoag. Evidently he was not very happy there, and from the day he met the Pilgrims he never left them.

Nothing could have been more fortunate. Without Squanto and his native skills and knowledge of the country, the Pilgrims would almost certainly have perished or been forced to flee the plantation, for they would have had no crops. As it was, the gaunt specter of starvation haunted them day and night for years, and they just barely managed to pull through. Squanto showed them how to plant their corn—the seed corn pilfered on the Cape—in small properly-spaced hillocks, and "how to dress & tend it." If they were to get any kind of a crop "in these old grounds," they would have to fertilize the fields with fish, he warned them, adding that they could easily catch plenty as soon as the herring began their spring run up the brook, showing them how to build traps for the purpose. On each hillock in the cornfield, according to an old tra- dition, three herring were placed spoke-wise, with their heads toward the center, and for weeks the fields were guarded day and night to keep off the wolves. In other ways the new Saint (for he quickly embraced the Holy Discipline) was invaluable, serving as interpreter and adviser in all relations with the Indians, inform- ing his new brethren where supplies were to be had, acting as guide on their foraging and trading expeditions. Altogether, as the Pilgrims gratefully acknowledged many times, Squanto was "a speciall instrumente sent of God for their good beyond their expectation."

Another Indian soon joined the Pilgrims, Hobomok, one of Massasoit's men, a "pinese" of the tribe, a title signifying that he was "one of their cheefest champions or men of valour," a member of the Big Chief's council.[2] Though he never returned to his people, remaining with the Pilgrims till he died, Hobomok seems to have functioned almost as Massasoit's resident minister at Plym- outh, keeping his master informed of all that happened there. Bitter rivalry developed between Squanto and Hobomok. The former had been more or less adopted by Bradford; the latter be- came Standish's man. The Pilgrims deliberately encouraged the rivalry between them, pitting the one against the other, thinking in this way to obtain "better intelligence and make them both more diligente," a stratagem that backfired dangerously and almost cost them Massasoit's friendship, not to speak of Squanto's clever head.

In May, with the planting done, New Plimoth celebrated its first marriage—between Mrs. Susanna (Fuller) White, a widow of three months, and Edward Winslow, a widower of less than two. Governor Bradford performed the ceremony "according to ye laudable custome of ye Low-Cuntries," for in the eyes of the Saints marriage was only properly "performed by the magistrate, as being a civill thing, upon which many questions aboute inheritances doe depend, . . . and most consonante to ye scriptures, Ruth 4, and no where found in ye gospell to be layed on ye ministers as a part of their office."[3]

The summer at Plymouth passed quietly except for an Indian alarm to which the Pilgrims reacted instantly with somewhat excessive violence, the first of several such incidents reflecting the bolder and more confident spirit that now animated them. Squanto and Hobomok had gone on a visit to Nemasket, now Middleborough, about fifteen miles to the west, the main village of a subtribe of the Wampanoag. Just what happened there is not clear, but Hobomok came hurrying in a few days later "full of fear and sorrow," to report that Squanto was dead—murdered—and that his own life had been threatened by the Nemasket chief, Cauntabant, or Corbitant as the Pilgrims always wrote it. The latter had worked himself into a rage against the English and Massasoit, storming at the treaty between them and at Squanto for his part in it, suddenly seizing the latter.

"If he is killed," shouted Corbitant, whipping out his knife, "the English have lost their tongue," at which point Hobomok broke away and ran for it.

This was very disturbing news because the rumor was circulating that the powerful Narragansett had attacked and captured. Massasoit, and that Corbitant was in league with them. Bradford hurriedly called a council, and the Pilgrims agreed upon the most drastic action. Captain Standish was dispatched with fourteen men, all heavily armed, "to goe & fall upon them in ye night, . . . for if they should suffer their freinds & messengers thus to be wronged, they should have none to cleave unto them, or give them any inteligence, or doe them serviss afterwards, but nexte they would fall upon themselves."

Led by Hobomok, the party crept into the sleeping village and quietly surrounded the chief's large hut. At the arranged signal several muskets were fired and the Pilgrims burst in, shouting, "Is Corbitant here?" The Indians were speechless with terror, particularly the women and children, of whom there were many in the hut. Commanding all to remain inside and not make a move, the Pilgrims explained that they were looking for Corbitant to punish him for Squanto's murder and "other matters," such as speaking disdainfully of the English, assuring the Indians that they "would not hurt their women and children." Some of the more skeptical Nemasket dashed for a side door and escaped, "but with some wounds" as the Pilgrims' blunderbusses flashed and thundered in the dark. Hobomok climbed to the roof of the hut and shouted for Squanto, who soon came ambling along with many Indians behind him, all rather fearful and carrying the choicest of their provisions as a peace offering. In the morning the Pilgrims were served breakfast in Squanto's hut, and to them came "all whose hearts were upright." Corbitant and his faction had fled, so Standish and his men came away disappointed in their plan to cut off the chief's head and carry it home in triumph as they had been instructed.

"Although Corbitant has now escaped us," was their sharp warning upon departure, undoubtedly spoken by Standish in his grimmest manner, "yet there is no place shall secure him and his from us if he continues his threatening us and provoking others against us who have so kindly entertained him, and never intended evil towards him till now he so justly deserves it. . . . If hereafter he shall make any insurrection or offer violence to Tisquantum, Hobomok, or any of Massasoit's subjects, we shall revenge it upon him to the overthrow of him and his."

This armed demonstration at Nemasket, according to the Pilgrims, brought them "many gratulations from diverce sachems and

much firmer peace." Indeed, so Bradford interpreted the sequence
of events, it brought the sachems of nine tribes hurrying to Plym-
outh to make their peace and declare themselves loyal subjects of
King James. All of the Cape tribes were represented—the Nauset,
Cummaquid, Manomet, Pamet, and even the fierce Gayhead of
Martha's Vineyard. Although somewhat "shie" about coming to
Plymouth for some time, Corbitant also made his peace, being a
"notable politician," using Massasoit to patch things up.

Emboldened by their success, the Pilgrims now ventured farther
afield, setting off in the shallop to explore the coast to the north,
making their way into what is now Boston harbor. The many
islands clustered at its entrance they named the Brewsters in honor
of their virile Ruling Elder and his family; the long spit guarding
the harbor on the south was christened Point Allerton, and another
promontory was named Squantum—names they still bear, being
the sole memorials to these three Saints. The Pilgrims found the
harbor and surrounding fields far superior to those at Plymouth
and openly regretted that they had not settled here, a regret frequently expressed during the next few years, moving them on one
occasion to suggest a shift to the merchant adventurers. But as
Bradford once wistfully remarked, "it seems ye Lord who assignes
to all men ye bounds of their habitations, had appoynted it for
another use."

In coming away the Pilgrims were followed to the shallop by
many of the Massachusetts women, mostly younger women and
some older squaws, all clad in coats of beaver. Seeing the Pilgrims'
eyes covetously fixed on these, Squanto suggested that they overpower the women and strip them of their furs, arguing that the
Massachusetts tribe was really hostile and not to be trusted.

"They are a bad people," he said, "and have often threatened
you."

"Were they never so bad," replied the Pilgrims with a humanity
they sometimes forgot, "we should not wrong them or give them
any just occasion against us."

Squanto's advice was a bit gratuitous, as things turned out, for
when they were shown a few bright trinkets, the women eagerly

stripped themselves. For a handful of beads and a gaudy or two they sold the coats off their backs, tying branches about themselves to hide their nudity as best they could, "but with great shamefastnesse, for indeed they are more modest," as one observant Saint remarked, "than some of our English women are." The Pilgrims promised them to come again, and "they us to keep their skins."

Indian summer soon came in a blaze of glory, and it was time to bring in the crops. All in all, their first harvest was a disappointment. Their twenty acres of corn, thanks to Squanto, had done well enough. But the Pilgrims failed miserably with more familiar crops. Their six or seven acres of English wheat, barley, and peas came to nothing, and Bradford was certainly on safe ground in attributing this either to "ye badnes of ye seed, or latenes of ye season, or both, or some other defecte." Still, it was possible to make a substantial increase in the individual weekly food ration which for months had consisted merely of a peck of meal from the stores brought on the *Mayflower*. This was now doubled by adding a peck of maize a week, and the company decreed a holiday so that all might, "after a more special manner, rejoyce together."

The Pilgrims had other things to be thankful for. They had made peace with the Indians and walked "as peacably and safely in the woods as in the highways in England." A start had been made in the beaver trade. There had been no sickness for months. Eleven houses now lined the street—seven private dwellings and four buildings for common use. There had been no recurrence of mutiny and dissension. Faced with common dangers, Saints and Strangers had drawn closer together, sinking doctrinal differences for a time. Nothing had disturbed the peace but a duel, the first and last fought in the colony, with Stephen Hopkins' spirited young servants, Edward Dotey and Edward Leister, as principals.

As the day of the harvest festival approached, four men were sent out to shoot waterfowl, returning with enough to supply the company for a week. Massasoit was invited to attend and shortly arrived—with ninety ravenous braves! The strain on the larder was somewhat eased when some of these went out and bagged five deer. Captain Standish staged a military review, there were games of skill and chance, and for three days the Pilgrims and their guests gorged themselves on venison, roast duck, roast goose, clams and other shellfish, succulent eels, white bread, corn bread, leeks and watercress and other "sallet herbes," with wild plums and dried berries as dessert—all washed down with wine, made of the wild grape, both white and red, which the Pilgrims praised as "very sweete & strong." At this first Thanksgiving feast in New England the company may have enjoyed, though there is no mention of it in the record, some of the long-legged "Turkies" whose speed of foot in the woods constantly amazed the Pilgrims. And there were cranberries by the bushel in neighboring bogs. It is very doubtful, however, if the Pilgrims had yet contrived a happy use for them. Nor was the table graced with a later and even more felicitous invention—pumpkin pie.

The celebration was a great success, warmly satisfying to body and soul alike, and the Pilgrims held another the next year, repeating it more or less regularly for generations. In time it became traditional throughout New England to enjoy the harvest feast with Pilgrim trimmings, a tradition carried to other parts of the country as restless Yankees moved westward. But it remained a regional or local holiday until 1863 when President Lincoln, in the midst of the Civil War, proclaimed the first national Thanksgiving, setting aside the last Thursday in November for the purpose, disregarding the centuries-old Pilgrim custom of holding it somewhat earlier, usually in October as on this first occasion.

With the departure of the Wampanoag, surfeited for once, the Pilgrims began to dig in for the winter now fast approaching. Taking careful inventory of the stores in the Common House, they made the upsetting discovery that they had grossly overestimated their harvest. The meager weekly ration was drastically reduced again, being cut in half. Otherwise, there was no hope of stretching supplies till harvest the next year or at least till late in the spring, for they could not now reasonably expect a ship from home before that time. It was a dismal prospect, for they had already been more than a year without supplies or a ship from home. As they were making themselves snug and secure against the cold, an Indian messenger came in one day to report that a tall white sail had been sighted off Cape Cod, evidently making for Plymouth. Bradford and his council were alarmed, suspecting that it was a French vessel from the Canadian settlements far to the north, come to raid the town. The cannon on Fort Hill boomed a warning, Standish marshalled his force, and "every man, yea, boy, that could handle a gun was readie." The vessel hove in sight, heading straight for Plymouth, and at length ran up her colors, a white ensign bearing the red cross of England, to the amazement of the Pilgrims anxiously watching from Fort Hill.

She proved to be the *Fortune* of London, Captain Thomas Barton master, a ship of fifty-five tons, with some thirty-five passengers on board, all in good health, "which did not a litle rejoyce them." One of the first to come ashore was Deacon Robert Cushman, with his son Thomas, aged fourteen, a man of note in later years. The company included a few more from Leyden— Jonathan Brewster, now almost thirty, a widower at the moment; William Bassett, the much-married master mason, with his third wife; Thomas Morton, born at Harworth, a few miles up the Ryton from Scrooby; and two French-speaking Walloons, Philippe de la Noye [Delano], a youth of nineteen, and Moses Symonson [Simmons], both of whom had joined the Green Gate congregation.

But most of the passengers on the ship, as on the *Mayflower*, were "strangers" recruited at large by the merchant adventurers. Among them came a future governor, Thomas Prence, and another of Winslow's younger brothers, John, who soon married the orphaned Mary Chilton. There were a few women in the group; "Goodwife" Ford was delivered of a son the night she landed. For the most part, however, they were "lusty yonge men, and many of them wild enough, who litle considered whither or aboute what they wente." They, too, had talked mutiny off the tip of the Cape. With their pinch-penny policy the adventurers had sent them out without "so much as bisket-cake or any other victialls." Nor had they any bedding but "some sorry things" in their cabins, "nor pot nor pan to dresse any meate in, nor over-many cloaths." But all were welcome, said Bradford, though the planters could not refrain from audibly wishing that "many of them had been of better condition, and all of them better furnished with provisions."

Cushman brought a letter from Thomas Weston and another from John Robinson. "The death of so many of our dear friends and brethren," wrote the latter, "oh! how grievous hath it been to you to bear, and to us to take knowledge of." He promised the Saints that he would come to Plymouth as soon as he could and with as large a company as possible. Always outspoken, he concluded on a rather critical note. "Brethren," he said, alluding to the quarrels and dissensions in the company and with the merchant adventurers, "I hope I need not exhort you to obedience unto those whom God hath set over you, in church and commonwealth. God forbid, I should need to exhort you to peace, which is the bond of perfection."

The admonition was more timely than he knew, for the Pilgrims could scarcely contain themselves on reading the letter sent by Weston, their "very loving frend," as he signed himself. Speaking for the merchant adventurers, he asked many brusque questions in the most insulting manner. Did they or did they not intend to sign the amended articles of agreement? "If you mean, bona fide, to performe the conditions agreed upon, doe us ye favore to coppy them out faire, and subscribe them with ye principall of your names." And what did they mean by keeping the *Mayflower* so long and at such great expense, and then sending her back empty, with nothing in the hold? "That you sent no lading in the ship is wonderfull," he said, "and worthily distated. I know your weaknes was the cause of it, and I beleeve more weaknes of judgmente than weaknes of hands. A quarter of ye time you spente in discoursing, arguing, & consulting would have done much more, but that is past." If they would get down to business and do what was required, they could count on him, he said, underlining his words, for *"I promise you I will never quit ye bussines though all the other adventurers should."*

This biting letter reflected the sharply critical attitude of all the merchant adventurers. They were obviously in no mood to be trifled with, and Cushman considered the situation so serious that he had conquered his fear of becoming "meate for ye fishes" and come on a flying visit to straighten things out if he could. Weston declared that he had never dared tell his partners that the Pilgrims had refused to sign the amended articles of agreement. Otherwise, they would not have spent another ha'penny on the colony. This was true, said Cushman, warning his brethren that unless they reconsidered their refusal, they would have to shift for themselves with no prospect of obtaining aid elsewhere. Under the circumstances they might well starve. In the end, after much grumbling and querulous debate, the Pilgrim leaders yielded and signed the agreement which they still violently hated. They were the more reluctant to do this because of their fear of precipitating an internal crisis. Many of the planters, particularly the Strangers, were making more frequent and insistent demands that the cornfields and all common lands be divided up in equal shares and permanently allotted to the individual settlers to hold as their private property. This directly violated the terms of the agreement. To quiet the agitation, Cushman was persuaded to address the company and impress upon all the necessity of honoring the agreement as a matter of moral obligation and practical expediency. Late in November or early in December, 1621, the company crowded into the Common House to hear Deacon Cushman expound *The Dangers of Self-Love.*

"Why wouldst thou have thy particular portion?" he asked in a sermon that could scarcely be repeated today without cries of anguish and irate protest from many quarters. Was not the reason simple—"because thou thinkest to live better than thy neighbor and scornest to live as meanly as he? But who, I pray, brought this particularizing into the world? Did not Satan, who was not content to keep that equall state with his fellows, but would set his throne above the stars?"

Let the planters not fall as Lucifer had done out of pride and arrogance, selfish ambition and greed. Beware! he concluded, for nothing in the world "doth more resemble heavenly happiness than for men to live as one, being of one heart and one soul; nor does anything more resemble hellish horror than for every man to shift for himself, for if it be a good mind and practice thus to affect particulars, *mine* and *thine,* then it should be best also for God to provide one heaven for thee and another for thy neighbor."[4]

The sermon temporarily silenced the clamor of the land-hungry planters, and Cushman departed on the *Fortune.* As he planned to return and settle as soon as affairs were untangled at London, he left his son in Bradford's care. Stung to the quick by Weston's sarcastic remarks about their delay in dispatching the *Mayflower* and her want of cargo, the Pilgrims worked hard to load up the *Fortune* as well and quickly as they could. Departing on December 13th, about a month after arrival, she was filled up with hardwood timber, wainscoting, and "good clapboard," and was carrying several hogsheads of beaver and otter pelts obtained from Massasoit's men and the giggling women of the Massachusetts. Altogether, the cargo was valued at £500, almost half of what the merchant adventurers had advanced them, and certainly enough to put the latter in good humor and convince them of their good faith—perhaps enough to persuade them to make another advance.

Cushman was carrying with him the signed agreement, a manuscript which he hoped to get published, and a letter from Bradford to Weston. He and his friends and brethren, wrote Bradford, had no apologies to make either for themselves or poor John Carver, their late governor, to whom Weston's sarcasms had been addressed. Carver had been at such pains "for ye commone good, both ours and yours, as that therewith (it is thought) he oppressed himselfe and shortened his days, of whose loss we cannot sufficiently complaine." What if the adventurers were temporarily out of pocket? That loss could be recovered, but nothing could repair the loss of "honest and industrious" men whose lives "cannot be vallewed at any prise." Bradford was particularly incensed by the charge that he and other leaders spent all their time consulting, holding conferences, and quarreling among themselves—a report sent back on the *Mayflower* by some of the disaffected Strangers. As for these critics, "their harts can tell their tongues, they lye.

They cared not, so that they might salve their owne sores, how they wounded others. Indeede, it is our callamitie that we are (beyond expectation) yoked with some ill conditioned people who will never doe good, but corrupte and abuse others, &c."

And whose fault was that but the merchant adventurers'!

"And now to be so greatly blamed for not fraighting ye ship, doth indeed goe near us, and much discourage us. But you say you know we will pretend weaknes; and doe you think we had not cause?" asked Bradford with scarcely concealed indignation. "Many of our armes & leggs can tell us to this day we were not necligent."

14

COLD
COMFORT
FOR HUNGRIE
BELLIES

> But all proved but wind . . . And well might
> it make them remember what ye psalmist
> saith, . . . Psa. 146. *Put not your trust in princes*
> (much less in marchants) *nor in ye sonne of*
> *man, for there is no help in them.*
>
> —WILLIAM BRADFORD

NOTWITHSTANDING WESTON'S CRUSTY LETTER, THE "FORTUNE"
seemed to be a good omen, an earnest of better things to come.
And the cargo she was carrying back would certainly brighten the
eyes and perhaps might even open the purses of the merchant
adventurers. But the Pilgrims never had any luck with ships, and
the *Fortune* was no exception, being as ill-starred and ill-named
in her way as the *Speedwell*. On the way home she was captured
by a French privateer and taken to a small island off the coast of
Poitou, where her cargo was confiscated—to the Pilgrims' great
loss and the blasting of their hopes. Cushman and all on board

were robbed and imprisoned. With not a "hat to their heads or a shoe to their feet," they lived for weeks on "light, livers, and entrails," as the long-suffering deacon complained. Stripped of almost everything having any value, even of the sheet anchor and some of her sail, the *Fortune* was allowed to proceed and in time made her way up the Thames.

Affairs in London had gone from bad to worse, Cushman discovered. The adventurers were bitterly quarreling among themselves. The *Fortune*'s misfortune upset them, and their tempers were not improved on reading Bradford's caustic reply to Weston's letter. It was well for the harassed Pilgrims that they did not learn till some months later just how alarming the situation was. Cushman informed the adventurers, as he had been instructed, that the planters would surely starve unless supplies were sent at the first opportunity. But Weston and his partners were too engrossed in their own problems and conflicts to be much concerned. Cushman patiently did what he could to keep the adventurers together and make sure that something was done, meantime seeing through the press a manuscript entrusted to him at Plymouth. Published by John Bellamie at the sign of the Two Greyhounds, near the Royal Exchange, it was entitled *A Relation, or Journal, of the Beginning and Proceedings of the English Plantation settled at Plymouth, in New England.* Signed by a mysterious "G. Mourt", it is now generally known as Mourt's *Relation.* But from internal evidence it is clearly the work of Bradford and Winslow, written in what they called their "plain and rude manner." To it Cushman appended an interesting essay on "The Lawfullness of Plantations."

Obviously designed to attract as many colonists as possible, the Pilgrim leaders laid great store by this small book as a means of building up their strength and easing their problems, and naturally they painted the country and their own accomplishments in the fairest possible colors. The climate, they said, was wonderful— or at least as good as England's, which was not hard to believe and did much to establish the authors' credibility at the outset. "By the goodness of God," they wrote, "we are so far from wante that we

wish you partakers of our plenty . . . For fish and fowl, we have
great abundance. Fresh cod in the summer is but coarse meat with
us." And during the winter tender clams and other shellfish all but
crept in at their doors. In the spring and fall they merely had to
go out and gather in Nature's bounty. Such was the Pilgrims'
"brief & true" declaration of their "joyfull building of and comfortable planting in the now well defended Town of New Plymouth."

The country, Winslow concluded, "wanteth only industrious
men to employ, . . . and if we have once but kine, horses, and sheep,
I make no question but men might live as contented here as in
any part of the world." But in hastening to New Canaan, let them
take heed of certain things. They should set aside, said the Pilgrims,
profiting from their experience on the *Mayflower*, "a very good
Bread-room" in which to store their biscuits so that these would
not become moldy or be devoured by rats and weevils. Only iron-
bound kegs should be used for beer and water. And let them bring
along plenty of beer and as much fresh meat as possible, allowing
the sailors to salt it for them. "Bring juice of lemons and take it
fasting . . . For hot waters, Anniseed Water is the best, but use
it sparingly. If you bring anything for comfort in the country,
butter or sallet oil, or both, are very good." Also, they should provide themselves with paper and linseed oil to use as windows in
their houses, and cotton yarn for their lamps. Above all, they
should not fail to bring plenty of clothes and bedding, and "every
man a musket or fowling piece," preferably one very long in the
barrel. "Fear not the weight of it, for most of our shooting is from
stands . . . Let your shot be most for big fowls, and bring store of
powder and shot."

In his appended essay Cushman quoted liberally from Scripture
to prove that men need not always live where they were born.
It was "lawfull" for them to live elsewhere, even among the
heathen if they brought the "true" gospel with them, for in the
wilderness a "drop of the knowledge of Christ is most precious."
It was their duty to go to the Indians and convert them, as the

latter could not come to them. Lastly and most important, men would find peace and plenty in the New World, which would remove the most frequent source of strife among them. The economic motive, as Cushman plainly saw, was the main drive of this migration, as it was to be of the successive waves of emigration that followed down to our own day.

Opportunity in the Old World was so restricted, Cushman observed, that "each man is fain to pluck his means, as it were, out of his neighbor's throat. There is such pressing and oppressing in town and country about farms, trades, traffic, &c., so as a man can hardly set up a trade but he shall pull down two of his neighbors." The towns were filled with unemployed men, and the almshouses and hospitals with the old. "The rent-taker lives on sweet morsels, but the rent-payer eats a dry crust, often with watery eyes; and it is nothing to say what one in a hundred hath, but what the bulk, body, and communalty hath—which, I warrant you, is short enough," observed the wise and humane deacon. "Multitudes get their means by prating, and so do numbers more by begging. Neither come these straits upon men always through intemperacy, ill husbandry, indiscretion, &c., as some think; but even the most wise, sober, and discreet men go often to the wall when they have done their best. . . . Let us not thus oppress, straiten, and afflict one another, seeing that there is a spacious land, the way to which is through the sea."

At Plymouth there was no rest for the weary Pilgrims. Half-starved as they were, they spent the winter at heavy labor, for a curious incident had seriously alarmed them. One day, soon after the departure of the *Fortune,* a strange Indian had walked into town bringing an enigmatic message from Canonicus, sachem of the powerful Narragansett, the People of the Small Point, traditional enemies of the Wampanoag. Carrying a sheaf of arrows bound with a large snakeskin, he had inquired for Squanto, who happened to be absent for a few days. Upon learning this, the messenger left the arrows to be delivered to him and was in haste to depart. But Bradford, his suspicions aroused, detained him, turning him over to Standish, Stephen Hopkins, and Winslow to see if they could get to the bottom of this mysterious business, instructing them "to use him kindly." They obtained some vague assurances of friendship and finally released the Indian who hurried away.

When shown the arrows and rattlesnake skin upon his return a few days later, Squanto promptly declared them a sign of hostility, "no better than a challenge." The Pilgrim leaders as promptly resolved to give the "braving" Narragansett a "round answere," sending "ye sneake-skine back with bullits in it." This so terrified Canonicus, according to Winslow, that he dared not touch the snakeskin. Nor would he "suffer it to stay in his house or countrie," and at length, "having been posted from place to place a long time," it came back to Plymouth unopened.

Still, the Pilgrims deemed it wise to improve the fortifications of the town, being all too well aware of the disparity between their actual strength and their "high words and loftie looks" toward the formidable Narragansett, able quickly to muster several thousand braves. They decided "to inclose their dwellings with a good strong pale, and make flankers in convenient places, with gates to shut, which were every night locked and a watch kept, and when neede required there was also warding in ye day time." Eleven feet high and almost a mile in circumference, the stout wooden "palizado" ran up the brook, around Fort Hill, down the far side of the clearing, and along the high bank above the beach— Cole's Hill—to the brook again. It was a herculean undertaking for so few hands, but it was prosecuted with great vigor and "very cherfully," for the most part, although there was some difficulty when the company was called to work on Christmas morning. Most of those who had come on the *Fortune* and a few of the *Mayflower* group "excused themselves and said it wente against their consciences to work on that day." Very well, said Bradford, if they made it a matter of conscience, he would excuse them "till they were better informed."

But at noon, when he and his work gang came in for dinner, he found the Strangers "in ye streete at play, openly; some pitching ye barr, & some at stoole-ball, and shuch like sports. So he wente to them, and tooke away their implements, and tould them it was against his conscience that they should play & others worke. If they made ye keeping of it matter of devotion, let them keepe their houses, but there should be no gameing or revelling in ye streets, since which time," observed Bradford some years later, "nothing hath been attempted that way, at least openly."

At this time, too, Standish reorganized the Pilgrim army, dividing it into four companies and appointing a commander for each —probably Bradford, Allerton, Winslow, and Hopkins. A company was assigned to guard each of the four walls of the stockade in case of danger. After the newcomers had received some instruction in handling arms, Standish ordered a general mobilization to test his disposition of forces and his men's acquaintance with their duties. At a given signal, the companies quickly assembled and marched in good order to their posts where the soldiers raised their pieces and fired a volley to honor their commanders. Accompanying them home, they again "graced them with shott, and so departed." One of the more reliable companies was chosen for special service in case of fire, the first precaution of the kind yet taken. These trusted men—probably Saints, for the most part— were to encircle the burning building with their backs to the fire, their muskets primed and ready, "to prevent treacherie if any were in that kind intended"—an open reflection upon the loyalty of some of the Pilgrims. The suspicion was not unfounded, it would seem, for mysterious fires occurred from time to time, and one attempt at least was made to burn New Plimoth to the ground. A fire broke out and destroyed four houses, a good part of the town, starting next to the Common House which, "if it had been lost, ye plantation had been overthrowne," for all their provisions were stored there. In the midst of their frantic efforts to check the blaze with water and wet cloths, "when ye tumulte was greatest," they heard an unrecognized voice say:

"Look well about you, for all are not friends that are near you."

After the fire had been brought under control at length by "ye great dilligence of ye people," smoke suddenly came pouring out of the lean-to built against the Common House. Running to quench this blaze, they found a "long firebrand of an ell longe, lying under ye wall on ye inside, which could not possibly come there by cassualtie, but must be laid there by some hand, in ye judgement of all that saw it. But God kept them from this danger, whatever was intended."

Even with the protection of their new stockade the Pilgrims remained uneasy and apprehensive. And now, quite innocently, they found themselves at odds with Massasoit in the most dangerous quarrel they ever had with him. Early in the spring of 1622, eager to resume their profitable beaver trade, they decided to sail north once again to skin the women of the Massachusetts. While preparations were under way, Hobomok came to Bradford and warned against the expedition, saying that the Massachusetts were hostile and leagued with the Narragansett in a plot to cut off the trading party and fall upon Plymouth, adding that Squanto was involved in the conspiracy. The latter had been holding secret powwows with other Indians in the woods, according to Hobomok, who complained that he had been excluded, arguing from this that his rival was obviously up to mischief.

"When they mean plainly," said Hobomok, "it is the manner of the Indians to deal openly."

Taking counsel with Allerton and Standish, Bradford hurriedly called in such Pilgrims "as, by them, were thought most meete for advice in so weighty a business." After careful consideration they decided to proceed with the expedition. They "had ever manifested undaunted courage and resolution," they said, and if the Indians now saw them "dismayed," they would be "encouraged to prosecute their malicious purposes with more eagerness than ever they intended." Besides, they could not afford to "mew" themselves up in the town. They would starve unless they could go hunting and travel freely about the countryside, for their "Store was almost emptie." With ten men, all heavily armed, Standish pushed off in the shallop, taking both Squanto and Hobomok with him because of "ye jelocie betweene them."

The boat had no sooner disappeared behind Gurnet's Nose, the bulbous end of the spit at the far side of the harbor, than one of Squanto's Indian friends came running breathlessly into a cornfield with blood streaming from his face. Repeatedly glancing behind him as if he were being closely pursued, he urged the men at work in the field to hasten home with all speed. He had been at Nemasket, he said, and had barely managed to escape, "not without danger," to warn them that "many of ye Narihgansets, with Corbytant, and he thought also Massasoyte, were coming against them."

At Bradford's order the military companies quickly took their posts and the cannon on Fort Hill fired three warning shots, which were heard by the men in the shallop. Standish immediately put back to find Plymouth in great alarm. All that day and throughout the night the Pilgrims kept strict watch without observing any sign of danger, with Hobomok insisting that the alarm was a hoax, assuring them of "Massassowat's faithfulness," telling Bradford that as a member of the Big Chief's council he would have been informed by the sachem before any such enterprise was undertaken.

"I should be very sorry if any just and necessary occasions of war should arise between us and any of the savages, but especially Massassowat—not that I fear him more than the rest," said Bradford, "but because my love more exceeds towards him than any."

Sure of himself, Hobomok offered to send his wife to Sowams on pretext of business to see what was going on there. Everything was quiet until the squaw informed Massasoit of the alarm at Plymouth and the reports that had been circulated about him, whereupon the Big Chief exploded with rage against Squanto, rightly suspecting him of being the author of the plot to serve some purpose of his own. Returning thanks to Governor Bradford for his "good thoughts" of him, Massasoit reiterated his intention of abiding by the treaty of peace and once more specifically promised to "send word and give warning when any such business was towards." Thus reassured, Standish and his men set sail to visit the Massachusetts and again had "good store of trade."

The Pilgrims now began to see that Squanto "plaid his owne

game by putting ye Indeans in fear, . . . making them beleeve he could stur up warr against whome he would, & make peace for whom he would," demanding gifts from the Indians as the price of his good offices in their behalf. As the peace with Massasoit hurt business, he had therefore raised this false alarm, hoping to provoke hostilities "whilst things were hot in the heat of blood," believing that once the Big Chief were out of the way, no serious rival would stand "between him and honour, which he loved as his life & preferred before his peace." Squanto's strongest hold on the Indians, it appears, came from their great terror upon learning from him that the Pilgrims kept the plague buried under the Common House and "could send it amongst whom they would" —at Squanto's direction, of course. This fear was given credence by the fact that the Pilgrims kept their powder buried under the Common House. One day, as they were digging up a barrel, Hobomok chanced to come by and stopped.

"What are they doing?" he asked Squanto.

"This is the place where the plague is buried," whispered the latter. Hobomok turned to some of the Pilgrims and inquired if this were true, and could they command it as he had been told?

"No, but the God of the English hath it in store," they said, modestly dispelling the Indians' simple notions about such things, "and can send it at His pleasure to the destruction of His and our enemies."

When Standish and his party returned from the north, they found Massasoit at Plymouth, still furious with Squanto, having come to ask that the culprit be delivered into his hands for punishment as required in Article II of the peace treaty. Bradford succeeded in pacifying him by explaining that Squanto had been most severely censured. But on the way home the Big Chief's ire began to rise again and he sent the messenger back to urge Bradford "to give way to the death of Tisquantum, who had so much abused him." Admitting that Squanto deserved to die, Bradford shifted ground and appealed to Massasoit not to deprive the English of "their tongue." This plea fell on deaf ears, and the messenger hastened back with a peremptory demand that the planters evince their intention of abiding by the terms of the treaty by surrendering Squanto forthwith. As evidence that the Big Chief wanted action, many braves in their war paint accompanied the messenger, bringing with them a quantity of beaver pelts. Drawing out a long knife, Massasoit's own, their spokesman declared that they had been instructed by the sachem to cut off Squanto's "head and hands and bring them to him," offering Bradford the beaver skins if he would consent.

"It is not the manner of the English to sell men's lives at a price," declared the governor, declining to trade. Yet the Pilgrims saw no way out of their dilemma. They could not deny the validity of Massasoit's claim, and it was far too dangerous to break the treaty and defy him. In the end they summoned Squanto, who threw himself upon their mercy, placing himself in Bradford's hands "to be sent or not, according as he thought meet," all the time moaning and cursing Hobomok as the "author and worker of his overthrow." It was a hard and trying decision to make, but there was no escape, and the Pilgrim council rose to hand Squanto over to his eager executioners when suddenly an alarm sounded. A strange boat had been sighted far out in the bay, beyond the harbor. Coming from the north, it crossed in front of the town and disappeared behind the towering headland to the south. There had been rumors of hostile Frenchmen along the coast, but the disturbing apparition was a relief in one respect at least. It provided an excuse for not surrendering Squanto till the mystery of the boat was cleared up. "Mad with rage and impatient of delay," Massasoit's warriors departed "in great heat" to inform the Big Chief, who was angrier than ever and continued "to frown on them" for some time.

The mysterious boat, a friendly one, at length put into the harbor, having failed to note the tiny scraggy settlement on the high bench above the brook as it sailed by. Coming from the coast of Maine, from the ship *Sparrow,* a fishing vessel sent out by Thomas Weston on his own account, the shallop had on board seven passengers, many letters from home, "but no vitails, nor any hope of any," as the Pilgrims learned to their dismay from

another of Weston's "tedious & impertinent" letters. The situation
of the planters was truly desperate, more critical than it had ever
been, for their "store of victuals was wholly spente, having lived
long before on a bare and short allowance"—and here it was only
May, at least four months yet till harvest.

The *Sparrow,* Weston blandly explained, had been hired by
him and John Beauchamp, salter of London, another of the adventurers, partly to recoup some of their heavy losses on the Plymouth
enterprise and "partly, it may be, to uphold ye plantation."* The
passengers from the ship were not colonists. They were not to work
for the joint account but for his and Beauchamp's private profit.
And their still "loving freind" had the effrontery to ask the Pilgrims to house and feed these men, to supply them with seed corn
and anything else they needed, so that they might immediately go
about their business, which was to erect a salt works right in the
Pilgrims' front yard, "on one of ye litle ilands in the bay." Not
to do this would be "extreme barbarisme."

Nor was this the worst of it. In a second letter Weston informed
them that the merchant adventurers' company, split by quarrels
and dissensions, was rapidly nearing an end. The articles of agreement allowed "ye adventurers & planters, upon just occasion, to
breake off their joynte stock," and the principal stockholders had
decided at a recent meeting "to breake it off, and doe pray you to
ratifie and confirme ye same on your parts." If the planters agreed,
a few of the "forward" in London might advance more money,
perhaps a third of their original investment. But here, at least,
Weston made no promises. "I find ye generall so backward and
your friends at Leyden so cold that I fear you must stand on your
own leggs and trust (as they say) to God and yourselves."

All of this, as the Pilgrims complained, was "but cold comfort
to fill their hungrie bellies." Plymouth was in such dire and apparently hopeless straits that Bradford took it upon himself to conceal
these letters, showing them only to "some trustie freinds for
advice." All agreed with him that there was "some misterie in

---

* On the margin of the letter Bradford acidly remarked, "I know not
which way."

ye matter," sharing his fear that if the articles of agreement were broken and Weston came over on his own account with the shipping he had ample means to provide, most of the planters would go with him "to ye prejudice of themselves & ye rest of the adventurers, their freinds." It now occurred to them that Weston had sent out the wild and lusty young men on the *Fortune* for some such purpose, which caused the latter to be suspect for some time, doing nothing to promote harmony at Plymouth. In spite of all, however, the Pilgrims took pity on the men from the *Sparrow* and "gave them as good as any of their owne."

Strangely, the boat from the *Sparrow* proved a godsend in disguise, and from a most unexpected quarter. On it had come a letter from a stranger, addressed to his "good freinds at Plimoth," written by one Captain John Huddleston, master of one of the English fishing vessels in Maine waters. He wished to inform them, he said, that three or four hundred settlers in Virginia had just lost their lives in a great Indian uprising. "Therefore I intreat you (allthough not knowing you) that ye old rule which I learned when I went to school, may be sufficiente. That is, Hapie is he whom other mens' harmes doth make to beware."

Presuming upon this friendly letter, Winslow collected a party and set sail for the Maine fishing grounds, almost 150 miles to the northeast and through waters none of them knew, ostensibly to thank the captain for his kindness and solicitude, but really to see if they could buy, beg, or borrow provisions from the English ships there, for "famine begane now to pinch them sore." Huddleston gave them all the stores he could spare and refused payment of any kind for them, urging other skippers to do the same, many of whom responded. With the shallop low in the water, Winslow returned as quickly as possible—to find the planters and their wives staggering with hunger as they went about their exhausting daily chores, some of them now reduced to skin and bones, others painfully puffed and swollen. Though the supply so providentially acquired in Maine brought "a present refreshing," it came to very little when divided among so many. "It arose but to a quarter of a pound of bread a day to each person, and ye Governour caused it to be dayly given them; otherwise, had it been in their owne custody, they would have eate it up & then starved."

And now, said Winslow in fending off criticism of the extravagant reports of plenty that he and others had sent back on the *Mayflower* and the *Fortune,* some captious person might rise to ask, "If the country abound with fish and fowl in such measure as is reported, how could men undergo such measure of hardness except through their own negligence? I answer, Everything must be expected in its proper season. 'No man,' as one saith, 'will go into the orchard in winter, to gather cherries.' "

October to April was the season for fowl, "but these extremities befell us in May and June." Of course, as the number of fowl decreased during the warmer months, the fish began to run, and their very abundance was a "a great cause of increasing our wants." The bay and the creeks were "full of bass and other fish, yet for want of fit and strong saynes and other netting, they, for the most part, brake through and carried all away before them. And though the sea were full of cod, yet we had neither tackle nor hawsers for our shallops. And indeed, had we not been in a place where divers sorts of shell fish . . . may be taken with the hand, we must have perished."

This was quite true and frank enough, but not a word about it was whispered in the *Relation* now just off the press.[1]

With a frown still clouding Massasoit's brow and the Narragansett and other tribes making "insulting speeches, glorying in our weakness," the enfeebled Pilgrims saw no choice but to undertake another major work of fortification, neglecting their crops to complete it as rapidly as possible. On the high knob where Standish had his cannon mounted, they erected a "strong & comly" fort of heavy oak timbers, a one-storied square structure with a flat roof, where the cannon were now mounted, their muzzles grimly pointing from openings in the battlements, guarded day and night by a sentry. It was undertaken "with great eagerness" and for decades served the Pilgrims also as a town hall, jail, court of justice, and meeting house.

On the Sabbath and every Thursday, which was Lecture Day, the Pilgrim Fathers with their families assembled "by beat of drum, each with his musket," in front of Standish's house at the foot of Fort Hill. Placing themselves three abreast, all with their best cloaks on, they were marched briskly up the steep slope "without beat of drum," led by a sergeant. "Behind comes the Governor, in a long robe," so the scene was described by a Dutch visitor a few years later. "Beside him, on the right hand, comes the preacher, with his cloak on; and on the left hand, the captain, with his sidearms and cloak on, and with a small cane in his hand; and so they marched in good order, and each sets his arms down near him." Plymouth's was a Church Militant in more than one respect, and for more than a half century the Saints in the Old Colony continued to go to the meeting house with a flintlock in one hand and a Breeches Bible in the other.

About the middle of the summer hope bounded up when the tall white sails of two ships were sighted in the bay. Surely, here was supply at long last! The vessels were the *Charity,* of 100 tons, and the *Swan,* a pinnace of thirty tons, both crowded with passengers, bringing some sixty men in all. But to their utter consternation, the Pilgrims quickly learned that the ships had brought them nothing but more letters of criticism, exhortation, and gratuitous advice. Weston coolly informed them that he was no longer one of the adventurers, "so I am quit of you," he said, "& you of me, for that matter." This dropped among the Pilgrims like a bombshell, and they were equally upset upon learning that he had obtained a patent to establish a colony close by, at the lower end of Boston Bay, where he planned to settle those who had come on these two vessels and the *Sparrow.* And would the planters please take care of them while the *Charity* went on to Virginia to discharge some freight and passengers there?

"If you are as freindly as we have thought you to be, give us ye entertainment of freinds, and we will take nothing from you, neither meat, drinke, nor lodging, but what we will, in one kind or other, pay you for. . . . I have charged ye master of ye ship

Sparrow not only to leave with you 2,000 [lbs.] of bread, but also a good quantite of fish,* &c."

Beware, beware! Cushman warned in a letter secretly sent on the ships. Weston's men "are no men for us," he declared, "wherefore I pray you entertaine them not, neither exchainge man for man with them, excepte it be some of your worst." Sell them nothing but what could be well spared. If they borrowed anything, "let them leave a good pawne." Above all, dispatch Squanto immediately to inform the Indians that Plymouth could not be held responsible for anything they did, making the point quite clear that "they are a distincte body from us, and we have nothing to doe with them."

There was another letter from London, also secretly sent, but Weston had intercepted it, finding it sewed inside the sole of one of the passenger's shoes. It was signed by two of the adventurers, one being Edward Pickering who had formerly been a member of the Green Gate congregation. Weston's withdrawal, they assured the Pilgrims, was all for the best. His London partners were very glad to be rid of him, for he "thought himselfe above ye generall, and not expressing so much ye fear of God as was meete . . . in a matter of so great importance." They, too, warned against Weston's designs and particularly against his brother Andrew, who was in charge of one of the ships, "a heady yong man & violente, and set against you there & ye company here, ploting with Mr. Weston their owne ends, which tend to your & our undooing in respecte of our estates there. . . . P.S. I pray conceale both ye writing & deliverie of this letter, but make the best use of it. *We hope to sett forth a ship ourselves within this month.*"

Weston, of course, was infuriated by this "treacherous" letter. It might have caused "ye hurt, if not ye ruine, of us all," he declared, "for I doe beleeve that in shuch a case . . . not only my brother, but others also, would have been violent and heady against you." And now, said Weston, "though I have nothing to

---

* "But he left not his own men a bite of bread," Bradford noted.

pretend as an adventurer amongst you, yet I will advise you a litle for your good, if you can apprehend it."

No one knew the adventurers and their motives as well as he. From the beginning they had been animated by nothing but hope of profit, whatever their other pretensions, and it was vain to expect anything more of them till sizeable profits began to come in. Besides, he said in accurately forecasting more trouble, "most of them are against ye sending of them of Leyden, for whose cause this bussiness was first begune." Therefore, if the planters wanted his advice, they should break off the joint stock as they had "warente to doe, both in law & conscience, for ye most parte of ye adventurers have given way unto it by a former letter." Then, by expanding their trade and with the help of friends, they might be able to transport Robinson and his people, "and when they are with you, I make no question but by God's help you will be able to subsist of yourselves."

For once, Weston's was good advice, and had the Pilgrims followed it, they would have spared themselves almost twenty years of nagging worry and needless sacrifice, for in the end they were heavily imposed upon and brazenly cheated. But they regarded it as "neither lawfull nor profitable" and reproached Weston for deserting them in their extremity when they had "neither vitals, nor anything to trade with." Worse, he would now set up a rival settlement close by and cut into the Indian trade which alone could provide the means of buying absolutely indispensable supplies. Weston's large promises had come to naught. They "proved but wind," and all of their high hopes in him were now "layed in ye dust."

Even so, the Pilgrims took in his men and lodged them in their already overcrowded houses, partly for Weston's sake, "considering what he had been unto them & done for them, & to some more espetially," and partly out of pity for those who found themselves in the wilderness without the slightest idea of what to do. Soon Plymouth was loud with complaints against the "unjust and dishonest walking of these strangers." They often went into the fields on the pretext of helping with the corn but "spared not, day and night, to steal the same." In fact, all the Pilgrims ever had from them, said Bradford, were "secret backbitings, revilings, &c.," and it was a happy day at Plymouth when the *Charity* returned from Virginia and sailed north with the *Swan* into Boston Bay, where Weston's men began to build the town of Wessagusset, now the city of Weymouth.

For months the Pilgrims had been looking forward to the welcome time of harvest when they hoped to have "their hungrie bellies filled." But again they had a disappointing crop. They had not yet mastered the art of growing corn, they had neglected their crop to build the fort, often they were too starved "to tend it as they should have done," and alas! some of the Pilgrims, too, had taken to stealing corn, and though many had been "well whipt (when they were taken)," yet hunger drove others "to venture." Never had the planters faced a blacker prospect, for it "well appeared that famine must still insue ye next year allso" unless a miracle happened. After Weston's letters they could not count on supplies from home. "Markets there was none to goe to," and they could obtain nothing from the Indians, for they had exhausted their stock of beads and other trading commodities.

"Behold now another providence of God: a ship comes into ye harbor . . ."

She was the *Discovery* of London, homeward bound from Virginia, and she happened to have on board a large supply of knives, beads, and assorted trinkets of value in the Indian trade. Quickly sensing the situation, the skipper took advantage of the Pilgrims in their great need, refusing to sell his wares except in bulk and at extortionate rates. In their extremity the Pilgrims traded excellent coat beaver at 3s. a pound, furs that ordinarily brought six or seven times that amount. The planters growled a bit at such piracy, but they were "glad of ye occasion and faine to buy at any rate."

The grasping skipper, it turned out, was an old hand at piracy. He had been seized in 1617 for attacking an East Indiaman, getting off lightly for want of evidence. In 1625, three years after his visit here, he turned up in Virginia with a Spanish frigate, saying that he had captured her in the Caribbean. The authorities had good reason to believe that he had been plundering English ships as well, but before inquiry could be pressed, the captain died.

In reporting the arrival of the *Discovery,* Bradford noted that "one Captain Jons [Jones] was cheefe therein," and with only this to go on it was confidently asserted for centuries that the pirate, Thomas by name, was also the skipper of the *Mayflower.* Many were not convinced, but as the Christian name and subsequent career of the Pilgrims' friend were unknown, the story had an air of credibility. In 1904 the musty records of the British Admiralty revealed that the Jones of the *Mayflower* was Christopher, not Thomas. It was later discovered that he had gone to his grave soon after his return home, another victim of that terrible first winter at Plymouth. Dying at Rotherhithe, Surrey, his birthplace, he was buried there on March 5, 1622, nine months before the *Discovery* dropped anchor at Plymouth. Yet the legend still persists, woven deep in the Pilgrim saga, that the able skipper of the *Mayflower* again came to Plymouth and ended his career flying the Jolly Roger.[2]

But posterity has reason, too, to remember the pirate and his ship. But for their chance visit to Plymouth, the Pilgrims would have found their plight worse "than ever it had been, or after was." Once again they could truck with the Indians for maize, beans, and other things. When Weston's men at Wessagusset heard of this, they proposed a joint trading expedition in the *Swan,* which had been left behind when the *Charity* sailed for home. The Pilgrims agreed, proposing a long voyage around the forearm of Cape Cod to the South Shore. After some delay the *Swan* put out from Plymouth, only to be driven back by a winter gale. She had to turn back a second time when Standish fell seriously ill with a fever. Pilgrim needs could not wait, and Bradford went instead, with Squanto as guide and interpreter.

With the Pilgrim shallop in tow, the *Swan* rounded the tip of the Cape and headed along the dangerous outer shore. Squanto insisted that he knew how to thread the "deangerous shoulds & roring breakers" at the elbow of the Cape, having passed that way twice before, once with the French and again with Captain Dermer. But the *Swan* was soon in trouble as the *Mayflower* had been, and bore up for the harbor at Monomoy, now Chatham. Bradford led a party ashore here where Champlain and his French had met stiff resistance upon landing some twenty years before. On this occasion the Indians kept out of sight until Squanto found some of them and allayed their suspicions. Coming out of hiding, they welcomed the whites and "refreshed them very well with store of venison and other victuals, which they brought them in great abundance, promising to trade with them." Altogether, the party obtained from them corn and beans enough to fill eight hogsheads, a most encouraging start.

This gain, however, was more than offset by an irreparable loss. Squanto was suddenly stricken, laid low with a raging fever, bleeding profusely at the nose, "which ye Indeans take for a simptome of death." Within a day or two, in spite of everything the Pilgrims and local medicine men could do, the last of the Patuxet died, bequeathing his few treasured possessions to Bradford and other friends as "remembrances of his love," beseeching "ye Governour to pray for him, that he might goe to ye Englishmen's God in heaven." And it is to be hoped that he did, if that is where he really wished to go, as is likely, for he may well have feared what would happen if he chanced to meet Massasoit in the Happy Hunting Grounds.[3]

Coming back from the Cape, the *Swan* proceeded to the country of the Massachusetts. There was no trade there, for the Indians were all sick with something "not unlike the plague, if not the same." Putting about again, the pinnace sailed south past Plymouth to the bottom of Cape Cod Bay, dropping anchor off Cummaquid, a name retained by one of the shore villages in the township of Barnstable. They were well received by Iyanough, the local sachem, whom the Pilgrims had met and been so impressed with the year before. A young man in his twenties, he was "personable, gentle, courteous, and fair conditioned; indeed, not like a savage save for his attire. His entertainment was answerable to his parts, and his cheer plentiful and various." So it was again, and Iyanough undertook to gather as large a supply of provisions as the Cummaquid could spare.

Meantime, anxious to obtain all they could to feed the starving at Plymouth and Wessagusset, the party sailed farther along the Cape to the country of the Nauset, with whom friendly relations had been established through their sachem, "stately" Aspinet. Enough beans and maize were obtained here to fill ten hogsheads, but before these could be loaded, a gale hit the coast and almost wrecked the *Swan*, snapping the towline to the Pilgrim shallop which drifted away and was smashed on the beach. Without the shallop it proved impossible to load the pinnace. Heaped up in a round stack, the corn was covered with Indian mats and sedge, and Bradford "gave the Indeans charge not to meddle with it," saying that he would soon come back for it and the battered shallop. If both were found in good order, "he would take it as a signe of their honest and true friendship," he said, and if not, "they should certainly smart for their unjust and dishonest dealing."

Weston's men and the Pilgrims decided to part company here at Nauset. Led by Bradford, the latter set out on foot for Plymouth, some forty miles distant, stopping at Cummaquid to ask Iyanough to guard the precious supplies assembled there until a boat could be sent to fetch them. The Wessagusset men sailed for home in the *Swan*, putting into Plymouth to unload four of the eight hogsheads of provisions obtained at Monomoy, which was all the expedition had to show for several weeks of toil and danger on stormy wintry seas.

Upon his return, Bradford immediately proceeded with a small party to some of the inland villages. First they visited Nemasket and from Corbitant's people obtained additional corn. Hiring some squaws to carry it to Plymouth, he crossed overland to the shoulder of the Cape, to the village of Manomet, now Bourne in the township of Sandwich. Here, too, Bradford was much impressed with the local sachem, "grave" Canacum, who "used the Governour very kindly." More corn and beans were obtained here, but in want of transport these had to be left behind for a time.

The results of the foraging expeditions and the friendly welcome and generosity of the Cape Indians warmed the hearts but did little to fill the "hungrie bellies" of the Pilgrim Fathers and their suffering families. All were thin, distraught, and irritable, a prey to many harrowing fears. Many must have wondered at times if they would ever lay the gaunt specter of famine. Weston's men had promised to return in the *Swan* "with all conveniente speed" to pick up the supplies left on the Cape, but they did not come. As the Pilgrims soon learned, things had gone from bad to worse at Wessagusset, generating a dangerous crisis in both settlements.

15

LIQUIDATION
OF
WESSAGUSSET

It is a thing more glorious in men's eyes than
pleasing in God's, or conveniente for Christians, to be a terrour to poore barbarous
people.

—JOHN ROBINSON

FROM THE START THE PILGRIMS HAD LOOKED UPON WESSA-
gusset with a jaundiced eye. It lay uncomfortably close to Plymouth, and they feared it as a rival in the Indian trade. They
equally feared it as a source of moral and spiritual contagion, for
Weston's men—so far as they were religious at all—professed the
Anglican creed. They were "not fitt for an honest man's company,"
so one of the adventurers had said, and even Weston granted that
they were "rude fellows." But he hoped, he said, "not only to
reclaime them from ye profanenes that may scandalize ye vioage,
but by degrees to draw them to God, &c." Little came of this pious
hope, it appears, and now it was reported—"how truly I know

not," said Bradford, hastening as always to pass along a salacious and damaging bit of gossip—that their governor was "keeping Indean women." Even worse, he had "wasted" supplies on them.

Weston's men were, by all accounts, a reckless and improvident lot, and quickly "made havoc of their provisions." Soon they were selling the Indians their blankets, even the clothes off their backs, for a bite to eat. Some, "so base were they," went to work for the savages and would "cutt them woode & fetch them water for a capfull of corne." Others took to "plaine stealing, both night & day," searching out the Indians' buried stores and breaking into them as the Pilgrims had done at Corn Hill. Many were well whipped and sentenced to the pillory for this, but still the larceny continued. At length, "to give ye Indeans contente," one repeated offender was condemned to die, which gave rise to a story that long plagued the Pilgrims. This was not the first or last time they were castigated for the sins of others. The condemned thief, so the story ran, was a strong able-bodied young man, and as the weakened colony could ill afford to lose him, a feeble old man was substituted for him on the gallows. In their ignorance, most people in England drew no distinction between Plymouth and Wessagusset, assuming that both were Brownist colonies, and the satirist Butler in his *Hudibras* seized upon the story to blast the Separatists:

> Our brethren in New England use
> Choice malefactors to excuse,
> And hang the guiltless in their steed [stead],
> Of whom the churches have less need. . . .

As the winter wore on, Weston's men reached the end of their rope. They had consumed all of their stores, even their seed corn, and could not buy, beg, or borrow any more from the Indians. The latter declared that they had scarcely enough maize and beans for their own needs, but some of the colonists refused to believe this, persuading themselves that the Massachusetts were hoarding corn out of sheer malice. At this point John Sanders, second gov-

ernor of Wessagusset, called his council together and decided upon
a foolhardy and fatal course of action. He had all but one of the
gates in the palisade about the town nailed up and, by Indian
runner, dispatched a note to Plymouth to inform Bradford of his
plan.

Wessagusset was starving, said Sanders, and therefore he was
sailing immediately for Maine to see if he could procure supplies
from the English fishing fleet in those waters, an idea doubtless
inspired by the Pilgrims' tale of their success there. It was doubtful,
however, if his men could hold out until his return unless supplies
were meantime obtained from the Indians. As the latter would not
sell their corn, he was "resolved to take it by violence and waited
only the return of the messenger, which he desired should be
hastened, craving advice therein, promising to make restitution
later"—again an echo of a Pilgrim phrase.

This threat thoroughly alarmed Bradford, who hurriedly called
in Allerton, Standish, Winslow, and several others for consultation. First, they questioned the Indian messenger, pretending that
they were in the market for corn, asking if the Massachusetts had
any to spare. No, came his reply, for they had "already spared all
they could." Convinced of the truth of this, the Pilgrim leaders
rushed back to Wessagusset a strong letter of protest, signed by
all of them.

"We altogether dislike your intendment," they declared, warning Weston's men not to count on them for any help in this or any
such action. It was plainly "against the law of God and Nature."
Why couldn't they do what those at Plymouth had often done
and were now doing in want of corn? It was quite possible to "live
on groundnuts, clams, mussels, and such other things as naturally
the country affordeth." What if they did manage to seize a little
corn? How would that help? They would soon be worse off than
before, for with the Indians in arms against them they could not
move about in search of supplies. And had it ever occurred to
them that their raiding party might be repulsed and smashed, for
they were weak from hunger, "swelled and diseased in their

bodies?" All would probably be scalped by the Indians, and those who escaped would surely be punished by His Majesty's officers for such an unprincipled attack and could "expect no better than the Gaol House." Besides, said the Pilgrims, "all of us might smart for it," and they should consider, too, that it would blast all hope of spreading the "glad tidings of Salvation."

Though Sanders was diverted from his foolhardy course, the fat was in the fire, for word of the plot reached the Massachusetts with unfortunate consequences for all concerned. "Yea," exclaimed Bradford indignantly, "so base were some of their company as they wente & tould ye Indians that their Govr. was purposed to come and take their corne by force." Why it was "base" to warn friendly neighbors against the rankest kind of treachery on the part of a misguided few is not quite clear.

At this time, having recovered from his fever, Standish sailed for the Cape to bring back the supplies bought there by Bradford. Putting in at Nauset, he found that Aspinet had kept his promise to guard the stack of corn and the damaged shallop. As he was leaving, Standish discovered that "certain beads, scissors, and other trifles" on the shallop were missing. At the head of an armed party he marched back and angrily delivered an ultimatum to Aspinet. The beads and other missing articles were to be returned immediately, he declared, "or else he would revenge it on them before his departure, and so took leave for that night, . . . refusing whatsoever kindness they offered."

Used to the gentler and more politic ways of Bradford and Winslow, Aspinet was quite taken aback and hurried to the beach early the next morning, "accompanied with many men, in a stately manner." He saluted the Captain by licking his hand from wrist to fingertips, "withal bowing the knee, striving to imitate the English gesture," as Squanto had taught him to do, but "in so rude and savage a manner as our men could scarce forbear to break out in open laughter." According to the story brought back by Standish, or at least attributed to Standish in the Pilgrim chronicles, the chief handed back the missing "trifles" with many apologies, saying that the thief had been "much beaten," and as a peace offering fed the Pilgrims delicious cornbread baked by his squaws during the night.

Standish and his men next proceeded to Cummaquid. Overtaken by a blizzard, they spent the first night there in the open boat (frozen fast in the harbor), suffering cruelly from the bitter cold. In the morning Iyanough and his braves spied them, brought them in, and took them to their houses, inviting them to spend the night as the storm was still raging. As at Nauset, the Indians here had carefully guarded the Pilgrims' supplies and even agreed to sell them more corn, volunteering to carry it down to the beach and help them load it in the shallop.

The Pilgrims weighed anchor and were about to depart when, curiously enough, the Captain again missed some trinkets from the shallop and in high dudgeon marched off to deliver another ultimatum. Throwing a ring of heavily armed men about the sachem's lodge, which was crowded with people, Standish loudly demanded the return of his beads, "threatening to fall upon them without further delay if they would not forthwith restore them." Even more astonished than Aspinet, "gentle" Iyanough came out to discover the cause of the tumult and suggested to the Captain that his precious beads might perhaps have been mislaid, "desiring him to search whether they were not about the boat." A man was sent to the shallop where the beads were found "lying openly upon the boat's cuddy." But to Standish this merely proved the Indians' "knavery," for he chose to believe that Iyanough had somehow managed to have the thief surreptitiously return them. Notwithstanding all of their kindness, the Cummaquid were only "pretending their wonted love."

Quite possibly there was some friction along the Cape, for trouble usually attended the Captain's contacts with the Indians— and with many of the whites, too, for that matter. But the curious story of the beads, if true and not fabricated after the event, was a flimsy foundation for the Pilgrims' later attempt to prove a conspiracy against them in their anxious effort to justify a quite indefensible action. If Aspinet and Iyanough had been engaged in a diabolical plot against Plymouth, as the Pilgrims tried to

represent, they would scarcely have begun by stealing a few beads
when they had in their possession the supplies that meant life or
death to the plantation. Nor would they have offered them more
corn and beans from their own very limited stock and carried
them down to the beach to see them quickly and safely loaded.

Standish soon returned to the Cape, going to Manomet, where
Bradford had been so well received not long before and had come
away with such a favorable impression of the "grave" Canacum.
Though he obtained the supplies he sought, the Captain was not
at all impressed. On the contrary, he was very much annoyed,
"not finding the entertainment he found elsewhere, and the Governor had here received." As he had doubtless heard of the martial
antics at Cummaquid and Nauset, perhaps the sachem was a little
cool. And he had even better reason than that to be somewhat
reserved and on his guard.

Word had come, spreading like wildfire through the forests, of
Sanders' proposed treachery at Wessagusset, which reminded the
Cape tribes of many sad experiences with white marauders. They
were aware that Sanders had been in communication with Bradford about his plan. They knew that Weston's men had lived at
Plymouth for months, and was it not obvious from their joint
foraging expeditions in the *Swan* that the planters at Plymouth
and Wessagusset were partners? The wonder is that Standish and
his party were received at all.

During the Pilgrims' visit, and to their great embarrassment,
two Indians walked in—both from Wessagusset! One was a
"notable insulting villain," Wituwamat by name, a renowned
Massachusetts brave, who held a very low opinion of the whites,
it appears, for he "derided their weakness, especially because, as
he said, they died crying, making sour faces, more like children
than men." And after making such insulting speeches, his "entertainment much exceeded the Captain's," which was simply insup-
portable, and Standish was so angry with his hosts that he "scorned
at their behaviour, and told them of it."

Ignoring the purplish Captain, Wituwamat drew out a long
knife, presented it to Canacum, and began a long speech "in an

audacious manner, framing it in such sort as the Captain, though he be the best linguist amongst us, could not gather anything from it." But Standish did not like the sound of Wituwamat's remarks, and in some mysterious manner it was "afterward discovered" just what had been said. The Massachusetts were resolved to "ruinate" Weston's colony and felt confident of success, being thirty or forty strong. But they feared Plymouth, persuaded that the planters there "would never leave the death of their countrymen unrevenged." Therefore they were come to persuade the Cape tribes to join their attack on Plymouth, for none could be safe "without the overthrow of both Plantations." As Captain Standish and his men were providentially at hand, why not begin with them?

Nothing happened.

Another visitor came in, one of the Pamet tribe, who had always been "very affable, courteous, and loving, especially towards the Captain." To all appearances he remained so, "making many signs of his continued affections." But this, it seems, was merely "to avoid suspicion," for he had "now entered into confederacy with the rest." Taken to the Pilgrim camp, he would have murdered Standish in his sleep but for the wit of the Captain, who paced up and down before the fire till dawn, the night being extremely cold. Yet the Pamet was invited to accompany the party to Plymouth the next day, and there he persuaded the Captain to go with him to the tip of the Cape to obtain more corn. They set sail together but did not arrive, being driven back by a storm.

The plot thickens, and now the scene shifts to Sowams.

During Standish's absence at Manomet, the Pilgrims had received the disturbing news that Massasoit was dying. Winslow immediately departed for Sowams with Hobomok. Along the way, in Corbitant's country, they were informed that the Big Chief was dead, to the alarm and anguish of both.

"Neen womasu Sagimus, neen womasu Sagimus!" wailed Hobomok. "My loving sachem, my loving sachem! Many have I known, but never any like thee. Whilst you live," he said, turning to Winslow, "you will never see his like among the Indians. He was no liar. He was not cruel and bloody like other Indians. In anger and passion he was soon cooled, easy to be reconciled towards such as had offended him, ruled by reason in such measure as he would not scorn the advice of mean men and governed his men better with a few strokes than others did with many, truly loving where he loved. Yea! I fear you have not a faithful friend left among the Indians."

Uneasy about the rumor that the new chief would probably be "that notable politician" Corbitant, always somewhat reserved toward Plymouth, Winslow thought it wise to visit him and be the first to offer his congratulations. He therefore proceeded to Corbitant's winter headquarters at Mattapuyst, now the town of Mattapoisett, on the western shore of Buzzards Bay. Corbitant was not at home, having gone to Sowams, and Winslow sent a messenger ahead to inform him of his coming. The messenger returned at sunset to report that the Big Chief was not dead but sinking fast, and if they wished to see him alive, they would have to hurry. Winslow and Hobomok pushed on, stumbling along the forest track in the dark, and at length arrived late at night to find the sachem's lodge so full of people that they could scarcely get in and "making such a hellish noise," said Winslow, "as it distempered us that were well." The medicine men were "in the midst of their charms for him," dancing about and chanting at the top of their lungs, while the Big Chief's squaws were frantically rubbing his legs and arms.

"Oh, Winslow, I shall never see thee again!" groaned Massasoit, explaining that he had lost his vision, that everything was black before his eyes, and he was very pleased when Winslow offered to treat him. The latter had brought along a "confection of many comfortable conserves" and gave some of this to the Big Chief, feeding it to him on the point of a knife which he had great difficulty in forcing between his teeth, for the patient's jaws were almost locked. A slip here might have had serious consequences, but no blood flowed. Winslow then washed out the sachem's mouth, which was "exceedingly furred," and scraped his enormously swollen tongue. Learning that the Big Chief "had not slept in two days . . . and had not had a stool in five," he gave him more confection. Within a half hour, to the amazement of all, "his sight began to come back to him." Impressed with Winslow's talents, Massasoit begged him to tend all his ailing people, "saying they were good folk." Winslow agreed and washed out their mouths also, though he found it a most offensive chore, "not being accustomed with such poisonous savours."

Now the Big Chief wanted soup, some of that "good English pottage such as he had eaten at Plymouth." Winslow brewed up corn, strawberry leaves, and sassafras root into something so palatable that the sachem asked for more—but with a duck or a goose in it. To humor him, Winslow shot a mallard and tossed that into the pot. When it was ready, he ordered Hobomok to skim off the fat before serving, but Massasoit would not hear of this and in spite of every warning "made a gross meal of it," suffering a violent relapse, heaving and retching, again losing his sight, bleeding profusely at the nose, to the great alarm of the Wampanoag. Winslow quieted their fears, and his own, by assuring them that he was so weak and exhausted that he would now sleep, "which was the principal thing he wanted." The sachem suffered another relapse, but within a day or two was again on his feet, "lustie" as ever, having quite forgotten his resentment at being denied Squanto's head.

"Now I see the English are my friends and love me," he told his people, "and whilst I live, I will never forget this kindness they have showed me."

Departing, Winslow accompanied Corbitant to Buzzards Bay and spent the night at his lodge there. Far from being an ogre, Corbitant proved upon acquaintance to be a very pleasant fellow, "full of merry jests and squibs, and never better pleased than when the like are returned again upon him." With a wry smile, alluding to the rumpus and shooting at Nemasket, the chieftain asked if the Pilgrims would come to physic him if he were sick. Assured of this, he then inquired if Winslow were not afraid to come alone among the Indians.

"Where true love is," he was told, "there is no fear."

"But if your love be such and bring forth such fruits," Corbitant objected, "how cometh it to pass that when we visit Patuxet, you stand upon your guard with the mouths of your pieces towards us?"

"It is the most honorable and respectful entertainment we can give you," Winslow explained, trying to make sense of the military salute.

"I like not such salutations," the chief remarked and began to talk of other things. Why was it, he asked, that grace was said not only before but after meals at Plymouth? This offered a splendid opportunity for an exposition of "God's works of Creation and Preservation, of his Laws and Ordinances, especially of the Ten Commandments," and Winslow made the most of it. Corbitant and his men listened attentively and observed that they "believed almost the same things," taking exception only to the Seventh Commandment, according to Winslow, "thinking there were many inconveniences in it, that a man should be tied to one woman, about which we reasoned a good while."*

The Pilgrim ambassador thoroughly enjoyed his stay and "never had better entertainment amongst any of them." Regretfully taking his leave, he set out for Plymouth next morning, and along the trail that day Hobomok told him an extraordinary story, or so Winslow reported. Massasoit, it appears, had called Hobomok aside before his departure and "privately" informed him that the Massachusetts Indians planned to destroy Wessagusset and then fall upon Plymouth. They had persuaded the Nauset, Cummaquid, Manomet, Pamet, and even the Gayhead of Martha's Vineyard to join them in the attack. Hobomok was therefore to inform his friends at Plymouth that if they wished the Big Chief's advice, they should instantly proceed against the "authors of this intended mischief" and kill them. There was not a moment to lose if they valued the lives of those at Wessagusset and their own "after-safety."

* Their conclusions, unfortunately, have been lost.

Such was the remarkable story offered by the Pilgrims as main and conclusive proof of a widespread conspiracy against them, as complete vindication of their decision to liquidate Wessagusset and put the Indian leaders to the sword. And the more one thinks about it, the more remarkable this story becomes, and the more amazing it is that the tale should ever have been taken seriously, as it always has been, even by critical historians. First, why should Massasoit have informed Hobomok "privately" about matters so vital to Plymouth when Winslow was with him, at his elbow day and night? Under the circumstances, he might at least have offered to assist the Pilgrims as the terms of the peace pact required. And why, if the Cape tribes were involved in the conspiracy, did he not offer to call them to heel, for they were his subjects and looked to him in all things? The inclusion of them in the Pilgrims' story undoubtedly was an afterthought, inserted to explain away several embarrassing events on the Cape—and it was a blunder. If the Cape tribes had actually been in league with the Massachusetts, then they were in revolt against Massasoit, which would have been genuinely startling news. But there is not a shred of evidence anywhere to suggest that this was true.

Was the story Hobomok's perhaps? Was he up to Squanto's trick of putting words in others' mouths to promote devious purposes of his own? It is interesting that Hobomok waited till he was two days along the trail before he told Winslow his story. But this fact must be set against another that is even more significant. One would suppose that Winslow, upon hearing such alarming news, would hasten home with all speed. Instead, he loitered along the way, stopping to spend the night at Nemasket, quite as if nothing had happened. And the next morning, while proceeding in a leisurely fashion, he met two friendly Indians coming from Plymouth who told him something which, carelessly left in the rather skilfully edited record, casts a most revealing light upon this entire business:

"Captain Standish was, that day, gone to the Massachusetts."

The decision to proceed against Wessagusset had been taken before Winslow arrived to tell Bradford what Hobomok had told him about what Massasoit had said to him "privately." Thus, unwittingly but quite effectively, the Pilgrims themselves exploded their official thesis that the attack on Wessagusset was preventive and inspired by Winslow's story. The truth is, plainly, that the tale was fabricated after the event in an effort to justify a series of treacherous actions of which the Pilgrims were always a little ashamed.

The shallop bearing Standish and his men was forced by strong head winds to turn back, arriving just as Winslow did. Then, according to the sequence of events in the Pilgrim chronicles, Bradford hurriedly called a council to discuss the terrifying news brought home by Winslow. As the governor had no authority to declare war "without the consent of the Body of the company," the question was laid before a general meeting of the planters. The latter were quite surprised by the sudden crisis, evidently not having the slightest suspicion that anything was wrong. As they hemmed and hawed, possibly rising to ask some embarrassing questions, their leaders pressed them to stop talking and make up their minds, declaring that it was "high time to come to resolution, how sudden soever it seemed to them." In the end they decided that as "every man was not of sufficiency to know nor fitness to judge," and as there should not be another dangerous leak of information to the Indians as at Wessagusset, the decision should be left to the discretion of Bradford, Allerton, and Standish, who were to choose such others as they desired.[1]

This committee quickly drew up a secret plan of action. On pretense of trade, Standish was to go to Wessagusset with as many men as he thought necessary to deal with the Massachusetts. He was to acquaint the governor of the real purpose of his coming, but there was to be no declaration of war. Rather, he was to show himself very friendly toward the Indians until he "could take them in such traps as they lay for others." In particular, and probably at his own suggestion, he was to make sure of "that bloody and bold villain," Wituwamat, who had so insulted him at Manomet and was given to making such disparaging remarks about the prowess of the English and their childish manner of dying—

"making sour faces," indeed! The wretch's head was to be cut off and brought back to Plymouth as a "warning and terrour to all of that disposition."

While preparations were under way, one Phineas Pratt arrived from Wessagusset to report that things were in a sad state there, requesting permission to stay in Plymouth for a time. Weston's men were in a pitiable condition and scattered all about the countryside in their desperate search for food. He felt sure, he said, that he had been followed from Wessagusset by one of the Massachusetts who planned to kill him along the way. But he escaped, according to the Pilgrims, because the Indian got lost in the woods!—missing Plymouth by so wide a margin that he ended up at Manomet, miles away. On his return the savage came through Plymouth, "still pretending friendship," and Bradford promptly lodged him in the Fort, chaining him to a post in the Guard Room, where he would have to be "content to remain," he was told, "till the return of Captain Standish from the Massachusetts." The Pilgrims did not propose to allow him any opportunity to wreck their plans by sounding the alarm.

With Hobomok and eight heavily armed men,[2] not taking more for fear of arousing suspicion, Standish again set sail and at Wessagusset found the *Swan* anchored in the harbor with not a soul on board, with "not so much as a dog therein." After the Pilgrims had fired a volley or two, the skipper and some of the crew appeared on the beach, having gone ashore to gather clams and groundnuts. How did they dare to live in such insecurity and leave their vessel thus unguarded? they were asked.

"We fear not the Indians," they replied, "but live with them and suffer them to lodge with us, not having sword or gun, or needing the same."

"If there is no cause, I am the gladder," said Standish with scarcely disguised contempt for these men "senseless of their own miserie." Marching his men into Wessagusset, he informed the governor of the purpose of his coming. Weston's men made a feeble protest but soon gave in, saying "they could expect no better." Forbidding anyone to leave the town "on pain of death" (three men preferred the Massachusetts to the Pilgrims and escaped), Standish waited patiently for the moment to strike, trucking for furs with the Indians, carrying things "as smoothly as he possibly could," but not altogether successfully. An Indian returned from Wessagusset to tell his people that from his eyes he could see the Captain was "angry in his heart." A few days later an exceptionally tall and powerful brave named Pecksuot came in to visit Hobomok. He was aware, he said, that Standish had come to kill him and others.

"Tell him we know it, but fear him not. Neither will we shun him, but let him begin when he dare." Turning to Standish on another occasion, he remarked, "Though you are a great Captain, yet you are but a little man, and though I be no sachem, yet I am a man of great strength and courage."

Wituwamat also came in and was as contemptuous as ever, drawing out and caressing a long sinister knife with the carving of a woman's face on the handle.

"I have another at home wherewith I have killed both French and English," he said, "and by and by the two must marry." All such "insulting gestures and speeches" Standish carefully noted and "bore with patience for the present." But his patience was wearing thin. Failing in his attempt to "get many of them together at once," he decided to start with Pecksuot and Wituwamat.

These two and another brave, together with Wituwamat's brother, a boy of eighteen, were lured one day into Pilgrim head-quarters—by an invitation to a feast, an enemy asserted. Whatever the lure, the Pilgrims were quite shockingly frank about what happened there. At a signal, the door was made fast and Standish leaped at the huge Pecksuot who had belittled him. Snatching the latter's knife from the string about his neck, he plunged it into his breast. Wituwamat and the other braves were done to death by the blades of Standish's men after a fierce hand-to-hand struggle, and even Standish remarked his admiration of the courage and strength of the trapped Indians as they hopelessly fought for their lives, saying that it was "incredible how many wounds they received before they died, not making any fearful noise, but catching at their weapons and striving to the last." Only one of the Indians escaped being cut to pieces, the Indian boy, "whom the Captain caused to have hanged."

The attack so took the Massachusetts by surprise that many of them, principally women, were caught in town. Placing these in charge of Weston's men, Standish commanded the whites to put to death every Indian warrior they could find. Weston's men killed two, Standish and his men added another, but a fourth escaped through "negligence"—what a pity!—"and crossed their proceedings." Thoroughly aroused, the Captain marched his forces out of town, "still seeking to make spoil of them and theirs." He encountered and drove back a band of the Massachusetts, who let "fly their arrows amain" as they slowly retreated from tree to tree, concentrating their attack upon Standish and Hobomok. Losing his temper, the latter stripped off his coat and "being a known Pinese, chased them so fast our people were not able to hold way with him." The Massachusetts finally took refuge in a swamp, hurling curses and insults at the whites as they came up, and Standish got nothing but "foul language" when he challenged their leader "to come out and fight like a man, showing how base and woman-like he was in tongueing it as he did."

Returning to Wessagusset, Standish asked Weston's men what they wished to do now, for they were afraid to stay where they were. They could come to Plymouth if they desired. Rather, they chose to sail for Maine in the *Swan*, hoping to hear of Weston there or to arrange to work their passage home in the vessels of the English fishing fleet, which most of them succeeded in doing. With troublesome neighbors out of the way and the Indians cowed, Standish and his men set sail and were "received with joy" at Plymouth as they came triumphantly home bearing Wituwamat's head. The bloody trophy was carried to the Fort and stuck on a spike on the battlements there for all to see, one of the sights of Plymouth for many years. But they brought nothing else with them, as the Pilgrims were at pains to point out. They had refrained from looting Weston's men, "not takeing ye worth of a penny of anything that was theirs." Nor had they stripped the once giggling women of the Massachuetts when the latter were prisoners of war. Resisting temptation, Standish ordered their release and "would not take their beaver coats from them."

King Beaver, it is likely, had more of a hand in this plot than appears at first sight. The fur trade was the life blood of Plymouth, its sole profitable enterprise. It alone could provide the revenues needed to buy supplies and pay off debts. The Pilgrims did not intend to sit quietly by and see this artery of commerce cut or blocked, and Wessagusset was strategically placed for such a purpose, as that shrewd trader Weston doubtless realized in choosing the site. The town was settled only a few months before the Pilgrims noted that it was already upsetting the corn and beaver trade. On their last visit to the Massachusetts they observed that "little good could be done there," for Weston's men were "giving as much for a quart of corn as we used to do for a beaver's skin." The Pilgrims had a way of representing the Indians as subtle and dangerous whenever it served their purpose, according to a later rival in the beaver trade. "I have found the Massachusetts Indians more full of humanitie than the Christians," he declared after years of experience with both, "and have had much better quarter with them." By creating fear and mistrust of the Indians, he said, the Pilgrims hoped to keep neighboring settlers from scattering and freely going about the countryside, with the aim of bringing them "under their Lee, that none might trade for Beaver but at their pleasure."[3] Certainly the Pilgrims wept no tears when Weston's men abandoned Wessagusset and sailed for home. The scheme of their "loving freind" to dispossess them had come to naught.

When news of the "huggery" at Wessagusset reached the tribes along Cape Cod, they were terror-stricken, recalling Standish's displeasure with them and his ultimatums. They were so "amazed" that they "forsook their houses, running to and fro like men distracted, living in swamps and other desert places." Many took sick and died, including "grave" Canacum of the Manomet, "stately" Aspinet of the Nauset, and "gentle" Iyanough of the Cummaquid, who had been so helpful and friendly, winning the respect and trust of every Pilgrim leader except Standish.

Well aware that recent events needed a deal of explaining, the Pilgrims entrusted their defense to the always plausible Winslow, who cleverly presented their case in *Good Newes from New England,* published in London the next year. Blandly observing that the accounts of the action at Wessagusset would no doubt be "various," as they certainly were—the Pilgrims were soon complaining about the "vile and clamorous" reports of the dispossessed Wessagusset men—Winslow apologized for the length of his story by saying that he durst not be too brief lest he "rob God of that honour, glory, and praise which belongeth to him. . . ."

But there was one Saint, and the greatest of them, who failed to discern any sign of God's handiwork in the treacherous and bloody business and who raised a mighty voice to place responsibility squarely where it belonged.

"Concerning the killing of those poor Indians," wrote John Robinson in phrases that cut the Pilgrims to the quick, "oh! how happy a thing it had been if you had converted some before you killed any; besids, where blood is once shed, it is seldome stanched off a long time after. You will say they deserved it. I grant it, but upon what provocations and invitments by those heathenish Christians? Besids, you being no magistrates over them, were to consider not what they deserved, but what you by necessitie were constrained to inflicte. Necessitie of this, espetially of killing so many (and many more, it seems, they would if they could), I see not, . . . and indeed I am afraid lest, by these occasions, others should be drawne to affecte a kind of rufling course in the world. . . .

"Upon this occasion let me be bould to exhorte you seriously to consider of ye dispossition of your Captaine, whom I love and am perswaded ye Lord in great mercie and for much good hath sent you him, if you use him aright. He is a man humble and meek amongst you and towards all in ordinarie course. . . . But there may be wanting that tendernes of ye life of man (made after God's image) which is meete. . . .

"It is a thing more glorious in men's eyes than pleasing in God's, or conveniente for Christians, to be a terrour to poore barbarous people."

16

THE SEASON
OF GENTLE
SHOWERS

*. . . and ye face of things was changed, to ye re-
joysing of ye harts of many, for which they
blessed God.*
——WILLIAM BRADFORD

THOUGH IT REMOVED A POTENTIALLY DANGEROUS RIVAL, THE
overthrow of Wessagusset solved none of the Pilgrims' immediate
problems. Starvation seemed just around the corner. The hungry
planters and their families seldom went to bed at night knowing
where they would find breakfast in the morning. They were worse
off than before, in fact, for they no longer dared to go on the
foraging expeditions by which they had managed to survive the
winter. Hardy Spanish *conquistadores* had been praised, said Bradford, for living four or five days at a time on a few grains of corn.
When the Pilgrims had that much, he exclaimed, they "thought
it as good as a feast," occasionally going two or three months

together with neither "bread nor any kind of corne." But it was a lie, he protested, that they ever ate toads or dogs that died in the street, for the Lord kept "his people ... from these extremities."

In the spring of 1623, with the aim of stimulating production of corn, an important shift occurred in Plymouth's basic economy. The majority of the company had never been reconciled to tilling the fields in common. Cushman's sermon on Self-Love had only temporarily silenced the clamor of the land-hungry planters to be given fields of their own to cultivate. Such a change, they argued, would make all hands more industrious. Though Bradford and other leaders personally shared this view, they hesitated to take a step so patently contrary to the articles of agreement, fearing that the adventurers might cut off their supplies. But the pressure within the company was so great that a compromise was forced. Every man was to set corn "for his owne perticuler," but the acres allotted for the purpose were "only for present use" and not for permanent possession.

Each household was granted a tract commensurate with its size. In general, an acre was allowed for every member. It is clear from a study of the records, however, that other considerations were given weight. Though there were four in the family, the "prophane" Billingtons received only three acres, the number allowed Bradford, who was now alone. Standish, who was also alone, received two acres. Altogether, sixty-nine acres fell to the surviving fifty-one members of the *Mayflower* company while thirty-three were distributed among the thirty-five who had come on the *Fortune*. The *Mayflower* group also did rather better in choice of sites, evidently so arranging it that their lands formed a compact unit along both banks of Town Brook. The acres of the *Fortune* people lay beyond these to the north. Assignments within these reserved areas were made by having the planters draw lots. Subject only to a tax for the support of "Public Officers, Fishermen, &c., who could not be freed from their Calling without greater inconveniences," each household was to keep for its own use all of the corn and other produce it managed to grow on its plot.

Once the spring planting was done, the men of the company

organized themselves into groups of six or seven, each of which was trained as a crew for the shallop. Now rudely equipped as a fishing vessel, the boat was kept almost constantly at sea trailing schools of cod and other fish. As soon as one crew returned, another shoved off, and none came back without a catch, often staying out a week or more in the worst of weather, for there was nothing at Plymouth and the men felt that "to goe home emptie would be a great discouragemente to ye rest." On their days ashore, they hunted deer and waterfowl. Men, women, and children prowled the beach for shellfish and gathered groundnuts in the woods. And "all this while no supply was heard of, neither knew they when they might expecte any."

Unknown to the Pilgrims, a ship had set sail for Plymouth months before—the *Paragon*, carrying supplies and many new recruits. But, like the *Speedwell*, she began to leak dangerously under the pounding of heavy seas and had to turn back. Repaired at considerable cost, she again set out but in mid-Atlantic was forced to head for home once more, stripped of mainmast and upper works, having all but foundered in a terrific storm during which her wretched passengers were often at a loss to know whether they were "within bord or withoute." The ship had been chartered by one of the more active adventurers, John Pierce, cloth merchant of London, and when the Pilgrims learned of his designs upon them, they felt that his heavy losses on the ship were richly deserved, a direct intervention of God to foil his nefarious schemes.

For almost a year the Pilgrims had been squatters and interlopers. They had no formal legal right to the lands they occupied until Cushman arrived on the *Fortune* with a patent signed by Sir Ferdinando Gorges and his partners in the Council for New England, as the reorganized Second Virginia (Plymouth) Company was known. The patent was made out to John Pierce and his associates in the company of the merchant adventurers, who were to hold it in trust for the settlers until a final settlement was made under the articles of agreement. But Pierce had meantime been quietly at work obtaining another patent to supersede the first. This new grant gave all of the country about Plymouth to him, his heirs, and assigns forever, depriving the other merchant adventurers of their rights, reducing the settlers to a position where they would "hold of him as tenants and sue to his courts as cheefe Lord." But the *Paragon* had been such a disappointment that he lacked the financial means to pursue his scheme, and he finally agreed to sell his "royall Lordship." He had paid £50 for it but now demanded £500, which the merchant adventurers paid, charging half of it to the Pilgrims under the joint account.

And who should now appear, in "ye disguise of a blackesmith," but their old friend Thomas Weston! He arrived with not much more than the shirt on his back, having been shipwrecked along the coast to the north and stripped of everything he owned by the Indians, being lucky to escape with his life. Weston was all smiles and easy promises, as usual, but the Pilgrims could see, they said, that resentment at the overthrow of Wessagusset was "still boyling in his mind." Anxious to recoup his losses, he asked to borrow a quantity of beaver, saying that one of his ships was on the way and the planters might have from it anything they wanted in exchange. The Pilgrims did not believe a word he said, protesting that they had no beaver to spare and that to grant his request would be "enoughe to make a mutinie among ye people, seeing there was no other means to procure them food which they so much wanted, & cloths allso." But in the end, because they "pitied his case and remembered former curtesies," the Pilgrim leaders secretly loaned him about two hundred pounds of beaver. So they set him again on the road to fortune, but all they ever had in return, according to Bradford, were "reproches and evill words," for he remained a "bitter enemie unto them upon all occasions," being such an ingrate that he divulged their secret to "some that were none of their best freinds," boasting that at last he had the planters where he wanted them, for he could use the surreptitious loan of beaver to "set them all together by ye ears."

Nor was the next ship of good omen. Late in June the *Plantation* came in under the command of Captain Francis West, recently

appointed Admiral of New England by Sir Ferdinando Gorges
and his partners, who had sent him out to stop all fishing along
the coast except by those who had paid the Council for New
England a good fat fee to obtain a license. Nothing came of this
scheme, for the "Admiral" found the fishermen to be "stuberne"
fellows and much too strong for him. He had on board two hogsheads of peas to sell and "seeing their wants," demanded £9 each
for them. But the Pilgrims were "stuberne" fellows, too, and told
him that as they "had lived so long without," they would go on
thus "rather than give so unreasonably."

On the high seas, so West reported, the *Plantation* had spoken
a ship bound for Plymouth "with sundrie passengers," and he was
surprised, he said, that she had not arrived, "fearing some miscarriage, for they lost her in a storme." Having reason to believe
that many of their families and friends were on board, the Pilgrims
spent an anxious week and then another before a large vessel was
sighted far out in the bay. She proved to be the *Anne* of London,
a ship of 140 tons, with supplies and some sixty passengers. She
had set sail from England with another vessel, the *Little James,* a
fine new pinnace of forty-four tons, built by the merchant adventurers "to stay in ye cuntrie." But the *Little James* had not been
seen since the storm at sea. Hope for her was almost dead when
she came limping in ten days later, the captain bitterly cursing
the crew, swearing that he would never put to sea again with the
green hands hired by the adventurers, for they "cared not whitch
end went forwardes."

In this second large wave of immigration there were, all told,
just ninety-three persons.[1] As on previous ships, Strangers constituted the larger part of the passengers.* From London came
the wife and five daughters of Richard Warren of the *Mayflower*
company, and from Chester the wife and two small children of
the young vintner, William Hilton, who had arrived on the
Fortune. The widowed Captain Standish had wooed and won

* For the names of the passengers, see Appendix A.

another bride, by mail, and she now came to the marriage, one Barbara; nothing more is known about her, though family tradition has it that she was a sister of the Captain's first wife, Rose. One of the merchant adventurers had decided to become a settler, Timothy Hatherly, "a very profitable and beneficial instrumente." The Strangers included several others of note—Francis Sprague, who soon added to the amenities of life at Plymouth by establishing the first tavern in New England; and young John Faunce of Purleigh, Essex, who sired a younger John, the third and last ruling elder of the Pilgrim church and the source of the story of Plymouth Rock as it has been handed down to us.

The Saints on board numbered thirty-two, almost as many as on the *Mayflower*. The Brewsters were again united with the arrival of their daughters, Patience, now a woman of twenty-three, and Fear, a girl of seventeen, who soon married Isaac Allerton. There was also another of the original Scrooby congregation on board—the last ever to reach Plymouth—the prosperous merchant, George Morton, "a pious gracious servante of God," who had brought his wife, four children, a nephew, and his wife's sister, Mrs. Alice Southworth, widow of Cushman's friend, Edward Southworth, the silk worker. Alice had come at Bradford's invitation, it would seem, for they were almost immediately married.[2] Allerton's sister, Sarah, widow of Degory Priest of the *Mayflower* company, had taken a third husband, Godbert Godbertson (Cuthbert Cuthbertson), a hatter, and they now came with five children of various marriages. There were three children with Francis Cooke's wife, Hester (Mayhieu), a Walloon; and three with Sarah Jenney and her husband John, the brewery worker, "a godlie though otherwise a plaine man, yet singular for publicness of spirit," builder of Plymouth's first mill.

But welcome as these and others were, many in the town were heartsick that their beloved pastor had not arrived to comfort them in his wise and gentle way. The merchant adventurers had given repeated assurances that they would send Robinson over at the first opportunity. "We will deal fairly and squarely answer your expectations to the full," they wrote on this occasion. But the Saints were beginning to suspect—and events bore out their misgivings—that there was a conspiracy in London to prevent his coming.

The ships had brought a third quite distinct group, the only one of its kind sent to Plymouth. It consisted of ten persons led by John Oldham, "a man of parts, but high-spirited and extremely passionate." The members of this group were not ordinary settlers, having come "on their perticuler." They made no contributions to the common store and had no rights in the joint stock, enjoying an independent economic status on the lands assigned to them. They were forbidden to engage in the Indian trade and were "subject to ye general Government," but their only specific obligations were military service and the payment of a nominal tax of a bushel of corn a year. Conceived by the merchant adventurers, this was an ill-advised and ill-defined arrangement, and sparks were soon flying from the friction that resulted.

Hastening ashore, eager to taste the felicities of New Canaan so rosily pictured in letters home and publicized in Mourt's *Relation,* the newcomers were appalled by the "very low condition" of the settlers, finding them pale, haggard, and in rags, some "litle better than halfe naked." Many were so "danted and dismayed" that they openly wished themselves at home again. Others "fell a-weeping, fancying their owne miserie in what they saw now in others." For their part, the planters were not altogether pleased with what they saw, frankly disliking the looks of much of the company. Some were "very usefull persons," but others were "so bad as they were faine to be at charge to send them home againe ye next year." Cushman had sent along a letter to disclaim responsibility for the character of the company.

"It greeveth me to see so weake a company sent you, but had I not been here, it had been weaker," he wrote from London. "You must still call upon the company here to see that honest men be sente you, and threaten to send them back if any other come. We are not any way so much in danger as by corrupte and noughty persons." The trouble, as always, was lack of funds, he said, for desirable new recruits "come flying in upon us, but moneys come creeping in . . . And because people press so hard upon us to goe, and often shuch as are none of ye fittest, I pray you write ernestly to ye Treasurer and directe what persons should be sente."

Tension almost immediately developed between the recent arrivals and the Old Comers, as the *Mayflower* and *Fortune* groups now began to call themselves. The newcomers could not become self-supporting for a year or more, not until they had planted a crop and harvested it the next fall; they were afraid of starving meanwhile, fearing that the hungry planters might quickly consume all the supplies brought on the ships, leaving them little or nothing. On the other hand, the Old Comers feared that the new company might prove to be an intolerable drain upon their own scanty supplies, the fruit of their conscientious labor in the meersteads along the brook and the fields in the clearing. The latter went to Bradford with the proposal that the newcomers be allowed to keep all of the supplies on the ships if they promised to stretch them until they could gather a harvest of their own and waived all right to share in the Old Comers' supplies. Both parties agreed with alacrity, and the compromise gave "good contente."

Laden with beaver and otter pelts, clapboard, and hardwood wainscoting, the *Anne* departed for home after a stay of six weeks. Edward Winslow went with her, having been chosen to report to the adventurers on the "encouraging" progress of the colony and to arrange for more ample and regular supplies. Under his arm he was carrying the manuscript of *Good Newes from New England, or a True Relation of things very remarkable at the Plantation of Plimoth in New England,* published in London the next year. It was well titled, for it contained some truly remarkable things, especially Winslow's Preface and Epistle Dedicatory. Both were largely an attack upon Weston's men and their conduct at Wessagusset. They had made "Christ and Christianity stink in the nostrils of the poor infidels," he declared, forgetting that they at least had not treacherously killed any in cold blood. Weston's men had been driven out, it now appeared, because the Pilgrims disapproved of their "lives and manners amongst the Indians" and were resolved "not to foster them in their desired courses," for which Wituwamat was scarcely to blame. Winslow was also at pains to defend the optimistic reports sent home about New Plimoth. Only men of "discontented passions and humours," only those "with their mouths full of clamours," complained of having to drink water in New Canaan. How could anyone, he asked, be "so simple as to conceive that the fountains should stream forth wine or beer, and the woods and rivers be like butchers' shops and fishmongers' stalls, where they might have things taken to their hand?" How, indeed, unless perchance they had read his own effusions in Mourt's *Relation.*

And now another ship put in to give the Pilgrims a fright. It had on board Captain Robert Gorges, son of Sir Ferdinando, who had brought along a shipload of immigrants, a patent to a large tract of land just to the north, and a commission from the Council for New England "to be generall Governor of ye cuntrie." Bradford was to be deprived of office, though he was to serve temporarily as an assistant. Even more alarming than this, if possible, was the presence in the Captain's *entourage* of one William Morrell, a man of "fine classical taste." But that interested the Saints far less than the fact that he was wearing Anglican vestments and came armed with "authority of superintendencie" over all churches in New England. Here was the intervention that had long been feared. While at Plymouth, Gorges summoned Weston to answer certain charges against him, probably inspired by the Pilgrims, for they chiefly concerned "ye ille carriage of his men at ye Massachusetts." Weston's sharp tongue got him into trouble, but at the intercession of Bradford and others he was finally freed and sailed away in the *Swan,* giving them this quip "(behind their baks) for all their pains, That though they were yonge justices, yet they were good beggers." Going to Virginia, Weston became a member of the House of Burgesses in 1628, moved to Maryland and served in the Assembly there in 1642, soon returning to England where he died a few years later, at the port of Bristol. He may have been a "staff of reed" to the plantation, but there is nothing in Weston's earlier or later career to bear out the Pilgrims' more malicious comments about him.

Gorges and his party soon sailed north and occupied the abandoned town of Wessagusset. But the Captain "scarcely saluted ye
cuntrie in his Governmente," finding that the state of things in
the wilderness did not "answer to his quallitie & condition." With
him went some of the discontented at Plymouth, largely those
who had come "on their perticuler," and also Timothy Hatherly,
who had lost his house in a conflagration that for a time threatened to consume the town. Within a short time Wessagusset was
again abandoned, some of the settlers returning to England, others
moving to Virginia. With the former went the Reverend William
Morrell, who had spent his time composing a long Latin poem on
New England, being particularly impressed with its "ghusts of
wind." He had made no attempt to exercise his "superintendencie"
over the churches—perhaps, as Bradford said, because he "saw it
was in vaine." It was so much pleasanter to pursue tripping dactyls
in Latin verse than to go poking about a hornet's nest.

The year 1623 had been a bitter one, the most difficult of all
in many respects, but it ended with rejoicing. The crops had prospered, and for the first time the Pilgrims enjoyed a bountiful
harvest. They had mastered at last the art of growing corn. Then,
too, the new system of tillage had worked well. More acres had
been planted, and the "women now wente willingly into ye field
and took their litle-ones with them to set corne, . . . whom to have
compelled would have been thought great tiranie and oppression."[3] But the more pious attributed the fine crops mainly to
prayer.

Early in the summer a drought had set in and continued for
weeks, with not a drop of rain, till even the most sanguine lost
hope. Their corn and beans wilted on the stalk and turned brown.
In desperation the Saints appointed a "solemne day of humiliation." They assembled in the morning and prayed eight or nine
hours under a hot clear sky, and it seemed that the drought was
"as like to continue as ever it was." But the meeting had no sooner
adjourned, so Winslow reported, than clouds began to pile up on
the horizon and during the night—and for two weeks thereafter—
"distilled such softe, sweete, and moderate showers . . . as it was

hard to say whether our withered corne or drooping affections were most quickened and revived." Hobomok and other Indians had noted their preparations for the meeting, and as it was not the Sabbath, had inquired the reason for it. When they saw the results, they were most impressed. It showed them, said Winslow, "the differance between their conjurations and our invocation on the name of God for rain, theirs being mixed with such storms and tempests as sometimes, instead of doing them good, it layeth the corn flat on the ground to their prejudice, but ours in so gentle and seasonable a manner as they never observed the like." The Pilgrims promptly set aside another day to thank the Lord for his "mercies towards his Church and chosen ones."

Whatever the cause, "ye face of things was changed to ye rejoysing of ye harts of many." All had raised enough to carry them through till the next harvest. Some of the more industrious had corn and other produce to sell, and Plymouth never again knew "any general wante or famine." Many another colony had cracked up under far less strain and hardship. The always "answerable courage" of the Pilgrims had stood them in good stead. They were at last securely established in the wilderness, thanks to their own tireless efforts, for it is true, as Bradford declared, that the supplies brought on the *Fortune* and later ships never did more— and often did less—than provide for the needs of the additional settlers who came on these ships. It had been a terrific uphill struggle, often against apparently hopeless odds. It had been fraught with tragedy, marked by many slips and egregious blunders, but the battle had been won. The Pilgrims could now confidently "stand on their owne leggs," as Weston had so often gratuitously advised them.

17

UNSAVORIE
SALTE

I purposed before I came, to undergoe hardness, therefore I shall, I hope, cherfully bear
ye conditions of ye place, though very mean;
and they have chainged my wages ten times
allready.

—JOHN LYFORD

WITH THE APPROACH OF MARCH 25, 1624, WHICH ON THE PIL-
grim calendar was New Year's Day, the planters met for their
regular annual election of officers. Having nursed the infant colony through its painful teething period, Governor Bradford tried
to beg off, asking to be relieved of office, saying that "if it was any
honour or benefite, it was fitte others should be made pertakers
of it; if it was a burthen (as doubtles it was), it was but equall
that others should help bear it." The Pilgrims would not hear of
this, however, and finally persuaded him to continue by agreeing
to increase the number of assistant governors to five. Isaac Allerton
remained the first and chief of these. The records do not reveal

the names of the others, but Winslow and Standish were almost certainly chosen. The remaining two probably were Richard Warren and Stephen Hopkins. The five assistants and the governor made up the Council, which performed all functions of government, not only executive but legislative and judicial as well, with the governor having a "duble voyce" in all matters.*

A week or two later the *Charity* reappeared in the harbor, again under the command of Captain William Peirce, renowned as the "ferryman of the North Atlantic" because he brought across so many of New England's early settlers, later settling down himself at Boston. On board was Edward Winslow, returning from his visit to London with a few provisions, articles for the Indian trade, a quantity of hooks and nets and other fishing gear, a ship's carpenter, a saltmaker, the Reverend John Lyford, and "3 heifers & a bull, the first begining of any catle of that kind in ye land." In a letter to his brethren, Cushman apologized for not sending such "comfortable things as butter, sugar, &c." There was no money for that. Rather, all available funds had been spent to provide Plymouth with the means of establishing itself in the fishing, saltmaking, and boatbuilding trades. Once that were done, the planters could take care of themselves and be freed from dependence upon irregular and uncertain shipments of supply. Let them give the ship's carpenter "absolute command over his servants & such as are put to him," Cushman advised, suggesting the immediate construction of two ketches, a lighter, and six or seven shallops. Let others be assigned to work with the saltmaker, "a skillfull & industrious man," so that they might quickly learn the "misterie" of it.

And in heaven's name, Cushman added, let some discretion be used in writing letters home. Some pictured New Plimoth as a virtual paradise. On the other hand, "some say you are starved in body & soule; others, that you eate piggs & doggs that dye alone; others, that ye things here spoken of, ye goodnes of ye cuntry, &c., are gross and palpable lyes ... It is a miserie when ye whole state

* For the officers of Church and State at Plymouth, see Appendix B.

of a plantation shall be thus exposed to ye passionate humors of some discontented men."

Discontent, in truth, was rising to the boiling point both at Plymouth and in London. The adventurers were again bitterly quarreling among themselves, and one occasion it seemed that the company had broken up. But the treasurer, James Sherley, brought his partners together again at his goldsmith's shop on London Bridge and they had, he wrote Bradford, "ye loveingest and frendlyest meeting that ever I knew, and our greatest enemies offered to lend us £50. So I sent for a potle of wine (I would you could doe ye like), which we dranke freindly together. Thus God can turne ye harts of men when it pleaseth him."

But the conversion was short-lived, for some of the Strangers were filling the adventurers' ears with loud complaints that they were denied the sacraments at Plymouth, religious disputes were incessant, family duties were neglected on the Lord's Day, children were not taught their catechism and not even taught how to read, many in the colony were thieves and many more were incurably lazy, the water was unwholesome and the country barren, and the plantation was much annoyed by foxes, wolves, and mosquitoes. "These are the cheefe objections . . . made against you and countrie," wrote Sherley, always friendly to the Pilgrim leaders. "I pray you consider them and answer them by the first conveniencie."

Bradford was furious and drafted a spirited but somewhat disingenuous reply. There had never been any controversy or opposition about religion, "either publicke or private (to our knowledge)," he declared—and he might have added that it was a good thing no opposition had presumed to show its face, for the Saints demanded as strict uniformity of belief and observance as ever the Anglican bishops had under James or Elizabeth. The settlers did not enjoy the sacraments, Bradford acknowledged, but "the more is our greefe," he said, "that our pastor is kept from us, by whom we might injoye them, for we used to have the Lord's Supper every Saboth, and baptisme as often as there was occasion." Plymouth had "no commone school for want of a fitt person, or hithertoo means to maintaine one, though we desire now to begine"—the first was not established till more than a half century later. Meantime, most parents were at pains to teach their children what they could. To say that many of the settlers were lazy and shirked their work was "not wholy true, for though some doe it not willingly, & others not honestly, yet all doe it." There were thieves among them, of course, but if "London had been free from that crime, then we should not have been trobled with these here; it is well knowne sundrie have smarted well for it, and so are ye rest like to doe, if they be taken." But it was quite false to say that the country was barren and without grass. As for the quality of the water, "if they mean not so wholsome as ye good beere and wine in London (which they so dearly love), we will not dispute with them, but els, for water, it is as good as any in ye world (for ought we knowe)." And who were those that complained about the mosquitoes! "They are too delicate and unfitte to begine new plantations and collonies that cannot enduer the biting of a muskeeto," he concluded scornfully, and it would be well for "such to keepe at home till at least they be muskeeto-proofe."

Winslow had found among the adventurers a "strong faction" opposed to the Saints and "ye coming of ye rest from Leyden." News of this had reached the congregation at the Green Gate, where the deepest gloom prevailed. "Our hopes of coming unto you be small and weaker than ever," wrote Robinson. "The adventurers, it seems, have neither money nor any great mind of us, for ye most parte. They deny it to be any part of ye covenants betwixte us that they should transporte us; neither doe I looke for any further help from them till means come from you."

The adventurers, according to him, were split into three factions. Five or six could be relied upon. An equal number were their "bitter professed adversaries." As for the rest, though they were honest men and friendly enough, still they were Puritans and were naturally interested in promoting "forward" preachers of that school. "They of all others are unwilling I should be transported," Robinson was convinced, "as thinking if I come there, their market will be marred in many regards . . . Whether any larned man will come unto you or not, I know not; if any doe, you must *consiliu capere in arena.*"

As Robinson feared, a "larned" man had been sent in his stead, the Reverend John Lyford, a graduate of Magdalen College, Oxford, who arrived with his wife and five children. Now in his late forties, he had spent many years ministering to small parishes in England and Ireland. To conciliate the adventurers, Winslow and Cushman had raised no objections, seeing "no hurt in it but only his great charge of children," saying that Lyford impressed them as an "honest plaine man though none of ye most eminente and rare."

"About chusing him into office," wrote Cushman, "use your owne liberty & discretion; he knows he is no officer amongst you, though perhaps custome & universallitie may make him forget himselfe."

Lyford's coming pleased the Strangers, and it is plain that he also made a most favorable first impression upon the Saints. On coming ashore he bowed and scraped and "would have kissed their hands if they would have suffered him; yea, he wept & shed many tears, blessing God that had brought him to see their faces." From the way he carried on, said Bradford, he seemed to be "made all of love, and ye humblest person in the world." The Pilgrims gave him the best quarters in town, the largest food allowance, and a servant to tend his every need. As it was customary to ask Ruling Elder Brewster to sit with the Council on important matters, so now Lyford was invited to consult with them "in their waightiest bussinesses."

Within a week or two, which was most flattering, Lyford asked to be admitted to the church. He was so thankful, he said, "for this opportunitie of freedom & libertie to injoye ye ordinances of God in puritie among his people." At last he could purge himself of "many corruptions which had been a burthen to his conscience." Making a fulsome confession of faith, he acknowledged his "former disorderly walking," which, so far as the Saints knew, consisted of nothing more serious than his dereliction in being an Anglican clergyman. That was serious enough, but the church welcomed him, pleased to have made so distinguished a convert in such record time, and soon he was sharing the pulpit with William Brewster, "teaching" every Sabbath.

Within a short time, however, the Saints noted with increasing concern that all the malcontents in town, particularly those who had come on the *Anne* with John Oldham, were forming a group about Lyford. "Were they never so vile and profane," the minister would listen to their complaints and encourage them. Everywhere there were "private meetings and whisperings among them." A birth in the family of young William Hilton, of the *Fortune* group, precipitated a crisis. As the Hiltons were Anglicans, their child could not be baptized at Plymouth—at least not until the parents joined the Pilgrim church, which they were not disposed to do. In desperation they appealed to Lyford, who arranged a private baptism, "signing the babe with a sign of the Cross on the forehead." There was an immediate outcry. The hated Sign of the Cross at Plymouth! And made by their own pastor at that, the "dissembling Ishmaell!" But the Saints, however outraged, were not yet ready to move against him.

After a fishing voyage to the north, the *Charity* was again at Plymouth, preparing to return home, and it was reported by some prying brother that Lyford was spending a lot of time at his desk writing letters. Others observed that when he met his intimates, there was much whispering and nodding of heads. Every now and again he dropped a remark that made them "laugh in their sleeves." This laughter was ill-advised, as it usually was at Plymouth.

The *Charity* weighed anchor late one afternoon, and that night Governor Bradford secretly pushed off in a shallop and overtook the ship far out in the bay, beyond sight of Plymouth. A search of the passengers and crew brought to light many letters written by Lyford, more than twenty in all, "full of slanders & false accusations, tending not only to their prejudice, but to their ruine &

utter subversion." Bradford also found several written by Oldham. Though the latter was "so bad a scribe that his hand was scarce legible," Bradford and his men patiently made copies of all the letters, retaining the originals of several so that evidence in the culprits' own hand might be produced against them in case they attempted a denial.

When Lyford and his party learned of Bradford's mysterious journey during the night, they were "somewhat blanke at it." But when nothing happened for several weeks, they assumed that Bradford had merely gone to dispatch some letters of importance, and soon the malcontents were "as briske as ever, thinking nothing had been knowne." This, too, was ill-advised, for they greatly underestimated the guile of the Saints, who were merely letting "things ripen, that they might ye better discover their intents and see who were their adherents." Open conflict was not long delayed. Called to stand watch in his turn, Oldham refused and quarreled with Standish.

"Rascal! beggarly rascal!" he shouted, drawing his knife on the Captain. Hearing the tumult, Bradford ran out and tried to restore the peace, without avail, for Oldham "ramped more like a furious beast than a man, and cald them all treatours, and rebells, and other such foule language." Hustled to the Fort, he was clapped in chains and left there "till he came to himselfe." This merely provoked more determined resistance. In throwing down the gauntlet, the opposition could scarcely have chosen any issue better calculated to rouse the Saints to full fury. For Lyford and his adherents, "without ever speaking one word either to ye Governor, Church, or Elder, withdrewe themselves"—quite as if they were Separatists themselves—"& set up a publick meeting aparte, on ye Lord's day!"

The Saints had had enough of such "insolente cariages." If they were "to prevente further mischeefe," it was high time to call these "Hedghoggs" to book. Lyford and Oldham were summoned to stand trial for "plotting against them and disturbing their peace, both in respecte of their civill & church state, which was most injurious, for both they and all ye world knew they came hither to injoye ye libertie of conscience and ye free use of God's ordinances."

All of Plymouth attended the trial. At the head of several military companies under arms, Captain Standish, sword in hand, escorted the prisoners up the street and into the Fort, past the bleaching skull of Wituwamat grinning at them from a corner of the battlements, a grim reminder of the stern code of Pilgrim justice. Inside, the gloom was broken only by a few narrow shafts of light from the loopholes, and the chill silence of the one large room was accentuated by the heavy tramp-tramp-tramp of the sentry pacing his rounds overhead.

Seated at a large table with his assistants on either side of him, Governor Bradford at length rose and read the indictment against the minister and his accomplice. They had complained that the church did its best to prevent any but Separatists from coming to Plymouth. That was false. They welcomed any honest men who were willing to "carry themselves peacably and seek ye commone good, or at least doe them no hurte." Strangers were not denied the consolations of religion; they were "free" to attend the Pilgrim church as often as they wished. Oldham had pretended that the Pilgrim leaders were trying to ruin those who had come "on their perticuler." That was not so; the Council had merely stopped their traffic in "stolne goods." They claimed to have noted "exseeding great waste of tools & vesseles." The most they could have seen was an "old hogshed or two fallen to peeces, and a broken hoe or two left carlesly in ye feilds by some." Nor was it true that there had been unjust distribution of supplies so that some men received sixteen pounds of meal a week while others received only four, leading Lyford to the sarcasm, "it seems some men's mouths and bellies are very little & slender over others." There had been some inequality in allowances as a result of the bargain struck with those who came on the *Anne,* Bradford explained, but that was only temporary. Besides, who was Lyford to complain? Had not he and his family always had the highest allowance?

Neither of the accused seemed to take the proceedings very seriously. Both were "stiffe & stood resolutly upon ye deneyall of most things, and required proofe." With his fine sense of dramatic situation, Bradford must have rather enjoyed the scene as he produced the copies of the letters he had made on the *Charity* and began to read them aloud. The dominant clique at Plymouth, so Lyford informed his friends among the adventurers, carried everything with a high hand and "matched the Jesuits for policie." There was only one way to break their hold on the colony— overwhelm them by sheer numbers. As many non-Separatists as possible should be sent over with the clear understanding that they were to have "voyces in all courts & elections, and be free to bear any office." Quite as important, "ye Leyden company (Mr. Robinson & ye rest) must be kepte back, or els all will be spoyled." And the hair on at least one head must have stood straight up when Bradford came to this passage:

"If that Capten you spoake of should come hither as a generall, I am persuaded he would be chosen Capten, for this Captaine Standish looks like a silly boy, and is in utter contempte."

Lyford was struck dumb by this undeniable evidence of his perfidy, but not Oldham. "A mad Jack in his mood," as even friends admitted, he stormed at Bradford and his assistants for daring to intercept and open his letters, "threatening them in very high language," trying in the boldest manner to raise the town against them, finally raising the standard of open revolt.

"My masters," he cried, turning to the assembly, "where is your harts? Now show your courage. You have oft complained to me of this and that. Now is the time if you will do anything! I will stand by you."

Not a man moved, not a voice was raised in the tense hushed room until Lyford, suddenly bursting into tears, began to wail that John Billington and others had deceived him with their constant complaints. He now saw that everything he had written was "false and nought, both for matter & manner." He had traduced and vilified men who had treated him with every kindness, and he feared that he could never make amends for the wrongs he had done them, moaning that he was a "reprobate, . . . unsavorie salte, &c."

The Council agreed and ordered both men to leave Plymouth, a drastic punishment on the wild frontier. Still scornful and defiant, Oldham was commanded to get out immediately though his wife and children, if they wished, might stay until he could "remove them comfortably." Going north some thirty miles, Oldham established a settlement at Nantasket, now the town of Hull, on the lower shore of Boston Bay. With him went a number of the discontented, including several persons of note. One was Roger Conant, salter of London, who had arrived about a year before, perhaps coming with Weston on his unwelcome visit. Now in his early thirties and by all accounts a "pious, sober, and prudent gentleman," Conant later founded Salem and subsequently made a name for himself in the Massachusetts colony. The William Hiltons journeyed even farther north, joining David Thompson, a Scottish trader, who had established himself at the mouth of the Piscataqua River, on the outskirts of the present city of Portsmouth, New Hampshire. Hilton and his brother Edward, fishmonger of London, later founded the now busy city of Dover, about fifteen miles up the river, and were prominent in the early history of New Hampshire.

Because he was so shamefaced and contrite, Lyford was granted six months' grace with the thought that his sentence might be lifted "if he caried himselfe well in the meane time, and his repentance proved sound." It seemed to be genuine enough, especially after he had repeated it by confessing "his sin publikly in ye church, with tears more largely than before." Like Lucifer, he had fallen from "pride, vaineglorie, & self love," he said, and it would be only just if God made him a "vacabund in ye earth, as was Caine." Deacon Samuel Fuller and "other tender-harted men" were so touched that they went down on their knees to beg his forgiveness, which was granted. Such good thoughts were conceived of him again that he was soon admitted "to teach amongst them as before."

What was their consternation to discover only a month or two

later—"a rarer president can scarse be showne"—that he was
again at the business of writing letters! Pouring out his woes to
the adventurers, he admitted that his previous letters had been
somewhat indiscreet. But "take notice of this," he said, "that I have
written nothing but what is certainly true, and I could make so
appeare plainly to any indifferente men, whatsoever colours be
cast to darken ye truth." And there were some at Plymouth "very
audatious that way." He would have returned to England long ago
if he had not had such regard for the adventurers' interests. He
had expected to endure hardships in the New World but nothing
quite so "mean" as the conditions at Plymouth. "They have
chainged my wages ten times allready." Signing himself "John
Lyford, Exille," he notified his friends that he did not intend to
remain unless he received "better incouragemente from you than
from ye church (as they call themselves) here." The truth was,
of course, that they had no proper church, and no ministry "but
such as may be performed by any of you, . . . whatsoever great
pretences they make, for herein they equivocate as in many other
things they doe."

Pains were taken to intercept this letter, and again Lyford was
on the carpet. What did he mean by belittling the church at Plymouth? "Our Reverend Elder hath laboured diligently in dispencing
the word of God unto us, . . . and be it spoaken without osten-
tation, he is not inferrirour to Mr. Lyford (& some of his betters)
either in gifts or lerning." And what was this nonsense about
wages? They had "never agreed with him for any wages, nor made
any bargen at all with him." The last straw was added at this
point when Lyford's wife, "a grave matron," came to one of the
deacons and complained that her husband "had wronged her"
before marriage. And afterwards, the poor woman sighed, she
could keep no maids because he "would be medling with them."
On occasion she had taken him "in ye manner as they lay at their
bed's feete, with shuch other circumstances," said Bradford, "as I
am ashamed to relate."

The Lyfords were ordered out, but they were still at Plymouth
several months later when John Oldham boldly reappeared, which

he had been forbidden to do. There was an immediate clash. Attempts to quiet him were only "oyle to ye fire." He was again locked up in the Fort "till he was tamer." Standish then marched him to the beach where two lines of soldiers were drawn up to receive him. As Oldham passed between them, each gave him a "bob upon the bumme," a good sound "thump on ye brich," with the butt end of his musket, and with that they tossed Oldham into a waiting shallop and bade him "goe & mende his manners." This and the fairness of the trial so impressed most of the Strangers, according to Bradford, that many now asked to join the church and became Saints, "which was looked at as a great worke of God."

The pariahs gathered at Nantasket, but the Pilgrims had not yet seen the last of them. Winslow had brought over a patent to a small tract on Cape Ann, in the vicinity of the present city of Gloucester, about sixty miles to the north. The Pilgrims planned to establish a fishing station there and in the spring of 1624 sent a party to explore the possibilities. A rough wharf, or stage, was erected at a convenient spot, but their catch that season was poor, for the captain of their vessel did nothing "but drink, & gusle, and consume away ye time & his victails."

On the Pilgrims' return in the spring of 1625, who should they find in possession of their stage but Lyford, Oldham, and company! The latter had moved up from Nantasket at the invitation of one of the Saints' critics among the adventurers, the Reverend John White, founder of the Dorchester Company and later identified with the Massachusetts colony. Roger Conant was superintendent of the settlement, with Lyford as pastor and Oldham as overseer of trade. In characteristic manner Captain Standish demanded the surrender of the stage "very peremptorily." Those on the wharf rolled up hogsheads as a barricade and laughed at him, claiming the Pilgrim patent was worthless, as it was.[1] Standish almost exploded with rage and, as an early chronicler remarked, there would certainly have been blows, if not blood and slaughter, had not Roger Conant and Captain William Peirce intervened. They finally arranged a compromise under which the Pilgrims abandoned their fishing stage and were assisted to build another.

The Pilgrims did their best to make a success of the venture. From Plymouth they sent the "skillfull & industrious" saltmaker brought over by Winslow to provide the colony with the means of curing fish. He was industrious enough but had never produced any salt, proving to be an "ignorante, foolish, selfwilld fellow," making a "grat misterie" of his business. He had first insisted upon building a warehouse and for a year kept eight or ten men busy digging holes that would not hold water. Here at Cape Ann he set up his pans with a great flourish and had another warehouse built. By the end of the summer he had burned it down, destroying his pans in the process, "and this was ye end of that chargable bussines." Fishing was "always a thing fatal to them," as Bradford said, and the season was so unprofitable that the Pilgrims never returned, abandoning Cape Ann to their rivals.

The latter did not long use the Pilgrim fishing stage. The next year, led by Conant, they moved back down the coast some fifteen miles and began building the town of Salem, first known as Naumkeag. Oldham became a prosperous trader and soon made his peace with the Pilgrims, being granted "libertie to go and come, and converse with them, at his pleasure." But the Saints never forgave Lyford. The unhappy Episcopal "exille" occupied the pulpit at Naumkeag for several years, until the arrival of Endecott's Puritans in 1628, when he departed for the more congenial atmosphere of Virginia, dying there a year or two later. As of Weston, so of Lyford and Oldham it should be noted that there is nothing in their earlier or later careers to bear out the slanders heaped upon them by the Saints.

It is a harsh thing to say of the Pilgrims, but there is some truth in the charge of an enemy who had felt the weight of their hand and the edge of their tongue, that the "first precept in their Politiques is to defame the man at whome they aime, and then he is a holy Israelite in their opinions who can spread that fame brodest, like butter upon a loafe. No matter how thin, it will serve as a vaile, and then this man (whom they have thus depraved) is a spotted uncleane leper; he must out lest he pollute the Land, and them that are cleane."

18

THE UNDERTAKERS

The Pilgrim saddle is always on the Bay horse.
—*Old folk-saying*

THE LYFORD-OLDHAM AFFAIR, WHATEVER SATISFACTIONS IT offered the Saints, had devastating consequences. When word of it reached the merchant adventurers, the company "broake in peeces." Winslow had been sent across to explain, but to no avail. Most of the adventurers washed their hands of the business, and even the friendliest were exasperated. It had been their hope, they said, to settle the colony comfortably and make a little money for themselves, or at least recoup some of their heavy losses. That now seemed to be quite impossible.

"The slothfulnes of one part of you and the weaknes of the other part is such that nothing can well go forward," wrote Sherley

in a letter signed also by William Collier, subsequently a Pilgrim
Father himself, and by their old friend of Leyden days, Thomas
Brewer, shortly to go to jail for the rest of his days, spending
fourteen years in King's Bench Prison for being a "Perfect Brownist." They did not credit all of the tales that came from Plymouth,
they said. Yet surely something was amiss in light of the charges
brought against the leaders there "not without some colour of
truth."

"You are (as they affirm) Brownists, condemning all other
churches and persons but yourselves and those in your way, and
you are contentious, cruel, and hard-hearted among your neighbors
and towards such as in all points, both civil and religious, jump
not with you." The Saints had deceived both the King and the
merchant adventurers in pretending that their doctrines and practices were those of the French Reformed church. They were reported to be "negligent, careless, wasteful, and unthrifty." They
allowed affairs "to go at sixes and sevens," and spent their time
"in idleness and talking and conferring, and care not what be
wasted, worn, and torn out." In a final withering comment Sherley
and his colleagues expressed a fear that they might be sinning
"against God in building up such a people."

Even so, it might still be possible, they said, to save "your lives
& our monies." But they would undertake to go on only upon
certain conditions. First, they were to have a direct voice in governing the colony, a right granted the adventurers by the patent.
Second, the French discipline was to be strictly followed, "to take
away ye scandallous name of Brownists, and other church differences." Third, Robinson and his people were not to come to
Plymouth "unless he and they will reconcile themselves to our
church by a recantation under their own hands."

Not knowing what to do, Bradford and his council simply
ignored these demands though they heatedly denied that they had
dissembled with His Majesty and the adventurers about their
religious tenets, protesting that they did follow the French discipline—at least "in effecte & substance." To demand that they
follow it "in every circumstance" would be insufferable insolence

and tyranny. "The French may erre, we may erre, and other churches may erre, and . . . it is too great arrogancie for any man or any church to thinke that he or they have so sounded ye word of God to ye bottome as precislie to sett down ye church's discipline . . . so that no other without blame may digress or differ in anything from ye same"—a profound truth never more eloquently expressed, though Plymouth did not practice it for generations. The battle for religious tolerance and freedom was won elsewhere.

More galling than these demands were the pious lectures the adventurers read the Saints on how to conduct themselves and bring up their children. "Walk close with God," they admonished them. They should live together in love "without secret whisperings and undermining one of another, and without contempt or neglect of such as are weak and helpless. . . . Freely and readily entertaine any honest men into your church, estate, and society, . . . taking heed of too great straitness and singularity." Above all, let them have an eye to their children to see that they were properly instructed "in the knowledge and fear of God, restraining them from idleness and profanation of the Sabbath!" It was, said Bradford, a "longe & tedious" letter.

In the end, largely through Cushman's untiring efforts, a handful of the adventurers—Sherley, Collier, Timothy Hatherly, and a few more—agreed to carry on if the joint stock arrangement were continued. The goods in the common store, they warned the planters, were not to be "dispersed or imbeseled away for any private ends or intents whatsoever." The settlers should first make provision for their own immediate needs. Once that were done, they should collect all the valuable goods they could find and ship them to England to pay off their debts. These now amounted to £1,400 ($70,000), which to the penniless Pilgrims must have seemed an almost astronomical sum.

"Goe on, good freinds," wrote the adventurers from their easy chairs in London, "pluck up your spirits and quitte yourselves like men in all your difficulties." The work the planters had in hand was so much to the glory of God and the honor of His Majesty that a man might more happily devote his life to it than live as long as "Mathusala in wasting ye plentie of a tilled land, or eating ye fruite of a growne tree."

It was not a difficult decision for the Pilgrims to make. They had no choice but to go on. Nor had they much choice in the matter of buying at simply exorbitant rates the cattle, cloth, shoes, stockings, and other supplies sent on the *Charity*. These were not for the common store. Rather, they were to be sold for the profit of Sherley and his partners, who appointed Allerton and Winslow as their agents. The goods, though none of the best, had been marked up seventy per cent for profit and risk outward and home-ward bound, "a thing thought unreasonable by some and too great an oppression upon ye poore people," but there was no help for it. Necessity compelled them to buy. Perhaps to ease his conscience, or it may have been simply a token of good will, Sherley sent Bradford a cheese and presented the plantation with a heifer "to begin a stock for the poor."

Stowed with fish, the *Charity* was now ready to set sail with the *Little James,* a constant source of trouble since the day she first put in with her many fancy trimmings, with flags and pennons flying. At the time some of the Saints had remarked that the pinnace was rather too "bravely set out," expressing their fear that the adventurers "did over-pride themselves in her." The crew had been mutinous from the start. Sent to fish Maine waters, she had piled up on the rocks there and gone to the bottom, drowning the skipper. She had since been raised with the aid of English fishermen and was now loaded with cod and all of the Pilgrims' beaver, valued at £277, enough to pay a large part of their debts. Captain Peirce of the *Charity* wished to load the furs on his larger vessel, but Winslow objected, for he was under bond to send them on the *Little James.* With the latter vessel in tow, the *Charity* departed and had an uneventful voyage until deep in the English Channel where the ships ran into a gale which forced the skipper to cut the pinnace loose. Pirates prowling north from the Barbary coast immediately pounced on the *Little James* and sailed her away to Sali (Sallee), Morocco, where the Pilgrim furs brought the pirates 4d. apiece. All on board were auctioned off on the slave block. Captain Standish, bound for England on an important mission, happened not to suffer that unkind fate only because he had decided at the last moment not to keep watch over the furs on the *Little James,* as arranged, but to go in greater comfort on the *Charity.*

"Thus was all their hops dasht, and the joyfull news they ment to carry home turned to heavie tidings." Nothing more was ever heard of the *Little James,* her passengers or cargo, to the great loss of the Pilgrims and the adventurers alike, although there was not much sympathy at Plymouth for the latter. "Some thought this a hand of God for their too great exaction of ye poore plantation, but God's judgments are unseerchable," Bradford hastily added, "neither dare I be bould therwith; but however it shows us ye uncertainty of all humane things. . . ."

Standish had been chosen to go to London "for sundrie reasons." The chief probably was the fact that he was not one of the Saints now in such disfavor. It may have occurred to some that the Captain's sense of diplomacy perhaps left something to be desired—that it would never do if he were to bring back the head of some "impertinent" adventurer to place on a spike beside Wituwamat's. Still, they evidently felt that he could do no worse than Winslow, who on his last visit had stirred up a great row about the Lyford business. Standish had been insistently warned not to alienate the few remaining adventurers. He was to make it plain nevertheless that the planters wanted better goods at cheaper prices, for they could never "bear such high interest or allow so much per cent." He was to urge the Council for New England to take some action against the unfriendly adventurers who had forsaken the planters but still kept them bound by the articles of agreement. They should be made to "come to some faire end by dividente or composition," and they should be forbidden to encroach upon the colony's rights as they had at Cape Ann.

"We will never build houses, fence grounds, or plant fruits for those who not only forsake us but use us as enemies, lading us with reproach and contumely," Bradford confidentially informed Cushman. "Nay, we will rather ruine that which is done than that they should possess it." In the same letter Bradford thanked Cushman for the spices he had sent and warned him to be on the lookout for Oldham, reported to have sailed for England. "Beware of him, for he is very malicious, and much threatens you. . . . Billington still rails against you, and threatens to arrest you, I know not wherefore; he is a knave, and so will live and die. . . . Your son and all of us are in good health (blessed be God). He received the things you sent him. I hope God will make him a good man." He did, for young Thomas Cushman eventually succeeded Brewster as ruling elder.

In London, where he remained several months, Standish accomplished very little. Plague was raging in the city, all with means had fled into the country, and it was practically impossible to transact any business. But "with much adoe" he managed to borrow £150—at fifty per cent!—and "spent a good deal of it in expences," said Bradford, who was inclined to be critical of the Captain's judgment in business affairs, remarking that in such matters he had the "least skill."

Standish returned, by way of Maine, brimming with news. And all of it was bad. Sherley and his partners were on the edge of bankruptcy from the loss of the *Little James* and other reverses. James I was dead, and nothing could be expected from Prince Charles whose policy in church and state would undoubtedly be based upon even higher doctrine than his father's. Of more immediate and grievous concern, the Pilgrims had lost "their right hand with their freinds ye adventurers," good Deacon Cushman, "ye stay & life of ye whole bussines," struck down by the plague. This was a heavy blow, but Standish had worse to report:

John Robinson was dead!

In all the troubled career of the Saints nothing ever quite so stunned them. Their darkest hours had been lighted by the hope that their beloved pastor would soon join them and they might again sit at his feet and be comforted as they had been with such content at Leyden. His eloquent letters with their serene faith, their clear-eyed grasp of fundamentals, their warm quick sympathy and understanding, had given them heart to go on when they were on the brink of despair, when all things seemed to be united in a conspiracy to overwhelm them. Now he was gone when not yet fifty, when at the very height of his powers, carried off by a "continuall inwarde ague." Taken sick on a Saturday, he had insisted upon preaching twice the next day, reluctant to disappoint his brethren. "The physick he tooke wrought kindly in man's judgmente, but he grew weaker every day," dying a week later, "feeling litle or no paine and sensible to ye very last," departing "this vaell of tears" on March 1, 1625. Four days later the greatest of the Saints, one of the great men of the age, was buried with simple ceremony under the pavement in the main aisle of the Pieterskerk, the immense stone cathedral that loomed so high above the Green Gate, quite overshadowing the humble meeting house just across Bell Alley where an always "loving & faithfull" pastor had lived and laboured for so long.

"And if either prayers, tears, or means would have saved his life," came the anguished cry from Leyden, "he had not gone hence." The grief of the Saints at Plymouth was as great. "Though they had esteemed him highly whilst he lived & laboured amongst them, yet more after his death when they came to feele ye wante of his help, and saw (by woefull experience) what a treasure they had lost to ye greefe of their harts and wounding of their sowls," wrote Bradford in a moving tribute. "Yea, such was ye mutuall love & reciprocall respecte that this worthy man had to his flocke, and his flocke to him, that it might be said of them, as it once was of that famous Emperour Marcus Aurelious and ye people of Rome, that it was hard to judge wheather he delighted more in haveing shuch a people, or they in haveing such a pastor."

It was a marvel, said the Pilgrims, that all their woes and troubles did not entirely "sinck them." But they gathered up their spirits and were so helped by the Lord, "whose worke they had in hand, as now when they were at their lowest, they begane to rise againe." As corn was the staple of their diet and the common medium of exchange, they diligently cultivated their fields and in off seasons extended their operations in the fur trade, pushing ever farther afield, usually by sea. The ship's carpenter sent with Lyford

had completed two shallops and a lighter, the first vessels built
in a region later famed throughout the world for its strong trim
craft, and he was working on two large ketches when he died of
a fever. Recalling that they had an "ingenious man that was a
house carpenter," the Pilgrims faced him with the problem of providing them with a sizeable vessel. The latter took a shallop, cut
it in two, lengthened it six or seven feet, put in a new waist, laid
on a deck, and fitted it up into a "comfortable" vessel, though the
master and his crew had to stand out at all times no matter how
rough and bitter the weather.

This vessel was badly needed, for competition in the corn and
beaver trade was increasing. Scattered settlements were now beginning to appear along the coast. Eager to enter the fur trade, they
"wente & filld ye Indeans with corne and beat down the prise,"
offering twice what the Pilgrims ever had, as the latter complained,
and "undertraded in other commodities allso." As a consequence,
the Pilgrims had to carry that much more corn to make a profitable
voyage. Hearing that a fishing station on Monhegan Island was
breaking up, a party was sent under Winslow to see what bargains
might be found there. The Pilgrims traded corn for trucking stuff
valued at £400 and from the wreck of a French ship obtained other
goods—chiefly Biscay rugs. This stuff in turn was traded to the
Indians, and the party returned with much beaver and a "parcell
of goats" picked up at Monhegan.

By hard and dangerous work, the Pilgrims had collected enough
peltry to pay off the money borrowed by Standish and a few scattered debts. They sent the furs to London by Isaac Allerton, now
Brewster's son-in-law, who had just recently married Fear, the
ruling elder's youngest daughter, a girl of twenty, bringing her
three children by his first marriage. Allerton was carrying a commission formally made out "under their hands & seals" to represent
the Pilgrims in all their business dealings with the adventurers,
a sensible plan designed to concentrate the management of business affairs in the hands of one man. But like all of the Pilgrims'
sensible plans, it went awry and ended in disaster. Allerton's first
duty was to persuade the adventurers to come to some under-

standing with the planters on the rights and claims of each. If he could manage to do so at a reasonable interest rate, he was to borrow £100—and not a penny more! If any of the Pilgrims had been endowed with second sight, they might have discerned trouble ahead. Allerton did as he pleased and borrowed £200—at thirty per cent. But he brought home a formidable legal document which cleared up many of the uncertainties that had long worried the planters.

In this document, signed by forty-two of them in all, the merchant adventurers agreed to surrender all their rights in the colony and free the planters of debt for a sum of £1,800 ($90,000), to be paid in nine annual instalments of £200. As the adventurers had now laid out some £7,000, this represented a considerable loss to them. But the Pilgrims' offer was a fair and reasonable one, according to that experienced colonial promoter, Captain John Smith, who pointed out that the First Virginia Company had sunk £200,000 ($10,000,000) in that colony without receiving so much as a sixpence in return.

Still, the £1,800 "bargen," however small it may have seemed to the adventurers, was large enough to give the Pilgrims pause. They were at once so poor and so few. The settlement had not grown since the arrival of the *Charity* and the *Little James* in 1624 when the population numbered about 180 persons, young and old. Plymouth now had thirty-two houses, but it was not properly a town, scarcely a village, wholly dependent upon a meager corn crop and an erratic fur trade. The purchase price amounted to £100 ($5,000) for every man, woman, and child in the colony. It was a great risk, obviously, but they signed the agreement "fairly ingrossed in partchmente," and seven or eight of the leaders undertook to guarantee payment in behalf of the rest.

At last the planters "owned" Plymouth—subject to the mortgage, of course. And now what was to be done? How were the "stocks, shares, lands, marchandise, and chatles" to be distributed? For a time Bradford and his council toyed with the idea of excluding the "untowarde persons mixed amongst them from the first"—in other words, many of the Strangers who had come on the *Mayflower* and later ships. This would have touched off a terrific explosion, but wiser counsel finally prevailed. As all had borne the hardship and toil of building Plymouth, all should share equally in the division—at least all "of abillity, and free, and able to governe themselvs with meete descretion." Indentured servants were to receive nothing but what their masters were disposed to give them or what "their deservings should obtaine from ye company afterwards."

Trade and commerce, as formerly, were to be conducted for the joint account to help pay the debts. All else was to be divided. Each family was to receive as many shares as it had members, including men, women, children, and servants. Each man retained the house and garden allotted to him along the street, but those who obtained the better houses were to compensate those who fell heir to the worse. An exception was made for Governor Bradford and four or five "speciall" men—Brewster, Standish, Winslow, and Allerton, it would seem—who were presented with their houses and gardens in recognition of the many services they had performed without salary. The livestock was rounded up, appraised "for age & goodnes," divided into equal units, and assigned by lot. A unit consisted of several swine, a cow, and two goats for every thirteen persons. Next, the clearings on both sides of Town Brook were divided into farms or "great lots" of twenty acres each, and these were assigned by lot. As some lay relatively far from town, those with farms close by agreed to allow others to share their fields for four years. Considerable farm land was reserved to provide for future settlers. No meadows were assigned at this time, for Plymouth had few good pastures and hay fields.

Shares carried obligations as well as rights. Assessments could be levied against them to help pay the mortgage and other debts. But all of the shareholders—or "purchasers"—were well pleased with the exception of Bradford, Allerton, and the others who had signed the mortgage and were responsible both collectively and individually for its payment. Under the circumstances it seemed only fair to them that they be granted exclusive direction and control of the money-raising enterprises of the colony. Besides, they hoped thus to secure means to bring over the rest of the congregation at Leyden. But this, like so much else at Plymouth, was kept secret, for Bradford and his colleagues well knew that most of the Purchasers did not care a straw whether any more of the Saints came or not, and they feared that the shareholders might violently object to laying out money for such a purpose.

To accomplish these ends, a scheme was soon born, probably Allerton's brain child, and "after some agitation of the thing" it was adopted in 1627. A monopoly in the colony's trade was granted to Bradford, Allerton, and Standish, who were given the right to choose whomsoever they wished to become partners—or "undertakers"—with them. The Undertakers were empowered to do what they liked with all the furs, corn, beads, hatchets, knives, and other "trucking stuffe" in the common store. They alone were to use the colony's trading posts and boats. Every year each Purchaser was to pay them three bushels of corn or six pounds of tobacco, whichever was stipulated. In return for such sweeping privileges, the Undertakers were to pay all of the colony's debts, both the money owed the adventurers and other scattered debts, amounting to £600. In addition, they agreed to supply Plymouth each year with £50 worth of shoes and hose, to be traded for corn at six shillings a bushel. The arrangement was to continue for six years, at which time all rights and privileges were to revert to the Purchasers, twenty-seven of whom signed the contract. Among the signers were such "old standards" as Stephen Hopkins, Edward Dotey (now a freeman), Deacon Samuel Fuller, Peter Browne, Francis Cooke, Francis Eaton, Cuthbert Cuthbertson, William Bassett, and John Billington.

As partners the three Undertakers chose William Brewster, Edward Winslow, John Alden, John Howland, and Thomas Prence. All went energetically to work in an effort to promote trade in every possible way. From the fact that the contract ran only for six years, which meant that they hoped to pay the nine instalments on the mortgage within that time, it is evident that the Undertakers were in an optimistic mood. Pushing far to the north, they established a trading post along the Kennebec, on the present site of Augusta, Maine.[1] With John Howland in charge, a brisk trade for beaver, otter, and other furs was carried on here with the Abnaki Indians in exchange for "coats, shirts, ruggs, & blankets, biskett, pease, prunes, &c."

At the same time the Pilgrims pushed their trade to the south and west by means of another trading post built twenty miles to the south on the outer shore of Cape Cod, at Aptuxcet, now the village of Bourne, almost on the spot where "grave" Canacum of the Manomet had so hospitably received the Pilgrims and been hounded to death for his pains. Here the Cape was almost cut from the mainland by the Scusset River on the near side and the Manomet River flowing westerly into Buzzards Bay. Both were navigable by small craft, and as there was short easy portage between, the Pilgrims used this route—now that of the Cape Cod Canal[2]—to avoid the long dangerous voyage around the Cape. Here on the banks of the Manomet, just above Buzzards Bay, they built a stout trading post of hewn oak timbers and kept two agents there winter and summer. They also built a pinnace and kept it at the post, using it to push their trade and explorations along the southern New England coast into Long Island Sound. It was by way of Aptuxcet that relations were established with the Dutch at New Amsterdam.

A letter arrived from Governor Peter Minuit, written in Dutch, addressed to the "Noble, Worshipful, Wise, and Prudent Lords, the Governor and Councillors in New Plymouth, our very Good friends," wishing their "Lordships, worshipful, wise, and prudent, happiness in Jesus Christ our Lord, with prosperity and health, in soul and body. Amen." Bradford quoted this much of the letter and remarked that he would translate the rest into English, "leaving out the repitition of superfluous titles."

Speaking through Isaac de Rasieres, secretary and chief trader at Fort Amsterdam in "ye Manhatas," Minuit congratulated the Pilgrims on their "prosperous and praiseworthy undertakeings," offered to be of service "in all frendly-kindnes & neighbourhood," and inquired if Plymouth had any beaver or other articles to sell, saying that his agents were willing to pay "ready money" for them. The reply of Bradford and his council was as "freindly tender." They recalled how they had lived in Holland for many years "with freedome and good contente," as some of their brethren still did, and they and their children would "never forgett ye same." At the moment they had everything they needed, they said, "both for cloathing and others things; but hereafter it is like we shall deal with you, if your rates be reasonable." What did the Dutch pay for beaver by the pound, and otters by the skin, they asked, and "what other commodities from us may be acceptable unto you, as tobaco, fish, corne, or other things, and what prises you will give?" But the New Netherlands Company, they gave warning, was not to trade with the Indians "in this bay, and river of Narragansett and Sowams, which is, as it were, at our doors."

Some months later the bark *Nassau,* coming from the Hudson, dropped anchor at Aptuxcet, and De Rasieres came ashore "accompanied with a noyse of trumpeters" and many attendants. Hearing that it was a twenty-mile walk to Plymouth, the portly burgher wrote Bradford to ask him to provide some easier means of transportation. He had not walked so far "this three or four years," he said, "whereof I fear my feet will fail me." A shallop was sent for him and brought him comfortably to the pier just inside the mouth of Town Brook. The Pilgrims found the *Opper Koopman* (chief trader) of the Dutch a "man of fair and genteel behavior," and he for his part was quite impressed with Plymouth and its somewhat curious ways, its manner of worship, its fish traps and eel pots, the use of herring to manure the stony fields, the broad Street about a cannon shot long, and their "stringent laws and ordinances upon the subject of fornication and adultery, which laws they maintain and enforce very strictly indeed, even among the tribes which live amongst them."

"Their houses are constructed of hewn planks," he noted, "with gardens also enclosed behind and at the sides with hewn planks, so that their houses and court-yards are arranged in very good order, with a stockade against a sudden attack, and at the end of the streets there are three wooden gates. In the center, on the cross street, stands the Governor's house, before which is a square en- closure, upon which four patereros are mounted, so as to flank along the streets. . . . Their farms are not as good as ours because they are more stony and consequently not so suitable for the plough. They apportion their land according as each has means to contribute to the 18,000 guilders which they have promised to those who sent them out, whereby they have their freedom without rendering an account to any one. . . . They have better means of living than ourselves because they have the fish so abundant before their doors."

De Rasieres had brought with him some fine Holland clothes, linen, and a chest filled with white sugar, for which the Pilgrims gave tobacco; this was the beginning of a prosperous trade that continued for some years until destroyed by competition from Virginia tobacco planters. De Rasieres also offered the Pilgrims some "sewan," or wampum, saying that it was in great demand among the tribes along the Hudson and undoubtedly would be so in New England. But the Pilgrims were skeptical, especially when the Dutch asked 5s. ($12.50) a fathom for these strings of white and purple beads. Fashioned of periwinkle and quahog shells, they seemed merely to serve a decorative purpose and to fall into the class of "gay apparel," something not to be encouraged even among the Indians. The Pilgrims were finally persuaded to take £50 of the stuff and for a time were resentful at being cheated. But the wampum, "though it stuck at first," soon worked a miracle in their trade, giving them for the first time a convenient currency. No longer did they have to do business upon a clumsy barter basis with corn as the standard medium of exchange. Wampum stimu- lated both domestic and "foreign" trade, for the Wampanoag, the Indians along the Cape, the Massachusetts, and the tribes in Maine soon so coveted it that they could not get enough of this *wampum- peag* ("white strings of money"). For several years, until their rivals learned the secret and found a source of supply, the Pilgrims enjoyed a practical monopoly of the New England fur trade, cutting "off the trade quite from ye fisher-men and in great part from other of ye stragling planters."

Early in 1628, on his annual visit to England, Allerton persuaded four of the adventurers to become Undertakers with the eight Plymouth partners—the haberdasher Richard Andrews, the salter John Beauchamp, the felt maker Timothy Hatherly, and the goldsmith James Sherley, "the only glue of the company," as Cushman called him. Sherley was also persuaded to become the Pilgrims' agent in London though he protested that he was weak, "both for abillities and body," and that if things did not turn out well, they had only themselves to blame for making "no better choyce." In addition, he generously offered to forgive the planters the high interest rate on his last loan of £50, adding that Beauchamp and Andrews were willing to do the same: "I say we leave it freely to yourselves to allow us what you please, and as God shall blesse."[3]

Allerton had brought with him enough beaver to pay not only the first instalment on the mortgage but another £200 to various creditors, thus reducing their debts by a sixth within a year. It now seemed that the remaining £2,000 could be quickly liquidated, within five years at most. Allerton returned with this good news and an adequate supply of goods at reasonable prices, which encouraged everybody at Plymouth. The Undertakers were particularly elated, confident that they had glimpsed at last the end of a long hard road. It was a mirage, unfortunately, but the prospect seemed so fair that they now proceeded to carry out their secret plan for bringing over the remainder of the Green Gate congregation. The London partners agreed to share in the expense of transporting "the next year without fayle . . . a competente number of them," to the delight of those at Leyden who, with a patience rare among the Saints, had been awaiting this call for almost ten years.

Sherley crossed to the Low Countries and remained there three months on this and other business. A small group from the Green Gate returned with him, and early in 1629 ten of these embarked

at Gravesend on the *Mayflower,* the second Pilgrim ship of that
name,[4] with Captain William Peirce in command. Several weeks
earlier thirty-five servants had been dispatched on the *Talbot.* By
and large, it was "but a weak company," Sherley apologized, "yet
herein is a good parte of that end obtained which was aimed at."
As the majority of passengers on both ships were Puritans recruited by the recently organized Massachusetts Bay Company,
the vessels did not proceed to Plymouth, but to Naumkeag; here
Captain John Endecott had arrived with the Puritan vanguard
about a year before, immediately coming into conflict with Conant
and Lyford, soon driving both out.

After some delay the Saints were fetched to Plymouth by boat.
This group of Pilgrims included Thomas Blossom, "a holy man
and experienced sainct," later a deacon, who arrived with his wife
and two young children. Blossom, originally of Cambridge, was
one of those who had turned back with Cushman when the *Speedwell* began to leak like a sieve. A wife and two children likewise
accompanied Richard Masterson, wool carder of Sandwich, also
a deacon in later years, "a man of rare abilities, a second Stephen
to defend the truth against gainsayers, and one who had expended
most of his estate for the publick good." Another newcomer
of ability and even greater enterprise was young Thomas Willet, of
Yarmouth, who would one day become the first English mayor of
New York City. Passage on the *Mayflower* had been arranged for
Bridget Robinson and three of her children—Isaac, Mercy, and
Fear. But for some reason the pastor's widow drew back at the last
moment and did not embark. Three years later, when twenty-two,
Isaac came alone and made a name for himself in a curious way,
being the only member of Robinson's large family to reach
New Canaan.

Again the next year, in the summer of 1630, a party from the
Green Gate crossed to England and set sail, embarking on the
Handmaid, which dropped anchor at Plymouth three months later
with sixty on board. There had been much trouble along the way,
and the company arrived with many complaints of neglect and
ill-usage, being especially critical of Allerton. "Believe them not,"

wrote Sherley. "Indeed, they have been unreasonably chargeable, yet grudge and are not contented. Verily their indiscreet carriage hath so abated my affection towards them [the remaining Saints at Leyden] as, verily, were Mrs. Robinson well over, I would not disburse one penny for the rest."

Nor were the brethren at Plymouth altogether pleased with this company. They were Saints of the "weakest and poorest" sort, they declared, "without any of note and better discretion and government amongst them." This doubtless accounts for the fact that the company is now anonymous. Their names were not preserved, and it is quite impossible to identify any of them. They had been chosen against the advice of those at Plymouth by the London Undertakers, who argued that "if these were got over, the others might come when they would." But as things turned out, it was a grave error to send these feeble grumblers. "Yet they were such as feared God," said Bradford with a sigh, "and were both welcome and useful, for the most part."

The cost of bringing over the ninety odd Saints increased Plymouth's debts by £550 ($27,500)—or so Allerton later brought in the account. In addition, it had been necessary to provide the newcomers with houses and lands, help them plant crops, and feed them for many months until they could gather a harvest of their own, "a rare example of brotherly love, for they never demanded, much less had, any repayment of all these great sums thus disbursed." But it was an example of individual rather than general virtue, for when the majority of the planters—not merely the Strangers, but some of the Saints—learned of the great expense incurred in carrying out the Undertakers' secret design, they "begane to murmure and repine" at being taxed three bushels of corn a year for such a purpose. To silence criticism and allay discontent, the Undertakers promised to waive the tax if they could possibly get along without it. Consequently, no more corn was paid in, and the whole weight of the colony's obligations fell upon the shoulders of the Undertakers. For years they staggered under an intolerable burden of debt which, no matter what they did, went on steadily increasing, thanks in large part to one of their own members whose skill in the higher reaches of finance was not yet suspected.

A few more of the Leyden brethren strayed in from time to time, but all subsequent settlers came as individuals. The *Handmaid* was the last of the Pilgrim ships. Largely because of poverty, organized efforts to colonize Plymouth came to an end just as the well-financed Puritan migration to the north got under way. In 1630 alone thirteen ships crossed to Massachusetts Bay with 1,000 settlers, three times as many as had come to Plymouth in a decade. Now, for the first time, the Pilgrims had serious and formidable rivals close at hand. They could no longer hope to dominate New England and keep out "interlopers." But the influence of New Plimoth was to be decisive in many ways.

In 1628, on his arrival at Naumkeag on the *Abigail,* Captain John Endecott had been seriously alarmed by the state of health of his company. Scurvy and infectious fever had broken out at sea, as on the *Mayflower* eight years before. Carried ashore, disease soon cut the Puritan vanguard in half and claimed many of Conant's company as well. In desperation Endecott appealed to Plymouth for help, having heard that someone there had "skill in such diseases." The Pilgrims sent Deacon Samuel Fuller, their "physition & chirurgeon." It was a momentous visit, for Deacon-Doctor Fuller tended not only the ailing bodies but the troubled souls of his patients. Though more and more critical of the Anglican church and its ways, these hesitant Puritans had never dared separate and go their way. They continued a nominal conformity, partly because they had ideological objections to "schisme," but chiefly because they were trimmers without the courage of their convictions. They were deterred by fear of the heavy hand of the bishops and the magistrates, as the event proved, for with that pressure removed, Fuller had no difficulty in converting them to Brownism. They quickly joined the Separation and embraced the Holy Discipline though for politic reasons they still protested— a feeble rationalization—that they had separated not from the Church of England but its "corruptions."[5]

"God's people are all marked with one and ye same marke, and

sealed with one and ye same seale, and have for ye mayne one
& ye same hart, guided by one & ye same spirite of truth; and
where this is, there can be no discorde; nay, here must needs be
sweete harmonie," Endecott wrote Bradford. "I acknowledge myselfe much bound to you for your kind love and care in sending
Mr. Fuller among us, and rejoyce much that I am by him satisfied
touching your judgments of ye outward forme of God's worshipe.
It is, as farr as I can yet gather, no other than is warrented by ye
evidence of truth, . . . being farr from ye commone reporte that
hath been spread of you touching that perticuler."

Shortly after the arrival of the *Talbot* and *Mayflower* in 1629,
which brought "many godly persons," including several "forward"
preachers, Endecott decreed a "solemne day of humilliation for
ye choyse of a pastor & teacher." The forenoon was spent in prayer
and exhortation. With the ground prepared, the company proceeded to the election of officers, having first narrowed its choice
to two candidates—Samuel Skelton of Lincolnshire and Francis
Higginson of Leicester, both graduates of Cambridge. As they
were Anglican clergymen, they "were demanded concerning their
callings." Both acknowledged that there was a "two-fold calling,
the one an inward calling, when ye Lord moved ye heart of a man
to take that calling upon him and fitted him with giftes for ye
same; the second was an outward calling, which was from ye
people, when a company of beleevers are joyned togither in a
covenante, to walke togither in all ye ways of God; every member
(being men) are to have a free voyce in ye choyce of their officers, &c." Satisfied on this score, the company took a secret ballot
which revealed that the "most voice" was for Skelton as pastor
and Higginson as teacher.[6] With three or four grave members
assisting, Higginson then laid hands on Skelton, "using prayers
therewith," and the latter in turn laid hands on Higginson. Elders
and deacons were subsequently chosen. In a long letter to Bradford, obviously sent with a desire to have his approval, Deacon
Charles Gott carefully described every step in the proceedings and
expounded the reason thereof.

"And now, good Sir," Gott concluded, "I hope that you & ye

rest of God's people . . . will say that here was a right foundation layed, and that these 2 blessed servants of ye Lord came in at ye dore, and not at ye window."

The Saints were most flattered, eagerly accepting an invitation to be present at a second day of humiliation set aside for the acceptance of a covenant and a confession of faith. Bradford, Brewster, Fuller, and several more set sail in the shallop. Cross winds so delayed them that they did not hear their new brethren solemnly swear "in the presence of God to walke together in all his waies, according as he is pleased to reveale himself unto us in his Blessed word of truth." But they arrived before the assembly broke up and in time "to give them the Right Hand of Fellowship." Two brothers Browne, one a lawyer and the other a substantial merchant, both members of the Massachusetts Bay Company, vehemently objected to these proceedings, particularly the bann on the Book of Common Prayer. Governor Endecott proved himself a likely Saint, however new his calling, by promptly shipping them back to England as "schismatiques."[7]

Again in 1630, as the tide of Puritan immigration rose, Deacon-Doctor Fuller was called in for consultation on religious matters, this time by Governor John Winthrop, who had landed at Naumkeag—or, as it was now called, Salem (from the Hebrew *sholom*, peace, after sharp fights that soon led Roger Conant and the Old Planters to move across the North River and found Beverly—"Beggarly," the new Saints dubbed it).

Not liking Salem, Winthrop departed with a large company to settle Charlestown, soon crossing to the other bank of the Charles River to found Boston and its famed First Church. The latter radiated wide influence and was almost the Vatican of early Massachusetts, especially in the days of the great John Cotton, "his head an Index to the Sacred volume."

Before their departure from England, Cotton had counselled Winthrop and his company "to take advice of them at Plymouth." This and general sickness in the company occasioned Fuller's visit. The Deacon-Doctor did not accomplish much for the ailing, but he was as persuasive as ever, and now these Boston settlers embraced the Holy Discipline and made a solemn covenant "to walk in all ways according to the Rule of the Gospel, and in all sincere conformity to his Holy Ordinances and in mutual love and respect each to other, so near as God shall give us grace."

John Robinson's prophecy had come true.

"There will be," he had said, "no difference between uncomformable Ministers and you when they come to the practice of the Ordinances out of the Kingdome."

With the Pilgrim saddle on the Bay horse, the Saints had cause to rejoice. Though the Bay horse would later throw them, giving them a nasty jolt, this was their hour of greatest triumph.

The coming of the *Handmaid,* second *Mayflower,* and other ships had been a "duble blessing." Not only had they brought more friends from Leyden "when all their hops seemed to be cutt off." But here, close by, "to ye admiration of many and allmost wonder of ye world," was "ye begining of a larger harvest unto ye Lord."

19

PURGE
OF JOYLITY

. . . dancing and frisking togither (like so
many fairies, or furies rather), and worse
practises.
—WILLIAM BRADFORD

FIVE YEARS EARLIER, IN 1625, SHORTLY AFTER OLDHAM'S DIS-
missal with a "bob upon the Bumme," a shipload of colonists had
arrived on the *Unity,* under the command of one Captain Wollaston, "a man of pretie parts." Composed largely of indentured
servants, the company established itself about twenty-five miles
to the north in what is now the city of Quincy, just beyond
Weston's old settlement at Wessagusset. Here was another brazen
trespass upon what the Pilgrims regarded as their domain. But
if the idea of liquidating Mount Wollaston occurred to them, they
did nothing about it at the moment, for behind the Captain and

his partners could be seen the busy figure of Sir Ferdinando Gorges.

Within a short time it seemed likely that the nuisance would be self-abating, that Mount Wollaston might liquidate itself. The raw settlement did not answer the expectations of the Captain and his lieutenants, who had dreamed of becoming "great men & rich all of a sudaine," but as many at Plymouth had discovered, their hopes were "castls in ye aire." In 1627, Wollaston gathered up some servants, sailed for Virginia, and there sold them to local tobacco planters for the period of their indenture. Realizing a handsome profit, he wrote back asking for more. Mount Wollaston might soon have been deserted, to the immense relief of the Pilgrims, had not this nefarious traffic been stopped by one of the partners, Thomas Morton. No wonder Plymouth was angry with him, denouncing him as a "pettifogger" and striving to belittle him in every way, asserting that he was "scorned even by ye meanest servants." It was Morton who remarked of the Saints that the "first precept in their Politiques is to defame the man at whom they aime, and then he is a holy Israelite who . . . can spread that fame brodest"—and in this, particularly toward Lyford and Morton, Pilgrim historians have been *sanctissimi.*

Bradford was at his malicious best on Morton, dismissing him as a nobody, "a kind of petie-fogger of Furnefell's Inne." As a matter of fact, Morton was an aristocrat, probably a graduate of Oxford, born of a line of distinguished soldiers who had won for the family, truly *arma gerens,* the right to bear a coat-of-arms. Trained for the law, he had practised as a member of Clifford's Inn, London, but this was the least of his interests and accomplishments. He was widely read in Latin literature and classical lore, quoted frequently and at length from the ancient poets, dabbled in verse himself, wrote an ornamental well-paced prose, knew the great Ben Jonson, and apparently sang, drank, and rollicked with him and his cronies at the immortal Mermaid Tavern. The Pilgrims were hardly the ones to appreciate this, and if aware of it, doubtless put it down to his discredit. So

far as Morton was interested in religion at all, he seems to
have been an Anglican of conventional views, knowing little
and caring less about the Separatists and the rigors of the Holy
Discipline.

That Morton was a scapegrace cannot be denied. In 1620 he
had married for money, courting an elderly widow, one of his
clients. When called upon by her sons for an accounting of the
estate, he dropped from sight for a time. According to his own
story, he visited New England in 1622, which is not improbable.
If so, he came with Weston's company, perhaps returning on the
Charity when she sailed for home late in the year. Nothing more
is seen of him until he appears as one of Wollaston's lieutenants,
arriving on the *Unity* "with 30 servants and provisions of all
sorts fit for a plantation." All went well until he and his partners
fell out about breaking up the settlement.

When Wollaston departed for Virginia, Morton invited the
remaining servants to a feast and—"after strong drinck & other
junkats," according to the Pilgrims—made them a long speech,
concluding with the remark that he would offer them "some
advice." They had seen many friends carried off to be sold as
slaves in Virginia, and a similar fate awaited them unless they took
steps to prevent it. If they were disposed to drive out the lieutenant
left in charge by Wollaston, he would not object. In fact, he
would help them.

"I, having a parte in the plantation, will receive you as my
partners and consociats," he promised, "so you may be free from
service, and we will converse, trade, plante, & live togeather as
equalls, & supporte and protect one another."

There was more craft than honesty in this, the Pilgrims complained, and it is doubtless true that Morton was not wholly
actuated by humanitarian motives—as who is? He planned to
profit from the arrangement, and he did. But regardless of motive,
few today will be disposed to find fault with him for releasing his
own servants from bondage and protecting others against heartless
masters eager to sell them for whatever they would bring. Even
that hard-bitten trader Thomas Weston opposed this unprincipled

slave traffc. In New England servants were "sold upp and Downe like horses," he protested, and for that reason he "held it not law-full to carie any."

Morton's advice was "easily received," Wollaston's agents were driven out, and so began a unique settlement, one of the gayest that ever graced our shores. Shrieks of laughter and snatches of song soon rang through the forest and echoed as far away as Plymouth—to the mounting concern of the Saints. They con-fidently expected God to rebuke such levity at any moment. Instead, Satan seemed to hold undisputed sway there and so blessed the revellers that they lived in "riotous prodigallitie," with no thought of the morrow, "quaffing & drinking both wine & strong waters in great exsess, and, as some reported, £10 [$500] in a morning."

To break with the past, Morton renamed the community. Fond of bad puns and showing off his Latin, he called it "Ma-re Mount," or Mountain by the Sea, but the Pilgrims were not altogether wrong in mistaking it for "Merie Mount." The rechristening of the town was a gala affair, fittingly celebrated in "a solemne manner, with Revels and merriment after the old English cus-tome." A straight thin pine eighty feet tall was cut down and trimmed for use as a Maypole. Hauled to the summit of the hill to the sound of drums, pistols, guns, and "other fitting instru-ments," it was raised with a pair of antlers secured at the top as a "faire sea marke for directions how to finde out the way to mine Host of Mar-re Mount." A barrel of beer to be consumed "with all good cheare" was brewed for the occasion, and all in the neigh-borhood were invited to attend—men and women, whites and Indians alike. Morton looked upon the latter with considerable curiosity and affection, having satisfied himself that there were Latin and Greek words in their language, which proved to him that the Indians were "some of the scattered Trojans" who had been dispersed "after such time as Brutus left Latium."

Morton composed two poems "to make their Revells more fashionable." The longer was tacked to the Maypole for all to read and enjoy if they could:

> Rise, Oedipus, and if thou canst, unfould
> What means Caribdis underneath the mould
> When Scilla sollitary on the ground
> (Sitting in forme of Niobe) was found . . .

The poem went on at great length in this vein. What it all
meant, if anything, is a secret that died with its author. Even
Morton confessed that it was somewhat "enigmaticall" and suggested that the Pilgrims' inability to understand it was one cause
of their consuming rage against him. They were always bothering
their heads about "things that were immaterial." But Bradford
pretended to see far enough into it to be sure that it tended "to ye
detraction & scandall" of the Saints. The latter certainly could
not mistake the drift of the other of Morton's poems. What it
meant was all too plain as it was chanted in chorus by Morton's
men and laughing Indian maids dancing hand in hand about the
Maypole "whiles one of the company sung and filled out the good
Liquor, like Gammedes and Jupiter."

> Drinke and be merry, merry, merry, boyes;
> Let all your delight be in Hymen's joyes;
> Iô to Hymen, now the day is come,
> About the merry Maypole take a Roome.

> Make green garlons, bring bottles out,
> And fill sweet Nectar freely about.
> Uncover thy head and feare no harme,
> For here's good liquor to keep it warme.

> Then drinke . . .

> *   *   *

> Give to the Nymphe that's free from scorne
> No Irish stuffe nor Scotch over-worne.
> Lasses in beaver coats, come away,
> Ye shall be welcome to us night and day
> > To drinke and be merry, merry, merry, boyes;
> > Let all your delight be in Hymen's joyes . . .

All of this, said Morton, was "harmlesse mirth by young men
who desired nothing more than to have wives sent over to them

from England." But he quickly learned that this was not the view
of those in control at Plymouth, who did not intend to put up
with his "idle or idoll May-polle" and "lasciviouse rimes." What
made him think that he would be allowed to revive in New Canaan
the "feasts of ye Roman Goddess Flora, or ye beastly practises of
ye madd Bacchinalians!" Under this "lord of misrule" the settlement was nothing but a "schoole of Athisme," with Morton and
his men "pouring out themselves into all profanenes, . . . inviting
the Indean women for their consorts, dancing and frisking togither
(like so many fairies, or furies rather), and worse practises." And
without a blush of shame and quite heedless of their neighbors—
"as if this joylity," growled Bradford, "would have lasted ever."

No doubt the Saints were seriously concerned about the morals
of their neighbors, as they always were, whether they lived next
door or at a greater distance. But their concern had other aspects.
Merry Mount did more than frolic, it appears, for it was a serious
competitor in the beaver trade, not only locally, but in Maine.
Morton had followed the Pilgrims there in 1625, and when they
returned to the Kennebec the next year, they found that Morton
had anticipated them and picked up almost everything of value.
According to Morton, one of his men made £1,000 in the fur trade
within a few years—a profit that would have paid half of the
Pilgrims' debts and provided badly needed supplies. These "interlopers," the Pilgrims felt, were snatching bread right out of
Plymouth's mouth.

Furthermore, Morton's trade was based upon his "vilanie" in
selling the Indians powder, shot, muskets, and "strong waters,"
which seriously impaired the trade in corn and other things. The
Undertakers had laid in a large stock of cloth, knives, beads,
trinkets, and similar goods, which suddenly and sharply declined
in value. Having armed the Indians and taught them how to shoot,
Morton then employed them to hunt for him, with great profit,
for they were far better in the woods than the whites. More than
once the Pilgrims met an Indian prowling the forest with a
blunderbuss, which sent cold shivers running up and down their
spines, and they decided to take action. Arms were being sold to

the Indians also by English fishermen and the French, but these
mischief-makers were beyond the reach and power of the Pilgrims.
But Morton, they concluded, was not.

Besides, as Bradford remarked in one of his always illuminating
asides, the Pilgrims could not hope to keep their servants unless
Merry Mount were destroyed, for Morton "would entertaine any,
how vile soever, and all ye scume of ye countrie or any discontents
would flock to him from all places." Such a free community was
obviously a danger so close at hand, and there was always the
possibility that some of the younger and less hardened Saints might
slip off through the woods to spend a few days with "mine Host
of Ma-re Mount," who was always ready to pleasure them with
"claret sparklinge neate" in the company of personable young
squaws.

Either because they felt themselves too weak to act alone, or
more probably from a desire to have others bear some of the
responsibility, the Pilgrims approached the smaller scattered settlements along the coast to urge that all unite "to suppress Morton
& his consorts before they grewe to further head and strength."
Some of these promised moral support and some financial aid—
notably, David Thompson's post at Piscataqua; Roger Conant, who
was still at Naumkeag; and the former Pilgrim, William Hilton,
of Dover (N.H.), who contributed £1 ($50) each. Bradford later
tried to make out that the initiative in the business had come from
them, but the Pilgrims' modesty in this deceived no one, least of
all Morton's friend and patron, Sir Ferdinando Gorges.

Carefully choosing their best ground for complaint, the Pilgrims wrote in a "friendly & neighborly way" to warn Morton
against selling arms and drink to the Indians. Morton denied the
liquor charge, protesting that in all his commerce with the savages
he had never sold them a drop; "nay, I would hardly let any of
them have a dram unless hee were a Sachem, or a Winnaytue,
that is a rich man," for he knew from experience that the Indians
would "pawne their wits" for a drink. He confessed to selling
them a few old muskets and some shot and powder. But what of

that? he asked "in scurillous terms full of disdaine." A second letter sharply commanded him to be better advised and "more temperate in his termes," for Plymouth did not intend to put up with the arms traffic which James I had forbidden by proclamation six years before.

"Proclamations are no lawes and enforce no penalties," answered Morton, the barrister, twitting them about their ignorance of the niceties of the law, mockingly asking what punishment he might suffer.

"Greater than you can bear—His Majesty's displeasure!"

"The King is dead," Morton replied, "and his displeasure with him."

There was nothing to do now, the Saints decided, but take him by force. Not to proceed would only make him "farr more hautie & insolente." Consequently, Captain Standish was dispatched with nine men to put a stop to Morton's "disorderlie walking" and teach him better manners.

The Battle of Merry Mount will ever remain as obscure as Morton's Oedipian ode. Both Standish and Morton left an account of what happened there, and one is as fantastic as the other. According to Standish, Morton and his men locked themselves up in a house with plenty of powder and shot, and might have done some damage if they had been sober. They answered the command to surrender with "scofes & scorns," but soon came running out to charge the Pilgrims. They were so drunk, however, that they could not even lift their pieces to their shoulders, let alone aim them. With a carbine "overcharged & allmost half fild with powder & shote," Morton ran at Standish, who calmly "stept to him, & put by his peece, & tooke him." By Standish's report the skirmish resulted in a single casualty, and that occurred when one of Morton's staggering crew fell against a Pilgrim sword, which punctured his nose and relieved him of some of "his hott blood."

Morton's was a very different story. As a son of distinguished soldiers, he had only contempt and ridicule for the "nine worthies of New Canaan" who, under "Captaine Shrimpe (a quondam

drummer)," came blundering into danger "like a flocke of geese."
And a pity it was, he said, paraphrasing Ben Jonson, that he could
not style them "Knights," for

> ... they had brawne and braine, and were right able
> To be installed of Prince Arthur's table;
> Yet all of them were Squires of low degree
> As did appear by rules of heraldry.

They had not dared attack Merry Mount when it was fully
manned, but had slyly waited until most of the partners were off
trading and hunting. On their arrival Morton happened to be
visiting Wessagusset a few miles away. They went after him,
"tayled together" like colts on their way to a fair, and posted a
guard around the house where he was staying. Pleased to have so
easily captured "this Monster of a man," the Pilgrims fell to
tippling and were soon in a happy daze, enabling Morton to slip
away and return home. In the morning Standish "took on most
furiously and tore his clothes for anger to see the nest emptie and
their bird gone." Trailing him to Merry Mount, they loudly ordered
his surrender. Morton refused, but seeing that great bloodshed
would result if he "played upon them out of his port holes," he
finally consented to parley. At length, according to his account,
it was agreed that he would give himself up. But he was to retain
his arms in token of honorable surrender, his goods were not to
be confiscated, and no harm was to be done to the town. Even the
Pilgrim account suggests the probability of voluntary surrender.
As Morton had only two men with him, resistance would have
been foolhardy.

When he stepped out the door to give himself up, so Morton
complained, he was assaulted by Standish, "the first Captaine in
the Land (as he supposed)," who rushed up, snatched away his
sword, threw him down, and pinned him to the ground. Others
came running, and "so eagerly was every man bent against him
(not regarding any agreement made with such a carnall man)
that they fell upon him as if they would have eaten him; some
of them were so violente that they would have a slice with a

scabbert, and all for haste." By this "outrageous riot" the Pilgrims made themselves masters of Merry Mount, for "this they knew (in the eyes of the Salvages) would add to their glory and diminish the reputation of mine honest Host. . . . But marriage and hanging (they say) comes by destiny."

Morton was not hanged, nor did he suffer the fate of Wituwamat, as he may well have feared, for when hauled before Governor Bradford and his council, he heard Standish speak long and earnestly for his execution. Instead, it was decided to ship him back to England, and "he was not thought a good Christian that would not lay out much for that imployemente." Meanwhile, to prevent any mischief, he was sent in the shallop to the Isles of Shoals, off the mouth of the Piscataqua. The Pilgrims left him there in winter weather with no clothes but the "thinne suite" on his back, without a gun, without even a knife, so Morton declared in a bitter denunciation of the "precise Seperatists," remarking that they made a "great shewe of Religion, but no humanity." Within a month or two, late in 1628, he was dispatched to England in the custody of another "malicious" character, John Oldham, who had been entrusted with letters of complaint against Morton addressed to Sir Ferdinando Gorges and the Council for New England.

In these letters, framed by Bradford and signed by other settlements, Morton was described as the "head of a turbulente & seditious Crewe" that lived "without all fear of God or common honesty, some of them abusing the Indean women most filthily, as is notorious." They lewdly spent their time and means "in maintaining drunkenness, riot, and other evils amongst them: yea, and inveigling of men's servants away from them, so as the mischiefe began to grow intolerable, and if it had been suffered a while longer, would have been incurable." Morton's traffic in firearms with the Indians had "spoiled the trade in all other things" and was little short of murder. The Pilgrims had therefore been compelled, they said, "for the safety of ourselves, our wives, and innocent children, to apprehende him by force (though with some peril)," and insisted that steps be taken to protect them against the "cankered covetousness of these licentious men."

The Pilgrims were elated by their easy triumph, convinced that the "habitation of the wicked should no more appear in Israel," but they were much mistaken. Perhaps nothing in the history of Plymouth ever caused quite such consternation as Isaac Allerton's landing upon his return from England early the next year, because their business manager and assistant governor, Brewster's son-in-law and a proper Saint, had brought with him—as his secretary!—none other than "mine Host of Ma-re Mount." Not satisfied with bringing "that unworthy man & instrumente of mischeefe" back to the country, he brazenly led him right into town and lodged him at his own house, "as it were to nose them," said Bradford. As soon as the brethren recovered from their "terrible amazement," they sent Morton packing, and he went to his "old nest in ye Massachusetts." Their many complaints against him, they discovered, had been ignored in England. "He was not so much as rebukte for ought was heard," so that it came as no surprise when they presently learned that the "lord of misrule" was at it again—firearms, firewater, Indian maids, Maypole, and all.

The Pilgrims had never pretended to legal jurisdiction over Merry Mount. They were aware that their weak and faulty patent could not be stretched so far. They considered Morton's presence undesirable and therefore decided to purge the land of him, "and if not in one way, then in another," as remarked long ago by one of the Commonwealth's most distinguished sons, Charles Francis Adams, who added that Morton's case "is not singular in Massachusetts annals; it is merely the first of its kind."[1] The status of Merry Mount had meanwhile changed. The recent Massachusetts grant embraced it, and Governor John Endecott therefore spoke with some authority in commanding Morton to appear at Naumkeag to swear an oath of allegiance and give surety for his good behavior. Deacon Fuller had already visited the Puritans there and brought them into the fold.

Morton evidently met the good deacon and was not impressed with him either as a Saint or a surgeon, remarking that he wore a "longe beard and a Garment like the Greeke that begged in Paul's Church [St. Paul's, London]." Properly enough, Fuller had been "bred a Butcher" and was always ready to practice his trade upon the unsuspecting. Nor was his physic any good. "He takes a patient and the urinall, eyes the State there, findes the Crasis Symptomes and attomi Natantes, and tells the patient that his disease was winde, which hee had taken by gapeing feasting overboard at Sea." In short, he was seasick. Still, Fuller had worked a marvelous cure for Endecott, that "great swelling fellowe, of Littleworth, . . . the Cow-keeper of Salem." He had "cured him of a disease called a wife; and yet I hope this man may be forgiven if she were made a fitting plant for heaven." The "Quacksalver" then treated other ailing Saints, some forty in all, who had no complaints to make, for all went promptly to heaven.[2]

The authorities asked Morton, as all others in the jurisdiction, to subscribe to a set of articles drawn up by their new pastor, "Master Eager." As paraphrased by Morton, these stipulated that "in all causes, as well ecclesiastical as political," they should follow the "rule of God's word." Morton agreed if they would add the proviso, "So as nothing be done contrary or repugnant to the laws of the kingdom of England," which gave offense. Nevertheless, Endecott offered to make him a partner in the company's fur trading monopoly, according to Morton. This offer was declined, for Morton felt that he could do better alone. Evidently he did— to the concern of his rivals, for he outstripped the monopoly "six and seaven for one." It was not long before "Captaine Littleworth," spurred by the Pilgrims, marched on Merry Mount, cut down the Maypole, "rebuked them for their profannes," burned his house to the ground, confiscated his goods, and "admonished them to looke there should be better walking," changing the name of the place to Mount Dagon, carrying out the Pilgrims' threat to make it a "woefull mount."[3]

Taken to Naumkeag, Morton was tried on a charge of harming the Indians and alienating their friendship, whereas the plain truth was that he got along with them only too well. First sentenced to the bilboes, he was again shipped back to England, "where he lay a good while in Exeter Gaole, for besids his miscarriage here, he was vemently suspected of ye murder of a man that had adventured moneys with him when he came first into New England," said Bradford in another of his libels.

Morton, on the contrary, went to work for Sir Ferdinando Gorges, with the specific assignment of voiding the Plymouth and Bay patents. And what a joy that must have been for "mine Host of Ma-re Mount"—almost as satisfying as that he found in pillorying the Saints in *New England Canaan,* one of the liveliest, wittiest, and most informative books of the day. Though it is not to be taken too literally, for it is obviously a satire, most solemn historians are simply stupid in dismissing the book as worthless.

Morton's portrait of the Saints contains as much truth—and as little—as theirs of him. Both are caricatures. Between them there is nothing to choose—except, perhaps, that his is etched with a more practised hand and an even sharper tool than Bradford's.

20

INTO YE
BRIERS

And thus they were kept hoodwinckte, . . .
and no better than bought and sold, as it
would seeme.

—WILLIAM BRADFORD

IF THE FIRST FRUIT OF PILGRIM-PURITAN COLLABORATION WAS
the purge of "joylity," the second was a hanging—and of a Pilgrim
Father at that. John Billington was in trouble again. He had
unquestionably been one of those mixed up in the mutiny on the
Mayflower. In 1621, as revealed in one of the first entries in the
Old Colony records, he had been foolish enough to show his contempt for Captain Standish, assaulting him "with opprobrious
speeches," for which he was sentenced "to have his neck and heels
tied together." By humbling himself and offering an apology, he
managed to beg off. Three years later he had joined the Lyford-
Oldham faction. In calling upon the colonists to revolt, Oldham

had appealed to him by name. Now, in 1630, Billington was at the end of his rope. After a bitter quarrel about some trifle, he had waylaid one John Newcomen, a recent arrival, and blown him to pieces with his blunderbuss.

The authorities did not know quite what to do in the case. By the first law recorded in the Pilgrim statute book, passed late in 1623, it had been decreed "by the Court then held that all criminall facts, and also all matters of trespasses, and debts betweene man and man, should be tried by the verdict of twelve honest men to be empanelled by authority in forme of a jurie upon their oath." Billington was accordingly tried "both by grand & petie jurie" and found guilty of "willfull murder by plaine & notorious evidence." But there was some question in the Pilgrims' minds about their authority to carry out the death sentence. They sought the advice of Governor John Winthrop and "ye ablest gentle-men in ye Bay of ye Massachusetts." Upon their concurrence that the murderer "ought to dye and ye land be purged from blood," Plymouth decided to proceed and poor unhappy John Billington was duly hanged, drawn, and quartered by his friends.

But "ye profanest" of the Pilgrim Fathers has a far more impressive memorial than most of the Saints—Billington Sea, as a small lake behind Plymouth is still known, named for its discovery by Francis, the younger of his two sons. The older had died of gangrene a few years before his father. Billington's widow, Ellen, later remarried, and Francis in time raised a numerous family, having eight children, and the family does not appear to have become more saintly with the years, to judge from the mention of it in the records: "June 27 [1703]. Abigail Billington (who was Churchell) was called before ye church openly for fornication with her new husband, Francis Billington, before her marriage to him."

While the novice Saints on the Bay were a comfort to the Pilgrims, they were also a problem. It was obvious from the start that they would be serious rivals in trade. Thanks to a storm that drove their ship into the harbor, Plymouth discovered that some of them were already trespassing, carrying on a surreptitious trade with Cape Cod. Bradford sent the ship back to Boston with the warning that such attempts would be resisted, "even to the spending of our lives." The Pilgrims were afraid, too, that the Puritans might encroach from the north and even claim all of their territory. The Bay had a proper charter, but the Pilgrims' claim rested largely upon priority of settlement, for their patent was vague and faulty. Plymouth's boundaries had never been sharply defined. Their powers of government were derived from no higher authority than the Mayflower Compact and might be seriously challenged at any time.

Since 1628 Allerton had been trying on his visits to London to secure an enlarged grant along the Kennebec. He was now instructed to enlist Sherley in an effort to obtain a royal charter for New Plimoth. Upon his return from England in 1630, Allerton brought back a charter made out by the Council for New England to William Bradford as trustee for the colony. Bearing the signatures of Sir Ferdinando Gorges and the Earl of Warwick, this patent granted to Plymouth all of New England southeast of a line running roughly from the lower shore of Boston Bay to the head of Narragansett Bay. It also widened the Pilgrims' strip along the Kennebec. It was designed, wrote Sherley, "to make you a corporation and so inable you to make & execute lawes in such large & ample manner as ye Massachusetts plantation hath it." Now they "might bear such sway & government as were fitt for the ranke & place that God hath called you unto, and stope ye moueths of base and scurrulous fellowes that are ready to question & threaten you in every action you doe."

But the patent, to the dismay of the Pilgrims, was not in proper order, for it did not bear the Great Seal. The fault was not Allerton's, Sherley hastened to assure them, for he had strictly followed instruction in the matter and been "so turrmoyled about it as, verily, I would not nor could not have undergone it if I might have had a thousand pounds." There had been many riddles to solve and many locks to open "with ye silver, nay, ye golden key."[1] Yet the time and money had been well spent, for His Majesty's assent would surely be obtained. A charter could have been obtained at this time, it appears, if Allerton and Sherley had not stubbornly insisted on inserting a clause exempting the colony from payment of customs duties for a period of years, "but covetousnes never brings ought home, as ye proverbe is, for this oppertunytie being lost, it was never accomplished." As a consequence, the Old Colony lived out its brief existence without a royal charter, ultimately a fatal weakness, and the Pilgrims were out of pocket £500 on this business, which did nothing to improve their tempers or their regard for the judgment of their business agent.

This was the time Allerton chose to appear with Thomas Morton, "that unworthy man," as his secretary. Nor was this his only offense. He had established the practice of bringing back goods to sell "for his owne private benefite, which was more than any many had yet hithertoo attempted." When called on the carpet, he argued that this also benefited the community by supplying it with more goods and without doing any harm to the Undertakers' trade, for his goods did not compete with theirs. Allerton's private trade grew larger from year to year, and his partners noted that his goods and theirs were always packed together and indiscriminately mixed so that if lost at sea, they could be charged wholly to the Undertakers' account. Whenever a shipment was unpacked, "what was most vendible and would yeeld presente pay, usually that was his." Also, he began to expand his operations to other parts in spite of the agreement that only the Undertakers as a group were to engage in foreign trade. Many were now beginning to suspect that Allerton, like Squanto, "plaid his owne game." It was an embarrassing situation, for in 1626 the aging Assistant Governor had married twenty-year-old Fear Brewster and naturally was defended by her "beloved & honoured" father, "whom they were loath to greeve or any way offend, so as they bore with much in that respecte." Then, too, Sherley was always praising their "honest & discreete agente, Mr. Allerton," saying that he knew his way around London and none could do as well as he. Yet it was plain that things were going very badly. Every year the Undertakers sent a large quantity of peltry and other commodities to England, and every year they fell deeper in debt. It was all very strange, "yet because love thinks no evill, nor is susspitious, they tooke his fair words for excuse."

Allerton returned from London in 1630 to report that he and the Undertakers there had procured a patent to a tract along the Penobscot River, about fifty miles up the Maine coast from the Pilgrim trading post on the Kennebec. They had done this on their own initiative, without consulting anybody at Plymouth. "Now if you please to be partners with us in this," the London Undertakers wrote Plymouth, "we are willing you shall." The idea was Allerton's, another of his money-making schemes, and it was to be a private venture.

Bradford and his associates did not like this business but were in a dilemma. A trading post on the Penobscot undoubtedly would cut into their profitable business on the Kennebec unless they joined the enterprise and attempted to control it. On the other hand, it was not likely that God would prosper a trading venture directed by such a man as Sherley had hired, one Edward Ashley, who had been in the country before and was not unknown to the Pilgrims. He had "wite & abillitie enough to menage ye bussines," Bradford confessed, "yet some of them knew him to be a very profane yonge man." He had lived "amonge ye Indeans as a savage," it appears, "& wente naked amongst them." Yet they swallowed their scruples and signed up, furnishing Ashley and his four or five "lustie fellowes" with corn, wampum, cloth, beads, and other trucking stuff, and a bark to transport them to Maine, where a trading post was built at Pentagoet, now Castine. The Pilgrims took the precaution of sending along a "discreete" young Saint, Thomas Willet, to "keep Ashley, in some good measure, within bounds."

The Pilgrims soon discovered that Ashley was much better supplied than themselves, for Allerton had again violated instructions and brought over virtually no trading goods. They were forced to buy cottons, kerseys, and other things out of his private stock "to their great vexation." Allerton "prayed them to be contente," assuring them that they might have what they wished the next year. He had also borrowed large sums at Bristol at fifty per cent, "which he excused, that he was forcte to it." Along the way, evidently in Maine, Allerton had picked up a bargain in salt and was about to sell it at a handsome profit when Winslow intervened, offering a suggestion that led to endless and almost disastrous complications. Why not keep the salt and hire a fishing ship to come out in the spring and use it? On her voyage out, in place of salt, she could carry "bread, peas, cloth, &c., and so they might have a full supply of goods without paying fraight, and in due season." Picking up the salt, she could then go fishing and turn a neat profit. It was hailed as a brilliant idea by all but Governor Bradford, who protested that they "had allways lost by fishing." But the rest were so earnest about it that he finally gave way, and Allerton departed for England with detailed instructions on just what should and should not be done.

Months passed with no word from London. While anxiously awaiting their annual spring shipment of supplies, the Pilgrims were forced to send more corn to Ashley. The latter refused to pay for it, telling them to charge it to Sherley's account, and shipped all beaver directly to England. At length, in the summer of 1631, word came that the *Friendship,* their fishing ship, was at Boston with one of the London partners, Timothy Hatherly, on board. Confident that here was supply at last, they sent a bark to fetch it. To their blank surprise the ship was filled up with baggage and goods for the Bay colony. There was nothing for them on board but two bundles of "Bastable ruggs" and two hogsheads of metheglin, or mead, a potent drink fermented of honey, most of which had been "drunke up under ye name of leackage and so lost."

Hatherly seemed "something reserved and troubled in himself," and a letter from Sherley threw light on this. Hatherly had been sent over, the Pilgrims were informed, to be "a comforte to Mr. Allerton, a joye to you, . . . and a great stay to ye bussines." In the past the London Undertakers had been willing to entrust all matters to those at Plymouth and their capable agent, Isaac Allerton, "who, without flaterie, deserveth infinite thanks & comendations both of us & you, for his paines, &c." That had been all very well when losses were small, but now Sherley and his colleagues were out as much as £1,500 ($75,000) each. It therefore seemed only prudent to send Hatherly, "your and our loving freind," to look into the accounts and general conduct of affairs.

"I would not have you take anything unkindly," Sherley concluded. "I have not written out of jeolocie of any unjuste dealing."

In Boston the Pilgrims learned that Allerton had bought a second ship, the *White Angel,* and was in Maine waters with a "wicked and drunken" crew fishing for bass, which upset them, for they regarded bass fishing "as a vaine thing that would certainly turne to loss." Totally in the dark about all this, they quickly sent Winslow off to London to "look into matters, and if he found things not well, to discharge Mr. Allerton from being any longer agent for them."

Allerton soon brought the *White Angel* to Boston, picked up Hatherly, and sailed for Plymouth, running her aground on Gurnet's Nose in trying to enter the harbor. The ship was carrying a large quantity of "linen cloath, bedticks, stockings, tape, pins, ruggs, &c.," valued at £500, which Allerton offered the local Undertakers. They declined to accept them and rebuked their agent "very much for runing into these courses, fearing ye success of them." As plausible as ever, Allerton somewhat satisfied his still credulous brethren with promise of future profits and his explanation of the tortuous ways of high finance. The *White Angel* represented a private venture, he said, and they need not "have anything to doe with her excepte they would." Hatherly confirmed this and added that the London partners would bear any loss on the *Friendship* inasmuch as the vessel had not been used to bring the Pilgrims supplies and for fishing purposes as originally planned.

Having examined the accounts and looked into the state of things at Plymouth to his "good contente and satisfaction," Hatherly went on an inspection tour of the Pilgrims' trading posts. He proceeded first to the Kennebec and then to the Penobscot, where Ashley already was in trouble. Although under a £500 bond not to

do so, he had been "trading powder & shote with ye Indeans."
Also, he had managed to give Willet the slip and commit
"uncleannes with Indean women." Otherwise, he had done very
well at Pentagoet, acquiring more than a thousand pounds of
beaver and otter, but the Pilgrims dismissed him and shipped him
back to England as a prisoner.

Once more Allerton was sent to London, sailing on the *White
Angel* with Hatherly and everything that Plymouth had collected
for export. But his partners immediately regretted their decision
to continue him in office. They now saw, though not yet suspecting
the worst, that transactions in London were "foulded up in ob-
scuritie, & kepte in ye clouds, to ye great loss & vexation of ye
plantation, who in ye end were (for peace sake) forced to bear
ye unjust burthen of them, to their allmost undoing." They hastened to revoke Allerton's commission and in his stead appointed
Winslow, who was in London and who soon reported that things
were in a dreadful mess. Sherley and his colleagues refused to bear
the heavy losses on the *Friendship* and the *White Angel,* placing
them on the general account, contrary to Allerton's and Hatherly's
assurances. Why should he and those in London shoulder the
expense? Sherley angrily asked. The *Friendship* had been hired
under instructions from Plymouth. The *White Angel* had been
bought by the Pilgrims' agent. Did the Plymouth partners now
propose to wiggle out of their engagements? Let them take care
not to act unreasonably and "so hasten that fire which is a-kindling
too fast allready." If Allerton exceeded his authority, whose fault
was that?

"I looke for bitter words, hard thoughts, and sower looks from
sundrie, as well for writing this as reporting ye former," wrote
Winslow. "I would I had more thankfull imploymente, but I hope
a good conscience shall make it comefortable."

What he and the Pilgrims needed far more than a good conscience was a mathematical genius to unravel Allerton's accounts.
It took two years to bring them into any kind of order, and then
it was discovered that their floating debt had risen from £400
($20,000) to £4,770 ($238,500) within four years! In addition, they

still owed £1,000 on the mortgage. There was no way of accounting for the expenditure of many large sums. In several instances the Pilgrims had been charged twice for goods delivered by him. He had inflicted intolerable interest charges and other expenses upon them—"£30 given at a clap, and £50 spent in a journey"—and under pretence of friendship cheated his brethren. "Yea, he scrued up his poore old father-in-law's accounte to above £200 and brought it on ye generall account . . . because he knew they would never let it lye on ye old man, when alass! he, poore man, never dreamte of any such thing," assuming that the goods "had been freely bestowed on him & his children by Mr. Allerton." Nor were the goods worth £200, for the sum had been "blown up by interest & high prises, which ye company did for ye most parte bear." Allerton's private trade had netted him such profits that within a year or two he cleared £400 and invested it in William Collier's brewery, "at first under Mr. Sherley's name."

To cap all, Allerton now brought in a claim that his partners owed him some £300 and demanded immediate payment!

The truth was, as later established, that the Pilgrims' "go-getter" had got into his partners for £2,000, and thus were they "hoodwinckte till now they were so deeply ingaged, . . . abused in their simplicitie, and no better than bought & sould, . . . so that which before they looked at as a heavie burthen, they now es-teemed but a small thing and a light matter." Hatherly came over and tried to collect the £2,000 from the Plymouth partners on the ground that Allerton had been their agent. "But they told him they had been fool'd longe enough with such things."

Allerton's fall from grace left the Saints gasping and embar-rassed. They were, on the whole, inclined to Sherley's view that he was "honest, and that his desire and intente was good." He had not meant to harm the plantation and his partners, but had been led astray by hope of private gain, believing that he could at once make a fortune for himself and free Plymouth from debt. "I say charitie makes me thus conceive," wrote Bradford, and "with pitie and compassion (touching Mr. Allerton) I may say with ye apostle Timothy, I. Tim. 6. 9. *They that will be rich fall into many*

*temtations and snares, &c., and pearce themselves throw with
many sorrows, &c.; for the love of money is ye roote of all evill.
v. 10."*

Having led his brethren "into ye briers," Allerton now deserted
them. Worse, he became a competitor, "but God crossed him
mightily." Sherley let him hire the *White Angel* under bond of
£1,000. Overloading the ship so that she almost foundered, Allerton reached the Maine fisheries too late to make a catch. Enterprising as ever, he turned to trade, trucking with the Indians for
whatever he could get, even offering them credit as the Pilgrims
loudly complained. He recruited some "base felows" and organized them into a trading company "to rune into every hole,"
sending them up the Kennebec and beyond the Penobscot to cut
off Plymouth's commerce in those parts, setting up a trading post
at Machias, close to the present Canadian boundary. On a visit to
Plymouth "ye church called him to accounte for these and other
his grosse miscarrages; he confessed his faulte and promised better
walking." But he went doggedly on his way flouting his former
loving brethren, giving vague assurances that he would soon have
his accounts in order with the assistance of one Mr. "Fogge."

Sherley had suggested sending over an accountant to Plymouth,
but the Pilgrims tartly replied that "if they were well delte with
and had their goods well sent over, they could keep their accounts
here themselves." They raised no objections, however, when Sherley got hold of another of Edward Winslow's younger brothers,
Josiah, and after some instruction in the mysteries of bookkeeping
sent him over "to perfecte the accounts." Though he sweated for
years trying to get a balance, Josiah was no help, trusting too
much to memory, losing important papers, and in the end "let
things rune into such confusion that neither he, nor any with him,
could bring things to rights."

To make confusion worse confounded, Sherley now let Allerton
buy on credit the *White Angel* and all her accounts from first to
last, thinking that if he were enabled to make some money, he
might the sooner pay his debts. He had also extracted from Allerton a promise to settle his accounts within two years. "And verily,

notwithstanding all ye disasters he hath had, I am perswaded he hath enough to pay all men here and there," wrote Sherley. "Only they must have patience till he can gather in what is due to him there."

Patience! snorted Bradford. With a man who "broke his bonds, kepte no covenants, paid no hire, nor was ever like to keep covenants!" Why, Sherley might as well have given him the ship; "and not only this, but he doth as good as provide a sanctuary for him" by asking those at Plymouth not to interfere with him as he went about collecting "all monies due for fraighte and any other debts belonging either to her or ye *Friendship's* accounts, as his owne perticuler." Meantime, the brethren were to "doe nothing but looke on till he had made all away into other men's hands (save a few catle & a little land & some small matters he had here at Plimoth) and so in ye end remove, as he had allready his person," whatever assets he had within reach!

Matters went from bad to worse. Sherley's shop at the sign of the Golden Horseshoe was burned out by a great fire on London Bridge. A gale drove the *White Angel* ashore near Bristol, and Allerton had to borrow £100 from Sherley to get her off. "Verily, his case was so lamentable as I could not but afford him some help therein," the latter explained, doubtless entering the loan on the general account, a handy catch-all for such things. "Oh, the greefe & trouble that man, Mr. Allerton, hath brought upon you and us!" exclaimed Sherley, "I cannot forgett it, and to thinke on it draws many a sigh from my harte, and teares from my eyes . . . I pray you finish all ye accounts of reconings with him there, for here he hath nothing but many debtes . . . Oh, what shall I say of that man who hath abused your trust and wronged our loves!" Allerton would never pay them a penny, as Sherley well knew, so that there was a note of genuine fervency in his prayer "that great God, whose care & providence is everywhere, and spetially over all those that desire truly to fear and serve him, [will] direct, guide, prosper, & blesse you so as you may be able (as I perswade myselfe you are willing) to discharge & take off this great & heavie burthen which now Lyes upon me for your saks."

Reverses and retreats multiplied on other fronts. The French in Canada had always regarded the Pilgrims' trading post on the Penobscot as an encroachment on their territory. One day in 1632, a small French ship put into the harbor on the pretence that she had lost her way and was leaking badly, needing to be hauled ashore for repair. The officers were very polite, "and many French complements they used and congees they made" in asking permission of the post, which was granted by the three or four "simple" servants left in charge by the resident agent, Thomas Willet, who happened to be in Plymouth getting supplies. Learning this, the visitors began praising the muskets in racks along the walls of the post, taking them down and examining them. Suddenly they turned them on their hosts, robbing them of everything at hand—rugs, blankets, coats, biscuit, and beaver worth £500. They even compelled the servants to carry the loot on board and stow it down before they leisurely sailed away.

"When your master comes," was their final taunt, "tell him that some gentlemen from the Île de Rey have been here."

At this time, too, there was an alarm at the trading post established among the Wampanoag at Sowams. After a skirmish in the woods, some Massachusetts Indians had come running in with a number of Narragansett in pursuit. It was feared that the latter were about to attack in force. The Pilgrims had a garrison of four men at the post under the command of Captain Standish. As the Plymouth colony was short of powder, Standish dispatched a runner to Boston to see if some could be obtained there. The runner quickly returned with thirty pounds of "black stuffe," as much as he could carry, and the Narragansett withdrew. But Governor Winthrop was in trouble for supplying Plymouth in her need, so jealous had the two colonies already become.

Using Sowams as a base, the Pilgrims now began to push their trade to the westward. Several years previously the Dutch, "seeing them seated in a barren quarter," had spoken to them of the rich lands along the Connecticut River, but the Pilgrims were then more interested in Maine. In 1631 Bradford had been urged to establish a settlement in the valley by the chiefs of several tribes driven out by the powerful and warlike Pequot. Failing to interest Plymouth, the chiefs went to Boston and were also turned away there.

The next year, however, Winslow led an expedition to explore the territory. It obviously had possibilities, and the Pilgrims now proposed to the Massachusetts leaders that the two colonies establish a joint post there to trade for furs and "hemp." Governor Winthrop and his colleagues declined with the excuse that they did not have sufficient trading goods. When the Pilgrims offered to supply these on credit, the Bay leaders thanked them but still opposed the project, at length frankly saying that they "had no mind to it," fearing a violent reaction on the part of the Pequot, 3,000 or 4,000 strong. Very well then, said Winslow, who was serving his first term as governor of Plymouth, did they have any objections to Plymouth going ahead alone? No, said the Puritans, and so it was agreed that the Pilgrims should pioneer the "Conightecute."

First, a prefabricated fort was built so that it might be hastily erected upon landing. The frame of a small house was cut and loaded on a large new bark, together with nails, clapboard, and other necessary materials. While the Pilgrims were thus engaged, their Dutch friends stole a march on them, erecting a large fort and trading post, the House of Hope, where the city of Hartford now stands. When the Pilgrim bark came sailing up the Connecticut under the command of William Holmes, Standish's chief lieutenant, the Dutch turned two cannon on her and commanded her to strike her colors and drop anchor. Holmes replied that he and his company had been commissioned by the governor of Plymouth to go up the river, and up the river they would go, cannon or no cannon—and up the river they went, about ten miles, to the mouth of a sizeable river, now the Farmington. Here at Matianuck, in what is now the city of Windsor, they landed their supplies and "clapt up their house quickly," surrounding it with a stockade, and none too soon. A heavily armed force of seventy men marched from New Amsterdam "in warrlike manner, with collours displayed, to assaulte them." But seeing that Holmes and his men could not be dislodged without great bloodshed, the Dutch offered to parley instead and in the end left the Pilgrims in possession.

After all, said Bradford, they had done "ye Dutch no wrong, for they took not a foote of any land they bought, but went to ye place above them."

Yet when they were served a like turn on the Kennebec a few months later, the Pilgrims were outraged. Early in 1634 a bark came up the river under the command of one Hocking from David Thompson's old settlement at Piscataqua. Hocking brazenly encroached upon their territory, the Pilgrims complained, and "would needs goe up ye river above their houses . . . and intercept the trade that should come down to them." Assistant Governor John Howland, the resident agent, ordered him to move on, "but all in vaine; he could get nothing of him but ill words." John Alden, also an assistant governor, was present and agreed with Howland that if such trespass were quietly suffered, "they had better throw up all." This they were resolved not to do. Both were Undertakers under heavy obligations, and their post here at Cushenoc was the most profitable of their ventures. They could never pay their debts without it. During the past two years it had brought them more than 7,000 pounds of beaver and otter, much of it worth 20s. a pound.

When another parley failed to move Hocking, Howland sent two men in a canoe to cut the cables of his ship as it lay at anchor in the river. As the vessel swung round, Hocking fatally shot one of the men, Moses Talbot. His partner picked up a musket and killed Hocking. "This was ye truth of ye thing," according to the Pilgrims, who added that news of the tragedy spread quickly and "in ye worst manner," for many ugly stories were circulating. As Hocking was in the employ of Lord Say and Sele, his death by violence was a serious matter—"much condemned by all men," Governor Winthrop wrote Plymouth, for it "has brought us all and the gospel under the common reproach of cutting one another's throats for beaver." Also, it might provide the King with a pretext for sending over a royal governor to rule all of New

England with an iron hand. This was not an imaginary danger. Headed by Archbishop Laud of Canterbury, a fierce and determined bigot, a Commission for Regulating Plantations had just been established with authority to legislate in all civil and religious matters, regulate trade, examine property titles, review charters, and revoke them if they contained any liberties or privileges harmful to the Crown. This sent shivers down many a spine, for the Pilgrim charter lacked the royal seal and was invalid, and Massachusetts' had its weak points.

Putting in at Boston on the Plymouth bark, John Alden was arrested and locked up on a charge of murder. Governor Thomas Prence, who had succeeded Winslow after a year in office, quickly dispatched Captain Standish to demand Alden's release and provide the Massachusetts authorities with "true information" about the shooting. The mission failed, and the fuming Captain found himself bound over to appear in court with the Kennebec patent and other papers. Now thoroughly aroused, the Pilgrims angrily protested Boston's assumption of authority and jurisdiction over them. They heatedly denied its pretended right either to imprison Alden or to command Standish's appearance in court. Governor John Winthrop and Assistant Governor Dudley urged caution and discretion, pointing out the great evils that might come upon them from the Commission for Regulating Plantations.

"This unhappie contention between you and us, and between you & Pascattaway, will hasten them, if God with an extraordinarie hand doe not help us," Dudley wrote Prence. "I pray you therfore, Sir, set your wisdom & patience a-worke, and exhorte others to ye same, that things may not proceed from bad to worse."

The Pilgrims quieted down, and Winthrop suggested that the shooting affray should be investigated by a court composed of representatives from the Bay colony, Plymouth, and neighboring settlements. As stipulated by the Bible in matters involving "ye clearing of conscience," Winthrop proposed that ministers from the several settlements should attend to give their advice on points of conscience. Always jealous of their independence, the Pilgrims looked somewhat askance at the proposed general court, fearing that it might set a dangerous precedent. In the end they agreed, and letters were sent to Piscataqua, Salem, and elsewhere. But on the appointed day only the delegates from Plymouth and the Bay appeared. The Pilgrim representatives were Bradford and Winslow, assistant governors at the moment, and the Plymouth pastor, Ralph Smith. The Bay was represented by Governor Winthrop and the Reverends John Cotton and John Wilson.

The court agreed that the primary guilt was Hocking's. Fault was found with the Pilgrims, however, and they were given some "grave & godly exhortations and advice." These were "imbrased with love & thankfullness," said Bradford, and the Pilgrims finally acknowledged "themselves under guilt of the breach of the sixth commandment," which restored "love and concord" between the colonies—at least for a time. Winthrop, Dudley, and Endecott undertook to write in the Pilgrims' behalf to the Council for New England and addressed a long explanation of the Kennebec affair to Lord Say and Sele in the hope of pacifying him, which it did in part.

The situation seemed so ominous, however, that the Pilgrims sent Winslow to England to defend their cause if any steps were taken against them. He was also to notify their London friends that the agreement granting the Undertakers a trade monopoly at Plymouth had expired. Perhaps to divert attention from the Hocking case, Winslow presented a petition to the Commission for Regulating Plantations. Pointing to the French attack upon their Penobscot post and their trouble with the Dutch in Connecticut, the Pilgrims declared that they could not resist such encroachments upon His Majesty's domain unless they were granted a special warrant to "defend themselves against all foraigne enemies," by arms if necessary. This petition was most ill-advised, as Winthrop declared, for it endangered their freedom of action. It tended to establish a precedent that nothing could be done without the authority of the Lords Commissioners. No doubt Standish agreed with Winthrop in this—as if the Pilgrims had ever had to have a special warrant to use arms against their "enimies!" The petition had other unfortunate effects—above all, for Winslow.

When the petition was presented, Sir Ferdinando Gorges began raising difficulties, aided and abetted by "ye archbishop of Counterberies." Gorges was already possessed of a huge tract between the Kennebec and the Piscataqua, and had never abandoned hope of acquiring all of New England as a vast feudal manor with himself as overlord. The Council for New England had been forced to surrender its charter, and Sir Ferdinando now had himself appointed governor-general of the territory. He was already making preparations to come over with 1,000 soldiers and scores of Anglican clergymen to "reform" the settlements, especially their churches, in light of the high doctrine laid down by that most regal and pigheaded of the Stuarts, Charles I, now fast traveling the road to revolution and the executioner's block. In these proceedings Archbishop Laud and Gorges were effectively aided by "Mine Host of Ma-re Mount," who was suddenly brought into the council chamber to badger poor Winslow about the Pilgrims' faulty patents and their "abhominable" religious practices. Morton charged that Winslow, a layman, was guilty of "teaching in ye church publickly, . . . and gave evidence that he had seen and heard him doe it." Worse, the wretch had desecrated the sacraments by daring to marry people.

Archbishop Laud was interested and took up the questioning. Yes, said Winslow, he had sometimes exercised "his gifte to help ye edification of his breethren, when they wanted better means, which was not often," and as a magistrate had performed the marriage ceremony on occasion. After all, marriage was "a civille thinge, and he found nowhere in ye word of God that it was tyed to the ministrie." Nor was this a new or unusual practice, for he had been so married in Holland by the burgomasters at Leyden.

In a rage Laud had Winslow thrown in jail, and for months the Pilgrims' usually discreet ambassador lay in the noisome Fleet, doubtless recalling with anxiety the tragic fate of John Greenwood, Henry Barrow, John Penry, and other martyrs who had been locked up here and elsewhere in London almost a half century before. Upon his release Winslow did not tarry to discuss the *White Angel* or any other matter, hastening home on the first ship, and such was "ye end of this petition, and this business," with the Pilgrims out of pocket as usual. Their only solace was that the designs of Gorges and Laud were frustrated by shipwreck and the growing crisis in England.

Misfortune continued to pile upon misfortune. In August, 1635, the tail of a West Indies hurricane did great damage at Plymouth and Aptuxcet. In the same month the French again attacked their trading post on the Penobscot and this time dispossessed them, sending Willet and his men back to Plymouth with only their shallop and a few provisions. Two years previously the French had fallen upon Allerton's post at Machias and destroyed it, killing two men and capturing three others. Far from protesting, the Pilgrims were rather pleased, feeling that it served Allerton right for trying to cut into their trade. Now the shoe was on the other foot, and the loss of Pentagoet "did much move them," inspiring a resolve to teach the French a lesson. The Bay colony was asked to participate on the ground that French "encroachment" had to be resisted for the safety of all, but the Bay as usual offered only moral support.

The Pilgrims met one Captain Girling, master of the *Great Hope,* a large ship of 300 tons, "well fitted with ordnance," and agreed with him that he was to have 700 pounds of beaver if he recaptured the post—and nothing if he failed. With the *Great Hope* went the Plymouth bark bearing Captain Standish, twenty of his men, and the promised beaver. Off Pentagoet, Standish suggested a parley to see if the French could be persuaded to withdraw by threat of superior force. But Captain Girling was "so rash & heady as he would take no advice," and while still so far out that he could do no damage, began shooting "like a madd man." Standish was "much greeved," ordering him to stand in, saying that the ship could safely lie broadside within pistol shot of the fort. After long argument Girling stood in, but now all of his powder was gone "so he could doe no good" and had to move off again. Standish was furious, for the French were lying snugly behind earthen breastworks laughing at them. It was this perhaps more than any hope of victory under Girling that led Standish to agree to go for sufficient munitions to pulverize the French. These he forwarded on another vessel and sailed back to Plymouth with his men and beaver, for he suspected that Girling planned to seize all. Ample supplies reached Girling and were a virtual gift from the Pilgrims, for the *Great Hope* sailed away without firing another shot.

Disappointed in this, the Pilgrims again tried to persuade the Puritans to help them dislodge the French. When the latter expressed mild interest, Standish and Thomas Prence went to Boston to see if Winthrop and his colleagues could be prevailed upon to put up some money, always a difficult task. The Puritans listened sympathetically and offered to assist in recruiting and outfitting an expedition if the Pilgrims would bear the entire expense. This was bad enough, complained Bradford, but some of their merchants immediately went to Pentagoet and began a profitable trade with the French there, "so as it is no marvell that they still grow, & incroach more & more upon ye English, and fill ye Indeans with gunes & munishtion, to ye great deanger of ye English." Under the circumstances the Pilgrims had no choice but to accept the loss of their post, which became for a time the seat of French power in upper Maine.

But this loss "Way Down East" at Castine was nothing compared with the blow now struck them in Connecticut—the unkindest and most disconcerting of all, for they were smitten not by the French, or the Dutch, but by their own God-children, the newly converted Saints of the Bay. The Pilgrims had been doing very well at Matianuck, their trading post on the Connecticut River, under the able management of Jonathan Brewster, now a man in his forties. The Puritans soon began casting a covetous eye in that direction even though they had rejected just a few years before the Pilgrims' suggestion for joint occupation. Led by John Oldham, ten men came from Watertown in 1634 and settled at Pyquag, soon named Wethersfield, a few miles below the Dutch post, planting great fields of onions "under the very noses of Fort Goed Hoop, insomuch that the honest Dutchmen could not look toward that quarter without tears in their eyes." The next year, annoyed by "King" Winthrop and his often arbitrary rule, Pastor John Wareham led many of his congregation from Dorchester and chose to settle virtually on Jonathan Brewster's doorstep. Bradford sharply warned them that they were trespassing, telling Brewster to be kind but firm with them in pointing out the error of their ways.

"I shall doe what I can to withstand them," Brewster promised and treated them very well indeed, to the Undertakers' great charge. The first arrivals would have starved if he had not fed them for many days. He went with them to the Dutch to see if the newcomers would be allowed to settle near them. The Dutch objected and wrote for aid in checking the English.

"And what trouble & charge I shall be further at, I know not, for they are comming dayly," wrote Brewster, saying that he simply could not persuade the Dorchester group to move on, which inspired a lively correspondence between Boston and Plymouth. It was God in His providence, said the Puritans smugly, who had tendered them these lands, which were "ye Lord's waste, . . . voyd of inhabitants."

"We tould you before," replied the Pilgrims angrily, "and (upon this occasion) must tell you still, that our mind is otherwise, and that you cast rather a partiall, if not a covetous eye, upon that which is your neighbour's, and not yours . . . Looke that ye abuse not God's providence in such allegations."

If Connecticut was the Lord's waste, who had made the first settlement there? Who had kept the Dutch from gobbling up the entire territory? And now because the tangled state of affairs at Plymouth prevented them from making any large colonizing effort at the moment, did the Bay have a right "to goe and take it from them"? Winthrop and his colleagues knew very well that the lands about Plymouth were barren, said Bradford, and that "neither they nor theirs could longe continue upon ye same."

It was an outrage that pretended friends, simply because they had more ample means, should deprive them of lands which they had acquired at such expense and danger and which they "intended to remove to as soone as they could & were able!"

But the Massachusetts Saints were not to be diverted, which left the Pilgrims in a quandary. To expel the intruders by force was out of the question. They had had "enough of that about Kenebeck, and to live in continuall contention with their freinds & brethren would be uncomfortable, and too heavie a burden to bear." A peace was patched up, as usual at the expense of the Pilgrims. They retained their trading post and two small lots at Matianuck. The interlopers agreed to reimburse them for the remainder of the tract they had bought from the Indians. Fratricide was averted, "but the unkindnes not soone forgotten."

Little more than a year later the Bay turned to Plymouth and without so much as a blush insistently asked for aid in a war to be waged—of all places!—in Connecticut. Ironically, too, hostilities had been precipitated there by the scalping of two men whom the Pilgrims had no cause to love—John Oldham and one Captain Stone, who had tried to run off on one occasion with the Pilgrim bark and later made an attempt to stab Winslow. Stone and eight men had been killed along the Connecticut in 1634 by the powerful Pequot, "a very false people." Two years later, while on a trading expedition to Block Island, Oldham was "knockt on ye head with a hatched."

Without notifying Plymouth or the settlers along the Connecticut, Captain John Endecott was sent with a small force "to take revenge" and badly managed the affair. He ravaged Block Island and then crossed to the mainland to demand the surrender of the guilty and great quantities of wampum. Not receiving immediate satisfaction, he fell upon the Pequot, killed a score or more, seized their supplies, burned and destroyed whatever he could—and then withdrew, leaving the scattered settlements to face the enraged Indians alone. For months the latter swept up and down the valley, plundering and killing. An alliance

between the Pequot and the Narragansett against all of the English
was foiled only by the persistent efforts of Roger Williams, recently cast out by Massachusetts and driven into the wilderness,
taking refuge with Canonicus, sachem of the Narragansett. As
the situation in Connecticut grew more desperate, Winthrop and
his colleagues appealed to Plymouth for help.

The Pilgrims were willing to consider the matter, Bradford
replied, but what about the Puritans' failure to aid Plymouth
in recovering its post on the Penobscot? It was well known
that Boston merchants were not only trading there but surreptitiously carrying on business along the Kennebec. If the Pilgrims
took a hand in this enterprise, what assurance had they of receiving assistance when they needed it? Why had Massachusetts
plunged into the war without consulting anybody, and why
should neighbors now be called upon to rescue them from their
own bungling? And had they forgotten their highhanded procedure in arresting Alden and forcing Standish to appear in court
at Boston? Finally, what had they to say about their virtual con-
fiscation of Pilgrim lands in this same Connecticut which Plymouth was now asked to defend?

Winthrop's reply was a masterpiece of its kind. Nothing could
have been more disingenuous. There was no parallel between
the present case and the French seizure of Pentagoet, he declared,
"yet we cannot wholly excuse our failing in that matter." Boston
merchants were not trading with the French—or at least, he had
no official knowledge of it. Winthrop quickly escaped to higher
ground and appealed to the Pilgrims' self-interest. If Massachusetts should be defeated by the Pequot, Plymouth would be in
dire peril and have to spend great sums to defend itself. If seasonable aid were given, the war would soon be over, which would
put an end to the one great fear that discouraged immigration.
Winthrop concluded with a scarcely veiled threat.

If Massachusetts were denied help from Plymouth, "it may
breed such ill thoughts in our people towards yours," he remarked,
"as will be hard to entertaine such opinione of your good will

towards us as were fitt to be nurished among such neighbours & brethren as we are. And what ill consequences may follow, on both sids, wise men may fear & would rather prevente than hope to redress."

Winthrop's curiously perverted "good neighbor" policy did not immediately resolve the Pilgrims' doubts, but a few months later they offered to send sixty men under the command of Lieutenant William Holmes, who knew Connecticut. Just as they were leaving on the bark, word came that the campaign was virtually ended. A combined Massachusetts and Connecticut force had wreaked a terrible vengeance upon the Pequot. Trapping some seven hundred of them—men, women, and children—near the mouth of the Mystic River, the English under Captain John Mason, one of the interlopers at Matianuck, fell upon the encampment with fire, sword, blunderbuss, and tomahawk. Only a handful escaped, and few prisoners were taken. Flames consumed almost all, and it was a fearful sight, said the Pilgrims in phrases quoted with delight and without acknowledgement by Cotton Mather, "to see them thus frying in ye fyer, and ye streams of blood quenching ye same, and horrible was ye stinck and sente thereof; but ye victory seemed a sweete sacrifice, and they gave prayse therof to God."

From this shattering blow the proud Pequot, lords of the New England forests, never recovered. Their chief sachem, Saccacus, fled to the Mohawk, who killed him and sent his head to Boston. Remnants of the tribe took refuge among the Mohawk and the Narragansett, and were adopted by them. Male prisoners were shipped to the West Indies and sold as slaves. Young squaws and maidens were divided among the soldiers. "There is a little squa that Stewart Calacot desires, to whom he hath given a coate," wrote Colonel Israel Stoughton, the commander-in-chief. "Lifetenant Davenport also desires one, to witt, a tall one that hath three stroakes upon her stummack, thus!!!." Winthrop informed Bradford that he had taken personal charge of the wife of a Pequot sachem, a woman "of a very modest countenance and behavior," whose only request was that the English "not abuse her body."

In the midst of all these distractions and defeats the *White Angel* popped up again. As Sherley once remarked, all would have been infinitely better off if they had sunk the ship the day they bought her at Bristol. After his imprisonment in the Fleet in 1635, Winslow returned home without the accounts so long promised, to the great disappointment of his partners. The latter were resolved to send no more goods to England until the accounts were received, having refrained from making any shipment the previous year. But Winslow contended that everything would soon be straightened out if they evidenced their good faith by continuing to send beaver. They thought his arguments "but weake," as they were, but yielded and forwarded three large shipments of peltry to London.

"Blessed be God for ye safe coming of it," wrote Sherley. He said nothing about the accounts, however, and filled up his letter with complaints about the sad state of affairs in England. There had been a great drought. Plague was sweeping London. It was impossible to do any business. The beaver could not be sold. Even if he had offered it at 8s. a pound, there would have been no customers so that it would have to be held for a better market. As a consequence, he was short of money. His partners Beauchamp and Andrews would not lift a finger to help. Altogether, it was the "miserablest" time he had ever known, with "preaching put downe in many places, not a sermone in Westminster on ye saboth, nor in many townes aboute us . . . Thus desiring you to remember us in your prayers, I ever rest, Your loving friend."

The Pilgrims frankly were not interested in Sherley's troubles, or England's either, having sufficient nearer home. Late in 1636 they discharged Sherley as their London agent and again demanded a financial statement. During the past five years, according to their accounts, they had sent him 12,530 pounds of beaver and thousands of otter, black fox, mink, and other skins. At a conservative estimate the beaver was worth £10,000. This repre-

sented net profit, for the otter and other peltry had paid all
freight charges. As their debts had totaled £5,770 in 1631 and the
value of all goods subsequently received did not exceed £2,000,
"they conceived their debts had been paid" and sent no more
beaver.

Now came a complaint from Beauchamp and Andrews that
since 1631, when each had been out £1,100, they had not received a penny in repayment. It was a strange business, remarked
the Pilgrims, referring them to Sherley. Everything shipped to
London was for all the partners, and if Beauchamp and Andrews
"did not looke after it, it was their own falts." But they could
get nothing from Sherley, they protested. Sherley explained that
his partners had abandoned him and saddled him with all the
bills, and these were far from paid. Besides, said he, posing the
question shrewdly, why should he satisfy these greedy claimants
when his first obligation was to salvage what he could for his
friends at Plymouth?

As usual, the blame was laid upon the Pilgrims for shipping
all goods to Sherley. Andrews made such a piteous story of his
reverses that a cargo of beaver was forwarded direct to him and
Beauchamp. The latter sold his share for £400, but through his
own indiscretion Andrews suffered a loss, which he promptly
charged to the Pilgrims, an invariable and invaluable formula
for the solution of all financial ills. He who had discovered that
formula, Isaac Allerton, had since vanished from the scene. His
property had been seized to satisfy the many claims against him.
Some of his cattle were now sold and the proceeds sent to Andrews and Beauchamp in the hope of silencing them. The Undertakers disposed of their post on the Kennebec and sold the bark
employed there.[2] Part of this money was also sent to Andrews
and Beauchamp, "yet this did not stay their clamors."

Sherley now urged them to send some one to England, preferably Winslow, to wind up the business once and for all. Most
of the local Undertakers thought this a wise course. But in light
of "bitter and threatening" letters from London, Winslow refused to go, "for he was perswaded, if any of them wente, they

should be arested, and an action of such a summe layed upon
them as they should not procure baele, but must lye in prison,
and then they would bring them to what they liste; or otherwise, they might be brought into trouble by ye archbishop's
means, as ye times then stood." England was teetering on the brink
of revolution, with Charles I and Laud making a last desperate
effort to hold back the rising tide of revolt.

The majority of Winslow's partners felt that Sherley's offer
should not be rejected. When Standish offered to go, probably
with the thought that as a non-Separatist he might avoid trouble,
it was decided to ask Boston's advice in the matter. Winthrop
strongly counselled them against it, and they wrote Sherley to
suggest an alternate course. The case should be referred to "some
gentle-men and marchants" of the Bay colony known to both the
London and Plymouth partners. All evidence, written and unwritten, should be submitted to these men for final review and
decision. Whatever it was, they at Plymouth promised to accept
the award "though it should cost them all they had in ye world."
They were tired, they said, of "ye clamours and aspertions raised
& cast upon them hereaboute," especially in the Bay colony. They
also feared a fall in the price of cattle, now their principal wealth,
which was not a groundless fear as things turned out. Furthermore, they were "loath to leave these intanglements upon their
children and posteritie, who might be driven to remove places,
as they had done; yea, themselves might doe it yet before they
dyed."

Sherley made a counterproposal. If Winslow feared to come
to England, why not arrange for a meeting in France, Holland,
or Scotland? "Let each give way a little," he urged, for otherwise the business would drag on endlessly. If the Pilgrims forced
him to sue for his money, they could expect no mercy, and only
the lawyers would stand to gain. He and his partners were prepared to accept compromise. Let the Pilgrims offer one, and it
would not be refused.

"Ye gospell suffers from your delaying," he declared, "and
causeth ye professors of it to be hardly spoken of, that you, being

many & now able, should combine & joyne togeather to oppress
& burden me."

At length, in 1641, after much backing and filling and many
reproaches, Sherley accepted the Pilgrims' suggestion and gave
power of attorney to a friend, John Atwood, assistant governor
of the colony in 1638, apparently a well-considered choice, for
he was a "godly man, singularly endowed with the grace of Patience." Joined with him for counsel and advice was Assistant
Governor William Collier, the brewer, formerly an adventurer
and a London Undertaker, who had come over to settle in 1633.
Still another assistant governor acted with them, Edmund Freeman, Beauchamp's brother-in-law, who had arrived in 1635. With
these the Plymouth Undertakers finally came to an agreement.
An inventory was made of what remained of the joint stock—
trading posts, boats, livestock, beads, hatchets, cloth, furs, and
other things. These were valued at £1,400, which was divided
equally among the partners. In addition, the Plymouth Undertakers put themselves under bond to pay their London partners
a sum of £1,200 ($60,000), to be paid £400 down and the re-
mainder at £200 a year. When all had been paid, the Plymouth
partners—Brewster, Bradford, Winslow, Standish, Prence, Alden,
and Howland—were to be "fully and absolutly aquited & discharged of all actions, suits, reconings, accounts, claimes, and
demands whatsoever concerning ye generall stock of beaver trade,
payment of ye said £1,800 for ye purchass," and all charges incurred by the *White Angel* and *Friendship* on any of their
voyages, "made or pretended, whether just or unjuste, from ye
world's beginning to this presente."

Bradford and his friends were encouraged, but they were not
yet in the clear. Sherley accepted £110 as his share of the settlement and sent them a release, expressing his pleasure that they
were ending as they had begun, "with peace and love." A sum of
£500 was paid to the haberdasher, Richard Andrews, now a member of the Massachusetts Bay Company and a resident of Boston,
who used his share to buy cattle and make other provision for the
relief of the poor in the Bay colony—as if there were no poverty

at Plymouth! Andrews put in an additional claim for £44, which the Pilgrims finally paid to be rid of him.

But Beauchamp refused to sign a release, demanding £400 more than he was offered. Both of his partners declared that he was not entitled to any such sum. Andrews advised Plymouth not to accept Beauchamp's account unless "on oath in chancerie." In the last of his letters the aging Sherley wrote the Pilgrims that they should not pay Beauchamp more than £100, and at that he was cheating them. But as always, the Pilgrims paid. In 1645, to satisfy Beauchamp's claims, the local partners pledged their estates as security, and in making a final settlement a few years later Bradford had to sell a large farm, Standish and Alden 300 acres each, while Prence and Winslow sacrificed their houses.

He who had led them "into ye briers" was now a prosperous merchant at New Haven, Connecticut. Allerton apparently left Plymouth in 1633 after the death of Fear Brewster, his second wife, though he was still listed as a freeman of the town two years later. On the eve of his departure, as the tax rolls revealed, he was much the richest man in the colony—which certainly came as no surprise to his brethren. In 1633 he paid a tax of £3 10s. ($175). Winslow's came next at £2 5s., while Bradford followed with £1 16s. The only others to be assessed £1 or more were William Brewster, Jonathan Brewster, Thomas Prence (a Brewster-in-law), Deacon John Doane, John Alden, Stephen Hopkins, and Edward Dotey, who had served his indenture and risen rapidly in the world. In the matter of worldly goods he had outstripped most of those who had come as freemen, even Captain Standish, who was rated at a mere 18s.

Upon retiring in disgrace, Allerton went to live at Marblehead with his daughter Remember, who had married Moses Maverick, the local pastor. His other children remained behind in Plymouth. His eldest son, Bartholomew, eventually returned to England and died there. Mary married Robert Cushman's son, Thomas, Bradford's ward, who in 1649 became ruling elder of the church. A young son by his second wife, Isaac, was brought up by the Brewsters and sent to Harvard. At Marblehead, "the greatest

Towne for fishing in New England," Allerton did very well, having eight vessels in neighboring waters. But the Massachusetts authorities soon commanded him to move on, evidently at the instigation of his former brethren. He "hath too great familiarity with our common adversaries," Winslow wrote Boston. "The truth is he loveth neither you nor us." Allerton is next seen at New Amsterdam in 1643. Two years later he established himself as a merchant in the young and growing town of New Haven, then five years old. Here he married again and pursued his speculations with seeming profit and success, building a "grand house on the creek, with four porches." In 1659, at the age of seventy-three, he died and was buried in the town square, leaving an estate of £120 ($6,000), large for the day. He had many debts, however, and it soon transpired that he had died insolvent, leaving his creditors with only the pleasure of weeping in their beer—which doubtless would have inspired Bradford to a fitting moral on the ways of "marchants" and the perils of higher finance if he had survived the enterprising and always plausible Allerton, first of the Yankee traders.

21

DIASPORA

And thus was this poore church left like an anciente mother, growne olde, and forsaken of her children, . . . like a widow left only to trust in God.

—WILLIAM BRADFORD

THOUGH THE PILGRIMS REACHED OUT INTO DISTANT PARTS of New England and established trading posts far and wide, from upper Maine to the Connecticut River, they made no attempt during the 1620's to establish any permanent settlements. They were too few in number and too poor to spread out from Plymouth and attempt any colonization. The Puritans, on the other hand, soon had a number of flourishing towns—Salem, Charlestown, Boston, New Towne (Cambridge), Watertown, Lynn, Roxbury, and Dorchester. Within two years the Bay had attracted several thousand settlers, six times as many as the Old Colony, which caused a sudden shift of weight in all New England affairs. The center of gravity was no longer at Plymouth, but at Boston, and the effects of this were immediately felt along Town Brook. The presence of the larger population to the north profoundly and permanently altered the Pilgrims' primitive economy. With economic change came fundamental shifts in the general social pattern, which in turn affected the frame of government and all institutions, even the church.

A staple of their diet from the first, often the famished Pilgrims' only food, corn had acquired a new value in 1623 when it became a principal medium of exchange in the beaver trade. As the Indians were always hungry for corn and eager to barter for it, the Pilgrims planted as much of it as possible. But its value as a trading commodity began to decline and production fell off with the introduction of wampum in 1627. For several years the planters followed agriculture only for home needs, having no market for surplus grain, cattle, hay, and other produce. Now all this was suddenly changed. The rapidly growing Puritan settlements wanted and had the means to buy everything the Pilgrims could produce. Corn was soon selling at 8s. a bushel. Milk goats brought £4 a head, calves £10, while beef cattle brought as much as £28 ($1400) a head. The Pilgrims went eagerly to work to increase their crops and livestock, "by which many were much inriched"—a quite unfamiliar state of affairs for most of them.

"No man now thought he could live except he had catle and a great deale of ground to keep them, . . . and having oxen growne, they must have land for plowing & tillage." Again there was a clamor for division of the common lands. It became so loud and insistent that the authorities gave way in 1632, distributing thousands of acres among the fifty-eight Purchasers in proportion to the number of shares each held in the colony. As the better farm lands and meadows lay in that direction, most of the assignments were made to the north of town. Bradford and John Howland were given large tracts along the Jones River, about five miles distant, in what is now Kingston. Grants were made even farther away, clear around the upper shore of the harbor. Anxious to develop their new farms and profit from soaring prices, people began moving out of Plymouth at an alarming rate.

"And if this had been all," said Bradford, "it had been less, though too much," for now "ye church must also be divided, and those that lived so long togeather in Christian & comfortable fellowship must now part and suffer many divisions."

The pull of larger and more fertile fields was so strong that many of the Old Comers, including some eminent Saints, were drawn across the harbor to Duxbury, the first of Mother Plymouth's daughters. The venerable William Brewster, now approaching seventy, went to live there with his two younger sons, Love and Wrestling, the only members of his family still living with him. His brave and patient wife Mary had died five or six years before. His daughter Fear was having her troubles as Mrs. Isaac Allerton, while Patience had married the ambitious and rapidly rising Thomas Prence, soon to be governor. Jonathan Brewster was off exploring Connecticut with Winslow. The ruling elder's neighbors included George Soule, Philip Delano, Moses Simmons, John and Priscilla Alden with five small children, and Myles Standish, who had his farm at the foot of what has long been known as Captain's Hill. With the latter came his "dearly beloved wife Barbara," several children, and Squanto's old rival, Hobomok, who braved the "enticements, scoffs, and scorns" of his people and lived in the Standish household till he died in 1642, always loyal to the Pilgrims and still "seeking after their God, . . . leaving some good hopes in their hearts that his soul went to rest."

According to an old and generally accepted tradition, the town was named for Duxbury Hall, later discovered to be one of the properties of the powerful Standish family from which the Captain claimed descent. Unfortunately for the tradition, Duxbury Hall was not so named until many years after the town was founded. Indeed, for a half century the town was not known as Duxbury at all, but as Duxburrow (often written "Ducksburrow"), which would suggest that it was named for the large

flocks of waterfowl that nested in the extensive salt marshes along
its shores.

For several years the Duxburrow people journeyed to Plymouth
every Sabbath to attend the meeting there, probably crossing the
harbor in the shallop whenever the weather was good, for it was
an exhausting ten miles' journey by land. And it had to be made
on foot or on the back of plodding oxen, for there were as yet
no roads and no horses in the colony. Stephen Hopkins appears
to have owned the first horse in the Old Colony, a mare, and she
does not appear in the records until twelve years later, in 1644.
Trails were rough and often muddy, and there was constant complaint about "dangerous and hazzerous" bridges, which were
usually just a few trees felled across a stream and difficult to
manage even on foot. Soon the distant brethren were complaining
that it was a "great burthen" to bring their wives, children, and
servants to the meeting at Plymouth every Sabbath and asked to
be allowed to "become a body of themselves." They sued for their
dismission, which was finally granted in 1637, "though very un-
willingly," for Plymouth had recently lost many of its abler men
and more experienced Saints.

In 1633 an "infectious fevoure" had swept the town, raging
throughout the summer. More than twenty people died—both of
Brewster's daughters, Fear Allerton and Patience Prence; Cuthbert Cuthbertson and his wife Sarah (Allerton); Francis Eaton,
the ship's carpenter of Bristol, who had lost his first wife in the
General Sickness and since been married twice; John Adams
of the *Fortune* company; and Peter Browne, "Goodman" John
Goodman's partner when they had gone hunting deer with a
sickle and had their dreadful encounter with "lyons." The church
lost all three of its deacons, "anciente friends" from Leyden days
—Thomas Blossom, Richard Masterson, and the faithful Samuel
Fuller, their doctor, "who had been a great help and comforte
unto them, ... a man godly and forward to doe good, being much
missed after his death." For decades Plymouth was left without
a doctor or anyone with even a smattering of medical lore.

To check the diaspora of the Saints, it was decided "to give out

some good farms to spetiall persons . . . lickly to be helpful to
ye church or commonewelth," if they would promise to live in
town and arrange matters so that their servants might cultivate
their fields and tend their livestock. Accordingly, large tracts of
fine meadow land were staked out beyond Duxbury, at a place
called Green's Harbor, soon named Marshfield, and were bestowed upon some of the "Old Standards," including Edward
Winslow and William Thomas, "a well-approved and well-
grounded Christian, well read in the Holy Scriptures, and other
approved authors."

"But alass! this remedy proved worse than ye disease." As soon
as their farms were developed, these also broke away, "partly by
force, and partly by wearying ye rest with importunitie and pleas
of necessitie," for those at Plymouth were getting tired of living
"in continuall opposition and contention." This encouraged still
others to plead "their owne conceived necessitie" and depart,
"which will be ye ruine of New England, or at least of ye churches
of God there," so Bradford believed, "& will provock ye Lord's
displeasure against them." At Marshfield the Winslows established what was almost a feudal manor, naming it Careswell for
their home in England, a large estate later occupied in part by
Daniel Webster, who was laid to rest there in the old Winslow
Burying Ground.

Beyond Marshfield, almost halfway to Boston, there was another Old Colony town, Scituate (Ind. *satuit*, cold brook). It was
not an offshoot of Plymouth but was populated by Saints of a
closely related school. The merchant adventurer Timothy Hatherly had settled there about 1633, and two years later a large company arrived from England under the Reverend John Lothrop,
a man "indowed with a Competent measure of Gifts," according
to the Pilgrims, "and eminently Indowed with a Great Measure
of brokenes of hart and humillitie of sperrit." Lothrop was a
disciple of Henry Jacob, founder of English Congregationalism,
once an exile in Holland, where he often conferred with Robinson. Returning home in 1616, Jacob organized a Separatist congregation at Southwark, across the river from London. His church

differed from Robinson's only in the view that the individual churches should be subject to some general supervision. With Jacob's departure for Virginia in 1624, Lothrop succeeded to the pulpit at Southwark and occupied it for ten years. At length, despairing of England under Archbishop Laud, he and most of his congregation decided to migrate to New England. Scituate evidently did not please them, for they soon packed up and moved down to Cape Cod, settling at Barnstable in the territory once ruled by the "gentle" Iyanough, sachem of the Cummaquid.

Another company had settled there a few months previously, led from Weymouth (Wessagusset) by the Reverend Joseph Hull, who dealt in real estate and cattle when not saving souls. As the raw hamlet of Barnstable obviously could not afford two pastors, Hull was soon forced out and moved a few miles down the Cape to where another Pilgrim town, Yarmouth, was being hacked out of the wilderness. Stephen Hopkins built a house here but soon turned it over to his son Giles and returned to Plymouth. In the other direction, at the shoulder of the Cape, the town of Sandwich had been settled by a group led by Edmund Freeman, soon made an assistant governor, brother-in-law of John Beauchamp, salter of London, Sherley's cantankerous partner. This group frankly avowed the purpose of its enterprise, which was "to worship God and make money."

The growth of these and other towns raised many puzzling new problems. Technically, all of Plimoth Plantation belonged to Bradford, for the patent of 1630 stood in his name. He now agreed to surrender it, signing over his rights to "ye freemen of this corporation of New Plimoth," having first set aside several huge tracts of land for the exclusive use of the Purchasers. Though some of these had been Strangers at first, almost all were now Saints and it was they who really owned the colony. They controlled the electoral machinery, and it was their voice that spoke through the governor's council. The rank and file of the Pilgrims, as Bradford had frankly declared years before, were allowed to share in the government "only in some weightie matters, when we thinke good." Long accustomed to shaping policy and directing affairs, the Purchasers did not now propose to let control slip from their hands. Still, it was evident that the old frame of government was inadequate and would have to be expanded to provide proper administration of the new towns. The latter contained many exemplary Saints and were already demanding representation. Accordingly, in 1636, a committee was appointed—four representatives from Plymouth, two each from Duxbury and Scituate—to consider this problem and the matter of drawing up a general code of laws. Previously, law had been improvised as occasion demanded. A few scattered enactments had been placed on the books, but for the most part the Pilgrims used the Scriptures, the Mosaic Code in particular, as legal writ.

Many drastic changes were made in the hitherto unwritten constitution. The Pilgrims took occasion to draw up a Declaration of Rights, stating that they would recognize only such laws as were enacted "by the consent of the body of freemen or associates, or their representatives legally assembled, which is according to the free liberties of the free-born people of England." Officers were to be elected annually as before, but in addition to a governor and seven assistants they were now to elect a treasurer and a secretary, with a coroner, constables, and other lesser officers. As their first treasurer the Pilgrims chose a recent arrival, William Paddy of London, a tanner. Though a man of some wealth, he was "a precious servant of Christ, endued with a meek and quiet spirit, of a courteous behavior to all men, and . . . instrumental in his place for common good, both in the church (being sometimes by office a deacon of the church in Plimoth) and in other respects very officious." The secretary was another recent arrival, Nathaniel Souther, also of London. For the first time the governor was now paid a salary, £20 a year, but other officers received only their living expenses while on duty.

The right to vote was restricted to freemen, and it was not easy to attain that status. All had to pass a minute examination of their religious views and moral character. Massachusetts had early decreed that only "members of some of the churches within the lymitts of the same" could become freemen of the colony.

Plymouth did not explicitly discriminate in favor of the Saints but accomplished the same end by declaring that "no person or persons shall be permitted to live and inhabit within the government of New Plimoth without the leave and liking of the Governor, or two of the Assistants, at least." The authorities were very strict about this, and many a "stranger" was "warned out." In 1643, when the colony contained some 3,000 people, there were just 232 freemen. Nor were all of these entitled to vote. The franchise was limited to those with a rateable estate of at least £20 ($1,000). Though the Pilgrim leaders never took such high ground as those at the Bay, they shared some of "King" Winthrop's fear of "mere democracy."[1]

All governmental functions—executive, legislative, and judicial alike—were exercised by the governor and his seven assistants, who constituted the General Court. There was here no separation of powers, no constitutional system of checks and balances often so nicely adjusted that the machine stalled at dead center. That was a later theory of government elaborated by John Locke upon his quite mistaken analysis of the workings of the British system. To give them representation on the General Court, the towns elected two deputies—Mother Plymouth saw to it that she had four—"to join with the Bench to enact and make all such laws and ordinances as shall be judged to be good and wholesome for the whole." Like the freemen, the deputies had to be acceptable to the General Court. If the latter found them to be "insufficient or troublesome," they could be sent back and the town ordered to hold another election, which was an effective check on local presumption. All town affairs were closely watched, and the central authorities never hesitated to interfere. No one could own land or build a house without their approval. In 1639, disliking some of the settlers at Sandwich, the General Court forbade the town "to dispose of any more land." And woe betide the town that did not promptly install an orthodox minister, or that chose one deemed "weak or unsafe."

Mother Plymouth clashed with her daughters now and again, but they were generally inclined to be dutiful. They, too, had an aversion to "strangers" and were quick to "warn them out." For years the towns were not civil communities at all, but private corporations run for the benefit of the principal stockholders— the local Proprietors, to whom the General Court made the original grants of land. Under the eagle eye of Plymouth they sold or donated lots to desirable settlers, scrutinized the credentials of all newcomers, set aside common fields and pastures, and were responsible for putting in roads, bridges, and other public improvements. Except at Plymouth, there was no representative local government until 1651 when Sandwich won the right to govern itself by an annually elected board of selectmen, an institution soon established in all the Pilgrim towns.

The criminal code adopted at this time was quite simple[2] and, for its day, remarkably humane in the matter of capital offenses. England inflicted the death penalty for hundreds of offenses, down to thefts of 5s. or more. Plymouth limited the number to seven —treason, murder, witchcraft, adultery, rape, sodomy, and arson —and actually took life for only two, murder and sodomy. Contrary to popular belief, the Pilgrims never hanged a witch, leaving that to the better-schooled but more benighted men of Massachusetts.

The only town touched by the witch hysteria was Scituate, and there it was quickly scotched. Mary Ingham was tried and acquitted when charged with causing one Mehitable Woodworth "to fall into violent fitts, and causing great paine unto severall parts of her body att severall times, soe as shee, the said Mehittable Woodworth, hath bin almost bereaved of her sencis." The wife of William Holmes, Standish's lieutenant, was likewise tried on complaint of one Dinah Sylvester.

"What evidence have you of the fact?" the Sylvester woman was asked by the presiding magistrate, John Howland.

"She appeared to me as a witch."

"In what shape?"

"In the shape of a bear, your honor."

"How far off was the bear?"

"About a stone's throw from the highway."

"What manner of tail did the bear have?"

"I could not tell, your honor, as his head was towards me."

To discourage such nonsense, Dinah was fined £5 and whipped. And that was the end of witchcraft in the Old Colony, though the law against it long remained on the books. The Pilgrims' common sense here is the more remarkable in light of the gross superstitions of the day and the almost universal belief in the supernatural powers of those "possessed by Sathan." The nineteen "witches" hanged or crushed to death at Salem Village during that dark summer of 1692 were few compared with the 40,000, so it has been estimated, who were put to death in England during John Alden's lifetime.[3]

Nor did the Saints execute Quakers and "other Notoriouse heretiques," or pass laws against "gay apparel," as was done at Boston. So far as the last was concerned, perhaps the Millinery War had taught them a salutary lesson. Still, the Pilgrims were never ones to spare the rod and spoil the child, and now that they had a statute book, they rapidly filled it up with enactments of all kinds. They were imbued with a naïve confidence, part of their legacy to us, that if anything went wrong, the sure cure was to pass a law against it. For firing a gun "at night, save at a wolfe or for a man lost"—later amended to read, "excepte at an Indean or a wolfe"—the fine was 20s. Swearing cost the profane 12d. for each offense, or three hours in the stocks, or three days in jail, "according to the nature and qualitie of the person." In this as in all discretionary sentences, the higher the station of the culprit, the less the punishment, for the Pilgrims were not equal before the law.

It was forbidden to make "motion of marriage to any man's daughter or maid-servant, not having first obtained leave and consent of the parents or master so to do." The penalty was a fine, or corporal punishment, or both, as young Arthur Howland discovered in his pursuit of Governor Prence's daughter Elizabeth, whom he finally won after much travail. Wages were strictly controlled. No worker was to be paid more than 12d. a day with board or 18d. without. The General Court kept a sharp lookout for "idlers," and anyone not able to give a satisfactory account of himself was subject to forced labor "according to the wisdom of the government."

Young Francis Billington was one of the first to pay 10s. for violating the ordinance against smoking—or, as the phrase went, for "drinking tobacco . . . in a very uncivill manner openlie in the towne streets, and as men pass upon the highways, as also in the fields, and as men are at work in the woods and fields, to the neglecte of their labours and to the great reproach of the Government." No liquor was to be sold "either within doors or without, excepte in inns or victualling-houses allowed." Only the most respectable could keep a tavern, for "mine host" was personally responsible for the sobriety of his guests, and care was taken that no license was issued to a man who "drinks druncke himself."

James Cole soon opened an ordinary on Cole's Hill, just above Plymouth Rock, later removing his casks and bottles to more ample quarters in Winslow's house, formerly Brewster's, conveniently situated in the very center of town, at the corner of the Street and the Highway. At the same time one of the *Fortune* group, Francis Sprague, said to have been of "ardent temperament," obtained leave "to keepe a victualling on the Duxburrow side," having his license suspended for a time the next year for "drinking overmuch" and tolerating too much jollity. His son John was a spark off the old flint, it appears, and spent hours in the stocks for "highly misdemeaning himself in the house of James Cole of Plymouth, near unto or on the evening before the Sabbath Day, in drinking, gameing, and uncivill revelling, to the dishonor of God and the offense of this govment, by his gameing and bringing of his mare uncivilly into the parlour of James Cole aforesaid." Among the more staid tavern keepers were Bradford's stepson, Constant Southworth, and Assistant Governor William Collier, brewer of London, now the richest man in the colony; nor should one forget Isaac Robinson, son of the Leyden pastor.

Nothing was too large or too small to escape the attention of the General Court. For telling a lie, "though not a pernicious lie, only inadvisedly," Goodwife Crispin escaped the usual fine of 10s. But a fine and also the lash were laid upon John Till "for lying & allureing John Bryan to drinking and slandering his dame Emerson, saying he would goe whome & lie with her." Up for "dealing fraudulentlie about a flitch of bacon," Edward Dotey paid an extra 50s. for calling the complainant "a rogue." The General Court, it must be said, did not spare its own members. Granted leave to build a grist mill on the banks of Town Brook, near Billington Sea, Assistant Governor John Jenney was called on the carpet in 1638 "for not grinding well and seasonable." After his death a few years later his wife was cited for not keeping the mill clean. In 1635 Assistant Governor Stephen Hopkins was fined £7 for assault—in 1637, £2 for "suffering servants and others to sitt drinkeing in his house . . . and to play at shovel board & such like misdemeanours," and as if that were not enough, "upon the Lord's day, before the meeting be ended"—in 1638, £1 on each of five counts for selling beer, wine, and "strong waters" above established ceiling prices; and for talking back to his colleagues, £3 for contempt; and for protesting that, spent four days in jail —in 1639, £3 for selling liquor without a license and a mirror for 16d., "the like of which is bought at the Bay for 9d." Deacon John Doane, formerly an assistant governor, and James Cudworth of Scituate, soon to become one, were both fined in 1640 for selling liquor without a license.

In that year the General Court decreed that "in every Constablerick there be a paire of stocks erected and a whipping post."[4] To judge from the first three entries in the records for 1633, the Saints evidently recognized a great and growing need of these:

Act. 1. John Holmes* was censured for drunkeness, to sitt in the stocks, & amerced in twenty shillings fine.

2. John Hewes & Jone, his wife, adjudged to sitt in the stocks because the said Jone conceived with childe by him before they were publickly married, though in the time of contract.

* Messenger to the austere General Court.

> 3. John Thorp & Alice, his wife, likewise adjudged to sitt
> in the stocks, & amerced in forty shillings fine, because his
> wife conceived with childe before marriage.

The Thorps were so poor that they were granted a year's grace
in which to pay their $100 fine—altogether, a remarkably lenient
sentence, for at this time it was usual for the husband also to be
well whipped in sight of his red-faced and anguished wife.

With the entire community watching eagle-eyed for evidences
of sin, many a hapless young couple went to the stocks "for having
a childe before the natural time of women after marriage," which
the Pilgrims assumed to be exactly nine months.[5] Occasionally
they made an allowance of a few days, but never more than a
week or two. The phenomenon of premature birth was not recognized in their book, and the advent of a child in the seventh or
eighth month of marriage was always a disaster—conclusive
proof of illicit relations before marriage and always promptly
punished as such, for "fornycation" was a legal as well as a moral
offense. After a time, learning something of the facts of life, the
Pilgrims liberalized their attitude, adopting the "seven months'
rule," but only after hundreds of innocent couples, as is now evident, had suffered public shame and disgrace for natural causes
quite beyond their control.

But from the records it is also evident that many of the younger
generation were as curious as Adam and Eve to taste forbidden
fruit. And with the many opportunities afforded them under a
curious institution long in favor among the Saints, the wonder is
that more did not indulge—or, at least, did not get caught.

The institution was known as Pre-contract, and under it an
enamored pair could assure themselves of an unusual degree of
privacy by appearing before two witnesses and formally announcing their intention to marry in due course. This was more than
an engagement, carrying almost the weight of marriage before
a magistrate.[6] Essentially, it was a semi-marriage, entitling the
betrothed to almost all of the intimacies of wedlock—all but the
last and most intimate. But this exception, as might have been
expected, was often more than aroused desire could brook, a fact

recognized even by the Saints, who drew a distinction between a lapse "in time of contract" and plain fornication, so to speak. The latter was far more severely punished, ordinarily with the stocks, the lash, three days in jail, and a £10 ($500) fine.

This, however, did not seriously dim the bright lustre of Satan's wares, and many succumbed to temptation. On the roster of confessed sinners appears many a familiar name—Isaac Robinson, grandson of the Leyden pastor; Peregrine White, Governor Winslow's stepson, the first white child born in New England; Thomas Cushman, son and namesake of Brewster's successor as ruling elder; Thomas, son of Philip Delano; and the two sons of Assistant Governor James Cudworth. "Uncleannesse" continued to be a felony up to 1703, thereafter being subject only to public censure and repentance in the meeting house. But by that time the moral fibre of the Saints had grown soft.

Violation of the marriage vow was, of course, a far more heinous offense. The law prescribed death for adultery, but that penalty was never exacted in the Old Colony though it was at the Bay and in Connecticut. The usual punishment was severe enough, however. For seducing an Indian, "Goodwife" Mendame of Duxbury was sentenced "to be whipt at a cart's tayle through the town's streets, and to weare a badge with the capital letters AD cut in cloth upon her left sleeve, . . . and if shee shall be found without it abroad, then to be burned in the face with a hott iron."

At this time, too, the Pilgrims passed a number of measures to stimulate economic activities. Towns were urged to improve and extend their roads, to build bridges and keep them in good repair. Steps were taken to promote the fishing industry by encouraging boat building, salt making, and the manufacture of barrel staves. Other measures were designed to stimulate agriculture and the breeding of livestock. For several years, with many circumstances favoring, the Old Colony enjoyed unusual prosperity.

Suddenly, everybody in the colony was poor or at least in financial straits. The boom stimulated by the steady immigration of the 1630's collapsed almost overnight. As luck would have it, the bubble burst just after the Pilgrims had signed their final compromise agreement with Sherley and his partners to clear themselves of debt. They had estimated their capacity to pay in terms of prevailing prices, which were fantastically inflated. Many had distrusted their unparalleled prosperity, fearing that it was too good to last, but they expected that the fall in prices would come "by degrees and not from ye highest pitch at once to ye lowest, as it did . . . and that so souddanly as a cowe that but a month before was £20 ($1,000) and would so have passed in any paymente, fell now to £5 and would yeeld no more; and a goate that wente at £3 or 50s. would not yeeld but 8 or 10s. at most . . . which was greatly to ye damage of many, and ye undoing of some."

The collapse had been caused by momentous events at home in England. More than ever resolved to have his way and crush all dissent, whether political or religious, Charles I had closed the ports of the kingdom to the many Puritans in flight from the rising storm, for the King and Archbishop Laud had no desire to strengthen the "heretics" in New England. As the tide of immigration declined to a trickle, the pressure on prices was removed, and the last props of inflation were swept away when the tide turned and began to flow back with the outbreak of the Civil War.

"Now, blessed be God, ye times be much changed here," Sherley had written his friends at Plymouth. "I hope to see many of you returne to your native land againe, and have such freedome & libertie as ye word of God prescribs. Our bishops were never so near downfall as now; God hath miraculously confounded them, and turned all their popish & Machavillian plots & projects on their owne heads."

The first skirmish in the conflict had been fought at Edinburgh, in the great church of St. Giles'. Bent on forcing episcopacy upon the stiff-necked Presbyterian Scots, Archbishop Laud and his prelates had drawn up a new liturgy with more Roman trimmings than had been used for a century. Many high dignitaries were present to enjoy the first service to be held under the new ritual. The Dean of St. Giles' had scarcely started before a devout parishioner, one Jenny Geddes, rose in her wrath and tossed a stool at him, narrowly missing the mitred head of the Bishop of Edinburgh. Pandemonium broke loose, and there was a great crash of glass as sticks and stones began to fly through the windows from the angry crowd gathered outside. Within a short time all of Scotland was united against the King and his fatuous ministers.

The latter were as resolutely opposed by the Puritan wing of the Anglican church and by a small but rapidly growing body of English Independents. In 1640, desperate for money, having exhausted all legal, extra-legal, and illegal means of raising revenue, Charles I called his first Parliament in eleven years, the renowned Long Parliament. But he soon dismissed it and at length, in the summer of 1642, he raised the royal standard at Nottingham, calling upon all "loyal" subjects to aid him in putting down "these base and unruly people."

Already, the King had been forced to abolish the hated Court of High Commission and the Star Chamber, and to sacrifice the Earl of Strafford, his chief minister, who had gone to the block in 1641.[7] And now the Long Parliament impeached Archbishop Laud and other high ecclesiastics. In 1643, soon after the outbreak of hostilities, Cromwell defeated the royal forces at the battle of Gainsborough, fought only a few miles from Scrooby, in one of the Roundheads' few early victories.

In the ranks of the rebels a dangerous split was growing wider every day, with the majority in Parliament favoring Presbyterianism and hoping to establish it as the state religion. Against them stood Cromwell and his army, who were Independents, the spiritual descendants of Robert Browne, more immediately of John Robinson, who "first struck out the Congregational or Independent form of church government," as all contemporaries agreed.[8] Though the two groups later quarrelled and came to blows, they remained united long enough to overwhelm their enemies.

In 1644, at Marston Moor, Cromwell smashed the Cavaliers with great slaughter, reporting that "God made them as stubble before our swords." With the next year came the execution of

Laud, the overthrow of the episcopacy, and the conclusive victory at Naseby.[9] All of this filled the Pilgrims with delight, inspiring Bradford to the most exclamatory passage he ever wrote.

"Full little did I thinke that ye downfall of ye Bishops, with their courts, cannons, & ceremonies, &c., had been so neare when I first begane these scribled writings . . . or that I should have lived to have seene or heard of ye same; but it is ye Lord's doing and ought to be marvelous in our eyes! . . . May not the people of God now say (and these poore people among ye rest), the Lord hath brought forth our righteousnes: come, let us declare in Sion the work of the Lord our God. Jer. 51. 10 . . .

"Doe you not now see ye fruits of your labours, O all yee servants of ye Lord that have suffered for his truth, and have been faithfull witnesses of ye same, and yee litle handfull amongst ye rest, ye least amongst ye thousands of Israll? You have not only had a seede time, but many of you have seene ye joyfull harvest; should you not then rejoyse, yea, and againe rejoyse, and say Hallelu-iah, salvation, and glorie, and honour, and power be to ye Lord our God, for true and righteous are his judgments. Rev. 19. 1, 2 . . . Hallelu-iah."

The revolution was not an unmixed joy, however, for it brought serious concerns to Plymouth and her neighbors. They feared that the Indians, or the French, or the Dutch, or all three, might take advantage of England's weakness and attack them. As early as 1637 Connecticut had proposed a league of mutual defense, but nothing was done about the matter until hostilities began at home. A meeting was called at Boston in 1643 to discuss the possibilities of alliance. Delegates were present from Massachusetts, Plymouth, Connecticut, and the recently organized New Haven colony, with Assistant Governors Edward Winslow and William Collier representing the Old Colony.

The alliance, it was decided, was not to embrace all of New England. When Roger Williams inquired about the project, he was bluntly told that Rhode Island was not eligible, and he was advised to join the colony to one or another of its neighbors.

New Hampshire and Maine were likewise excluded, the latter having recently become the vast feudal estate of Sir Ferdinando Gorges, now a leader in the King's party and obviously ineligible.[10]

Under the Articles of Confederation signed in September, 1643, the colonies of Massachusetts, Plymouth, Connecticut, and New Haven pledged themselves to a "firme & perpetuall league of friendship & amitie, for offence and defence, mutuall advise and succore, . . . both for preserving & propagating ye truth (& liberties) of ye Gospell, and for their owne mutuall saftie and wellfare." Each of the United Colonies of New England, as they called themselves, was to be represented by two commissioners. The latter had to be "in church fellowship" and were to "bring full power from their severall Generall Courts respectively to hear, examene, waigh, and determine all affairs of warr, or peace, leagues, aids, charges, and numbers of men for warr, divissions of spoyles & whatsoever is gotten by conquest." No decision was valid unless six of the eight commissioners concurred. In case of danger each colony was to provide a specified number of armed men. As Massachusetts was much the largest, the Bay was to provide a hundred soldiers; each of the others had to furnish forty-five.

From the start Massachusetts dominated the Confederacy, taking the lead here as in the American Revolution more than a century later. The Bay had made it a treasonable offense for anyone "by word, writing, or action . . . to disturb our peace, directly or indirectly, by drawing a party under pretence that he is for the King of England." Trade relations were broken off with Virginia, Bermuda, and the Barbadoes for supporting the royalist cause. Conscious of its relative strength, the Bay was somewhat overbearing toward its associates. At its insistence the commissioners met twice as often at Boston as elsewhere, and Massachusetts' delegates demanded and were finally granted precedence over others in signing documents and occupying the better seats —not "as a matter of right," the smaller colonies made plain. but out of courtesy.[11] The latter gave Massachusetts a sharp rap over the knuckles when it reached out for Pilgrim territory at Seekonk along Narragansett Bay.

In the midst of these distractions Plymouth was greatly weakened by death. Nathaniel Souther, the secretary of the colony, and John Atwood, John Jenney, and Stephen Hopkins, all men of strength, died in 1644. But the most grievous loss had been suffered the year before—on April 16, 1643—when the gentlest and most beloved of the Saints, "sweet" William Brewster, now almost eighty, "dyed in his bed, in peace, amongst ye mids of his friends, who mourned & wepte over him." He was not long sick, being up and about the day he died. Stricken in the afternoon, he lingered till evening, and "some few minutes before his last, he drew his breath long, as a man fallen into a sound sleep, without any pangs or gaspings, and so sweetly departed this life unto a better." As Bradford said of the always kindly man who had befriended and adopted him under such different skies and so long ago, Brewster did more for the gospel of simple human brotherhood in a year than most men in a lifetime.

"What though he wanted ye riches and pleasures of ye world of this life, and pompous monuments at his funerall? yet ye memoriall of ye just shall be blessed, when ye name of ye wicked shall rott (with their marble monuments). Pro. 10. 7."

Brewster's later years had been darkened by the dubious enterprises of his son-in-law, Isaac Allerton, and by the loss of so many of his family—his wife Mary, his daughters Fear and Patience, and his son Wrestling. But to the end he retained his "cherfull spirite" and served his brethren as ruling elder to their "comfortable edification." Though the oldest in the company, he had willingly labored in the fields and bore the "burthen with ye rest, living many times without bread, or corne, many months together, having many times nothing but fish, and often wanting that also; and drunke nothing but water for many years togeather, yea, within 5 or 6 years of his death." Always a contemplative and scholarly man, he spent more and more of his time in his study as old age crept upon him, finding pleasure and solace in a library that was quite remarkable for its day. It contained some 400 volumes, almost a third again as many and revealing quite as discriminating a taste as that more renowned collection which John Harvard left as a principal endowment to the college named for him.

Most of the volumes on Brewster's shelves dealt with religion in general, with Separatist doctrine in particular, and included the major works of Robinson, Barrow, Browne, John Smyth, Perkins, Ainsworth, and others, as well as copies of the books he had published at the press in Choir Alley. But the shelves held other things at once more interesting and revealing—Aristotle, Machiavelli's *Princeps,* Francis Bacon's *Advancement of Learning,* books on silk worms and medicine, W. Hornsby's *Scyrge of Drunkards,* something in verse entitled *A Good Wife: or, a rare one among Women,* and a copy of the *Tragedy of Messalina, the Roman Emperesse,* "as it hath been acted with generall applause, divers times, by the Companie of his Majestie's Revells. London, 1640." The ruling elder's taste, it would seem, had become more catholic with the years and his brethren, if they knew of it at all, must have been more than a little upset to find him in his old age consorting with that seductive Roman empress, imaginatively sitting in on "his Majestie's Revells," for the stage and everything about it had always been and would long continue to be anathema to the Saints.

Just at this time, while mourning their losses and struggling against adversity, the Pilgrims received a most unexpected visit. They could not have been more surprised if Satan himself had come to jeer at their reverses and mock them in their grief. It was almost impossible to believe their eyes, but there could be no mistaking the insolent though somewhat subdued leer of that "lord of misrule," Thomas Morton of Merry Mount, "starved out of England" by the turn of events there. The Pilgrims did not quite know what to do with "this sarpint," for he still had friends of influence at home, having come out as agent of several powerful Lords with vast properties in New England. After serious debate Bradford allowed him to spend the winter at Plymouth if he would "be gone as soon as winter breaks up." This greatly offended Morton's old enemy, "Captaine Shrimpe," who objected "especially that he is so neer him at Duxburrow, & goeth sometimes a-fowling on his ground." When not annoying Standish, who threatened to shoot him, Morton spent his time trying to recruit settlers, promising them generous grants of land at New Haven, but he was scorned by everybody, according to Winslow. He persuaded only one man to go with him, and that was no loss, for the fellow was "old, weake, & decreped, a very atheist, & fitt companion for him."

Early in 1644 Morton departed, going to Gloucester by sea. Hearing of this, the Massachusetts authorities issued a warrant for his arrest. "It is most likelie," they declared, "that the Jesuites, or some that way disposed, have sent him over to doe us mischiefe, to raise up our enemies round about us, both English & Indean." Morton escaped to Maine but was later seized, carried to Boston, and thrown in jail there—to prove, said Winthrop, "the justice of our [former] proceedings." No charges whatever were lodged against him, and after a year "in irons, to the decaying of his limbs," he was heavily fined and released, eagerly seizing an "opportunitie to go out of the jurisdiction." Morton withdrew to Agamenticus [York], Gorges' headquarters in Maine, where he lived "poor and despised," dying there two years later, "old and crazy," according to his enemies whose scorn dogged him to his grave. On his last visit, they observed, he had sunk so low that he was "content to drinke water."

Far from getting better, things at Plymouth went from bad to worse. With trade at a standstill there was a growing restlessness along Town Brook. One family after another packed up and left the town. In 1644, the "church begane seriously to thinke whether it were not better joyntly to remove to some other place than to be thus weakened and, as it were, insensibly dissolved." There was much conferring and discussing, as in the old days, for opinion was evenly divided. Many could not bring themselves to the thought of leaving Plymouth, tearing up roots again after all they had been through. They were no longer young, and it would be too much of a wrench to break up their homes and abandon the now comfortable houses they had so painfully built with their own hands, where their children had been born and they themselves had found rest and peace after so many trials and tribulations. It was possible to live comfortably at Plymouth, they protested, if men "would be contente with their condition" and not always be thinking of "enriching themselves."[12] Quite as many, on the other hand, were convinced that the possibilities of Plymouth were exhausted and flatly announced that "if ye church did not remove, they must."

The latter party prevailed, and the painful decision was made to undertake another pilgrimage, a general exodus of town and church to Nauset, halfway along Cape Cod. But some now began to waver, pointing out that Nauset was far off the beaten path, "remote from all society," and so limited in extent that it would "not be competente to receive ye whole body, much less be capable of any addition or increase." The question was reconsidered, and the decision reversed. But the leaders in the agitation had already staked out fields and started building houses on the Cape, and insistently asked permission to proceed, which at length was granted. Assistant Governor Prence, now married to Mary Collier, led the exodus to Nauset, or Eastham, as it was renamed. With the Prences went the families of Deacon John Doane, Richard Higgins, John Smalley, Edward Bangs, Josiah Cook, and Nicholas Snow, who had arrived on the *Anne* and married Constance, the eldest of Stephen Hopkins' daughters—almost all of which are still familiar names up and down Cape Cod.

"And thus," grieved Bradford, "was this poore church left like an anciente mother, growne olde, and forsaken of her children, (though not in their affections), yett in regarde of their bodily presence and personall helpfullness. Her anciente members being, most of them, worne away by death and these of later time being like children translated into other families, and she like a widow left only to trust in God. Thus she that had made many rich became herselfe poore."

Two years later, in 1646, Plymouth was almost a ghost town

but did not quite expire, thanks again to a pirate, one Captain Cromwell, luckily driven into the harbor by a storm. Laden with Spanish loot, his three vessels were manned by a lusty crew of eighty men, "very unruly," who came ashore and stayed six weeks rioting through the town, drinking "like madd-men." Their pockets filled with pieces of eight, they scattered a great deal of money among the people, said Bradford, "and yet more sine (I fear) than money." But wild as they were, they apparently liked the Saints and "gave freely to many of the poorer sort." Captain Cromwell was tried and acquitted for bashing in the head of one of his crew in a drunken brawl. Plymouth had never seen such goings-on but under the golden shower was apparently willing to blink them. The Pilgrims were not prepared to quarrel with the "divine Providence" which, as Winthrop remarked, directed the pirates to Plymouth "for the comfort and help of that town which was now almost deserted."

A few months later Edward Winslow departed for England, never to return. Sailing on a mission for the Bay,[13] he planned to be away only a short time. "But by reason of the great alterations in the State, he was detained longer than was expected, and afterwards fell into other imployments there, so as he hath now been absente this 4 years," wrote Bradford in 1650, "which hath been much to the weakning of this governmente, without whose consent he tooke these imployments upon him."

And on that melancholy note Bradford's history ends. Too deep in despair to continue, the patient chronicler of the Pilgrims' deeds, the faithful mirror of their hopes and fears, abandoned *Of Plimoth Plantation* and turned to other things, apparently weary of reporting only losses and defeats and what he regarded as the fatal scattering of the Saints.

Arriving in England, Winslow found it very different from what it had been on his last visit eleven years before when he had been summoned to the Privy Council and been so mercilessly badgered by Thomas Morton and Archbishop Laud, "that antichristian monster," who had ended by having him locked up in the Fleet. The royalist forces, while not yet crushed, were everywhere in retreat, and the Independents under Cromwell's aegis were rapidly rising to power. With a show of force they purged the Long Parliament of appeasers, expelling those Presbyterians disposed to compromise with the King. Enunciating the doctrine of popular sovereignty, declaring that "the people, under God, are the original of all just power," they appointed a High Court of Justice to try Charles I for high treason. Condemned to death, he went to the block in 1649 in the palace yard at Whitehall where he had long held despotic sway. A week later, because of its opposition to the trial, the House of Lords was abolished as "useless and dangerous." England was now a Commonwealth, stripped of feudal trimmings in Church and State, with Cromwell well on his way to supreme command as Protector.

"I am a poor weak creature," the latter wrote John Cotton at Boston, "and not worthy the name of a worm," yet happy nevertheless to have been "accepted to serve the Lord and his people." In one of his first acts he appointed a commission of Independents, Presbyterians, and Anabaptists to examine and regulate ecclesiastical affairs. It was primarily charged with seeing that every pulpit in the land was occupied by a pastor chosen "for the grace of God in him, his holy and unblameable conversation, and also for his knowledge and utterance, able and fit to preach the Gospel"—which was Pilgrim doctrine, almost word for word, now triumphant throughout the kingdom.[14]

Chosen for his "abilities of presence, speech, courage, and understanding," Winslow was his usual adroit self in defending the interests of both Massachusetts and Plymouth before the Commission for Foreign Plantations. "Heretics," in New England had lodged several serious complaints against them, but "this Hercules was accustomed unto the crushing of that sort of serpents," blasting them with *Hypocrisie Unmasked* (1646) and *New England's Salamander* (1647). Two years later he published *The Glorious Progress of the Gospell among the Indeans in New England,* which helped in organizing the Society for the Propagation of the Gospel in New England. Dedicated to converting the "heathen," it proved quite useful in later years in keeping the "praying" Indians at heel.

Winslow failed to obtain a proper charter for Plymouth, but in all else he was successful, rising from honor to honor and evidently enjoying himself. His oldest son Josiah, a youth in his early twenties, joined him and in 1651 persuaded his father to sit for his portrait. Though spurious daubs of one or another of the Forefathers hang on many a wall, this is the sole authentic Pilgrim portrait.* And certainly there is little of the typical Pilgrim as ordinarily conceived in the aspect of this serious but pleasant-looking man (the almost quizzical expression about the eyes suggesting a sense of humor), dressed in doublet with gold buttons, ruffled wrist-bands, and a broad starched collar held in place by a looped gold cord with tassels. With his moustache and the imperial on his chin he might almost be mistaken for one of Van Dyck's amiable Dutch burghers.

Cromwell soon noted Winslow's finesse in negotiation and in 1654 made him chairman of a joint English-Dutch committee to assess damages against the Dutch for attacking English vessels in neutral Danish ports. Winslow carried this off so well that he was appointed chief commissioner of an expedition dispatched to drive Spain from the West Indies. Attacking Santo Domingo, the invaders were repulsed with heavy loss, and as the ships drew off to storm and capture Jamaica, Winslow fell sick, evidently of a tropical fever. A few days later, in his sixtieth year, on May 8, 1655, he died on the flagship and was buried at sea, with a salvo of forty-two guns. Perhaps it was just as well that he died when he did, while the lustre of his fame was still bright, for upon their return to England his fellow commissioners, General Venables and old Admiral Penn, father of a more famous William, were committed to the Tower for their part in mismanaging the expedition.

Little more than a year later—on October 3, 1656—Captain Standish "expired his mortal life," having passed his seventieth

---

* Reproduced as the frontispiece.

birthday. "He, growing anciente, became sicke of the stone, or stranguary, whereof, after his suffering of much dolorous paine, he fell asleep in ye Lord, and was honourably buried at Dux-burrow," being laid away, as he had requested in his will, "as near as conveniente to my two dear daughters, Lora Standish, my daughter, and Mary Standish, my daughter-in-law." His "dearly beloved wife Barbara" and four sons—Alexander, Myles, Josiah, and Charles—survived him. Though he and his wife had never joined the church, they were obviously not averse to having their children do so. Alexander was a deacon at Duxbury, the town clerk as well, and soon opened a store in his father's house. In light of Longfellow's "Courtship of Miles Standish," based upon a pleasant but apocryphal story, it is curious that the Captain's oldest son married an Alden, young Sarah, John and Priscilla's second daughter. The Captain's second son, Myles, also married a Sarah, daughter of John and Mary (Chilton) Winslow, now residents of Boston, having followed Deacon William Paddy there. Standish had succeeded Paddy as treasurer of the colony after the latter's resignation to accept church office in 1644, and for five years the fiery little Captain collected taxes, paid out vouchers, and kept books, which must have been tedious business to one used to more wholesome and exciting pursuits.

For more than thirty years, until 1653, when age forced him to retire from active duty, Standish was commander-in-chief of the small but formidable Pilgrim army. It was ridiculously small, even in comparison with the forces that the local Indians could have brought against it, but in his hands it was always an ade-quate instrument for the purpose employed, never suffering a defeat. Though easily provoked and not to be trusted in matters of high policy, for his judgment was often warped by his quick temper and the boundless suspicions and fears of the professional military mind, yet Standish proved himself an always capable and inspiring leader in the field, and no one ever challenged— at least, not with impunity—his resolution as a commander or his personal courage. And it must be said of Standish that he took criticism well. After the Wessagusset affair he had received from

John Robinson such a stinging rebuke as few men would have been disposed to forgive or forget. The Captain bore no rancor, however, and in his will left £3 to "Marcye Robinson, whom I tenderlie love," he declared, "for her grandfather's sake."

Standish had prospered in the New World, leaving an estate of £258 ($13,000), which was large for the time. As executors, he had chosen none of the Saints, but Timothy Hatherly and James Cudworth of Scituate, two of the most liberal men in the colony, both of whom were later disenfranchised for protesting the violent bigotry of some of the Saints. Among his assets were listed five horses, two saddles, a bridle and pillion, fourteen head of cattle, a flock of sheep, some swine, three muskets, four carbines, two smaller guns, a sword, a cutlass, a warming pan, a dozen trenchers, three beer casks, a malt mill, a churn, and a small library. In its way this library was as interesting as Brewster's, reflecting the tastes of a man of the world. Volumes on religion were few, and there was none on purely Separatist doctrine. Among other things it contained, in addition to "three old Bibles" and a translation of the Iliad, a history of the world, a volume on the state of Europe, a chronicle of England, a history of Queen Elizabeth's reign, a Turkish history, a German history, *The Swedish Intelligencer,* a book on farming, a dictionary, *The Physician's Practice,* Bariffe's *Artillery,* and a well-thumbed copy of Caesar's *Commentaries.*

Little more than six months later, in the spring of 1657, William Bradford "expired his breath" and was buried "with the greatest sollemnities . . . many deep sighes, as well as loud volleys of shot," and was honored with a threnody by a local bard:

> The ninth of May, about nine of the clock,
> A precious one God out of Plimouth took; . . .
> A man approv'd in town, in church, in court, . . .
> Sweet Brewster, he is gone some time before;
> Wise Winslow, whose death we lament so sore;
> And faithful Standish, freed from horrid pain,
> To be with Christ, in truth, the greatest gain;
> Now blessed holy Bradford, a successor

> Of blessed holy Bradford, the confessor,
> Is gone to place of rest, with many more
> Of precious ones, whom I might name, great store ...

To the end Bradford continued in office, struggling to keep the ship of state and the ark of the covenant afloat, though he had been in failing health for some months. "Yet he felt himself not what he counted sick" till the day after he had seen a startling vision in the night, which "so filled his mind with ineffable consolations that he seemed little short of Paul, rapt up unto unutterable entertainments of Paradise. The next morning he told his friends that the good Spirit of God had given him a pledge of his happiness in another world and the first-fruits of his eternal glory; and on the day following he died ... in the sixty-ninth year of his age."

Bradford was the richest man in the colony at his death, leaving an estate of £900 ($45,000), which included a 300-acre farm on the Jones River, a house with gardens and orchard at Plymouth, a large library containing almost 300 volumes, a great silver "beer bowle," two silver wine cups, four Venice glasses, a dozen or more silver spoons, silver and pewter candlesticks, and many pewter dishes, pots, and flagons—but no forks, for the Pilgrim Fathers and their families, like everybody else at the time, ate with their fingers or their knives. In addition to "2 hattes, a blacke one & a coullered one, and 4 fine shirts," the governor's personal effects included a "stuffe" suit and a "lead coullered cloth suit," both with silver buttons; a turkey-red grogram suit and cloak; a cloth cloak, "faced with taffety"; a broadcloth cloak; and an "old violett coullered cloake, and an old green gowne."

Bradford had prospered both as a farmer and as an enterprising trader, and among his assets were listed £153 "upon the Dutch account att the Westward" [Aptuxcet] and £256 in trucking stuff at the old Pilgrim trading post on the Kennebec, which he, Prence, and others had leased from the colony a few years before. The estate was left in varying proportions to his wife Alice, "a blessed mother in Israell," who survived him thirteen years; to their daughter Mercy and their two sons, William and Joseph; to Bradford's two stepsons, Thomas and Constant Southworth; to his former ward, Thomas Cushman, now ruling elder in Brewster's stead; and to his son John, only child by his first wife Dorothy May. Left behind at Leyden as a small boy, he was finally sent for in 1627 but lived his life in almost complete obscurity, first at Plymouth, later at Duxbury and Marshfield, finally removing to Norwich, Connecticut, where he died in 1678.

Of Plimoth Plantation fell to Bradford's oldest son by his second marriage, and it was handed down in the latter's family for several generations, as attested by this somewhat illiterate notation on a fly leaf in the manuscript volume: "This book was rit by goefner William Bradford, and gifen to his son mager William Bradford, and by him to his son mager John Bradford, rit by me [his son] Samuel Bradford, Mach 20, 1705." But the author less prized this magnificent piece of work than other of his writings, for Bradford did not lay down his pen upon abandoning his chronicle. In 1648 he penned the first of three dialogues "betweene some yonge-men borne in New-England and some Anciente men which came out of Holand and old England, concerning the Church." The first dialogue was, in large part, a disingenuous defense of Francis Johnson and the scandalous Ancient Brethren, Ruling Elder Studley and all. Evidently stories about them had reached Plymouth to pique the curiosity of the younger Saints. Obviously to protect the good name of the Separatists, Bradford presented the Amsterdam congregation as very pious folk. The second dialogue has been lost. The third was a blistering attack on the "corrupte" Roman and Anglican churches, a mild criticism of the Presbyterian, and a complete vindication of the "Congregationall Way." But Bradford laid greatest store by the poetry—or at least, the rhymed couplets (when they did rhyme)—to which he turned in his declining years, especially recommending to the wisdom and discretion of his heirs "sundrie usefull verses . . . to be improved as you shall see meet." Wisely, they did nothing with them though they have since been published and have some interest as *curiosa*. The most ambitious of these lyrics, entitled "Some Observations of God's Mercifull Dealing with us in this Wildernesse, and His Gracious Protection over us These Many Years, Blessed be His Name," opens with these lines:

> In this wildernesse we lived have here,
> In happy peace this four and thirty year...

and goes on in this wise:

> All sorts of roots and herbs in gardens grow,
> Parsnips, carrots, turnips, or what you'll sow,
> Onions, melons, cucumbers, radishes,
> Skirrets, beets, coleworts, and fair cabbages...
> Nuts and grapes of several sorts here are,
> If you will take the pains them to seek for...

What led Bradford astray here is not clear. But there is the fact that in middle life, thinking that he had missed something in the schooling denied him as a youth, he took to reading philosophy and studying strange tongues, Latin and Greek, but especially Hebrew, for he had a great desire, he said, to see with his own eyes the language of God and the angels, and "how the words and phrases lye in the holy texte . . . and what names were given to things from the creation."

Talented and indefatigable, passionately devoted to the welfare of New Plimoth, Bradford was unquestionably the greatest of the Pilgrims, one of the greatest figures of seventeenth century New England—indeed, of our whole colonial period. His death marked the end of an era, and he went to his grave, as Cotton Mather said with none of his usual extravagance, "lamented by all the colonies of New England, as a common blessing and father to them all."

As his successor, the Pilgrims unanimously chose Thomas Prence, already twice a governor, a member of the General Court for more than twenty years. It was expected that he would occupy the Governor's House at Plymouth, but he declined, coming only on occasion, preferring to remain at Eastham, virtually the capital of the Pilgrim empire until 1665 when Prence was lured back with the gift of a large farm near by. Plain Dealing, he chose to name it.

By this time all contact with the Leyden church had been lost. Wanting a pastor, weakened by the exodus to the New World, the congregation at the Green Gate rapidly disintegrated. As has been noted, Bridget Robinson engaged passage for herself and three children on the second *Mayflower* in 1629 but for some reason did not embark. The only one of the pastor's family to reach the New World was Isaac, who came in 1632 as a youth in his early twenties, settling at Scituate. Many of those at the Green Gate soon joined the local English-speaking unit of the Dutch church, "complaining of a lack of appropriate exercises since his [Robinson's] death, so that they cannot be edified in the way they might were they members of some other church provided with a pastor." Others returned to England, including Bridget Robinson's brother-in-law, Ralph Tickens, the looking-glass maker of London, and her eldest son John, who had studied medicine at the University of Leyden and was now a doctor. Still others moved back to Amsterdam to join the Ainsworthians there. Ainsworth had died of a "fit of gravel" some years before, in 1622, but his church survived for almost eighty years, outliving its Leyden rival by half a century.

In 1643 Bridget Robinson died and in 1655, two years before Bradford's death, what little remained of the Green Gate congregation was absorbed by the local English-speaking unit of the Dutch church.[15] As payments on the mortgage were too heavy for the impoverished congregation to bear, the Groenepoort itself had passed into other hands in 1637 and was torn down about forty years later to make way for a Walloon hostel, Pesyn's Hof, which still stands in Bell Alley facing the towering Pieterskerk.

John Robinson's last years, it has recently transpired, had been discouraged and unhappy ones. It was not only that he was kept from Plymouth by the machinations of the dominant Puritan faction among the merchant adventurers. Nor was it altogether the fact that he found his congregation greatly weakened in character and resources by the exodus of the stronger part. The source of his unhappiness lay much deeper, at the very heart of his faith. Toward the end he had come to entertain serious doubts about the rigid course of Separation chosen by himself and his brethren.

From the beginning the Brownists had manifested the usual faults of all small sects in revolt against the established order. They were single-minded zealots, fanatically eager to work their will upon the world. Their narrow concentration of aim was at once their main strength and chief weakness. Their difficulties were, in large part, of their own creation. Driven to extremes by general hostility and violent unprincipled opposition on the part of selfish vested interests, they were unwilling to cede an inch of their position, no matter how extreme. Too weak to allow the slightest deviation in the group, any latitude in belief or behavior, they demanded the strictest conformity in all things and incessantly quarreled among themselves about minutiae of doctrine, ritual, morals, and manners. The conflicts and schisms in Robert Browne's church, in John Smyth's, in Francis Johnson's, had been symptomatic of the ills that represented the negative and weaker side of the Separation.

All of this pained Robinson. In his reasonable and peaceable way he had been moving steadily toward more liberal views. As early as 1617, according to a contemporary, he "so far came back [from the Separation] that he approved of communion with the Church of England, in the hearing of the word and prayer (though not in sacraments and discipline), and so occasioned the rise of such as are called Semists, that is Semi-Separatists, or Independents." This doctrine Robinson elaborated in a completed manuscript found upon his desk at the time of his death. This work, entitled *The Lawfullnesse of Hearing Ministers in the Church of England,* aroused so much opposition among the brethren that it was suppressed for nine years.

Shortly after its publication in 1634, several Leyden Saints on a visit to London "heard some of the ministers in England preach," which precipitated a row at the Green Gate. The more bigoted demanded that the church deal roundly with them "as for sin."

If they declined to repent, they should be excommunicated. As the congregation was "not willing to consent" to such drastic measures, the bigoted withdrew in a huff, making a "rent in the Church," and removed to Amsterdam to join the Separatists there under John Canne, Ainsworth's successor. The latter fully shared their views and issued a blast against the late Leyden pastor in *A Stay Against Straying*.

It was this exclusive and smug self-righteousness, this sectarian and bitterly contentious spirit, that Robinson always found so hard to bear. And in recent years the archives at Leyden have yielded several documents which quite clearly reveal his troubled state of mind. In one of these, Antonius Walaeus, theological professor at the University of Leyden, deposed that Robinson had often talked with him "concerning the separation between their congregation [at the Green Gate] and other English congregations in this country, and . . . was disposed to do his utmost to remove this schism." He was averse, so Walaeus reported, "to educating his son for the work of the ministry in such congregations, and much preferred to have him exercise his ministry in the Dutch churches; that to this end, by the help of Domine Teellinck[16] and myself, he had also begun to move some good people in Middelburg to provide some decent support for his son's studies for a few years." But Robinson, it appears, was not hopeful of accomplishing either aim, for he "found in his congregation so many difficulties . . . that he, with a good part of his congregation, was resolved to remove to the West Indies, where he doubted not that he should be able to accomplish his desires."

The Saints at Plymouth apparently knew nothing of this, and it was well for their peace of mind that they did not—that they remained blissfully unaware of their beloved pastor's final resolve not to come to them, but to go elsewhere, far away to the south, to one of the islands in the Caribbean, to found there another rather different colony, one far less rigid and exacting in its religious views.

22

MINISTER
TROUBLE

... ministers, compared with other Christians,
have little to joy in in this world.

—COTTON MATHER

NOTHING IN THE HISTORY OF THE OLD COLONY IS MORE
ironic than the acute minister trouble that afflicted it from first
to last. It was almost as if the Fates wished to see how much the
Pilgrims could endure, as if they were determined to find out
once and for all just how far human patience could be stretched
before it snapped under the strain and men were driven mad with
exasperation.

The congregation had had its share of minister trouble before
it reached the New World. In the beginning William Brewster
and his friends had worshipped for a time at Gainsborough under
the brilliant but erratic John Smyth, whose later excursions into

Se-Baptism and other "hellish errours" so scandalized his one-time
brethren and caused all of the English Separatists such pain and
embarrassment. After the Gainsborough group had amicably
divided and the Saints along Scrooby Water formed a congregation of their own, they enjoyed great spiritual content for a year
or two under the "grave & reverend" Richard Clyfton, who
brought many benighted souls to the light by his "paines and
dilligens." Then had come that distressing period at Amsterdam
with the scandalous Ancient Brethren when the company sat
each Sabbath at the feet of the touchy Francis Johnson and had
to endure the moral admonitions and fetching leer of that con-
summate rogue, Ruling Elder Daniel Studley. In their panicky
flight to Leyden they lost their pastor, for Clyfton refused to go
and abandoned his flock, preferring the company of the "Franciscans." While hurt and upset by this, the congregation quickly
dismissed him as a renegade and soon regarded his defection as
a blessing in disguise, for it enabled John Robinson to step forward and come into his own as the greatest of the early Separatist
leaders. The Saints at Leyden enjoyed his "able ministrie & prudente governmente" for more than ten years, a period none of
them ever forgot, for it was the happiest and most wholly satisfying of their lives. They would never know another like it.

When the decision was made that Robinson would not accompany the first group to set out for the New World, someone had
managed to enlist as "teacher" the Reverend John Wincob, a
chaplain in the service of the Dowager Countess of Lincoln,
prominent in Puritan circles of the day. As the Pilgrims had taken
their first patent in his name, Wincob had evidently given positive
assurance that he would embark on their "waighty vioage," but
"God so disposed as he never went."

In June, 1620, just a month before the *Speedwell* left Delft
Haven, Deacon Cushman reported from London that a "Mr.
Crabe" had been approached to take Wincob's place. "He hath
promised to goe with us," wrote Cushman, "yet I tell you I shall
not be without feare till I see him shipped, for he is much opposed;
yet I hope he will not faile." Again the Pilgrims were disap-

pointed, for when the *Mayflower* sailed, there was no minister on board.

Plymouth remained without a minister for more than three years, to the concern of Saints and Strangers alike. In want of a pastor, the sacraments could not be administered. There could be no baptisms and none could partake of the Lord's Supper, which gave weight to the Strangers' complaint that the "means of salvation" were grossly neglected at Plymouth. Expecting Robinson to join them soon, the Saints were not prepared to accept anyone in his stead and raised a question about Ruling Elder Brewster's powers, asking if he might not administer the sacraments meanwhile. But John Robinson thought not, saying that he "judged it not lawfull . . . nor convenient if it were lawfull."

Plymouth was indebted to the *Charity* for its first minister, "that dissembling Ishmaell," the Reverend John Lyford, who came ashore early in 1624, bowing and scraping, weeping with joy and praising everything he saw, "as if he had been made all of love and ye humblest person in ye world." If he had not been so addicted to letter writing and so fond of telling his cronies such things as "made them laugh in their sleeves," he might have gone far in subverting the unpopular minority rule of the Saints. As it was, his vanity undid him, and he and "mad-jack" Oldham were driven into the wilderness.

Not many months later Captain Standish brought back the staggering news that John Robinson was dead. This entirely changed the complexion of the problem. A new minister would have to be found if Plymouth's spiritual needs were not to suffer indefinitely. But the Saints were so stunned by their loss that they did nothing about the matter for several years.

In 1628, on his own responsibility, Isaac Allerton engaged a "yonge man for a minister" and shipped him across on the *White Angel*, perhaps hoping to put that vessel to some profitable use. As the congregation had not been consulted, the Saints were very skeptical about the business, for they "had bene so bitten by Mr. Lyford as they desired to know ye person well whom they should invite amongst them." The new preacher, a "Mr. Rogers," proved to be a lamentable choice, for it was "perceived, upon some triall, that he was crased in his braine." As a consequence, the Pilgrims were at the expense not only of bringing him over,[1] but of shipping him back the next year. Again in England poor Rogers "grue quite distracted, and Mr. Allerton was much blamed that he would bring such a man over, they having charge enough otherwise."*

In the fall of 1629, while on a voyage in the shallop, a small Pilgrim party happened to put in at Nantasket (Hull), where Lyford and Oldham had taken refuge for a time. While there, the Pilgrims met a bedraggled man in his middle thirties, who introduced himself as the Reverend Ralph Smith and told them a sad story. He had arrived at Salem earlier in the year, coming on the *Talbot* with the Reverends Skelton and Higginson, who had since become officers of the church there, leaving Smith out in the cold. Worse, the more conservative of the Massachusetts Bay adventurers, upon learning that he was an avowed Separatist, now loudly protested his presence in the town.

"Passage was granted to him before we understood his difference of judgment in some things from our ministrie," they wrote Governor Endecott, "and though we have a very good opinion of his honesty, we give you this order, that unless he will be comfortable to our government, *you suffer him not to remain within the limits of your grant.*"

Forced to leave Salem, Smith came to Nantasket and now begged the Pilgrims to take him and his family to Plymouth, "having before heard that there was liklyhood he might procure house-roome for some time till he should resolve to setle there, if he might, or els-where as God should dispose, for he was werie of being in that uncoth place, & in a poore house that would neither keep him nor his goods drie." Though they "had no order for any such thing," the visiting Pilgrims agreed to transport him, "seeing him to be a grave man . . . & a minister." At Plymouth he was "kindly entertained & housed, & had ye rest of his goods & servants sente for, and exercised his gifts amongst them, and

---

* It was just a year later that Allerton brought over Thomas Morton of Merry Mount as his "secretary."

afterwards was chosen into ye ministrie, and so remained for sundrie years."

Thus, quite by chance, Plymouth had a settled minister at last, one of the Puritans' castoffs. Born at Belton, Lancashire, and a graduate of Cambridge with great but absurd pretensions as a scholar, Smith was quite pleased at first with his "studdie in new Plimmouth in new Ingland," spending much time there in literary composition, strewing his pages with Greek and Latin phrases, often indiscriminately mixed.

Smith soon had a most illustrious colleague, the great Roger Williams, who came to Plymouth late in 1631 or early the next year to become the Pilgrims' "teacher." Williams was still very young, being less than thirty at the time, but he had already made a name for himself. Arriving at Boston in 1630 with his wife and two small children, he had been invited to Salem to become "teacher" of the church there as successor of Francis Higginson, who had recently died. The Bay authorities immediately raised objections. While at Boston, it seems, Williams had refused to take communion with Governor Winthrop and his brethren because they were an "unseparated people." The least they could do to clear the stain on their conscience, he said, was to "make public declaration of their repentance for having taken communion with the churches of England while they lived there." Also, he questioned the right of the magistrates to punish breaches of the Sabbath and similar offenses. It was improper for them to meddle in such matters. Hearing of Salem's choice of Williams, "King" Winthrop wrote the authorities there to express his amazement that they "would choose him without advising with the Council, and withal desiring them that they would forbear to proceed till they had conferred about it." As Williams had already been inducted into office, the Salem church ignored Winthrop's protest. But the pressure of the Bay authorities was so constant and such an annoyance that Williams decided to remove to Plymouth to enjoy the Holy Discipline in the company of a "separating" people who had always had the courage of their convictions and had never been trimmers either soon or late.

Williams was "friendly entertained, according to their poore abilitie," and made a great impression upon the Pilgrims as "a man godly & zealous, having many precious parts." His teaching was "well approoved," as Bradford declared years later, and "for ye benefite wherof I still blese God and am thankfull to him, even for his sharpest admonitions & reproufs, so farr as they agreed with truth." Williams in turn always spoke well of the "prudent and Godly Governour, Mr. Bradford, and others of his Godly Council." During his stay Governor Winthrop, Captain Endecott, and Pastor John Wilson of Boston came on their first visit to Plymouth, sailing across the Bay to Wessagusset and proceeding thence on foot through the woods. Met outside the town by Bradford, Brewster, and others, they were escorted with great ceremony to Governor Bradford's house to be lodged and entertained there. On the Lord's Day, bright and early, they climbed the steep winding path up the hill to take communion with the Pilgrims in their combination fort-jail-townhall-meeting house, returning in the afternoon to enjoy the "prophecying," or informal "teaching," which in want of books and because of widespread illiteracy was very popular among the Saints. Governor Winthrop, as a new convert, was much impressed, leaving a graphic picture of the scene:

"Mr. Roger Williams, according to the custom, proposes a question, to which the pastor, Mr. Smith, speaks briefly; then Mr. Williams prophecies (or explains); and after, the Governor of Plymouth (who has studied the Hebrew language and antiquities) speaks to the question; after him, the elder (a man of learning); then two or three more of the congregation. Then the elder (agreeably to Acts xiii. 14, 15, &c.) desires Governor Winthrop and Mr. Wilson to speak to it, which they do. When this is ended, the deacon, Mr. Fuller, puts the congregation in mind of their duty of contribution, whereupon the governor and all the rest go down to the deacon's seat, and put it in the bag, and then return."

It was this "prophecying" that led Morton of Merry Mount to

remark of the Separatists with a sneer that there was not one among them, "though he be but a Cow keeper, but is allowed to exercise his gifts in the publick assembly on the Lord's Day, so as he doe not make use of any notes for the helpe of his memory, for such things, they say, smell of Lamp oyle, and there must be no such unsavory perfume admitted to come into the congregation."

One man, Morton declared, would rise and talk like a grocer, weighing everything. He would be followed by a second, "of a more cutting disposition," who would tailor a close-fitting religious garment and urge his audience to put it on and love it for being "of such a fashion as doth best become a Christian man." Still others talked like tapsters, "filling up the cup of repentance," or like cobblers, exhorting the careless to mend their ways and walk upright in the paths of the righteous. And usually there was one who took up the text and ran off with it so fast—"doubtless his father was some Irish footman"—that no one in the congregation could follow him.

At Plymouth, Roger Williams was paid so little that he had to devote much of his time to scratching out a bare subsistence. As he said, he had to labor "day and night, at home and abroad, on the Land and water, at the How [hoe], at the Oare, for bread." But he also found time to go among the Indians, frequently visiting Massasoit and other sachems, for God had been pleased, he said, "to give me a painful patient spirit, to lodge with them in their filthy smoky holes, and (even while I lived at Plymouth and Salem) to gain their tongue."

God had also been pleased, others said, "to put a windmill in his head," and Williams was not long at Plymouth, so Bradford complained, before he fell "into some strang oppinions, and from oppinion to practise, which caused some controversie betweene ye churche & him, and in ye end some discontente on his parte, by occasion whereof he left them something abruptly."

Williams had written and privately circulated a tract denying the validity of the settlers' patents and charters. As the land belonged to the Indians, he declared, neither the King nor the

Council for New England had a right to dispose of any part of it.[2] This was obviously true but very disturbing doctrine. Williams had also become increasingly impatient with all limitations upon religious freedom. To him "liberty of conscience" meant just that, without any "ifs" and "buts," and this is his title to honor as one of the greatest of Americans. He was the first to proclaim and, better yet, to practice that civilized doctrine on our shores, following in this the first of the Saints, Robert Browne, who long ago had written that "to compell Religion, to plant churches by Power, and to force a Submission to ecclesiasticall Government by laws and penalties, belongeth not to them [the magistrates], neither yet to the Church."

These radical views found some acceptance at Plymouth, it appears, especially with Winslow, who always remained one of Williams' close friends, and with Deacon Samuel Fuller, who left a clause in his will that two acres on Strawberry Hill were to go to his son "if Mr. Roger Williams refuse to accept of them as formerlie he hath done." Wishing to keep their "teacher," some of the Saints were eager to patch up their differences with him, but Ruling Elder Brewster advised against it, "fearing that his continuance amongst them might cause divisions." In 1634 Williams asked to be dismissed to the church at Salem, and his request was granted, though "with some caution to them concerning him."

"I hope he belongs to the Lord," remarked Bradford with scarcely veiled doubts, adding that Williams was "to be pitied and prayed for" with the hope that the Lord might yet "shew him his errors, and reduse him into ye way of truth, and give him a settled judgment and constancie in ye same."

Upon Skelton's death the Salem church chose Williams as its pastor, again over the protests of the Bay authorities. But the latter were not to be denied this time and late in 1635 ordered his banishment from Massachusetts. He was to depart within six weeks and "not to return any more without license from the Court." When granted leave to remain till spring, Williams went on preaching, which so angered the magistrates that they hatched a plot to seize him and ship him back to England. Getting wind of this, Williams abandoned his family and fled into the wilderness, being "sorely tossed for fourteen weeks in a bitter winter season, not knowing what bread or bed did mean." Making his way to the country of the Wampanoag, he settled at Seekonk, a few miles north of Sowams, where he was joined by a few of his Salem friends. Here they "began to build and plant," but Williams halted work when the Pilgrims complained.

"I received a letter from my ancient friend, Mr. Winslow, then Governor of Plymouth, professing his own and others' love and respect for me, yet lovingly advising me, since I was fallen into the edge of their bounds, and they were loath to displease the Bay, to remove but to the other side of the water; and then, he said, I had the country before me, and might be as free as themselves, and we should be loving neighbours together."

With five faithful disciples Williams moved across Narragansett Bay and there founded Providence, expressing a hope that it would always be "a shelter for persons distressed for conscience." His friend Canonicus, sachem of the Narragansett, feared and loathed by the Pilgrims and Puritans as a bloodthirsty savage, gave him land for his settlement and treated him with the utmost kindness, cherishing him as a son. More than once Williams acknowledged his indebtedness and gratitude to the proud old sachem, the most powerful in the region, saying that he could have accomplished little without him. A remarkably democratic community from the first, Providence never altogether forgot its heritage and influenced all of Rhode Island. Williams gave it a minimum of government, a maximum of civil liberties, and absolute religious freedom for all. There was here no formal separation, no division whatever between Saints and Strangers. One man's faith was as good as another's, and he was as free to follow it as the next. For some time it was the habit of the settlers to address one another as "Neighbor," which reflected the friendly and cooperative spirit of the town.

In advising against Williams' retention at Plymouth, Ruling Elder Brewster had voiced a fear that he "would run the same course of rigid Separation and Anabaptistry which Mr. John Smyth, the se-baptist at Amsterdam, had done." And so it was, though he did not imitate Smyth in re-baptizing himself. He had it done, appropriately enough, "by one Holyman" of Salem. Williams then performed the rite on his baptizer and a dozen followers, and together they formed the first Baptist congregation in America. But Williams soon began to question the validity of his second baptism, precisely as Smyth had done, and within a few months left the church to become a "Seeker," rejecting all formal creeds and rituals. Every man should establish his own individual relation with God, and none should prescribe the form of his worship. The Pilgrims scowled at this, but "it pleased the Father of mercies," said Williams, "to touch many hearts with relenting, among whom that great and precious soul, Mr. Winslow, melted and kindly visited me at Providence, and put a piece of gold into the hands of my wife, for our supply."

Two years later Anne Hutchinson and her followers were expelled from Massachusetts "for ignorance of Christ" on eighty-two points—"some heretical, some blasphemous, some erroneous, and all incongruous," according to Cotton Mather. In seeking a refuge their eyes turned toward the island of Aquidneck, or Rhode Island, in Narragansett Bay. Thinking that it lay within the bounds of the Plymouth grant, they wrote to ask if they might settle there, a request which the Pilgrims granted, "considering they were their countrymen and fellow-subjects that were thus distressed and destitute of habitation, although they held their errours in as great dislike as those from whence they came." An offshoot of this colony founded Newport. Through Roger Williams a patent was soon obtained uniting these settlements with Providence as the colony of Rhode Island; this was shortly expanded to include Shawomet, or Warwick, founded by a London clothier, Samuel Gorton, who had also been at Plymouth and in trouble there.

Signing himself "Professor of the Mysteries, and De Primo," Gorton was a Familist, one of a sect rejecting formalism and exalting the untrammeled spirit of divine love. There is much

that is modern and enlightened in his point of view. But Gorton
was a "most prodigious Minister of exhorbitant Novelties," it must
be confessed, and the Pilgrims found him "blasphemous, . . . a
proud and pestilent seducer . . . a subtle deceiver, courteous in
his carriage to all at some times for his own ends, but soon moved
with passion, and so lost that which he gained upon the simple."
Like Williams, he challenged the authority of the magistrates,
but for a different reason. No colonial government had any legal
foundation unless its form had been reviewed by the King and
given royal sanction, and none of those in New England had.
Nor could the magistrates forbid what the Common Law of
England allowed, having no right whatever to pass laws of their
own devising.

If this was bad, Gorton's religious views were worse. "Faith
and Christ is all one," so they understood his doctrine. Sermons
were "lies, tales, and falsehoods"—churches, "devised platforms"
—baptism, "a vanity and abhomination"—and the Lord's Supper,
"vanity and a spell!" As for ministers, they were "magicians."
Gorton was such a "beast," the outraged Saints declared, that he
urged men to make the most of this life and take what joy they
could in it, for there might not be another. All this and more
Gorton later set forth in a rather ambitious work entitled *An In-
corruptible Key,* "composed of the CX Psalme, wherewith you
may open the Rest of the Holy Scriptures" and discover, among
other things, the truth about "Fall and Resurrection, Sin and
Righteousness, Ascension and Descension, Height and Depth,
First and Last, Beginning and Ending, Flesh and Spirit, Wisdome
and Foolishnesse, Strength and Weakness, Mortality and Immortality, Jew and Gentile, Light and Darknesse, Unity and Multipli-
cation, Fruitfullness and Barrenness, Curse and Blessing, Man and
Woman, Kingdom and Priesthood, All-Sufficiency and Deficiency,
God and Man."

Trouble began when Pastor Smith, who had been boarding
Gorton and his family, ordered them out of his house, allegedly
for "unworthie and offensive speeches." But, so Gorton said, it
was really because the pastor's wife preferred his prayers to her

husband's, which was not at all unlikely in light of the Pilgrims' own complaints about the services. Matters reached a crisis when the Gortons' maid was caught smiling in church and was threatened with banishment. Gorton rushed into court to defend her and committed several costly indiscretions. He addressed the presiding magistrate (probably Bradford) as "Satan" and invited him to "come down from Jehoshuah's right hand." Heavily fined for contempt of court, he was commanded to get out of the Old Colony within two weeks.[3]

"You see, good people, how you are abused in your liberty!" exclaimed Gorton, turning to the assembled Pilgrims as Oldham had done on a somewhat similar occasion. "Stand for your liberty!"

None responded, and with only two converts, who soon became "very atheists, looking for no more happiness than this world affords," Gorton departed. Going to the settlements along Narragansett Bay, he made himself very unpopular there, trying the patience of all, even of Roger Williams, a feat that no one had ever performed. In a dispute about a pig he was roundly censured by the easy-going Providence court for referring to the chief justice as a "lawyer" and to his colleagues as "just-asses." Hostilities between him and the Pilgrims continued. Gorton was one of those whom Winslow was sent to England to combat in 1645, for he had lodged several well-grounded complaints against Plymouth and Massachusetts for disturbing him at Shawomet in a most presumptuous manner. But after a time, again like Oldham, he and the Pilgrims were reconciled and many years later, when a man of eighty, he acted as Plymouth's interpreter in a last desperate effort to avert King Philip's War.

Meantime, in 1634, Pastor Smith had married one of the Saints, the widow of Deacon Richard Masterson. If he had hopes that this would strengthen his position in the town, he was quite mistaken. The Saints found him dull and uninspiring, "a man of low gifts," and in 1636 Smith "layed down his ministrie, partly by his owne willingnes, as thinking it too heavie a burthen, and partly at the desire and by ye perswasion of others; and the church sought out for some other, having often been disappointed in their hops and desires heretofore."

For his part, the pastor complained of much hard usage. He had been batted about from pillar to post, he declared, being forced to move from house to house at least a dozen times in six years. Writing to his wife's friends at Leyden, he urged them to sell a house she owned there and forward the funds immediately, for he and his family were almost starving. "It hath pleased God to tire us by great losses by fire, watr, and theeves (often) in this wilderness, so that it's a mercie I yet live & have bread and water to drinke." His house had been rifled five times by burglars. "I am sore weakened & unable to labor as formerlie," he groaned. Still, there was one thing to be thankful for—"I have got freedome . . . of that intollerable charg pressing mee nigh 7 yeares, but with all my small means went."

On his visit to England in 1635, Winslow had been instructed to bring back "some able & fitt man for to be their minister." He engaged and spent considerable money outfitting one Mr. Glover, "a godly and a worthy man." But on the eve of departure Glover "fell sick of a feaver and dyed," so that Winslow was at the trouble and expense of finding another. At length he persuaded the Reverend John Norton to accompany him, though the latter refused to commit himself to remaining at Plymouth until he had seen it. Norton wrote "pure elegant Latin," it is said, but that was scarcely a recommendation to the Saints. They were much more interested to learn that he was a "hard student" and "much in prayer; he would spend whole *days* in prayer." In his youth, so he liked to relate, he had been a wild one, much addicted to playing cards. But he had early seen the light and reformed, being now inclined to see sin and Satan in almost everything. A graduate of Cambridge, he and Brewster must have spent many pleasant hours reminiscing, for both had been at Peterhouse. Though "courteously and earnestly" invited to become the Pilgrim pastor, Norton declined, for he had the itch of ambition, a rich wife, and Plymouth did not answer his expectations, offering too narrow a field for his morbid interests and choleric talents.

John Norton, so Bradford has it, remained about a year, "teaching" every Sabbath. The fact is that he stayed only four months, just long enough to receive a call from Ipswich, "where were many rich & able men, and sundry of his acquaintance, so he wente to them." The Pilgrims had laid out £70 to bring him over, with the understanding that he was to repay it if he did not remain. In their hunger for good sermons, having heard none for sixteen years, the Saints forgave him half the charge "for ye pains he tooke amongst them." Norton went on to become one of the most powerful clerics in New England. In 1653 he was called from Ipswich to the First Church, Boston, to succeed that "bright star," John Cotton, and to become a leader in the witch hunts and Quaker persecutions that brought shame upon the Bay colony, uniting his fanatic zeal with that of his colleague, the Reverend John Wilson, "very much a man of God, with a certain prophetical afflatus." Together, they were as arrant and bloodthirsty a pair of bigots as ever ramped through New England inciting the ignorant and the credulous. The Pilgrims, though disappointed at the moment, were well spared the "pure, sublime, scholastical" John Norton,

> Zealous for order, very critical
> For what was truly congregational.

Once again the whole burden of "teaching" fell upon the aging William Brewster. Hearing of his arrival at Boston, Plymouth tried to interest the Reverend Richard Mather,[4] distinguished in his own right though perhaps better known as the father of Increase and the grandfather of Cotton Mather, the "compleat" Puritan. But Mather chose to go to Dorchester, "the greatest Towne in New England," later removing to Boston.

Soon after, however, the Pilgrims managed to engage a "faithfull laboriouse preacher," one John Reyner of Yorkshire,[5] another graduate of Cambridge, who occupied the pulpit for many years—to the general satisfaction of the Saints, who found him "wise, faithfull, Grave, sober, a lover of Good men, not Greedy of matters of the world, Armed with much faith, patience and meekness, mixed with Currage for the cause of God, . . . sound in ye truth, and every way unreprovable in his life & conversation" —an implied but pointed comment upon most of his predecessors.

About two years later the church also acquired a "teacher," the Reverend Charles Chauncy, a man in his middle forties. Like Norton, he was of Hertfordshire, a graduate of Cambridge, and was destined to make a name for himself elsewhere. Chauncy had taught Greek and Hebrew at the university for a time before accepting a parish in his native shire, where in 1629 he was cited for saying that the Anglican church was "full of Idolatrie, atheism, popery, Arminianism, and heresy." William Laud, then bishop of London, ordered him "to make a submission in Latin," which he did. Six years later, he was summoned before the Court of High Commission for opposing the erection of a rail around the communion table in his church, objecting to it as an "innovation and a snare to men's conscience." Suspended from office until he formally recanted, Chauncy hesitated but finally announced that he thought the rail a "decent and convenient ornament." His recantation was "greatly dishonourable," as his son admitted, and "made him often uneasy to his dying day." When trouble again threatened, for his refusal to read the Book of Sports, he fled to the New World and made his way to Plymouth, arriving in 1638. Though he struck some of the Saints as conceited and opinionated, he was elected to office, for he gave the congregation what it wanted in the pulpit, "an exceeding plaine preacher," and all were pleased to note that he spent even more of his time in prayer than Norton, devoting not merely days but weeks to private prayers and fasting.

The Saints at Duxbury had done even better by themselves, obtaining as their pastor the Reverend Ralph Partridge, who had arrived at Boston in 1636. For years one of the most respected ministers in the colony, this Partridge "had not only the innocency of a *dove* . . . but also the loftiness of an *eagle* in the great *soar* of his intellectual abilities," wrote Cotton Mather in one of his excruciating puns, carefully underscoring every point so that it could not possibly escape the dullest reader, "and so afraid was he of being anything that looked like a *bird* wandering from his *nest* that he remained with his poor people till he took *wing* to become a *bird of Paradise,* along with the winged *seraphim* of heaven."

At Marshfield was the Reverend Richard Blinman, "a Godly able Minnester." Lothrop was at Barnstable dispensing the Word there, "willing to spend and to be spente for the cause of the church of Christ." Though not too pleased with him, Yarmouth had the Reverend Joseph Hull. The Duxbury church gave up its "teacher," William Leverich, when he received a call from Sandwich, and the Saints at Eastham were granted their request when they asked for the "teacher" at Barnstable, the Reverend John Mayo. Several settlements had been established west of Plymouth —at Taunton, Rehoboth, Swansea, and Dartmouth (New Bedford). Each of these had a small but growing congregation. The pastor of Taunton, William Hooke, soon returned to England to be honored by Oliver Cromwell and was succeeded by Nicholas Street, who was "pious, judicious, and modest, and no inferior preacher." The Rehoboth minister, Samuel Newman, was conscientious and spent his leisure hours writing a concordance, "which he revised by the light of pine knots." Thus the Lord was pleased "richly to accomplish and adorn the colony of Plimouth ... with a considerable number of godly and able gospel preachers ... burning and shining lights," and the churches might have been "greatly happy and prosperous," according to Nathaniel Morton, "had not sin and Satan's envy interposed."

Chauncy had been at Plymouth only a short time before he justified the fears of some of the Saints by precipitating controversy on several important points, stubbornly refusing to acknowledge himself "in errour." It was indefensible, he said, to celebrate the Lord's Supper at the Sabbath morning service. The proper time to serve supper was in the evening. He also raised a question about baptism, "he holding it ought to be by dipping, and putting ye whole body under water, and that sprinkling was unlawfull."

Though Robinson had been a "sprinkler," the church "yealded that immersion, or dipping, was lawfull, but in this cold country not so conveniente." They vehemently denied, however, that sprinkling was "unlawfull & a human invention," and asked Chauncy if he would accept a compromise "so as there might be no disturbance in ye church hereaboute." If they allowed him to dip, they inquired, would he "peaceably suffer Mr. Reinor" to go on baptizing in the old way?

No! said Chauncy. How could they expect him to yield in so vital a matter of conscience?

Ralph Partridge was now summoned from Duxbury to demolish Chauncy and his arguments in public debate, "which he did sundrie times, very ablie and sufficiently," it seemed to Bradford. Chauncy was not much impressed, however, so the Saints wrote the most eminent divines in Massachusetts, Connecticut, and New Haven, and invited them to join the fray, receiving "very able & sufficiente answers, as they conceived." But nothing could bring the "larned Mr. Chancy" around, and in 1641 he departed to become pastor at Scituate where he continued his dipping—first, with two infants of his own. As it was bitter winter weather, as cold within the unheated meeting house as in the icy gale without, the children swooned away—which proved at least one of the Pilgrims' points.

Perhaps because of its experience with Chauncy and Roger Williams, or simply because the town was now too poor to bear the cost, Plymouth never had another "teacher."

The echoes of this controversy had scarcely died away before the ministers of New England were deep in a subject even more interesting than the finer points of baptism, however engrossing these might be. A servant on Love Brewster's farm at Duxbury, a youth of seventeen, had slipped into strange and sinful ways— "Horrible it is to mention," exclaimed Bradford, "but ye trueth of ye historie requires it"—and was indicted for his transgressions.

Fortunately, the Pilgrims knew just how to proceed, for several similar offenses had recently been committed in Massachusetts, and the authorities had written Plymouth for advice. Bradford in turn had consulted a few distinguished divines to ask their opinions on three questions—(1) should death be inflicted for unnatural sins, (2) how far can the magistrates go in forcing a confession from the accused, and (3) is one witness sufficient to convict of a capital offense? In brief depositions Reyner and Partridge agreed that death was a proper penalty for such sins, as evidenced by the Scriptures; that the magistrates could not employ force or torture to extract a confession; that at least two witnesses were required for conviction in a capital crime. While agreeing on the first point, the "larned Mr. Chancy" was not of their opinion on the others, and from Scituate came a long disquisition on every phase and mode of "carnall copulation," running on page after page, studded with dozens of citations in support of every point, such an exhaustive treatise as might have have been expected of one about to become a college president, even though the subject was somewhat esoteric:

"Ye judicials of Moyses, . . . grounded on ye law of nature, or ye decalogue, are immutable and perpetuall, which all orthodox devines acknowledge; see ye authors following . . . [After filling up ten lines] And more might be added. I forbear, for brevitie's sake, to set downe their very words." None could deny that the Mosaic code prescribed death for "adultry, Levit: 20. 10., Deut: 22. 22., Esech: 16. 38, Jhon: 8. 5 . . . So incest is to be punished with death, Levit: 20. II, 22. Beastiality likewise, Lev: 20. 15., Exod: 22. 19. Rapes in like manner, Deut: 22. 25. Sodomie in like sort, Levit: 18. 22, & 20. 13. And all presumptuous sins, Numb: 15. 30, 31 . . . as discovering of nakedness, Levit: 18. 20., which is retegere pudenda, as parts per euphemismum (saith Junius), or detegere ad cubandum, (saith Willett) . . . Abulensis says that it signifies omnes modos quibus . . . Add to this a notable speech of Zepperus de legibus (who hath enough to end all controversies of this nature) . . . Againe, some sinnes of this nature are simple, others compound . . . but when there is a mixture of diverce kinds of lust, this is capitall, double & triple. Againe, when adultrie

... is committed by professors or church members, I fear it comes too near ye sinne of priests' daughters, forbidden and comanded to be punished, Levit: 21. 9 ... Againe ... Once more ... But I must hasten to ye other questions."

A confession should never be forced by putting the accused on oath, but on occasion—and this was one—the magistrates "may proceede so farr to bodily torments as racks, hot-irons, &c." While it was a good thing to have more than one witness, that was not essential. "Lastly, I see no cause why in waighty matters, in defecte of witnesses & other proofes, we may not have recourse to a lot as in ye case of Achan, Josu: 7. 16., which is a clearer way in such doubtfull cases (it being solemnely & religiously performed) than any other that I know of."[6]

Lots were not cast in this instance "in defecte of witnesses & other proofes." Nor was there need of resorting to "racks, hot-irons, &c.," for in the end the youth confessed and was summarily executed for his sins, "according to ye law, Levit: 20. 15."

How was it, Bradford asked himself, that such things could be in New Canaan? There had been an alarming outbreak of "sundrie notorious sins ... espetially drunkenness and unclainness; not only incontinencie betweene persons unmarried, for which many, both men & women, have been punished sharply enough, but some married persons allso." Reviewing the moral progress in the colony during the past twenty years, he saw little to encourage him, admitting that it was a "question whether ye greater part be not growne ye worser."

The "mixt multitude" of Strangers, as usual, got most of the blame, an aspersion not borne out by the Pilgrim records. For another thing, said Bradford, "ye Divell may carrie a greater spite against the churches of Christ and ye gospell here by how much ye more they indeavour to preserve holyness and puritie amongst them, and strictly punisheth the contrary when it ariseth either in church or commonwealth ... I would rather think thus than that Satan hath more power in these heathen lands, as some have thought." Finally—and here Bradford laid a finger upon a profound truth—"it may be in this case as it is with waters when their streames are stopped or dammed up, when they gett passage they flow with more violence, and make more noys and disturbance, than when they are suffered to run quietly in their own channels. So wickedness, being here more stopped by strict laws and ye same more nearly looked unto so that it cannot run in a commone road of liberty as it would and is inclined, searches everywhere and at last breaks out where it getts vente."

But wise as he was in his observation, Bradford did not favor loosening the reins of authority. If sin raised its head, clamp on more restraints. So, too, with heresy—stamp it out. The religious issue was becoming acute. Popular resistance to intolerance was growing, stimulated in part by the large measure of religious freedom prevailing in England as a result of the revolution there. In 1645 a petition was presented to the General Court asking the removal of religious discrimination and all civil disabilities based upon it. At the same time a similar petition was presented to the General Court at Boston. Both were the work of William Vassall of Scituate, once a magistrate in Massachusetts and a man with powerful connections at home, his brother being a member of the Commission for Foreign Plantations.

The Plymouth petition was well received, and a motion made to grant "full and free tolerance of religion to all men that will preserve the civil peace and submit unto the government." There was to be "no limitation or exception against Turk, Jew, Papist, Arian, Socinian, Nicolaitan, Familist, or any other."

The majority of the deputies favored the measure. The General Court was equally divided. Against it stood Governor Bradford, Thomas Prence, William Collier, and Edward Winslow, once sympathetic with Roger Williams but now grown conservative. Toleration had the support of Standish, John Browne, Timothy Hatherly of Scituate, and Edmund Freeman of Sandwich, and the motion would have passed if Prence had not prevented it from coming to a vote by parliamentary maneuvering. The measure was finally buried when Winslow obtained postponement of action on the plea that he wished time for further consideration, writing his friend Winthrop at Boston to remark his disgust with many of the brethren:

"You would have admired to have seen how sweet this carrion relished to the palate of most of the deputies!"[7]

This defeat of the liberals seeking toleration marks another turning point in Pilgrim history. Always more tolerant, humane, and discerning than the Puritans, the Saints now began to trail them closely in calling upon the constables to act where the ministers had failed, substituting force for persuasion. Such a policy is always a confession of weakness, and here was the first certain symptom that the rule of the Saints was doomed. A law was passed imposing a fine of 10s. for neglect of public worship on any pretext whatever. Another threatened corporal punishment for "such as shall deney the Scriptures to bee the rule of life." Still another denied the rights of citizenship to all, whether freemen or not, who were "opposers of the good and wholesome lawes of the colony, or manifeste opposers of the true worship of God . . . or such as shall speak contemptuously of the lawes." These measures, of course, did not increase the popularity of the meeting house, and in an effort to silence criticism a law was aimed at those who "shall villifie by approbrious tearmes or speaches any church or minestry or ordinance." This necessitated another law inflicting a fine of 20s. "for speakeing evill of one of the magistrates."

All of this merely increased tension and resistance, and in 1654 Pastor Reyner resigned because of dissensions in the church, withdrawing to Dover, New Hampshire. As Dover was always a rather liberal town, this suggests that he may have been opposed to the new rigor at Plymouth. Whatever the cause, his departure left the "poor forlorne flock of Christ Groning under the want of Gospell ordinances," and it long remained so. Invitations were extended to many ministers, "accompanyed with fasting and prayer frequently," but none would accept. As a consequence, "much Ignorance Inseued in the Towne of Plimoth amongst the voulgare, and also much lysensiousnes and prophanes amongst the younger sort," notwithstanding the conscientious labors of

Brewster's successor, Ruling Elder Thomas Cushman, "a good man (as was said of Barnabas), & full of the holy Goast."

Religious affairs were in a sad state throughout the Old Colony. Almost all towns were without a "ministeryall shephard." John Lothrop died at Barnstable in 1653 and was not immediately replaced. Yarmouth had no pastor. John Mayo left Eastham because of dissensions there and went to Boston to serve with Richard Mather as "teacher" of the Second Church, the famous Old North, best known for the lantern that was hung in the belfry to signal Paul Revere. With the death of Partridge the pulpit at Duxbury was unoccupied for some years. Troubles at Marshfield led to the resignation of Blinman, who sought a quieter life among the Indians in Connecticut. His successor remained only a short time before departing for Massachusetts to accept a call there.

In 1654, weary of hardship and poverty, the "larned Mr. Chancy" left Scituate with the intention of returning to England. While awaiting passage in Boston, he was approached by a committee appointed by the Harvard Overseers to find a president for the college to succeed the cultivated and conscientious Henry Dunster, forced out for holding "antipaedo-baptistical principles" —meaning, in simple English, that he had followed John Smyth, Roger Williams, and others in rejecting infant baptism. As Harvard was the citadel of orthodoxy, the consistory of the Holy Discipline, the shock was profound. Fearing the wrath of the Bay authorities, Dunster withdrew to Scituate, where he was not molested by the Pilgrims. In time he took Chauncy's place in the pulpit there, and Scituate certainly suffered no loss by the exchange.

Meantime, at Boston, Richard Mather and John Norton, acting for the Harvard Overseers, had come to terms with Chauncy, demanding of him a promise that he would "forbear to disseminate or publish any tenets concerning the necessity of immersion in baptism and celebration of the Lord's Supper at evening." On this occasion Chauncy's conscience did not trouble him, and he yielded "without reluctance." Becoming the second president of

Harvard, at a salary of £100 a year, he directed its affairs for seventeen years, introducing a "stiff regimen of prayer, catechism, and repeating sermons," occasionally going himself to deliver a lecture to the "nasty salvages" in the Indian College, originally planned as a principal part of the institution.[8]

Two years later, in 1656, so many pulpits in the Old Colony were empty that Massachusetts became alarmed, bringing the situation to the attention of the United Colonies. "Our neighbour colony of Plymouth, our dear brethren, in great part seems to be wanting to themselves in a due acknowledgmente of and encouragement to the ministers of the Gospel," the Bay authorities complained. "As many pious ministers of the Gospel have (how justly we know not) deserted their stations, callings, and relations, our desire is that some such course might be taken as that a pious orthodox ministry may be reinstated amongst them, that so the flood of errour and principles of anarchy which will not long be kept out where Sathan and his instruments . . . prevail to the crying down of ministry and ministers, may be prevented."

What a blow to Bradford's pride, what a bitter pill for him to swallow in the last year of his life! To be publicly rebuked for want of zeal by the novices at the Bay, and with himself in the chair as president of the Confederacy! The old governor, deeply humiliated, almost cried out with pain.[9]

Yet there was no denying the ground of the complaint. As the condition could no longer be ignored, the Saints took an unprecedented step, reversing a historic policy. The "true" church, they had always contended, was a purely voluntary fellowship, a free association of like-minded Christians, to which each contributed what he would or could. Abandoning this fundamental of their faith, they now made support of the church compulsory, a legal obligation upon all—one of the "tyrannies" they had found so intolerable in the Anglican church. Each town was ordered to appoint officers to rate the estates of all inhabitants for the new pulpit tax.

This measure was greeted with much audible groaning and

several vehement protests. Dr. Matthew Fuller of Duxbury spoke the minds of many when he declared—for which he drew a 50s. fine—that surely the "Divill sat in the stern" when the General Court passed this "wicked" law establishing a virtual tithe system.

Unhappily for the ministers, who were otherwise pleased, the law contained a rather mean joker. The civil authorities set the rates, but the pastors had to collect their own salaries. This, as one of them plaintively remarked, "was attended with much trouble and often impaired his usefulness." Parishioners were always in arrears, sometimes for years at a time. When they saw the minister coming to make a call, they were never sure whether he was more interested at the moment in their souls or their pocketbooks, and they naturally resented being dunned. Yet the poor pastor could not be expected to sit idly by and watch his family starve.

Altogether, the General Court seems to have been rather unsympathetic about the ministers' problems and took only one immediate step to ease their hard lot. This was to recommend that it would be a "thing very commendable and beneficial" if the seaside towns were to set aside for the "Incurragement of an able Godly Minnestry amongst them" a small part of the oil and flesh of all drift whales that came ashore within their bounds. In his *Cape Cod,* that most charming of books, Thoreau has left us an affecting picture of a poor pastor sitting forlornly on a high bleak sand dune, with a bitter wind howling about him, as he scans the sea to the farthest horizon for sight of some expired leviathan that might possibly drift his way and be the means of providing beans and bacon for his hungry brood at home.

Such a vigil was seldom rewarding, of course. And yet, "for my part," said Thoreau, "if I were a minister, I would rather trust to the bowels of the billows, on the back side of the Cape, to cast up a whale for me, than to the generosity of many a country parish I know."[10]

Stung to the quick by the criticism of the Bay, outraged at the suggestion that the Old Colony was incapable of managing its affairs and should be taken in hand as a ward of the Confederacy,

Plymouth redoubled its efforts to secure a minister and avoid further scandal. For a time the pulpit was occupied by one James Williams, "an able Gospell preacher," but he soon departed for England. Several years later came William Brimstead, "a well accomplished servante of Christ." Eager to hold him, the Pilgrims offered him a salary of £70 a year, "besides his fierwood." He declined and removed to Massachusetts, preferring to minister to the town of Marlborough.

Now thoroughly alarmed, both town and church authorities bestirred themselves with greater vigor and practicality to make the local pulpit more attractive. All wood on Clark's Island, Saquish, and Gurnet's Nose was set aside for the pastor's use. Deacon Samuel Fuller's widow and son donated a choice lot on the Street and the congregation appropriated £60 to build a parsonage, the first at Plymouth. Another £60 was appropriated to finish and furnish it as comfortably as possible. But still, in spite of frequent prayers that the Lord would be pleased to send a likely occupant, the house stood empty for some time.

At length, in 1667, after "perishing without vision" for thirteen years, Mother Plymouth had a settled minister again, welcoming a "man of strong parts & good abillities to preach the word of God," the son and namesake of the great John Cotton of Boston. Still in his twenties, young Cotton had been offered the post once before and refused it, choosing rather to go to Martha's Vineyard to work there with Thomas Mayhew, "Lord of the Islands," as a missionary among the Gayhead Indians.* The two missionaries frequently clashed, and Cotton was summoned to explain before the commissioners of the Confederacy. The latter flatly declared, after looking into the situation, that "no good could be expected of their labours when by their mutuall contentions and invectives, they undid what they taught the natives." Young Cotton thereupon agreed to come to Plymouth, at a salary of £50 a year—a third to be paid in wheat or butter; an equal amount in rye,

---

* In 1685 Cotton edited the second revised edition of old John Eliot's Indian Bible.

barley, or peas; and the remaining third in Indian corn—and "so to continue," read his contract, "till God in his Providence shall so impoverish the town that they shall be necessitated to abridge the sum."

Though something of a scapegrace during his student days at Harvard, having been excommunicated by his father's church on one occasion, the young pastor entered upon his new duties in a sober frame of mind and with the rather officious zeal characteristic of all the Cottons. Trailing Ruling Elder Thomas Cushman, he went through the "whole towne, from family to family, to enquire into the state of soules," applying "counsells, admonitions, exhortations, & incouragements" to shame sinners and awaken sluggards "to attend upon the means of grace, & to minde the concernments of their soules, & practise family prayer more constantly."

All in all, it was a fruitful mission, it seemed to Cotton, who noted a "considerable reviving in the work of God"—and certainly there was need. In all the town, he had been shocked to discover, there were just forty-seven proper Saints! Only that number were members of the church in good standing, in sufficient state of grace to take communion. And the pastor suspected that even some of these were sinners—or, as he liked to call them, "offending church-seed."

To stimulate the revival, Cotton introduced regular catechizing. For this purpose he used a brief text entitled *The Foundation of the Christian Religion, gathered into six Principles,* which, so the preface explained, were "to be learned by ignorant people, that they may be fit to heare Sermons with profit, and receive the Lord's Supper with comforte." The text had been written almost a century before by William Perkins, who had so profoundly influenced both Brewster and Robinson at Cambridge. To it Robinson had added an appendix of forty-six questions and answers, all of which were now to be mastered.

Next, turning to intemperance, "a growing scandal," Cotton and Cushman addressed a remonstrance to the General Court:

"The multipling of ordinaries, or places of strong drinck, we judge to be as the digging or opening of a pit . . . We are very confident that, in the middle of the town, one public house is very sufficient for the entertainment of travelers; and yet within your sight, when you are in the place of justice, you may behold at least four or five houses where, not only at Court times (which there may be need of), but all the year long, more or less strong drinck is sold; whereby much precious time is spente and money lost by men's going from one drinking-house to another, till not only all appearance of religion, but reason, is in a manner lost; and not only English, but Indians, are greatly maintained in a course and way of drunkennesse."

There was also at this time stricter enforcement of the laws against profanation of the Sabbath "by doeing any servill worke or any such like abuses." Many were fined for "needles travelling upon ye Lord's Day." One man was "sharplie reproved" for writing a letter on the Sabbath, "or at least in the evening, somewhat too soon." Married couples were forbidden even to quarrel on the Lord's Day, two couples paying 40s. each in 1677 for unseasonable enjoyment of their usual pastime. The records of the day are filled with such entries as these: "A chh-child [churchchild] was publickly admonished for selling liquor to the Indeans . . . for scandalous words . . . for sinne . . . for being overtaken with Drinck . . . for prophaning the Sabbath by carrying grist from the mill . . . for having a childe before the natural time of woman . . ."

Cotton evidently held women to be the chief source of sin and was fond of lecturing them, frequently summoning "female chhchildren" to the parsonage to scold them about "pride, increase of sensuality, too much neglect in the education of children, not duly catechizing them, not calling upon them to remember at sermons, suffering them to play on Sabbath evenings."

During Cotton's pastorate Plymouth built a new meeting house. The old oak bastion on Fort Hill had served the Pilgrims for almost thirty years, until 1649, when it ceased to be used for

religious purposes upon completion of a proper meeting house
at the foot of the hill, on the north side of Town Square. This was
a most unpretentious structure, more like a barn than a church,
and deliberately designed so, for in their revolt from the past the
Pilgrims, like all the Separatists, rejected traditional forms of
church architecture. The beautiful old Gothic and Romanesque
structures handed down from the Middle Ages were scorned by
them as "idol-temples" and "steeple-houses," and they strove to
make their places of worship as unecclesiastical as possible.

The Pilgrims' first meeting house was a small unpainted structure, of clapboard on a heavy oak frame. Inside, there was no
paint, plaster, or ornament of any kind. As at Leyden, the congregation sat on hard wooden benches, and the "pulpit" was
simply a low dais with a plain wooden table in the center of it.
A few narrow openings in the walls, protected with "shuts" on
the outside, admitted a little light—enough for Reyner to read
his Bible, but nowhere near enough to dispel the pervading gloom.

Plymouth's second meeting house was somewhat larger and
incorporated a few improvements and refinements. Erected in
1683 with funds from the sale of Indian lands confiscated after
King Philip's War, it had windows of glass with diamond panes
and a shingled pyramidal roof, with a small cupola rising from
the point and housing a bell to call the faithful to worship. These
early meeting houses were plain and crude, but from them evolved
by slow degrees the white churches that dot New England's older
towns, as beautiful in their proportions, their knowing workmanship, their utter simplicity, and fine sharp line, as any the world
has seen.

In one of the first changes within the meeting house the long
wooden benches gave way to pews, not without protests from
traditionalists who pronounced them "wicked and unworthy,"
serving only to allow sinners to slide down inside them during
the long services and take a nap without detection. There was
some ground for this complaint, for the pews were built higher
and higher as time went on, until they offered a secure retreat

for tired and often sleepy plowmen—provided they did not snore. That baleful sound was always fatal not only to their blissful dreams but to their waking dignity, for it brought down upon their skulls with a sharp rap the bone-headed rod of the ubiquitous tithingman, a sort of ecclesiastical constable, ever on the prowl for just such sinners.

With the introduction of pews the always touchy question of social rank entered the meeting house and caused much bitter complaint, for the Saints were no longer equal before the pulpit, whatever might be the case before God. Each family built its own pew and the wealthier, especially those who had contributed substantially to building the meeting house, demanded the better places up front. To quiet envy and discontent, the Old Colony towns tried many different systems of seating the meeting house, and none was altogether satisfactory. Some towns used the tax rates—the bigger the taxpayer, the better the seat. Others sat by "age, office, and estate, Negroes excepted." But a younger man, if his estate were large enough, was permitted to add twenty years to his age for this purpose. The rule at Plymouth was (1) dignity of person, (2) age, and (3) "what charge they have been at in building the meeting house." Indians and Negroes were placed off by themselves, as were children, who sat in the gallery, wherever there was one.

The rise of the minister from a low dais almost on a level with his audience to a towering position above them took place by gradual stages. The pulpit rose in height and grew in size until the preacher, excitedly striding up and down it as he directed the battle against Satan, resembled in his formidable black clothes some fierce warrior of old pacing a medieval battlement. Over his head, amplifying the thunder of his commands and his warnings, was a large canopy, or sounding board, a favorite nesting place for bats, which were aroused now and again by all the sound and fury and came forth to do battle themselves, darting and diving about the house and creating pandemonium.

But the pests that more sorely tried the ministers' patience

were not the bats but "ye wretched Boys"—"young vipers," hissed
Jonathan Edwards, that great breather of hell fire—"yea, infinitely more hateful than vipers to God." Their character had not
changed much for the better, it seems, since that day long ago
when Martin Luther had sadly observed that "public sermons do
very little edify children."

Youngsters at Plymouth, particularly the boys, stood charged
with many "indecencies" in the meeting house. They fidgeted in
their seats—they stamped their feet—they pinched one another
—they giggled—they even "larfed out loud" when the tithingman
smartly used his rod upon sleeping elders. They were guilty, too,
of "frequently passing and repassing by one another in the Galleries," of sitting down during two-hour prayers, of sitting with
their hats on "during ye whole exercise," of "running out of ye
meeting house before prayer be done and ye Blessing pronounced,"
even of sneaking out during the always exhaustive sermon.

And the girls were not much better, it appears. They fidgeted
in their seats—stamped their feet—pulled one another's hair—
giggled—"larfed out loud" at the boys' "indecencies"—and were
even caught making eyes at them—all in the meeting house!

By 1676, during King Philip's War, the situation had become
so bad that Pastor Cotton ascribed the Indians' fury to God's displeasure with the unconscionable ways of New England youth.
There was no unanimity of opinion about this, however. Old John
Eliot, the Indian missionary, attributed it rather to the new fashion
of wearing wigs, which was an "Abhomination," he declared,
"unseemlie in the sight of God."

In any case, the almost continuous hubbub in the galleries
could no longer be tolerated, and every parish appointed Inspectors of Youth to put an end to it. Armed with birch rods, these
special officers did their best to keep some semblance of order
"in ye pue of ye wretched boys." They had strict instructions "to
see that they behave comlie, and to use such raps and blows as
shall be meet." They were to stop all "Smiling and Larfing and
Intiseing others to the same Evil," as well as "whispering and

Larfing in the meeting house betweene meetings." The switch was conscientiously applied, but the boys went on with their "indecencies"—to the shrill delight of their pig-tailed admirers, with the result that Inspectors of Youth were commanded to strike harder and on the least provocation, receiving specific instructions "that the same course be pursued with the Girls."

For the most part, Cotton's was a profitable ministry and the longest that Plymouth had yet enjoyed. But, like so many others, it ended abruptly, terminating in a scandal that shook all of New England, for no name carried greater weight among the Saints everywhere than that of Cotton, no other having quite its odor of sanctity. A natural fondness for "female chh-children" (women parishioners) had apparently led the Pilgrim pastor astray. The matter was hushed as much as possible, with old Judge Sewall coming down from Boston to smooth things over with his tact, good sense, and sympathetic understanding of human frailty.

"Upon the fourth day of the Week, Septr. 29, 1697," reads Sewall's diary, "a Council met at Plimouth . . . They published their Advice, that Mr. Cotton should make an orderly secession from the Church. Adv's'd the Church to dismiss him with as much Charity as the Rule would admit of, and provide for themselves. This was for his Notorious Breaches of the Seventh Commandment, and Undue Carriage in chusing Elders. Thus Christ's words are fulfilled. Unsavoury Salt is cast to the Dung-hill. A most awfull Instance!"

Perhaps the greatest mystery about early Plymouth is how, for so long, Pastor Cotton went on committing "Notorious" adulteries among the ewes of his flock in a very small town where everyone, not merely as a risible pleasure but as a matter of solemn religious duty, was peeking out the window curtains to watch what everybody else was doing and happily reporting derelictions to the Deacons or the Elders—not, in this instance, to the Pastor.

Allowed to resign after he had made a "full and penetentiall Aknoledgment of those evels," Cotton departed early in 1698 to become pastor of a small church at Charleston, South Carolina, dying there the next year.

For more than two centuries the Plymouth pastors moved so far and so fast, for one reason or another, that only two were buried in the town—the first not until 1723, more than a century after the landing.

23

THROWN
BY THE
BAY HORSE

... the whole of New England's interest seems
designed to be loaded on one bottome, and
her particular motions to be concentric to
the Massachusetts tropic.

—ICHABOD WISWALL

THE BURDEN THAT FELL UPON PRENCE AFTER BRADFORD'S
death in 1657 was a heavy one, and the new governor's policy was
ill designed to lighten the load. Now in his fifty-seventh year, a
man of no education but of considerable natural ability, he had
worked closely with Bradford for some years and probably was
the latter's choice as his successor, which accounts for the unanimous vote he received. Though "very amiable & pleasante" in his
private life, Prence was harsh and overbearing as a magistrate,
sitting the bench with a "countenance full of majestie," being a
strict and often cruel disciplinarian. As the church records rather
ambiguously phrased it, he was "an awfull frowne of God upon

this church & colony." Once a Stranger himself, he had become one of the narrowest and most bigoted of the Saints. The colony was seething with discontent, but Prence refused to listen to grievances or attempt to redress them, pleased to be known as a "Terrour to evill doers." And almost anyone who opposed him was "evill."

At Prence's right hand sat John Alden, now almost sixty but hale and hearty, still quite able to carry on his carpenter's trade. Alden had succeeded his old friend Standish as treasurer of the colony and held office till 1659, at which time he was so "low in his estate" that he was voted a grant of £10 for his public services. There were four other older men on the General Court—Captain Thomas Willet, now returned after living for a time in New Amsterdam; Prence's father-in-law, William Collier, one of the original merchant adventurers; still another adventurer, Timothy Hatherly, of Scituate; and Captain James Cudworth, also of Scituate, a son of the Reverend Ralph Cudworth, fellow of Emmanuel College, Cambridge, where so many of the Puritans at the Bay had gone to school. Captain Cudworth was a liberal and in the Old Colony's last years showed far more wisdom and tolerance than most of his colleagues, suffering much in his uncompromising fight against religious persecution, a course which John Robinson would have applauded.

But with so many of the Old Standards gone, a younger generation began to rise in the higher councils. On the General Court now sat Josiah Winslow, not yet thirty, Edward Winslow's oldest son, and two of the Bradford family—the younger William, in his early thirties and "eminente in grace," and Bradford's stepson, Lieutenant Thomas Southworth, "rarely Indowed both in Sacred and Civill Respects." After Brewster's death, when it was a question of naming his successor as ruling elder, the choice lay between Southworth and Thomas Cushman, who had also grown up in the Bradford household, and the old governor virtually made the choice himself by directing his stepson toward the magistracy. Southworth's younger brother, Constant, Prence's brother-in-law through marriage to another of the Colliers, also served frequently as an assistant governor in later years. There was one more of note in the younger group—Thomas Hinckley, once of Scituate and now of Barnstable, a future governor and, like Bradford, addicted to writing "poetry."*

Events in England presented the new regime with several delicate problems. With the restoration of the Stuarts in 1660, the Anglican bishops were again in the saddle and tracking down their enemies. The skies had suddenly darkened, no one knew what to expect, and all the news was bad. "Episcopacy, common prayer, bowing at the name of Jesus, the sign of the cross in baptism, the altar, and organs are in use, and like to be more," a Massachusetts agent reported from London. "The Lord keep and preserve his churches, that there may not be fainting in the day of trial."

It proved to be not too difficult to make peace with Charles II, partly as a result of the canny policy the Pilgrims and the Puritans had pursued during the Civil War. They had not committed themselves too explicitly to the new order of things. On Cromwell's triumph, it is true, Plymouth had decreed a "day of public thanksgiving throughout the Colony . . . to give thanks for the great victories granted to the Army in behalf of Parliament and the Commonwealth of England." But the Pilgrims had maintained a discreet official silence about the execution of Charles I. They had not formally congratulated Cromwell when he was proclaimed Protector. Any laments for his death were carefully kept off the record.

Plymouth drew up a declaration of loyalty to Charles II, assuring him and his heirs that they did "most humblie and faithfully submit and oblige themselves for ever." The declaration was forwarded to London with a letter from Prence to the younger John Winthrop, entreating the latter "with all exspideton to present the inclosed to my Lord [Say and Sele], as also the vewe of our hombel petishon, craving his lordship's help and furtheranc ther in." As for the "petishon," wrote Prence, "I hop you will not

---

* For the Old Colony officers during these and later years, see Appendix B.

find anything in it which will be offensive, exsep our rude ex-preshons, for which we crave your hellp also to ecskuse us . . . We would not be to tedious, but leav our case with you, and count both you and it, and all other pore waighty ocations, to the blessing of the Lord our God, who is our hop, and in hom we ever desir to rest." As Charles was too busy consolidating his position at home to be much concerned at the moment about the colonies, Plymouth's "hombel petishon" was graciously received at Whitehall.

Though the Pilgrims remained somewhat apprehensive and disposed to keep a weather eye in that quarter, they had more immediate and vexing problems closer home, on their very door-step, laid there by a swarm of "Notoriouse heretiques," chiefly Quaker, who began to appear in New England in 1656. In the Friends the Saints met for the first time a people as courageous and stubbornly determined as themselves, possessed of the same passionate devotion to their principles, and they were somewhat taken aback, not quite knowing what to do with these "pests."

The Quakers stood at the extreme left of the Separation, rep-resenting its final revulsion against a religion of sacrament and spectacle. They went beyond the Saints in their aversion to "idol-temples" and "steeple-houses" with their tolling bells—"like a market-bell, to gather the people that the priest may set forth his wares to sell." They rejected all formal ritual. They had as small respect for magistrates, the Pilgrims' included, as the Saints had shown for those in England. Quite as disturbing was the latitude they allowed women. They actually allowed them to speak at meeting. This not only violated the Pauline injunction against such freedom but might lead to no end of trouble in other respects. Altogether, their doctrine was the "grossest collection of blas-phemies and confusions that ever were heard of." The Friends were angrily denounced as "madmen, lunaticks, daemoniacks," and their behavior lent some color to this charge, for they were not the quiet, gentle, and unobtrusive people they later became. As always happens, ruthless opposition drove them to extremes. One burst into the meeting house at Cambridge with two bottles in his hand. "Thus," he shouted at the pastor, crashing the bottles to the floor, "will the Lord break you in pieces." The congregation at Newbury was electrified one Sabbath morning when a comely young woman walked into the meeting house quite nude—"to show the people," she said, "the nakedness of their rulers."

At a meeting in 1657, the council of the United Colonies urged prompt steps to rid the country of Quakers by driving them into the wilderness. At the same time a letter was dispatched to Rhode Island to insist that they not be allowed to take refuge there. As the Confederacy refused to admit Rhode Island and constantly snubbed it, this was sheer impudence, and one of the Plymouth representatives, James Cudworth, refused to sign the letter, objecting to other of the proceedings as well. Faithful to Roger Williams' principles, Rhode Island rejected the "request," adding an observation that should have given the commissioners pause. They had no law "whereby to punish any for only declaring by words, &c., their minds and understandings concerning the things and ways of God, as to salvation and an eternal condition." And it was their experience, they said, that where these people "are most of all suffered to declare themselves freely . . . there they least of all desire to come . . . They begin to loathe this place."

At Boston the next year, under the presidency of Governor John Endecott, the United Colonies recommended more violent measures. Quakers and all other heretics were to be banished from each of the colonies "under pain of death, and if afterwards they presume to come again into that jurisdiction, then to be put to death as presumptuously incorrigible." As Cudworth had been dropped as a commissioner because of his opposition to such measures, Plymouth was represented by Prence and Josiah Winslow. Both signed the recommendation,[1] and it was quickly adopted by all of the colonies although Massachusetts alone exacted the extreme penalty of Quakers.

Fearing "these wolves in sheep clotheing," detesting their "horred and damable tenetts," the Pilgrims decreed early in 1657 that no one should bring in "any quaker, rantor, or other Notoriouse heretiques" on pain of a 20s. fine for each week that such "strangers" remained in the colony—a penalty almost immediately increased to a £5 fine or the lash, or both. The workhouse was declared the proper place for Quakers and "all such vagrants as wander upp and down without any lawfull calling, and alsoe all Idle persons or rebellious children, or servants that are stubborne." Prisoners received only what they could earn by their own labors in the workhouse, but as there was no House of Correction at the moment, they were punished by "stocking or whiping." People were encouraged to seize and hand over to the constables anyone suspected of heresy. Hereafter, those seeking admittance as freemen were to be placed on probation for an extended period, to "stand one whole yeare propounded to the Court," to make sure that no "corrupt" persons crept in. These laws were aimed at Baptists as well as Quakers, for the former had been making converts. And to keep Anglicans in their place, it was now a crime—previously it had been only a social error though serious enough—to celebrate Christmas by "forbearing of labour, feasting, or in any other way."

In 1659, when six Friends were banished on pain of death, John Alden nodded assent as Prence remarked that, "in his conscience," all Quakers deserved "to be destroyed, both they, their wives and their children, without pity or mercy." But most Pilgrims rejected this view. Nor did they follow the Puritans in slicing off the Quakers' ears, branding them with hot irons, flaying them with tarred ropes, beating them senseless with iron rods, burning their books, and confiscating everything they owned in guise of a fine.

Seized at Plymouth, one Humphrey Norton was "found guilty of divers horred errours, and was centanced speedily to depart." After a few weeks in Rhode Island he returned and was again hauled before the General Court, with Governor Prence presiding and in a great rage against the prisoner, charging him with "many offenses against God."

"Thou lyest, Thomas, thou art a malicious man," Norton interrupted. "Thou art like a scolding woman, and thy clamorous tongue I regard no more than the dust under my feet."

Asked to take an oath before he testified, the prisoner refused.

Sentenced to be whipped, he escaped punishment by declining to pay the marshal his customary fee for such exertions. Finally released—for what could one do with such people?—Norton delivered a parting blast in a letter to Prence and another to Alden.

"John Alden," he wrote, "I have weighed thy ways, and thou art like one fallen from thy first love; a tenderness once I did see in thee, and moderation to act like a sober man, which through evil counsel and self-love thou are drawn aside from . . . like a self-conceited fool puffed up with the pride of his heart because he hath gotten the name of a magistrate. . . . In love this is written, to dishearten thee in time before the evil day overtake thee; let it be so received from thy friend."

After some months in jail two other "Incendiarys of mischiffe," William Leddra and a friend, were offered their freedom if they would engage "without any sinestery reservation . . . to depart, and to come into this Collonie noe more, and pay their fees to the jayler." They refused, though Leddra added, "It is like if I were at liberty out of prison, I might depart in the will of God ere long." Seeing nothing better to do than make experiment of this, they turned Leddra loose and, sure enough, he departed, going to Salem where he was promptly seized and carried to Boston. The Bay authorities offered him his freedom if he would return to England, which Leddra declined with the remark that he had no business there. Brought to trial, he was sentenced to death.

Massachusetts had already hanged three Quakers for "rebellion, sedition, and presumptuous obtruding themselves," including Mary Dyer, wife of the secretary of Rhode Island, whose ghost, it is said, still walks Boston Common, clad in the simple gray in which she died. At the trials there had been the most revolting scenes, with Governor Endecott and most of the ministers crying for blood, led by John Wilson, "very zealous against known and Manifest evills," Norton's colleague at the First Church.

"I would carry fire in one hand, and fagots in the other, to burn all the Quakers in the world. . . . Hang them!" cried Wilson. "Or else—," and he drew a finger across his throat. Norton rushed into print to defend these proceedings, but there was deep and growing opposition. Sensing this, the authorities took the precaution of calling out troops at the executions. Now came Leddra's turn, but his was the last. Though one more Quaker was condemned to die, the authorities dared not execute the sentence in face of the rising indignation in all classes of people, especially among the rank and file.[2] The dominant theocrats and idealogues in Massachusetts here suffered a significant reverse, beating their first retreat before the common sense of the common people who would one day shatter their autocratic power.

Opposition in the Old Colony was even more articulate and determined among both Saints and Strangers. Secretary Morton tried to pretend that the Quakers had little or no influence in the colony, and that few were "leavened with their fixions and fantacyes." In truth, as the records reveal, there was much open sympathy throughout the colony for the poor harassed Friends, and the latter made many converts by their bravery of spirit, a quality the Pilgrims always admired. Their neighbors often went to great lengths to protect them from the authorities, as at Barnstable which remembered the liberal doctrine it had been taught by John Lothrop. The latter had accepted all, even Anabaptists, who professed faith in God and promised to keep the Ten Commandments. A special state constable had to be sent to Sandwich to enforce the laws against heretics. The fellow was one George Barlow, "the Quaker Terrour," who worked on a commission basis, so to speak, and ruthlessly began to plunder the town, heavily fining many suspects and their "manifest encouragers," including eight freemen, all of whom were disenfranchised. The stouter citizens of Sandwich gave him no peace until he was in the stocks for immorality, his three stepdaughters for beating him up in a domestic fracas, and his wife for selling rum to the Indians.

Duxbury was another heretical center, harboring Baptists as

well as Quakers. Prence's policy met stiff opposition here, led by John Howland's brother, Arthur, and the sons of Joseph Rogers of the *Mayflower,* seconded by the local pastor, the Reverend John Holmes. For outspoken criticism of the authorities, young Henry Howland was up on the malicious charge of "improperlie entertaining" a neighbor's wife. His brother Zoeth was put in the stocks for saying that he "would not goe to meeting to hear lyes, and that the Divill could preach as good a sermon as the ministers," with which many townspeople seemed to agree, choosing to pay a fine rather than attend public worship.

And what was Governor Prence's amazement to discover at just this time that another of his chief enemy's sons, young Arthur Howland, was surreptitiously courting his daughter Elizabeth. As the law forbad "making motion of marriage" to a girl without her parents' consent, the irascible old governor promptly hauled the "impudent" youth into court and fined him £5 for "inveigeling" his daughter. The young lovers were not discouraged and remained constant, for seven years later Arthur was again in court for having "disorderlie and unrighteously endeavored to obtain the affections of Mistress Elizabeth Prence." Elizabeth's affections were already his, it is evident. All he wanted were those of her father, and once more Arthur was fined and put under bond of £50 "to refrain and desist."

But the younger Saints were quite as stubborn as their fathers, and the couple continued to behave "disorderlie and unrighteously," finally breaking the iron will of the old governor. The next year he had to capitulate, and in good time the names of Thomas Howland and Prence Howland were inscribed on the baptismal roll of the church.[3]

But the strongest resistance came from Scituate, articulated by Assistant Governors James Cudworth and Timothy Hatherly. The latter had served on the General Court almost continuously for more than twenty years. He was now dismissed and disenfranchised for his opposition. When the people of Scituate elected him as a deputy and sent him back to Plymouth, the Court refused to seat him. Captain Cudworth had already lost his post as commissioner to the United Colonies. "Our Civil Powers," he complained, "are so exercised in matters of religion and conscience that we have no time to effect anything that tends to the promotion of the civil weal; but must have a State religion, and a State ministry, and a State way of maintenance." He expressed his surprise that John Alden favored such a course, remarking that the latter had "deceived the expectations of many, and indeed lost the affections of such as I judge were his cordial Christian friends." Nettled and angry, the Court now called upon Cudworth to explain his presence at Quaker meetings.

"I thought it better so to do," he replied, "than with the blind World to Censure, Rail at, and Revile them when they neither saw their Persons nor knew any of their Principles. But the Quakers and myself cannot close in divers things, and so I signify to the Court that I am no Quaker. . . . But withal I tell you that as I am no Quaker, so I will be no Persecutor." Cudworth was dismissed as assistant governor, deprived of his military command, and disenfranchised. As all of this had little effect but to swell the chorus of protest, the authorities drew back somewhat and decided to try a more reasonable policy. They would overpower the Quakers by showing them the error of their ways. In every town several reliable Saints were appointed "to repair to their meetings, together with the marshal or constable of the town, and to use their best endeavors by argument and discourse to convince or hinder them."

Constant Southworth and William Peabody religiously went to all Quaker meetings in Duxbury, with what success does not appear. But elsewhere the new policy backfired in the most surprising way. Appointed to spy on heretics at Plymouth, Deacon John Cooke, son of Francis of the *Mayflower* company and of the original Scrooby congregation, had to be excommunicated for turning Baptist; he withdrew to Dartmouth at the western limit of the colony, close to the Baptists in Rhode Island, followed by several of the Howlands. One of the four men named to reason with the Quakers at Sandwich was Isaac Robinson. As the son of John Robinson, he was regarded as eminently sound. But it was the Quakers, it seems, who reasoned with him, for he soon joined them. Charged with "sundrie scandels and falsehoods," he was dismissed from the offices he held in the town and deprived of his rights as a freeman. With a group of Quakers, Robinson crossed the Cape to settle at Succanesett (Falmouth), where he opened a tavern which he ran for many years.

In the end the Friends defeated the Saints as they had the Puritans. The General Court finally let it be known that if Quakers and other "rantors" would remove to the western boundary of the colony along Narragansett Bay, they would not be molested there. In 1681 the town of Sandwich granted heretics the right to vote in the disposal of town lands and levying of taxes "soe long as they carry themselves civilly and not abuse their libertie." Other towns granted them similar privileges though for some years all disabilities were not removed.

Charles II had intervened in the conflict, ordering the colonies to cease persecuting Quakers and ship them home for trial there, an order which was blandly ignored though it did something to discourage official violence. In 1664, with complaints of injustice still pouring into London, the King appointed a commission to visit New England and look into affairs there, a step regarded by all of the colonies as a most alarming intrusion. They had reason to be uneasy, for one of the commissioners was Samuel Maverick, a staunch Anglican, one of the early settlers in New England, whom the Massachusetts authorities had driven off Noddle's Island in Boston Bay and imprisoned during the Civil War. Always critical of the Separatists, he was a dangerous adversary, for he was a shrewd observer and from his long stay in the country knew all the ins and outs of Puritan and Pilgrim policy.

Four ships of the line—the *Guinea* carrying thirty-six guns, with the *Elias, Martin,* and *William and Nicholas*—put in at Boston, the first appearance of the Royal Navy in the harbor. On board were the four royal commissioners and about four hundred troops, sent out to dispossess the Dutch along the Hudson. One of Plymouth's assistant governors, Captain Thomas Willet, was assigned to this expedition "for counsel and advice," an appointment for which he was well qualified, and he readily accepted, though somewhat treacherously, for he had lived at New Amsterdam for some years and been most hospitably entertained there, honored as one of Governor Peter Stuyvesant's trusted agents. With a show of force the English troops overawed the Dutch, Stuyvesant capitulated, and the red cross of St. George went up along the Hudson. New Amsterdam became New York, with Willet, a Leyden Saint, as its first English mayor, serving three years before returning to receive Plymouth's congratulations. He and the latter day Saints had forgotten or chose to ignore Bradford's assurance to De Rasieres and the Dutch at New Amsterdam many years before.

The Saints, Bradford had written, wanted only the friendship of the Dutch and would always remember the kindness they had received in Holland, "haveing lived there many years with freedome and good contente . . . for which we and our children after us are bound to be thankful to your Nation, and shall never forgett ye same but shall hartily desire your good & prosperity, as our owne, for ever."

The royal commissioners, though a nuisance, caused no great disturbance. They found Plymouth the most tractable of the United Colonies, largely because the Pilgrims now were, as Governor Prence confessed, "the meanest & weakest, least able to stand of ourselves, and litle able to contribute any helpfullnes to others and we know it, though none should tell us of it." Eager to obtain a proper patent at last, the Pilgrims acceded, tongue in cheek, to most of the commissioners' demands and received a flattering letter from the King.

"Your carriage," wrote His Majesty, "seems to be set off with the more lustre by the contrary deportment of the Colony of Massachusetts, as if, by their refractoriness, they had designed to recommend and heighten the merit of your compliance."[4]

Plymouth was, Maverick noted on his visit, "a poor small Towne now, the People being removed into Farmes in the country." In all the colony there were "about twelve small townes, one sawmill for boards, one bloomary for iron, neither good river nor good harbour, nor any place of strength; they are so poor they are not able to maintain scholars to their ministers but are necessitated to make use of a gifted brother in some places." The commissioners had been instructed to look into the state of education in the colonies, and their interest at last stimulated some action at Plymouth in regard to schools.

Though New England had no public school system worthy of the name for almost two centuries, New Haven early took steps to encourage education, passing its first school law in 1638. Massachusetts followed four years later, "it being one chief project of that old deluder, Satan, to keep men from the knowledge of the Scriptures" by keeping them ignorant so that the "true sense and meaning of the original might be clouded by false glosses of saint-seeming deceivers." The Pilgrims had announced their intention of providing a common school as early as 1624, excusing their delay by saying that they had been prevented by "want of a fitt person or hithertoo means to maintaine one." Whatever their intentions, nothing was done about the matter for almost a half century.

What little instruction youngsters received was obtained at home from their parents, many of whom were illiterate. For the wealthier and more ambitious, a few persons conducted what were virtually small private schools. In 1635 young Benjamin Eaton, son of shipwright Eaton of the *Mayflower* company, was "put to Bridget Fuller, being to keep him att schoole two years, & employ him after in such service as she sees good and he may be fitt for." The Winslows and others at Marshfield clubbed together and hired a teacher for their children. Bradford appears to have run a select school in politics and public administration for his three sons, his two stepsons, young Thomas Cushman, his ward, and Nathaniel Morton and other nephews. Not for his daughter Mercy or his nieces, of course, for the world was still a jealously guarded male world, and the masters of it were agreed that it should remain so. As legal chattels of their liege lords, women had no voice in Church or State. Long ago, in the early years of settlement, Bradford had denied the "libel" that women had acquired any new rights or privileges at Plymouth.

"Touching our governemente," he wrote indignantly, "you are quite mistaken if you think we admite weomen . . . to have to doe in the same, for they are excluded, as both reason and nature teacheth they should be."

Education of girls was a vain and idle thing, the Pilgrim Fathers agreed.[5] At best, it was a silly affectation; at worst, a danger to the established order. Women should mind their own business, and that business was cooking, spinning, washing, sweeping, and bearing children—often. Consequently, as more than one foreign visitor noted, the women of New England were all "pittifully Tooth-shaken" and apt to look much older than their years.

"*Uxor praegnans est,*" reads an almost annual entry in Judge Sewall's diary, and in this regard his was not an unusual family.[6] Always, as the day of delivery drew near, there was a great bustle in the house as relatives and neighbors prepared a plentiful supply of "groaning cakes" and "groaning beer." And on the infant's first Sabbath, winter or summer, it was carried without fail to the meeting house to be baptized even if the minister had to break ice in the font to perform the rite.

Along with the high birth rate went an appalling infant mortality—the result of cold and drafty houses, bad diet, want of medical knowledge and surgical care, and congenital weakness born of too frequent parenthood. Of Sewall's fourteen children, only three survived him; of Cotton Mather's fifteen, only two. The rate of maternal mortality also ran high. The old burying grounds of the Saints, as anyone can verify, are filled with stones to young wives who went to their graves prematurely, worn out by childbirth, and often with five or six of their infants buried beside them.

Yet life in the Old Colony was now much easier than it had been for the Pilgrim Mothers. Except in the new towns springing up along the Cape and in the wilds to the west, the primitive "booths" of early days, constructed of two upright rows of saplings with rubble between, roofed with marsh grass and having only the bare earth as floor, had given way to new and larger houses. The better of these houses were, in general, very similar to the Howland House (1667), which still stands in Plymouth—a two-storied clapboard structure with a shingled roof, built around a massive central fireplace, with the "great room" in the southeast corner, as was traditional. Glass had replaced oiled paper in the window openings. As plaster had not come into general use, interior walls were panelled, usually with pine. Ceiling rafters were left uncovered. The floors of wide hand-hewn boards, always well-scrubbed and usually bare except for a small hooked rug or two, were sanded for more special occasions. Furniture was simple, serviceable, and uncomfortable—homemade beds, with ropes or slats supporting thin straw ticks; homemade chairs, stools, benches, and tables; a number of large wooden chests, and at least one heavy cradle on rockers, normally in use and within reach of the housewife's foot. More prosperous families had a few better pieces of furniture—serrated cabinets, chests, and cupboards, well designed and skilfully wrought by Plymouth's two master carpenters, John Alden and Kenelm Winslow, the coffin-maker.[7]

All cooking was done in the wide stone fireplace with its built-in brick oven, and went on almost continuously from early morning to late at night. A usual breakfast consisted of rye pudding and bread, or hasty pudding ("ye Indean porridge"), plus pea or bean soup, or stew, flavored with pork or salt fish. At dinner in the middle of the day the Saints again had bean soup, or pork and beans, with stewed peas, squash, turnips, onions, or other vegetables. Supper was much like breakfast, with the addition of gingerbread, cake, cheese, or pie—all washed down with beer, which was drunk at all meals, even by younger children. Milk was reserved for babies. There was butter on the tables of the wealthier families, and fresh fish was often served, though seldom beef or mutton, which was reserved for sale in the larger town markets.

For her endless round of duties in kitchen, scullery, and nursery, no "book larnin" was required, and only an occasional

woman—Alice Bradford and Bridget Fuller were exceptions—
could read and write. Of the younger women born at Plymouth,
all seem to have been illiterate. When called upon to sign a deed,
the daughters of Nathaniel Morton, secretary of the Old Colony,
could do no more than make their mark. Even "ye wretched
boys" were taught little more than the three R's, with some proper
homilies from the Bible.

The General Court first concerned itself with education in
1663 by recommending for "serious consideration that there may
be a schoolmaster in each Towne to teach the children in reading
& writing." Of more practical effect was the decision seven years
later to lease the Cape Cod fishery and use the funds to provide
Plymouth with a common school, a policy later extended to all
larger Pilgrim towns. The subsidy was ridiculously small, being
limited to not more than £5 ($250) a year. Though these schools
were not free, they were open to all and the tuition was low.

Plymouth's was opened in 1671 when John Morton, nephew
of the secretary, was hired to teach the young how "to read and
write & cast up accounts." There was much criticism of this narrow program on the part of parents who felt that they were not
getting their money's worth, and the next year Morton was succeeded by Anmi Ruhamah Corlet, distinguished as the first Harvard graduate to have a middle name. Fault was found with his
teaching also. It inclined toward the "higher learning," and the
Saints felt that far too much time was spent on Latin and Greek.
It was enough if children knew how to write, cipher, and read
the Bible. Ordered to keep within those bounds, Corlet resigned,
and Plymouth was without a schoolmaster for almost twenty
years. Finally, in 1699, another was hired, and it was about time
if one is to judge from the Town Fathers' decree in regard to the
rates to be charged:

"Every scollar that Coms to wrigh or syfer or to lern latten,
shall paye 3 pence pr. weke; if to Read onlie, then to pay 3 half
pence per weke."

Plymouth's first schoolhouse was built six years later, by public subscription. All Pilgrim towns containing seventy or more families were now under compulsion to maintain a grammar school or be fined £5 a year. Many took the cheaper way of paying the fine rather than provide the requisite space and hire a schoolmaster at the prescribed minimum salary, which was "at least £12 [$600] in current merchantable pay, to be raised by rate on all the inhabitants of such towne."

Efforts had meantime been made to educate the Indians, largely with the aim of bringing back into the fold "these poor natives, the dregs of mankind," almost universally regarded as the "degenerate" remains of the ten lost tribes of Israel. It was also hoped that they could be taught to "labour and work in building, planting, &c.," not to speak of wearing proper clothes. The leader in the work was the Reverend John Eliot, "teacher" at Roxbury, a man of "exemplary mortification," who was disturbed that the Indians were "so stupid and senseless" that they would not even inquire of the English the road to salvation. Mastering their language, he translated the Lord's Prayer and the Decalogue and set out on his mission, making such encouraging progress around Boston that he went on to translate the Bible. Even earlier, Roger Williams had mastered the Algonquin tongue and thought of embarking on a missionary project, but soon dismissed it as presumptuous.

Eliot came into the Old Colony, visiting Yarmouth, "speaking with and preaching to the poor Indians in the remote places about Cape Cod." To the south the Thomas Mayhews, father and son, proprietors of Martha's Vineyard, had made some converts there among the Gayhead. Steps were taken to arouse interest in the work among the devout in England, largely through Edward Winslow, then in London; he did so well that in 1649 the Parliament blessed the formation of the Society for the Promoting and Propagating of the Gospel of Jesus Christ in New England. Funds were to be solicited in England and expended at the direction of the commissioners of the United Colonies. Within seven years more than £1,700 ($85,000) was transmitted to the commissioners, who spent the money paying salaries, building an Indian College at Harvard, providing a few scholarships, printing Indian catechisms, and giving presents to "deserving" Indians, such as the sagamore of Agawam, who was given a "coat of about three yards of the coarsest cloth . . . to encourage him to learn to know God, and to excite other Indians to do the like."

Strangely, most of the Indians showed no gratitude whatever, especially those in the Narragansett, Mohegan, Nipmuck, and stronger tribes. Even some of the lesser remained quite unmoved by the "glad tidings of Salvation." When Eliot asked the weak Podunk, near Hartford, if they would accept Christ as their savior, the old men flatly declared:

"No! We have lost most of our lands, but we are not going to become the white man's servants."

Most of the converts in the Old Colony were made among the broken tribes along Cape Cod. Those on the upper arm found an unusual friend in Richard Bourne, a prosperous layman of Sandwich, through whose efforts fifty square miles of territory were set aside for the Praying Indians in what still exists as the "Kingdom of Mashpee," just south of the town. Here they enjoyed a large measure of self-government and the sage counsel of Bourne, who, becoming a minister, preached to them till his death in 1685. The Indians farther along the Cape were in the care of Samuel Treat, pastor at Eastham, "a Godlie able man," son of Governor Treat of Connecticut, the oldest of twenty-one children, in time having fourteen himself. He soon trained four native schoolmasters and an equal number of dusky preachers and kept them busy under his supervision, writing sermons for them in Indian, translating the Confession of Faith for their use. Treat did much to aid his charges materially and spiritually, but what most impressed them was the boom of his voice. He could make himself heard a half mile off, it was said, even when a stiff northeaster was howling through the pines and across the sand dunes of his bleak parish.[8]

But the missionaries had no success whatever with the Wampanoag, largely because of Massasoit's influence. The Big Chief had remained a faithful ally since that day so long ago when he had signed the treaty of mutual assistance with Carver. Pledges were again exchanged in 1639 when Massasoit agreed not to sell or give away lands to anyone without the Pilgrims' consent. But he stoutly resisted conversion. In 1653, when conveying a large tract around the town of Swansea to the Pilgrims, he asked the latter to promise that they would never attempt to draw his people away from their gods, but the Saints would give no such assurance.

Upon the Big Chief's death in 1661 he was succeeded by Wamsutta, his older son. The new chief soon came to Plymouth with his brother Metacom to confirm the peace treaty. On their visit they asked the Pilgrims to give them English names. The one became Alexander and the other Philip, probably being named for those famed "barbarians" of the old Greek world, Philip and Alexander the Great of Macedon.

Not many months later a rumor came to Plymouth by way of Boston that Alexander was plotting against the Pilgrims. When he failed to answer a summons to appear before the General Court and explain, Major Josiah Winslow was dispatched with ten armed men to fetch him from Sowams. Along the way they discovered that he was at a hunting lodge near Taunton. Breaking in upon him, they commanded him at pistol point to accompany them, dragging him off as if he were a common felon whereas he and his father had always regarded themselves as sovereign allies. Pilgrim apologists have made much of the fact that he was honorably treated along the way by being offered a horse to ride, an offer which Alexander declined, saying that he would not ride so long as the women with him had to walk on this forced march. Taken to Assistant Governor Collier's house at Duxbury, then to Josiah Winslow's at Marshfield, he was sharply questioned by Governor Prence and finally released, desperately sick of fever, brought on by a sense of guilt and "inward fury," according to some. A day or two later Alexander died at Plymouth, and in solemn procession his men carried him on their shoulders to Sowams for burial there among his people.

His brother Philip succeeded him and came to Plymouth to

confirm the treaty of peace once more. As time went on, however, it became evident that a storm was brewing. Both the Pilgrims and the Wampanoag were restless, full of complaints against one another. The mutual trust that had marked their relationship gave way to brooding suspicion. Basically, the conflict sprang from their very different and incompatible ways of life. What was good for one was not good for the other. The more the English settlements grew and expanded, the more they impinged upon the hunting grounds of the Indians who, in spite of every effort made to "civilize" them, preferred the nomadic life of their fathers, not because they were ignorant and perverse but because, like most of us, they preferred what was familiar and were wedded to their old ways. Men cannot change their culture patterns over-night, even when offered the "glad tidings of salvation," a fact which escaped the early settlers and most Americans until recent years.

The fundamental cause of conflict lay in the opposed land systems of the whites and the Indians. The right of private property entitling the owner to its exclusive use—or non-use, if he chose—was a concept quite foreign to the Indians. The latter had personal property, such as bows, arrows, blankets, pots, and such things, usually fashioned by their own hands. If they tilled a plot of ground, the crop they grew was theirs. But the land in general —the woods, streams, and everything on it—belonged to every-body and was for the use of all. If a brave shot a deer in the forest, or brought a pot of water from a stream, that deer and that water were his. But no one could assert an exclusive proprietary right to all the deer in the forest or all the water in the streams. The Indians did not understand the symbolism of fences. When they "sold" lands for a few beads or other trinkets, it was often with a misconception of what was involved. In their minds they were merely selling the whites the right to use the land as they them-selves used it and did not anticipate being entirely dispossessed, which explains the ridiculously small price they were prepared to accept in such transactions. Captain Standish, Constant Southworth, and Samuel Nash obtained a tract fourteen miles square at Bridgewater for seven coats, eight hoes, nine hatchets, ten and a half yards of cotton cloth, twenty knives, and four "moose" skins. One day, when exploring the Cape beyond Eastham, a party of Pilgrims pointed to a particular section and asked the Indians who owned it.

"Nobody," was the Indians' reply, meaning everybody.

"In that case," said the Pilgrims, "it is ours."

But the English attitude toward the natives' rights was never more succinctly expressed than by a town meeting at Milford, Connecticut, in 1640: "Voted, that the earth is the Lord's and the fulness thereof; voted, that the earth is given to the Saints; voted, that we are the Saints."

The Indians had other complaints to make against the whites than their insatiable hunger for land. They were treated, even at best, with an ill disguised contempt that hurt their pride—as if they were a blight upon the face of the earth, to be removed as quickly as possible. Special laws were passed against them to keep them in their place. After 1643 no "stray" Indian was allowed in the Old Colony. If an Indian were guilty of theft, he was to make fourfold restitution; if unable to do so, he was to work it off at the rate of 12d. a day, or "be sold for his theft." Each colony early took steps to monopolize the trade of the Indians living within its claim, which placed the latter at a great disadvantage when any bargaining was to be done. Nor would the whites sell the Indians many of the things they most desired. In 1656, for example, Plymouth decreed that no boats or sail or rigging, and "no horse or mare Coult or foale," were to be sold to an Indian. None of the colonies, of course, would sell them liquor or firearms. Yet there was an illegal traffic in both, which greatly alarmed the whites, especially the traffic in arms. Bradford had complained of this, saying that the Indians were no longer content to eat the colonists' "garbage," but went out and shot deer and other game for themselves, "a most desperate mischeef." But what most infuriated the Saints was that Philip, like his father, objected to their proselytizing. When John Eliot attempted to convert him, Philip reached over and took hold of a button on the old missionary's coat.

"I care no more for your gospel," he said, "than that."

Irritation became acute in 1671 when the Wampanoag complained that the Pilgrims were encroaching on their hunting grounds. According to rumors reaching Plymouth, King Philip and his men were gathering near by in large numbers from time to time, repairing their guns, sharpening their knives and hatchets. Asked about this, Philip suggested a conference at Taunton with representatives from Massachusetts as mediators. Governor Prence had some difficulty in preventing the townspeople from falling upon the Indians, but the parties finally sat down together in the meeting house, the English on one side, the Wampanoag on the other, both armed and suspicious. Philip declared that his military preparations were aimed at the Narragansett. Denounced as a "caitiff . . . a fiend . . . a hell-hound," he broke down at length and "confessed," according to the English, and agreed to surrender his firearms to the Plymouth authorities "to be kept by them for their securitie so long as they shall see reason."

The General Court immediately took steps to assure the loyalty of the Praying Indians along the Cape, theoretically still under King Philip's sway. Though the hand of the ministers is plain, the records pretend that the Indians drew up the document in which they declared that "forasmuch as the English and wee, the poor Indians, are of one blood, as Acts 17th, 26., for wee doe confess wee poor Indians in our lives were as captives under Sathan and our sachems, doeing theire wills whose breath perisheth, as Psalmes 146. 3,4; Exodus 15. 1,2, &c.; but now wee know by ye word of God that it is better to trust in the great God and his strength, Psa. 118. 8,9; and besides, wee were like unto woulves and lyons, to destroy one another . . . therfore wee desire to enter into covenant with the English respecting our fidelitie, as Isai: 11. 6."

Philip was in no hurry to surrender his firearms. He turned in a few which were distributed among the settlers along his boundaries. When the flow of arms ceased, the Pilgrims promptly sent him an ultimatum, forwarding a copy to Boston. Philip now went to Boston himself and convinced the authorities there that he had no hostile intentions. Massachusetts wrote to Plymouth to suggest that another meeting be held to iron out misunderstandings. Bent on proceeding against Philip without delay, Prence and his colleagues refused, whereupon the Bay flatly declared that as there was no just occasion for war, it would take no part in hostilities. Staggered by this, the Pilgrims drew back and agreed to a conference at Plymouth. Here Philip was forced to acknowledge himself not only a subject of the King but of the "governmente of New Plimouth." He was to pay an indemnity of £100, a yearly tribute of five wolves' heads, and not to make war anywhere without the colony's permission. The final pledge exacted of him was quite as humiliating—"I doe promise not to dispose of any of the lands that I have at presente but by the approbation of the Governour of Plimouth." Philip agreed to this on the Pilgrims' promise that no more settlers would be allowed to bother him for at least seven years—in particular, that none would come to disturb him on Montaup, or Mount Hope Neck, south of Sowams, where the Wampanoag were now concentrated. This promise was not kept.[9]

The next year, in 1673, Governor Prence died in his seventy-third year and was succeeded by Josiah Winslow, now forty-four, "a worthie and well-accomplished gentleman, deservedly beloved by the people, being a true friend of their just liberties, generous, facetious, affable, and sincere, qualities incident to the family." Educated at Harvard, married to Penelope, daughter of Herbert Pelham, treasurer of the college, he had been an assistant governor since 1657, a commissioner of the Confederacy since 1658, and in the next year became commander-in-chief of the Pilgrim army, a post unfilled since Standish's death three years before. Major Winslow had a taste for ceremonial and military display, and it was decreed that four halberdiers in full panoply, with their great axes on their shoulders, should attend the governor and his assistants on election days, and two during sessions of the General

Court. "King" Winthrop, to the displeasure of many at the Bay, had been so attended as early as 1637.

Notwithstanding its novel military trappings, Winslow's regime was far more liberal than Prence's. The new governor immediately restored the civil rights of all who had been deprived of them during the Quaker troubles. Through his influence James Cudworth again took his seat among the assistant governors, Timothy Hatherly having died in 1664. But it was Winslow's fate to be known less for this enlightened policy than for the great conflict and tragedy that marked his short term of office. Relations between the whites and the Indians had reached a point where no accommodation of interest was possible. It was now war to the death, with Philip engaged in building as grand an alliance as an Indian chief ever conceived, rallying to his standard almost all the Indians of New England, revealing the highest order of diplomatic skill in breaking down jealousies and prejudices of long standing, uniting the tribes in one last desperate fight for their heritage, all the more tragic because the struggle was now so hopeless. Their opportunity had long since passed.

The uneasy truce came to an end with the mysterious death of a Praying Indian named Sassamon, once a student at Harvard, more recently King Philip's secretary. He had renounced Christianity but now experienced a change of heart and was again baptized. To manifest his sincerity, he "secretly" informed the Pilgrim magistrates of Philip's designs. The latter was summoned to Plymouth to be examined. Though still suspicious, the Pilgrims had to release him for want of evidence. Sassamon soon disappeared and after a time his body was found in a frozen pond, with his hat and gun on the bank as if he were a suicide. Buried near by, his remains were later exhumed and carried to Plymouth where an autopsy revealed "bruises" and other marks which heightened the Pilgrims' suspicion of murder. Philip was again examined and released.

Months later, after determined search and "by a strange Providence," they found an Indian who declared that he had witnessed the murder from a hill. On his charges a warrior in Philip's council and one Tobias were arrested, as well as the latter's son. All were brought to Plymouth and tried before a jury of twelve whites with six "grave" Indians added to the panel. In the end the youth "confessed," pinning the blame on his father and Philip's councillor. But the most convincing proof of their guilt, according to Dr. Increase Mather, "teacher" at the Old North in Boston and one of the "larned Mr. Chancy's" successors at Harvard, was that whenever Tobias was brought near the corpse, "it fell a-bleeding as fresh as if it had been newly slain, albeit it was buried a considerable time before that." Tobias and his friend were promptly hanged, and if the youth hoped to escape by impeaching his father, he was disappointed, for he was shot a few weeks later "in view of Philip's operations."

The Wampanoag accepted this challenge for what it was. Roger Williams and Samuel Gorton made attempts to avert war but without success. Reports flooded into Plymouth from towns along the frontier that Philip's men "were giving frequent alarums by drums and guns in the night . . . and that their young Indians were earnest for war." Annoyed by their trespasses, a settler at Swansea shot and wounded an Indian in June, 1675, the beginning of one of the great Indian wars of our history. Plymouth immediately set aside a day of fasting to entreat the Lord "to goe forth with our forces, and blesse, succeed, and prosper them; delivering them from the hands of his and our enemies; subduing the heathen and returning them all in safetie to their families and relations againe."

A small force was dispatched to Swansea under Major James Cudworth, now past seventy,[10] with Major Bradford as his aide. Here they were joined by forces from the Bay. Forced to withdraw from Mount Hope Neck, Philip swung back into the Old Colony to strike at Dartmouth, Taunton, Middleborough, and other towns, later sweeping in to the outskirts of Plymouth, sacking and burning Scituate. The flames of war quickly spread throughout New England as one tribe after another joined Philip. Everywhere there was panic, even on remote Cape Cod, where the most drastic measures were taken against the Praying Indians. Their squaws were seized as hostages. No Indian was to approach nearer to Plymouth than Sandwich on pain of instant death. Indians elsewhere in the colony were herded into Plymouth and isolated on Clark's Island in the harbor. In spite of all this the Cape tribes proved to be faithful and very useful allies, serving both as scouts and on the firing line.

Massachusetts took even sterner measures against its Praying Indians after a company of two hundred converts deserted to Philip. They were driven from their towns, their fields were ravaged, many were placed in close confinement, and some were put to death on the flimsiest of suspicions. When these measures were protested by old John Eliot and Captain Daniel Gookin, superintendent of the Praying Indians and one of the Bay's assistant governors, they were subjected to vitriolic abuse and Gookin was so threatened that he was "afraid to go about the streets."

Taking concerted action at last, the United Colonies agreed to raise a large force of 1,000 men, appointing Josiah Winslow as commander-in-chief at a salary of £100 a year. Plymouth was to provide 158 soldiers. Connecticut's quota was 315 while Massachusetts' was 517, more than half the army. Each soldier had to provide his own arms. Another force of equal size was raised a few months later when it was decided to proceed against the Narragansett. At this point the Plymouth General Court threw the whole responsibility of recruiting upon the towns. Any able-bodied man refusing to serve was to be fined £5, "or in want thereof should be compelled to run the gauntlet, or both." When this failed to fill up the ranks, town constables were authorized to press men for service. They went about their job ruthlessly, and several were heavily fined for sending cripples.[11]

From the start of the war the attitude of the Narragansett had been equivocal and a source of grave concern. For a price they had promised to hand over for summary execution all Wampanoag and other hostile Indians taking refuge with them. Many had done so, but none had been surrendered, and inquiries brought only surly replies. Learning that the Narragansett were assembled on a fortified island in the Great Swamp near Kingston,

Rhode Island, a combined force from Plymouth, Massachusetts, and Connecticut, with a band of Mohegan allies, made a forced march there and on a bitter winter morning—a Sabbath morning, too—took the encampment by surprise and fell upon it with fire and sword, slaughtering many hundreds, not only men, but women and children, shattering forever the power of the once mighty Narragansett. The remnants that escaped fled to join other tribes. There can be little doubt that the Narragansett planned to join the war and were making preparations, intending to open hostilities in the spring of 1676 as Philip had originally planned. Their delay was fatal both to themselves and Philip, for if they had put their large forces in the field at the start, the Indians probably would have triumphed everywhere from the Penobscot to Long Island Sound, as informed contemporary observers acknowledged.

The fighting now shifted to the west and north, into Connecticut and Massachusetts. Town after town was plundered and burned with heavy loss of life—Lancaster, Medfield, Mendon, Weymouth, Marlborough, Springfield, and Sudbury. A column from Scituate consisting of fifty townsmen and twenty Praying Indians walked into an ambush from which only one of the English and eight of the Indians escaped. Plymouth decreed a solemn day of prayer and humiliation, and then another and another. Finally it was decided to renew the church covenant. The ministers were everywhere busy trying to discover the cause of the trouble, the root of all the Saints' defeats and woes. The Plymouth pastor, John Cotton, laid the blame upon the young, calling the children together for a sermon, castigating them for being "haughty in spirit, in countenance, in garbe, & fashion . . . stubborne and rebellious against God & disobedient to parents . . . very dull & sloathfull & irreverent in the time of worship." John Eliot, as has been remarked, proclaimed the war a judgment on the people for wearing wigs, an even worse abomination than long hair. Pastor Holmes of Duxbury was quite frank in saying, to the shock of many, that their troubles were of their own making —a just punishment, he declared, "for our dealing with the

Quakers," and on his deathbed he repeated that he was "of the same minde as to that matter as formerlie."

In the spring of 1676 the tide of battle began to turn. The Indians had insufficient stores to carry on sustained warfare. Pressed on all sides, they had to keep on the move and out of sight in forests and dismal swamps. Always hungry, becoming weak and diseased, Philip's allies began to desert his standard and surrender.

"I have eaten horse," complained one of these ailing deserters, "but now horse is eating me."

In all the campaigning no glimpse had yet been caught of Philip, who was like a phantom in the forests, striking terror wherever his presence was reported. As his fortunes rapidly declined in the summer of 1676, he returned to the land of his fathers on Mount Hope Neck, a fact soon known to the Pilgrims. A force was sent against him under the command of one of the most skilled captains developed by the war, Benjamin Church, born at Duxbury in 1639, son of Richard Church, the carpenter who had designed Plymouth's first meeting house. Married to a Southworth and descended from the "grave" Richard Warren, Church belonged to the ruling clique, but he had had his troubles. Persuaded that the only way to fight the Indians was to adopt their mode of warfare, an idea shared by George Washington a century later, he criticized formal military tactics and had twice resigned from the Pilgrim army because of quarrels with the high command which constantly interfered with him and rejected his ideas "with some marks of contempt." Now given a free hand, he "made havoc among the Indians like another Scanderbeg," cutting down five or six hundred within a few months.

Closing in on Philip, now almost alone, Church captured his wife and son, killed others of his family and many of his council. A traitor from Philip's camp came with an offer to lead him to the sachem's hiding place. Church and his men crept up at dawn, covering every avenue of escape, and when the alarm sounded, the surprised Indians fled in all directions. A few of the faithful gathered about Philip, who dismissed them, urging them to flee for their lives. Picking up his musket, the sachem struck out along a narrow woods path. Caleb Cook and one Alderman, a Praying Indian, were lying in wait for him. Jumping up, they fired point-blank. Cook's gun did not go off, but Alderman's sent a ball crashing through Philip's heart, and he "fell upon his face in the mud and water, with his gun under him." Church denied him burial. After his head and hands had been cut off, his body was quartered and left for the wolves. The hands were sent to Boston, arriving the same day, while the head was carried in triumph to Plymouth where, like Wituwamat's, it was placed on a pike on the brick watch tower hurriedly built to replace the old wooden bastion on Fort Hill. For more than twenty years the bleached skull remained there, a favorite nesting place for wrens, and in time Increase Mather delightedly carried away the jawbone of "that blasphemous leviathan." Alderman obtained possession of one of the hands, preserved it in a pail of rum, and carried it up and down the country exhibiting it for several years. The lock of the gun that killed Philip is one of the showpieces of the Massachusetts Historical Society.

Plymouth now proclaimed a "day of publick Thanksgiving for the beginning of revenge upon the enemy," and the revenge was terrible. Two of Philip's chief lieutenants, Anawan and Tispiquin, surrendered themselves and their bands to Church on his promise that their lives would be spared. Over Church's vehement protests Anawan was immediately beheaded. The Plymouth commander thought so highly of Tispiquin that he wished to make him a captain in his Indian brigade, but he was overruled. As a *pinese,* Tispiquin was said by the Indians to be invulnerable to bullets, "but upon triall he was found penetrable by the English guns, for he fell down upon the first shot, and thereby received the just reward of his former wickedness." How far the authorities were responsible for such monstrous equivocation is not clear, but they could not disclaim responsibility for much else almost as reprehensible. Early in the war Captain Church had persuaded the Indians around the town of Dartmouth not to join Philip but to follow him to Plymouth; here they were seized and shipped

off to Tangiers to be sold as slaves. Church resigned his command
in great anger, and the treachery did much to prolong the war,
costing the Old Colony many lives, for it drove all of the wavering
tribes to Philip's banner.

As Indian captives—men, women, and children—continued
to pour into Plymouth, all were sold into slavery, some to local
planters, the majority in the West Indies. One likely Indian boy
was picked out by Pastor John Cotton and sent as a gift to his
brother-in-law, Dr. Increase Mather, who was all pleasure at such
thoughtfulness. Now the question arose about what to do with
Philip's son, a boy of nine. After some debate the matter was
referred to the ministers. Cotton and Samuel Arnold of Marshfield agreed in principle that a child should not be punished for
the sins of its parents, "yet, upon serious consideration, we humblie
conceive that the children of notorious traitors, rebels, and mur-
therers, especially such as have been principal leaders and actors
in such horrid villainies, and that against a whole nation, yea, the
whole Israel of God, may be involved in the guilt of their parents,
and may, *salva republica,* be adjudged to death, as to us seems
evident from the Scripture incidents of Saul, Achan, Haman, the
children of whom were cut off by the sword of justice for the transgressions of their parents." Increase Mather slyly made the same
point. The only Pilgrim pastor to make a plea for mercy was the
Reverend James Keith of Bridgewater. In the end the life of
Philip's son was spared but it might better have been taken, for
he, too, spent the remainder of his days in chains, a slave in
Bermuda.

"The design of Christ in these last days is not to extirpate
nations but to gospelize them," exclaimed John Eliot in bitter
protest against these and similar acts throughout the United
Colonies. "To sell souls for money seemeth to me a dangerous
merchandise."[12]

All of the Wampanoag lands were seized and sold "so as to
settle plantations thereon in an orderly way to promote the publick
worship of God, and our owne publick good." The Bradfords and

others obtained large tracts on the beautiful promontory of Mount Hope. Funds from the sale of lands went to pay debts and provide relief for crippled soldiers and those who had been impoverished by the war. There was scarcely a family in the colony that was not grieving for someone lost on the battlefield or in an Indian raid. Many had been left in dire straits by the loss of their husbands and fathers, their houses and cattle. But the payment of debts came first, and these were staggering—more than £27,000 ($1,350,000).

Only one part of New England escaped devastation. Most of the Rhode Island towns escaped unscathed though the bitterest fighting had taken place around them. Throughout the war Roger Williams lived quietly and unmolested in the heart of the Indian country, at his trading post near North Kingston, where he died about eight years later, a "seeker" to the end.

The Old Colony had weathered its worst storm, but its days were numbered. King Philip was no sooner disposed of than King Charles raised his head, and there was small prospect of posting it on Fort Hill. Edward Randolph was sent over as a special royal agent to bring Massachusetts to heel and inquire minutely into the state of affairs in all the colonies. The Bay received him with its usual caution and reserve, and gave him little satisfaction. He was pleased with Plymouth, however, finding Governor Winslow a "gentleman of loyal principles." According to Randolph, the latter "expressed his great dislike of the carriage of the Magistrates of Boston to his Majesty's royal person and his subjects under their government," even volunteering his private opinion that "New England could never be secure, flourish, nor be serviceable to his Majesty until the several colonies and plantations were reduced under his Majesty's immediate government."

As Winslow had learned the devious ways of diplomacy at his father's feet, it is uncertain how far such expressions represented his actual views. His frank dislike of Massachusetts was probably real enough, for the Old Colony had reason to fear its grasping

ways. The Bay had just entered a most impudent claim to Mount
Hope Neck, always accepted as lying within the Pilgrims' bounds.
In the back of their minds lurked the uneasy suspicion that at the
first opportunity Massachusetts would gobble up Plymouth as the
small New Haven colony had been swallowed by Connecticut
some ten years before in direct violation of the terms of the Confederacy, a bit of power politics which brought strong protests
from Plymouth and broke up the United Colonies for a time.
As protection against such a fate, the Pilgrims were still hoping
to obtain a proper charter, and Winslow so beguiled Randolph
that the latter promised to do everything he could to obtain one
for such a "loyal colony." In his recommendations to the King,
the latter urged Winslow's appointment as commander-in-chief
of the combined militia of New England. To ingratiate himself,
Winslow sent His Majesty a "few Indian rarities, being the best
of their spoils, and the best ornaments and treasure of Sachem
Philip, the grand rebel, . . . being his crown, his gorge, and two
belts of their own making of their gold and silver."

In the midst of negotiations Winslow died in his fifty-third
year "after sore Pain with the Gout and Griping," and was honored with a £40 ($2,000) funeral, the most elaborate yet seen at
Plymouth.[13] His successor was Thomas Hinckley of Barnstable,
an older man of sixty-two, one of those who had removed from
Scituate to the Cape with Pastor Lothrop in 1639. Having been an
assistant governor for twenty-two years, Hinckley took office in
1681, with James Cudworth as his deputy. The latter immediately
departed for England to prosecute the charter business, carrying
an address to the King and a letter of appeal. If any colony was
entitled to a royal charter, Plymouth was, said Hinckley, for it
was "the first that broke the ice and underwent ye brunt . . . for
the inlargemente of his Majestie's dominions in this heretofor
most howling wilderness, amidst wild men and wild beasts." Cudworth shortly died of smallpox in London, and after several years
another agent was dispatched, the Reverend Ichabod Wiswall of
Duxbury, married to one of John Alden's grand-daughters. A day

of fasting was decreed on which to pray that God might "prosper his way to the other England and give them to find favor in the eyes of their lord the King, and in due season return a comfortable answer to their desires." Wiswall obtained many promises of action, but things were moving at a snail's pace when they took a sudden turn for the worse in 1685 with the death of the Merry Monarch and the succession of his glum brother.

James II came to the throne with the scarcely concealed design of restoring Catholicism and returning the kingdom to Rome. For a year or two he confused many of those who were potentially his bitterest enemies by urging toleration of all religious sects in England, a stratagem to allow Catholics to organize.[14] There is no reason whatever to believe that toleration would have continued twenty-four hours after the Roman rite was re-established, for that was not in the books of the Holy See or in James' mind either. The deluded King, the most errant of the wrongheaded Stuarts, had other schemes as well, one of which caused consternation throughout New England. A pliant tool, Sir Edmund Andros, governor of New York for many years, was commissioned "Governor-in-Chief in and over the territory and dominion of New England," his sway later being extended to include all English territory north and east of the Delaware.

Sir Edmund put in at Boston in great style in December, 1686, accompanied by sixty Redcoats "to keep the country in awe; a crew that began to teach New England to drab, drink, blaspheme, curse, and damn . . . committing insufferable riots amongst a quiet and peaceable people," so the colonists complained. Andros summarily scrapped the existing machinery of government in all the colonies. After the magistrates had been unseated, some were invited to sit on the governor's council. From Plymouth came Governor Hinckley and his deputy, Major William Bradford, with three assistant governors and Nathaniel Clarke, secretary of the colony since the death the previous year of Nathaniel Morton, "of some learning and of much industry . . . a very good writer, whose sincere piety breaks out in many places." All officers held their appointments from the King, for there were to be no more elections, no slightest pretence of self-government. At last the stiff-necked colonists were going to be called to account and made to do what they were told. All authority was concentrated at Boston in the person of the royal governor. Increased taxes and special assessments were arbitrarily imposed. When the selectmen at Taunton objected, declaring that they did "not feel free to raise money on the inhabitants without their own assent by an Assembly," the town clerk was fined and locked up several months for daring to submit such an impudent document.

For himself and his friends Andros requested the use of a meeting house, which was refused by the Boston ministers, led by Increase Mather, who declared that they could not "in good conscience" allow any to be used "for the Common-Prayer worship." Andros thereupon forced his way into the Third Church, later renowned as the Old South, and held Anglican services there. The parishioners were outraged to have their meeting house defiled with "leeks, garlic, and trash." Those who scrupled to "kiss the Book" when taking an oath were fined and imprisoned —to the howl of the Saints about the injustice and tyranny of it all, unmindful of their own recent practises upon the Quakers. Some of the Strangers may have found a grim irony in this, but even they were alarmed when Andros challenged the colonists' title to their lands, refusing to recognize the validity of any Indian deeds—of "no more worth," he declared, "than a scratch with a bear's paw."

As in Massachusetts, where a few were found willing to betray the principles of their fathers to advance themselves, so Andros found a traitor at Plymouth, and it was most embarrassing, for he was the secretary of the Old Colony, Nathaniel Clarke, whose father Thomas had come on the *Anne.* The governor rewarded his creature by granting him Clark's Island in the harbor. Valuable for its pasturage, its timber, and its salt works, it had been set aside for the support of Plymouth's pastor and the poor of the town. Deacon John Faunce, the town clerk, and Pastor Wiswall of Duxbury were so angered that they began soliciting funds to carry the matter to the courts. Arrested on the charge of levying taxes upon His Majesty's subjects without the governor's consent, they were ordered to stand trial at Boston. Wiswall requested a delay, explaining that he was "lame in both feet with the gout, fitter for bed than a journey." But he had to go not only once but three times, bringing on an almost fatal illness. The only reason he recovered, Wiswall remarked in an acid comment upon ministers' salaries, was the sudden realization that if he died, his family was so poor that it would immediately starve.

In the spring of 1689 John Winslow, son of the older John and Mary (Chilton) Winslow, put in at Boston with the still unconfirmed news that James II had been overthrown and been succeeded by William and Mary. Two weeks passed quietly and then on a Thursday, Lecture Day, a usual time for everybody to assemble to hear the exercises in the churches at noon, there was a strange excitement in Boston, an air of great expectancy. Crowds began to gather at both ends of town, soon there was a beating of drums through the streets, and by noon all of Andros' minions were in jail, followed by the royal governor, who was soon shipped back to England. At Plymouth the Saints pounced on Nathaniel Clarke and sent him along with Andros to answer to the new monarchs for his "high crimes and misdemeanors."

Hinckley, Major Bradford, and their colleagues were restored to office, and things went on as before, with the charter business as great a source of worry as ever. With good Protestants like William and Mary on the throne, prospects seemed much more hopeful than they had been for a long time. During Andros' reign Increase Mather had managed to slip out of Boston in disguise to carry the colonists' complaints to England, his ketch lying at Plymouth two days before making a rendezvous at sea with the *President.* Hinckley now conveyed him his thanks for presenting Plymouth's case and informed him that Wiswall was coming over as its agent. All of the colonies lacked charters, and in the race for favors Mather had the inside track, as Wiswall soon discovered. As usual, the Bay was asking for everything within reach —New Hampshire, Maine, and even Nova Scotia. Learning that

New York had included Plymouth in its charter, Mather "procured the dropping of it" and with no authority whatever incorporated it in the Massachusetts charter on the pretext that the Old Colony had no hopes of obtaining one of its own. The clause was angrily stricken out by Wiswall—"the Weasel," Mather called him for balking his design, nettled by the pastor's remark that Plymouth would roundly curse him for his presumption.[15]

Always energetic, ambitious and bumptious, never one to hide his talents, Dr. I. Mather had a great advantage on this occasion —a fat purse. On his mission he spent almost £1,700 ($85,000). "I found it necessarie," he later reported, "to gratifie severall persons, some with £20, some with £30, some with £50, some with 50 guineas, &c., as allsoe to bestow dayly gratifications—on Servants belonging to persons of Quallitie, and—manie Visitts on Lawyers, &c., in all which and—in all other accidentall Necessarie Charges not less than £1,000."

Wiswall kept writing for funds. "Why Plymouth, under its present circumstances, should sit silent so long (may I not say sleep secure) is a riddle," he declared. In February, 1691, the General Court ordered that the people in the Pilgrim towns be called together and asked to subscribe £500 "to keep their independence." Pastor John Cotton, Mather's brother-in-law and from the Bay himself, urged Hinckley to go over, saying that all men "of wisdome, prudence, and pietie" were opposed to any scheme of union with Massachusetts. But Hinckley was halfhearted about the enterprise at best, and the campaign for funds failed.

"The people are suspicious and irritable," he informed Mather. "The authoritie of the Governmente is not only doubted but denied by those who dislike its proceedings. Not being in a capacitie to make rates for an equall defraying of the charge, I see litle or no likeliehood of obtaining a Charter for us unless their majesties, out of their Royal bounty and clemencie, graciously please to grant it, *sub forma pauperis,* to their poor and loyal Subjects of this collonie."

The General Court decreed days of prayer and fasting, but to no avail. "All the frame of heaven moves upon one axis," wrote Wiswall in despair, "and the whole of New England's interest seems designed to be loaded on one bottome, and her particular motions to be concentric to the Massachusetts tropic. You know who are wont to trot after the Bay horse."

In October, 1691, Massachusetts obtained a charter under which New Plimoth was included within its bounds, largely through the "rashness and impudence," said Wiswall, "of one at least, who went from New England in disguise by night." Perhaps Mather could not have saved Plymouth. It was small and weak, thinly populated and with few resources, and Mather's apologists have certainly made the most of this. Yet Rhode Island, even smaller and quite as weak, obtained a charter and retained its independence. Whatever may be said in his defense, it is plain that Mather always placed the interests of the Bay above those of the Old Colony, and it is difficult to forget his early gratuitous motion to dispose of Plymouth as he thought best. He may not have rejoiced but certainly shed no tears to see the Pilgrims thrown at last by the Bay Horse.

The Old Colony expired in its seventy-third year, less than the span of many a life. Two members of the *Mayflower* party survived it—John Cooke, the former deacon, now a Baptist preacher at Dartmouth, and Mary (Allerton) Cushman, widow of Ruling Elder Thomas Cushman, who had died in 1691 at the age of eighty-four, and "much of God's presence went away from this Church when this blessed pillar was removed." John Alden narrowly missed the final debacle, dying in 1687 in his eighty-ninth year, outliving many of his children, being buried beside Priscilla on his farm near Eagle Tree Pond in Duxbury. To the last he was a bold and hardy man, "stern, austere, and unyielding," hating change and innovations, walking steadily in the ways of the Saints he had learned as a youth.

Early in July, 1692, the Plymouth General Court met once more and as its final act set aside the last Wednesday of August "to be kept as a day of sollemne fasting and humilliation." The

Saints had had so many—and never one that had been quite so humiliating.[16]

And yet, in their despondency, they glimpsed a ray of hope. It might have been worse, and some months later they proclaimed a Thanksgiving "for the Preservation of the King & Queen, &c.; for our Gospel-mercies, health, harvest, destroying caterpillars last summer, saving ours in storms, & for that the Governmente over us is yet in the hands of Saincts."

24

APOTHEOSIS

> ... all great & honourable actions are accompanied with great difficulties, and must be both enterprised and overcome with answerable courages.
>
> —WILLIAM BRADFORD

FROM BEING THE POOR BUT PROUD CAPITAL OF THE PILGRIM empire, Plymouth sank to the status of a county seat—and not a very important one at that. Its interests shrank until they were contained within a radius of a few miles, and the scale of its affairs diminished accordingly. There were no special envoys now to be dispatched to London almost as from one sovereign state to another. There were no more petitions to the Parliament to frame, no more addresses to the King. Debates on high policy were to be heard only in Boston.

Yet Mother Plymouth's day was not done. In time she would wield greater influence and enjoy a wider fame than ever she had in the heyday of her temporal power. She would shape the ideas, manners, customs, ways of life, and moral values of millions of Americans. Her instrument was the Brownist meeting house and the essentially democratic concepts that underlay it. She gave the meeting house to the stronger Puritans at the Bay, for at home the latter had known nothing like it. From Massachusetts its influence radiated far and wide, to the remotest parts of the country to contribute as much as any other single influence to the creation of an American *mythos* and *ethos.* Both the Pilgrims and the Puritans repeatedly sinned against the basic concepts of their faith, but the democratic equalitarianism implicit in it was never killed and has constantly grown stronger.

Notable in no way, lying quite outside the main currents of the day, its heroic origin all but forgotten and of interest to few, Plymouth was just another sleepy country town in 1769 when a handful of young men, all from its better families, decided to organize a gentlemen's club to elevate the social tone of the town. They had, they said, "maturely weighed and seriously considered the many disadvantages and inconveniences that arise from inter-mixing with the company at the taverns in this town."

The Old Colony Club, as it was named, never had more than thirteen members. Though young, most of them being in their late twenties, all were soon to win fame or infamy. Apparently the club was promoted by an eligible but lonesome young bachelor of the town, Isaac Lothrop, a prosperous merchant, descended from the Reverend John Lothrop of Barnstable, for Isaac became the Old Colony's first president, with his younger brother Thomas as secretary. The other five charter members were of equally prominent families—Elkanah Cushman, a descendant of old Deacon Robert Cushman, more immediately of Mary (Allerton) and Ruling Elder Thomas Cushman; John Thomas, great-grandson of Assistant Governor William Thomas of Duxbury; two Winslows, young Edward and his cousin Pelham, both descended from Governors Edward and Josiah Winslow; and John Watson, a Winslow-in-law.

The families of the two Winslows were probably the richest

and most distinguished in town. Edward's father, another Edward, a large landowner and prosperous lawyer, had recently erected a mansion "in a style of elegance far superior to any previously erected in the Old Colony," a house which still stands on Cole's Hill, just above Plymouth Rock, commanding a view of the whole harbor. Young Pelham was the son of Major General John Winslow, who enjoys the dubious fame of being the British officer who carried out the rape of the Evangeline country in Nova Scotia.[1] Scattered far and wide, with many families irreparably broken, most of the simple and inoffensive Acadians were shipped to Louisiana and settled in the swamp lands there. But early in 1756 almost a hundred were brought to Plymouth, some remaining in the town, settling along the Jones River, while others went to live in Duxbury and Marshfield.

The founders of the Old Colony Club soon asked five others to join—Cornelius White, Pelham Winslow's brother-in-law, descended not only from Peregrine White, the first Edward Winslow's stepson, but also from John Howland and John Tilley of the *Mayflower* company; Thomas Mayhew, whose great-grandfather had been "Lord of the Islands," proprietor of Nantucket and Martha's Vineyard, and missionary among the Indians there; Oakes Angier, son of the pastor at Bridgewater, descended from the Pilgrims' sixth governor, Thomas Hinckley, and from the Reverend Uriah Oakes, president of Harvard College; Alexander Scammell, who kept the local grammar school; and Pelham's and young Edward Winslow's cousin, James Warren, a merchant and another of those who traced his ancestry back to the *Mayflower* group. Almost half of the members were recent graduates of Harvard.

Eager to honor the Forefathers, feeling the first stirrings of that filial piety which has chiefly distinguished so many of their descendants, the young gentlemen of the Old Colony Club looked about for some suitable occasion to celebrate. But what? There was an old tradition in the Alden family that the first landing at Plymouth had been made on a rock, with young John as the hero of the story. Unfortunately for the tradition, a reading of

Mourt's *Relation* revealed that John Alden was not on that first exploring expedition but miles away on the *Mayflower,* off the tip of the Cape, tending the Pilgrims' precious barrels of beer. As handed down in another family, the story had a heroine, Mary (Chilton) Winslow, who gathered up her skirts and hopped from the shallop to the rock. But there had been no women, of course, on the Third Discovery or any of the early explorations.

It was all very vague and confusing, and the Old Colony Club was quite at a loss, for there was no mention of a rock in Bradford, Winslow, or any contemporary. And there were those among the seafaring men of the town who declared that if the shallop was steered for the rock and beached there on that cold blustery December day, instead of being headed into the sheltered mouth of Town Brook opening so invitingly only a few hundred yards away, then those in command of the shallop should themselves have been beached for all time.

Just when the members of the club were most discouraged, Deacon Ephraim Spooner came forward with a curiously interesting story. Many years before, in 1741, he happened to be on the beach one day, he said, and though only a boy of six, he would never forget how Ruling Elder Thomas Faunce, an "aged and godly" man in his ninety-fifth year, had been brought there in his wheelchair from his home at Eel River several miles to the south. To a handful of people gathered on the beach Faunce related how, as a boy, he had been told by his father, who had heard it in turn from some who had come of the "Thievish Harbour" expedition, that the Pilgrims had made their first landing at Plymouth on a rock—and, shaking with palsy, he pointed out *the* rock.

Then, with tears coursing down his face, the old man bade it a last farewell, for he and everyone had reason to fear that it was about to be destroyed. It stood in the way of several local enterprisers who had just been granted "Libertie to Whorfe downe into the sea."[2] If dynamite had been known at the time, the boulder undoubtedly would have been blown to pieces. As it was, after several futile attempts at removal, the wharf was built over and around the rock, which stood so high that it came up through the planking, leaving its top exposed, and for years heavy carts and barrows bumped over it, chipping it and grinding it down.[3]

Delighted with Deacon Spooner's story, the Old Colony Club prepared to celebrate the historic landing made by the Forefathers on December 11th, Old Style. Meantime, in 1752, Britain and her colonies had belatedly discarded the old Julian for the more accurate Gregorian calendar, at which time the difference between them amounted to eleven days. The club made that allowance and set the celebration for December 22nd, New Style.

Festivities began in the morning with a salvo of cannon and the raising of an "elegant silk flag." The members of the club and a few guests then repaired to the tavern kept by Thomas Southworth Howland on Cole's Hill, on the site of Plymouth's first ordinary, to pay their forbears fitting honors. The banquet board was "dressed in the plainest manner, all appearances of luxury and extravagance being avoided," but the dinner itself was ample, consisting of nine courses (which must have caused many a Forefather to sigh in his grave). It began with a large baked Indian whortleberry pudding, followed by a dish of "sauquetash,"[4] a dish of clams, a dish of oysters and codfish, a haunch of venison "roasted on the first jack brought to the Colony," a dish of sea fowl, a dish of "frost-fish" and eels, apple pie, cranberry tarts and cheese, interspersed with the singing of a few stanzas of John Dickinson's stirring ode, "In Freedom We're Born," then sweeping the colonies:

> Our worthy forefathers, let's give them a cheer,
> To climates unknown did courageously steer;
> Thro' oceans to deserts for Freedom they came,
> And dying bequeath'd us their freedom and fame.
>
> In Freedom we're born and in Freedom we'll live.
> Our right arms are ready,
> Steady, friends, steady!
> Not as slaves, but as Freemen, our lives we will give.

Late in the afternoon, no doubt after much frank regurgitation, as was then allowed in the politest company, the club adjourned to its quarters on Main Street, "in Mr. Jonathan Diman's front room." Marching hand in hand, led by Elkanah Cushman, steward of the club, carrying a folio volume of the Old Colony laws, they paid their respects to the rock en route and along the way were greeted with cheers and a volley of small arms; and the children of the private school kept by Peleg Wadsworth of Duxbury, another young man of note, "came into the street and sang a song appropriate to the day." In the club, with President Lothrop occupying a "large and venerable chair," reputedly Governor Bradford's, the company extolled the virtues and principles of the Forefathers and recounted their brave deeds until almost midnight when the meeting adjourned, with another salvo of cannon. About a month later, in what must have been Plymouth's first remotest contact with the theater, the young blades of the club entertained a "company of about forty gentlemen and ladies" at a reading of a comedy, *The Provoked Husband,* one of Colley Cibber's worst even though "newly revamped."[5]

Forefathers' Day had been so successful that it became an annual event, being celebrated the next year on December 24th, again at Howland's and the club room on Main Street. The proceedings were somewhat more formal, with a song written especially for the occasion by Alexander Scammell and a prepared address by Edward Winslow, Junior. Their fathers, said he, little realizing that his phrases would rise to haunt him, had always loved freedom and fiercely resisted tyranny, "and if we, their sons, act from the same principles and conduct ourselves with the same noble firmness and resolution when our holy religion or our civil charters are invaded, we may expect a reward proportionate."

Though not specifically mentioned in his address, Winslow and all present were thinking of the Boston Massacre which had occurred not many months before in the shadow of the old State House, with repercussions felt sharply and immediately throughout the colonies. Conflict with the mother country was daily

becoming more acute. Passions were rising on both sides of the
water, and within the colonies as well. Momentous issues, soon
to be decided on the battlefield, were splitting communities in
two. Everywhere men were talking politics, arguing, disputing,
often quarrelling, and the questions of the day soon forced themselves into the Old Colony Club. The conservative majority was
disturbed and tried to smother discussion and debate by passing
a resolution that the club had only one purpose—"to hold weekly
meetings for the mutual advantage of each other, to enjoy the
refined pleasure of social and unrestrained intercourse, unalloyed
with the disputes and contentions of parties."

To hope to enjoy such idyllic pleasures in the midst of a social
hurricane was Utopian, declared the two Lothrops and James
Warren, who had thrown in their lot with the rebels. A selectman
of the town, Warren had already been in communication with
Sam Adams and other leaders of the popular party in Boston, all
members of the mysterious Long Room Club, the center of opposition and the directing brain of a larger and even more mysterious
organization, the Sons of Liberty.[6] Their enemies knew them as
the "Sons of Licentiousness," made up of "obscure pettifogging
attorneys, bankrupt shopkeepers, and outlawed smugglers, . . .
ignorant bricklayers and carpenters"—altogether, "the foulest,
subtlest, and most venomous serpent ever to issue from the egg
of Sedition." Warren was not too sanguine about what could be
done locally, reporting that the Old Colony towns were "Dead,
and the Dead can't be raised without a Miracle."

Sam Adams believed in miracles.

"I wish our Mother Plymouth would see her way clear to have
a meeting and second Boston by appointing a Committee of
Communication and Correspondence," Adams wrote Warren
early in November, 1772. The latter went out with a petition
asking the selectmen to call a town meeting and quickly obtained
a hundred signatures. At this meeting a Committee of Correspondence was elected, with Warren as chairman and Isaac
Lothrop as secretary. Led by the elder Edward Winslow, with his

son and his nephew Pelham assisting, the more staid and respectable tried to poohpooh the action of the meeting, circulating the report that only a handful of people—and none of the best—had attended, which led Adams to complain of the Tories' "scurvy trick of lying," evidently congenital with the breed, as the Saints had discovered for themselves long ago.

As Forefathers' Day was approaching, the Committee of Correspondence wrote the Old Colony Club to suggest that the celebration be made a public affair, with all of the town participating in a patriotic demonstration. Tentative plans had been made, the committee said, and it was hoped that the club would approve and be willing "to join with and conform thereto."

The celebration of Forefathers' Day, the committee was informed, was none of its business. The day would be celebrated as usual; the club had no need of gratuitous advice and presumptuous suggestions. The proposed plan, they declared, "is so great an invasion of the liberties and privileges of the town of Plymouth and the Old Colony Club that we cannot approve or comply with the same." The day came and went without incident, but there were no cheers as the members marched to their quarters to hear a sermon by the Reverend Charles Turner of Duxbury, who discreetly chose a non-controversial subject, being content to declare himself against sin.

The next year, in 1773, a few days after "Indians" from the Old South Meeting House had staged the Boston Tea Party, Plymouth called a meeting at Warren's instigation and praised the work at Boston in a series of strong resolutions "highly applauded by all the Friends of Liberty." Again the Winslows tried to block the meeting and questioned the proceedings, drawing up a long legalistic protest. The town refused to have it read, but it gained wide circulation elsewhere. The authorities at Marlborough took notice of it in a letter to say that they regarded all who did "not oppose the present unconstitutional Measures of the Administration (especially Edward Winslow & others of the ancient and honorable Town of Plymouth, who, without giving one Reason, have protested against the Proceedings of the said Town), as inimical to the Interests of America, and they ought to be despised by all the human Race."

Agreeing with Adams that Plymouth, like Boston, "should strike some bold stroke and try the issue," the Committee of Correspondence again addressed the Old Colony Club on the subject of Forefathers' Day and once more was advised to mind its own business.

"As we were the first institutors of this festival," came the impudent reply, "and as no event has taken place to lessen our dignity or consequence as a club, we shall hold the celebration as before."

Not feeling that Forefathers' Day properly came under the head of private property, the plain people of the town took matters into their own hands the next year. The Committee of Correspondence did not even bother to communicate its plans to the few remaining members of the Old Colony Club, which had gone into a rapid decline and soon disbanded.

Early on December 22, 1774, led by Warren and the two Lothrops, the Liberty Boys of the town appeared on the beach with thirty teams of oxen. Securing chains around the rock, they proceeded to wrest it from its age-old bed in the sand, handling it so roughly that the rock broke in two. The larger part fell back into the gaping hole in the sand, to be buried there in time by the sweep of wind and tide. With shouts of triumph, the crowd dragged the smaller part up Broad Street (originally The Street, later Leyden Street) to Town Square, where with great ceremony it was placed beside a large elm used to support the "memorable Liberty Pole erected on that exciting occasion,"

> To wake the sons of Plymouth to oppose
> The daring insults of our country's foes.

"Even our Tory protesters hang their ears," Warren wrote Boston, though opposition was still devious and active, led by his two cousins, young Pelham and Edward Winslow, "of Impudent and as they think, Shineing Talents."

Less than four months later the "shot heard 'round the world" was fired at Lexington. And young Edward Winslow was the man who guided Lord Percy to Lexington and Concord when the latter was sent with reinforcements to aid Major Pitcairn's command as it was desperately fighting its way back to Boston with fearful loss.[7] Winslow had his horse shot from under him by some "embattled farmer" not as steady in his aim, unfortunately, as most of his neighbors. Pelham Winslow had also fled to Boston to offer his services to General Gage and take the field against his old friends and neighbors.

Fighting had almost broken out at Marshfield two years earlier. The local Tories had petitioned General Gage for troops to suppress the Marshfield Committee of Correspondence, and a company of the Queen's Guards had been sent under a Captain Balfour, who was a frequent guest at Careswell, the Winslow estate there. On one occasion the Captain asked those assembled at a gay dinner party what they thought of sending troops to Plymouth to put down the rabble and seize their arms. The Winslows at least knew the spirit of the town and advised against it, declaring that the people "would fight like devils."[8]

But for that, "the shot heard 'round the world" might well have been fired in Plymouth.

As soon as news of Lexington was received at Plymouth, a detachment marched on Marshfield, a notorious Tory center, and was joined along the way by the burly seamen from the crews of sixty vessels lying in the harbor. The detachment moved on to Roxbury, soon joining the Continental Army. Plymouth sent Warren and Isaac Lothrop to represent it in the Provincial Congress of Massachusetts, Warren becoming president of the body after Dr. Joseph Warren had fallen at the Battle of Bunker Hill. In March, 1776, the town gave its representatives these clear and forthright instructions, revealing that the spirit of the Forefathers was not dead or in any way enfeebled:

"1. That you, without hesitation, be ready to declare for independence of Great Britain, in whom no confidence can be placed, ... and we, for our parts, do assure you that we will stand by the determination of the continental congress in the important and, as we think, necessary measure, at the risk of our lives and our fortunes.

"2. We wish you to use your influence that such form of government may be adopted as may appear most salutary . . . In particular, we recommend it to you to use your influence that the executive and legislative offices in the government do not meet in the same person."

Independence was generally received with enthusiasm throughout the Old Colony. Though under the guns of British ships, the towns along the Cape were not cowed, and the descendants of the old Pilgrim stock, having long since turned to the sea to become as skilled a lot of blue-water salts as the world has ever seen, pushed off in small boats and played havoc with enemy shipping, swooping down and capturing his vessels when they were becalmed, cutting them off at night as they passed along the back of the Cape on their way to New York and ports to the south. The first American privateer, the *Independence,* was launched at Kingston, on the Jones River. Six privateers operated from the harbor and did so prosperously that the whole town, according to Warren, was "privateering mad." But the only local shooting occurred when the fort hastily built at the entrance to the harbor, on Gurnet's Nose, exchanged shots with H.M.S. *Niger.*

Six members of the Old Colony Club supported the colonial cause. The two Lothrops and Mayhew remained active at Plymouth while Oakes Angier led the rebels at Bridgewater. One member made a name for himself as a soldier—Alexander Scammell, the schoolteacher, who early joined Washington's army and rose to be a major general, dying of wounds received at Yorktown. Another of Plymouth's schoolmasters, Peleg Wadsworth, joined up and came out of the war a brigadier, on one occasion severely criticizing Captain Paul Revere, who demanded a court-martial on charges of insubordination and was acquitted. James Warren went on to become Paymaster General of the Continental Army, leaving his affairs at Plymouth in the hands of his wife, Mercy (Otis), a remarkable woman in her own right. Poet, dramatist, and historian of the Revolution, Mercy Warren early supported the Liberty Boys and was one of the first to lead a campaign against the ancient laws that kept women in chattel bondage. She anticipated Mary Wollstonecraft in championing the cause of free and equal rights for all, regardless of sex. Her brother was the renowned James Otis, of Barnstable, whose great Writs of Assistance speech in 1761 was, as President John Adams later declared, "the first act of opposition to the arbitrary claims of Great Britain. Then and there, the child of independence was born . . . I do say in the most solemn manner that Otis's oration . . . breathed into this nation the breath of life."

Among its ancestors the Otis family numbered Edward Dotey of the *Mayflower* company, and both James and Mercy were true descendants of that spirited youth, Stephen Hopkins' indentured servant, who almost certainly was one of the rebel group that so boldly and alarmingly announced, as the *Mayflower* dropped anchor, "that when they came ashore, they would use their owne libertie."

The church as well as the town of Plymouth was split by politics. Many absented themselves from the meeting house to avoid contention. Called to book for this, a communicant excused himself by saying that the "people of the town in general treat me with contempt, calling me a Tory." One of the deacons, Thomas Foster, was charged with being an "Advocate for ye Destructive Doctrines of Passive Obediance & Non Resistance." He had publicly denounced the Liberty Boys as "Rebels, & of consequence deserving ye Punishment of such." Worse, he had called the wife of one of them a "cursed murderous Bitch." The church voted "almost unanimously (20 Members present, all but 2 Voted) that they could not contentedly communicate with him at ye Lord's Table."[9] On the other hand, Deacon Foster's colleague, Ephraim Spooner, staunchly supported the rebels, proving himself a clever negotiator, more than once obtaining large loans from wealthy Tory gentlemen when the town was without funds to equip and pay its ragged soldiers. The local pastor, Chandler Robbins, served for a time as a chaplain in the Continental Army.

But there were hundreds in the Old Colony of very different sentiments. The less principled Tories humbled themselves and made peace with their neighbors. Some of those at Marshfield who early asked General Gates for troops had since fled the town —among others, three of the Winslow-Whites, three of the Tilden family which had come on the *Anne,* and Elisha Ford, descended from Widow Ford who had arrived on the *Fortune.* These now petitioned the authorities for permission to return. They had signed the letter to Gage "through inadvertencie," they declared, and were very anxious "to come back and go to work rather than they should be Confind in a Gaol, wharefore Considering you will take a Compassionate Regard to this petition, we Beg Leve to Subscribe ourselves your Humbel Servents."

The Tories at Duxbury had likewise offered their services to General Gage in a letter signed by Captain Gamaliel Bradford, Gideon Bradford, Major Briggs Alden, and Abijah White. These and others, including Wrestling Brewster and Thomas Foster, son of the Plymouth deacon, appeared at a town meeting to make a public recantation, and humbly asked the "forgiveness of the town of Duxbury and all the inhabitants of the Province."

But there were others of stronger convictions who refused any compromise. Frankly despising the "Separation," rejecting the "heresy" of democracy and all its works, five members of the Old Colony Club now or later fled the country, while a sixth, John Watson, a Tory sympathizer, retired to Clark's Island and by a discreet silence rode out the storm. Elkanah Cushman, Cornelius White, and John Thomas accompanied the British forces to Halifax upon their evacuation of Boston and never returned. Pelham Winslow campaigned against the Continentals and died at Brooklyn in 1783, leaving his wife Joanna (White) and two children in Plymouth, where they lived poor but unmolested. Young and ambitious Edward Winslow steadily advanced in rank until he was Muster Master General of all Loyalist forces operating with the Redcoats. Later fleeing to Canada, he was rewarded for his very useful services by being named a member of the King's Council and a justice of the Supreme Court of New Brunswick, dying at Fredericton in 1815. His elderly father also fled Plymouth, and his mansion there was confiscated.[10] The latter joined the staff of Sir Henry Clinton in New York and was granted a pension of £200 a year, with all expenses for his "family, servants, & slaves," later joining the exodus to Halifax. Another to depart was the friend and frequent host of the Old Colony Club, Thomas Southworth Howland, the tavernkeeper.

All told, more than 1,000 native Tories fled Massachusetts with General Gage or in later years, including one William Bradford, of the Harvard class of 1760, who became an officer of the Crown in the Bahamas. But none of the descendants of the more prominent Pilgrim families quite so distinguished himself as Dr. Benjamin Church, scion of Southworths and Colliers, grandson of Plymouth's ablest captain in King Philip's War. Church lived in Boston but maintained an elaborate house at Raynham, about twenty miles west of Plymouth. A member of the Long Room Club and of the inner circle of patriot leaders, he was always the most vociferous in denouncing British "tyranny" and demanding bold and violent action—until he was discovered to be in the pay of General Gage. Tried and ordered to leave the country, Church embarked for the West Indies and was never heard of again.

Under the circumstances it is not strange that a half century passed before the more self-conscious Pilgrim descendants again dared lift their heads. And when the day for this came, after sufficient time had elapsed to allow many things to be forgotten and forgiven, it was a member of the Old Colony Club who took the initiative—John Watson, the Tory sympathizer, who in 1819 organized the Pilgrim Society and became its first president. It was not an exclusive social club, but open to all interested in perpetuating the fame of the Forefathers "by durable monuments to be erected at Plymouth," and able to pay a membership fee of $10, which entitled one to an "appropriate diploma."

To the end of the Revolutionary War the plain people of Plymouth celebrated Forefathers' Day with fitting ceremony each year in Town Square, renamed Liberty Pole Square, but not again till 1793 when the Reverend Chandler Robbins preached a memorial sermon.[11] It was in no way remarkable but for one fact—thumbing through the old church records, particularly those yellowed pages on which Nathaniel Morton had copied long passages from Bradford's now "lost" manuscript, Robbins came upon the phrase, "they knew they were pilgrimes," and happily so named them. But not until the 1840's did the phrase begin to make its way into print and become the generally accepted designation of the heterogeneous group long known merely as the First Comers.[12]

At the celebration in 1802 the memorial address was delivered by John Quincy Adams. "No Gothic scourge of God—No Vandal pest of nations—No fabled fugitive from the flames of Troy—No bastard Norman tyrant appears among the list of worthies who first landed on the rock," the speaker thundered, keeping well within the bounds of truth. The occasion is rather more important for the fact that attention was here first drawn to the Mayflower Compact, and Adams' interpretation of its significance has become traditional. It was the "only instance in human history of that positive, original social compact," he declared, speaking straight out of Rousseau. "Here was a unanimous and personal assent by all the individuals of the community to the association by which they became a nation," Adams concluded, blinking several salient facts—above all, the circumstances that prompted the compact, which was plainly an instrument of minority rule.

In 1820, on the bicentenary of the historic landing, the celebration at Plymouth first began to assume more than local significance. On that occasion the Pilgrim Society made its bow to the public by organizing a large procession. Escorted by the Standish Guards, "an independent company lately organized," it marched through the streets to Town Square, halting near the fragment of the rock still lying there, to hear an address by the great Daniel Webster, even more famed in his day than now, later a son of the Old Colony by adoption, for he soon bought the Winslow estate in Marshfield. Mounting a platform in front of the meeting house, impressively attired in small clothes and a silk gown, looking every inch a statesman, and bursting with Ciceronian periods, Webster began:

"We have come to this Rock to record here our homage to our Pilgrim Fathers, our sympathy in their sufferings, our gratitude for their labours, our admiration of their virtues, our veneration of their piety, and our attachment to those principles of civil and religious liberty for which they encountered the dangers of the ocean, the storms of heaven, the violence of the savages, disease, exile, and famine, to enjoy and to establish . . . We seem even to behold them as they struggle with the elements and with toilsome efforts gain the shore. We listen to their chiefs in council; we see the unexampled exhibition of female fortitude and resignation; we hear the whisperings of youthful impatience, and we see . . . chilled and shivering childhood, houseless but for a mother's arms, couchless but for a mother's breast, till our own blood almost freezes"—and the orator is quite out of breath.

Webster's address, "full of the farina of thought and feeling," was published by the Pilgrim Society and did something to acquaint a wider public with the character and accomplishments of the Forefathers, and with the symbolism of Plymouth Rock, which as yet were scarcely known outside the Old Colony.

But here again, as had happened so often in their lives, it was coincidence of the strangest kind that brought the Pilgrims their first general recognition and meed of posthumous fame. Far off in the town of Rhyllon, Wales, a local greengrocer wrapped up a few small purchases in an old newspaper and delivered them to Mrs. Felicia Dorothea Hemans, a stranger in the town, the author of several sentimental romances and a prolific writer of pietistic verse. As she unwrapped the package, she began to read the old newspaper which by some odd chance had found its way here from Boston. Even more curiously, the few remaining pages contained an account of the celebration of Forefathers' Day in 1824. Mrs. Hemans was fascinated, never so much as having heard of the Forefathers before. As described, their every act and sentiment and gesture struck a responsive chord, and she promptly sat down to compose the ode that has become the Pilgrims' and her own chief memorial. All of us know it, remembering it well from our days in school, particularly the scene of the landing, with the roar of the wind in the forest and the wild waves dashing high "on a stern and rock-bound coast"—

> Ay, call it holy ground,
>   The soil where first they trod!
> They have left untouched what there they found—
>   Freedom to worship God.

As Mrs. Hemans knew little of the Pilgrim story and nothing about Plymouth, the poem was wholly imaginative in many of its more graphic details; and fault has often been found with it on that score. There is the story of one of the always somewhat pontifical Channings who, on a voyage to England, went to visit the poetess and offer his congratulations. Having said a few nice things about her stirring hymn, he began in a most literal-minded way to pick her lines to pieces. "The soil where first they trod" was not at Plymouth, he pointed out, but at the tip of Cape Cod. And the Pilgrims had been seeking something more than "freedom to worship God"; they had enjoyed that in Holland. Nor was the *Mayflower* a "bark"; she was a ship, square-rigged throughout, though she may have been carrying a lateen on the mizzen. And the sandy low-lying coast at Plymouth was, of course, anything but "stern and rock-bound"—whereupon the poetess burst into tears and fled the room. But there was no need for her to be so upset, for she had done more than any other to bring the Pilgrims their meed of fame, and none would have her influence in shaping their saga. It is her conception of the Pilgrims that prevails today, though other influences have been at work, too.

In pursuit of its principal aim, the Pilgrim Society built Pilgrim Hall, an enduring granite monument, Greek Revival in style, which still stands on Plymouth's main street. In it was collected a great assortment of Pilgrim memorabilia, both authentic and not—a Geneva Bible handed down by Bradford, a chair allegedly Carver's which had been rescued from a local barber shop, a Winslow chair, one of Standish's swords, an empty pocketbook "which always belonged in the Church family," together with Malay daggers, South Sea shells, Chinese coins, Algerian pistols, a sword of Peregrine White's grandson, a pitchfork from Bunker Hill, and the bones of Iyanough, sachem to the Cummaquid. The amount of "authentic" *Mayflower* furniture in the hall, as a member of the Pilgrim Society early remarked, was enough to have sunk that vessel. Altogether, according to a judicious local historian, Pilgrim Hall was a "receptacle of rubbish," though it has since been reasonably well cleaned out. At the end of the hall is a group portrait entitled "The Landing of the Fathers in 1620," painted and presented by Henry Sargent of Boston. Often reproduced, usually to be seen on at least one wall in every schoolhouse, it has done much to shape the popular conception of the Pilgrims.

"We must do Mr. Sargent the justice to say," observed a distinguished citizen of Plymouth at the time of the presentation, "that he has not disgraced the noble story."

Looking about for other things to add to its collection, the eyes of the Pilgrim Society fell upon the fragment of Plymouth Rock lying under a great elm in Town Square. It had shrunk and been considerably damaged down the years, for souvenir hunters had been chipping away at it relentlessly. In his travels through the country in the 1830's, De Tocqueville noted "bits of it preserved in several towns in the Union." Some of the more enterprising at Plymouth apparently made a business of mutilating the rock, one shopkeeper of the time advertising, "A few small specimens are for sale, a piece the size of a common hen's egg costing $1.50. These take a very fine polish."[13]

On July 4, 1834, what remained of the fragment of the rock was placed on a cart, decorated with flowers and bearing a miniature of the *Mayflower*. Drawn by six boys and followed by a cheering crowd, the cart descended Leyden Street to Cole's Hill, along Carver Street, and back up to Pilgrim Hall, where with a volley of shot by the Standish Guards, it was dumped into a pit, where it remained for almost fifty years, with an iron fence around it to protect it from pious and impious vandals.

And now a very embarrassing question arose to plague the Pilgrim Society for decades, another of those curious misadven-

tures that dogged the Pilgrims in their life and followed them
even in their graves. The landing of the Forefathers had been
completely ignored for a century and a half—and now, as a proud
descendant cried out in distress, it was being celebrated on the
wrong day!

When the calendar change from Old Style to New Style had
been made in 1752, the difference between them amounted to
eleven days, and the Old Colony Club had set Forefathers' Day
accordingly. But this was an error, for at the time of the landing
in 1620 the difference between the calendars was only ten days.
Therefore, as the landing had been made on December 11th, Old
Style, it was plain that it should be celebrated on December 21st,
New Style. Or was it?

First raised in 1832, the question was debated, often rather acri-
moniously, for almost twenty years. While agreeing that the
mathematics were right, many doubted the propriety of making
a change and created a formidable opposition, declaring in a
gem-like phrase that should be inscribed upon the banners of
traditionalists everywhere, "We much prefer established error to
novel truth."

To which a true son of the Forefathers replied that if the
Pilgrims had harbored any such notion, there would have been
no landing to celebrate.

At length, in 1849, the Pilgrim Society appointed a committee
to remove the subject from interminable debate, and on its recommendation Forefathers' Day was celebrated the next year on
the proper day for the first time. But it was back again on December 22nd by 1862. Moved forward once more in 1870, it slipped
back again in 1882, when the Pilgrim Society concluded that
December 22nd was the preferable date "in view of the speeches
consecrating that day by Winslow [the Tory exile], Webster,
Everett, Adams, and Seward."

Meantime, the Pilgrim Society had inspired others with its zeal,
and the Old Colony towns were soon strewn with monuments,
from the decorative to the monstrous, the worst being reserved

for Captain Standish at Duxbury. Attention at Plymouth turned
more and more to Burial Hill, rising steeply behind the meeting
house, a beautiful and impressive spot, increasingly the Mecca
of the faithful. Dominating the town, the palisaded Fort Hill of
early days, it had become a burial ground some time after King
Philip's War, first being remarked by old Judge Sewall of Boston
on a visit to Plymouth in 1697. "I walk out in the morn. to see
the Mill," he noted in his diary, "then turn up to the Graves,
come down to the Meetinghouse, and seeing the door partly open,
went in and found a very convenient Opportunity to pray, the
wind being very cold."

Though the oldest stone goes back only to 1703, a few of the
Mayflower company and those on the other Pilgrim ships may
be buried here, but their remains were shown no reverence whatever until well along in the nineteenth century. These now famous
"Eternity Acres" were first fenced during the American Revolution when Pastor Robbins decided to pasture his cows here. In
1789 the town had to take steps to prevent desecration of the
graves by "wanton or imprudent men or boys," at the same time
urging the pastor "not to have more horses there than shall be
really necessary." As they raced up and down and round the hill,
perhaps pursued by protesting ghosts at night, the animals were
knocking down many old stones with their flying hoofs, breaking
and chipping others. Worse, some of the townspeople made use
of Burial Hill as a quarry whenever they needed a slab for a
doorstep or some similar purpose, carrying off the fallen or broken
stones heaped up in a corner of the burial ground. And there
were some who did not hesitate to pull down standing stones if
these seemed to serve their purpose better. "In various parts of
the town today," wrote an outraged son in 1884, "may be found
gravestones, fifty or seventy-five or a hundred years old, utilized
as covers of drains and cesspools."

A stop was put to this, and new and more elaborate monuments began to appear on Burial Hill, erected in memory of
Forefathers whose graves had been lost—one to Mrs. Alice Brad-

ford, "a godly matron," and two of her sons, Major William and
Joseph Bradford, and another to the first Cushmans, Thomas and
Mary (Allerton). Still another was erected by his descendants
to the memory of John Howland and his wife Elizabeth, who
was, according to the inscription, "the daughter of Gov. Carver,"
for that was the long established tradition in the family. From
generation to generation the story had been told—an early American success story—of how young John Howland, a servant in
the Carver household, had wooed and won his master's daughter,
inheriting his wealth and rising steadily to become a power at
Plymouth, dying there in 1672 in his eightieth year, "a good olde
disciple."

There was considerable fluttering among the genealogically-
minded when the fact came to light in 1855 that Howland had
not married his master's daughter, but Elizabeth Tilley, daughter
of a humble silk worker. Even more startling was the fact that
there had been no such person as Elizabeth Carver at all, for the
Pilgrims' first governor had died childless.[14]

What exploded the Howland legend and many another myth
was the unexpected recovery, under strange circumstance, of
Bradford's long-lost manuscript, which after many wanderings,
had apparently vanished into thin air almost a century before.
Of Plimoth Plantation, as already remarked, had been written by
the old governor with no thought of publication, and upon his
death it "was gifen to his son majer William Bradford, and by
him to his son mager John Bradford, rit by me Samuel Bradford,
Mach 20, 1705." Not long after this illiterate note was written,
the manuscript passed into the hands of old Judge Sewall of
Boston, as was learned in 1728 by a collector of old manuscripts,
Thomas Prince, pastor of the Old South Church, Boston.

The grandson of the Old Colony's last governor, Thomas
Hinckley, and deeply interested in the early Plymouth records,
Prince came to visit the Bradford homestead along the Jones
River, and Major John gave him, as Prince noted on the flyleaf
of the history, *"several Manuscript Octavoes* which He assured

me were written with his said Grandfather Govr. Bradford's own
Hand. He also gave me a *little Pencil Book,* wrote with Blew-
lead Pencil by his said Father ye Dep. govr. And He also told me
that He had sent & only lent his said Grandfather Govr. Bradford's History of Plimouth Colony, wrote by his own Hand also,
to Judg Sewall; and desired me to get it of him or find it out, &
take out of it what I think proper for my New England Chron-
olgy, which I accordingly obtained; and This is ye said History,
which I find wrote in ye same Hand-writing as ye Octavo Manuscripts above said . . . I also mentioned to him my Desire of
lodging this History in ye New England Library of Prints &
Manuscripts, which I had then been collecting for 23 years, to
which He signified his willingness—only that He might have
the Perusal of it while he lived."

Excerpting a few passages for publication in his brief annals,
Prince placed the chronicle on the shelves of his library high up
in the steeple of the Old South, where it remained for a half
century, at least until 1774, when in seeking material for his
history of New England it was consulted by Massachusetts' governor, Thomas Hutchinson, soon to flee the country as a Tory
refugee. From that time till the day of its recovery, nothing is
known of the travels of the manuscript, but from subsequent
events it is possible to hazard a guess.

With the outbreak of the American Revolution, the Old South
was commandeered by the British and used as a riding rink by
the Queen's Light Dragoons, "Gentleman Johnny" Burgoyne's
favorites. After the royal forces evacuated Boston, sailing away to
Nova Scotia with hundreds of native Tories in tow, many from
Plymouth and Marshfield, it was found that Prince's library had
been looted, and that all of Bradford's manuscripts were gone.
One of them, Bradford's "Letter-Book," suddenly turned up in a
shop at Halifax in 1793, as previously remarked, and was rescued
before it was altogether destroyed by the grocer who was using
its precious pages as wrapping paper. There was a lingering hope
for a time that *Of Plimoth Plantation* might also turn up in the
town, but as the years dragged on, that hope faded and finally

died. Even the most sanguine were now persuaded that the missing manuscript had disappeared forever.

Fate, for once, was kind to the Pilgrims.

In 1844, in compiling material for his *History of the Protestant Episcopal Church in America,* the Lord Bishop of Oxford, Samuel Wilberforce, consulted various unprinted sources in the library of his colleague, the Lord Bishop of London. His history was sufficiently well received to go into a second printing in 1849, but the startling clues it contained escaped notice for eleven years—until 1855, when these were picked up almost simultaneously by two students and writers of Massachusetts history, John Wingate Thornton and the Reverend John S. Barry, the latter making his discovery in a copy of Wilberforce's history borrowed from a friend. Thumbing through the book, he came upon several unknown passages attributed merely to a "MS. History of the Plantation of Plymouth," and instantly recognized that they could have been written only by Bradford.[15] And in answer to an excited query there soon came a letter from London saying, "There is not the slightest doubt that the manuscript is Governor Bradford's own autograph . . . The written pages are 270, the number named by Prince . . . as the number of pages in the long-lost volume."

How the manuscript came to be on the shelves of the library in Fulham Palace, on the outskirts of London, is not clear. Perhaps some British soldier of a literary or historical turn of mind removed it from the Old South. Or perhaps—which is more probable—it was carried off by Governor Hutchinson when he fled, for examination of the Fulham library revealed several other volumes from Prince's collection, with notes along the margins in Hutchinson's handwriting.

Of Plimoth Plantation, fascinating in its every detail, altogether an extraordinary human document, was given to the world in 1856 when a transcript was published at Boston. For the first time in their posthumous lives the Pilgrims stood out strong and clear, in three dimensions, rather than as thin silhouettes in black and gray. They began to breathe once more—and love, and hate, and fight, as only they could. It became unmistakeable that, in spite of their revolt against many aspects of it, they had gone to Holland and had come to the wilderness trailing the glory of Elizabethan England, that age of towering imagination and high bold enterprise. In addition, Bradford's pages filled in many huge gaps in the Pilgrim story, opening up new and unsuspected scenes, brightly illuminating many incidents that had been tantalizingly obscure before.

Yet the facts in Bradford's authentic and engrossing chronicle have never made much headway against the mass of fancy, legend, and folklore that had already crystallized in the Pilgrim saga. And just two years later, in 1858, that saga was immeasurably reinforced by the publication of "The Courtship of Miles Standish," by Henry Wadsworth Longfellow, grandson of Peleg Wadsworth, the former Plymouth schoolmaster, whose forbears had early settled at Duxbury. From him Longfellow had heard many tales of the Old Colony,[16] and one of his favorites took form in the story of the fiery Standish's curiously diffident wooing. The poem was phenomenally well received. More than 10,000 copies were sold the day of its appearance in London. Its immediate popularity at home was as great, and it has since become a part of the growing American *mythos,* with the natural consequence that in thinking of the Pilgrims most of us have difficulty in recalling the names of any but Myles Standish, John Alden, and Priscilla Mullins. Yet these were scarcely typical of the men and women who most clearly reflected the character and motives of the First Comers, and Longfellow's painting of the general background is fantastic.[17]

Having completed a towering monument in 1859, the Pilgrim Society turned to search for the lost half of Plymouth Rock and found what seemed to answer its description down on the dilapidated waterfront, serving as a doorstep to an abandoned warehouse. The old building was torn down, the environs were cleaned up, and a stone canopy—an Italianate baldachino—was erected over the precious relic. Some bones had recently been uncovered by workmen installing water pipes along Cole's Hill, long used by the Indians as a burying ground and also by the Pilgrims during the General Sickness, according to another tradition from the lips of old Ruling Elder Thomas Faunce. Assured by Dr. Oliver Wendell Holmes that these were Pilgrim bones, the Society packed them into a small box and mortared them into the ceiling of the canopy directly above the rock.

At length, in 1880, it was decided to reunite the rock, and the fragment in front of Pilgrim Hall was dragged down to the beach. The two parts did not fit very well—perhaps because it was a strange marriage, or more probably because of the hard usage each had received. But they were joined after some difficulty and at last Plymouth Rock was one again. Its double identity had been rather confusing to the faithful and to casual sightseers who were beginning to crowd the town.

New honors and growing recognition came in the 1890's. The rock had become a national institution, an international symbol, the pivot of the entire Pilgrim story. In 1895 the Commonwealth of Massachusetts settled the controversy about the proper time to celebrate Forefathers' Day by setting aside December 21st as a legal holiday. The next year the Society of Mayflower Descendants was founded, which gave a paid secretary and many idle women pleasant employment. And in 1897, on the last leg of a long and mysterious pilgrimage, Bradford's manuscript came back to our shores.

The question of its return had been raised a few years after its discovery by the Reverend Dr. John Waddington, an English clergyman, and again in 1860 by the Massachusetts Historical Society. The legal authorities of the Crown anticipated no difficulties in arranging this, but the Lord Bishop of London raised objections, saying, "The difficulty of alienating property of this kind could, I believe, only be got over by an Act of Parliament." Seven years later, finding itself in possession of some manuscripts that did not properly belong to it, the Philadelphia Library returned the documents to the British Archives from which they had presumably been stolen. The circumstances were brought to the attention of our ambassador at London, the historian John

Lothrop Motley, who tactfully suggested that *Of Plimoth Planta-tion* might be sent back in return, but without result. The question was again raised in 1877, and once more in 1881, after the Arch-bishop of Canterbury had restored to France the original of Napoleon's last will and testament, found in the church archives, and had been sustained by the Parliament when the legality of his action was questioned.

Finally, in 1896, a number of distinguished Americans ad-dressed a petition to our ambassador in Britain, asking him to explore every possible avenue that might open a way for the return of Bradford's chronicle. After some discussion the church authorities suggested a plea to the Consistory Court of the Diocese of London. Such a plea was framed, with the usual legalistic abracadabra, and the chancellor of the court was much impressed. "Had this mss. been solely of historical value," he said, it would have been very difficult indeed to see any good reason for its removal. Fortunately, there was a much more compelling argu-ment for granting the plea, and that was the "necessity of pro-tecting the pecuniary interests of the descendants of the families named in it, in tracing and establishing their rights to succession of property."

And so, as a mere title deed and not as a superlative historical document, *Of Plimoth Plantation* came back to us at last—but not home to Plymouth, going to Boston instead, where it was presented to the governor of Massachusetts and lodged in the State House, in a glass case, where it is still to be seen.

With the approach of 1920, the tercentenary of the landing, Plymouth began to lay plans for a great celebration, and the town fathers turned their attention to a matter that had been of serious concern to them for some time. If Plymouth Rock had ever rested at the water's edge, it was there no longer and now lay some little distance up the beach, far above tidewater. Many—too many— visitors were apt to smile when shown the rock and told the story of the landing, and the more skeptical simply dismissed it as a fake, asking how the Pilgrims could possibly have landed there? —to which there was no easy answer.

The town fathers were determined to put a stop to this, fearing its effect upon the tourist trade. The Italianate stone canopy over the rock was torn down. A steam shovel was driven down to the beach to excavate around the rock and lay it bare. With chains fast around it, the boulder was lifted high in the air—whereupon, evidently tired of all this business, it fell apart, breaking up in many pieces. Put together again, it was swung down the beach and dropped at tidewater where it as yet remains, in a pit hollowed in the floor of the Grecian temple hurriedly constructed over and around it, the generous but not very happy inspiration of the Colonial Dames of America.

But all of this took time, and 1920 came and went without a celebration at Plymouth. Festivities had to be postponed till the following summer, allowing the sponsors to make elaborate preparations for the occasion. It was to be not merely a national but an international event, and Plymouth made ready to receive a great influx of visitors—plain people come to visit an historic shrine, distinguished men and women to address the multitude, officers and devoted members of patriotic societies, thousands of Pilgrim pedigree, and the usual throng of the curious, eager to enjoy the spectacle and the excitement. Procession after procession wound through the streets. A giant sarcophagus was unveiled on Cole's Hill, and in it was placed the small box of Pilgrim bones unearthed a half century before. The late Professor George P. Baker presented a pageant, *The Pilgrim Spirit,* with the Forefathers in conventional roles. But the climax of the celebration came when another *Mayflower* slowly sailed into the harbor— the presidential yacht, bearing Warren Gamaliel Harding and a large party, escorted by four battleships and six destroyers. The party included three Old Guard members of the United States Senate and one of the more honest in Harding's Cabinet, Secretary of War Weeks.[18] The President's "specially prepared address" was cabled round the world.

"The germ of progress is doubtless universal," he declared, "but requires favorable conditions for its development. Conditions were favorable in the New World ... The men and women who came here to found in a wilderness, across a thousand leagues of ocean waste, a new State came with high and conscious purpose of achieving a great human end . . . Some have seen in this nothing more than the basis for an indictment on the ground of zealotry, bigotry, even fanaticism. But bigotry, extremism, fanaticism never found their fruition in noble ends achieved, in freedom established, in mankind emancipated, in great States raised up as guardians of unshackled thought and unchained souls . . . We stand today before the unknown, but we look to the future with confidence unshaken . . . We welcome the theories wrought out in new hope, but we cling to the assurance founded on experience. All that is, is not bad; all that is to be, will not be ideal . . . We are slowly but very surely recovering from the wastes and sorrows and utter disarrangements of a cataclysmal war. Peace is bringing its new assurances; and penitent realization and insistent conscience will preserve that peace . . . The international prospect is more than promising, and the distress and depression at home are symptomatic of early recovery. Solvent financially, sound economically, unrivaled in genius, unexcelled in industry, resolute in determination, and unwavering in faith, these United States will carry on!"

The Pilgrims would have smiled at the smugness of this. And they would have laughed aloud when a large bronze statue of Massasoit was donated to the Pilgrim Society and unveiled with great fanfare by the Improved Order of Red Men. The Forefathers were never ones for mummery and ceremonial. They had no use for precedent and tradition, and deliberately flouted both. They were innovators, revolutionaries, never being restrained by the dead hand of the past. They were interested in the immediate scene about them and in trying to make it better, even at the cost of their lives. They had no time for ancestor worship, no taste for monuments. Rather, they had the supreme human qualities—an intelligent awareness of the things about them, a sensitive desire to do something to bring them closer to their heart's desire, and an absolutely indomitable spirit in pursuing their own high purposes.

"True it was," they had said when discussing the question of leaving Leyden to plunge into the unknown, "that such attempts were not to be made and undertaken without good ground & reason; not rashly or lightly as many have done for curiositie or hope of gaine, &c . . . It was granted ye dangers were great, but not desperate; the difficulties were many, but not invincible. For though there were many of them likly, yet they were not certaine; it might be sundrie of ye things feared might never befalle; others by providente care & use of good means might in a great measure be prevented; and all of them, through ye help of God, by fortitude and patience, might either be borne or overcome. . . .

"Yea, though they should lose their lives in this action, yet they might have comforte in the same . . . all great & honourable actions are accompanied with great difficulties, and must be both enterprised and overcome with answerable courages."

And the Pilgrims' courage, that of Saints and Strangers alike, was always "answerable"—let that be their epitaph.

Appendix A

THE PILGRIM
COMPANY

Who should properly be included in the Pilgrim Company?

The question is almost wholly one of definition. Many lists have been drawn, some more inclusive than others. By the criteria I have chosen to use, which are as broad as they can reasonably be made, the company includes:

a) all "saincts," "strangers," hired hands, and indentured servants who came on any of the Pilgrims' ships—*Mayflower, Fortune, Anne, Little James, Talbot, Handmaid,* or second *Mayflower;*

b) all members of the Green Gate congregation who came at any other time, either soon or late;

c) those of the merchant adventurers who settled in the colony;

d) all others who settled at Plymouth and were granted land there before 1631 (such as Phineas Pratt, a refugee from Wessagusset, and those who came with John Oldham "on their perticuler").

With the exception of the "Straggling Saints" and "Merchant Adventurers," the several groups are listed under the name of the ship on which each came.

An asterisk (*) indicates the remarkably few Pilgrims from Scrooby.

Those addressed as "Master" (sometimes written "Mister," occasionally "Mr.") were relatively the aristocrats of the company—in general, those with means to bring indentured servants.

For the special meaning of "Purchaser" and "Undertaker" as used in the notes below, see pp. 282–283.

I. MAYFLOWER—of Harwich (180 tons); Christopher Jones, master; out of London, mid-July, 1620, dropping anchor off tip of Cape Cod, November 11th, Old Style, with 102 passengers, including Oceanus Hopkins, born at sea.

(Names in italics are of those who died in General Sickness or within six months of landing.)

A. SAINTS

(17 men, 10 women, 14 children)

Allerton, Master Isaac (c.1586-1659) —of London, tailor

"the first Yankee trader"

Probably one of Ancient Brethren, Amsterdam; citizen, Leyden, 1614; asst. governor, Plymouth, 1621-c. 1631; married, 1626, to 2nd wife, Fear Brewster (see *Anne* Saints); 1 child; Purchaser, 1626; Undertaker and London business agent, 1627-c. 1631; dismissed in disgrace, went to Marblehead, operating fishing fleet until asked to leave by Mass. authorities, c.1635; merchant, New Amsterdam, c.1636-46; married, c.1644, to 3rd wife, Joanna ———; merchant, New Haven, c.1647-59, making fortune in Virginia and West Indian trade; died insolvent.

———, *Mrs. Mary (Morris)* (c. 1588-1621) — of Newbury, Berks

Married, Leyden, 1611; died on *Mayflower* in Plymouth harbor several days after being delivered of stillborn child at height of winter gale.

Bartholomew (c.1612-   )
After father's disgrace, returned to England, becoming minister there.

Remember (c.1614-c.1655)
Married, c.1633, to Moses Maverick, pastor at Marblehead; 6 children.

Mary (c.1616-1699)
Married, c.1635, to Thomas Cushman (see *Fortune* Saints); last survivor of *Mayflower* company; 4 children.

*Bradford, Master William (1589-1657)—of Austerfield, Yorks.; fustian maker

"a commone blessing and father to them all"

Early orphaned and virtually adopted by Brewster, c.1602; silk worker, Amsterdam, 1607-09; citizen, Leyden, 1612; governor or asst. gov., Plymouth, 1621-57; Purchaser, 1626; Undertaker, 1627-41; leader in opposing attempt to establish toleration, 1646; presiding officer of United Colonies, 1648 and 1656; left £900 estate.

———, *Mrs. Dorothy (May)* (1597-1620)—of Wisbeach, Cambridgeshire; daughter of Henry May, elder of Ancient Brethren and later of Ainsworthians, subsequently joining Leyden church

Married, Leyden, 1613; drowned at tip of Cape Cod, "falling" from *Mayflower* while at anchor; 1 child, John (see Straggling Saints, p. 485).

*Brewster, Master William (c.1566-1643)—probably born in Scrooby or vicinity

"wise and discrete and well spoken ... qualified above many"

Peterhouse College, Cambridge, 1580-c.1583; employ of Sir William Davison, c.1583-89; postmaster and bailiff-receiver, Scrooby, 1590-1607; instrumental in organizing Scrooby congregation, 1606-07; Amsterdam, 1608-09; tutoring and odd jobs, Leyden, 1609-1616; ruling elder, 1609-43; operated Choir Alley Press, 1616-19; flight and hiding in England, 1619-20; Purchaser, 1626; Undertaker,

1627-41; argues against Roger Williams' retention as "teacher," 1633.

*———, Mrs. Mary (Wentworth?) (c.1568-1627)—perhaps daughter of Thomas Wentworth, Brewster's predecessor at Scrooby Manor
Married, Scrooby, 1591; died Plymouth; 5 children.

Love (1611-1650)
Married Sarah Collier (see Merchant Adventurers), 1634, and early removed to Duxbury where he died.

Wrestling (1614-c.1635)
Went to Piscataqua (Portsmouth), N. H., as young man and soon died there.

Carver, John (c.1586-1621)—of Doncaster, Yorks.; merchant
"Of singular piety, and rare for humilitie"
First appears in Leyden records as connected with church, 1616; negotiations with merchant adventurers and purchasing of supplies, 1617-20; deacon, c.1617-21; died of sunstroke while toiling in cornfields.

———, Mrs. Catherine (White) (c. 1580-1621)—of Sturton le Steeple, eldest sister of Bridget, John Robinson's wife
Married George Leggatt, 1596; 1 child, Marie, who evidently died young; married Carver, c.1600; died "of a broken heart" soon after husband; no children.

Minter, Desire (c.1600-   )— daughter of Thomas Minter, member of Green Gate congregation, citizen of Leyden
Returned to England, c.1625, and died there.

*Cooke, Francis (1577-1633)—wool comber, of Blyth, Notts

Amsterdam, 1607-09; Leyden, 1609-20; Purchaser, 1626; died Plymouth (for family, see Anne Saints).

John (1612-1695)
Married Sarah Warren (see Anne Strangers), 1634; deacon, c.1634; deprived of office and excommunicated for turning Baptist during religious troubles, 1657; removed to Dartmouth (New Bedford) and became occasional Baptist preacher there.

Crackston, John (   )—of Colchester
John (-1628)
Lost himself in woods and froze feet, dying of gangrene.

Fletcher, Moses (   )—smith, of Sandwich
Married Mrs. Sarah Dingby, Leyden, 1613.

Fuller, Master Samuel (c.1585-1633) —serge maker, of Redenhall, Norfolk; Pilgrims' "physition & chirurgeon"
"a great help & comforte unto them" Leader of seceding Ancient Brethren, 1609; deacon, c.1609-33; married Agnes Carpenter, 1613; married Bridget Lee, 1617; Purchaser, 1626; "bled" and converted Puritans at Salem and Boston, 1628-30 (for wife, see Anne Saints).

Goodman, John (c.1595-1621)—linen weaver
Married, Leyden, 1619, to Sarah Hooper. Brought only dogs on ship, large mastiff bitch and small spaniel; Peter Browne's companion on deer and "lyon" hunt.

Priest, Degory (c.1580-1621)—hatter, of London
Married, Leyden, 1611, to Mrs. Sarah (Allerton) Vincent; citizen, Leyden, 1615.

Rogers, Thomas ( )—camlet merchant
Citizen, Leyden, 1618.

Joseph (c.1608-1678)
Married Hannah (——) and removed to Eastham, 1644; 7 children.

Tilley, Edward (-1621)—cloth maker, of London
Joined with Captain Standish "for counsel and advice" on First Discovery; almost froze on "Thievish Harbor" exploration.

———, *Mrs. Anne* (——) (1621)
Brought along two small "cousins," Humility Cooper and "Henery" Samson (see Strangers below).

Tilley, John (-1621)—silk worker, of London
On Third Discovery, probably on First and Second as well.

———, *Mrs. Bridget (van der Velde)* (-1621)—native of Leyden, converted to Brownism
Married, Leyden, 1615.

Elizabeth (1606-1687)—child of previous marriage
Married John Howland (see Servants below), c.1624; died at Swansea; 9 children.

Tinker, Thomas (-1621)—wood sawyer
Citizen, Leyden, 1617.

———, *Mrs.* (——) (-1621)
——— (son) (-1621)

Turner, John (-1621)—merchant
Citizen, Leyden, 1610.

——— (son) (-1621)
——— (son) (-1621)

White, Master William (c.1592-1621)—wool carder

Perhaps related to White family of Sturton le Steeple, into which Carver and Robinson married.

———, *Mrs. Susanna (Fuller)* (c. 1594-1680)—sister of Deacon Samuel Fuller (see above)
Married, Leyden, 1612; became 2nd wife of Edward Winslow (see below), 1621.

Resolved (c.1615-1680)
Married Judith Vassall of Scituate, 1640, and settled there, removing to Marshfield, 1662; died at Salem; 5 children.

Peregrine (1620-1703)
Born on *Mayflower* month after arrival; 1648, married Sarah Bassett (see *Fortune* Saints); granted 200 acres by General Court, 1665, "in respect that he was the first of the English that was born in these parts"; captain of militia, 1673; did not join church till 1698, in 78th year; died at Marshfield; 6 children.

Winslow, Master Edward (1595-1655)—of Droitwich, Worcestershire; printer
Assistant printer at Choir Alley Press, 1617-19; member of parties sent out to explore Cape Cod and environs; married, Plymouth, 1621, to Mrs. Susanna (Fuller) White (see above); diplomatic mission to Massasoit, 1621; author of "come-on" literature to attract settlers; agent to England, 1623; opened trade along Kennebec, 1625; member of General Court as governor or asst. governor, 1624-46; Purchaser, 1626; Undertaker, 1627-41; jailed in London by Archbishop Laud, 1635; removed to Marshfield, 1637; commissioner to New England Confederacy, 1643-44; sailed for London, 1646, and

never returned; chairman of joint English-Dutch commission to assess damage done English ships by Dutch in neutral Danish ports; chief of 3 commissioners appointed by Oliver Cromwell to conquer Spanish West Indies; died of tropical fever on flagship off Jamaica, buried at sea with salvo of cannon.

————, Mrs. *Elizabeth (Barker)* (c. 1597-1621)—of Chester or Chatham
Married, Leyden, 1618; no children.

B. Strangers

(17 men, 9 women, 14 children)

Billington, John (c.1590-1630)—of London
"one of ye profanest families amongst them"
Tied up by neck and heels for cursing Standish when called to perform military duty, 1622; mixed up in Lyford-Oldham "mutiny," 1624; Purchaser, 1626; hanged for murder, 1630.

————, Mrs. *Ellen* (c.1592-   )—of London
Married, Plymouth, 1638, to Gregory Armstrong.

Francis (c.1612-   )
Almost blew up *Mayflower* by shooting off squibs near powder kegs; discovered Billington Sea, small lake behind Plymouth; married, Plymouth, 1634, to Mrs. Christian (Penn) Eaton (see *Anne* Strangers); removed to Yarmouth and died there; 9 children.

John (c.1614-c.1628)
Lost himself in woods and turned up on Cape Cod, 1621, leading to first acquaintance with Cape tribes.

Britteridge, Richard (-1620)

Browne, Peter (c.1600-1633)—of Great Burstead, Essex
John Goodman's companion on deer and "lyon" hunt; married, Plymouth, 1623, to Mrs. Martha Ford (see *Fortune* Strangers); Purchaser, 1626; married to Mary ————, 1628; 2 children by 1st marriage and 3 by second.

Chilton, James (c.1563-1620)—of Canterbury, tailor

————, *Mrs.* ———— (————) (- 1621)

Mary (c.1605-1679)
Reputedly first Pilgrim to step foot on Plymouth Rock; married, Plymouth, 1624, to John Winslow (see *Fortune* Strangers); removed to Boston, 1655, and died there; 10 children.

Clarke, Richard (-1621)

Cooper, Humility (c.1612-   )—of London
One of two small "cousins" brought along by Edward Tilleys (see above); "was sent for into England, and dyed there."

Eaton, Francis (c.1595-1633)—of Bristol, carpenter and shipwright
Married, Plymouth, c.1622, to 2nd wife, ———— ————; married Christian Penn (see *Anne* Strangers), c.1626; 4 children.

————, *Mrs. Sarah* (————) (c.1590-1621)—presumably of Bristol

Samuel (1620-   )—arrived in mother's arms, "a suckling child"
Married, Plymouth, to Elizabeth ————, c.1647; in 1661, to Martha Billington, daughter of father's third wife by her second husband, Francis Billington (see above).

Fuller, Edward (-1621)—of Redenhall, Norfolk

Probably Deacon Samuel Fuller's brother, but apparently not of the Leyden congregation.

———, Mrs. Ann (———) (-1621)

Samuel (c.1616-1683)
Removed to Barnstable, c.1640, and married Jane Lothrop, local pastor's daughter; 3 or more children.

Gardiner, Richard (c.1600-1621)— of Harwich, Essex, John Alden's home town

Hopkins, Master Stephen (c.1585-1644)—of Wotton-under-Edge, Gloucestershire
Shipwrecked on Bermuda while on way to Virginia and condemned to death for leading mutiny there, 1609-10; joined to Captain Standish for "counsel and advice on First Discovery," being only one of passengers with any knowledge of New World; accompanies Winslow on visit to Massasoit at Sowams, 1621; Purchaser, 1626; asst. governor, 1633-36, and probably 1624-32; frequently in conflict with authorities in later years.

———, Mrs. Elizabeth (———) (-c.1640)—Hopkins' second wife
Bore five more children at Plymouth (Giles and Constance were Hopkins' children by 1st wife).

Giles (c.1607-c.1690)
Married, Plymouth, 1639, to Catharine Wheldon, and removed to Yarmouth; died Eastham; 7 children.

Constance (c.1605-1677)
Married, Plymouth, c.1627, to Nicholas Snow (see *Anne* Strangers); died at Eastham.

Damaris (c.1617-c.1627)

Oceanus (1620-   )
Born at sea on *Mayflower,* dying before 1627.

Margeson, Edmund (-1621)

Martin, Master Christopher (c.1575-1621)—of Great Burstead, Essex
"he so insulteth over our poore people, with shuch scorne & contempte, as if they were not good enough to wipe his shoes"
Named by merchant adventurers to represent Strangers in purchase of provisions for voyage, 1619-20; treasurer of emigrant company and "governour" of passengers on *Mayflower;* accounts found to be in great disorder, the beginning of Pilgrims' extended financial troubles.

———, Mrs. ——— (———) (-1621)

Prower, Solomon (-1620)
Martin's stepson.

Mullins, Master William (c.1580-1621)—shopkeeper, of Dorking, Surrey

———, Mrs. Alice (———) (-1621)
Probably Mullins' 2nd or 3rd wife.

Priscilla (c.1602-c.1685)
Married John Alden (see Hired Hands below), c.1622; 9 children.

Joseph (c.1614-1621)

Rigdale, John (-1621)—of London

———, Mrs. Alice (———) (-1621)

Samson, Henry (-1684)—of London
Married Ann Plummer and removed to Duxbury; 8 children.

Standish, Captain Myles (c.1584-1656)—probably of Chorley, Lancashire

"a little chimney is quickly fired"
Soldier in English forces sent to aid Dutch, c.1600-02; leader of First Discovery, 1620; saves Pilgrim party in "huggery" at Eastham, 1620; organizes Pilgrim army and explores Mass. Bay, 1621; brings Wituwamat's head home in triumph from Wessagusset, 1623; married, Plymouth, 1623, to 2nd wife, Barbara —— (see *Anne* Strangers); vainly attempts to recover Cape Ann, 1625; sent to England and returns with news of Robinson's death, 1626; Purchaser, 1626; Undertaker, 1627-41; arrests Thomas Morton at Merry Mount, 1629; removed to Duxbury, c.1632; asst. governor almost continuously from 1633, and probably from 1624; favors religious toleration, 1646; treasurer, 1652-55; left estate of £360; alone of Pilgrim leaders, never joined church.

——, *Mrs. Rose* (——) (1621)
Nothing whatever is known of Standish's wife

Warren, Master Richard (c.1580-1628)—of London, merchant
"a usefull instrumente"
Member of exploration parties along Cape Cod; probably asst. governor, 1624-28 (for family, see *Anne* Strangers).

Williams, Thomas (-1621)— of Yarmouth, Norfolk

Winslow, Gilbert (1600-)— Edward Winslow's third brother
Returned to England, c.1646, and died there.

C. Hired Hands
(5 men)
Alden, John (1599-1686)—cooper, of Harwich, Essex

"a hopfull yong man"
Married, c.1622, to Priscilla Mullins (see Strangers above); removed to Duxbury, c.1632; asst. governor, 1633-39, 1651-86, and probably 1631-32; arrested at Boston for murder, 1634; opposes religious toleration, 1646; leader in Quaker and Baptist persecutions, 1657; treasurer, 1656-58; being "low in his estate," granted £10 in consideration of his public services, 1660.

Allerton, John (-1621)—mariner
Hired to go back for those at Leyden.

Ellis, —— ( )—sailor
Engaged to remain a year in colony, returned to England on *Fortune*.

English, Thomas (-1621)— mariner
Hired to take charge of Pilgrim shallop.

Trevore, William ( )—sailor
Returned to England with Ellis and spread lavish tales about richness of Plimoth Plantation.

D. Servants
(11 men, 1 woman, 6 children)

Allerton's—
Hooke, John (-1621)—"a servante boy"

Brewster's—
More, Richard (c.1613-c.1684) —of London
One of family of orphaned waifs forced, as was common practice at the time, to become indentured servants under auspices of church and Lord Mayor of London; was living with one of adventurers, Thomas Weston, when "transported"; later changed name to Mann; married Christian Hunt

and Jane Hollingsworth; died Salem; 4 children.

More, —— (-1621)—Richard's brother

Carver's—

More, Jasper (-1620)

Wilder, Roger (-1621)— "Man-servant"

——, —— ( )—"Maid-Servant"

Catherine Carver's "maid servant maried, & dyed a year or two after, here in this place."

Latham, William (-c.1645) —servant boy

After more than 20 years at Plymouth, returned to England and thence to Bahamas, where, "with some others, was starved for want of food."

Howland, John (1592-1672)—of London

"a plaine-hearted Christian"

Evidently inherited Carver's estate and immediately bought his freedom; married Elizabeth Tilley (see Saints above), c.1624; Purchaser, 1626; Undertaker, 1627-41; asst. governor, 1633-35, and probably 1629-32; in charge of Kennebec trading post at time of Hocking murder, 1634; apparently held somewhat to blame, for never again entrusted with public office; died Swansea; 9 children.

Fuller's—

Butten, William (1598-1620)— of Austerfield

Died before land was sighted, and buried at sea.

Hopkins'—

Dotey, Edward (c.1600-1655)— of London

Perhaps one of leaders of mutiny

on *Mayflower;* with Leister (see below), fought first and last duel in colony, 1621; Purchaser, 1626; married —— —— and then Faith (Clarke), c.1635; died at Yarmouth; 9 children.

Leister, Edward (c.1600-)— of London

". . . after he was liberty, went to Virginia, & there dyed"

Martin's—

Langemore, John (-1620)

Mullins'—

Carter, Robert (-1621)

White's—

Holbeck, William (-1621)

Thompson, Edward (-1620)

Winslow's—

More, Ellen (-1621)—"a little girle that was put to this family"

Story, Elias (-1621)—man servant, of London

Soule, George (c.1600-1680)—of Eckington, Worcestershire

Married Mary Becket (see *Anne* Strangers), c.1627; died Duxbury; 7 children.

II. FORTUNE—of London (55 tons); Thomas Barton, master; out of London early July, 1621, arriving Plymouth, November 11th, with "35 persons to remaine & live in ye plantation."

A. SAINTS

(9 men, 2 women, 1 child)

Bassett, William (c.1590-c.1655)— master mason, of Bethnal Green, Middlesex

Married, Leyden, 1611, to 2nd wife, Margaret Oldham; later married 3rd wife; Purchaser, 1626; removed to Bridgewater, 1649.

————, Mrs. Elizabeth (————) ( )

Bompass, Edward (-c.1655)— native Leydener
Removed to Duxbury, married Hannah ————; later to Marshfield; 8 children.

*Brewster, Jonathan (1593-1659)— ribbon maker, of Scrooby
Amsterdam, 1608-09; Leyden, 1609-21; married, c.1615, to ———— ————, losing wife and child four years later; citizen, Leyden, 1617; married, Plymouth, 1624, to Lucretia Oldham (see *Anne* Strangers); Purchaser, 1626; removed to Duxbury, c.1632; agent at trading post on Connecticut River, 1635-36; removed to New London, Conn., 1649, founding trading post by Thames River on present site of Groton; deputy to Conn. General Court, 1650, 1655, 1658; 8 children; 2 oldest sons returned to England, c.1656, and Brewster seriously contemplated going with them.

Cushman, Robert (1578-1625)— wool comber, of Canterbury
"their right hand with their freinds, ye adventurers"
Married, Canterbury, 1606, to Sarah Reder; deacon, c.1609-1625; married, Leyden, 1617, to Mrs. Mary (Clarke) Singleton, widow of Canterbury shoemaker; negotiations in London for removal to New World, 1617-20; sailed on *Speedwell*, 1620, but abandoned voyage when vessel put back 3rd time; sermonized on "Danger of Self-Love" soon after arrival of *Fortune;* returning to England to compose quarrel about amended articles of agreement, captured by French pirates; planning to settle in colony,

died suddenly, London, 1625, probably of plague.

Thomas (1607-1691)
"very studious & sollicitous for the peace & prosperity of the church, & to prevent & heale all breaches"
Left with Bradford during father's absence and adopted by him after latter's death; married, Plymouth, c.1636, to Mary Allerton (see *Mayflower* Saints); Brewster's successor as ruling elder, 1649-91; 7 children.

De la Noye, Philippe (Delano) (1602-c.1680)
"born of French parents, . . . and proving himself to be come of such parents as were in full communion with the French churches, was hereupon admitted by the Church of Plymouth"
Removed to Duxbury, c.1632; married, 1634, to Esther Dewbury; removed to Bridgewater, 1649; married, 1657, to Mrs. Mary (Pontus) Glass (see Straggling Saints); 9 children.

*Morton, Thomas ( )—of Harworth, Notts; brother of George Morton (see *Anne* Saints)
Died or left colony before 1627.

Nicholas, Austin ( )
Died or left colony before 1627.

Symonson, Moses (Simmons) ( )
"a child of one that was in communion with the Dutch church at Leyden"
Removed to Duxbury, c.1632; married ———— ————; 2 children.

Wright, William (-1633)
Purchaser, 1626.

————, Mrs. Priscilla (Carpenter) (1597-1689)—sister of Mrs. Juliana Morton (see *Anne* Saints)

Married, Leyden, 1619; died, Duxbury; 1 child.

B. STRANGERS
(17 men, 2 women, 4 children)

Adams, John (-1633)
Married, c.1625, to Ellen Newton (see *Anne* Strangers); Purchaser, 1626; 3 children.

Beale, William ( )
Died or left colony before 1627.

Briggs, Clement (-1649)—of Southwark, fellmonger
Married Joan Allen, c.1630, and removed to Dorchester; 5 children.

Cannon, John ( )
Died or left colony before 1627.

Conner, William ( )
Died or left colony before 1627.

Deane, Stephen (-c.1636)—of Southwark, miller
Married Elizabeth Ring; Purchaser, 1626; granted leave to build Plymouth's first mill, but died before work began; 3 children.

Flavell, Thomas ( )—of London
Died or left colony before 1627.
——— (son) ( )
Died or left colony before 1627.

Ford, Mrs. Martha (———) (-c. 1626)—probably of London
"delivered of a sonne the first night she landed, & both are doing very well"
Widow of leather dresser, of Southwark, who evidently died at sea; married, 1623, to Peter Browne (see *Mayflower* Strangers); 5 children.
William ( )
Returned to England but came back to settle at Duxbury, c.1632; married Ann ———; 4 children.
Martha ( )

John (1621-1693)
Married Hannah ———; died Marshfield.

Hicks, Robert (-1648)—of Southwark, dealer in hides
Purchaser, 1626 (for family, see *Anne* Strangers).

Hilton, William (c.1600-1675)—vintner, of Northwich, Cheshire
Left colony at time of Lyford-Oldham troubles, 1624, going to New Hampshire and there founding Dover with brother Edward, fishmonger, of London; removed to York, Maine, c.1648, and died there (for family, see *Anne* Strangers).

Morgan, Benedict ( )—of London, mariner
Died or left colony before 1627.

Palmer, William (-1638)—of London, nailer
Purchaser, 1626; removed to Duxbury, c.1632; 3 children (for wife, see *Anne* Strangers).
William (-c.1661)
Married, Scituate, 1633, to Elizabeth Hodgkins; removed to Yarmouth, c.1640; to Dartmouth, 1652; to Newton, Rhode Island, 1656, where he died a member of Baptist church.

Pitt, William ( )—of London, armorer
Died or left colony before 1627.

Prence, Thomas (1600-1673)—carriage maker, of London
"a terrour to evill-doers"
Married, 1624, to Patience Brewster (see *Anne* Saints); 5 children; Purchaser, 1626; Undertaker, 1627-41; married, 1635, to Mary Collier (see Merchant Adventurers); 4 children; member of General Court, 1633-73; governor, 1634, 1638, 1657-73; re-

moved to Eastham, 1644; opposes religious toleration, 1646; leader in Quaker and Baptist persecutions, 1657; married, Eastham, 1662, to Mrs. Apphia (——) Freeman; induced to move back to Plymouth by gift of large farm at "Plain Dealing"; married Mrs. Mary (——) Howes, c.1667.

Stacey, Hugh (   )
Removed to Dedham, then Salem, finally returning to England.

Steward, James (   )
Died or left colony before 1627.

Tench, William (   )
Died or left colony before 1627.

Winslow, John (1597-1674)—of Droitwich, Worcestershire; Edward Winslow's second brother
Married, Plymouth, c.1627, to Mary Chilton (see *Mayflower* Strangers); agent at Kennebec, 1651-54; removed to Boston, 1655, and died there; 10 children, daughter Sarah marrying Myles Standish, Jr.

III. SHALLOP FROM SPARROW, arriving early in 1622, bringing seven men who joined those sent out later by Weston on *Charity* and *Swan* and went north with them to found Wessagusset.

Pratt, Phineas (1593-1680)—probably of London
Fled Wessagusset to Plymouth before Standish's liquidation of Weston's "disorderly" colony, 1623; Purchaser, 1626; married, Plymouth, 1630, to Mary Priest (see *Anne* Saints); removed to Mass., c.1650; died Charlestown.

IV. ANNE—of London (140 tons); William Peirce, master; and LIT-

TLE JAMES (44 tons); John Bridges, master; arriving July-August, 1623, with "about 93 persons for ye generall, some of them being very usefull persons, . . . and some were so bad as they were faine to be at charge to send them home againe ye next year."

A. SAINTS
(5 men, 9 women, 18 children)
*Brewster, Patience (1600-1634)— ruling elder's oldest daughter
Amsterdam, 1608-09; Leyden, 1609-23, probably living with Robinsons, 1620-23; married, 1624, to Thomas Prence (see *Fortune* Strangers); died, Plymouth, in smallpox epidemic; 5 children.

*Brewster, Fear (1606-1634)—born on eve of flight from Scrooby
Amsterdam, 1608-09; Leyden, 1609-23; married, 1626, to Isaac Allerton (see *Mayflower* Saints); died, Plymouth, of smallpox; 1 child, Isaac Allerton, Jr., first Plymouth student at Harvard, who later migrated to Virginia.

Cooke, Mrs. Hester (Mayhieu) (c. 1592-1675)—Walloon, wife of Francis Cooke (see *Mayflower* Saints)
Married, Leyden, c.1613.
  Jane (c.1615-1666)
  Married, Plymouth, c.1638, to Experience Mitchell (see below); died at Bridgewater; 7 children.
  Hester (c.1616-c.1666)
  Married, Plymouth, 1644, to Richard, son of William Wright (see *Fortune* Saints); 3 children.
  Jacob (1618-1675)
  Married, 1646, to Damaris Hopkins; 1669, to Mrs. Elizabeth (Lettice) Shurtleff; 6 children.

Godbertson, Godbert (Cuthbert Cuthbertson) (c.1590-1633)—Walloon; hat maker, of Leyden
Married, Leyden, 1617, to Elizabeth Kendall; Purchaser, 1626; died, Plymouth, "of infectious fever."

———, Mrs. Sarah (Allerton) (c. 1590-1633)—of London; widow of John Vincent, of London, and Degory Priest (see *Mayflower* Saints)
Married, Leyden, 1621; 5 children by her husband's two and her own three marriages.

   Mary Priest ( )
   Married, Plymouth, 1630, to Phineas Pratt (see *Sparrow* above).

   Sarah Priest ( )
   Married John Coombs.

   Samuel Godbertson ( )
   Removed to Dartmouth, c.1652.

———

Fuller, Mrs. Bridget (Lee) (- 1664)—3rd wife of Deacon Samuel Fuller (see *Mayflower* Saints)
Married, Leyden, 1617; opened small private school, 1634; donated lot for parsonage on the Street, 1663; 2 children.

Jenney, John (c.1594-1644)—of Norwich, brewery worker
Granted "libertie to erect a mill for grinding and beating of corne upon the brook at Plimoth," 1636; asst. governor, 1637-40.

———, Mrs. Sarah (Carey) (- c.1655)—of "Moncksoon"
Married, Leyden, 1614; 5 children.

   Samuel (-c.1690)
   Removed to Dartmouth, c.1652; married Ann Lettice; 2 children.

   Abigail ( )
   Married Henry Wood.

Sarah ( )

Mitchell, Experience (1609-1689) Purchaser, 1626; married, c.1628, to Jane Cooke (see above); removed to Bridgewater, 1649, and died there; 7 children.

*Morton, George (1585-1624)—merchant, of well-to-do Roman Catholic family of Harworth, near Scrooby
"a pious gracious servante of God"
As "G. Mourt," signed Bradford and Winslow's *Relation* (1622); organized *Anne* and *Little James* company; died impoverished not long after landing, his brother-in-law Bradford providing for his family.

———, Mrs. Juliana (Carpenter) (1584-1665)—of Wrington, near Bath, Somersetshire; daughter of Alexander Carpenter, member of Ancient Brethren
Amsterdam, -1609; married, Leyden, 1612; married, Plymouth, 1627, to Menassah Kempton (see Strangers below).

   Nathaniel (1616-1685)
   "very religiously tender & carefull in his observations of the Sabbath day & of speaking truth"
   Brought up by uncles Bradford and Fuller, becoming former's clerk and agent, 1634; married Lydia Cooper, 1635; secretary of Old Colony, 1647-85; town clerk, 1674-79; *New England's Memorial*, 1669; secretary of Pilgrim church, copying many passages of Bradford's *Of Plimoth Plantation* into church records; granted many tracts of land for services and died one of wealthiest men in colony; 8 children.

   Patience (1616-1691)
   Married, 1634, to John Faunce

(see Strangers below); 9 children, including Ruling Elder Thomas Faunce (see Appendix B).

John (1616-1673)
Married, c.1636, to —— Lettice; removed to Middleborough, c. 1670; 8 children.

Sarah (1618-1694)
Married, 1644, to George Bonum, or Bonham; 4 children.

Ephraim (1623-1693)
Born on voyage; married, 1644, to Ann Cooper; deacon, 1669-93; 8 children.

Morton, Thomas, Jr. (   )—young son of Thomas Morton (see *Fortune* Saints)
Died or left colony before 1627.

Southworth, Mrs. Alice (Carpenter) (c.1590-1670)—of Wrington, near Bath, Somersetshire; sister of Mrs. Juliana Morton (see above)
"a godlie matron"
Amsterdam,   -1609; married, Leyden, c.1610, to Edward Southworth of Sturton le Steeple, silk worker; 2 children, Constant and Thomas Southworth (see Straggling Saints); married, Plymouth, 1624, to William Bradford; 3 children by second marriage—William (see Appendix B), Mercy, and Joseph.

Tracy, Stephen (   )—say maker
Purchaser, 1626; removed to Dartmouth, c.1652; returned to England, 1654.

——, Mrs. Tryphosa (Lee) (   )
Married, Leyden, 1620; 5 children.

Sarah (1621-   )
Married, Duxbury, 1638, to George Partridge, brother of local pastor; 6 children.

B. STRANGERS

(23 men, 18 women, 17 children)

——, Barbara (-c.1650)
Married, 1623, to Captain Standish; nothing is known of her antecedents, though by family tradition she was younger sister of Rose, Standish's 1st wife; 5 children.

Annable, Anthony (-c.1655)— of Cambridge
Purchaser, 1626; removed to Scituate, c.1632; to Barnstable, 1639; 3 wives and 5 children.

——, Mrs. Jane (Momford) (-1643)
Married, Cambridge, 1619.

Sarah (c.1620-   )
Married, 1638, to Henry Ewell.

Hannah (c.1622-   )
Married, 1645, to Thomas Freeman.

Bangs, Edward (c.1592-1678)— shipwright, of Panfield, Essex
Purchaser, 1626; married, c.1627, to Lydia Hicks (see below); removed to Eastham, 1644; 10 children.

Bartlett, Robert (1603-1676)— cooper
Married, c.1627, to Mary Warren (see below); 8 children.

Becket, Mary (c.1605-1676)
Married, c.1627, to George Soule (see *Mayflower* Servants); died, Duxbury; 7 children.

Burcher, Edward (   )—of Southwark
——, Mrs. —— (——) (   )
Burchers died or left colony before 1627.

Clarke, Thomas (1599-1697)—carpenter
Married, c.1630, to Susanna Ring; to Alice Nichols, 1664; 6 children; grave probably oldest on Burial Hill.

Conant, Christopher (c.1596-   )
  —of London, grocer; brother of
  Roger Conant (see below)
Left colony at time of Lyford-Old-
ham troubles, 1624, withdrawing to
Nantasket (Hull).

Conant, Roger (c.1592-1679)—of
  London, salter
"a pious, sober, and prudent gentleman"
One of those who came "on their
perticuler" with Oldham (see below); withdrew to Nantasket (Hull)
with Oldham, 1624; governor of
Pilgrims' rival settlement on Cape
Ann, 1625; founded Naumkeag
(Salem), 1626; supplanted as governor by John Endecott, 1628; withdrew to found Beverly, 1636; son
and namesake married, 1644, Elizabeth, daughter of Thomas Weston,
merchant adventurer.

———, Mrs. Sarah (Horton) (c.
  1600-c.1642)
Married, London, 1618; 9 children.
  Caleb (c.1620-   )
  Returned to England, c.1644, and
  died there.

Dix, Anthony (-1638)
Left colony before 1627, probably
in Lyford-Oldham exodus, 1624;
shipmaster, Charlestown, c.1630;
drowned in shipwreck off Cape Cod,
1638.

———, Mrs. Tabitha (———)
  (   )
Married, c.1640, to Nathaniel Pit-
man.

Faunce, John (c.1610-1687)—probably of Purleigh, Essex
Married, 1634, to Patience Morton
(see Saints above); 9 children, including Ruling Elder Thomas Faunce
(see Appendix B).

Flavell, Mrs. Elizabeth (———)
  (   )—wife of Thomas Flavell
  (see Fortune Strangers)
Died or left colony before 1627.

Flood, Edmund (   )
Died or left colony before 1627.

Heard, Thomas (   )
Died or left colony before 1627.

Hicks, Mrs. Margaret (Morgan)
  (   )—wife of Robert Hicks
  (see Fortune Strangers)
Married, Southwark, c.1606; 4 chil-
dren.
  Lydia (c.1608-   )
  Married, c.1627, to Edward Bangs
  (see above); 10 children.
  Phebe (c.1610-   )
  Married, c.1635, to George Wat-
  son; 2 children.
  Samuel (c.1615-c.1675)
  Removed to Eastham, 1644; mar-
  ried, 1645, to Lydia, daughter of
  Deacon John Doane; removed to
  Barnstable, c.1650; to Dartmouth,
  c.1670; 2 children.

Hilton, Mrs. Mary (———) (c.1600-
)—wife of William Hilton
  (see Fortune Strangers)
Left colony with family, 1624; 5
children, one born at Plymouth, its
baptism by Anglican rite precipi-
tating Lyford-Oldham rumpus.
  William (c.1618-   )
  Removed from Dover, N. H., to
  Newbury, Mass., c.1648; to
  Charlestown, c.1667; twice mar-
  ried; 10 children.
  Mary (c.1620-   )

Holman, Edward (   )—of Clap-
  ham, Surrey
Returned to England, coming back
in 1632; removed to Dartmouth,
1652.

Kempton, Menassah (c.1600-1663)
—of Colchester, Essex
Purchaser, 1626; married, 1627, to
Mrs. Juliana Morton (see Saints
above); removed to Dartmouth,
1652; no children.

Newton, Ellen (1598-1681)
Married, Plymouth, c.1625, to John
Adams (see *Fortune* Strangers);
3 children; married, 1634, to Ken-
elm Winslow (see 2nd *Mayflower*
Strangers); 4 children.

Oldham, John (-1636)—probably of Lancaster
"a mad jack in his mood"
Organized group to come not as partners in settlement, but "on their
perticular" (see Oldham's Company
below); expelled with Reverend Lyford for trying to establish Anglican
rite and incite insurrection, 1624,
retiring to Nantasket (Hull); returned and again driven out "with a
bob upon the bumme," 1625; trading agent of group which seized Pilgrims' fishing stage on Cape Ann,
1625, later making peace with
Saints; Thomas Morton of Merry
Mount sent to England in his charge,
1628; settled Watertown, Mass., 1630,
and grew rich in Indian and coastal
trade; representative in Mass. General Court, 1632, 1634; overseer of
shot and powder for colony, 1633;
one of committee to consider problem raised when Asst. Governor
John Endecott cut red cross of St.
George out of English flag, 1635;
killed by Indians while on trading
expedition to Block Island, 1636, precipitating Pequot War.

———, Mrs. Lucretia (———)
( )
Lucretia (c.1606-)
Married, 1624, to Jonathan Brew-

ster (see *Fortune* Saints); 8 children.

Christian ( )

Oldham's Company—granted 10
acres in assignment of lands, 1623,
presumably one each for every
person in Oldham's family and
for the following:

Conant, Roger (see above)

Penn, Christian (see below)

———

———

———

Palmer, Mrs. Frances (———) ( )
—wife of William Palmer (see
Fortune Strangers)

Penn, Christian (c.1608-)—
one of those who came with Oldham "on their perticuler"
Married, c.1626, to Francis Eaton
(see *Mayflower* Strangers); 4 children; married, 1634, to Francis
Billington (see *Mayflower* Strangers); died Yarmouth; 9 children
by 2nd marriage.

Pratt, Joshua (-c.1656)—brother of Phineas Pratt, who came to
Plymouth from Wessagusset
Removed to Dartmouth, 1652; married Bathsheba ———; 3 children.

Rande, James ( )—of Southwark
Died or left colony before 1627.

Ratcliffe, Robert ( )
———, Mrs. ——— (———) ( )
Ratcliffes died or left colony before
1627.

Snow, Nicholas (c.1605-1677)—of
Hoxton, Middlesex
Married, c.1626, to Constance Hopkins (see *Mayflower* Strangers); removed to Eastham, 1644; town clerk,
1646-62; 11 children.

Sprague, Francis (c.1600-1676)
Licensed to "keepe a victualling on the Duxburrow side," 1638; ran tavern till 1669, when succeeded by son John.

————, Mrs. Anna (————) (c.1602-c.1660)
Four children; died Duxbury.

Mercy (   )
Married William Tubbs.

Tilden, Thomas (   )—of London
Left colony before 1627, probably returning to England.

————, Mrs. ———— (————) (   )
———— (child) (   )

Wallen, Ralph (   )—of London

————, Mrs. Joyce (————) (   )

Warren, Mrs. Elizabeth (March) (c.1583-1673)—wife of Richard Warren (see *Mayflower* Strangers)
Married, London, c.1605; 7 children.

Mary (c.1608-1680)
Married, c.1627, to Robert Bartlett (see Strangers above); 8 children.

Ann (c.1612-   )
Married, 1633, to Thomas Little; 8 children.

Sarah (c.1614-c.1676)
Married, 1634, to John Cooke (see *Mayflower* Saints); 5 children.

Elizabeth (c.1616-1670)
Married, 1636, to Richard Church; 12 children, including Benjamin Church, Plymouth's captain-general in King Philip's War.

Abigail (c.1618-   )
Married, 1639, to Anthony Snow; 6 children.

C. SERVANTS
(1 man, 2 unidentified)
Brewster's —
Long, Robert (   )

Captain Peirce's —
————
————

V. MAYFLOWER (not the original Pilgrim ship); William Peirce, master; out of London, March, 1629; arriving Salem, May 15th, with many Puritans for Bay colony and a few passengers for Plymouth.

A. SAINTS
(3 men, 2 women, 4 children)
Blossom, Thomas (-1633)—of Cambridge
"a holy man & experienced sainct"
Shipped on *Speedwell*, 1620, turning back with Cushman, discouraged by mishaps; deacon, 1629-33.

————, Mrs. Ann (Elson, or Alston) (   )—of Cambridge
Accompanied husband on *Speedwell;* married, 1633, to Henry Rowley.

Thomas, Jr. (   )
Married, 1645, to Sarah Ewer of Charlestown; 2 children.

Elizabeth (   )
Married, 1637, to Edward Fitz-Randolph.

Masterson, Richard (c.1590-1633) —of Sandwich, wool carder
"a second Stephen"
Citizen, Leyden, 1612; deacon, 1629-33.

————, Mrs. Mary (Goodall) (c.1600-c.1650)—of Leicester
Married, Leyden, 1619; married, Plymouth, 1634, to Pastor Ralph Smith (see Appendix B); died Boston.

Nathaniel (c.1620-   )
Removed to Salem, later to Boston, c.1660, being sheriff there, 1665.

Sarah (c.1622-   )
Married, c.1640, to Henry Atwood (subsequently Wood).

Willet, Thomas (c.1610-1674)—
born, Leyden, son of Thomas Willet, of Yarmouth, Norfolk
"an honest yonge man"
Agent at Kennebec, 1629-34; agent
at trading post on Penobscot, 1635;
married, Plymouth, 1636, to Mary
Browne (see Straggling Saints below); at New Amsterdam, 1650, acting as agent for Peter Stuyvesant;
asst. governor, 1651-64; in command
of company on expedition against
Dutch along Hudson River, becoming first English mayor of New York
City, 1664-67; died Swansea; 12
children.

B. STRANGERS
(1 man)

Winslow, Kenelm (1599-1672)—
carpenter and cabinet maker, of
Droitwich, Worcestershire; brother of Edward Winslow (see *Mayflower* Saints)
Married, 1634, to Mrs. Ellen (Newton) Adams (see *Anne* Strangers);
official coffin maker; designer and
builder of only fine furniture in early
colony, many pieces being preserved
in Metropolitan and other museums;
removed to Marshfield, 1641; encouraged settlement of Yarmouth
and other Cape Cod towns; jailed 4
weeks, 1646, "for opprobrious words
against the church of Marshfield,
saying they were all lyars, &c." Died,
Salem; 4 children.

VI. TALBOT—of London; Thomas
Beecher, master; out of London, mid-
May, 1629; arriving Salem, July

29th, with company of servants for
Plymouth, "being 35 persons."
None of this group can be identified.

VII. HANDMAID—of London;
out of London, mid-August, 1630;
arriving Plymouth, Oct. 29th, with
some sixty passengers, chiefly from
Leyden, "of ye weakest & poorest
sort."
Nor can any of this group be identified.

VIII. STRAGGLING SAINTS
(6 men, 3 women, 2 children)

Bradford, John (c.1615-1678)—
born, Leyden, only child of William and Dorothy (May) Bradford (see *Mayflower* Saints)
Arrived, c.1627; married, c.1640, to
Martha Bourne; removed to Duxbury, 1645; to Marshfield, 1653; to
Norwich, Conn., 1660; no children.

Browne, John (-1662)—broth-
er of Peter Browne (see *Mayflower*
Strangers)
Arrived and settled Duxbury, 1632;
asst. governor, 1636-55; removed to
Taunton, 1643; commissioner to
New England Confederacy, 1644-
55; died Rehoboth.

——, Mrs. Dorothy (——)
(-1674)
Died Swansea; 4 children.

Mary (c.1616-c.1670)
Married, 1636, to Thomas Willet
(see 2nd *Mayflower* Saints); 12
children.

Carpenter, Mary (1577-1667)—sister of Mrs. Alice (Carpenter)
Southworth (see *Anne* Saints)
"a godlie old maid, never married"
Amsterdam, c.1600-09; Leyden, 1609-

c.1635; living in England, 1646, when sent for by William and Alice Bradford, arriving Plymouth, c.1647.

Pontus, William (c.1583-c.1653)— of Dover, fustian maker
Arrived, Plymouth, c.1633, settling along Eel River several miles south of town.

————, Mrs. Wybra (Hanson) (c. 1590-   )—perhaps of Austerfield
Married, Leyden, 1610; 2 children.
  Mary (c.1612-   )
  Married, Plymouth, 1644, to William Glass; married, Duxbury, 1657, to Philip Delano (see *Fortune* Saints); 4 children.

  Hannah (c.1614-1690)
  Married, 1644, to John Churchill; to Giles Rickard, 1669.

Robinson, Isaac (c.1610-1704)— born, Leyden, son of John and Bridget Robinson, only one of pastor's family to come to New World
Arrived, Scituate, c.1632; married, 1636, to Margaret Hanford, niece of Timothy Hatherly (see Merchant Adventurers below); removed to Barnstable, 1639; married, c.1650, to ———— ————; disenfranchised for opposing Quaker and Baptist persecutions, 1659-72; licensed to keep tavern at Succanesett (Falmouth), 1665; removed to Tisbury, Martha's Vineyard, 1673; returned to Barnstable, 1701, and died there; 10 children.

Southworth, Constant (c.1615-1679) —born, Leyden, son of Alice (Carpenter) Southworth (see *Anne* Saints)
Arrived, Plymouth, c.1628; married, 1637, to Elizabeth Collier (see Merchant Adventurers below); treasurer of colony, 1659-79; asst. governor, 1670-78; died, Duxbury, "of feavor & jaundice"; 8 children.

Southworth, Thomas (c.1616-1669) —born, Leyden, brother of Constant (see above)
"rarely Indowed both in Sacred and Civill Respects"
Arrived, Plymouth, c.1628; married, c.1637, to Elizabeth, daughter of Pastor Reyner (see Appendix B); agent at Kennebec, 1651-54, representing stepfather Bradford's interests; asst. governor, 1652-53, 1657-69; commissioner to New England Confederacy, 1659-61, 1664, 1667-69; 1 child.

IX. MERCHANT ADVENTURERS
(3 men, 1 woman, 5 children)
Collier, William (c.1585-1670)—of London, brewer
"lived a godly and holy life until old age"
Arrived 1633; asst. governor, 1634-37, 1639-51, 1654-65; commissioner to New England Confederacy, 1643; took liberal side in attempt to establish religious toleration, 1646.

————, Mrs. Jane (————) (c.1590-   )—presumably of London
  Rebecca (c.1610-1698)
  Married father's apprentice, Job Cole.

  Sarah (c.1612-1691)
  Married, 1634, to Love Brewster (see *Mayflower* Saints); married, c.1652, to Richard Parks of Cambridge, and removed there; 4 children.

  Mary (c.1614-c.1662)
  Married, 1636, to Thomas Prence

(see *Fortune* Strangers); died, Eastham; 5 children.

Elizabeth (c.1616-   )
Married, 1637, to Constant Southworth (see Straggling Saints); 8 children.

Hatherly, Timothy (-1666)—
of Southwark, felt maker
Came on *Anne,* 1623, returning to London when house burned down; settled at Scituate, 1632; married, 1642, to Mrs. Lydia (——) Tilden; asst. governor, 1636-57; deprived of office and disenfranchised for opposing Quaker and Baptist persecutions, 1658; died Scituate; no children.

Thomas, William (c.1573-1651)—
of Yarmouth, Norfolk; merchant "a well-approved and well-grounded Christian"
Arrived, 1637, settling at Marshfield; asst. governor, 1642-44, 1647-50; 1 son.

Nathaniel (c.1608-   )

SUMMARY

		SAINTS	STRAN-GERS	HIRED HANDS	SERV-ANTS	UNIDEN-TIFIED	TOTAL	SUM-MARY
MAYFLOWER	MEN	17	17	5	11		50	
	WOMEN	10	9		1		20	
	CHILDREN	14	14		6		34	
	(INCL. 2 BORN ON SHIP)	41	40	5	18		104	104
FORTUNE	MEN	9	17				26	
	WOMEN	2	2				4	
	CHILDREN	1	4				5	
		12	23				35	35
SHALLOP from SPARROW	MEN		1				1	
	WOMEN							
	CHILDREN		1				1	
			2				2	2
ANNE and LITTLE JAMES	MEN	5	23		3		31	
	WOMEN	9	18				27	
	CHILDREN	18	17				35	
		32	58		3		93	93
Second MAYFLOWER	MEN	3	1				4	
	WOMEN	2					2	
	CHILDREN	4					4	
		9	1				10	10
TALBOT	MEN				?			
	WOMEN				?			
	CHILDREN				?			
					35		35	35
HANDMAID	MEN					?		
	WOMEN					?		
	CHILDREN					?		
						60	60	60
Straggling Saints	MEN	6					6	
	WOMEN	3					3	
	CHILDREN	2					2	
		11					11	11
Merchant Adventurers	MEN		3				3	
	WOMEN		1				1	
	CHILDREN		5				5	
			9				9	9
Totals		105*	133	5	56	60		359

* Of these, only nine Saints came from Scrooby, and four were children at the time.

Appendix B

OFFICERS OF
THE OLD COLONY
AND OF THE
PILGRIM CHURCH

Biographical notes are given only for the more important of those not numbered in the Pilgrim Company (Appendix A).

I. OFFICERS OF THE OLD COLONY—

A. GOVERNORS

Carver, John, 1620-21

Bradford, William, 1621-32, 1635, 1637, 1639-43, 1645-57

Winslow, Edward, 1633, 1636, 1644

Prence, Thomas, 1634, 1638, 1657-73

Winslow, Josiah, 1673-80

"a true picture of wisdome, courage, and generosity"

Born, Plymouth, 1629, oldest son of Edward Winslow and 2nd wife, Mrs. Susanna (Fuller) White (see *Mayflower* Saints, Appendix A); student at Harvard College, departing without taking degree to join father in England, c.1650; asst. governor (see below); married, Boston, 1657, to Penelope Pelham, daughter of

Herbert Pelham, asst. governor of Bay colony and treasurer of Harvard; commissioner to New England Confederacy, 1658-80; Standish's successor as commander-in-chief of Pilgrim army, 1659; established Plymouth's 1st public school, 1674; commander-in-chief of United Colonies' forces during early phases of King Philip's War, relinquishing command because of ill health, 1676; sold Indian captives into slavery; died, Plymouth, 1680; 3 children, son Isaac marrying a Prence and siring Major General John Winslow who conducted rape of the Evangeline country.

Hinckley, Thomas, 1681-86, 1689-92

Born, Scituate, c.1635; asst. governor (see below); commissioner to New England Confederacy, 1667, 1673-

86; councillor under 1st royal governor, Sir Edmund Andros (see below), 1687-88; half-hearted in attempts to obtain royal charter, 1689-91, accepting Old Colony's absorption by Massachusetts without protest, 1692; died, Barnstable, 1706; 5 children.

Andros, Sir Edmund, 1687-89
First royal governor; driven out after Revolution of 1688 which unseated James II and brought in William and Mary.

B. DEPUTY GOVERNORS
[Post of deputy governor was created in 1680.]

Hinckley, Thomas, 1680 (see above)

Cudworth, James, 1681
Born, London, c.1605; arrived, 1632, settling at Scituate; commissioner to New England Confederacy, 1655, 1657, 1681; deprived of office and disenfranchised for opposing Quaker and Baptist persecutions, 1657; rights restored by Josiah Winslow, 1673; captain of Plymouth forces in early skirmishes of King Philip's War; sent to England to obtain royal charter, 1681, soon dying there of smallpox.

Bradford, William (younger), 1682-86, 1689-92
"eminente in grace"
Born, Plymouth, 1624, oldest son of Governor William Bradford by 2nd wife, Mrs. Alice (Carpenter) Southworth (see *Anne* Saints); asst. governor and treasurer (see below); as major, commanded two Plymouth companies in King Philip's War, being seriously wounded in massacre of trapped Narragansett in Great Swamp fight; commissioner to New England Confederacy, 1682-86; councillor under Sir Edmund Andros, 1687-89; twice married; 15 children.

C. ASSISTANT GOVERNORS
[There was only one assistant governor, 1621-23; number increased to five in 1624, to seven in 1633. With exception of Allerton, names of those who served before 1633 are unknown, but there is ground for reasonable conjecture—*(   ) indicates probable years of service before 1633. Names are listed chronologically in order of first year of election to office.]

Allerton, Isaac, 1621-c.1631

Warren, Richard, *(1624-28)

Standish, Myles, *(1624-32), 1633-35, 1637-41, 1645-56

Hopkins, Stephen, *(1624-32), 1633-36

Howland, John, *(1629-32), 1633-35

Alden, John, *(1631-32), 1633-39, 1651-86

Bradford, William, 1633-34, 1636, 1638, 1644

Doane, John, 1633

Gilson, William, 1633

Winslow, Edward, *(1624-32), 1634-35, 1637-38, 1641-43, 1645-47, 1650

Collier, William, 1634-37, 1639-51, 1654-65

Prence, William, 1635-37, 1639-57

Hatherly, Timothy, 1636-37, 1639-57

Browne, John, 1636, 1638-45, 1647-55

Jenney, John, 1637-40

Atwood, John, 1638

Freeman, Edmund, 1640-46
Born, Pulborough, Essex, c.1594; brother-in-law of John Beauchamp, merchant adventurer; arrived, 1635, and settled in Mass.; to Plymouth,

1637, and on to Cape Cod to found Sandwich with 10 others sharing desire "to worship God and make money"; died, Sandwich, 1682; 4 children.

Thomas, William, 1642-44, 1647-50

Willet, Thomas, 1651-65

Southworth, Thomas, 1652-53, 1657-69

Cudworth, James, 1656-57, 1674-80

Winslow, Josiah, 1657-72

Bradford, William (younger), 1658-81

Hinckley, Thomas, 1658-80

Brown, James, 1665-66, 1673-83

Freeman, John, 1666-86, 1689-92

Bacon, Nathaniel, 1667-73

Southworth, Constant, 1670-78

Smith, Daniel, 1679-86, 1689-92

Lothrop, Barnabas, 1681-86, 1689-92

Thacher, John, 1682-86, 1689-92

Walley, John, 1684-86, 1689-92

Cushing, John, 1689-92

D. SECRETARIES

[Until 1636 the governor was also secretary-treasurer of the colony.]

Souther, Nathaniel, 1636-44

Morton, Nathaniel, 1645-84

Clarke, Nathaniel, 1685-86
Son of Thomas Clarke (see *Anne* Strangers); became Sir Edmund Andros' "creature" and rewarded with grant of Clark's Island in harbor, 1687; shipped back to England with Andros to answer for "high crimes and misdemeanors," 1689; later returned to Plymouth, dying there 1717.

Sprague, Samuel, 1689-92
Grandson of Duxburrow tavernkeeper, Francis Sprague (see *Anne* Strangers).

E. TREASURERS

Paddy, William, 1636-51
"He, having a great temporal estate, was occasioned thereby to have abundance of business upon him, . . . a precious servante of Christ."

Skinner, of London, arrived 1635; deacon (see below); married, Plymouth, 1639, to Alice, daughter of Edmund Freeman (see Assistant Governors above); removed to Boston, 1651, dying there two years later; 5 children.

Standish, Myles, 1652-55

Alden, John, 1656-58

Southworth, Constant, 1659-79

Bradford, William (younger), 1680-86, 1689-92

II. OFFICERS OF THE PILGRIM CHURCH TO 1692

A. PASTORS

Smyth, John (at Gainsborough), 1606
"wanton of wit"

Born, c.1572, perhaps at Sturton le Steeple; Christ's College, Cambridge, c.1586-93, studying under Francis Johnson (see below); "lecturer," city of Lincoln, 1603-05; organized Gainsborough congregation, 1606; led migration to Amsterdam, 1607; baptized himself, 1608, to become Se-Baptist of history; renounced sebaptism, causing split in the Brethren of the Separation of the Second English Church at Amsterdam; spurned by local Mennonite church when he and few followers sought admission; sick and impoverished, died Amsterdam, 1612, in Jan Munter's Great Cake House; disciples absorbed by Dutch Mennonites, 1615.

Clyfton, Richard (at Scrooby), 1607-08
"a grave & reverend preacher"
Born, 1553, at Normanton, Derbyshire; rector at Babworth, 1586-1606; arrived, Amsterdam, in August, 1608; declined to join exodus to Leyden, 1609, remaining with Ancient Brethren; sided with Francis Johnson (see below) when church split, 1610, becoming "teacher" of "Franciscans" in place of Ainsworth (see Teachers below); published Ruling Elder Studley's "Answer" to critics, 1612, and immediately had to retract; died, Amsterdam, 1616; 3 sons, two living and dying at Amsterdam, third returning to England, 1653.

*[Johnson, Francis (at Amsterdam), 1608-09
"the most solemn in all his administrations"
Born, 1562, son of mayor of Richmond, Yorks.; student and fellow, Christ's College, Cambridge, 1579-89; twice jailed and deprived of fellowship for preaching militant Puritan sermons, 1589; became minister to English merchants at Middelburg, Holland, 1590; dramatic conversion to Separatism, 1591, resigning post at Middelburg, becoming pastor of Barrowist congregation in London; jailed by Archbishop Whitgift, 1592-96; married, 1594, to Thomasine Boys, well-to-do widow of Fleet Street haberdasher, precipitating Mil-

linery War; ordered transported to America, 1597, with brother George and Ruling Elder Daniel Studley (see below); escaped with companions to Amsterdam, organizing Ancient Brethren, alias Brethren of the Separation of the First English Church at Amsterdam; scandalous quarrel with Reverend Thomas White, 1604; doctrinal quarrel with John Smyth, former pupil, 1608; withdrawal of Scrooby exiles to Leyden, their pastor Clyfton deserting them for Ancient Brethren, 1609; split with "Teacher" Ainsworth, 1610, wrecking church; led migration of "Franciscans" to Emden, 1613; died, Amsterdam, 1618, being spared final catastrophe to "Franciscans" on way to Virginia, 1619.]

Robinson, John (at Leyden), 1609-25
"a man not easily to be matched for all things"
Born, Sturton le Steeple, c.1576; student, fellow, Reader in Greek, and finally Dean of Corpus Christi College, Cambridge, 1592-1603; married, 1604, to Bridget White of Sturton le Steeple, and resigned fellowship; assistant minister at St. Andrew's, Norwich, 1604, being deprived of office later in year for "branding the ceremonies"; persuaded to join Separation by John Smyth (see above); "teacher" of Scrooby congregation, 1607; organized exodus from Amsterdam to Leyden, 1609; entered Leyden Univ., 1615, as student of divinity; agreed to remain behind with majority of Green Gate congregation, 1620; blocked from coming to Plymouth by strong Puritan majority among merchant adventurers, 1621-24; died, Leyden, March 1, 1625, evidently of plague.

* Johnson was not a Pilgrim pastor, but the Scrooby exiles were members of his church for more than a year, sitting at his feet every Sabbath.

Lyford, John, 1624
"unsavorie salte"
Born, c.1574, and probably graduate of Magdalen College, Oxford; sent to Plymouth by dominant Puritan faction among merchant adventurers; baptized child of William Hilton (see *Fortune* Strangers) by Anglican rite, "with the sign of the cross on his forehead," precipitating fearful row, 1624; discovered writing critical letters to adventurers; tried and ordered banished; forgiven and restored to office, only to be discovered writing more critical letters; driven out, withdrew to Nantasket (Hull); with Oldham and Conant (see *Anne* Strangers) on Cape Ann, seized Pilgrims' fishing stage there, 1625; helped found Naumkeag (Salem), 1626, being pastor there till Endecott's arrival, 1628; withdrew to Virginia and died there, 1629.

Rogers, ——, 1628
Brought over by Allerton, "but they perceived, upon some triall, that he was crased in his braine"; sent back to England, 1629, and "grue quite distracted."

Smith, Ralph, 1629-36
"a dull man"
Born, Denton, Lancashire, c.1593; Christ's College, Cambridge, 1610-13; arrived with Puritan company on *Talbot,* 1629; forced from Salem at insistence of Bay colony adventurers, withdrawing to Nantasket (Hull), 1629; found there in miserable condition by Pilgrim party and brought to Plymouth, succeeding "crazy" Rogers; married, 1634, to Deacon Masterson's widow, Mary (Goodall) (see 2nd *Mayflower* Saints); virtually forced to resign pastorate, 1636; removed to Mass., c.1640; died, Boston, 1661.

Reyner, John, 1636-54
"an able, faithfull, laboriouse preacher"
Born, c.1605, at Gildersome, Yorks., about 35 miles from Scrooby district; Emmanuel College, Cambridge, 1622-25; arrived, Boston, c.1635; resigned because of doctrinal disputes, 1654, removing to Dover, N. H., where he died 1669.

Williams, James, 1659
"an able Gospell Preacher"
Departed for England after few months' trial of Plymouth.

Brimstead, William, 1665
"a well accomplished servante of Christ"
Harvard College, c.1651-55; accepted call to Marlborough, Mass., 1666, dying there 1701.

Cotton, John (younger), 1667-97
"a man of strong parts"
Born, 1640, son of famed John Cotton, pastor of First Church, Boston; schooled at Harvard; missionary among Indians on Martha's Vineyard, 1664-67; introduced catechizing, 1669, going about town "to inquire into the State of souls," noting "considerable revival"; attributed King Philip's War to impiety of youth; complained of "multiplying of ordinaries, or places of strong drinck," 1681; dismissed, 1697, for being on too familiar terms with one of women parishioners, or "female church-children," as he liked to call them; died, Charleston, S. Carolina, 1699.

B. TEACHERS

? (at Gainsborough), 1606

Robinson, John (at Scrooby), 1607-08

[Ainsworth, Henry (at Amsterdam), 1608-09

"taught well without tossing & turning the book"
Born, 1571, near Norwich, Norfolk; Caius College, Cambridge, c.1589-91, leaving without taking degree because of religious scruples; joined Barrowist congregation in London, 1592, and English Separatists at Amsterdam, c.1595; "teacher" of Ancient Brethren, 1597-1610; split with Pastor Francis Johnson because of latter's autocratic views, 1610, forming church of his own; published *Book of Psalmes,* 1612, used by Pilgrim church till 1692; died, Amsterdam, 1621.]

――――― (at Leyden), 1609-20
Green Gate congregation had no "teacher."

Williams, Roger (at Plymouth), c. 1631-34
"had the root of the matter in him"
Born, c.1603, son of well-to-do merchant tailor of London; Pembroke College, Cambridge, 1624-29; arrived, Boston, 1631, and declined pastorate of First Church because they were "unseparated" people; "teacher" at Salem, 1631, accepting call to Plymouth later in year; early mastered Indian language, often visiting them in their "smoky holes"; wrote tract denying English right to appropriate Indian lands, alarming Plymouth and Bay authorities; pastor at Salem, 1634-35, until sentenced to be banished; fled into wilderness, founding Providence, Rhode Island, 1636, as haven for those who believed in religious and political liberty; rejected all formal religious tenets and became Seeker, 1639; repelled Mass. encroachments and obtained royal charter for R. I., 1644; frequently mediated conflicts between Indians and authorities of Bay and Plymouth colonies, making last desperate effort to avert King Philip's War, 1675; died, 1683.

Norton, John, 1636
"his temper had a tincture of choler in it"
Born, 1606, at Bishop's Stortford, Hertfordshire; Peterhouse College, Cambridge, 1624-27; arrived, Boston, 1636, coming to Plymouth with Edward Winslow; ambitious for larger and richer congregation, removed to Mass., 1637; pastor at Ipswich, 1637-55; succeeded the great John Cotton as pastor of First Church, Boston, 1656; led persecution of Quakers and Baptists, crying for summary execution of all "heretics"; died, Boston, 1663.

Chauncy, Charles, 1638-41
"the larned Mr. Chancy"
Born, 1592, at Yardley-Bury, Herts; Trinity College, Cambridge, 1611-17; conflict with ecclesiastical authorities, 1629; jailed by Archbishop Laud for heretical opinions, 1634, later recanting; arrived Boston, 1638; parted ways with Plymouth congregation for insisting upon "dipping" in baptism and celebrating Lord's Supper in evening; pastor at Scituate, 1642-54; planning to return home to England, stopped in Boston when offered presidency of Harvard College if he would abandon notions about baptism and Lord's Supper; president of Harvard, 1654-1672; died, Cambridge, 1672.

C. RULING ELDERS
? (at Gainsborough), 1606
? (at Scrooby), 1607-08

[Studley, Daniel (at Amsterdam), 1608-09
"fitter for the stewes than to be an elder in any Christian society"

Elected elder of Barrowist congregation in London, 1591; jailed and sentenced to death, 1592, for smuggling Separatist manuscripts out of prison to be printed in Holland; sentence commuted and shipped to America, 1597; escaped with Francis Johnson to Amsterdam, being elected ruling elder of Ancient Brethren; charged with gross immorality by Reverend Thomas White, 1604, and again by Christopher Lawne, 1612; wrote "Answer" to critics, published by Clyfton, who immediately had to retract; finally expelled by "Franciscans," 1612.]

Brewster, William (at Leyden and Plymouth), 1609-43

Cushman, Thomas, 1649-91

Faunce, Thomas, 1699-1746
"aged & godlie"
Born, Plymouth, 1647, son of John Faunce (see *Fortune* Strangers, Appendix A) and Patience, daughter of George Morton (see *Anne* Saints); brought up in family of Bradford's stepson, Thomas Southworth (see Straggling Saints); deacon, 1686-99; story of Pilgrims' first landing on Plymouth Rock based upon tale related by Faunce in 1741, more than 120 years after event; died, Eel River, 1746, in 99th year, Plymouth's 3rd and last ruling elder.

D. DEACONS

? (at Gainsborough), 1606

? (at Scrooby), 1607-08

[Bowman, Christopher (at Amsterdam), 1608-09
"Judas, the Purse Bearer"
Born, London, c.1561; goldsmith, of West Smithfield; jailed, 1588-92, for petitioning Queen Elizabeth for right to liberty of conscience; elected deacon of Barrowist congregation, London, 1592; Amsterdam, c.1595-1618; died, 1619, on disastrous voyage of "Franciscans" to Virginia.]

Cushman, Robert (at Leyden), c. 1609-25

Fuller, Samuel (at Leyden and Plymouth), c. 1609-33

Carver, John (at Leyden and Plymouth), c.1617-21

Masterson, Richard, 1629-33

Blossom, Thomas, 1629-33

Doane, John, 1634-44

Paddy, William, c.1634-51

Cooke, John, c.1634-51

Finney, Robert, 1669-87

Morton, Ephraim, 1669-93

Faunce, Thomas, 1686-99

NOTES

CHAPTER 2

1. The tablet contains not only an error of omission but one of commission as well, and it might as well be corrected here as later, to avoid any confusion. Brewster died in 1643 and not in 1644, as has been commonly reported since the mistake was first made three centuries ago by Nathaniel Morton in copying a passage from Bradford's history into the Plymouth church records.

2. Skilled workers at the time received 1s. a day, which on the scale used here (roughly a ratio of 1:10) would be the present equivalent of a daily wage of $2.50, or $15 for a six-day week. More than a half century later, when labor at Plymouth was scarce and regarded as "excessive" in its demands, the Pilgrims forbad anyone paying workers more than 1s. a day ($2.50) with board, or 1s. 6d. ($3.75) without.

3. From a book of etiquette of the day, the scene being a typical country tavern as at Scrooby:

Traveler (to chambermaid)—My shee frinde, is my bed made?—is it good?

Jane (the chambermaid)—Yea, sir, it is a very good federbed; the scheetes be very cleane.

Traveler—Pull off my hosen and warme my bed; drawe the curtines

. . . My shee frinde, kisse me once and I shal sleape the better. I thank you, fayre mayden.

4. Henry Brewster had been vicar at Sutton-cum-Lound since 1565. In 1584 a James Brewster became master of the "hospital" (poor farm and old folks' home) at Bawtry, a mile above Scrooby, and in 1598 succeeded Henry Brewster as vicar at Sutton-cum-Lound. Though previous researchers failed to find any connection between the various Brewsters in and around Scrooby, the latest and most exhaustive student of the old local records (Walter H. Burgess, *John Robinson, Pastor of the Pilgrim Fathers.* London, 1920) is convinced that all were related, suggesting that James Brewster was young William's older brother. If so, it is curious that the Pilgrims' ruling elder never once alluded to the vicars of the neighboring hamlet.

Burgess also believes that a close connection existed between these Brewsters and those of Wrentham Hall, Suffolk, a prosperous family of landed gentry with strong Puritan leanings. One of its sons, Robert Brewster, enrolled at the University of Leyden in 1619. Cf. Burgess, pp. 80-1, pp. 338-40.

5. On one occasion Da Silva, the Spanish ambassador, accompanied

Elizabeth to St. Paul's to hear a sermon by Dean Nowell, "an ornament to the art of angling," according to Izaak Walton, for the good Dean spent a full tithe of his time at it. Noting the presence of the Queen and casting about for a subject sure to take her fancy, Nowell began to denounce the use of "idols," for Henry VIII had always risen to that bait.

"Leave that alone!" came a sharp command from the royal pew. Quite taken aback, the Dean stammered a few words and obviously misunderstanding the cause of the interruption, circled cautiously round and began fishing again in the same waters.

"To your text, Mr. Dean, to your text!" thundered the Queen. "Leave that! We have heard enough of that! —to your subject!"

And with that, Elizabeth swept out of the cathedral on the arm of Da Silva, who gleefully reported the incident to his masters at Madrid and Rome.

It may or may not be a *non-sequitur,* but the good Dean's nephew, Increase Nowell, migrated to New England to become an elder of the church at Boston.

CHAPTER 3

1. English schoolmen (Anglicans, for the most part) have belatedly recognized Browne's creative thinking and intellectual stature, usually with the gratuitous and obviously inaccurate remark that his contributions to religious thought and ecclesiastical theory were second only to those of Richard Hooker, the philosophic apologist of the old order, whose *Lawes of Ecclesiasticall Politie* began to appear in 1593. Browne spoke for the future, Hooker for the past and naturally took exception to the Holy Discipline, reflecting the feudal view.

"It may justly be feared," he wrote, "whether our English Nobility, when the matter came in trial, would contentedly suffer themselves to be always at the call and to stand to the sentence of a number of mean persons, assisted with the presence of their poor teacher, a man (as sometimes it happeneth) though better able to speak, yet little or no whit apter to judge than the rest."

The nobility and landed gentry, as a rule, certainly had no fear of "sentence" from the Anglican clergymen they placed in the church livings within their gift. A parson who did not know his place was soon removed.

2. Burgess (*John Robinson,* p. 81) suggests that she may have been Mary Wentworth of Scrooby, daughter of Thomas Wentworth, whom the older William Brewster had succeeded as bailiff-receiver of "Scrowbie Manor."

3. For the best account of Penry's exciting career, for the most plausible but not altogether convincing identification of the mysterious Martin Mar-prelate, see William Pierce's *John Penry* (London, 1923), which also contains an excellent bibliography on the more relevant aspects of Elizabethan England.

CHAPTER 4

1. Sabbatarianism, as we know it, was the brain-child of the English Puritans—"to their immortal honour," one of them remarked—for

the "divine authority of the Sabbath" was not recognized by Martin Luther, John Calvin, or any of the early reformers. Even that dour Scot, John Knox, merely noted the fact without comment when, on a visit to Geneva, he found his friend and master Calvin bowling on a Sunday.

The Puritans first attacked the time-honored way in which the English celebrated certain religious festivals, notably Whitsuntide, at which time the wardens of the parish brewed ale to be sold in the church to raise money for various purposes, as is now somewhat more sedately done by church suppers, bazaars, and pin-ball machines.

At these Whitsun-ales it was usual for the "wild-heads" of the parish, decked out in bright scarves and ribbons, their legs gartered with bells, riding hobby-horses and dragons, to dance into church and up the aisle, piping and playing, as the congregation climbed up on the pews to cheer and laugh at their antics.

Agitation against this sort of thing grew so rapidly that early in the next reign James I issued a proclamation known as the Book of Sports (1604). In this, to the great offense of the Puritans, the King declared that Englishmen were not to be "disturbed or discouraged from dancing, archery, leaping, vaulting, having May games, Whitsun-ales, Morrice dances, setting up May Poles, and other sports therewith used, or any other harmless recreations, on Sundays after divine service."

The Book of Sports was one of the first casualties of the Puritan revolution under Cromwell. In 1643 the House of Commons ordered it to be "forthwith burned by the hand of the Common Hangman in Cheapside and other usuall places."

2. The best account of Smyth, a restless and always interesting character, is found in Walter H. Burgess' *John Robinson* and in his *John Smith, the Sebaptist, . . . with fresh light upon the Pilgrim Fathers' Church* (London, 1911). These works have at last cleared up considerable confusion about the identity of Smyth, his antecedents, and the facts of his life.

3. As with Smyth, so in Robinson's early career there has long been a tangle. Here again, by painstaking and extensive search of old local records, Burgess (*supra*) has apparently unraveled the knot.

Interestingly, he suggests the possibility and offers much convincing evidence to support his conjecture that John Smyth, like Robinson, was born and brought up at Sturton le Steeple. Cf. *John Robinson*, pp. 409-17.

CHAPTER 5

1. Cf. F. J. Powicke, *Henry Barrow, the Separatist* (London, 1920).

Though able and imaginative, Barrow was a "hot brain" and often needlessly injured himself and his cause. Called before the Privy Council in 1588, he was asked if he knew the Bishop of London.

"I know him not as a bishop," he replied, "but as a wolf, a bloody persecutor, and an apostate," adding that the Archbishop of Canterbury was "a monster, a miserable compound, . . . neither ecclesiastical nor civil—even the second Beast that is spoken of in the Revelations."

"Thou art a fantastical fellow, I

perceive," remarked Burghley as he sent him back to jail. From prison Barrow wrote the great Lord Treasurer a letter framing several profound truths most eloquently:

"Deal tenderlie with tender consciences; we are yet persuaded that we should show ourselves disobedient & unthankfull to our Master except we hold fast this (our) cause. ... Why should our adversaries wish to persuade the civil magistrates to deal with us by the *sword* and not by the *Word,* by *prisons* and not by *persuasions?* As for dungeons, irons, close prison, torment, hunger, cold, want of means to maintain families —these *may* cause some to make shipwreck of a good conscience, or to lose their life, but *they are not fit ways to persuade honest men to any truth or dissuade them from errours."*

2. George entitled his work *A Discourse of some Troubles and Excommunications in the banished English Church at Amsterdam.* Unfortunately for the curious reader, this is a rare book, there being only three copies, so far as I know—one at Trinity College, Cambridge; another at Sion College, London; a third at the Library of Congress, Washington.

3. Lawne wrote a second book entitled *Brownisme Turned the Inside Outward, being a Parallel between the Profession and Practice of the Brownists' Religion* (London, 1613). For the literature of the doctrinal and other troubles at Amsterdam, cf. Edward Arber, *The Story of the Pilgrim Fathers, 1606-1623,* p. 112 et seq.

CHAPTER 6

1. The Saints did their distracted best to sing such verses as these:

And th'earth did shake and quake and styrred bee
grounds of the mount: & shook for wroth was hee
Smoke mounted, in his wrath, fyre did eat
out of his mouth; from it burned with heat.

Nor can anything much be said for the *Bay Psalm Book* (1640), later taken over by the Pilgrims from the Puritans of Massachusetts Bay. This was the latters' "improved" version of the 137th Psalm:

The rivers on of Babilon
there when we did sit downe:
Yea even then we mourned, when wee remembered Sion.
Our harpe wee did hang it amid, upon the willow tree,
Because there they that us away led in captivitee,
Requir'd of us a song, thus askt mirth: us waste who laid,
Sing us among a Sions song unto us then they said.

No wonder some of the Pilgrims and the Puritans got into trouble "for speaking contemptuously of singing psalms."

For students of American culture there is much of interest in Waldo Selden Pratt, *The Music of the Pilgrims* (Boston, 1921); Percy A. Scholes, *The Puritans and Music in England and New England* (Oxford, 1934); and S. Lothrop Thorndike, "Psalmodies of Plymouth and Massachusetts Bay" (Colonial Soc. Pub., I, pp. 228-38).

2. Though the birthplace of the Southworths has not been conclusively established, W. H. Burgess suggests the probability that they came from Sturton le Steeple, find-

ing an Edward Southworth there who was about Robinson's age. Jane Southworth, who fled Gainsborough with John Smyth, was doubtless a sister. The Carpenter family in which Edward found a wife (subsequently, the second Mrs. Bradford) had early joined the church at Amsterdam, coming from the West of England, probably with the Reverend Thomas White in 1604, so that the company at the Green Gate represented all of the warring groups among the Ancient Brethren.

3. A fascinating and scholarly account of Brewster's publishing activities appears in *The Pilgrim Press* by Rendel Harris and Stephen Jones (Cambridge, 1922).

For the varying list of titles ascribed to the Choir Alley Press, see Roland Usher, *The Pilgrims and Their History;* D. Plooij, *The Pilgrims,* etc.; H. M. Dexter, *England and Holland of the Pilgrims;* and Edward Arber, *Story of the Pilgrim Fathers.*

CHAPTER 7

1. A liberal in both his religious and political views, Sir Edwin Sandys was almost committed to the Tower in 1614 when, as a member of Parliament, he spoke his mind too freely about the abuse of the royal prerogative by James I. A leader of the "popular" party in the Virginia Company, Sir Edwin worked closely with the governor of the company, the Earl of Southampton, Shakespeare's patron.

CHAPTER 8

1. Clarke's first voyage had been made to Virginia in 1611. Captured by the Spanish, he was taken to Havana and later to Madrid. At this time he declared that he was "thirty-five years old and of the religion of his King," which was probably correct, though little more than a year later he changed his story and told his captors that he was forty and a Catholic, no doubt to please them with the hope of speeding his release. Finally freed in an exchange of prisoners, he returned to England in 1616.

2. This date is always given as November 9th, for so it appears in Mourt's *Relation*. But it would seem to be a slip of the pen. Either that, or another important date must be corrected.

In both Bradford and the *Relation* it is clearly stated that on the day the Pilgrims sighted land, they sailed down the coast till noon, then turned back, and "ye nexte day" tacked round the tip of Cape Cod and dropped anchor in what is now Provincetown harbor. Later that same day they drew up and signed the Mayflower Compact, which is dated "at Cap-Codd, ye 11 of November." Therefore the *Mayflower* must have made its landfall on the 10th, or the Compact is incorrectly dated.

CHAPTER 9

1. For the Bermuda troubles, see "William Strachey's Account" in J. H. Lefroy's *Memorials of the Bermudas* (i, pp. 22-54). Curiously, one of the leading mutineers was a certain John Want, who was, according to Strachey, "both seditious and a sectary in points of Religion . . . being suspected by our Minister for a Brownist," which suggests that some of the men's reluctance to go on to Virginia arose from a desire to be free of the Episcopal establishment.

The Bermuda incident has another interest. The story of the great storm, the shipwreck, the wonders and strange legends of the land as told by Strachey and in Silvester Jourdain's *A Discovery of the Barmudas, Otherwise called the Ile of Divels* (1610), was early passed along to Shakespeare by his friend and patron, the Earl of Southampton, an officer of the Virginia Company, and inspired one of his greatest plays, *The Tempest*.

2. The villain in the piece, if any, was probably Sir Ferdinando Gorges, enterprising leader of the Second (Plymouth) Virginia Company. A powerful noble of Somersetshire, related to Sir Walter Raleigh and Sir John Popham, the Lord Chief Justice, Gorges had been in earlier years a close friend and supporter of the young Earl of Essex, being involved in the latter's rebellion, withdrawing in time to betray the Earl and save his own neck.

In 1606, at the time its rival was preparing to found Jamestown, the Second Virginia Company had made an attempt to colonize New England, establishing a settlement on the Maine coast at the mouth of the Kennebec. The enterprise had failed, but the company was eager to try again.

Weston and the Leyden leaders had been in touch with Sir Ferdinando and his partners, as Bradford plainly intimates, saying that "aboute this time [early in 1620] they had heard, both by Mr. Weston and others, that sundrie Honourable Lords had obtained a large grante from ye king for ye more northerly parts of that countrie derived out of ye Virginia patente, and wholy secluded from their Governmente, and to be called by another name, viz., New-England. Unto which Mr. Weston, and ye cheefe of them, begane to incline it was best for them to goe, as for other reasons, so cheefly for ye hope of presente profite to be made by ye fishing that was found in that countrie."

But Gorges' company was not in a position to grant a patent, for it was being reorganized and had surrendered its charter, hoping to obtain a new and enlarged one from the King. On July 23, 1620, just a day or two before the *Speedwell* tied up at Southampton, the Solicitor General was instructed by royal warrant to prepare such a charter for His Majesty's signature. But the new charter of the company, renamed the Council for New England, did not pass the seals till November 3rd, two months after the *Mayflower* had sailed.

For the Pilgrims to have waited to obtain a patent from the Council would have been fatal. Under the circumstances there would seem to have been an understanding between Sir Ferdinando and his partners on the one hand, and the merchant adventurers and the Pilgrims on the other, that the emigrants would settle in New England, both sides agreeing that legal formalities could be straightened out later without difficulty, as indeed proved to be the case. And to avoid any embarrassing questions or the possibility of further dangerous delay, the Pilgrims pretended to be bound elsewhere.

This is not to say, however, that the change of plan was known to any but a few of the leaders on the *Mayflower*. Most of the Pilgrims were probably left completely in the dark on this, as on so many other vital matters, so that their surprise was genuine when they unexpectedly found themselves so far from their announced destination.

The "deangerous shoulds and roring breakers" that allegedly caused the *Mayflower* to turn back sound more like a phrase coined by Bradford than an objection to proceeding advanced by Captain Jones, a hardy and experienced old salt, who had braved the most tempestuous waters, having been engaged for a time in that roughest of all seagoing enterprises, whaling in the Arctic off Greenland shores.

Sir Ferdinando Gorges confessedly had designs on New England and spent his life trying to acquire it as a vast feudal estate with himself as overlord, and more than once almost succeeded. There is reason to suspect that he had a hand in guiding the Pilgrims' steps here, anxious to have them blaze a trail that he might follow to his own profit. In later years, at all events, the Pilgrims repeatedly found themselves entangled in the machinations of Sir Ferdinando, who gave Plymouth several bad frights.

Still, in spite of his always devious schemes and greedy ambitions, Gorges deserves to be well remembered for doing more than any other individual to promote the early colonization of New England.

CHAPTER 10

1. English and French (Breton) fishermen had been frequenting this coast for years. In 1616 or 1617 a French ship had been cast away here in a storm, and the yellow-haired man and the child were probably

from that vessel. There had been other survivors, several of whom were found among the Indians on the mainland by Captain Thomas Dermer, one of Gorges' men, while prowling along this coast earlier in the year, about six months before the Pilgrims arrived. Dermer had taken the Frenchmen on board and carried them to Virginia.

The Pilgrims' wanderings about the Cape, and their first contacts with the Indians, appear in engrossing detail in Mourt's *Relation.*

CHAPTER 11

1. See any good encyclopedia—the *Britannica,* for example.

CHAPTER 12

1. James I was of the same opinion. In the Great Patent granted the Council for New England in 1620, he noted the "wonderful plague among the salvages," declaring that the "appointed time is come in which Almighty God, in his great goodness and bounty towards us [James] and our people, hath thought fit and determined, that these large and goodly territories . . . shall be possessed and enjoyed" by the English.

CHAPTER 13

1. The Pilgrims made their first acquaintance with the formidable Nauset and neighboring tribes on the Cape in the summer of this year when young John Billington, a boy of six or seven, wandered off into the woods one day and got lost. After a week or more of fruitless search the Pilgrims gave him up as dead, probably a victim of wolves, when word came from Massasoit that the boy had been found on the Cape, more than twenty

miles to the south, and was safe among the Indians there. The youngster had been out in the open "some five days, living on berries and what he could find." Profane they may have been, but the Billingtons were always resourceful, endowed with a Cockney sharpness of wit (see the characterization of them in the late Stephen Vincent Benét's magnificent unfinished epic, *Western Star,* with its many vivid scenes of early Plymouth and Jamestown).

A party was sent in the shallop to rescue the boy. The Pilgrims first put in at Cummaquid, near the shoulder of the Cape, and were warmly welcomed by Iyanough, the young and "courteous" local sachem. The boy was farther down the Cape, he told them, "yet since we were there, they desired us to come ashore and eat with them, which, as soon as our boat floated, we did."

Pushing on, they came to the country of the Nauset, accompanied by Iyanough and two of his braves, and sent Squanto to find Aspinet, the sachem of the tribe. "After sunset Aspinet came with a great train and brought the boy with him, one bearing him through the water . . . There he delivered us the boy, behung with beads, and made peace with us, we bestowing a knife on him and likewise on another that first entertained the boy and brought him thither."

On their way home the Pilgrims stopped again at Cummaquid. As eager as ever to please, Iyanough helped his men carry water to the boat, and "in the mean time, the women joined hand in hand, singing and dancing before the shallop, the men also shewing all the kindness they could, Iyanough himself taking a bracelet from about his neck and hanging it upon one of us."

Altogether, the Pilgrims were much impressed by the honest dealing and simple friendliness of the Cape tribes, a fact to keep in mind in reading the Pilgrim account of subsequent events.

2. A "pinese" was at once a warrior, a priest, and a statesman. Only the bravest and strongest in the tribes attained such status after long and arduous training in their youth, all being "men of great courage and wisdom, . . . of greatest stature and strength," said Winslow, "and such as will endure most hardness; and yet are more discreete, courteous, and humane in their carriages than any amongst them." They were under the special protection of the gods and could not be wounded in battle, the Indians believed, "by reason whereof one of them will chase almost a hundred men, for they account it death for whomsoever stand in their way."

3. In 1708 there was much lifting of eyebrows when Hannah Sturtevant, granddaughter of Edward Winslow, was married with benefit of clergy, the first instance of the kind in the colony. Marriages were not recorded in the church registers until 1760.

4. Deacon Cushman took his text from I Corinthians 10. 24: "Let no man seek his own, but every man another's wealth." Published at London in 1622, the sermon was addressed "to His Loving Friends, The Adventurers for New-England, Together with all well-willers and well-wishers thereunto." It has since gone through

many editions—the second at Boston in 1724, the third at Plymouth in 1785.

CHAPTER 14

1. The seaman William Trevore, one of the hired hands on the *Mayflower,* had returned home on the *Fortune* and was telling highly embroidered tales about the richness of the new land across the sea. At this time, too, Captain John Smith published his *New England's Trials* (London, 1622), setting forth the "successe of 80 Ships employed thither within these eight yeares, . . . with the present estate of that happie Plantation [Plymouth], begun but by 60 weake men in the year 1620." In this he quoted from letters sent from Plymouth on the *Mayflower* and the *Fortune,* each affirming the "healthfulnesse of the aire, the richnesse of the soile, the goodnes of the woods, the abundance of fruits, fish, fowle in their season."

2. For a recent and elaborate repetition of the pirate myth that had been decently buried years before, see Marquis James, *They Had Their Day* (1926). The facts about Christopher Jones were discovered in 1904 by M. R. G. Marsden, editor of *Select Pleas in the High Court of Admiralty,* who published his findings in the English Historical Review (Oct., 1904), with new facts also on the *Mayflower* (*infra,* Note 4, Chapter XVIII).

John Clarke, the *Mayflower's* first mate, survived his skipper only a year. In a petition to the First Virginia Company at this time he asked to be made a Free Brother of the company and have lands assigned to him for his services to the colony.

An assignment was made, and Clarke arrived in Virginia early in 1623, and died there a few months later.

3. Among the many monuments and memorials that clutter up the Pilgrim towns there is none to Squanto that I have ever seen or heard of. His name has been given to a short dilapidated street in Plymouth; a promontory above Quincy is known as Squantum; and that is all the honor that has been paid to one of the most talented and useful of the Saints.

CHAPTER 15

1. The names of those chosen to serve on this committee are not known. But Winslow undoubtedly was one, and Stephen Hopkins probably another.

2. Captain John Smith's army in Virginia had been almost equally small. "When I had ten men able to go abroad, our common wealth was very strong," Smith declared, boasting that "with such a number I ranged that unknown country 14 weeks; I had but 18 to subdue them all, with which great army I stayed six weekes before their greatest Kings' habitations . . ."

3. This charge was made by Thomas Morton of Merry Mount, an avowed and bitter enemy. But it cannot be airily dismissed, as has been the fashion, with the remark that Morton was an "immoral" character. The affair at Wessagusset and subsequent events elsewhere clearly reveal that a lively concern about the beaver trade was strongly operative among the Pilgrims' motives on many occasions, which was only natural. After all, their very existence

depended upon it. One can only find fault with them for trying to cover needless barbarity with "moral" pretences—and all of us, seemingly, have a weakness for that.

CHAPTER 16

1. This was a substantial increase for Plymouth, almost doubling its size. But it was the merest trickle compared with the tidal waves of immigration that followed for two centuries, reaching a crest in 1907 when 1,285,349 "pilgrims" from all the lands of Europe and Asia hopefully landed on our shores.

2. This marriage was the fourth at Plymouth, Winslow's being the first. The second (1622?) was probably that of John Alden and Priscilla Mullins, who had been taken into the Brewster family when she was left an orphan by the General Sickness.

3. Neither the Pilgrims nor the Puritans who followed them to New England had any scruples about child labor. Soon after his arrival at Salem in 1629, the Reverend Francis Higginson, "teacher" of the church there, wrote in an enthusiastic letter to friends at home, "Little children here by setting of corne may earne much more than their owne maintenance." With eight children in the family, Higginson doubtless hoped to do very well.

CHAPTER 17

1. The patent, made out to Winslow and Cushman, was signed by Lord Sheffield, a member of the Council for New England, who was hoping to obtain Cape Ann in a contemplated division of the territory among the individual members of the company. But as this division had not taken place and was never attempted in want of royal sanction, the Pilgrims' patent was worthless. They were always wasting money on the most useless documents.

CHAPTER 18

1. With Winslow in command, the Pilgrims had first gone to the Kennebec late in 1625 with a shallop full of corn, coming back with seven hundred pounds of beaver and other peltry, an unexpected and encouraging success. Allerton obtained a patent to territory there in 1628, but it was "so straite & ill bounded as they were faine to renew & inlarge it the next year." This second patent gave them a strip fifteen miles wide on both sides of the stream, and they "erected a house up above in ye river in ye most convenientest place for trade, as they conceived, and furnished the same with commodities for that end, both winter & sommer."

2. The Plymouth colony talked of digging a canal here as early as 1676 when old Judge Samuel Sewall of Boston noted in his diary, after a visit to the Cape: "Mr. Smith rode with me and showed me the place which some had thought to cut for to make a passage from the south sea to the north. He said it was about a mile and a half between the utmost flowing of the two seas in Herring [Manomet] River and Scusset—the land very low and level."

The canal project interested General George Washington as a means of shortening his lines of supply during the Revolutionary War, but nothing was done about it until 1909, when August Belmont organized a company to start digging—which it did, for five years, at a cost of $13,-000,000. The Federal Government bought the canal at a discount shortly after World War I, but it remained a ditch until the Great Depression, when it was made into a proper waterway, thanks largely to the stupidly maligned W.P.A.

3. Sherley "hath cloven to us still amidst all persuasions of opposites," Cushman had written Bradford in 1624, "and could not be moved to have an evil thought of us for all their clamours." Offering to advance as much as £800 at a time to draw others on, he "hath indeed by his free-heartednesse been the only glue of the company . . . He hath sent you a cheese, &c. Also he hath sent an heifer to the plantation, to begine a stock for the poor."

Sherley had a relative at Plymouth, and asked Bradford on one occasion to give "my loving respect to my kinsman." But who this person was, I have no idea.

4. There is some doubt about the identity of this ship, which had been chartered by Thomas Goffe, for a time one of the Plymouth adventurers, now a member of the Massachusetts Bay Company. Some believe that she was the famous Pilgrim ship (cf. Rendel Harris, *Last of the Mayflower*, 1920), but it seems to me that this is unlikely. In the first place, there were more than twenty *Mayflowers* of English registry in 1620. Second, if she were the same ship, one would certainly expect Bradford or one of the Pilgrims to make at least some passing mention of the fact. Third, when last seen in 1624, the first *Mayflower* was lying

at Rotherhithe in very poor trim, being valued at £138 8s. with all her fittings and "one suit of worn sails."

5. Not only did the Puritans maintain this fiction, but for politic reasons the Pilgrims played down the report that they had made Separatists of their neighbors. Wrote Winslow (*Hypocrisie Unmasked*): ". . . 'tis falsely said they took Plymouth for their precedent as fast as they came; 'tis true, I confess, that some of the chief of them advised with us (coming over to be freed from the burthensome ceremonies then imposed in England) how they should do to fall upon a right platform of worship, and desired to that end, since God had honoured us to lay the foundation of a Commonwealth and to settle a Church in it, to show them whereupon our practice was grounded . . . We accordingly showed them the primitive practice for our warrant, taken out of the Acts of the Apostles and the Epistles . . . Which being by them well weighed and considered, they also entered into covenant with God and one another . . . So that here also thou mayest see they set not the church at Plymouth before them for example, but the primitive churches were and are their and our mutual patterns and examples, . . . a pattern fit to be followed of all that fear God."

6. Of Skelton's inclination toward Separatism, John Cotton later declared that he had been "studious of that way" before leaving England.

7. As Artemus Ward once remarked, "I believe we are descended from the Puritans, who nobly fled from a land of despotism to a land of freedom, where they could not only

enjoy their own religion, but prevent everybody else from enjoying *his*."

CHAPTER 19

1. For Adams' rather solemn view of the purge here and the affair at Wessagusset, see his *Three Episodes in Massachusetts History* (Boston, 1893).

2. Morton did not much exaggerate here in light of what passed for medicine at the time. A few years later Sir Kenelm Digby, "the universal genius of the age," wrote John Winthrop, Junior:

"For all sorts of agues I have of late tried the following magnetical experiment with infallible success. Pare the patient's nails when the fit is coming on, and put the parings into a little bag of fine linen or sarsanet, and tie that about a live eel's neck in a tub of water. The eel will die, and the patient will recover. And if a dog or a hog eat that eel, they will also die."

In the pharmacopeia of the day fox oil was prescribed for earache; "stones" of beaver, for palsy, trembling, and numbness of hands; vulture bones about the neck, for headache; dolphin teeth, mixed with honey, for teething children. "The gall of a Wolf is Soveraign for swelling of the *sinens;* the fiants or dung of a Wolf, drunk with white-wine, helpeth the Collick." And a good "fat" beaver tail worked magic as an aphrodisiac.

3. One of Morton's men, Edward Gibbons, soon made a name for himself in the Bay colony, serving frequently as deputy to the General Court, being captain of the Boston militia, and becoming a prosperous merchant in the Virginia and West Indian trade.

CHAPTER 20

1. Sherley suspected that Winthrop and others of the Massachusetts Company were working behind the scenes to prevent Plymouth from obtaining a proper patent (cf. Bradford's *Letter-Book,* Series I Mass. Hist. Soc. Collections, vol. 3, pp. 71-2).

2. Trade along the Kennebec was declining, and the Undertakers were about to abandon Cushenoc when Bradford and others, "being loath it should be lost by discontinuance," organized a private company and obtained a lease to the post there, paying the colony a sixth of the profits, "with ye first fruits of which they builte a house [the first brick structure in town] for a prison"—"one sign," remarked a nineteenth-century historian, "of the permanency of the settlement, which hitherto had been a matter of uncertainty."

The post was leased by another Pilgrim group in 1651 at a rent of £50 a year, reduced to £35 a year in 1654. Finally, in 1661, the Kennebec patent was sold for £400 to four Boston men, one of whom was John Winslow, Edward's second brother, who had left Plymouth some years before.

CHAPTER 21

1. "The best part is always the least, and of that best part the wiser part is always the lesser," Winthrop wrote Thomas Hooker, pastor at New Towne (Cambridge), to which that stout democrat replied, "In matters which concern the common good, a general council, chosen by all, to

transact businesses which concern all, I conceive most suitable to rule and most safe for relief of the whole."

But Hooker was an exception among the ministers at the Bay, most of whom were inclined to take very high ground. John Cotton preached that an elected magistrate somehow acquired a vested interest in office, saying that "a magistrate ought not to be turned into the condition of a private man without just cause, and to be publicly convict, no more than magistrates may turn a private man out of his freehold without like public trial." This doctrine so appealed to some of the "aristocrats" that they prevailed upon the Bay to appoint three Councillors for Life—Winthrop, Endecott, and Dudley. But the popular party in the General Court put an end to this in 1638, however, by stripping the office of all powers and authority, making it an honorary post. A second attempt to establish a Council for Life was scotched in 1642 by the opposition of Richard Bellingham, a former governor, and Assistant Governor Richard Saltonstall.

There was nothing comparable at Plymouth. The institution of annual elections was never challenged there. Far from being anxious to continue in office, Bradford and others repeatedly tried to beg off, the former finally succeeding in 1633, getting a breathing spell of two years. Indeed, matters reached such a point in Plymouth at this time that a law was passed imposing a fine of £20 upon anyone refusing to serve when elected as governor, unless he had served the previous year; and a fine of £10 similarly threatened those

who refused to serve as assistant governors.

2. Lawyers were allowed in court if defendants wished legal counsel. But they were merely tolerated, the law strictly enjoining them "not to mislead the Court, or darken the case," a salutary provision that might well be resurrected and placed again on the books.

3. The witchcraft mania began to assume serious proportions after Pope Innocent VIII issued a papal bull on the subject in 1484. One of his agents boasted a few years later that he himself had burned more than 900 poor wretches. James I made a contribution with his *Daemonologie* (1599). The first execution for witchcraft in New England took place in 1648 at Boston; two were hanged in Connecticut in 1650.

The hysteria came to an end in New England in 1696 when Judge Samuel Sewall, to his everlasting honor, rose in the Old South Meeting House in Boston and stood with bowed head as the pastor read his confession of shame for the part he had played in the Salem witch trials. The jurymen later acknowledged their error, to the outrage of Cotton Mather, who sought to justify his part in the proceedings by promoting another witch scare at Boston, playing a farce with a tipsy wench who was, it turned out, suffering nothing more serious than *delirium tremens*.

Increase Mather, president of Harvard, had done his part in exciting public credulity with his *Essay for the Recording of Illustrious Providences* (Boston, 1684). In this he collected all the gossip he could about the most incredible "supernatural" events. (For Mather's "scientific" approach to this mass of old wives' tales, see Kenneth Murdock's *Increase Mather,* a remarkable job of special pleading exhibiting all that could be asked in the way of a fine old "school-tie" spirit.)

With a few notable exceptions, everyone at the time was prey to the most repulsive superstitions. When Massachusetts was having trouble with that spirited rebel, Mrs. Anne Hutchinson, the rumor ran that a woman associated with her, Mrs. Mary Dyer, later hanged as a Quaker, had given birth to a "monster," and John Winthrop put it down as a visitation for her "sins." Hearing of this "monsterous & prodigious birth," Bradford wrote Winthrop, "If your leasure would permite, I should be much behoulden unto you, to certiffie me in a word or two, of the trueth & forme of that monster, &c." Comets, earthquakes, thunder, lightning, caterpillars, mildew, heavy rains, drought—everything had a "divine" meaning, and men literally cracked their brains trying to interpret these special messages from on High.

The Dutch were as infatuated with such notions as the English. On a visit to Leyden in 1641 the English diarist, John Evelyn, was shown a monument erected to the Countess of Holland for having had, at one birth, 365 children (apparently one for every day in the year). And as conclusive proof of the "miracle," he was shown the 365 silver basins in which the litter had been baptized.

4. The man who built the first stocks in Boston was, with poetic justice, the first to occupy them, being convicted of padding the bill he submitted to cover the costs of construction.

5. The Pilgrims believed that if a child were born on a Wednesday, it had been conceived on a Wednesday —which led to great embarrassment at times, for many a child was unhappily born on a Sabbath. Some ministers were disposed to question the propriety of baptizing children born on that day. One pastor loved to thunder on the subject—until his wife presented him with twins one Sabbath, just after the morning service, when it was the pastor's custom to retire for what the congregation had always presumed was rest and meditation.

6. The ring was not given either in the Pre-contract or the marriage ceremony. To the Saints it was "antichristian," a relic of popery, "a diabolicall circle for the Devill to daunce in."

7. On the same day that Strafford appeared before the House of Lords to answer impeachment charges, the Saints' old friend of Leyden days, Thomas Brewer, partner in the Choir Alley Press, was released from King's Bench Prison upon paying a fine of £1,000 ($50,000) and after spending more than fourteen years there, dying a month later, aged 65. Brewster might well have suffered his fate if he had been caught. In a posthumous work entitled *Gospell Public Worship* (1656), Brewer declared that he had published similar works "at Leyden in Holland, where he walked in communion with Master Robinson and also with Master Ainsworth."

8. Robinson's works went through many editions during these years. The most popular were *The People's*

Plea for the Exercise of Prophecy and his *Justification of Separation,* which was reprinted in 1639 and again in 1644, many copies being smuggled in from Holland, as in Barrow's and Brewster's day (cf. W. H. Burgess, *John Robinson,* p. 222 *et seq.*).

9. At this same time John Milton, soon to be secretary of Cromwell's Council of State, published his *Areopagitica,* a "Speech . . . for the Libertie of Unlicensed Printing." It is still the most eloquent and closely reasoned plea for freedom of the press in the language, and will repay a careful reading today. Milton was an Independent, but far more liberal than most.

10. Another of the King's men, incidentally, was Colonel Sir Henry Washington, ancestor of our first President, the commander-in-chief of the ragged Continental Army arrayed against the royal forces in the American Revolution more than a century later—which is interesting in view of the curious reversal of roles, not only within the Washington family but also among the Pilgrim descendants, many of whom, particularly those in the more prominent families, forgot their "rebel" origin and turned King's men during our struggle for Independence, several taking up arms against their neighbors.

11. One of the first acts of the Confederacy, again reflecting the influence of the Bay, was a recommendation that strong measures be taken "against excesse and disorder in apparell, drink, and all other loose and sinfull miscarriages not fitt to be named amongst Christians, by which the name of our holy God is much dishonored, and the churches of

Christ in these parts much reproached . . ."

In this same year, turning over the pages of his manuscript history, Bradford came upon a letter from Sherley in 1623, in which the latter described how he had calmed a storm among the adventurers by sending "for a potle of wine (I would you could doe ye like) . . ."

How times do change, Bradford remarked on the back of this page, "for what is now more plentifull than wine? and that of ye best, coming from Malago, ye Cannaries, and other places, sundry ships lading in a year. So as ther is now more cause to complaine of ye excess and ye abuse of wine (through men's corruption) even to drunkennes, than of any defecte or wante of ye same. Witnes this year 1646. The good Lord lay not ye sins & unthankfullnes of men to their charge in this perticular."

12. They might have quoted Robinson to the restless brethren: "That fools and idiots that know no better things should love money is not strange, for oxen love grass, and swine, draff; and every creature naturally the best thing which it knows; but that wise and learned men, & they who know the good things of the mind, . . . should so doat upon it, is most vile and monstrous" (*New Essays, or Observations Divine and Moral,* 1628).

13. Like Plymouth, Massachusetts was so poor at this time that to pay Winslow's expenses, as Governor Winthrop noted, the Bay had to borrow £100.

14. After conquering Ireland, Cromwell toyed with the idea of bringing in New England Saints to

impose the Holy Discipline upon the Irish—how the gore would have flowed!

15. Founded in 1609, just a few months before the Scrooby exiles' arrival from Amsterdam, the so-called Scottish Church continued to hold services for almost two centuries, not closing its doors until 1807.

16. William Teellinck, pastor of the Dutch church at Middelburg, had been active in Thomas Brewer's defense when the Choir Alley Press ran into trouble.

For a good detailed account of Robinson's last years and the diaspora of the Leyden church, see Walter H. Burgess, *John Robinson,* pp. 283-313, 348-59.

CHAPTER 22

1. The cost of an Atlantic passage at this time is indicated by the expense incurred in bringing over the "crazy" Rogers:

Passage	£1		
11 weeks dyatt			
at 4s. 8d.	£2	11s.	4d.
	£3	11s.	4d.—or

roughly the equivalent of $200 today.

2. "Why lay such stress upon your patent from King James? 'Tis but parchment," Williams wrote Bradford a few years later. "James has no more right to give away or sell Massasoit's lands, and cut and carve his country, than Massasoit has to sell King James' kingdom or send Indians to colonize Warwickshire."

3. "Being but poor and low in his estate," declared Winslow, "we took not above £8 or £10 [$400-500] of it, lest it might lie too heavy upon his wife and children." Many years later, when gathering material for his *New England's Memorial* (1669), Nathaniel Morton evidently questioned Gorton about several local matters, for the latter replied, "I would say something of the foundation of your Church at Plimouth if I thought it were not a matter too low to talke of, . . . because it consists of an Apostatized people fallen from the faith of the Gospell . . ."

4. Cf. Kenneth Murdock, *Increase Mather* (Cambridge, 1925). Richard Mather had a hand in fashioning the wooden *Bay Psalm Book,* and was one of three chiefly responsible for the Cambridge Platform drawn up for the New England churches in 1646.

At this Cambridge synod, incidentally, the New England churches first took the name Congregational.

5. Tradition has it that Reyner was the brother of Governor Bradford's wife, the former Mrs. Alice (Carpenter) Southworth. This cannot be so. Reyner was born at Gildersome, Yorkshire, not far from the Scrooby district, while Mrs. Bradford's family, the Carpenters, came from the village of Wrington, near Bath, hundreds of miles to the south. The tradition is undoubtedly based on confusion arising from the fact that Alice Bradford's son by her first marriage, Thomas Southworth, married Elizabeth Reyner, the pastor's daughter.

6. The Saints' objection to playing cards and to all games of chance was less the "moral" one that these might lead to "idle courses," but rather, as explained by Cotton Mather, that "lots, being mentioned in the sacred oracles of Scripture as used only in weighty cases and as an

acknowledgment of God sitting in judgment, . . . cannot be made the tools and parts of our common sports without, at least, such an *appearance of evil* as is forbidden in the word of God."

7. In defending his course Winslow heaped scorn upon Vassall, the author of this measure, attacking him bitterly in *New England's Salamander* (London, 1647). And he was a salamander, said Winslow, "because of his constant and many years' exercise and delight in opposition to whatsoever hath been judged most wholesome and safe for the weal-public of the country from whence he last came, either in politics or ecclesiastics."

This quarrel had other embarrassing aspects, for the two families were related through the marriage of Resolved White, Winslow's stepson, to Vassall's daughter. Resolved evidently sided with his father-in-law and shared his libertarian views, as did his brother Peregrine, "first white child born in New England." To the shock and chagrin of his elders, the latter showed a marked aversion to the church, stubbornly refusing to join it until he was almost eighty years old. Peregrine (from the Latin *peregrinus,* pilgrim) was well named, it appears, and wandered much in his life, often from the straight and narrow, preferring pleasant ambles down the primrose path, being "in the former part of his life extravagant, yet he was much reformed in his last years, and died hopefully."

8. In zeal at least, Chauncy left nothing to be desired, being a "glutton for pious observances" (see Samuel Eliot Morison, *Three Centuries of Harvard*). Rising at four every morning, winter and summer, he prayed for an hour, then went to the college hall to expound to the assembled students a chapter of Scripture, "with a short prayer before, and a long one after," hurrying home to expound another chapter to his family, with prayer. At eleven he withdrew for three quarters of an hour of silent devotions, and again at four. In the evening he expounded a third chapter in hall, with prayer; a fourth chapter at home, with prayer; and at nine retired for the night, after another hour of "secret prayer."

Chauncy once assured the restive students that they might have had a more "larned" president than he, "but none more affectionate towards you, or more zealous for your good."

The Harvard establishment at this time consisted of a "wooden college, and in the yard a brick pile of two bayes, for the Indians." But when they came on a visit in 1666, the royal commissioners could find only one Indian in it though the school authorities assured them that there were three others somewhere about.

The commissioners were not much impressed with the college except for its capacity for doing evil, reporting their fear that it "might afford as many schismatics to the Church, and the corporation as many rebels to the King, as formerly they had done, if not timely prevented."

Ten years later another royal commissioner found the Indian College turned into a printing house and a third building under construction, "New College, built at the public charge," containing "twenty chambers for students, two in a chamber; a large hall which serves for a chapel; over that a convenient library, with some few books of the ancient fathers and school divines . . . Here they teach Hebrew before they well understand Latin. No formalities or distinctions of habits, or other decencies as in England, much less those exhibitions and supports for scholars. They take no degrees above Master of Arts. Their Commencement is kept . . . in the meeting-house, when the Governor and Magistrates are present, attended with throngs of illiterate elders and church-members . . . The allowance of the President is £100 per ann., and a good house. There are but four fellowships. The two seniors have each £30 [$1,500] per ann., and the two juniors £15; but no diet is allowed. These are tutors to all such as are admitted students."

Harvard graduated its first class in 1642 when nine young men "performed their acts so as gave good proof of their proficiencie in the Tongues and Arts"—Latin, Greek, Hebrew, Chaldee, Syriac, arithmetic, geometry, logic, and divinity.

9. At this time, fingering through the pages of his manuscript history, Bradford came upon this passage written many years back in a letter from Leyden to Sir Edwin Sandys of the (First) Virginia Company:

"We are knite togeather as a body in a most stricte & sacred bond and covenante of the Lord, of the violation of which we make great conscience."

Turning the page, Bradford sadly added this note on the back:

"O sacred bond, whilst inviollably preserved! how sweete and precious were the fruits that flowed from ye same, but when this fidelity decayed, then their ruine approached. O that

these anciente members had not dyed, or been dissipated (if it had been the will of God), or else that this holy care and constante faithfullnes had still lived, and remained with those that survived and were in times afterwards added unto them. But (alass) that subtill serpente hath slylie wound in himselfe under faire pretences of necessitie and ye like, to untwiste these sacred bonds and tyes, and as it were insensibly by degrees to dissolve or in great measure to weaken ye same.

"I have been happy, in my first times, to see and with much comforte to injoye the blessed fruits of this sweete communion, but it is now a parte of my miserie in old age to find and feele ye decay and want thereof (in great measure), and with greefe and sorrow of hart to lamente & bewaile ye same."

10. The law requiring ministers to collect their own salaries was repealed in 1670, but it was nevertheless still true that they were the makers of their own felicity. For two centuries they were paid largely in kind, though a few of the more fortunate gathered in some hard money. In 1673 the Roxbury pastor, John Eliot, "Apostle to the Indians," was given thirty-four pounds of copper pennies, "the same being by estimation £1 13s. 4d. lawfull money."

The ministers were miserably poor, as a rule, and had to spend much of their time in reminding parishioners of the bargain struck between them. There is the story of the Reverend Timothy Alden, a descendant of John and Priscilla, who for fifty years preached lively and timely sermons to his flock at Yarmouth, down on Cape Cod, and kept them well pleased. Unlike so many others, the town was always prompt in paying him his meager salary, a large part of which consisted of "fat" firewood to warm the parsonage. But one winter came, with the coldest and rawest kind of weather, and still no firewood had been delivered. On the next Sabbath, Timothy is said to have been rarely eloquent on Proverbs 26. 20: "Where no wood is, there the fire goeth out."

The shepherd at Duxbury, poor John Robinson (not related to the Leyden pastor), had more than his share of woes, and his colleagues throughout the Old Colony followed his case with bated breath and the deepest sympathy, for they well knew what he was up against. For thirty-two years Robinson conscientiously tended his flock and at length, tired of being fobbed off with easy promises, unwilling to endure any more hunger and hardship, he sued the town for the money owed him—his salary for almost thirty years! The town fathers and most of his parishioners were outraged.

What did he expect? they indignantly inquired. Had they not given him thirty acres of upland to improve?

Yes, said Robinson, but the upland, if mowed with a razor and raked with a comb, "wouldn't yield enough to winter a grasshopper."

The town thereupon named a committee to draw up accounts with the pastor "from the beginning of the world to the present day—August 7, 1738," and at a town meeting two months later it was "Voted that ther meeting hous should be shot up so that Mr. John Robrson of Duxburrough may not get into said meeting

hous to preach anay more without orders from the towne."

Departing for Lebanon, Connecticut, the long-suffering pastor gave his parishioners a final benediction:

"Neighbors," he said, "I am going never to return, and I shake the dust from my feet as an everlasting testimony against ye, vipers that ye are."

CHAPTER 23

1. Winslow's name, though not on the official record of the proceedings, appears on the Connecticut copy as one of those subscribing to this action (Cf. Palfrey, *History of New England,* II, p. 470).

2. The Massachusetts authorities, with bland sophistry, washed their hands of the blood of Quakers by saying that the latter, having been warned to stay away, knew what their punishment would be if they came into the colony and were therefore *felones de se* (suicides), so why the clamor about the magistrates' "severity"?

3. Constant Southworth had his difficulties, too. In his will he left his daughter Elizabeth "my next best bed and furniture, with my wife's best bed, provided she do not marry William Tokes; but if she do, then to have 5s."

Like a sensible girl, Elizabeth chose to enjoy the 5s. with her lover rather than two beds—even the best and the next best—without him.

4. The stiff-necked Massachusetts authorities treated the royal commissioners with scant respect, having them up on one occasion for profanation of the extended Sabbath favored by the Saints. Making merry one Saturday evening at the *Ship Tavern* in Boston, Maverick and two of his

colleagues were ordered to be quiet and disperse by a town constable. They took their canes to him, drove him out, and then went on to another tavern, where a second constable came in and ordered them to stop their roystering. During the heated argument that followed, the constable swore that he would arrest the King himself if he found him noisy on a Saturday evening in Boston.

Maverick had the man up on charges of "maliciously uttering treasonable words," for which he was "admonished in a solemn manner by the Governor." The authorities immediately retaliated by summoning the royal commissioners to appear before them on a charge of "riotous and abusive carriage to one of his Majesty's officers, one of the constables of the town."

5. Plymouth opened its first "female" school in 1795, and it was conducted only during the summer months. Girls were not admitted to the Massachusetts public schools on an equal footing with boys until 1828.

6. Early New Englanders were, for the most part, remarkably prolific. In 1821 there died at Middleboro (Nemasket), aged 102, one John Alden, great-grandson of the first John and Priscilla, who had had during his long life 19 children, 62 grandchildren, 134 great-grandchildren, and 7 great-great-grandchildren—of whom 172 survived him.

An even more remarkable instance is attested by this tombstone in an old Connecticut "burying ground":

Here lies the Body
of Mrs Mary, wife of
Dr John Buell, Esq.

She died Nov. 4.th
1768. AEtatis 90
Having had 13 children
107 Grand Children
274 Great G. Children
22 Great G. G. Children
416 Total
336 Survived her.

7. For early Pilgrim workmanship and design, see Wallace Nutting, *Furniture of the Pilgrim Century*.

8. The missionaries had trouble with their converts as well. Many were given to asking the most difficult questions, wanting to know, for example:

Why did not God give all men good hearts, that they might bee good?

Why did not God kill the Devill who makes all men so bad, God having all power?

If a man should be inclosed in Iron a foot thick and be thrown into the fire, what would become of his Soule—whether could the Soule come forth thence or not?

Publishing these and other puzzlers in a tract lauding the missionaries' efforts, Thomas Shepard, pastor at Cambridge, informed his readers that he would not attempt to answer them—"lest I should clog your time with reading," he said.

In 1662 the great Irish-English scientist, Robert Boyle, "father of Chemistry," became president of the Gospel Society which, under the name of the London Society, continued its activities down to the American Revolution. Cotton Mather thought so much of its endeavors that he suggested using it "to spread the Gospel abroad" in all parts of the world—"among the Muscovites, Mahometans, Irish, and other benighted peoples." It was, he declared, "but proper charity."

9. A few months later, through his secretary, King Philip wrote Plymouth in this regard:

> To the honored governir, mr. thomas prince, dwelling at plimouth.
>
> honored sir.
>
> King Philip desires to let you understand that he could not come to the court, for tom, his interpreter, has a pain in his back, that he could not travel so far and philip's sister is very sick. philip would entreat that favour of you, and any of the magistrates, if any english or enjians speak aboute any land, he pray you to give them no answere at all. the last summer he made that promise with you, that he would not sell no land in seven yeares time, for that he would have no english trouble him before that time. he has not forgot that you promised him. he will come as sune as possible he can to speak with you, and so I rest your very loving friend, philip, dwelling at Mount hope nek.

10. Two years previously, in 1673, when appointed to command the Plymouth forces recruited for an expedition against the Dutch, Cudworth had declined to serve, not "out of any discontent in my spirit arising from any former difference," he said, "neither out of an effeminate or dastardly spirit; but am as freely willing to serve my king and country as any man whatsoever in what I am capa-

ble and fitted for; but do not understand that a man is so called to serve his country with the inevitable ruin and destruction of his own family . . .

"My wife, as is well known to the whole town, is not only a weak woman, and has so been all along; . . . never a day passes but she is forced to rise at break of day, or before; she cannot lay for want of breath, and when she is up, she cannot light a pipe of tobacco, but it must be lighted for her; and until she has taken two or three pipes, for want of breath she is not able to stir, and she has never a maid . . . And then in regard of my occasions abroad, for the tending and looking after all my creatures, the fetching home of my hay that is yet at the place where it grew, getting of wood, going to mill, and for the performing all other family occasions, I have none but a small Indian boy about thirteen years of age to help me."

11. The first of the Articles of War read:

> 1. Let no man presume to blaspheme the holy and blessed Trinity, God the Father, God the Son, and God the Holy Ghost, upon paine to have his tongue bored with a hotte iron.

The second forbad swearing; the third prescribed a heavy penalty for abstention from public worship and prayers. Under Article 13, death was the penalty for adultery. The other articles dealt, more or less, with military matters. Similar prohibitions had been written into the military code adopted by the Pilgrims in 1636.

12. There had been both Indian and Negro slaves in the Old Colony

as early as 1646, at which time the authorities announced their intention of selling Indians or exchanging them for Negroes as punishment for offenses. Upon Philip's defeat the Plymouth pastor, John Cotton, was presented with a captured Wampanoag as a slave, and he begged another to send to his brother-in-law, Increase Mather. Young Roland Cotton, pastor at Yarmouth, had an Indian slave who served as janitor of the meeting house, receiving £1 a year in wages, which his master pocketed. In 1706, Cotton Mather noted in his diary: "Received a singular blessing in the gift of a likely slave, which was a mighty smile of heaven on this family."

The Bay Colony had formally recognized the institution of slavery in its *Code of Fundamentals, or Body of Liberties,* adopted in 1641, being the first of the colonies to do so, anticipating even Virginia in this (cf. George H. Moore, *A Note on the History of Slavery in Massachusetts*). Three years later, the "peculiar institution" was implicitly recognized in the articles of confederation drawn up by the United Colonies.

Chief Justice Samuel Sewall—peace be to his gallant soul—was one of the first to speak out against human slavery. In 1700 he published *The Selling of Joseph, A Memorial,* which upset many of the conservative. The latter were even more shocked in 1719 when, at the trial of a man charged with killing his slave, the wise and benign old judge declared:

"The poorest Boys and Girls in this Province, such as are of the lowest condition, whether they be Indians or English or Ethiopians—they have the same Right to Religion and Life that the Richest Heirs have. And they who go about to deprive them of this Right, they attempt the bombarding of Heaven, and the shells they throw will fall down on their own heads."

When James Otis declared in his great Writs of Assistance speech in 1761 that slavery violated the inalienable rights of man—that all men should be free—John Adams "shuddered at the doctrine he taught."

Slaves continued to be sold at Boston as late as 1788, when the traffic at last was forbidden. Massachusetts shipmasters, of course, continued their slave traffic in the South and the West Indies, growing rich on the Triangular Trade—rum to Africa, slaves to the Caribbean and the southern states, molasses to New England, to be turned into more rum and slaves and molasses, with dividends in cotton and tobacco.

13. Burial, like marriage, was not a religious ceremony among the Saints for generations. No prayers of any kind were said over the dead until the eighteenth century, for the Pilgrims feared that this might lead to the practice of praying for the souls of the departed, which was associated in their minds with the hated doctrine of Purgatory. The next step, they feared, would be the burning of candles to the dead and all sorts of elaborate incantations.

Burial was nevertheless a solemn ceremonial. The deceased was laid out by family and friends in a simple coffin of oak or pine, either fashioned at home or ordered from John Alden or Kenelm Winslow, the official coffin-maker. With a crowd of weeping mourners in train, the coffin was carried to the "burying ground" on a bier covered with a black pall. There was no hearse at Plymouth until 1820, and in earlier years there were usually two sets of pallbearers—six honorary bearers, who walked to either side holding the tassels of the pall, and an equal number of under-bearers, either hired for the purpose or occasionally Indian and Negro slaves, who did the actual carrying, four of them shouldering the coffin at a time.

It early became a custom among the Saints to present each of the pall-bearers with a pair of black gloves. On his death in 1633 Deacon-Doctor Fuller directed that his sister Susanna, Edward Winslow's wife, should mourn him in a 12s. pair of gloves, adding that a certain Rebecca Prime, perhaps a family servant, should be provided for the purpose with a 2s. 6d. pair of gloves. It was also one of the pastor's perquisites of office to receive a pair of black gloves, and ministers received so many that they plied a rather brisk trade in them. One Boston pastor collected 2,940 pairs in thirty years, which he sold for £1,442, considerably augmenting his meager salary.

Later, the pastor and pallbearers were given not only black gloves but white linen scarves and black enam-elled gold rings, with the name, age, and date of death of the deceased in-scribed on the inside. And in time, as funerals became more and more elaborate, such articles were given to all of the invited mourners—some-times, in the case of local celebrities, to as many as 1,000 people. This practice finally became so ruinously expensive that in 1721, after the Bay had swallowed the Old Colony, Mas-sachusetts passed a law for the regu-lation of funerals, forbidding the gift on such occasions of "scarves, gloves (except six pairs to the bearers and one pair to the minister . . .), wine, rum, and rings."

In the early days, once the funeral procession reached the "burying ground," the corpse was laid away in complete silence, broken only by sobs and an occasional heart-piercing cry. There were many misgivings and much lifting of eyebrows when, in 1697, the first sermon over the dead was preached by Pastor Wis-wall of Duxbury, in burying Jon-athan, one of John Alden's sons. But by 1730 the ceremony at the graveside had become much like the Protestant service we now know.

After the dead had been laid away, it was long the custom at Plymouth—up to 1833, when "tem-perance" agitation began—for the mourners to return to the home of the bereaved or to one of the local taverns for what was virtually a wake, now and again rather riotous in nature. Food and drink to com-fort the mourners were always pro-vided, in accord with an old English custom, and these items constituted a large part of the cost of all funerals, as evidenced by this account paid at Plymouth in 1656:

For winding sheet, five yards of lock-orum and thread	8s.	5d.
Coffin	8s.	
Digging Grave	3s.	
Clarke of Court	2s.	6d.
	£1 1s.	11d.
Taverne Charges	12s.	d.
	£1 13s.	11d.

14. "Men are, for the most part, minded for or against tolerance of diversity of religion according to the conformity which they hold or hold not with the country or kingdom where they live," John Robinson had once sagely observed. "Protestants living in the country of Papists commonly plead for toleration of religion; so do Papists that live where Protestants bear sway, though few of either, specially of the clergy as they are called, would have the other tolerated where the world goes on their side."

15. The Mathers, Increase and Cotton, had a genius for making enemies, both being fond of heaping abuse upon all who opposed them, putting on an air of injured innocence whenever the latter replied in kind. Not liking the proceedings of the liberal Brattle Street Church in Boston, Increase Mather denounced its pastor, Benjamin Colman, as "a little thing, . . . a raw and unstudied youth, . . . of a very unsanctified temper and spirit." Thomas Brattle, treasurer of Harvard, retorted by calling Mather a "reverend scribbler, a moral heathen." Cotton Mather rushed to his father's defense to proclaim that all in the Brattle Street Church were "Ignorant, Arrogant, Obstinate, and full of malice and slander, and they fill the Land with Lyes," he whined, "in the misrepresentations thereof I am a very singular sufferer."

16. There was, too, a minor revolution in the church at this time. The Saints had been using Ainsworth's *Psalms* almost since the day of their publication in 1612, and Longfellow made use of them in his "Courtship of Miles Standish" to present a typical scene, portraying Priscilla as John Alden found her sitting at home when he came on a visit:

Open wide on her lap lay the well-worn psalm-book of Ainsworth,
Printed in Amsterdam, the words and the music together,
Rough-hewn, angular notes, like stones in the wall of a churchyard,
Darkened and overhung by the running vine of the verses.

Now, in 1692, Ainsworth's *Psalmes* were abandoned, over the protests of many, for the equally rough and even less inspired measures of the *Bay Psalm Book*.

CHAPTER 24

1. Major General John Winslow, great-grandson of the first Edward, was a spirited but poorly educated man, being scarcely literate. He held his rank not as a colonial officer, but in the regular British army. On September 5, 1755, he had issued a proclamation that all male Acadians, even lads of ten and up, should assemble in the church at Grand Pré to hear a communication. More than four hundred attended. Suddenly the doors were locked, and all were taken prisoner. Five days later they were placed on board five transports and shipped away. More than three hundred women and 1,000 children were later gathered up and transported, being forced to abandon houses, lands, and all but a few personal belongings. Perhaps through the General's influence, one shipload was sent to Plymouth.

Winslow was still alive in 1769, a venerable figure in the town, dying here at Plymouth five years later.

2. There was trouble in the church at this time, occasioned by the "Great Awakening." Jonathan Edwards began preaching his Hell-fire sermons at Northampton in 1734, but the movement at Plymouth began with the visit in 1740 of George Whitefield, the first itinerant evangelist of note in New England. He was so eloquent, it is said, that he could reduce his audience to tears merely by pronouncing the word "Mesopotamia." Benjamin Franklin heard him and was much impressed, coming to scoff and remaining to pray, emptying his "pocket into the collector's dish, gold and all."

Whitefield and his assistant Andrew Crosswell, so the orthodox complained, were "so lost to all sense of decency and decorum" that they "actually pressed women, negroes, and children into the pulpit to exhort the people." The community, as elsewhere in New England, was soon split between the "Old Lights" and the "New Lights," or "Come-outers." The local pastor, Nathaniel Leonard, "a clear & sound Gospell teacher, making Christ the Alpha & Omega in his preaching," was much pleased with the revival, saying that "after this, for a considerable time, the Taverns were much reformed, & the Children forsook their Plays in the Streets, and Persons of all Denominations, Excepte a few, gave themselves to Reading the Word of God & other Books of Devotion, to Meditation, Prayer, Conference, & other Religious Exercises, & refrained from their customary Vices."

Under the impulse of enthusiasm a new meeting house, Plymouth's third, was built in 1744, and Leonard exclaimed at its dedication, "O! that the Glory of this House may be greater than the former." But the Old Lights were not pleased with the meeting house or the new doctrines favored by Leonard. The faculties at Harvard and Yale were equally exercised and denounced these innovations. In 1746, led by Ruling Elder Faunce, still spirited in spite of his ninety-eight years, the Plymouth conservatives "separated" and built an Old-Light temple of their own, "a neat edifice of wood, with a tower and spire in front." This was the first serious split at Plymouth, and forty years passed before the dissidents returned to the fold.

3. Interestingly, the rock is not a native of Plymouth, but a "Stranger" —from the Laurentian Highlands in Labrador, transported thence during the last ice age some 35,000 years ago and dumped here on the beach when the glaciers melted and retreated northward.

4. As made at Plymouth, "sauquetash" (succotash) is a soup. Here is an old recipe for the dish (out of Arthur Lord's *Plymouth and the Pilgrims*): Boil two fowls in a large kettle, at the same time boiling in a second kettle a ½ lb. of lean pork and 2 qts. of common white beans till like soup. When fowls are boiled, skin off fat and add small pieces of corned beef, a turnip sliced and cut small, and 5 or 6 potatoes sliced thin. When tender, take out fowls and keep in oven with the pork. The soup of beans and pork should be added to water of fowls and beef. Add salt and pepper. Boil 4 qts. of hulled corn till soft and add to soup. Before serving, add meat of one fowl. Serve other fowl separately, with corned beef and pork.

Incidentally, the club's host on this occasion, Thomas Southworth Howland, came more or less naturally by tavernkeeping, numbering among his illustrious ancestors James Cole, who opened Plymouth's first public house.

5. With the aim of preventing "immorality, impiety, and contempt of religion," the Massachusetts law forbad the performance of any play before an audience of more than twenty people, which reflected the early Saints' prejudice against the theater. In 1792, when an attempt was made at Boston to present Shakespeare's *Richard III,* the players were hustled off to jail. This touched off such a hubbub, led by John Quincy Adams and Paul Revere, that the law was never again enforced, and Massachusetts finally legalized the theater in 1806.

6. For an excellent account of the Long Room Club and the Sons of Liberty, see Esther Forbes, *Paul Revere and the World He Lived In* (Boston, 1942).

7. See W. O. Raymond, *Winslow Papers, 1776-1826* (St. John's, New Brunswick, 1901).

8. See James Thacher, *History of the Town of Plymouth* (Boston, 1832), and Allen French, *General Gage's Informers* (Ann Arbor, 1932).

9. Deacon Foster was a conservative in all things. Five years before, in 1771, weary of the cacophony of the *Bay Psalm Book,* the Plymouth church had decided to make trial of the Tate and Brady *Psalm Book,* with Watt's hymns attached, beautiful and simple lyrics now known to millions. There was bitter opposition led by Deacon Foster, who declared that

"when Dr. Watts composed his Hymns, he was under the influence of ye Devill." Brought to book for this, the Deacon quibbled and was forgiven when he explained that his remarks about Dr. Watts were "with respect to his Psalms, though not Hymns," and harmony in the Pilgrim meeting house—at least in regard to song—was achieved at last, though many years passed before instrumental music was admitted.

10. Much "improved," though not quite spoiled, this old house still stands at the foot of North Street, overlooking the Doric temple that now shelters Plymouth Rock. The house was long the home of one of Mother Plymouth's most distinguished sons, Dr. Charles T. Jackson, co-discoverer of ether, and here his daughter Lydia was married in 1835 to Ralph Waldo Emerson, the mellowest of the latter-day Saints. Two years previously Emerson had talked at Pilgrim Hall on Socrates. But he was not half so well received as a wandering minstrel who appeared a few months later with kilt and bag pipes, and "Potter, the sword-swallower."

Another distinguished son of Plymouth of this generation was John Bartlett, descended from Robert Bartlett of the *Anne* company, who in 1856 published his *Familiar Quotations,* long since a classic.

11. Robbins was a liberal in his religious views and in 1796 was "constrained to lament the narrow policy of the church in excluding from its communion many exemplary Christians merely on account of their different conceptions of some points of doctrine about which learned and

good men have entertained a great variety of opinion, and this circumstance is more especially a source of regret at this enlightened period when the principles of civil and religious liberty are almost universally understood and practised."

This evidently was the feeling of the town, for in 1800, a year after Robbins' death, the First Church of Plymouth ceased to be Congregational and became Unitarian. Again there was a schism, with Deacon John Bishop seceding with a violently protesting minority to found the Church of the Pilgrimage. Thirty-three years later full freedom of religion was granted by Massachusetts when support of all churches was made voluntary. Those who finally established liberty of conscience in New England were the Quakers, Baptists, and Episcopalians, after a bitter struggle of two centuries to break the stranglehold of the Saints and the Congregational theocracy.

12. In 1802, less than ten years after Robbins first used it, the name "Pilgrims" appeared in a play written in blank verse, *A New World Planted,* by Joseph Croswell, a Plymouth shopkeeper. Six years later, at the Boston theater, the Pilgrims made their first appearance on the stage with the presentation on Forefathers' Day, 1808, of a "new Melo Drama . . . in 3 acts." It was so well received that it was again presented four days later and once more on January 2, 1809, "for the 3rd and last time this season . . . (with alterations)."

The play is interesting for several reasons. I have been unable to find a copy, but the handbill announcing its last performance is exciting and revealing, to say the least:

THE PILGRIMS

Or, the Landing of our Forefathers at

PLYMOUTH ROCK

In the course of the Melo Drama, the following Scenery, Incidents, &c.

A View of the Rock and Plymouth Bay, and the landing of the Pilgrims. The whole scene represents Winter, with a snow storm. After returning thanks to Heaven for their safe arrival, Carver orders one of the Pilgrims to cut on the Rock, DECEMBER 22nd, 1620, the day of their landing.

An alarm of Indians. . . .

A comic scene between an Irish Boatswain and an Indian Woman. The perilous situation of Juliana through the treachery of one of the Pilgrims. The act concludes with a GLEE and CHORUS.

In act II—Scene 1st Represents several half finished Houses . . . a shell sounds to announce the arrival of Massasoit. A Grand INDIAN MARCH. A Treaty of Peace and Amity. . . . The treachery of Samoset, who attempts to carry off the person of Juliana. She struggles and seizes his Tomahawk and pursues him—he implores her pardon—which she grants—he wrests the Tomahawk from her and aims a dreadful blow, when Winslow rushes in to her rescue —his gun misses fire—he draws his sword and a combat ensues— in the mean time Juliana takes the gun and fires at Samoset, without effect—Winslow is wounded, and Samoset pursues Juliana—who is seen ascending a rock—she reaches the summit, and as Samoset is following, she strikes him with the fuzee, and he falls headlong down the precipice. . . .

THE INDIAN METHOD OF LYING IN AMBUSH

And the act concludes with a Procession of Indians, carrying Winslow and Juliana on their boughs.
In act 3, The Indians preparing to sacrifice one of the Pilgrims.

Scene 2d.
A dreadful Combat with Clubs and Shields, between Samoset and Squanto

Scene last—A View of an Indian Encampment, A Marriage and Nuptial Dance,

AFTER WHICH

The Genius of Columbia descends in a Magnificent Temple, surrounded with Clouds

In addition to Standish, Carver, Winslow, Cushman, "Other Pilgrims," and the "Genius of Columbia," the *dramatis personae* included Boatswain Blunder and Yankee, an Indian woman. One of the "Other Pilgrims" was played by a Mrs. Poe, who was delivered of a child a week or two later—named Edgar Allan Poe—and those who believe in prenatal influence may find here some new light on the poet's chronic melancholia.

13. From the *New York Times,* Dec. 22, 1940: "A three-day celebration of the 320th anniversary of the Landing of the Pilgrims was opened yesterday with the transfer of a fragment of Plymouth Rock to the Plymouth Congregational Church of the Pilgrims, . . . Brooklyn, from the former Church of the Pilgrims . . . The rock fragment, weighing more than fifty pounds, had rested in a wall of the tower of the Church of the Pilgrims since Forefathers' Day, Dec. 22, 1844, the year the church was founded . . . The rock fragment will rest in a niche in the hall of paintings and relics of the Civil War . . ."

14. The article in the *Dictionary of National Biography* (1887, revised edition) is representative of a great deal written about the Pilgrims. It has Carver "the father of several children, one daughter being aged 14." The article then relates the old story that John Howland married this daughter, Elizabeth, and had a numerous progeny.

But down the page a few paragraphs, the article denies all this and rightly states that Carver "does not seem to have had any children."

Nor is the article in the *Dictionary of American Biography* much better. It baldly states as matters of fact a number of surmises that have, so far as I can discover, little or no warrant. It has Carver in London during the last years of Elizabeth's reign, making a fortune there; he appears in the Leyden records as a "merchant of York." He is credited with organizing the London group and hiring the *Mayflower,* which was obviously of Cushman's doing, for Carver was down at Southampton buying supplies. He did not "command the two boats sent out to spy the land" along Cape Cod; Captain

Christopher Jones was in command on the Second Discovery, and Captain Standish on the Third (see Mourt's *Relation*). Carver did not die on April 5, 1621. And it is highly questionable if "his chair and sword are among the few relics of undoubted authenticity" in Pilgrim Hall; there is good reason to believe that the Pilgrims did not bring a stick of furniture with them on the overcrowded *Mayflower*.

15. Seven years previously, in 1848, the Bradford manuscript had been identified as such by an Englishman, the Reverend James S. M. Anderson, in his *History of the Colonial Church*. It is inexplicable how the fact escaped notice both in England and on this side of the water.

16. Longfellow came naturally by his interest in the Pilgrims, for his line of ancestry ran back to John Alden, Ruling Elder Brewster, and Robert Bartlett of the *Anne* company. In writing of John Alden and Priscilla he was relating a family romance. His grandfather, the old general, was the one who also interested him in the story of the midnight ride of Paul Revere and, though Hawthorne had something to do with it, he may likewise have planted the germ of "Evangeline" by telling his grandson of the exploits of Major General Winslow and the sufferings of the Acadians who had come to live at Duxbury when he was a boy.

17. Of the general scene in "The Courtship of Miles Standish," local historians never tire of pointing out, among many other things, that John Alden married Priscilla late in 1621, or early in 1622, several years before there were any cattle at Plymouth—

least of all, a white bull with an "iron ring in its nostrils, covered with crimson cloth," to serve as the bride's palfrey.

As remarked in the Preface, Longfellow is responsible in large part for the continued popular confusion in identifying the Pilgrims with the Bay settlements, always referring to them as "Puritans."

18. This was an eventful summer in Washington, too. Not long before boarding the *Mayflower*, President Harding had issued an executive order transferring the administration of Teapot Dome and all other naval oil reserves from the Navy to the Department of the Interior under Secretary Albert B. Fall. The latter had already "leased" the Elk Hills Reserve to Edward Doheny, who, properly grateful, passed along to the Secretary a little black satchel containing $100,000 in cash, as a "loan." A few months later Teapot Dome was "leased" to Harry Sinclair. At the same time the Ohio gang was busily plying many lucrative rackets, from plain bootlegging to looting the Veterans Administration. They were much too busy to accompany the President on the *Mayflower*.

Four of our Presidents, incidentally, have numbered *Mayflower* immigrants among their ancestors:

Zachary Taylor was descended from William Brewster and Isaac Allerton;

U. S. Grant, from Richard Warren;

William Howard Taft, from Francis Cooke, of the Scrooby group;

Franklin Delano Roosevelt, from

Francis Cooke, Isaac Allerton, Richard Warren, John Howland, and John Tilley—the "Delano" in another branch of his family comes from Philippe de la Noye, the young Walloon who joined the congregation at the Green Gate and came on the *Fortune* in 1621.

SELECTIVE
BIBLIOGRAPHY

This list is for the general reader who may wish to explore for himself one or another corner of the Pilgrim field. For that purpose it is a waste of time and good paper to put down hundreds upon hundreds of books which contain a fact or two about the Pilgrims, but which no one in his senses would recommend as either interesting or important.

In compiling this list, I have omitted standard histories, genealogical registers, and other easily-found secondary sources. Where the same ground is more or less covered in a number of books, I have usually chosen to list only one. Books of interest only to specialists have also been omitted. Even so, the list is rather long, for the Pilgrim story has many facets.

My sole unqualified recommendation is—read what the Pilgrims themselves said of their aims, attributes, and accomplishments, and what their contemporaries, both friendly and hostile, had to say about them. For the rest, I have indicated which works seem to me to be most worth consulting. The code is simple:

*** altogether interesting and relevant

** informative

* relevant and/or interesting in part.

The works listed, with few exceptions, can be found in any large library.

I. PILGRIM WORKS AND DOCUMENTS

***Bradford, William. *Of Plimoth Plantation*. Boston, 1856.
Basic and fascinating from cover to cover. Available in many editions, the latest in 1912, ed. by Worthington Chauncey Ford.

**————. *Letter-Book,* in Series I Mass. Hist. Soc. Collections, vols. 3-4. Boston, 1794.
Contains some material not in

Bradford's chronicle, including letters from Deacon-Doctor Fuller when he was "bleeding" and converting the Puritans at Salem and Boston in 1629-30.

**————. *Letters to John Winthrop*, in Series IV Mass. Hist. Soc. Coll., vol. 6.
Other letters appear in scattered sources, but none is of primary importance except that of September 8, 1623, in *American Historical Review*, vol. 8, p. 295 *et seq.*

*————. *A Dialogue, or the Sum of a Conference betweene some Yonge-men, born in New England, and sundry Ancient-men, that came out of Holand and Old England* (1648), in Alexander Young, *Chronicles of the Pilgrim Fathers* (1841).

*————. *A Dialogue, or 3rd Conference*, etc. (1652). Ed. by Charles Deane, Boston, 1870.

**Church, Benjamin. *Entertaining Passages relating to Philip's War.* Boston, 1716.

***Cushman, Robert. *The Danger of Self-Love, and the Sweetnesse of true Friendship.* London, 1622 (various reprints)#

**————. "*The Lawfullness of Plantations*," appended to Mourt's *Relation* (see below).

**Hinckley Papers, in Series III Mass. Hist. Soc. Coll., vols. 5 and 7, and Series IV, vol. 5.
On last years of Old Colony and Mather's dubious agency.

**Leyden Documents Relating to the Pilgrim Fathers. Ed. by D. Plooij and J. R. Harris. Leyden, 1920.

***Morton, Nathaniel. *New England's Memoriall.* Cambridge,

1669 (various reprints, with *Supplement*, 1669-92)#
Particularly useful as first-hand account of the middle years of the Old Colony, 1647-69.

***Mourt, G. (William Bradford and Edward Winslow). *A Relation, or Journall, of the Beginnings and Proceedings of the English Plantation settled at Plimoth, in New England.* London, 1622 (various reprints)#
Engrossing day-by-day detail on Pilgrims' initial wanderings about Cape Cod, their "randevouse" at Plymouth, the General Sickness, visit of Massasoit, and first Thanksgiving.

**Plymouth Church Record, 1620-1859. 2 vols. Boston, 1920.
Far from dull, containing much graphic and amusing material not found elsewhere.

**Plymouth Colony Records. 12 vols., ed. by D. Pulsifer. Boston, 1861.

**Plymouth (Town) Records, 1636-1783. 3 vols. Plymouth, 1889-1903.

**Pratt, Phineas. *A Declaration of the Affairs of the English People that first Inhabited New England.* In Series IV Mass. Hist. Soc. Coll., vol. 4.
The story of Wessagusset by one of Weston's men.

*Robinson, John. *Collected Works.* 3 vols., ed. by Robert Ashton. London, 1851.
Largely theological, but Robinson had his moments.

Three Unknown Documents concerning the Pilgrim Fathers in Holland. Ed. by Albert Eekhof. The Hague, 1920.

***Winslow, Edward. *Good Newes from New-England*. London, 1624 (various reprints)#
The Pilgrims' foraging expeditions on Cape Cod and their obviously garbled account of the affair at Wessagusset.

*————. *Hypocrisie Unmasked*. London, 1646.
Winslow's defense of the cruel and unusual punishment meted out to Samuel Gorton.

*————. *New England's Salamander*. London, 1647.
Specious argument to justify the Saints' refusal to tolerate freedom of religion.

*————. *The Glorious Progress of the Gospell amongst the Indians in New England*. London, 1649.

Morton's *Memorial,* Winslow's *Good Newes,* and Cushman's sermon on *Self-Love* can be found in a volume of Everyman's Library, *Chronicles of the Pilgrim Fathers,* with an introduction by John Masefield.

Mourt's *Relation* and Winslow's *Good Newes* are included, with other interesting original material, in Edward Arber's *Story of the Pilgrim Fathers, 1606-1623* (see below under III).

II. OTHER CONTEMPORARY SOURCES

**Ainsworth, Henry. *The Book of Psalmes; Englished both in Prose and Metre*. Amsterdam, 1612. Reprinted in Waldo Selden Pratt (see below under III).

**Andros Tracts*. Ed. by W. H. Whitmore. Boston, 1874.
On conflict between first royal governor and "seditious sectaries" at Plymouth and the Bay.

Baillie, Robert. *A Dissuasive from the Errours of the Time*. London, 1646.

Ball, John. *A Tryall of the New Church Way in New England and Old*. London, 1644.

**Bay Psalm Book*. Cambridge, 1640 (facsimile reprint, with intro. by Wilberforce Eames, New York, 1903).

**Bishop, George. *New England Judged by the Spirit of the Lord*. London, 1667.
Quaker account of their persecutions at the hands of the Saints.

Brewer, Thomas. *Gospell Public Worship,* etc. London, 1656.

**Browne, Robert. *A Treatise of Reformation without Tarying for Anie*. Middelburg, Holland, 1582.
Foundation and first principles of Separatism, with many shrewd criticisms of Anglican church.

**————. *A Booke which sheweth the life and manners of all True Christians*. Middelburg, 1582.

**Calef, Robert. *More Wonders of the Invisible World*. London, 1700.
A Boston layman's demolishing attack upon the Reverend Cotton Mather's superstitions and his activities in the witchcraft hysteria; should be read with the latter's *Wonders of the Invisible World*.

Camden, William. *Annals of the Reign of Queen Elizabeth*. London, 1615.

Clarendon, E. *History of the Rebellion and Civil Wars in England*. London, 1702.

Collection of Historical Tracts. Ed. by Peter Force. Washington, 1836-46.

Contains both Pilgrim and Puritan documents.

Collection of Original Papers. Ed. by T. Hutchinson. Boston, 1769.

Cotton, John. *Spiritual Milk for Boston babes in either England, Drawn out of the breasts of both Testaments.* Cambridge, 1656 (photostat reprint, Boston, 1939).

Council for New England, Records of. Cambridge, 1867.

**Eliot, John. *A Briefe Narrative of the Progress of the Gospell amongst the Indians in New-England.* London, 1671 (various reprints).

Fairlambe, Peter. *The Recantation of a Brownist, or a Reformed Puritan.* London, 1606.

Gorges, Sir Ferdinando. *A Briefe Relation of the Discovery and Plantation of New England.* London, 1622 (in Series II Mass. Hist. Soc. Coll., vol. 9, pp. 1-25).

Hanbury, Benjamin. *Historical Memorials relating to the Independents or Congregationalists from their rise to A.D. 1660.* 2 vols. London, 1841.

Higginson, Francis. *New England's Plantation.* London, 1630.

Historical Collections consisting of State Papers. Ed. by E. Hazard. 2 vols. Philadelphia, 1792-94.

Hubbard, William. *General History of New England.* (1680). In Series II Mass. Hist. Soc. Coll., vols. 5-6.

***Johnson, Edward. *Wonder-Working Providence.* London, 1654.

Johnson, George. *Discourse of Some Troubles and Excommunications in the Banished English Church at Amsterdam.* Amsterdam, 1604.

**Josselyn, J. *Account of Two Voyages to New England, 1638 and 1663.* London, 1665.

***Lawne, Christopher, and collaborators. *The Prophane Schisme of the Brownists and Separatists,* etc. London, 1612.

*———. *Brownisme Turned the Inside Outward.* London, 1613.

**Lefroy, J. H. *Memorials of the Bermudas.* London, 1877.

For the Bermuda troubles, Stephen Hopkins' exploits, and the wild tales that inspired Shakespeare's *Tempest.*

*Levett, Christopher. *A Voyage into New England.* London, 1628.

Massachusetts Bay Colony Records. 6 vols. Boston, 1853-54.

***Mather, Cotton. *Magnalia Christi Americana.* London, 1702.

Adulatory biographies of the more eminent Saints in which Mather unwittingly paints his own portrait.

***Morton, Thomas. *New English Canaan.* Amsterdam, 1637. (Reprinted by Prince Society, Boston, 1883).

"Mine host of Ma-re Mount" had wit and was a shrewd observer, whatever his morals.

*New England's First Fruits. London, 1643.

Paget, John. *An Arrow against the Separation of the Brownists.* London, 1918.

Paget was pastor of the English-speaking unit of the Dutch Reformed church at Amsterdam.

Pagitt, Ephraim. *Heresiography, or a Description of the Heretics and Sectaries of these Latter Times.* London, 1647.

***Sewall, Samuel. *Diary.* Ed. by Mark Van Doren. New York, 1927.

To my mind the most intelligent, distinguished, and lovable Saint of seventeenth-century New England.

***Smith, Captain John. *Description of New England*. London, 1616.
Used by the Pilgrims in directing their course to New England and finding a place to settle there.

**———. *New England's Trials*. London, 1622.

———. *Generall Historie,* etc. London, 1624.

Stubbes, Philip. *Anatomy of Abuses.* London, 1583.

Taylor, John. *A Cluster of Coxcombes, or a Cinquepace of Five Sorts of Knaves and Fooles: Namely, the Donatists, Publicans, Disciplinarians, Anabaptists, and Brownists.* London, 1642.

Verax, Theodorus (Clement Walker). *Anarchia Anglicana, or the History of the Independency.* London, 1643.

*Ward, Edward. *A Trip to New England.* London, 1699.

Welde, Thomas. *A Brief Narration of the Practices of the Churches in New-England.* London, 1645.

White, Thomas. *A Discoverie of Brownism.* London, 1605.

***Winthrop, John. *A History of New England from 1630 to 1649.* 2 v., ed. by J. Savage. Boston, 1825-26.
Early history from the Bay point of view, based upon Winthrop's Journal.

**Wood, William. *New England's Prospect.* London, 1635.

III. GENERAL AND SPECIAL

Adams, Brooks. *Emancipation of Massachusetts.* Boston, 1887.

***Adams, Charles Francis. *Three Episodes in Massachusetts History.* Boston, 1892.
For a somewhat different view of the affairs at Wessagusset and Merry Mount.

**Adams, James Truslow. *The Founding of New England.* Boston, 1921.

**Andrews, C. M. *The Fathers of New England.* New Haven, 1919.

***Arber, Edward. *The Story of the Pilgrim Fathers, 1606-1623.* London, 1897.

Ayres, M. F. *Richard Bourne, Missionary to the Mashpee Indians.* Boston, 1908.

Bacon, Leonard. *Genesis of the New England Churches.* New York, 1874.

Baker, George P. *The Pilgrim Spirit: A Pageant,* etc. Boston, 1921.
For the tercentenary celebration at Plymouth, 1920.

***Banks, Charles Edward. *The English Ancestry and Homes of the Pilgrim Fathers.* Boston, 1929.

***———. *The Planters of the Commonwealth.* Boston, 1930.

Barclay, Robert. *Inner Life of the Religious Societies of the Commonwealth.* London, 1876.

*Bell, Margaret. *Women of the Wilderness.* New York, 1938.

***Benét, Stephen Vincent. *Western Star.* New York, 1943.
There is more about the Pilgrims in a dozen pages of this unfinished masterpiece than in a dozen volumes of conventional history.

***Bliss, William R. *Old Colony Town.* Boston, 1893.

***———. *Side Glimpses from the Colonial Meeting House.* Boston, 1894.

*Bolton, Charles Knowles. *The Real

Founders of New England. Boston, 1929.

***Burgess, Walter H. *John Robinson, the Pastor of the Pilgrims.* London, 1920.

*————. *John Smith, the Sebaptist ... with fresh light upon the Pilgrim Fathers' Church.* London, 1911.

Burrage, Champlin. *The Church Covenant Idea.* Philadelphia, 1904.

————. *The True Story of Robert Browne.* Oxford, 1906.

————. *Early English Dissenters.* 2 vols. Cambridge, 1912.

Crandom, Edwin Sanford. *Old Plymouth Days and Ways.* Attleboro, Mass., 1921.

Cuckson, John. *First Church at Plymouth.* Boston, 1902.

***Davis, William T. *Ancient Landmarks of Plymouth.* Boston, 1889.

*————. *Plymouth Memories of an Octogenarian.* Plymouth, 1906.

*————. *History of the Town of Plymouth.* Philadelphia, 1885.

*Dexter, Henry Martyn. *The Congregationalism of the Last Three Hundred Years.* New York, 1880.

*————. *Congregationalism as Seen in its Literature.* Boston, 1880.

***———— and Dexter, Morton. *The England and Holland of the Pilgrims.* Boston, 1905.

***Digges, Jeremiah. *Cape Cod Pilot.* Provincetown and New York, 1937.

The story of the Cape from the early days down to the intrusion of those strangest of "strangers," the summer tourists—a book with a rare sparkle.

Dow, G. F. *Domestic Life in New England in the Seventeenth Century.* Topsfield, Mass., 1925.

————. *Every Day Life in the Massachusetts Bay Colony.* Boston, 1935.

**Drake, S. G. *The Witchcraft Delusion in New England.* Roxbury, 1866.

**————. *History of King Philip's War.* Boston, 1862.

Dunham, H. C. *Old Houses in Plymouth.* Plymouth, 1893.

Dunnack, Henry E. *Maine Forts.* Augusta, Maine, 1924.

***Earle, Alice Morse. *The Sabbath in Puritan New England.* New York, 1893.

Edes, Henry H. "Society for the Propagation of the Gospel in New England," in *Colonial Soc. of Mass. Pub.,* vol. 6.

Ernst, James. *Roger Williams.* New York, 1932.

**Federal Writers' Project. *Massachusetts.* Boston, 1937.

**————. *Rhode Island.* Boston, 1937.

**————. *Connecticut.* Boston, 1937.

**————. *New Hampshire.* Boston, 1938.

**————. *Maine.* Boston, 1938.

***Forbes, Esther. *Paul Revere and the World He Lived In.* Boston, 1942.

For the stirring days of '76.

Foster, Frank Hugh. *Genetic History of New England Theology.* Chicago, 1907.

*French, Allen. *General Gage's Informers.* Ann Arbor, 1932.

Garçon, Maurice, and Vinchon, Jean. *The Devil. An historical, critical, and medical study.* London, 1929.
Witchcraft down the ages.

Gardiner, S. R. *History of the Commonwealth and Protectorate*. London, 1903.

**Goodwin, J. A. *The Pilgrim Republic*. Boston, 1888.

**Hare, Lloyd C. M. *Thomas Mayhew, Patriarch to the Indians*. New York, 1932.

Harrington, Thomas. *Dr. Samuel Fuller of the Mayflower*. Baltimore, 1903.

*Harris, James Rendel. *Finding of the Mayflower*. London, 1920.

*———. *Last of the Mayflower*. London, 1920.
Harris believes the first and second *Mayflower* to be the same.

***——— and Jones, Stephen. *The Pilgrim Press*. Cambridge, 1922.
Excellent account of the Choir Alley Press and its publications, with facsimiles of title pages.

Hart, Albert Bushnell. *Commonwealth History of Massachusetts*. 5 v. New York, 1927-30.
Latest and most inclusive history of the Commonwealth.

Hill, H. A. *History of the Old South Church*. Boston, 1890.

**Hunter, Joseph. *Collections Concerning the Church or Congregation of Protestant Separatists formed at Scrooby*, etc. London, 1854.

Hurd, D. Hamilton. *History of Plymouth County*. Philadelphia, 1884.

*Hutchinson, T. *History of the Province of Massachusetts Bay*. 3 vols. London, 1765-1828.
A Tory view of early New England.

*Kittredge, George Lyman. *Witchcraft in Old and New England*. Boston, 1929.

**Kittredge, Henry C. *Cape Cod, Its People and Their History*. Boston, 1930.

Jameson, J. F. *The History of Historical Writing in America*. Boston, 1891.
For the critically minded, on how "history" is made.

Jones, E. Alfred. *Loyalists of Massachusetts*. London, 1930.

Levermore, C. H. *Forerunners and Competitors of the Pilgrims*. 2 vols. Brooklyn, 1912.

Lord, Arthur. *Plymouth and the Pilgrims*. Boston, 1920.

Love, W. D. *The Fast and Thanksgiving Days of New England*. Boston, 1895.

Marble, A. R. *The Women Who Came in the Mayflower*. Chicago, 1920.

Marsden, J. B. *History of the Early Puritans*. London, 1850.

———. *History of the Later Puritans*. London, 1852.

Marsden, M. R. G. "Captain Christopher Jones and the Mayflower," in *English Historical Review*, Oct., 1904.
Marsden discovered the *Mayflower* papers in the Admiralty archives and dispelled the myth that the skipper was a pirate.

Mitchell, Nahum. *History of the Early Settlement of Bridgewater*. Boston, 1840.

Moore, George Henry. *Notes on the History of Slavery in Massachusetts*. New York, 1866.

***Morison, Samuel Eliot. *Builders of the Bay Colony*. Boston, 1930.

*———. *Three Centuries of Harvard*. Cambridge, 1936.
Rather special but worth reading.

Motley, John Lothrop. *Rise of the Dutch Republic*. New York, 1898.

*Murdock, Kenneth. *Increase Mather*. Cambridge, 1925.

A "school-tie" defense of the bumptious and inordinately ambitious Mather; absolves him from all blame for Plymouth's loss of its charter.

Neal, Daniel. *History of the Puritans*. London, 1732.

Nicolas, Nicholas Harris. *The Life of William Davison*. London, 1823.

Noyes, E. J. R. *Women of the Mayflower*. Washington, 1915.

Nutting, Wallace. *Furniture of the Pilgrim Century*. Framingham, Mass., 1924.

**Otis, Amos. *Genealogical Notes of Barnstable Families*. Barnstable, 1885.

Much interesting material on Yarmouth, Barnstable, and Sandwich, once famous for its glass.

***Parrington, Vernon Louis. *The Colonial Mind* (vol. I in *Main Currents in American Thought*). New York, 1927.

The best and sharpest analysis of the ideas and temper of early New England, though not without bias.

Patten, E. B. *Isaac Allerton*. Minneapolis, 1908.

**Perry, Ralph Barton. *Puritanism and Democracy*. New York, 1944.

Philleo, C. W. "A Pilgrimage to Plymouth," in *Harper's New Monthly Magazine*. Dec., 1853, and May, 1854.

***Pierce, William. *John Penry*. London, 1923.

Interesting not only for its exciting story but for the Elizabethan background.

*Plooij, D. *The Pilgrim Fathers from a Dutch Point of View*. New York, 1932.

Plumb, Albert H. *William Bradford of Plymouth*. Boston, 1920.

Porteus, T. C. *Captain Myles Standish*. London, 1920.

**Powicke, F. J. *Henry Barrow, Separatist*. London, 1900.

*———. *John Robinson*. London, 1920.

Pratt, Enoch. *History of Eastham*. Yarmouth, 1844.

Pratt, Harvey H. *Early Planters of Scituate*. Scituate, 1929.

**Pratt, Waldo Selden. *The Music of the Pilgrims*. Boston, 1921.

Prince, Thomas. *A Chronological History of New England in the form of Annals*. Boston, 1736.

Raymond, W. O. *Winslow Papers, 1776-1826*. St. John's, New Brunswick, 1901.

Reynard, Elizabeth. *The Narrow Land: Folk Chronicles of Old Cape Cod*. Boston, 1934.

*Rich, Shebnah. *Truro Cape Cod, or Landmarks and Seamarks*. Boston, 1884.

Russell, William S. *Pilgrim Memorials*, etc. Boston, 1864.

Sanford, Elias B. *History of Connecticut*. Hartford, 1922.

Sawyer, Joseph D. *History of the Pilgrims and the Puritans*. 3 vols. New York, 1922.

Scales, John. *Piscataqua Pioneers, 1623-1775*. Dover, N. H., 1919.

Scholes, Percy A. *The Puritans and Music in England and New England*. Oxford, 1934.

Shakespeare, J. H. *Baptist and Congregational Pioneers*. London, 1906.

Sherrill, E. Prescott. *The House of Edward Winslow*. Plymouth, 1931.

Steven, William. *History of the Scot-*

tish Church, Rotterdam, with Notices of the other British Churches in The Netherlands. Edinburgh, 1833.

**Strachey, Lytton. *Elizabeth and Essex.* New York, 1928.

*Straus, Oscar Solomon. *Roger Williams.* New York, 1894.
A more perceptive biography than most.

Swift, Charles E. *History of Old Yarmouth.* Yarmouthport, 1884.

**Tawney, R. H. *Religion and the Rise of Capitalism.* London, 1926.
The economic motives in the Reformation.

Terry, Roderick. *Early Relations between Rhode Island and Plymouth.* Newport, R. I., 1920.

Thacher, James. *History of the Town of Plymouth.* Boston, 1832.

Thatcher, B. B. *Indian Biography.* 2 vols. New York, 1832.

Thomas, M. A. *Memorials of Marshfield.* Boston, 1854.

***Thoreau, Henry David. *Cape Cod.* Boston, 1865.
Altogether charming account of the old and then still remote Cape about 1850.

Traill, H. D., and Mann, J. S. *Social England* (illustrated). London, 1904.

**Usher, Roland. *The Pilgrims and Their History.* New York, 1918.

Best conventional history though not without an Anglican bias, in my opinion.

Waddington, J. *Congregational History, 1567-1700.* London, 1874.

Walker, Williston. *History of the Congregational Churches in the United States.* New York, 1894.

Wayman, Dorothy G. *Suckanesset, a History of Falmouth.* Falmouth, 1930.

*Weeden, William B. *Economic and Social History of New England, 1620-1789.* Boston, 1890.

Wendell, Barrett. *Cotton Mather, the Puritan Priest.* New York, 1891.

Wertenbaker, Thomas Jefferson. *The First Americans, 1607-1690.* New York, 1927.

Winsor, Justin. *A History of Duxbury.* Boston, 1849.

*Winthrop, R. C. *Life and Letters of John Winthrop.* 2 vols. Boston, 1867.

*Woodhouse, A. S. P. *Puritanism and Liberty.* London, 1938.

Wright, Thomas Goddard. *Literary Culture in Early New England, 1620-1730.* New Haven, Conn., 1920.

Young, Alexander. *Chronicles of the First Planters of the Massachusetts Bay.* Boston, 1846.

————. *Chronicles of the Pilgrim Fathers.* Boston, 1844.

Index

Library of Congress Cataloguing in Publication Data

Willison, George Findlay, 1897-
Saints and Strangers.
Reprint. Originally published: Time Reading
Program special ed. New York: Time, 1964.
Bibliography: p.
Includes index.
1. Pilgrims (New Plymouth colony)
2. Massachusetts – History – New Plymouth,
1620-1691. I. Title.
F68.W75 1981   974.4′02   81-5795   AACR2
ISBN 0-8094-3635-3 (pbk.)
ISBN 0-8094-3634-5 (deluxe)